Tear out this answer mask and use it to cover the answers column in the "Completion" section in each chapter. Write in the missing words on the blank lines in those sections; then look at the answer.

Tear out this answer mask and use it to cover the answers column in the "Completion" section in each chapter. Write in the missing words on the blank lines in those sections; then look at the answer.

ECONOMICS

Study Guide

KAMERSCHEN/McKENZIE/NARDINELLI

ECONOMICS

Second Edition

Study Guide

Douglas W. Copeland

Avila College

Houghton Mifflin Company **Boston**

Dallas Geneva, Illinois Palo Alto Princeton, New Jersey

Cover photograph by Thomas Leighton.

Printed in the U.S.A.

Library of Congress Catalog Card Number: 88-81338

ISBN 0-395-49571-7

ABCDEFGHIJ-A-898

Dedicated to
my wife, Mette

Contents

Preface

From the beginning, I have intended that you come to view this Study Guide as a close and helpful companion. Therefore, it has been designed to fulfill two major goals. First, by complementing the material presented in Kamerschen/McKenzie/Nardinelli ECONOMICS, Second Edition, I hope to increase your understanding and appreciation of economics. If I am successful, you will be better equipped to respond intelligently to real-world economic issues that you read about and hear about every day. After all, many economic decisions made by businesses and political leaders have far-reaching implications for your personal life. Furthermore, a firm grasp of the principles of economics is invaluable to those of you who are pursuing careers in economics or business. Second, and possibly of more immediate and practical concern to you, this Study Guide has been designed to prepare you for your examinations. I am confident that if you work through each chapter of this Study Guide in its entirety after you have studied the chapter in the textbook, you will enter your tests with confidence and will score accordingly.

In order to fulfill these goals, I have attempted to make this Study Guide thorough and rigorous enough to be of real value. Each chapter consists of the sections outlined below.

Chapter Summary

I have recapitulated the principles, concepts, and issues introduced in the text as thoroughly — yet succinctly — as possible. However, out of necessity, many details are left out of the Chapter Summary. Remember, the Study Guide is not intended, nor should it be used as, a substitute for the text. To lead you back into the text when you need more explanation than the Study Guide can provide, the Chapter Summary is organized around the Key Questions used in ECONOMICS, Second Edition. As in the textbook, the Key Questions present the chapter material in a more organized and understandable manner. Each Key Question clues you in to what you should know by the time you finish reading each section of the text; the chapter material related to each question "answers" the question posed in the margin. I urge you to think in terms of the Key Questions when studying the chapter material.

Review Terms and Concepts

This lists the terms and concepts that are important for understanding the chapter material. You may want to look at this list before you read the chapter in the text. If you are unable to define or explain the terms, you should review them (use the index and glossary at the back of the textbook).

New Terms and Concepts

These are new terms and concepts you should familiarize yourself with. They are important for understanding the chapter material as well as material yet to come. Most of the New Terms are defined in the chapter and can be found in the Review of New Terms in the text (or in the glossary). I have also added some terms that I think are necessary for a greater understanding of the material.

Completion

This section enables you to test your understanding of — and to gain confidence in — the material and language of economics. It can also help point out to you areas in which you are weak and that you may need to correct.

Problems and Applications

This section enables you to become actively involved with the material — as opposed to passively listening to a lecture or reading your book — and is therefore designed to increase your understanding of the more technical aspects of economics. Basically, this section attempts to carry on a dialogue with you. Many times you will be asked to explain something or will be led step by step to a major conclusion or a realization of an important concept. In the more difficult chapters you may find this section to be increasingly important, because you will be asked to reason through a problem as an economist would.

True-False

This section tests your understanding of the material and requires you to reach conclusions independently. Many statements are false because of just one word. This is deliberate, and is designed to help you identify seemingly unimportant differences and to learn the language of economics. You are asked to correct false statements by rewriting them as true statements. This is designed to further aid you in the learning process.

Multiple Choice

This section also tests your understanding of the material. You are required to identify subtle differences in statements and to reach conclusions on your own. This section, as well as the True-False section, may be very helpful in preparing for exams, because most instructors give exams in the multiple choice/true-false format.

Discussion Questions

Many of the Discussion Questions go beyond the material in the chapter and are designed to stimulate thought. Many times, there is neither a "right" nor a "wrong" answer because of subjective value judgements based on what "ought to be." In this way, the discussion questions have been designed to show how the chapter material relates to the real world. The discussion questions are cross-referenced to the text Key Questions to help you determine the material each discussion question is related to, and therefore what might be a good answer. If you have difficulty understanding any of the Discussion Questions, the Key Question references can also lead you back into the text for further review of the material that's causing you difficulty.

Answers

Answers are provided for the Problems and Applications, True-False statements and Multiple Choice questions. I have tried to make the answers to the Problems and Applications thorough enough to facilitate fruitful dialogue, but only as thorough as the level of difficulty warrants. The answers to statements in the True-False section are provided, and all false statement are rewritten as true statements. The correct answers for the Multiple Choice questions are also provided. In addition, all Multiple Choice answers are cross-referenced to the text Key Questions that each question tests. If you answered any of the Multiple Choice questions incorrectly, you can easily refer back to the section of the text — indicated by the Key Question reference — that gave you trouble.

The order in which these sections appear in each chapter is deliberate, as are the references to the text Key Questions. This format is intended to maximize your understanding and therefore your ability to successfully tackle an exam, given your limited studying time. It should not take you too long to work through the Study Guide material for each chapter you are assigned. Considering the payoffs, I would urge you to do so! Incidentally, the chapter numbers in the Study Guide are those used the hardcover text; if you are using the paperback *Macroeconomics* or *Microeconomics*, please refer to the chart following this Preface for the appropriate Study Guide chapter.

I hope you find this Study Guide helpful. But regardless of the success of my undertaking, I also hope you come to appreciate the practical applications of economics, and find the study of economics both rewarding and interesting.

Doug Copeland

Contents in Brief

CHAPTER 1

The Economic Way of Thinking

Chapter Summary

Key Question 1: What is the central concern underlying economic analysis?

Key Question 2: What topics does economics cover?

Key Question 3: What role does theory play in economics?

Economics is the study of how we attempt to satisfy people's unlimited wants by maximizing the production of goods and services given our limited resources of land, labor, capital, and technology. Because we have an unlimited desire (demand) for products but only limited production capabilities, we are faced with scarcity. Scarcity means we are unable to have all we would like all the time. Indeed, economics may be defined as the study of scarcity. Since we are faced with scarcity, we must face some unavoidable questions and choices about how to allocate limited resources among competing wants. Markets emerge in direct response to the scarcity of goods and services.

An array of problems have their roots in scarcity and are therefore economic problems. Economists attempt to understand these problems by developing theories that are useful in explaining and predicting economic behavior. A theory (or model) is a generalization about how variables are related based on careful observation of facts. Theories are practical because they avoid unnecessary detail and enable us to explain and predict economic behavior reasonable well. Theories are realistic because they are based on facts.

Economic theories are simplified explanations of how the economy, or part of the economy, functions or would function under specific conditions. In turn, these theories are useful to governmental and business policymakers in deciding which course of action may be taken to solve, or avoid, a particular problem under consideration. In economics, deduction is the principal form of theorizing. Deduction moves from very general propositions to more precise statements or predictions.

Deductive economic theorizing incorporates three steps. First, a few very general premises or propositions about a relationship (or relationships) are stated. At this point, definitions and assumptions are also stated. An assumption is anything that is held to be true for the sake of analysis. Simplifying (or unproved) assumptions are made quite often in economic theorizing to make the discussion more manageable by focusing on the key features of a problem. Simplifying assumptions are permissible as long as they do not alter the problem under study or destroy its relevance to the real world.

The second step in economic theorizing is the process of logical deduction, in which one deducts what logically follows from the initial premises, definitions, and assumptions. Mathematics and graphic analysis are often very useful in deducting the consequences of premises. The logical consequence of a premise or proposition usually takes the form of "If x happens, then y will happen." To see if the prediction is a candidate for "truth," we must test it against observable experience (the facts). This takes us to the third and final step in the deductive process, the empirical test.

Empiricism can determine whether the deduction is *probably* true or not true. We can never be certain about the validity of a deduction because the prediction observed may have been caused by factors not considered. If the deduction is considered to be probably true, then it becomes a theory. However, even when the truth of a theory is accepted, it is only tentatively accepted because we are always awaiting further knowledge that may render the theory obsolete or because the facts (the real world) may change, rendering our theory inoperative.

Key Question 4: What are the major approaches to economic theory?

Economists develop theories in order to understand the world as it is, but many economists are also concerned with what ought to be. Therefore economic thinking can be divided into two categories: positive and normative. Positive economics is concerned with *what is,* and value judgments have no place in this branch of inquiry. Normative economics is concerned with *what ought to be* and relies heavily on value judgments. The textbook is primarily concerned with positive economics because we must first know what *is* before we can state with any credibility what ought to be. However, from time to time the issue of what ought to be will be presented by raising the proper questions, leaving you to make the decision based on your own value system.

Key Question 5: What are the two major branches of economics as a course of study?

Two major branches in the field of economics are microeconomics and macroeconomics. Both are forms of positive economics in nature. Microeconomics is concerned with some particular segment of the economic system. Macroeconomics is concerned with the overall economic system. The distinction between microeconomics and macroeconomics based on size is not sufficient. For instance, some firms in the United States take in more revenue than some Third World countries produce as a nation. Instead, the difference between microeconomics and macroeconomics is more correctly a matter of approach. That is, the distinction is more properly stated in terms of the questions that each branch addresses.

All of the questions addressed by either microeconomics or macroeconomics have prompted the development of theories to answer them. These theories can be and are applied to problems and issues of the real world. Throughout the text and this study guide, the practical applications of economic theory are examined in an attempt to equip you with the necessary tools to understand better the world in which we all live—a world in which scarcity is a universal reality.

New Terms and Concepts

Market
Entrepreneur
Resources
Land
Labor
Capital
Technology
Scarcity
Economics
Theory
Positive economics
Normative economics
Microeconomics
Macroeconomics

Completion

Economics can be defined as the study of how people cope with

scarcity, limited — ________________. In any economy, resources are ________________ (unlimited/limited); therefore the production of goods and services is

limited — ________________ (unlimited/limited). However, society has an

unlimited — ________________ (unlimited/limited) demand for goods and services; therefore we are faced with scarcity. Scarcity means that people are

unable — ________________ (able/unable) to have all they would like all of the time. Whenever a product is scarce, a market for the product will arise.

process — A market is really a ________________ (place/process). For a market to exist, there must be both a demand for and a supply of the product.

maximize — From society's point of view, we attempt to ________________
(maximize/minimize) the production of goods and services, given our
satisfy — limited resources, in an attempt to ______________ (reduce/satisfy)
Resources — society's unlimited wants. ______________ (Resources/Products) are
things used in the production of goods and services. Any society's
land, labor — resource categories include ______________, ________________,
capital, technology — ________________, and ______________. Land includes all things
found in nature, including the surface of the earth, that are useful in the
production process. Labor incorporates all physical and mental energy ex-
plant and equipment — pended by humans. Capital includes all types of ________________
(money/plant and equipment) used in the production process. Technology is the knowledge of how resources can be combined in productive
entrepreneurs — ways. Often considered a resource in themselves, ________________
are enterprising people who discover profitable opportunities and organize, direct, and manage productive ventures.

Because we are faced with scarcity, we must face some unavoidable
questions and choices about what should be produced and how goods
and services should be distributed. Economist attempt to find answers to
these question by studying what is and what ought to be. When
positive — economists study what is, they are thinking as ______________
(positive/normative) economists. When economists study what ought
normative — to be, they are thinking as ________________ (positive/normative)
economists. Value judgments are made when studying
normative — ________________ (positive/normative) economics, but no value
positive — judgments are made when studying ______________ (positive/
normative) economics.

Two major branches of positive economics are ________________ and ________________. When we are concerned with the overall economy, we are studying ______________ (microeconomics/ macroeconomics). If we are interested in some particular segment of the economy, we are studying ______________ (microeconomics/ macroeconomics). Although we have implicitly distinguished between microeconomics and macroeconomics on the basis of size, these sub-disciplines are best distinguished by the questions each addresses. (Can you list some of the question each addresses?)

All of the questions addressed by either microeconomics or macro-economics have prompted the development of theories to answer them. A theory is a ________________ (simplified/detailed) description or model of the real world. An economic theory is a ________________ (simplified/detailed) explanation of how the economy, or part of the economy, functions or would function under specific conditions. Economists derive theories to help ________________ and ________________ economic behavior. A "good" theory must do two things. It must ________________ well and it must give a ______________________________ why the predicted outcome will occur.

In economics, the principal type of theorizing is ________________ (deduction/induction) which moves from________________ (particular/general) propositions to more________________ (particular/general) statements or predictions. Deductive economic theorizing incorporates three steps. First, a few very ________________ (specific/general) premises or propositions are stated, along with a few

microeconomics
macroeconomics
macroeconomics
microeconomics
simplified
simplified
explain
predict
predict
reasonable explanation
deduction
general
particular
general

definitions and simplifying assumptions. The second step is to draw a tentative prediction or ______________________ from the premises. Mathematics and graphic analysis are often very useful in developing and describing the logical consequences of premises. To see whether the prediction is borne out in the real world, we must test it against observable experience. The ________________ is the third step in the theorizing process. Empiricism determines if the deduction can ____________ well and if it can give a ________________________ why the predicted outcome would occur.

logical deduction

empirical test

predict

reasonable explanation

If the deduction is not disproven by repeated testing, then it is accepted as a theory. However, we are ________________ (never/always) certain about the validity of a theory because the prediction observed may have been caused by factors not considered. A theory accepted as probably true is accepted__________________(forever/tentatively). This is because we are always awaiting further knowledge and because there is always the possibility that the facts (economic environment) may change, rendering the theory inoperative.

never

tentatively

Problems and Applications

1. For each of the following items, indicate whether the concern is an interest of microeconomics or macroeconomics.
   a. Consumption habits of an individual
   b. The total output of a firm
   c. The total output of a nation
   d. The total income of all farmers in the United States
   e. Government spending and taxation policies of the federal government
   f. Profits earned in the steel industry
   g. The money supply in an economy
   h. The forces that determine the mix of goods and services produced in an economy

2. Respond to the following statement: "Theory is of no use to me because it's not very practical. All I need is the facts because they speak for themselves."
3. How can an increase in technology help alleviate scarcity?
4. How can education and training of labor help alleviate scarcity?
5. For each of the following items, indicate whether the statement is positive or normative in nature.
   a. "The unemployment rate is 8 percent."
   b. "The unemployment rate is too high."
   c. "What this economy needs is fewer unions."
   d. "Unions can cause unemployment in that industry."
   e. "Our nation's income is primarily determined by control over resources."
   f. "We need to redistribute our nation's income more fairly."
6. Economists may disagree over normative aspects because they may have differing opinions of what ought to be. But we also find they sometimes disagree about positive aspects. Why is it that economists may sometimes disagree over what is?
7. The United States is the wealthiest nation on earth, yet our fundamental economic problem is scarcity. How can this be?

True-False

For each item, indicate whether the statement is basically true or false. If the statement is false, rewrite it so it is a true statement.

_____ 1. A theory (or model) is simplified version of reality.

_____ 2. To economize is to choose among alternatives.

_____ 3. The federal government attempts to maximize its economic objectives (goals) given its resources (budget).

_____ 4. Positive economics is concerned with subjective economic statements; normative economics is concerned with objective economic statements.

_____ 5. Human wants for any particular product are always unlimited.

_____ 6. Technology refers to the ways in which resources are converted into want-satisfying goods and services.

_____ 7. A theory must incorporate all details of the real world to which it applies.

_____ 8. Economists are concerned with the development of theories, not policy.

_____ 9. If two things occur together, this necessarily means one caused the other.

_____ 10. Our resource categories consist of land, labor, capital, and technology.

_____ 11. Wants are unlimited, but resources are limited.

_____ 12. Deduction moves from the general to the particular.

_____ 13. Scarcity means we are unable to have all we want all of the time.

_____ 14. For a theory to be a "good" theory, it must predict well but not necessarily explain why the predicted outcome is expected to occur.

_____ 15. Normative economic statements cannot be empirically tested to determine whether they are true, but positive economic statements can be determined to be true or not true.

_____ 16. An economic model is a utopian ideal for which we should strive.

_____ 17. Any statement that is held to be true for the sake of analysis is a positive statement.

_____ 18. In economics, capital is money.

Multiple Choice *Choose the one best answer for each item.*

_____ 1. The fundamental economic problem of any nation is to
   a. distribute income fairly.
   b. eliminate scarcity.
   c. conserve its resources.
   d. maximize production given limited resources.
   e. provide employment to those who are willing and able to work.

_____ 2. Which of the following is *not* an economic resource?
   a. Chemicals used to destroy particular plant life
   b. Money
   c. An economics professor
   d. The brick and mortar in a factory building
   e. Land used as a nuclear waste site

_____ 3. Economic theories
   a. are always correct in their predictions.
   b. once established as "true" are always "true."
   c. are generalizations based on careful observation of facts.
   d. always include as much detail as possible.
   e. are all of the above.

_____ 4. To an economist, capital is
   a. money held by the public.
   b. plant and equipment.
   c. stock in a company.
   d. money held by banks.
   e. any natural resource.

_____ 5. Positive economics is concerned with
   a. policy designed to achieve what ought to be.
   b. effective teaching techniques for economics professors.
   c. enhancing politicians' economic understanding.
   d. causal relations between economic variables—what is.
   e. redistributing income fairly.

_____ 6. Which of the following is a macroeconomic problem?
   a. Wage rates of electricians in Kansas City, Missouri
   b. The effects of agricultural price-support programs on the income of farmers
   c. The causes of unemployment
   d. How profits are maximized for a firm
   e. How the composition of output is determined in a capitalist economy

_____ 7. Which of the following is a possible definition of economics?
   a. A study of scarcity
   b. A study of how choices are made
   c. A study of how limited resources are allocated among competing wants
   d. A study of how something is maximized or minimized given some constraint or group of constraints
   e. All of the above are limited definitions of economics.

_____ 8. For a theory to be useful over time, it must be
   a. intellectually stimulating.
   b. checked and rechecked against the changing economic environment to see if it is still in accordance with reality.
   c. continually taught over time.
   d. based on an economist's idea of what ought to be happening over time.
   e. based on realistic assumptions.

_____ 9. The statement "What works well at the level of theory and what works in practice are two different things" is
   a. a fact because they cannot be compared.
   b. true of economics but not true of the physical sciences.

c. contradictory because theories help explain what happens in practice.
d. true of all sciences.
e. none of the above.

_____ 10. The notion of scarcity is
a. a synonym for poverty.
b. different for underdeveloped nations as compared to modern industrial states.
c. applicable to all people and all nations.
d. applicable only to nations that have an inadequate supply of natural resources.
e. not applicable if we had full employment.

Discussion Questions

1. Is scarcity a synonym for poverty? *(KQ1)*
2. Is the economic problem facing the United States the same economic problem facing less developed nations? *(KQ1)*
3. If two variables are highly correlated, does this mean that a change in one causes a change in the other? *(KQ3)*
4. Does economics teach us how to think, or does it give us a set of answers? *(KQ3)*
5. "Human beings are all unique. Each behaves differently. So economists cannot generalize about human behavior." How would economists respond to this statement? *(KQ3)*
6. Can we say that what is true for the part (micro) must be true for the whole (macro)? *(KQ5)*
7. Do you think the u.S. economy is allocating its resources in the best possible manner? In other words, do we need to devote more of our limited resources to some products and less resources to other products? *(KQ1)*
8. Are nuclear missiles an economic resource? *(KQ1)*
9. How can an unrealistic assumption be justified? *(KQ3)*

Answers

Problems and Applications

1. a. microeconomics b. microeconomics c. macroeconomics
   d. microeconomics e. macroeconomics f. microeconomics
   g. macroeconomics h. microeconomics
2. Theories are practical because they enable us to predict and explain why the predicted outcome is expected to occur. Facts by themselves may not be relevant to a particular problem and, even if they are relevant, they may appear to be unrelated without a theory or model to tie them together. One must systematically arrange, interpret, and generalize from facts by tying them together, thereby giving them order and meaning. Theory and facts are inseparable in the scientific process because theory gives meaning to facts and facts check the validity of theory.
3. Technology is a resource. An increase in resources enables us to produce more and thus help to alleviate scarcity. But because our wants are unlimited, we will always be faced with scarcity.
4. Education and training make labor more productive, enabling us to produce more and thereby helping to alleviate scarcity.
5. a. positive b. normative c. normative
   d. positive e. positive f. normative
6. Economists may disagree over what is when available data is insufficient to accept or reject competing hypotheses.
7. At first glance, this statement may appear to be inconsistent. But although we may be very well off, we are not as well off as we would like. We will always be faced with scarcity because our wants are unlimited.

True-False

1. T 2. T 3. T
4. F: Positive economics is concerned with objective economic statements; normative economics is concerned with subjective economic statements.
5. F: Human wants for all products as a group are always unlimited.
6. T
7. F: A theory does not have to incorporate all details of the real world to which it applies.

8. F: Economists are concerned with the development of theories and the implementation of policy.
9. F: If two things occur together, this does not necessarily mean one caused the other.
10. T 11. T 12. T 13. T
14. F: For a theory to be a "good" theory, it must predict well and explain why the predicted outcome is expected to occur.
15. T
16. F: An economic model is not a utopian ideal for which we should strive.
17. F: Any statement that is held to be true for the sake of analysis is an assumption.
18. F: In economics, capital is plant and equipment.

Multiple Choice

1. d *(KQ1)* 2. b *(KQ1)* 3. c *(KQ3)*
4. b *(KQ1)* 5. d *(KQ4)* 6. c *(KQ5)*
7. e *(KQ2)* 8. b *(KQ3)* 9. c *(KQ3, 4)*
10. c *(KQ1, 2)*

CHAPTER 2

Scarcity and Production Possibilities

Chapter Summary

Key Question 1: How are the concepts of scarcity and cost related?

Key Question 2: What are production possibilities curves and what does their downward slope imply?

Because we are faced with scarcity and unlimited wants, we must make choices about what to produce. The production possibilities curve is a graphical model of the basic economic problem of how to maximize our output given our limited resources. This model reflects the fact that because we are faced with scarcity we must make choices, and when we make choices a cost (or, opportunity cost) is incurred.

A production possibilities curve shows that if we employ our resources fully and efficiently, we will be maximizing our output given our limited resources. This is shown as a point on the production possibilities curve. Note that the production possibilities curve is downward sloping and bows out. This implies that greater production of one type of product can only be obtained at increasing additional cost in terms of the other type of product that must be foregone. If we do not employ our resources fully and efficiently, we will not be maximizing our output given our limited resources, and this is shown as a point inside the curve. Any point outside the curve represents a combination of products that is impossible to produce (at least in this time period). However, if we experience enough economic growth in the future, a point outside the curve may be obtainable over time.

The production possibilities curve helps us envision the types of choices we must make. For example, we have the choice of what combination of goods to produce. There are two basic types of products, consumption goods (consumer products) and investment goods (capital products). Consumption goods satisfy our present wants directly; investment goods satisfy our future wants indirectly because they use the capital products used to produce other products. It may be tempting to choose a whole lot of consumer products now (because they satisfy our wants now), but this decision means fewer capital products produced now. Relatively fewer capital products produced now means a less productive economy in the future (because workers will have fewer machines to work with in the future). A less productive economy in the future means lower production possibilities in the future—and less economic growth. In other words, the choice we make between the production of consumer products and capital products affects our economic growth, and our present location on the curve will determine the future location of the curve.

Key Question 3: What does investment do to future production possibilities?

Economic growth, shown as a rightward shift in the production possibilities curve, means that we can produce more of both consumer and capital products in the future. To experience greater economic growth (or greater increases in our production possibilities and a greater rightward shift in the curve) we need to devote a larger percentage of our limited resources to the production of capital products and fewer resources to consumer products. The only way to do this is to have greater investment in capital products. Therefore, we can say that greater investment increases our future production opportunities.

Whenever a choice is made, an opportunity cost is incurred. The opportunity cost of producing more investment goods is fewer consumption goods and vice versa. Moreover, because resources are not perfectly adaptable to alternative uses, the opportunity cost of shifting resources from consumer to capital products (or vice versa) increases. So we can see that the cost of higher and higher rates of economic growth is proportionately smaller and smaller amounts of consumer products that we can have now.

The actual choice between the production of consumer and capital products (and the consequent effect on economic growth) is determined by the market process, the political process (government), and the interaction between the two. But note that whatever choice we end up with cannot be judged to be "better" than another by economics alone. Such a decision requires political or social judgments as to what is best or what ought to be based on political or social goals. All an economist can say is that any choice actually made between consumer and capital products will have the predicted effect on economic growth.

Key Question 4: How do current choices between private and public goods affect future production opportunities?

The production possibilities curve can also illustrate the choices between public and private goods and the effect of these choices on economic growth. First, as before, there are increasing opportunity costs associated with providing more public goods at the expense of private goods (and vice versa). Second, the amount of economic growth depends on whether these public goods increase our nation's stock of plant and equipment by increasing people's tendency to produce, work, save, and invest, as compared to the affects on people and our stock of plant and equipment when resources are used by the private sector.

Key Question 5: How do people, acting individually and collectively, change their production possibilities?

Besides devoting a larger percentage of our resources to investment products, there are other factors that contribute to a rightward shift in the production possibilities. First, substituting relatively inexpensive new resources for scarce ones will increase society's production possibilities curve. Second, cost sharing reduces the inefficient use of scarce resources. Third, specialization of labor is also a more efficient use of resources that causes a rightward shift in the curve. Fourth, economies of scale decrease per unit costs of production and increase our production possibilities. These lower per unit costs can be viewed as lower opportunity costs in that fewer of other products have to be given up. (There is, however, a limit to economies of scale. That limit is reached when diseconomies of scale set in, which are usually associated with such a large scale of production that management has lost control of the operation.) Finally, specialization and trade based on comparative advantage increase our production possibilities. Money is used to facilitate specialization and trade and to escape the inefficiencies associated with a barter economy. Money is any generally acceptable medium of exchange that also acts as a store of purchasing power.

Key Question 6: Why do people benefit from trade?

Trade based on specializing and comparative advantage reduces the cost of production thereby increasing total production for all trading partners. Trade also increases the dependence of producers and consumers on one another. The circular flow of income model shows the interdependence of consumers and producers in the economy. In simplified form, the model depicts only the private sector of the economy. Consumers (resource owners) supply resources to producers (businesses), who use these resources to produce goods and services which they supply to consumers. In turn, consumers receive income (money) from producers for the use of their resources. In other words, producers demand these resources with money, which constitutes income to consumers. With this income, consumers demand goods and services. The integrated nature of the economy is symbolized by arrows pointing in opposite directions and by the interdependence of producers and consumers. This simple model can be expanded to include both government and international trade and to reflect more fully the complexity of exchange relationships in the economy.

Key Question 7: How are major sectors of the economy tied together?

Review Terms and Concepts

Resources
Scarcity

Economics
Market

New Terms and Concepts

Cost (opportunity cost)
Production possibilities curve (production possibilities frontier)
Economic growth
Investment goods (capital products)
Consumption goods (consumer products)
Private goods
Public goods
Specialization of labor
Economies of scale
Diseconomies of scale
Money
Comparative advantage
Circular flow of income

Completion

The production possibilities curve is a model that shows we are faced

scarcity, choices — with ________________, that ________________ have to be

opportunity cost — made, and that an ________________________ will be incurred

with any decision. This is the value of the most highly preferred alternative *not* taken. Scarcity is shown in the model by the fact that a point

outside — ______________ (inside/outside) the curve is unobtainable in this period of time.

We begin with two basic choices. The first is whether to employ our resources fully and efficiently. If we choose to employ our resources

on — fully and efficiently, this is shown as a point ________________ (inside/outside/on) the production possibilities curve. If we do not employ our resources fully and efficiently, this is shown as a point

inside — ____________ (inside/outside/on) the curve. Second, we have the choice of how to allocate our resources. If we devote a relatively high percentage of our scarce resources to the production of investment

greater — (capital) products, we will experience a __________ (greater/ smaller) rate of economic growth. Economic growth is shown graphically as a

rightward — ________________ (rightward or outward/leftward or inward) shift

	of the production possibilities curve. The reason economic growth occurs
capital	is because of increases in our ________________ (capital/consumer)
	stock. Therefore, the only way to increase the stock of plant and equip-
more	ment is to invest ______________ (more/less).
directly	Consumption goods satisfy our wants ________________ (directly/
present	indirectly) and in the ________________ (present/future). Investment
indirectly	goods satisfy our wants __________________ (directly/indirectly) and
future	in the ________________ (present/future). It may be tempting to choose
	many want-satisfying products now, but they will come at the expense of
lower	a _____________________ (lower/higher) rate of economic growth. So
	in making a choice between consumption goods and investment goods,
opportunity cost	an __________________________________ is involved. The oppor-
fewer	tunity cost of more investment goods is ________________________
	(fewer/more) consumption goods, and vice versa, for as we produce
	more and more of one type of product we will have to give up propor-
greater	tionately _________________ (greater/smaller) amounts of other
	products. That is to say, the opportunity cost of producing more and
increases	more of one type of product __________________ (decreases/increases).
not perfectly	This is because resources are _____________________ (perfectly/not
	perfectly) adaptable to alternative uses. Because of increasing oppor-
out	tunity costs, the production possibilities curve bows ______________
	(in/out) from the origin.

In reality, the actual choice between consumption goods and investment goods is determined by the market process, the political process (government), and the interaction between the two.

The production possibilities curve can also be used to show the choice
between public goods and private goods. But the essential concepts are
increasing — the same as before. That is, there are __________________ (increasing/
decreasing) opportunity costs associated with producing greater amounts
of one type of product. The choice between public and private goods and
the consequent effect on economic growth depends on the number of
capital products produced. In other words, producing more or fewer
public goods must be judged as contributing or not contributing to
increasing — economic growth on the basis of whether it is ____________________
(increasing/decreasing) our capital stock.

We know that increasing our nation's capital stock will cause
increases — economic growth and that economic growth _____________________
(increases/decreases) our production possibilities. Specialization and
increases — trade based on comparative advantage also _____________________
(increases/decreases) out production possibilities. For specialization and
money — trade to be efficient, we need a ____________________ (money/barter)
economy. Anything that is generally acceptable as a medium of ex-
money — change is __________________ (money/a resource). Money must also
store of purchasing power — act as a __________________________________ (store of purchasing
power/resource). Money facilitates specialization and trade based on
comparative — _____________________ (comparative/absolute) advantage.

A diagram that shows the interdependence between consumers
circular flow of income — (households) and producers (businesses) is known as the
____________________________________ model. This model shows
interdependent — the _______________________ (independent/interdependent) relations
broad — between ____________________ (narrow/broad) segments of the

producers (businesses)
consumers (households)
supply
goods and services
supply
producers
demand
households
demand

economy. A simple circular flow of income model incorporates only the private sector. The private sector consists of ____________________ and ____________________. As the ultimate owners of resources, consumers ____________________ (demand/supply) resources to producers. Producers use these resources to produce ____________________. Therefore, the producers ____________________ (supply/demand) goods and services to consumers. On the other hand, ____________________ (consumers/ producers) ____________________(supply/demand) resources from households in the form of money payments. The flow of money from businesses to households constitutes the income to households. With this income, the ____________________ (households/businesses) ____________________ (supply/demand) goods and services. However, because their control over resources is not equally distributed, a nation's income is not equally distributed. Therefore goods and services are not equally distributed.

demand
supply
demanding
supplying
supplying
demanding

For a market to exist, there must be a ________________ (demand/supply) for *and* a ________________ (demand/supply) of the item. From the simple circular flow model, we can see that, in the product market, households do the ____________________ (demanding/ supplying) while businesses do the ____________________ (demanding/supplying). In the resource market, households do the ____________________ (demanding/supplying) while businesses do the ____________________(demanding/supplying).

Problems and Applications

1. Consider the following production possibilities between products X and Y.

Product X	Product Y
0	20
1	18
2	14
3	8
4	0

   a. What is the opportunity cost of producing the first unit of X? The second unit of X? The third unit of X? The fourth unit of X?
   b. Is the opportunity cost of producing successively larger amounts of X increasing, decreasing, or remaining the same?
   c. What is the economic justification for increasing opportunity costs?
   d. If this production possibilities curve was graphed, would it be a straight line or would it bow out or in with respect to the origin?

2. Answer the following questions based on the production possibilities curve shown below.
   a. Which of the points shown would give the greatest rate of economic growth?
   b. What does point *D* represent?
   c. What does point *E* represent?
   d. What do points *A*, *B*, and *C* represent?

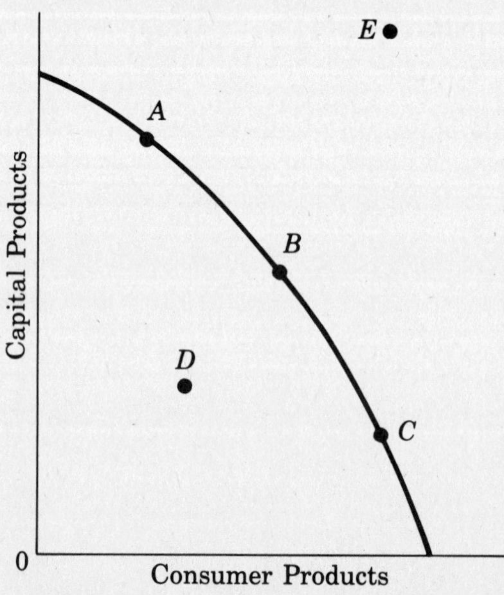

3. Consider the production possibilities of Dana and Julio shown below.

Dana						Julio					
Good X:	0	1	2	3	4	Good X:	0	2	4	6	8
Good Y:	8	6	4	2	0	Good Y:	32	24	16	8	0

a. Is increasing opportunity cost applicable for either Dana or Julio?
b. For Dana, what is the opportunity cost of X in terms of Y for each of the production possibilities? of Y in terms of X?
c. For Julio, what is the opportunity cost of X in terms of Y for each of the production possibilities? of Y in terms of X?
d. Who has the comparative advantage in the production of X? Of Y?
e. Assume Dana and Julio each specialize in the production for which they have a comparative advantage (Dana produces all X and Julio Produces all Y). However, both Dana and Julio would like to have some X and some Y. What would be fair terms of trade?
f. Would Dana and Julio both be better off by specializing in their comparative advantage and then trading?

4. Draw a simple circular flow of income model. Indicate by arrows who is doing the demanding and the supplying.
5. What would happen to our production possibilities if we could develop a very cheap synthetic fuel?
6. Use graphs to express a positive (direct) relationship and an inverse relationship between any independent and dependent variables. (*Note:* An independent variable goes on the horizontal, or *X*, axis and a dependent variable goes on the vertical, or *Y*, axis).

True-False

For each item, determine whether the statement is basically true or false. If the statement is false, rewrite it so it is a true statement.

_____ 1. Scarcity implies choice, which in turn implies opportunity cost.
_____ 2. Business supply goods and services to households.
_____ 3. An opportunity cost is the highest preferred alternative taken.

_____ 4. Allocating a relatively greater amount of our scarce resources to the production of consumption goods will give us a greater amount of economic growth in the future.

_____ 5. Unemployment is shown as a point outside the production possibilities curve.

_____ 6. Households demand resources.

_____ 7. Economic growth is shown as a leftward (inward) shift of the production possibilities curve.

_____ 8. Increases in our capital stock contribute to economic growth.

_____ 9. The actual choice between consumption goods and investment goods we end up with is determined by the market process, the political process (government), and by the interaction between the two.

_____ 10. Because resources are perfectly adaptable to alternative uses, we have increasing opportunity cost.

_____ 11. Specialization and trade based on comparative advantage increase our production possibilities.

_____ 12. Money is a resource.

_____ 13. A market exists if there is demand for the item.

_____ 14. The circular flow of income model consists of resources and money, which flow in the opposite direction.

_____ 15. There are only three general types of markets.

_____ 16. In the product market, businesses (producers) do the demanding.

_____ 17. Investment goods are synonymous with capital products.

_____ 18. Opportunity cost and cost are synonyms.

_____ 19. Our nation's distribution of income is determined by control over resources.

Multiple Choice *Choose the one best answer for each item.*

_____ 1. Society's production possibilities curve bows out because
   a. we are faced with scarcity.
   b. a point inside the curve represents unemployment.
   c. we attempt to maximize our output given our limited resources.
   d. of increasing opportunity cost.
   e. resources are perfectly adaptable to alternative uses.

_____ 2. The combination of consumption goods and investment goods that we end up with
   a. will have to be a point inside the production possibilities curve.
   b. will have to be a point on the production possibilities curve.
   c. is determined by the market process.
   d. is determined by the market process, the political process, and the interaction between the two.
   e. is none of the above.

_____ 3. With respect to the production possibilities curve, economic growth is shown by
   a. a point outside the curve.
   b. a movement along the curve toward more investment goods and fewer consumption goods.
   c. increasing opportunity cost.
   d. a leftward shift of the curve.
   e. a rightward shift of the curve.

_____ 4. A production possibilities curve
   a. represents different combinations of goods that can be produced if we employ all our resources fully and efficiently.
   b. bows out.
   c. shows we are face with scarcity.
   d. shows we are faced with increasing opportunity cost.
   e. is all of the above.

_____ 5. Which of the following may increase our production possibilities?
   a. Cost sharing
   b. Specialization of labor
   c. Economies of scale
   d. The use of money to facilitate trade
   e. All of the above

_____ 6. The three basic types of markets in a capitalist system are the
   a. product, resource, and money markets.
   b. private, government, and international markets.
   c. labor, capital, and technology markets.
   d. product, resource, and international markets.
   e. government, product, and resource markets.

_____ 7. Capitalism is characterized by
   a. the concept of private property.
   b. producers and consumers.
   c. economic activity coordinated through the market system.

d. a and b.
e. a and c.

_____ 8. Capital products
a. include plant and equipment.
b. contribute to economic growth.
c. satisfy our wants indirectly.
d. are produced at the expense of consumer products when we employ all of our resources fully and efficiently.
e. are all of the above.

_____ 9. Which of the following is true of opportunity cost?
a. It is stated in terms of dollars and cents.
b. It is incurred when moving from a point inside the production possibilities curve to a point on the curve.
c. It decreases as we move down along the production possibilities curve.
d. It is applicable to any choice that is made.
e. It is not applicable for government policymakers.

_____ 10. Which of the following will definitely increase our production possibilities?
a. More private goods and less public goods
b. Diseconomies of scale
c. More consumer goods and less capital goods
d. Specialization and trade based on comparative advantage
e. A greater reliance on the political process to allocate our resources

_____ 11. Which of the following would *not* be included in the product market?
a. Automobiles purchased by consumers
b. Bulldozers purchased by businesses
c. Home computers purchased by consumers
d. Steak purchased for consumption
e. Boots purchased by consumers

Discussion Questions

1. Is it possible to devote too many resources to investment goods? *(KQ3)*
2. We know that the range of "fair" terms of trade may be quite wide. What do you think determines the actual terms of trade between

two nations who have a comparative advantage in different products? *(KQ6)*

3. Is it possible to specialize labor too much? *(KQ5)*
4. Constant opportunity cost means resources are perfectly adaptable to alternative uses. Constant opportunity cost characterizes some alternative production processes, such as gasoline and heating oil in oil refineries. Can you think of any others? *(KQ2)*
5. Why is it that many doctors and lawyers share the same office and equipment? *(KQ5)*
6. Why has the Soviet Union experienced a higher rate of economic growth than the United States since World War II? *(KQ3)*
7. Why do public utilities operate on such a large scale? Would we all be better off with our own generating plants in our backyards? *(KQ5)*
8. The cost of higher education is usually associated with tuition and fees, books, room and board, entertainment, and so on. Is there another cost that one must consider? *(KQ1)*
9. What effect may population growth have on our production possibilities and our standard of living? *(KQ3, 5)*

Answers

Problems and Applications

1. a. Two units of Y; four units of Y; six units of Y; eight units of Y.
   b. Increasing.
   c. Resources are not perfectly adaptable to alternative uses.
   d. The curve would bow out from the origin.
2. a. Point A.
   b. We are not fully and efficiently utilizing our resources (we are not maximizing our output given our limited resources).
   c. Point *E* represents an unobtainable combination of consumer and capital products given our limited resources. However, point *E* may be obtainable at some time in the future if we experience enough economic growth over time.
   d. These points on the curve represent different combinations of consumer and capital products we can produce if we are utilizing our resources fully and efficiently.
3. a. No.
   b. The cost of 1X is 2Y; the cost of 1Y is ½X.

c. The cost of 2X is 8Y or of 1X is 4Y; the cost of 1Y is $^1/_4$X.
d. Dana has a comparative advantage in X; Julio has a comparative advantage in Y.
e. The range of fair terms of trade would exist anywhere between 1X = 2Y and 1X = 4Y; for instance, 1X = 3Y. (Alternatively, fair terms of trade exist between 1Y = $^1/_2$X and 1Y = $^1/_4$X; for instance, 1Y = $^1/_3$X.)
f. Yes. Dana would produce 4X because of her comparative advantage in X and Julio 32Y because of his comparative advantage in Y. Assume the terms of trade are 1X = 3Y. Dana could give up 2X to Julio and receive form him 6Y—a greater combination of X and Y than if she were to produce both products herself. Likewise, Julio would have to give up only 6Y to receive 2X form Dana, leaving him with 2X and 26Y-a greater combination of X and Y than if he were to produce both products himself.

4.

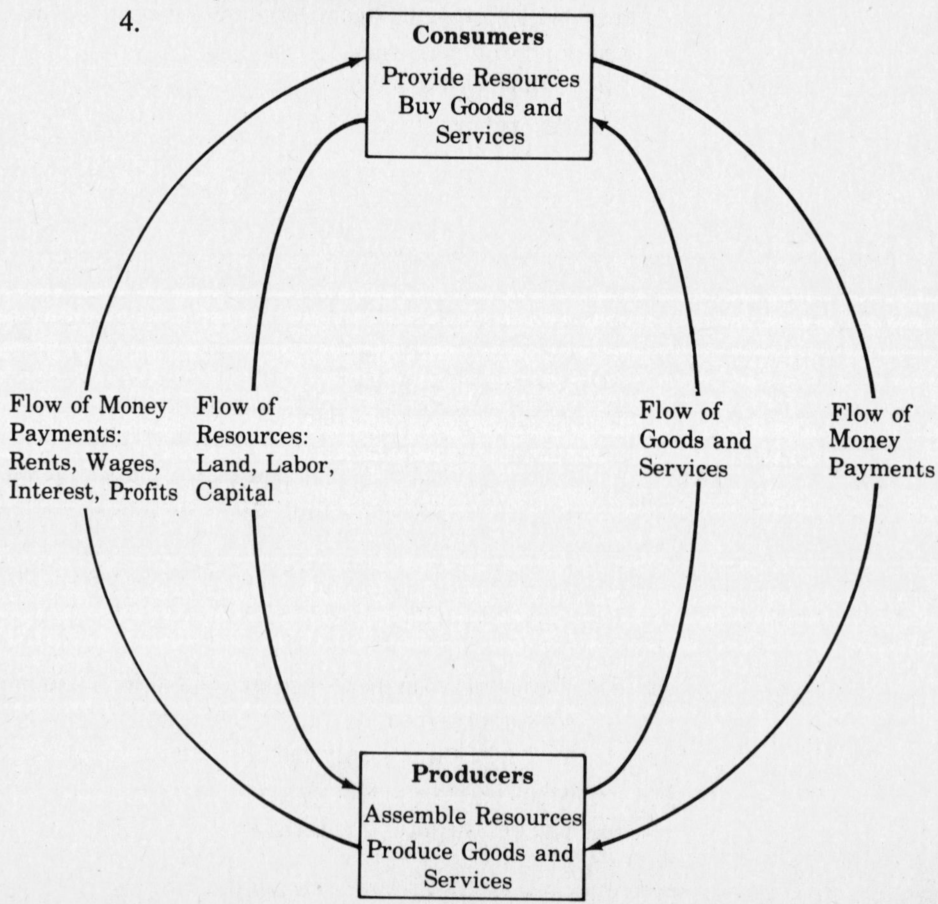

5. Substituting this cheap resource for the more scarce crude oil would increase our production possibilities.
6. A positive (direct) relationship is expressed graphically as a positively sloped line or curve; an inverse relationship is expressed graphically as a negatively sloped line or curve.

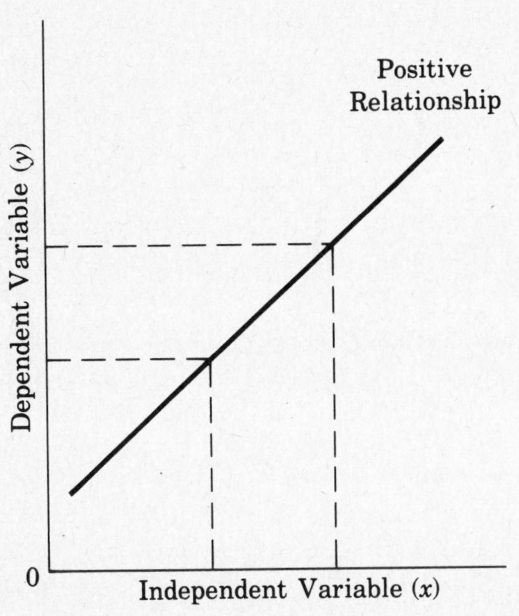

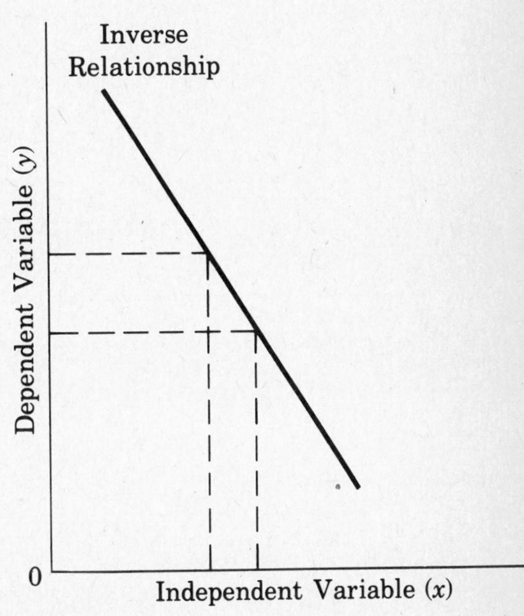

True-False

1. T 2. T
3. F: An opportunity cost is the highest preferred alternative not taken.
4. F: Allocating a relatively greater amount of our scarce resources to the production of investment goods will give us a greater amount of economic growth in the future.
5. F: Unemployment is shown as a point inside the production possibilities curve.
6. F: Households supply resources.
7. F: Economic growth is shown as a rightward (outward) shift of the production possibilities curve.

8. T 9. T

10. F: Because resources are not perfectly adaptable to alternative uses, we have increasing opportunity cost.

11. T

12. F: Money is not a resource but is anything that is generally acceptable as a medium of exchange and that acts as a store of value.

13. F: A market exists if there is demand for the item *and* supply of the item.

14. T 15. T

16. F: In the product market, businesses (producers) do the supplying.

17. T 18. T 19. T

Multiple Choice

1. d *(KQ2)* 2. d *(KQ1, 2)* 3. e *(KQ3)*
4. e *(KQ1, 2)* 5. e *(KQ5)* 6. a *(KQ7)*
7. e *(KQ7)* 8. e *(KQ3)* 9. d *(KQ1)*
10. d *(KQ6)* 11. b *(KQ7)*

CHAPTER 3

The Elements of Supply and Demand

Chapter Summary

Key Question 1: What is the competitive market process?

Key Question 2: What are the supply and demand curves, and how can they be used to understand the market process?

The competitive market process can be thought of as a system where the desires of buyers and the desires of sellers, each pursuing their own interests, interact to determine simultaneously the equilibrium price (market-clearing price) and the equilibrium quantity (the same quantity buyers want to buy and sellers want to sell). The desires of buyers are reflected in demand while the desires of sellers are reflected in supply, and we assume the interaction to be competitive. With respect to supply, competition can be based on price or nonprice factors (such as brand names, quality, color, and so on). Perfect competition means complete freedom of entry into and exit from the market, which is composed of so many buyers and sellers that no one individual buyer or seller has the ability to influence the price.

Demand is the inverse relationship between the price of a good or service and the quantity consumers are willing and able to buy during a given time period, all other things being equal. That is, as price increases, quantity demanded decreases, and as price decreases, quantity demanded increases. This inverse relationship between price and quantity demanded is known as the law of demand and is expressed graphically as a negatively sloped curve. Price and quantity are inversely related because of income and substitution effects of a price change. The income effect is the effect a price change has on the purchasing power of consumer incomes. The substitution effect is the effect a price change has on the relative prices of other substitutable products.

As the definition of demand indicates, consumers must be both willing and able to buy the product for their desires to be registered in demand. The definition also refers to some specified period of time with all other things being equal (constant). "All other things" refers to the nonprice determinants of demand. When one or more of these nonprice determinants change, demand also changes. A change in demand is reflected graphically as a shift of the demand curve.

An increase in demand results in a rightward shift of the demand curve, indicating consumers are willing and able to buy *more* at any given price during some period of time. An increase in demand also indicates that consumers are willing and able to pay a greater price to receive the same quantity. A decrease in demand results in a leftward shift of the demand curve, indicating consumers are willing and able to buy *less* at any given price during some period of time. A decrease in demand also indicates that consumers are no longer willing or able to pay as high a price to receive the same quantity.

A change in demand must be distinguished from a change in quantity demanded. An change in quantity demanded results from a change in price and is reflected graphically as a movement along a given demand curve. The direction of a change in quantity demanded given a change in price is known from the law of demand.

Supply reflects the desires of sellers. Supply is the direct (positive) relationship between the price of a product and the quantity producers are willing and able to produce and offer for sale during a given time period, all other things equal. This means that as price increases, quantity supplied increases, and as price decreases, quantity supplied decreases. This direct (positive) relationship between price and quantity supplied is known as the law of supply and is expressed graphically as a positively sloped curve.

As the definition of supply indicates, producers must be both willing and able to produce and offer the product for sale in order for their desires to be registered in supply. The definition also refers to some specified period of time with all other things being equal (constant). "All other things" are the nonprice determinants of supply. When one or more of the nonprice determinants change, supply also changes. A change in supply is reflected graphically as a shift of the supply curve.

An increase in supply results in a rightward shift of the supply curve, indicating producers are willing and able to produce and offer for sale a *greater* amount at any given price during some period of time. An increase in supply also indicates that producers are willing and able to accept a lower price to produce the same quantity. A decrease in supply results in a leftward shift of the supply curve, indicating producers are willing and able to produce and offer for sale a *lesser* amount at any given price during some period of time. A decrease in supply also indicates that producers must require a higher selling price to produce the same quantity.

A change in supply must be distinguished from a change in quantity supplied. A change in quantity supplied results from a change in price and is reflected graphically as movement along a given supply curve. The direction of a change in quantity supplied given a change in price is known from the law of supply.

Out of the competitive interplay of demand and supply we can determine market equilibrium. Market equilibrium is that price and quantity which, once achieved, will be sustained until there is a change in one or more of the nonprice determinants of demand or supply. In other words, equilibrium exists until demand or supply changes. Market equilibrium is characterized by the fact that there is neither a shortage nor a surplus. Equilibrium implies that quantity demanded is exactly equal to quantity supplied (equilibrium quantity), and this occurs at only one price (equilibrium price).

If, at a given price, quantity demanded exceeds quantity supplied, there will be a shortage of the product and market equilibrium will not be observed. The shortage is equal to the difference between the quantity demanded and quantity supplied. If a shortage exists, buyers would like to have more of the product than is currently being made available by producers at that price. Some consumers would be willing and able to pay a higher price than is currently being paid just to receive one of the products. If a shortage exists, then, we would expect buyers to competitively bid up the price. This bidding process illustrates the rationing function of prices. As the price is bid up, some consumers will be either unwilling or unable (or both) to purchase the product at the higher price. This causes a decline in quantity demanded. In addition, as the price is bid up, producers will increase quantity supplied. This process continues until equilibrium quantity is reached (where quantity demanded equals quantity supplied) at the equilibrium price. Said another way, a shortage implies price is below the equilibrium level.

If, at a given price, quantity supplied exceeds quantity demanded, there will be a surplus of the product and equilibrium will not be observed. The surplus is equal to the difference between quantity supplied and quantity demanded. If a surplus exists, producers are offering more of the product for sale than buyers are willing or able to purchase at that price. Producers will competitively bid down the price to rid themselves of their unsold products. As the price decreases, quantity supplied decreases, but quantity demanded increases. This process continues until equilibrium quantity and equilibrium price are reached. In short, a surplus implies price is above the equilibrium level.

In a competitive market, price fluctuates in response to either a shortage or a surplus. Note that competition among buyers eliminates a shortage while competition among sellers eliminates a surplus. A shortage or surplus is eliminated when quantity demanded equals quantity supplied and there is no tendency for price to change (market equilibrium). Graphically, equilibrium occurs where demand and supply curves intersect. Equilibrium can change only if demand or supply changes (causing a shift in one or both of the curves) due to changes in the nonprice determinants. If this occurs, we get a new point of intersection, or a new equilibrium price and quantity.

The market is not always allowed to operate freely to reach an equilibrium price and quantity. Sometimes government intervenes in the market process by setting legal prices called price ceilings and price floors. An effective price ceiling is set below the equilibrium price and causes a shortage. The price is a *ceiling* price because the price would otherwise rise due to the shortage. An effective price floor is set above the equilibrium price and causes a surplus. The price is a *floor* price because the price would otherwise decrease due to the surplus.

Key Question 3: When does the market operate "efficiently"?

The competitive market is said to operate efficiently if it fulfills two conditions. First, most of the time the amount produced equals exactly the amount consumers want. Second, the market system maximizes output.

Key Question 4: What are the many ways firms compete?

The competitive nature of the market system is not based solely on price. In reality, competition also takes the form of nonprice competition. Firms undertake nonprice competition to increase their profits. When some producers are successful, other firms will enter the market and imitate the successful products or develop their own variations of the product. The result is a very large variety of products from which consumers can choose. Therefore, nonprice competition increases consumer welfare. However, if entry into the market is restricted by monopoly power or government regulation, then the variety of products offered will not be as great as in a free (open, competitive) market. Thus, an argument for a free market is an argument for the optimal product mix. The argument for a free market becomes even stronger when we recognize that consumer preferences change over time (as do other market conditions), which changes the optimal product mix that most satisfies society.

Key Question 5: How do competitive markets adjust to changes in conditions in the "short run" and "long run"?

When investigating a free market we are always concerned with a specified period of time. If we change the period of time under consideration, we can compare short-run equilibrium with long-run equilibrium. In doing so, we can get a better understanding of how price and nonprice competition play a role in reaching long-run equilibrium.

Key Question 6: What are the shortcomings of competitive markets?

Although competitive markets may promote long-run improvements in product prices, quality, and output levels, there are a few shortcomings associated with them. Among these are: (a) an "unfair" distribution of income,

(b) pollution, (c) production of socially objectionable goods and services, (d) product proliferation, and (e) fraud.

Review Terms and Concepts

Market
Money
Circular flow of income
Public goods
Private goods
Consumer products
Capital products

New Terms and Concepts

Competition
Perfect competition
Nonprice competition
Demand
Decrease in supply
Law of demand
Law of supply
Inverse relationship
Positive (direct) relationship
Quantity demanded
Quantity supplied
Change in quantity demanded
Change in quantity supplied
Determinants of demand
Determinants of supply
Market surplus
Equilibrium price
Increase in demand
Decrease in demand
Supply
Increase in supply
Equilibrium quantity
Market equilibrium
Market shortage
Efficiency
Price ceiling
Price floor
Free market
Income effect
Substitution effect
Short-run equilibrium
Long-run equilibrium
Substitutes
Complements

Completion

buyers, sellers — A market implies that there are ______________ and ______________ willing to come together and engage in trade. The interaction between

market process — buyers and sellers is known as the ____________________________.

price — The market process relies on ______________ competition and

nonprice — ________________ competition. Perfect price competition allows for

entry and exit	complete freedom of ________________________ in the market.
	Perfect price competition also means that there are such a large number
buyers, sellers	of independently acting ____________ and ____________ that no one
buyer, seller	individual ______________ or ______________ has the ability to
price	affect the ______________. A competitive market results in an equi-
price, quantity	librium ______________ and an equilibrium ______________.
	Market equilibrium is determined by the intersection of the
demand, supply	______________ and ______________ curves.
demand	The desires of buyers are reflected in ______________ (demand/
supply	supply), and the desires of sellers are reflected in ______________
inverse	(demand/supply). Demand is the ______________ (inverse/positive)
	relationship between the price of a good or service and the
quantity, able	______________ consumers are willing and ______________ to
time	purchase during a given ______________ period, all other things
equal	being ______________. An inverse relationship between price and
demand	quantity demanded is known as the law of ______________
	(demand/supply). Graphically, a law of demand is expressed as a
negatively	______________ (negatively/positively) sloped curve. This inverse
substitution effect	relationship exists because of the ________________________
income effect	and ________________________ of a price change. The
	substitution effect is the effect a price change has on the
relative price of substitutable products	____.
	The income effect is the effect a price change has on the
purchasing power of consumer incomes	____.
price	When a demand curve is graphed, we put ______________ on the
quantity	vertical axis and ______________ on the horizontal axis.

	It is important to distinguish between a change in demand and a
quantity demanded	change in quantity demanded. A change in ____________________
	(demand/quantity demanded) is a result of a change in price while a
demand	change in ______________________ (demand/quantity demanded)
	results form a change in the nonprice determinants of demand. The
	direction of change in the quantity demanded is given by the law of
demand	________________ (demand/supply). A change in quantity demanded
movement along a given demand curve	is expressed graphically as a ____________________________
	(movement along a given demand curve/shift in the demand curve). So
	the real difference between demand and quantity demanded is that
demand	________________ (demand/quantity demanded) is associated with a
quantity demanded	whole set of possible prices while ____________________
	(demand/quantity demanded) is associated with a given price.
consumers	An increase in demand shows that ________________ (consumers/
more	producers) are willing and able to buy ________________ (more/less)
	at any given price during some period of time. Graphically, an increase
rightward	in demand results in a __________________ (rightward/leftward)
	shift of the demand curve. A decrease in demand shows that
consumers	__________________ (consumers/producers) are willing and able to
less	purchase ________________ (more/less) at any given price during some
	period of time. Graphically, a decrease in demand is expressed as a
leftward	________________ (rightward/leftward) shift of the demand curve.
sellers	Supply reflects the desires of ________________ (buyers/sellers).
direct or positive	Supply is the ______________________ (inverse/direct or positive)
price	relationship between the ______________ of a product and the
quantity, willing	______________ producers are ______________ and able to produce

time	and offer for sale during a given ______________ period, all other
equal	things being ____________. This direct or positive relationship means
quantity supplied	that if price were to increase, the __________________ (quantity
increase	demanded/quantity supplied) would ____________ (increase/decrease).
	This positive relationship between price and quantity supplied is know as
supply	the law of ______________ (supply/demand). Graphically, the law of
positively	supply is expressed as a _______________ (positively/negatively)
price	sloped curve. When a supply curve is graphed, we put ____________
quantity	on the vertical axis and ________________ on the horizontal axis.
	It is important to distinguish between a change in supply and a change
supply	in quantity supplied. A change in ________________ (supply/quantity
	supplied) is a result of a change in the determinants of supply and is
shift of	reflected graphically as a __________________ (movement along/
quantity supplied	shift of) the supply curve. A change in ________________ (supply/
	quantity supplied) is a result of a change in price and is expressed graphi-
movement along	cally as a _________ (movement along/shift of) the supply curve. The
	direction of change in the quantity supplied is given by the law of
supply	______________ (demand/supply). So the real difference between
quantity supplied	supply and quantity supplied is that _________________ (supply/
	quantity supplied) is associated with a particular price while
supply	_____________ (supply/quantity supplied) is associated with a whole
	set of possible prices.
producers	An increase in supply shows that _________________ (consumers/
greater	producers) are willing and able to produce a ________________
	(greater/lesser) amount at any given price during some period of time.
rightward	An increase in supply is expressed graphically as a _______________

(leftward/rightward) shift of the supply curve. A decrease in supply

lesser — shows that producers are willing and able to produce a ______________ (greater/lesser) amount at any given price during some period of time. A

leftward — decrease in supply results in a ________________ (leftward/rightward) shift of the supply curve.

When demand and supply are brought together on the same graph, representing that buyers and sellers are engaging in trade, we can determine

equilibrium — market ________________________. That is, we can determine

equilibrium — ____________________ price and quantity. Graphically, equilibrium price and quantity are located where demand and supply curves

intersect — _________________. This is because at the point of intersection there is neither a surplus nor a shortage of the product.

If at some price the quantity demanded exceeds the quantity supplied,

shortage — we will observe a _________________ (surplus/shortage). This means

consumers — there is a tendency for _________________ (consumers/producers) to

up — competitively bid ___________ (up/down) the price. If a shortage exists

quantity demanded — and the price is bid up by consumers, the ________________________ (quantity demanded/quantity supplied) decreases while the

quantity supplied — ___________________________ (quantity demanded/quantity supplied) increases until quantity demanded and quantity supplied are equal. When this occurs, we have reached market equilibrium at one price called the

equilibrium price — ___________________________.

If at some price the quantity supplied exceeds the quantity demanded,

surplus — we will observe a ___________________ (surplus/shortage). This means

producers — there is a tendency for ___________________ (consumers/producers)

down — to competitively bid _____________ (up/down) the price. As price

quantity demanded	decreases the ________ (quantity demanded/quantity
quantity supplied	supplied) increases while the ________ (quan-
	tity demanded/quantity supplied) decreases until quantity demanded and
	quantity supplied are equal. When quantity demanded equals quantity
quantity	supplied, this is known as the equilibrium ________. An
quantity demanded	equilibrium quantity exists only when ________
quantity supplied	equals ________. In summary, a
surplus	________ (surplus/shortage) is a result of a price that is above
shortage	the equilibrium level while a ________ (surplus/shortage)
	is a result of a price that is below the equilibrium level.
	A free market results in market equilibrium. Sometimes the market is
	not allowed to operate freely because the government intervenes by set-
price floors	ting legal prices called ________ and
price ceilings, price ceiling	________. A ________ (price floor/price
	ceiling) is a legal price set by the government that is below the equi-
price floor	librium level. A ________ (price floor/price ceiling) is a
	legal price set by the government that is above the equilibrium level. A
minimum	price floor is the ________ (maximum/minimum) legal price
surplus	for which a product can be sold. A price floor causes a ________
maximum	(surplus/shortage). A price ceiling is the ________ (maximum/
	minimum) legal price for which a product can be sold. A price ceiling
shortage	causes a ________ (shortage/surplus).
	The competitive market is efficient in at least two respects. First, most
consumers	of the time producers produce exactly the quantity that ________
maximizes	want. Second, the competitive market ________ (maximizes/
	minimizes) output.

The competitive nature of the market system is rarely based solely on
nonprice — price. In reality, competition also takes the form of ______________
competition. When we compare the short run with the long run, we are
price, nonprice — able to see how ______________ competition and ______________
competition interact. An important contribution of nonprice competition
consumer welfare — is that it adds to ______________________.

There are a few shortcomings in competitive markets. First, we may
income — not have a socially desirable distribution of ______________. Second,
costs of production may be imposed on members of society who are not
consumers — ______________ (consumers/producers) of the product in question.
undesirable — Third, the free market may give rise to socially ______________
(desirable/undesirable) goods and services. Fourth, opponents of the
product proliferation — market system contend that competition leads to ______________
waste — and ______________ in production and advertisement of goods and
services. Finally, producers may take advantage of customers'
ignorance, unethical — ______________ by engaging in ______________ business
practices.

Problems and Applications

1. Consider the following schedule for Product X.

Quantity Demanded	Price per Unit	Quantity Supplied
30	$5	130
50	$4	100
70	$3	70
90	$2	40
100	$1	10

a. Does this schedule represent demand and supply relationships?

b. When price equals \$2, what is the quantity demanded and the quantity supplied? Does a shortage, surplus, or equilibrium exist? If a shortage or surplus exists, what is it equal to? What would you expect to happen to the price and why?
c. When price equals \$3, what is the quantity demanded and the quantity supplied? Does a shortage, surplus, or equilibrium exist? If a shortage or surplus exists, what is it equal to? What would you expect to happen to the price and why?
d. When price equals \$4, what is the quantity demanded and the quantity supplied? Does a shortage, surplus, or equilibrium exist? If a shortage or surplus exists, what is it equal to? What would you expect to happen to the price and why?
e. Graph these relationships. What is the nature of the slope of the demand curve and of the supply curve?

2. Consider the market described by the graph below. Let the demand and supply curves D_1 and S_1 be the original curves.

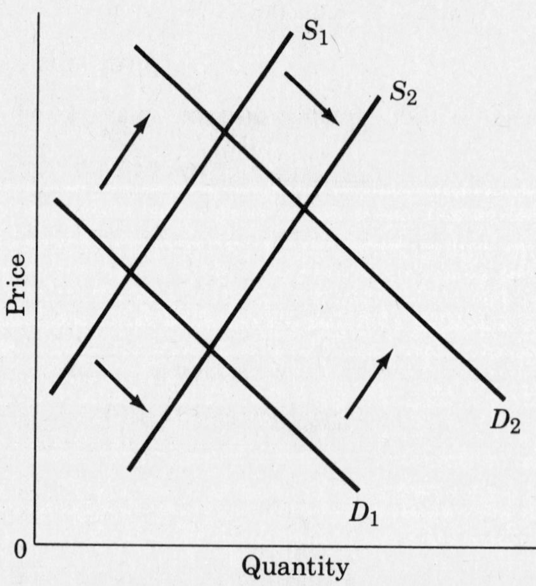

a. Where is the equilibrium price and quantity?
b. Would a shift from D_1 to D_2 represent a decrease in demand?

c. Where is equilibrium price and quantity given S_1 and D_2?
d. Would a shift from S_1 to S_2 represent an increase in supply?
e. Given S_2 and D_1, where would equilibrium occur?

3. Assume the following graph represents the market for beef.

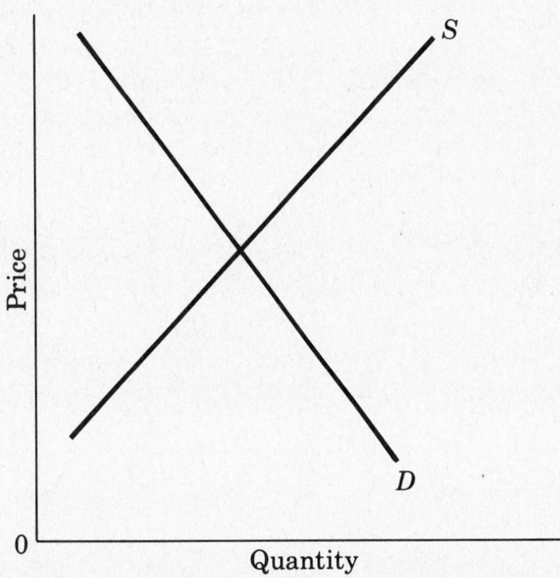

a. Locate the equilibrium price and quantity.
b. If consumer incomes increase, what happens to demand? Express the changing demand graphically. What happens to equilibrium price and quantity? Why would the changes in equilibrium price and quantity occur?
c. Suppose a deadly disease that affects cattle sweeps the Midwest. What would you expect to happen to the supply of beef?
d. Suppose government imposes a price floor on beef. What happens to quantity demanded and quantity supplied? Would this cause a surplus or a shortage?

4. Draw your own graphs to answer the following questions. Remember to begin each analysis with original demand and supply curves (an original equilibrium price and quantity).
   a. Suppose it has recently been determined that the consumption of grapefruit stops the aging prices. What would you expect to

happen to the price of grapefruit and the quantity of grapefruit bought or sold?

b. Suppose consumer incomes increase. Also suppose an early frost in Florida freezes a sizable percentage of the orange crop. What will happen to the demand for and supply of oranges? What will happen to equilibrium price and quantity?

c. Suppose the minimum wage has just been abolished. What would happen to the supply of lettuce? What would happen to equilibrium price and quantity?

d. Suppose it is now more profitable for farmers to produce soybeans. What would happen to the supply of corn? What will happen to the supply of soybeans? Also suppose there has been a substantial population explosion. What will happen to the demand for soybeans? Given the predicted change in the supply and demand of soybeans, what would you expect to happen to the equilibrium price and quantity of soybeans?

e. What would happen to equilibrium price and quantity given that there is a decrease in demand but an increase in supply?

f. What would happen to equilibrium price and quantity given that there is a decrease in demand and a decrease in supply?

g. Are hot dogs and hot dog buns most likely substitutes or complements? Given an increase in the price of hot dogs, what would you expect to happen to the demand for hot dog buns? What would happen to equilibrium price and quantity for hot dog buns?

5. How long is the short run? How long is the long run?
6. List the shortcomings of the market system. Can you add to the list?
7. The next time you go shopping, list as many nonprice competitive variables as you can. Your list should be quite long. (*Hint:* Consider everything from convenience to packaging to service and so on.)

True-False

For each item, decide whether the statement is basically true or false. If the statement is false, rewrite it so it is a true statement.

_____ 1. The law of demand states that consumers will buy more of a product when the price is high than when the price is low.

_____ 2. The substitution effect is the effect a price change has on relative prices of other substitutable products.

_____ 3. Automobiles and gasoline are complements.

_____ 4. A change in any of the determinants of demand will cause a change in quantity demanded.

_____ 5. A change in price always results in a change in the quantity demanded, the quantity supplied, or both.

_____ 6. The law of supply states that as price increases the quantity demanded increases.

_____ 7. An increase in productivity will result in an increase in supply.

_____ 8. The income effect is illustrated by this statement: "The price of chicken decreases, so consumers can afford to buy more chicken because the purchasing power of their income increases."

_____ 9. A surplus is a result of quantity demanded exceeding quantity supplied.

_____ 10. A decrease in demand shows consumers are willing and able to pay a higher price to receive any given quantity.

_____ 11. Equilibrium price and quantity are depicted graphically at the intersection of demand and supply curves.

_____ 12. An example of nonprice competition are advertisements stressing quality service after the purchase is made.

_____ 13. Price ceilings cause a surplus.

_____ 14. Demand is positively sloped while supply is negatively sloped.

_____ 15. If the price of product X increases and the demand for product Y increases, then X and Y are substitutes.

_____ 16. An increase in technology will increase supply.

_____ 17. A free market is a market where the product is free.

_____ 18. Short-run equilibrium is the price-quantity combination that will exist so long as producers do not have time to alter their production facilities.

_____ 19. Nonprice competition enhances consumer welfare.

_____ 20. One of the shortcomings of the market system is an unfair (inequitable) distribution of income.

_____ 21. Monopoly power or government regulation limiting freedom of entry and exit in a market is expected to increase consumer welfare.

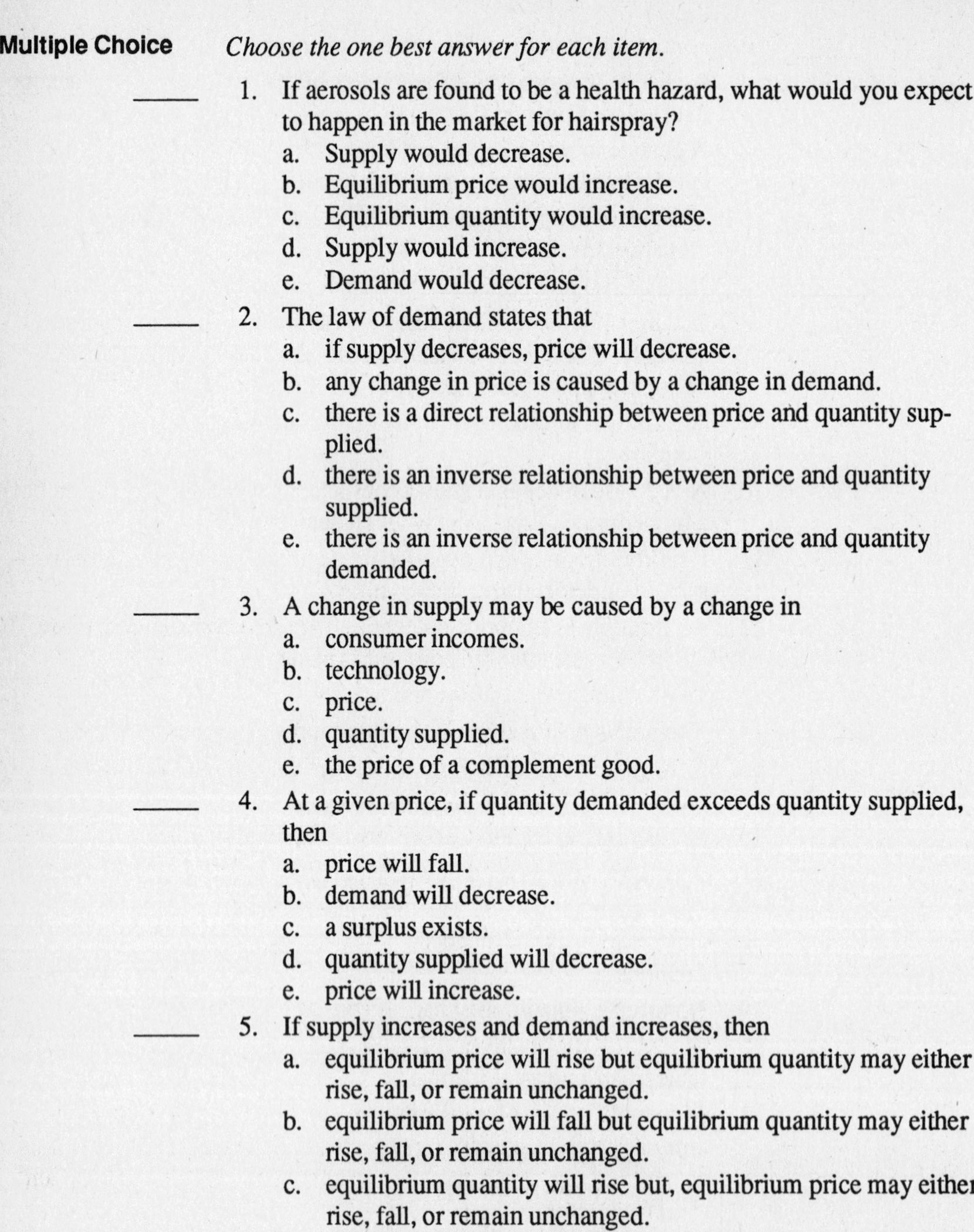

Multiple Choice *Choose the one best answer for each item.*

____ 1. If aerosols are found to be a health hazard, what would you expect to happen in the market for hairspray?
a. Supply would decrease.
b. Equilibrium price would increase.
c. Equilibrium quantity would increase.
d. Supply would increase.
e. Demand would decrease.

____ 2. The law of demand states that
a. if supply decreases, price will decrease.
b. any change in price is caused by a change in demand.
c. there is a direct relationship between price and quantity supplied.
d. there is an inverse relationship between price and quantity supplied.
e. there is an inverse relationship between price and quantity demanded.

____ 3. A change in supply may be caused by a change in
a. consumer incomes.
b. technology.
c. price.
d. quantity supplied.
e. the price of a complement good.

____ 4. At a given price, if quantity demanded exceeds quantity supplied, then
a. price will fall.
b. demand will decrease.
c. a surplus exists.
d. quantity supplied will decrease.
e. price will increase.

____ 5. If supply increases and demand increases, then
a. equilibrium price will rise but equilibrium quantity may either rise, fall, or remain unchanged.
b. equilibrium price will fall but equilibrium quantity may either rise, fall, or remain unchanged.
c. equilibrium quantity will rise but, equilibrium price may either rise, fall, or remain unchanged.
d. equilibrium quantity will fall but equilibrium price may either rise, fall, or remain unchanged.
e. any of the above could happen.

_____ 6. A change in price may cause
   a. movement along a given demand curve.
   b. movement along a given supply curve.
   c. a change in quantity supplied.
   d. a change in quantity demanded.
   e. all of the above.

_____ 7. The substitution and income effects explain
   a. why demand is negatively sloped.
   b. why as price decreases quantity demanded increases.
   c. the law of demand.
   d. why as price increases quantity demanded decreases.
   e. all of the above.

_____ 8. If the price of ink increases, then the
   a. demand for fountain pens increases.
   b. supply of fountain pens decreases.
   c. price of fountain pens decreases.
   d. substitution effect would increase.
   e. quantity demanded for fountain pens increases.

_____ 9. A popular rock star sets a new trend in hairstyles and haircare by having his head shaved. This would cause which effect in the market for haircuts?
   a. An increase in demand
   b. An increase in supply
   c. Equilibrium price to fall
   d. Equilibrium price to remain the same
   e. Equilibrium quantity to fall

_____ 10. A bountiful crop of coffee beans in Colombia will
   a. increase the supply of coffee.
   b. decrease the equilibrium price of coffee.
   c. increase equilibrium quantity of coffee.
   d. decrease the price of tea.
   e. cause all of the above.

_____ 11. A price ceiling
   a. is a legal price set by the government that is below the equilibrium price level.
   b. is a legal price set by government that is above the equilibrium price level.
   c. is the minimum legal price set by government for which a product can be sold.

d. causes a surplus.
e. has never been enacted by the Congress of the United States.

____ 12. Competition means that
a. there is only one seller of a product.
b. many buyers, in pursuing their own interests, are trying to outdo, outmaneuver, and outdistance each other.
c. many buyers and sellers, in pursuing their own interests, are trying to outdo, outmaneuver, and outdistance each other.
d. the government ensures that no one buyer or seller is able to influence the price.
e. buyers can pay and sellers can charge what they wish.

Use the following graph to answer questions 13-15.

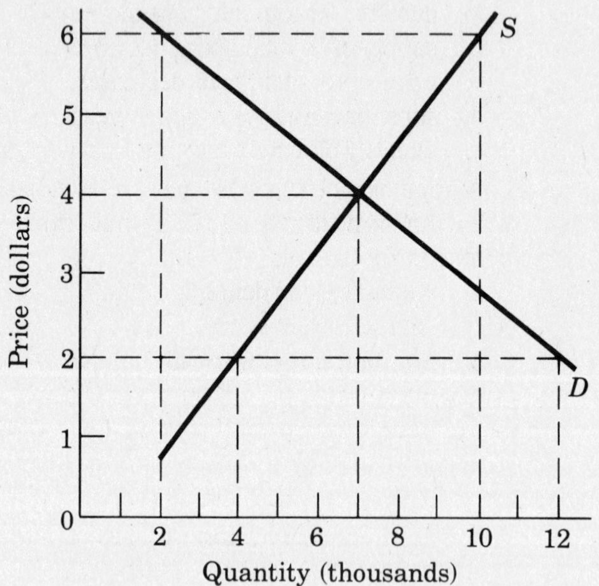

____ 13. Equilibrium price and quantity in this market would exist at
a. $6 and 3,000 units.
b. $2 and 12,000 units.
c. $4 and 7,000 units.
d. $4 and 3,000 units.
e. $6 and 7,000 units.

____ 14. If the current price is $6 per unit, then
a. a surplus of 8,000 units would exist.
b. this market would be in equilibrium.

c. quantity supplied would be 2,000 units and quantity demanded would be 10,000 units.
d. there would be a tendency for price to increase.
e. there would be a tendency for supply to decrease.

_____ 15. If the government imposes a price ceiling at $2 per unit, then
a. quantity supplied would exceed quantity demanded.
b. the quantity sold would be 12,000 units.
c. there would be an excess supply of 10,000 units.
d. there would be a shortage of 8,000 units.
e. there would be a surplus of 8,000 units.

_____ 16. Assume products Y and Z are complements. Given an increase in the price of Y, we can conclude that
a. the supply of Y will increase.
b. the supply of Z will decrease.
c. the demand for both Y and Z will decrease.
d. the demand for Z will decrease.
e. the quantity demand for Y will decrease and the demand for Z will increase.

_____ 17. Within a competitive market, equilibrium price and quantity are primarily determined by
a. demand.
b. quantity supplied.
c. production costs.
d. the interaction of supply and demand.
e. government regulation of businesses.

_____ 18. Which of the following will *not* cause the demand for oranges to change?
a. A change in consumer tastes
b. A change in consumer incomes
c. A change in the price of oranges
d. A change in the price of grapefruit
e. The expectation that the price of oranges will rise in the near future

_____ 19. Which of the following is *not* associated with nonprice competition?
a. Increased advertisements stressing quality
b. Lowering the price to attract more customers
c. Increased consumer welfare
d. Convenience for customers in terms of parking and increased hours that customers can shop

e. A greater variety of size and color from which the customer can choose

_____ 20. Which of the following is *not* considered a shortcoming of competitive markets?
a. They limit individual freedom by imposing prices consumers cannot control.
b. They are often characterized by an inequitable (unfair) distribution of income.
c. They can cause "overproduction" of some goods and services.
d. They can cause product proliferation.
e. They are sometimes characterized by unethical business practices.

Discussion Questions

1. Suppose in 1982 the price of Camaros was $14,000 and 500,000 of these automobiles were bought. Also suppose in 1983 the price was $15,000 and 700,000 were purchases. How can it be explained that as the price went up the quantity demanded also went up? (*Hint:* Equilibrium is determined by the interaction of both demand and supply.) *(KQ2)*
2. It has been said that supply influences quantity demanded in that as supply increases, people want more of the product. Explain. *(KQ2)*
3. The age distribution of our population is changing. The average American is older. On the average, we are not only living longer but we are also having fewer children. This trend is expected to continue. What effect do you think this will have on the demand for toys, educational services, resort areas, and houses and on the profit opportunities for firms in these industries? *(KQ2)*
4. A price ceiling has been imposed on the price of gasoline in the United States. What effect would you expect this to have on our country's oil imports? *(KQ2)*
5. The supply of food production in the United States has been increasing faster than demand for food. What would you expect to happen to the price (relative to other prices) of food in the United States and the consequent relative income of farmers? *(KQ2)*
6. A successful "drink more milk" advertising campaign is expected to have what effect on the price and quantity of milk bought and sold? *(KQ2)*

7. Recently the government has increased its efforts to curtail the importation of illegal drugs into this country. What would you expect to happen to the street price of heroin? What would you expect to happen to the number of crimes committed by those addicted to heroin? *(KQ2, 6)*
8. Time and again it is notice that fans line up (sometimes a day or two in advance) to buy tickets to see famous rock groups. What can be said about the price of these tickets? Are they below, above, or at the equilibrium level? Why do you thing rock groups price their tickets as they do? *(KQ2)*
9. "Aspirin is aspirin." Why, then, is there a difference in the price of aspirin? *(KQ4)*
10. It has been said that the distribution of income in the United States is not fair. Do you agree or disagree? Why? *(KQ6)*
11. "Government needs to limit entry into some markets to prevent product proliferation and waste in production and advertisement." Discuss the implications of this statement with respect to consumer welfare. *(KQ6)*

Answers

Problems and Applications

1. a. Yes, because the laws of demand and supply hold.
   b. Quantity demanded equals 90; quantity supplied equals 40. Shortage equals 50. Price would rise because buyers would competitively bid up the price.
   c. Quantity demanded equals 70; quantity supplied equals 70. Equilibrium exists.
   d. Quantity demanded equals 50; quantity supplied equals 100. Surplus equals 50. Price would decrease because sellers would competitively bid down the price.
   e. Demand is negatively sloped; supply is positively sloped. (See the graph on page 50.)

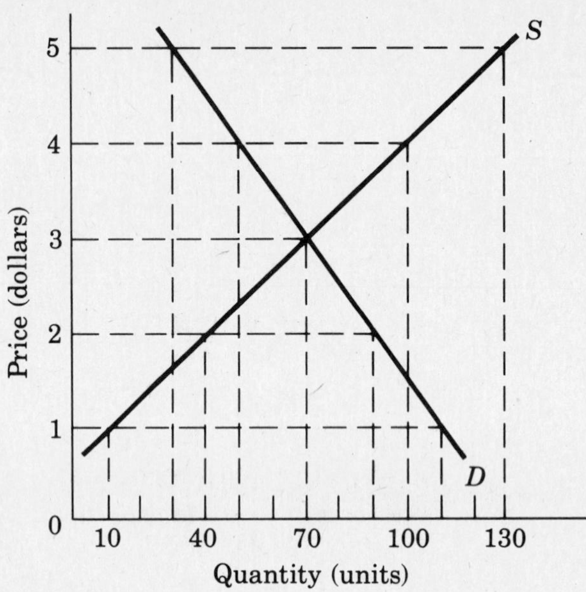

2. a. Equilibrium occurs at the intersection of D_1 and S_1.
   b. No, it would represent an increase in demand.
   c. Equilibrium occurs at the intersection of D_2 and S_1.
   d. Yes.
   e. Equilibrium occurs at the intersection of S_2 and D_1.
3. a. Equilibrium price and quantity occur where demand and supply intersect because there is no shortage or surplus.
   b. Demand would increase. An increase in demand is expressed graphically as a rightward shift. Both the equilibrium price and equilibrium quantity would rise because after the increase in demand the original equilibrium price would result in a temporary shortage. Therefore, price would be bid up by consumers, and consequently the equilibrium quantity would rise.
   c. Supply would decrease, causing equilibrium price to rise but equilibrium quantity to decline.
   d. A price floor is a legal price set above the equilibrium. The quantity demanded will decrease and the quantity supplied will increase. This would cause a surplus of beef.
4. a. Demand would increase, causing equilibrium price and quantity to rise. (See the graph on page 51.)

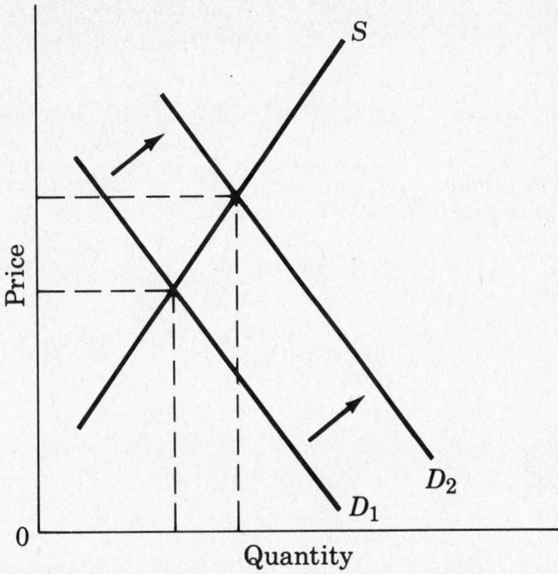

b. Demand will increase, but supply will decrease. Equilibrium price will rise, but we are uncertain as to the change in equilibrium quantity because it would depend on the magnitude of the changes in demand and supply.

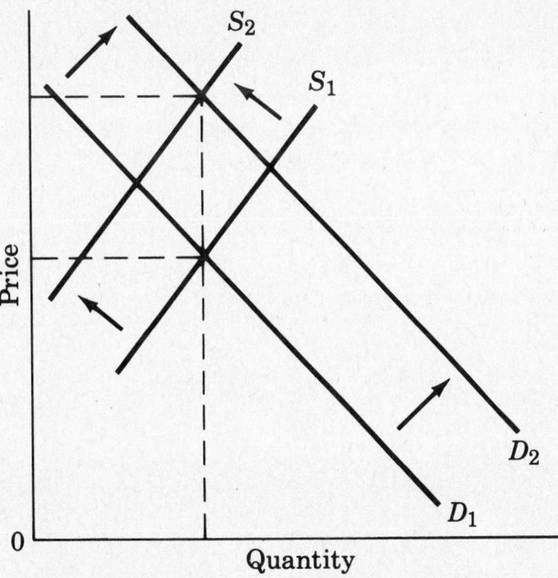

c. Supply would increase because businesses would now pay workers a smaller wage (businesses can now afford to produce a greater amount at any given price). Equilibrium price would decrease, but equilibrium quantity would increase.

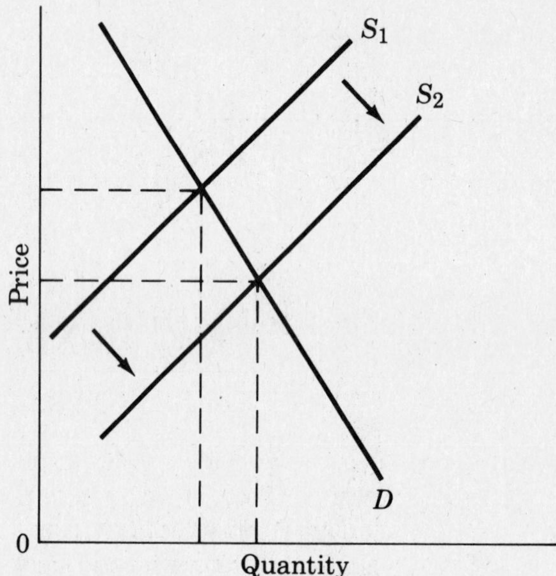

d. The supply of corn will decrease. The supply of soybeans will increase. The demand for soybeans increases. The equilibrium quantity will increase. This is certain. But we are not certain as to what will happen to the equilibrium price because it depends on the magnitude of changes in demand and supply. (See the graph on page 53.)

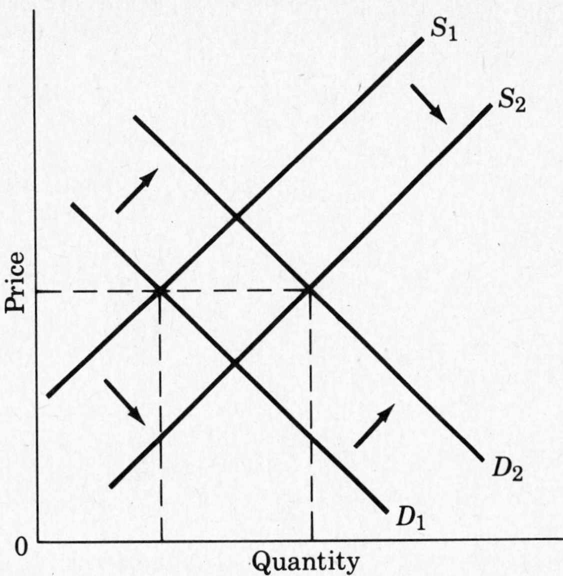

e. A decrease in equilibrium price is certain, but the change in equilibrium quantity is uncertain. The change in equilibrium quantity would depend on the magnitude of change in demand and supply.

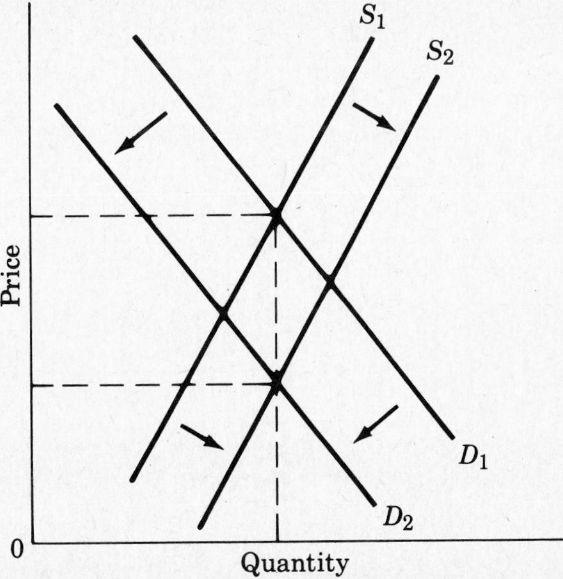

f. A decrease in equilibrium quantity is certain, but the change in equilibrium price is uncertain. The change in equilibrium price would depend on the magnitude of changes in demand and supply.

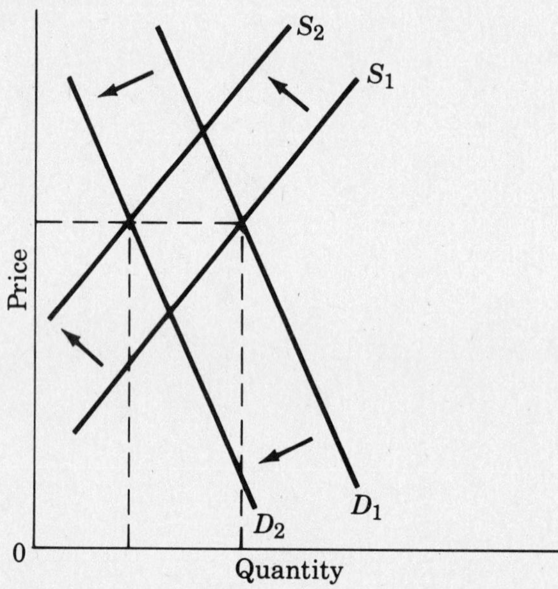

g. They are complements. The demand for hot dog buns would decrease. The equilibrium price and quantity would decrease. Can you explain why?

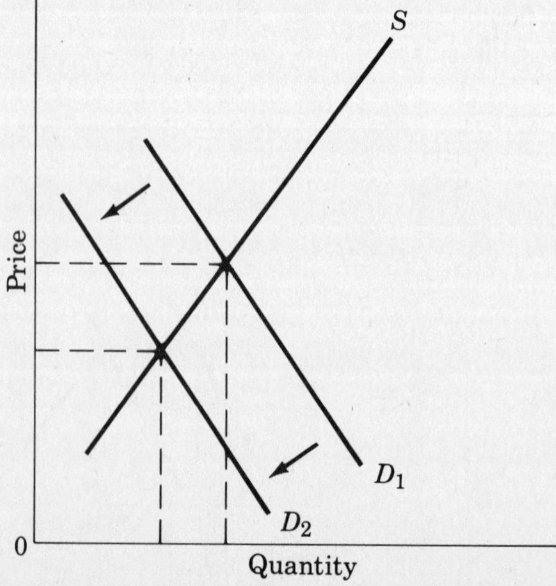

5. The calendar time associated with the short run or the long run will vary from industry to industry and from firm to firm within a given industry. The important thing to note is that the short run is any calendar time for which producers do not have the time to expand their production facilities. Any calendar time in which they can expand production facilities is the long run.
6. Income may not be fairly distributed, production costs may be imposed on people who do not consume a product, the market may produce socially undesirable products or services, competition may lead to product proliferation, or unscrupulous competitors may take advantage of customers' ignorance.
7. Examples could be: color and texture of packaging, after-sale service, status-appeal, convenience of location, and so on.

True-False

1. F: The law of demand states that consumers will buy more of a product when the price is low than when the price is high.
2. T   3. T
4. F: A change in any of the determinants of demand would cause a change in demand.
5. T
6. F: The law of supply states that as price increases the quantity supplied increases.
7. T   8. T
9. F: A surplus is a result of quantity supplied exceeding quantity demanded.
10. F: An increase in demand shows consumers are willing and able to pay a higher price to receive any given quantity.
11. T   12. T
13. F: Price ceilings cause a shortage.
14. F: Demand is negatively sloped while supply is positively sloped.
15. T   16. T
17. F: A free market is one in which equilibrium price and quantity are determined by the interaction of demand and supply.
18. T   19. T   20. T
21. F: Monopoly power or government regulation limiting freedom of entry and exit in a market is expected to decrease consumer welfare.

Multiple Choice

1. e *(KQ2)*	2. e *(KQ2)*	3. b *(KQ2)*
4. e *(KQ2)*	5. c *(KQ2)*	6. e *(KQ2)*
7. e *(KQ2)*	8. c *(KQ2)*	9. a *(KQ2)*
10. e *(KQ2)*	11. a *(KQ4)*	12. c *(KQ1)*
13. c *(KQ2)*	14. a *(KQ2)*	15. d *(KQ4)*
16. d *(KQ2)*	17. d *(KQ2)*	18. c *(KQ2)*
19. b *(KQ4)*	20. a *(KQ6)*	

CHAPTER 4

The Public Sector

Chapter Summary

Key Question 1: What does government do?

Key Question 2: What are the economic functions of government?

Key Question 3: Under what circumstances will markets "fail"?

Many economic decisions are made by government, whose policies strongly influence economic activity. Government involvement in our economy reallocates resources away form the private sector to the public sector (if we are at or near full employment). Government activity can also positively or negatively affect individual incentives to work, save, and invest for the future. In addition, several economic functions are the responsibility of government. These include: defining and protecting property rights; providing for public goods and services; reducing the inefficiencies associated with external costs and benefits; protecting common access resources; providing for health and income security; and providing macroeconomic stability.

Traditionally, one of the most important economic functions of government is to define and protect property rights, which are the permissible uses of resources, goods, and services. We are all better off with government protection of property rights because this frees human time and energy for specialization and trade based on comparative advantage and allows us to exchange the property rights to products in the market. Efficient trade, however, requires the use of money, and for money to be used, its purchasing power must remain relatively stable. Therefore a closely related governmental function is the establishment of a stable monetary system.

Another traditional role of government is to provide for public goods and services that would not otherwise be provided by the private sector. In this regard markets fail to produce enough public goods and services. Public goods and services are financed through forced taxation.

Still another function of government is to correct for externalities (spillovers). In the absence of government, the market system fails to allocate our resources efficiently when external benefits and costs are involved. That is, the market system fails by "overproducing" products that have external costs associated with them, and "underproduce" products that have external benefits associated with them.

External benefits are positive effects of production or consumption received by some third party not directly involved in the production or consumption of a good. Because of the external benefits associated with these goods or services, we as a society want more of them. So we call on government to correct for the underallocation of resources devoted to these goods and services by subsidizing their production and/or consumption. When the seller is subsidized, the supply curve shifts to the right. When the buyer is subsidized, demand increases. In either case, the equilibrium quantity increases, thereby increasing the amount of resources devoted to the item and its production. If the external benefit of some product is very large, the government itself may produce that product. If so, that product becomes a public good or service.

External costs are negative effects of production and consumption imposed on some third party not directly involved in the production or consumption of the product. When the external costs associated with these goods and services are considered, we as a society do not want as many of them. That is, they are being "overproduced." So we call on government to correct for the overallocation of resources devoted to these products by taxing or prohibiting their production and/or consumption (or by making the undesirable side effects illegal). If government taxes the production of the item, the supply curve will shift leftward equal to the amount of the tax. This leftward shift causes equilibrium quantity to decrease, thereby correcting for the overallocation. If the government makes production of the item illegal, we will experience the same result—the supply curve shifts to the left, correcting for the overallocation of resources devoted to production. If the government taxes consumption or makes consumption illegal, then demand shifts to the left, causing a decrease in the equilibrium quantity and correcting for the overallocation.

Key Question 4: Why are some resources overused and abused?

The market also fails to protect common access resources. The government attempts to protect common access resources through regulation. A common access resource will tend to be overused or abused if there is not enough of the resource to go around. A common access resource may also be overused or abused if people who use the resource do not account fully for the effects of their use of the resource on others because no one has the power to exclude users or to charge for their use.

Key Question 5: How can government-provided income-security programs be justified?

Another form of market failure is an inequitable (unfair) distribution of income. In recent years, the government has become involved in correcting for an inequitable distribution of income by providing income security and health insurance. Government attempts to redistribute income through taxation and the provision of welfare programs these taxes support. These efforts at providing greater security are justified as a means of providing the public good of poverty relief; in the absence of government poverty relief would be "unproduced."

Key Question 6: What can government do to stabilize the economy?

Another modern function of government is providing for macroeconomic stability. The federal government attempts to promote a high and stable level of employment, production, and prices by using the tools of macroeconomic policy. These tools are fiscal policy (the manipulation of federal spending and taxation policies) and monetary policy (the manipulation of the rate of growth in the nation's money supply). There is currently some debate over which type of macroeconomic policy is more effective in smoothing out the business cycle. Keynesians favor fiscal policy while monetarists argue that monetary policy is a more effective tool.

Key Question 7: What are the shortcomings of government actions?

Most of the economic functions of government are attempts to overcome the shortcomings of the market system. However, the government's track record has been less than perfect in correction for market failure. Even when government is able to correct market failure, such action may have undesirable side effects (excessively costly or monopolistic behavior). Like the free market system it attempts to correct, government also has its shortcomings.

Review Terms and Concepts

Market
Macroeconomics
Public goods and services
Private goods and services
Comparative advantage
Money

New Terms and Concepts

Private sector
Public sector
Budget deficit
Budget surplus
Property rights
Personal income taxes
Corporate income taxes
Excise taxes
Proportional tax system
Marginal tax rate
Average tax rate
Externalities
External benefits
External costs
Common access resources
Monopoly

General sales tax
Property tax
Progressive tax system
Regressive tax system
Macroeconomic policy
Fiscal policy
Monetary policy

Completion

	This chapter includes a discussion of the economic functions of govern-
public	ment in the ______________ (public/private) sector. The public sector
	entails the three levels of government—federal, state, and local. Govern-
	ment collects massive amounts of taxes and spends equally impressive
one third	amounts of money. The public sector accounts for nearly ____________
	(one half/one third) of the nation's output. The federal government's
personal income taxes	main source of receipts are ______________________ (personal income
	taxes/corporate income taxes) closely followed by social security con-
national defense	tributions. Its main outlay is for ______________________ (social
	security/national defense). At the state level, government's main source
state income and sales tax	of revenue is ______________________________ (state income and
	sales taxes/property taxes), most of which is spent on highways and
	schools. Local governments collect most of their receipts from
property taxes	______________________ (income taxes/property taxes) and spend
education	money primarily on ________________ (education/police and fire
	departments).
	Government is involved in the economy not only by collecting tax
regulation	revenues and spending this money but also through ________________
tax exemptions	and ______________________________. The effect of all this involve-
private	ment is to reallocate resources away from the ________________

public (private/public) sector to the ____________________ (private/public)
sector if we are at or near full employment. Other effects are to provide
incentives to work, save, and invest for the future.

The government is involved in the economy for many reasons. Some
of the functions the government undertakes are traditional; other functions are relatively new. But most functions are an outgrowth of
market __________________ (government/market) failure.

One of the most important traditional functions of government is to
property rights define and protect ________________________, which produces an
environment that is conducive to the market system. The market process
property rights is really the buying and selling of ________________________. It is an
orderly system. When people specialize in their comparative advantage
property rights and trade ________________________ in the market, this
increases __________________ (increases/decreases) our production possibilities
increases and __________________ (increases/decreases) our economic well-
being. But for specialization and trade based on comparative advantage
money to take place, we need _____________ to escape the inefficiencies of a
monetary barter system. Therefore, establishing a stable __________________
(monetary/fiscal) system is also a traditional function of government.

Another traditional function of government is to protect
common access ________________________ resources. Examples of such resources
regulation are air and water. These resources are protected by _______________
(regulation/people themselves). The protection of common access resour-
benefit ces also provides an external _______________ (benefit/cost) to the entire community.

Another traditional role of government is to provide for

public — ________________ (public/private) goods and services. These goods

would not — and services ___________________ (would/would not) be provided in

cannot — the absence of government, and individuals ____________ (can/cannot) be excluded form their benefits. These products, in other words, provide benefits to the entire community or nation as a whole.

Another function of government is to correct for externalities. Exter-

spillovers — nalities are also know as _________________________. An externality

benefit, cost — can be either a _______________ or a ________________. We call some products externalities because the benefit or cost associated with its production and/or consumption is external to the market. The market

does not — simply ________________ (does/does not) take into consideration the external cost or benefit. External costs or benefits spill over to some

third — ________________ (first/second/third) party. We can view this party as the entire community or nation. The other two parties are the

buyers, sellers — _________________ and _________________ of the product.

positive — External benefits have ____________ (positive/negative) effects on some third party when a particular product is bought and sold and the

does not — third party ____________ (does/does not) have to pay for the benefits. Because of the external benefits of such products, society would like to

more — have ____________ (less/more) of these products than have been provided by the market process. In other words, the market process has

underallocation — given rise to an ____________________________ (underallocation/ overallocation) of resources devoted to these products. The government can correct for this misallocation of resources by

subsidizing — _______________________ (taxing/ subsidizing) its production

and/or consumption. If the government subsidizes its production, this
increase would ________________ (increase/decrease) supply for this product,
increasing thereby ________________ (increasing/decreasing) the equilibrium quantity and correcting for the underallocation. If the external benefit of some product is very large, the government may provide for the product itself.
public Such a product is called a ______________ good or service.

negative External costs are __________________ (positive/negative) effects on some third party of the production and consumption of certain products.
less We want ______________ (more/less) of these types of products after we consider all of the negative side effects. Therefore, we can say the market
overallocation process has given rise to an ______________________ (underallocation/overallocation) of resources devoted to the production of these products. The government can correct for this misallocation of resources by
taxing ________________ (taxing/subsidizing) the producer and/or consumer or by making the undesirable side effects (or the production and/or con-
illegal sumption of the product) ______________ (legal/illegal). Consider pollution as an undesirable side effect in the production of some product. If we were to tax the producer or make illegal the emission of pollutants,
decrease this would cause a(n) ________________ (increase/decrease) in supply.
decrease The effect in the market is to ________________ (increase/decrease) the equilibrium quantity of the product, meaning that fewer resources would be devoted to the product, thereby correcting for the overallocation.

Another function of government is to correct for an inequitable distribution of income. That is to say, the government attempts to
income security provide for ______________________________________ and
health insurance ______________________________________. There are many methods

used. First, there is the progressive income tax, in which the percentage
increases — of income paid as taxes __________ (increases/decreases) as
income increases. The objective is to make after-tax income
more — __________ (more/less) equally distributed than before-tax
income. Other forms of taxes are also collected by the various levels of
government. The receipts are used in part to support the welfare system.

The final major function of government is to provide for
macroeconomic — __________ stability. Instability in economic
activity has always occurred and is commonly referred to as the
business — __________ cycle. The government attempts to smooth out
these periodic but recurring fluctuations in employment and production
macroeconomic — with the use of __________ policy. This can be broken down
fiscal, monetary — into __________ policy and __________ policy.
Fiscal — __________ policy is the manipulation of government spending
monetary — and taxation policies; __________ policy is the manipulation of the
growth rate in the nation's money supply. There is currently some debate
over which policy is most effective in smoothing out the business cycle.
fiscal — Keynesians argue for __________ (fiscal/monetary) policy, and
monetary — monetarists favor __________ (fiscal/monetary) policy.

Problems and Applications

1. List the major market failures and the corresponding governmental functions to correct for these failures.
2. Consider external costs (spillovers) and the methods government uses to correct for the overallocation of resources devoted to their production. Below is a list of goods and services that impose external costs. Determine which are taxed and which have had their undesirable side effects declared illegal. Also indicate whether it is the producing or consuming side that is taxed or made illegal or both.

(Can you think of the undesirable side effects associated with the production and/or consumption of these goods and services?)
a. burning trash within city limits
b. prostitution
c. tires
d. trucks
e. gambling casinos
f. littering the highway
g. liquor

3. a. What causes an inequitable distribution of income in the first place?
   b. Who determines what is a fair distribution of income in the United States?
4. The federal government has enacted antitrust laws and regulations throughout the years. Under which of the governmental functions would this activity fall?
5. a. Is university education an external benefit or cost service? Explain.
   b. What does government do to correct for the misallocation of resources devoted to its production?
6. a. Is cancer research an external benefit or cost service?
   b. What could government do to correct for the misallocation of resources devoted to its production?
7. Indicate whether each of the following products impose external benefits or costs.
   a. fireworks
   b. city, state, and national parks
   c. zoos
   d. water treatment plants
   e. polio vaccine
   f. public health clinics
8. Describe the different types of government failure.

True-False

For each item, indicate whether the statement is basically true of false. If the statement is false, rewrite it so it is a true statement.

F 1. Government activity reallocates resources from the public sector to the private sector.

____ 2. The market process is really the buying and selling of property rights.

____ 3. Air and water are examples of public goods and services.

____ 4. Making it illegal to sell fireworks (external cost product) within city limits is an attempt to decrease supply of fireworks within city limits, thereby correcting for the overallocation of resources devoted to fireworks.

____ 5. Public goods and services are a result of either of two situations: either (a) they would not be provided in the absence of government, or (b) there are very large spillover benefits associated with them, and therefore they would be grossly underproduced in the absence of government.

____ 6. The relative size of the public sector as compared to the private sector has remained relatively stable over the last forty years.

____ 7. Public goods and services are financed by voluntary contributions and are purchased by the private sector.

____ 8. A stable monetary system is needed to facilitate specialization and trade.

____ 9. More public goods means less private goods if we are at full employment (on our production possibilities curve).

____ 10. Resources will be misallocated in the market system if not properly adjusted by government in the case of external costs and benefits.

____ 11. Monetary policy is the manipulation of the public budget.

____ 12. The marginal tax rate is the rate at which additional income is taxed.

____ 13. A proportional income tax would mean people would pay the same percentage of their income as taxes regardless of their income levels.

Multiple Choice *Choose the one best answer for each item.*

____ 1. Goods and services from which no one can be excluded are

a. external benefit goods and services.
b. public goods and services.
c. common access resources.
d. welfare benefits.
e. all of the above.

_____ 2. The federal government spends most of its revenues on
   a. social security.
   b. education.
   c. income security.
   d. energy programs.
   e. national defense.

_____ 3. The progressive personal income tax
   a. is the major source of revenue to the federal government.
   b. is an income tax in which the percentage of income paid as taxes increases as income increases.
   c. is not the major source of revenue for state governments.
   d. tries to make after-tax income more equally distributed than before-tax income.
   e. is all of the above.

_____ 4. A budgetary deficit means
   a. receipts are greater than outlays.
   b. outlays are greater than receipts.
   c. outlays are equal to receipts.
   d. fiscal policy is greater than monetary policy.
   e. none of the above.

_____ 5. Efficiency in the use of society's resources may require
   a. government spending for goods and services that would not be provided at all by the private sector.
   b. government subsidizing of the production and/or consumption of external benefit goods and services.
   c. government regulation over the use of some resources.
   d. government macroeconomic policy to provide for higher rates of employment than would be provided by the private sector.
   e. all of the above.

_____ 6. The providing of national defense is primarily a responsibility of
   a. consumers.
   b. businesses.
   c. government.
   d. those who lose a war.
   e. monetary policy.

_____ 7. A monopoly
   a. is the sole seller of a good or service.
   b. is the sole buyer of a good or service.
   c. charges a competitive price.

d. cannot earn any more profit than a competitive firm.
e. has one competitor.

_____ 8. When using its taxation and spending powers to stabilize the macroeconomy, the federal government is using
a. market policy.
b. monetary policy.
c. political policy.
d. fiscal policy.
e. its powers to correct for externalities.

Refer to the following diagram to answer the next two questions. Assume we begin with demand durve D and supply curve S_1 and the government is not involved in this market.

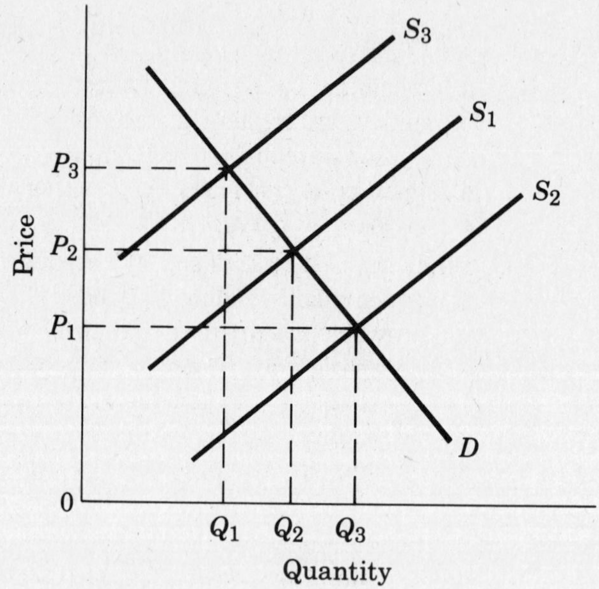

_____ 9. If a spillover cost is discovered for this product, the government should take steps to
a. shift supply from S_1 to S_2.
b. shift supply from S_1 to S_3.
c. control the price of the product at P_1.
d. increase the equilibrium quantity.
e. increase demand.

_____ 10. If a spillover benefit is discovered for this product, the government should take steps to

a. shift supply from S_1 to S_2.
b. shift supply from S_1 to S_3.
c. control the price of the product at P_3.
d. decrease the equilibrium quantity.
e. decrease demand.

_____ 11. Property rights are bought and sold
a. by government but not individuals.
b. by individuals but not government.
c. by both government and individuals.
d. abroad but not in the United States.
e. by none of the above.

_____ 12. Macroeconomic policy affects
a. the level of employment and production.
b. composition of employment and production.
c. distribution of the nation's output.
d. the general level of prices.
e. all of the above.

_____ 13. Which of the following is not a form of market failure?
a. Instability in the macroeconomy
b. An inequitable distribution of income
c. An inefficient allocation of resources with respect to externalities
d. Lack of public goods and services
e: All of the above are forms of market failure.

_____ 14. If government alters demand to correct for an external benefit, the result will be
a. a decrease in the equilibrium price of the product.
b. a decrease in the equilibrium quantity of the product.
c. an increase in the equilibrium quantity of the product.
d. fewer resources devoted to the production of the product.
e. increased taxes imposed on the consumption of the product.

_____ 15. Which of the following statements is true?
a. More government involvement in the economy reallocates resources away form the public sector to the private sector if we are at or near full employment.
b. Government involvement in the economy may affect people's willingness to work, save, and invest.
c. A progressive tax system has constant marginal tax rates.

d. The main source of revenue to the federal government is corporate income taxes.
e. The main expenditure for state governments is police and fire protection.

Discussion Questions

1. We know that public goods and services are a result of one of two situations. Either (a) they would not be provided by the private sector, or (b) they would be grossly underproduced by the private sector because of the very large external benefits associated with them. Let's consider the second situation more closely. There are external benefits associated with adequate medical care and adequate housing. Do you think these external benefits are large enough that medical care and housing should be supplied by government, or do you think the market system provides enough medical care and housing to the general public to be adequate? Put another way, should medical care and housing be provided through the market system (private sector) and allocated on the basis of ability to pay, or should they be provided by the government (public sector) so that no individual can be denied their benefits? (*Note:* The discussion may focus on whether medical care and housing is a privilege or a right.) *(KQ2, 3, 5, 7)*
2. If your neighbor puts up a fence between your property lines at his expense, is this a spillover benefit or cost to you? *(KQ3)*
3. If the person who sits next to you in economics takes very good notes and shares them with you, does this provide you with an external benefit or cost? If a benefit, should the school provide tutors in such classes? Is this why graduate teaching assistants are provided? *(KQ3)*
4. What do you think would be the consequences of a privately owned army? Why does the government provide for national defense? *(KQ3)*
5. What is your conception of a fair distribution of income? Is the distribution of income in the United States fair? What do you think the government should do in this regard? *(KQ3, 5)*
6. In the absence of governmental attempts to bring about a more equitable distribution of income, what do you think would happen to the distribution of income over time? *(KQ5)*

7. If we are below full employment (at a point inside the production possibilities curve), is it possible for more public goods to be produced without any decrease in the production of private goods? *(KQ3, see also Chapter 2, KQ4)*
8. Can we view price ceilings and price floors as a governmental attempt to redistribute income? For example, is a price ceiling such as rent control an attempt to prevent an undesired redistribution of income away from tenants to landlords? Is a price floor such as an agricultural price-support system an attempt to cause a desired redistribution of income away form the general public to farmers? *(KQ3,5)*
9. Can a progressive tax system add stability to the business cycle? *(KQ2)*
10. Can you explain why heroin is an external cost product? What has the government done to correct for the misallocation of resources devoted to its production? *(KQ3)*

Answers

Problems and Applications

1. Market failures
   –overuse of common access resources
   –lack of public goods and services
   –misallocation of resources with respect to externalities
   –business cycle

   Corresponding governmental functions
   –regulation of common access resources
   –to provide for public goods and services
   –to correct for misallocation of resources with respect to externalities
   –macroeconomic policy to smooth out business cycle
2. a. It is illegal to produce the smoke.
   b. It is illegal to produce (sell) and consume (buy) prostitutes in most areas of the world.
   c. Tire consumption is taxed (excise tax) because of the problems of disposing of them after they are used (such as the smoke associated with burning them or the space they take up at dump sites).
   d. Truck drivers have to pay highway taxes because of the congestion problem they pose (or would otherwise pose).

e. It is illegal to sell or buy the services of gambling casinos in most regions of the country.
f. It is illegal to produce this litter.
g. It is illegal to buy or sell liquor to minors, and its production and consumption is also taxed (retail excise tax) in many regions of the world.

3. a. An inequitable distribution of control over resources causes an inequitable distribution of income.
   b. We all do by way of the political process—we vote for those who most closely represent our views.
4. This activity does not easily fit any of the functions discusses in the text. However, antitrust laws and regulations do promote economic efficiency by fostering competition (inhibiting monopoly power), and their enactment is another function of government.
5. a. University education is an external benefit service for many reasons. For example, it enhances the culture and increases the productivity of our nation's people. With greater levels of education, a country usually experiences less crime and violence.
   b. The government subsidizes its production (most universities receive massive amounts of money from state legislatures) and its consumption (many students receive governmental financial aid assistance in one form or another).
6. a. Cancer research is an external benefit service.
   b. Government could subsidize its research.
7. They are all external benefit products except for fireworks. Fireworks are generally considered an external cost product when fired within city limits (because of the noise and the possibility of fire and physical injury to innocent bystanders). The government attempts to correct for the spillover costs associated with fireworks on the consumption and production sides of the market by making it illegal to buy and/or sell them or explode them within city limits. On the other hand, note that the external benefit products are either subsidized by government on the consumption or production sides of the market, or they are provided by government itself.
8. First, all government activity requires resources, but the government will not necessarily use these resources more efficiently than the private sector. Also, the government is itself a kind of monopoly. In addition, government may not always act in the best interest of the majority but may yield instead to special interest groups. Or

government may act to promote its own jobs or interests. Furthermore, vote-seeking politicians may act to promote short-term, clear-cut benefits to the detriment of long-term goals of the general public. Finally, there is the controversial issue concerning government intervention versus freedom.

True-False

1. F: Government activity reallocates resources from the private sector to the public sector if we are at full employment.
2. T
3. F: Air and water are examples of common access resources.
4. T
5. T
6. F: The relative size of the public sector as compared to the private sector has increased in the last forty years.
7. F: Public goods and services are financed by taxes and are purchased by the public sector.
8. T
9. T
10. T
11. F: Monetary policy is the manipulation of the rate of growth in the nation's money supply.
12. T
13. T

Multiple Choice

1. b *(KQ3)*	2. e *(KQ1)*	3. e *(KQ2)*
4. b *(KQ1)*	5. e *(KQ3)*	6. c *(KQ1)*
7. a *(KQ4)*	8. d *(KQ6)*	9. b *(KQ3)*
10. a *(KQ3)*	11. c *(KQ4)*	12. e *(KQ6)*
13. e *(KQ3)*	14. c *(KQ3)*	15. b *(KQ1, 7)*

CHAPTER 5

Measurements of the Macroeconomy

Chapter Summary

The measurements of macroeconomic activity introduced in this chapter are (1) gross national product (GNP), which is a measure of our overall output; (2) other measurements of output and income levels such as national, personal, and disposable personal income, which are measures of consumer buying power; (3) the unemployment rate; and (4) the inflation rate.

Key Question 1: Why is GNP the most common measure of economic production for the macroeconomy?

GNP is the most common measure of economic production for the macroeconomy because it is such a broad measure that can be calculated with relative ease and precision and with no subjective value judgments being made. GNP is defined as the *current* market value of all the *final* goods and services produced in the economy in a given time period, usually one year. GNP can be calculated by the expenditure approach or the resource cost-income approach. In terms of the expenditure approach, GNP is really a price-times-quantity calculation. If we were to take the current price of each final product times the quantity of that product produced and then add these dollar values together, we would get GNP.

That is, to compute GNP, we simply add all current purchases for final goods and services made by consumers, businesses, government, and international trade. These purchases include personal consumption expenditures (household purchass of consumer products); gross private domestic investment (business purchases of plant and equipment, inventories, and residential housing construction); government purchases of goods and services at the federal, state, and local level; and net exports. Net exports equal exports minus imports and can be positive or negative depending on our balance of payments. We can add all purchases to arrive at GNP because the total dollar amount of purchases spend on goods and services must equal the total dollar amount of production. That is, total expenditures must equal the total value of goods and services produced.

The resource cost-income approach simply sums the dollar income payments to all resource owners. Both approaches to calculating GNP yield the same results. This is because what is spent eventually ends up as someone's income.

Key Question 2: What are the deficiencies of GNP statistics?

There are several shortcomings of GNP. First, because of price changes due to inflation and deflation, comparisons of GNP over time are difficult to make. To eliminate the influence of inflation and deflation, GNP figures must be adjusted for price changes, which results in real GNP. Real GNP is calculated with the aid of the implicit GNP price deflator index and is often referred to as constant dollar, or inflation-adjusted, GNP. By comparing real GNP figures for different years, meaningful comparisons of actual production over time can be made. Note that absolute values of real GNP figures are less meaningful than the relative changes in real GNP over time.

GNP is also deficient in the sense that even if real GNP is increasing, the population may be growing even faster and people will be no better off. A better indication of whether production per person is increasing is to calculate per capita real GNP. However, this figure says nothing about how national output is distributed among the population.

Another deficiency of GNP is that it omits some production activity in the economy. GNP does not include nonmarket production, nor does it count production activity in the underground economy.

Still another shortcoming is that GNP is not, and was never intended to be, a measure of our social welfare. GNP simply measures our output level, but indicates nothing about how this output may be distributed. Other factors that affect our welfare which GNP does not measure include changes in our leisure time, changes in the quality of goods and services, and the undesirable side effects associated with economic activity and growth. The measure of (or net) economic welfare attempts to make adjustments in GNP for these factors to obtain a more accurate assessment of social welfare.

Key Question 3: What are other non-GNP measures productive activity in the macroeconomy?

There are other social accounts of our output and income levels that are useful measurements of macroeconomic activity. The net national product (NNP) measures new additions to our output level. But NNP does not tell us how much income was created in producing this output level. By making adjustments to NNP, we derive national income, or the total payment made to owners of productive resources for the use of those resources during a given time period. But because not all income earned is received and because not all income received is earned, modifications to national income must be made to arrive at personal income. Personal income is that part of national income paid to individuals as opposed to businesses. By subtracting personal income taxes from personal income, we get disposable personal income. Disposable personal income tells us how much money people have to spend or save after taxes. And it is disposable personal income that primarily determines the level of personal consumption expenditures.

Key Question 4: What does the unemployment rate measure?

Key Question 5: What are the shortcomings of unemployment rate statistics?

Another type of measure of economic activity is the unemployment rate. The unemployment rate is an indicator of lost production because unemployment represents a loss of potential output that can never be realized. However, the unemployment rate may not reflect the true rate of unemployment because of government procedures in calculating unemployment, voluntary unemployment, and unreported employment and unemployment. Furthermore, unemployment rate statistics don't reflect the full extent of social hardships associated with being out of work. Finally, there will always be some natural rate of unemployment and we cannot expect to even be able to reduce unemployment to zero.

Key Question 6: What is inflation and how is it estimated in the macroeconomy?

The final measure of economic activity discussed in the text is the inflation rate. It is defined as an increase in the general level of quality–adjusted prices over a period of time. The consumer price index (CPI), the producer price index (PPI), and the GNP implicit price deflator index are popular estimates of inflation. The CPI is often referred to as the cost of living index. However, the CPI does not give a true indication of changes in the cost of living for all consumers.

Review Terms and Concepts

Microeconomics
Macroeconomics
Positive economics
Normative economics
Economic growth

New Terms and Concepts

Gross national product (GNP)
Final goods and services
Intermediate goods and services
Value added
Expenditure approach
Resource cost-income approach
Underground economy
Measure of (or net) economic welfare (MEW or NEW)
Real (or constant dollar) gross national product
Net national product (NNP)
National income
Personal income
Disposable personal income
Unemployment rate
Labor force
Hidden unemployed
Underemployed workers
Labor force participation rate
Inflation
Consumer price index (CPI)

Nominal, money, or current dollar gross national product
Implicit GNP price deflator index
Consumer unit
Producer price index (PPI)

Completion

	Among the many ways of measuring macroeconomic activity, one of the
current	most important is GNP. GNP is defined as the ________________
final	(current/fixed) market value of all the ___________ (final/intermediate)
given	goods and services produced in the economy in a ___________
	(given/changing) time period. By intermediate goods and services, we
	mean those products that are purchased for resale or for further process-
	ing. By final goods and services, we mean those products that are pur-
consumption	chased for _______________ (consumption/further processing). We
final	count only ____________ (final/intermediate) products. To count inter-
overcounting	mediate products would be _________________ (overcounting/under-
	counting). If intermediate products were included in GNP, we would
overstate	__________________ (overstate/understate) our output level. Note also
current	that GNP is calculated using _________________ (current/fixed) prices.
	Because prices change over time, meaningful comparisons of GNP over
cannot	time _______________ (can/cannot) be made. To make meaningful com-
real	parisons of GNP, we must use ___________ (real/current) GNP figures.
	An inflation-adjusted GNP, or a constant dollar GNP, is synonymous
real	with ___________ GNP. We use real GNP because output levels of dif-
the same	ferent years are all stated in terms of __________________ (the same/
	different) base year's prices. Because prices are held constant, the only
output	reason real GNP changes is if there are changes in the ______________

(output/price) level. However, absolute values of real GNP are not impor-
relative tant. What is important are the ________________ changes in real GNP
over time.

To compute GNP in terms of the expenditures approach, we simply
add ____________ all purchases made by consumers, businesses, government, and international trade. That is, the total dollar amount of pur-
equal chases of goods and services must ______________ the total dollar
output (production) amount of ________________.

One of the shortcomings of GNP is that meaningful comparisons over
time cannot be made unless GNP is adjusted for price changes that occur
real over time. In other words, we must use ____________ (money/real)
GNP to make meaningful comparisons over time. There are other
shortcomings of GNP as a measure of economic activity. One of them relates to changes in population. To account for these changes, we use
per capita ________________ GNP, which is equal to real GNP divided by the
population level. If we have an increase in GNP but our population in-
decrease creases even more, then per capita GNP will ________________
(increase/decrease). However, useful per capita GNP may be in determining whether production per person is increasing, this measure still says
nothing about how that output may be distributed. This brings us to
is not another shortcoming of GNP. It ____________ (is/is not) a measure of
social well-being (or social welfare). Factors such as changes in our
leisure time, the quality of goods and services, and the production of undesirable side effects all affect our social welfare, and these factors
are not ____________ (are/are not) taken into consideration when calculating

GNP. Another shortcoming is that GNP omits some production activity in our economy.

There are other social accounts of our output and income levels that are of interest. Net national product (NNP) equals GNP minus the

capital consumption allowance

________________________. A capital consumption allowance is one big depreciation charge against the entire economy. It

replace

represents output that is used to __________ worn out plant and

subtracting

equipment. National income is derived from NNP by __________ (adding/subtracting) indirect business taxes and other items from NNP. National income represents the cost to businesses in producing this year's output. But not all income received is earned, nor is all income earned received. Adjustments to national income gives us

personal

__________ (personal/disposable) income. Disposable personal

personal income taxes

income is equal to personal income minus __________ (indirect business taxes/personal income taxes). Disposable personal income represents the amount of income consumers have at their disposal to consume or save as they wish.

The unemployment rate is another measure of economic activity that interests consumers, businesses, and government. It is equal to the

number of unemployed

________________________ (number of employed/number

labor force

of unemployed) divided by the __________ (population level/labor force). We would never expect the unemployment rate to get

5–6 percent

below __________ (8–9 percent/5–6 percent) for various reasons. There are problems in estimating the unemployment rate, but the government does the best it can. Voluntary unemployment would

overstate

__________ (overstate/understate) the real unemployment rate.

overstating
is not

Unreported employment, such as in the underground economy, results in the unemployment rate ________________ (overstating/understating) the real unemployment problem. However, underemployment creates hardships that ___________ (is/is not) measured is calculating the unemployment rate.

consumer price index (CPI)
prices
cost of living
divided
1967

Finally, the inflation rate is another important measure of economic activity. One way to estimate inflation is the ____________________ (consumer/government price index). Changes in the CPI reflect changes in ____________ (output/prices). The CPI is often referred to as the ______________________________ index and is equal to the cost of some representative market basket of goods and services in any one year ________________ (divided/multiplied) by the cost of the same market basket in some base year, all multiplied by 100. The base year for the CPI is ___________ (1972/1967).

Problems and Applications

1. National income is the total of payments made to owners of productive resources for the use of those resources. We know what our resource categories are. What particular payments constituting national income are made to each of the resource categories?
2. Consider the example of bread production discussed in the text and reprinted below, which demonstrates that only final goods and services are counted in calculating GNP.

Wheat sold to miller	$100
Flour sold to baker	200
Bread sold to the consumer	300
	$600

a. Which of these transactions should be included in calculating GNP?

b. If bread was the only product produced in this economy, what is GNP?
c. How much value was added at each stage of the production process?

3. We know GNP is a price times quantity calculation. Keeping this in mind, consider the economy described below. Assume the economy produced only three products: X, Y, and Z.

	Prices Per Unit		Output	
Production	1967	1988	1967	1988
X	$1	$1	10	15
Y	$2	$4	30	35
Z	$5	$6	20	20

a. What is GNP for 1967?
b. What is GNP for 1988?
c. Assume 1967 is the base year. Compute the CPI for 1967.
d. Assume 1967 is the base year. Compute the CPI for 1988.
e. What was the average percent increase in prices from 1967 to 1988?
f. If we assume that GNP divided by the CPI all multiplied by 100 equals real GNP, what is real GNP for 1967?
g. How would we interpret real GNP for 1967?
h. If we assume that GNP divided by the CPI all multiplied by 100 equals real GNP, what is real GNP for 1988?
i. How would we interpret real GNP for 1988?
j. What is the percent increase in GNP from 1967 to 1988?
k. What is the percent increase in real GNP from 1967 to 1988?
l. Why is the percent increase in GNP greater than the percent increase in real GNP?

4. Why are intermediate products excluded in calculating GNP?
5. In calculating GNP, we know total expenditures must equal the total value of goods and services produced. Why is it that net exports can be either positive or negative in calculating total expenditures?
6. What are some examples of nonmarket production and underground production activity, and why are they not added in calculating GNP?
7. What do we mean by the labor force? Why can we never expect to have 100 percent of the labor force employed?

True-False

For each item, indicate whether the statement is basically true or false. If the statement is false, rewrite it so it is a true statement.

_____ 1. NNP measures real growth in production rather than maintenance of existing productive capacity.

_____ 2. GNP can be computed by adding up the total market value of final goods and services sold but not by adding the total expenditures made on those final goods and services.

_____ 3. An underemployed worker is characterized in part as someone who is working part-time but would like to work full-time.

_____ 4. When calculating real GNP, we adjust for price changes so we can get a better estimate of the real output level.

_____ 5. Comparisons of real GNP figures over time are more valid when concentrating on absolute changes.

_____ 6. The base year in calculating a CPI is 1972.

_____ 7. If inventory levels increase for some year in an economy, then this should be added when calculating GNP.

_____ 8. Real GNP measures current output in current prices.

_____ 9. The labor force participation rate has increased in the last decade or so.

_____ 10. Government policy cannot affect the different social accounts.

_____ 11. Unemployment represents a loss of potential output that is lost forever.

_____ 12. The CPI is also known as a "misery index."

_____ 13. If I paid you to clean my house and you paid me to clean your house, GNP would increase.

_____ 14. If real GNP is increasing, the per capita GNP may increase, decrease, or remain the same.

_____ 15. National income can be viewed as the total cost of acquiring the resources to produce the output of a given period.

_____ 16. GNP is the dollar value of all the final goods and services produced in the economy in a given time period.

_____ 17. The labor force participation rate is the number of people in the labor force divided by the number of people who are not institutionalized.

_____ 18. The inflation rate could be coming down, but we may still be experiencing some inflation.

_____ 19. Including intermediate goods and services would result in a smaller GNP.

_____ 20. We count only final goods and services when calculating GNP.

_____ 21. Real GNP is a better measure of our real output level and must be used to compare output levels of different years.

Multiple Choice

Choose the one best answer for each item.

_____ 1. Full employment of labor exists when
   a. the unemployment rate is zero.
   b. when every member of the population above the age of sixteen who is not institutionalized is fully and efficiently employed.
   c. 5–6 percent of the labor force is unemployed.
   d. the unemployment rate is 3 percent.
   e. the unemployment rate is 8 percent.

_____ 2. Inflation is best defined as
   a. an increase in the price of a product.
   b. an increase in the purchasing power of money.
   c. an increase in real GNP.
   d. an increase in the general level of prices.
   e. all of the above.

_____ 3. If GNP is increasing, then
   a. real GNP must also be increasing.
   b. real GNP must be decreasing.
   c. the general level of prices must have increased.
   d. the national output level must be increasing.
   e. real GNP may be increasing, decreasing, or remaining the same.

_____ 4. In any given year, which of the following accounts would tend to be smallest?
   a. GNP
   b. NNP
   c. Disposable personal income
   d. Personal income
   e. National income

_____ 5. Which of the following is not a component in calculating GNP?
   a. Disposable income
   b. Personal consumption expenditures
   c. Gross private domestic investment
   d. Net exports
   e. Government purchases of goods and services

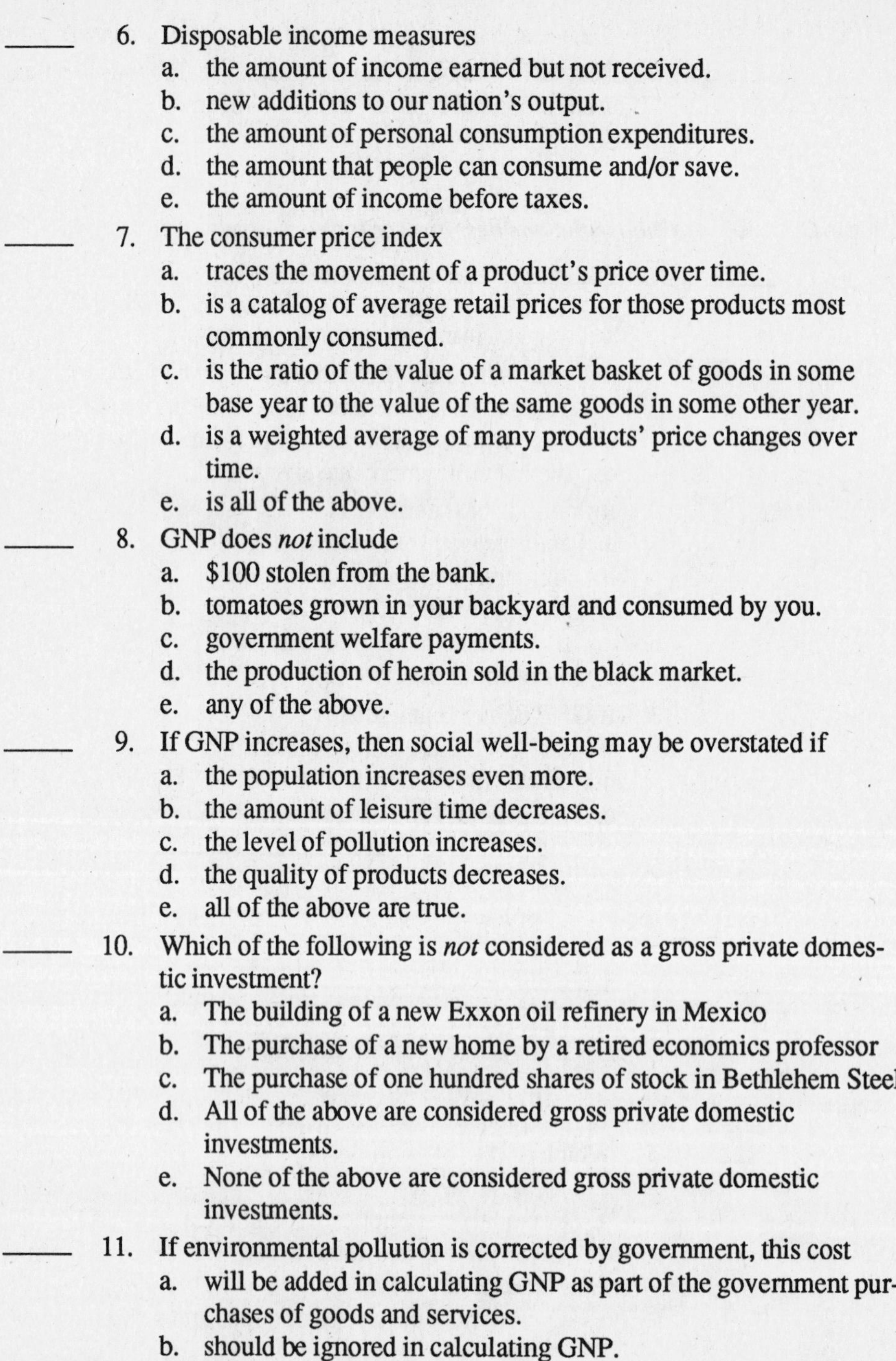

____ 6. Disposable income measures
   a. the amount of income earned but not received.
   b. new additions to our nation's output.
   c. the amount of personal consumption expenditures.
   d. the amount that people can consume and/or save.
   e. the amount of income before taxes.

____ 7. The consumer price index
   a. traces the movement of a product's price over time.
   b. is a catalog of average retail prices for those products most commonly consumed.
   c. is the ratio of the value of a market basket of goods in some base year to the value of the same goods in some other year.
   d. is a weighted average of many products' price changes over time.
   e. is all of the above.

____ 8. GNP does *not* include
   a. $100 stolen from the bank.
   b. tomatoes grown in your backyard and consumed by you.
   c. government welfare payments.
   d. the production of heroin sold in the black market.
   e. any of the above.

____ 9. If GNP increases, then social well-being may be overstated if
   a. the population increases even more.
   b. the amount of leisure time decreases.
   c. the level of pollution increases.
   d. the quality of products decreases.
   e. all of the above are true.

____ 10. Which of the following is *not* considered as a gross private domestic investment?
   a. The building of a new Exxon oil refinery in Mexico
   b. The purchase of a new home by a retired economics professor
   c. The purchase of one hundred shares of stock in Bethlehem Steel
   d. All of the above are considered gross private domestic investments.
   e. None of the above are considered gross private domestic investments.

____ 11. If environmental pollution is corrected by government, this cost
   a. will be added in calculating GNP as part of the government purchases of goods and services.
   b. should be ignored in calculating GNP.

c. should be subtracted from GNP because pollution reduces our social welfare.
d. will decrease our social welfare.
e. will be subtracted in calculating GNP as part of the gross private domestic investment.

_____ 12. GNP may decrease if
a. personal consumption expenditures increase.
b. gross private domestic investment decreases.
c. exports increase.
d. imports decrease.
e. government purchases increase.

_____ 13. Net exports may be defined as
a. total exports minus personal consumption expenditures.
b. government purchases minus taxes.
c. exports minus imports.
d. imports minus exports.
e. GNP minus imports.

_____ 14. Which of the following is a shortcoming of unemployment rate statistics?
a. They count the underemployed.
b. They count discouraged workers.
c. They measure foregone production.
d. They do not measure social hardship associated with unemployment.
e. They are adjusted for changes in the relative size of the labor force.

Discussion Questions

1. Why does unemployment represent a loss of potential output that can never be realized? *(KQ4, 5)*
2. We know the business cycle is the ups and downs in macroeconomic activity. If real GNP is dependent on time, what would a business cycle curve look like? *(KQ1)*
3. What negative effects may economic growth have on social welfare? What positive effects? *(KQ2)*
4. What problems may one encounter in comparing the GNP of two different economies? *(KQ2)*

Answers

Problems and Applications

1. Our resource categories are land, labor, capital, and entrepreneurial talent. Owners of land receive rental income. Labor receives wages and salaries. Capital receives interest income. The entrepreneur receives profit income. The total of all of these payments is national income.
2. a. Only the final transaction (the bread sold to the consumer) should be included.
   b. $300
   c. When the farmer produced the wheat to sell the miller, $100 of value was added to the bread. The miller added $100 of value to the bread because he bought the wheat from the farmer for $100 and sold the flour to the baker for $200. The baker added $100 to the value of the bread because he bought the flour from the miller for $200 and sold the bread to the consumer for $300.
3. a. $170
   b. $275
   c. 100
   d. 137.5
   e. 37.5%
   f. 170 = (170/100)100
   g. The dollar value of output in 1967 in terms of 1967 prices
   h. 200 = (275/137.5) 100
   i. The dollar value of output in 1988 in terms of 1967 prices
   j. 105/170 = 61.7%
   k. 30/170 = 17.6%
   l. Because real GNP has been adjusted for changes in the price level and GNP has not. In essence, real GNP holds prices constant and thereby only measures changes in the real output level.
4. If we include intermediate goods and services, we would grossly exaggerate our output level by overcounting. In addition, if we included intermediate products and experienced a change in the structure of an industry or industries, GNP would change for that reason alone and not because of any change in our output level. For these reasons, we include only final goods and services.
5. Net exports equals exports minus imports. Our exports is a positive number in calculating total expenditures because it represents spending by foreigners on our output. We subtract imports because this represents spending on foreigners' output—not spending on our output. Net exports can be a positive or negative figure

depending on our balance of payments. If we are running a balance of payments surplus, then net exports is a positive figure because we are selling more abroad than we are buying abroad. If we are running a balance of payments deficit, then net exports is a negative figure.

6. Examples of nonmarket production include food produced and consumed on the farm, home haircuts, homemaker services, and other home services. These things are excluded because it is difficult to put a value on services people provide for themselves when the quality of production varies from person to person and because it is difficult to determine what should not be included. Examples of production activity in the underground economy include bartering, selling goods and services for cash to avoid paying taxes, and sale of illegal items. These transactions are not included because we can't calculate how much of this activity actually takes place.
7. The labor force included all those who are willing and able to work who are sixteen years of age and are not institutionalized. We can never expect to have 100 percent of the labor force employed because there will always be people changing jobs, the jobs available may not be the type of work some people want, some people would rather collect unemployment compensation than work, and because some people may not have the skills necessary for even the simplest tasks. Some economists believe the unemployment rate will never get below 5-6 percent because of the effects of the minimum wage and unions.

True-False

1. T
2. F: GNP can be computed by adding up the total market value of final goods and services sold or by adding the total expenditures made on those final goods and services.
3. T 4. T
5. F: Comparisons of real GNP figures over time are more valid when concentrating on relative changes.
6. F: The base year in calculating a CPI is 1967.
7. T
8. F: Real GNP measures current output in some base year's prices.

9. T
10. F: Governmental policy can affect the different social accounts.
11. T
12. F: The CPI is also known as a "cost of living index."
13. T 14. T 15. T
16. T 17. T 18. T
19. F: Including intermediate goods and services would result in a larger GNP.
20. T 21. T

Multiple Choice

1. c *(KQ4)* 2. d *(KQ6)* 3. e *(KQ2)*
4. c *(KQ3)* 5. a *(KQ1)* 6. d *(KQ3)*
7. d *(KQ6)* 8. e *(KQ2)* 9. e *(KQ2)*
10. e *(KQ1)* 11. a *(KQ2)* 12. b *(KQ1)*
13. c *(KQ1)* 14. e *(KQ5)*

CHAPTER 6

Macroeconomic Problems and Policies

Chapter Summary

Our macroeconomic goals are full employment, price stability, and high and rising incomes provided by economic growth. Our major macroeconomic problems are inflation, unemployment, stagflation, and lagging economic growth.

Key Question 1: Is inflation a major macroeconomic problem in the United States?

Persistent high peacetime inflation is a relatively recent phenomenon in the United States. There are three general types of inflation: demand-pull, cost-push, and structural. To deal with inflation, one must first identify which type of inflation is at work because different types require different policy responses. The second major problem in dealing with inflation is to overcome any possible political objections to implementing the appropriate policies.

Key Question 2: Is unemployment a major macroeconomic problem in the United States?

Unemployment is a problem because of the human hardship it creates and because it represents a loss of potential output that can never be realized. In addition, an increase in unemployment can result in higher government spending for unemployment compensation and other types of welfare relief, which means higher taxes for the reduced working population. The GNP gap and Okun's law are useful in measuring some of the effects of unemployment.

There are three general types of unemployment: transitional (frictional), structural, and cyclical. Transitional unemployment occurs when people move from one job to another requiring similar skills. Structural unemployment results from changes in the structure of the economy. Structural and transitional unemployment will always exist, and these types of unemployment make up the 5-7 percent natural unemployment rate. Cyclical unemployment is caused by an insufficient demand for products and is not part of the natural unemployment rate. Different policies are required to combat the different types of unemployment.

Key Question 3: Are stagflation and lagging productivity major macroeconomic problems in the United States?

The third major macroeconomic problem is stagflation, or the persistence of high rates of unemployment and inflation at the same time. In the past, an increase in unemployment has been accompanied by a decrease in inflation, and vice versa. This inverse relationship is shown by the Phillips curve. But recent experience implies a positive relationship between unemployment and inflation that is particularly striking if the two rates are summed to obtain what is referred to as the misery index. Currently, economists disagree on how and why stagflation can occur.

Lagging economic growth is also a macroeconomic problem and refers to a slowdown in growth of worker productivity and real income. Because a nation's income is tied to workers' output level (their productivity), there can be no increase in people's incomes without an increase in productivity. The government could simply give people more money, but this would simply drive up prices.

Key Question 4: What are business cycles?

Our macroeconomic problems can be viewed in the context of the business cycle. The business cycle slopes upward over time, expressing the long-run trend of economic growth. But this long-run trend is punctuated by fluctuations in economic activity known as business cycles. Business cycles have four phases: a recession, a trough, a recovery, and a peak. Business cycles are measured from peak to peak, and they vary in intensity and in length of time, which makes predictions difficult to make. However, economists do forecast changes in the business cycle with some success by using leading economic indicators and the composite index.

Key Question 5: What are the major macroeconomic schools of thought?

Economists differ widely on what should be done to smooth out the business cycle because they disagree over what really causes these fluctuations. The classical, Keynesian, monetarist, supply-side, and rational expectations schools of thought stress different factors as the primary causes of macroeconomic problems.

Before the 1930s, the classical school dominated economic thinking. According to classical theory, an increase in unemployment would cause decreases in wage rates, and therefore businesses would hire more labor, correcting for the unemployment. Unemployment that is experienced must be due to laws or unions that prevent downward flexibility of wages and prices. Therefore, classical economists advocate minimal government intervention and the abolishment of all legal impediments to wage and price flexibility. Their belief is that lagging growth and productivity reflect consumers' unwillingness to forego current consumption in order to have greater rates of economic growth.

Keynesians believe that macroeconomic instability stems from changes in total spending. That is, if total spending is down, so is the level of economic activity (and vice versa). To correct for a recession, the government should increase expenditures, decrease taxes, or increase the money supply to reduce the interest rate (which would increase investment spending). The converse would be prescribed for inflationary pressures. Note, however, that Keynesian theory may be inappropriate for addressing simultaneously the dual problems of inflation and unemployment.

The monetarist school of thought views economic instability as a monetary problem. That is, inflation is a result of too many dollars pumped into the economy. To attack inflation, monetarists would advocate a decrease in the money stock. An increase in the money stock would help correct unemployment.

The supply-side school is appropriately labeled because it contends that most macroeconomic problems stem from the supply side of the economy. According to supply-side economists, the solution to unemployment, inflation, and lagging productivity is to reduce tax rates, thereby increasing people's willingness to work, save, and invest, which, in turn, will increase employment and output. And if the quantity of money in circulation stays constant (or increases less than the quantity of goods and services), then the increased supply of goods and services should exert downward pressure on prices. Finally, lower tax rates *may* increase government revenues because more people will be working and so more taxes can be collected.

The rational expectations theorists focus on what people have come to expect given certain government policies. This school of thought assumes that people will acquire some rationally determined amount of information about the impact of government activity and will act out of their own self-interest on that information. But in so doing, people's actions will negate the policies of government.

A macroeconomic model useful in analyzing and comparing the various schools of economic thought is the aggregate demand and aggregate supply model. The aggregate demand curve shows the inverse relationship between the general price level and the total desired spending on national output. The aggregate supply curve shows the positive relationship between the general price level and the total quantity of goods and services that will be produced during a given time period. The equilibrium price level and output level occur where the two curves intersect. By changing the level of aggregate demand (total spending) or aggregate supply (total output), we can predict what happens to the price level and national output. Indeed, changes in the business cycle may be viewed in the context of a shifting aggregate demand or aggregate supply curve.

Review Terms and Concepts

Macroeconomics
Economic growth
Real GNP
Unemployment
Inflation
Consumer price index
National income
Personal income
Disposable personal income
Labor force participation rate
Underemployed workers

New Terms and Concepts

Misery (or discomfort) index
Demand-pull or buyer's inflation
Cost-push or sellers' or suppliers' inflation
Structural inflation
Structural unemployment
Hidden unemployment
Natural rate of unemployment
Potential output (or GNP)
GNP gap
Okun's law
Phillips curve
Stagflation
Trend
Business cycle
Recession
Aggregate supply
Transitional (frictional or search) unemployment
Cyclical unemployment
Trough
Recovery
Peak
Leading indicator
Coincident indicator
Lagging indicator
Composite index
Neutrality of money
Classicism
Keynesian
Monetarist
Supply-side
Rational expectations
Aggregate demand
Real balances or wealth effect

Completion

Answers	
full employment price stability, economic growth	Three significant macroeconomic goals are ______________________, ______________________, and ______________________.
fiscal monetary	We attempt to realize these goals through ________________ policy and ________________ policy.
inflation, unemployment stagflation, lagging economic growth (or productivity)	Our major macroeconomic problems include ______________________, ______________________, ______________________, and ______________________.

There are three general types of inflation. Inflation characterized by too many dollars chasing too few goods and services is known as

demand-pull — __________ inflation. Cost-push inflation is a result of

increases — __________ (increased/decreased) production costs that

up — push prices __________ (up/down). Finally, structural inflation is due

structure — to changes in the __________ of the economy.

There are two major problems in dealing with inflation. First, one must

identify — __________ which type of inflation is the major problem

different — because different types require __________ (the same/ different) policy responses. The second major problem is to overcome

political — possible __________ objections to implementing the appropriate policies.

Unemployment is a macroeconomic problem because it creates human

hardship, loss — __________ and because it represents a __________ of

realized — potential output that can never be __________. Unemploy-

heavier — ment may also create __________ (lighter/heavier) tax burdens

increased — on the reduced working population to finance the __________ (reduced/increased) government spending for unemployment compensation and welfare payments.

There are three general types of unemployment. The two types that are

transitional (frictional) — considered natural (or normal) are __________

structural — and __________. Transitional unemployment is charac-

changing — terized by people __________ jobs. Structural unemployment

obsolete — occurs when workers' jobs have become __________ because of technological development. Together, transitional and structural un-

5–7 — employment account for the __________ percent natural

cyclical — unemployment rate. The final type of unemployment is ____________
recession — unemployment, which is the result of a ______________ (recovery/
different — recession). The three types of unemployment require ______________
(one/different) policy (policies) because each type of unemployment is
caused by different variables.

Another major macroeconomic problem is the persistence of high rates
of unemployment and inflation at the same time. This is known as
stagflation — ____________________. According to conventional wisdom, there
should be a trade-off between unemployment and inflation. The
Phillips curve — _________________________ is a graphical representation of the
inverse — ________________ (positive/inverse) relationship between unemployment and inflation. The conventional view is that changes in fiscal and
along the — monetary policy would move us __________________ (to a higher/
along the) Phillips curve. But experiences in the 1970s and 1980s sug-
positive — gest there may be a ___________________ relationship between the
unemployment rate and the inflation rate. In other words, we could have
higher — a higher unemployment accompanied by ___________ (lower/higher)
inflation. This long-run positive relationship is particularly striking if we
add the two rates together to obtain what is sometimes referred to as the
misery — ________________ index.

Finally, there is the macroeconomic problem of lagging growth in
economic growth — productivity and real income, or slower rates in __________________.
To achieve higher income levels, our economy must achieve
higher — ________________ (lower/higher) output levels. To achieve higher
increase — output levels, workers' productivity must __________________
(increase/decrease). In other words, higher income levels require greater

Answers	Text
productivity	__________________. And because we get greater output levels
	over time with greater productivity, achieving greater rates of economic
productivity	growth requires greater ______________. Therefore, productivity
	is the link to economic growth and higher income levels.
	The business cycle is a reflection of our major macroeconomic
economic growth	problems. It slopes upward over time, reflecting ______________.
	This is the trend. But the trend is punctuated by ups and downs in macro-
business	economic activity called ______________ (business/growth)
peak	cycles. A business cycle is measured from __________ to
peak, four	__________. There are _________ (four/six) phases to any
recession	given business cycle. The first phase is the ______________. By
six	definition, this phase must last at least _________ (six/twenty-four)
	months to be considered a recession. A very severe decrease in economic
15 percent	activity with unemployment of at least ______________ (15
depression	percent/20 percent) is called a ______________. A trough,
recovery	which is where the recession ends and the ______________
months	begins, may last for a few days or several ____________
increase	(months/years). A recovery is an ______________ (in-
may not	crease/decrease) in macroeconomic activity that ______________
	(will/may not) take us to full employment. A peak is where the recovery
recession	levels off and another ______________ begins. However, the
six	peak cannot be distinguished until a new recession is declared—at least
	_________ (nine/six) months after the decline in real GNP. Business
vary	cycles _________ (are the same/vary) in intensity and time. This
more difficult	makes forecasting ______________ (easier/more difficult).
	However, economists do attempt to forecast changes in

real GNP	__________ (GNP/real GNP) and the consequent effects on
	employment, inflation, and our nation's income. In other words,
business cycle	economists do attempt to predict the __________
economic indicators	with the use of leading __________.
	Economists also use a combination of leading economic indicators
composite index	known as the __________ of lead-
	ing economic indicators.
disagree	Economists __________ (agree/disagree) over what should
	be done to smooth out fluctuations in the business cycle because they
disagree	__________ (agree/disagree) over the causes of these fluctua-
	tions. Classical economists believe most fluctuations are due to
inflexibility	downward __________ (inflexibility/flexibility) of wages
laws, unions	and prices caused by __________ and/or __________.
less	Therefore, they advocate __________ (more/less) government
fewer	intervention in the economy and __________ (more/fewer)
demand	unions. The Keynesians emphasize the __________ (demand/
	supply) side of the macroeconomy as the key determinant of the level of
total spending (or total demand or aggregate demand)	economic activity. In other words, they believe that changes in __________ cause fluctuations in the business
more	cycle. Therefore, Keynesians advocate __________ (more/less)
	government intervention in economic affairs. The monetarist school of
money	thought focuses on __________ (expectations/money) as the
	key variable in macroeconomic activity. Monetarists advocate a
steady	__________ (steady/varying) growth rate in the money
supply	supply. The supply-side theorists emphasize the __________
lower	(supply/demand) side of macroeconomics. They believe __________

(lower/higher) tax rates will stimulate the economy toward full employment. Finally, the rational expectations school emphasizes the influence

rational — of people's ________________ (rational/irrational) expectations regarding the effects of certain government policies. The idea is that people acting out of their own self-interest will behave in such a manner as to

negate — ________________ (enhance/negate) government fiscal and monetary policy. In the extreme, this means government fiscal and monetary policy

incapable — is ________________ (capable/incapable) of correcting for the macroeconomic problems. Although economists belong to different schools of thought, they generally agree that money, expectations, total demand, and total supply are the principle variables in macroeconomic activity.

different — However, different schools of thought emphasize ________________ (different/the same) variables.

It has been argued that changes in the business cycle can be viewed in

demand — the context of changes in aggregate ____________________ and

supply — aggregate ____________________. Aggregate demand relates the

general price level, total desired spending — ________________________ to ________________________

inverse — on national output. This relationship is ________________ (positive/

positive — inverse). Aggregate supply is the presumed ____________________

general price level — (positive/inverse) relationship between the ____________________ and the total quantity of goods and services that will be produced during a given time period. The equilibrium price level and output level is located where the two curves

intersect — ____________________. By changing

can — aggregate demand and/or aggregate supply, we ____________ (can/cannot) predict what will happen to the price and output levels. How and

debatable

why aggregate demand and aggregate supply change is ______________ (known/debatable).

Problems and Applications

1. Assume we are faced with demand-pull inflation. What type of fiscal and monetary policies would you recommend to reduce this type of inflation?
2. Explain how demand-pull and cost-push inflation could be related. In other words, might these types of inflation feed upon each other?
3. What is the economic cost of unemployment?
4. List the different types of unemployment and indicate how long each type may be expected to occur.
5. What is one of the differences between transitional and structural unemployment?
6. What are some changes in the structure of the economy that could cause structural unemployment?
7. What type of fiscal and monetary policies would Keynesians recommend to reduce cyclical unemployment?
8. In the past, how have American workers increased productivity and economic growth?
9. We know that most economists agree that money, expectations, total spending, and the total supply of goods and services are the main variables that effect macroeconomic activity. List the modern schools of economic thought and, for each school, indicate which variable is emphasized as the principal cause of the business cycle.
10. In the context of the aggregate demand and aggregate supply model, determine what happens to the general price level and national output and income levels given the following changes.
    a. An increase in aggregate demand
    b. A decrease in aggregate demand
    c. An increase in aggregate supply
    d. A decrease in aggregate supply
    e. An increase in aggregate demand and an increase in aggregate supply
    f. An increase in aggregate demand and a decrease in aggregate supply

g. A decrease in aggregate demand and a decrease in aggregate supply
h. A decrease in aggregate demand and an increase in aggregate supply

11. What is the difference between a recession and a depression?
12. How are competition and structural inflation related?

True-False

For each item, determine whether the statement is basically true or false. If the statement is false, rewrite it so it is a true statement.

_____ 1. Demand-pull inflation is characterized by too many goods and services chasing after too few dollars.

_____ 2. Cyclical unemployment is considered "normal" in that it will always occur.

_____ 3. Persistent peacetime inflation has been particularly acute in the last decade or so.

_____ 4. One of the problems in dealing with inflation is to identify which type of inflation is politically objectionable.

_____ 5. Transitional unemployment can persist for years.

_____ 6. Stagflation is the combination of persistently high rates of unemployment and inflation.

_____ 7. Economic growth is one of our macroeconomic problems.

_____ 8. Price stability means no inflation.

_____ 9. Unemployment is a problem only because it represents a loss of potential output that can never by realized.

_____ 10. The Phillips curve expresses a positive relationship between unemployment and inflation.

_____ 11. A trend consists of many business cycles.

_____ 12. In a depression, the unemployment rate is 15 percent or more.

_____ 13. Economists agree on what should be done to address the macroeconomic problems.

_____ 14. Keynesians advocate active fiscal and monetary policy to smooth out the business cycle.

_____ 15. The monetarists emphasize the total supply of goods and services as the key variable affecting the business cycle.

_____ 16. If we had an increase in aggregate demand and an increase in aggregate supply, then the equilibrium national output and income level would rise, but we are uncertain as to what the equilibrium price level will do.

_____ 17. Cost-push inflation is characterized by an increase in the costs of production, which pushes prices up.

_____ 18. The natural rate of unemployment consists of transitional and structural unemployment.

Multiple Choice *Choose the one best answer for each item.*

_____ 1. Cyclical unemployment is a result of
   a. people voluntarily quitting their jobs and expecting to start their new jobs in a few weeks.
   b. a deficiency in total demand.
   c. an increase in real GNP.
   d. technological developments that render some jobs obsolete.
   e. a recovery in the business cycle.

_____ 2. A peak is
   a. an upward trend.
   b. the top of an inflationary spiral.
   c. when the recovery ends and a new recession begins.
   d. when the recession ends and a new recovery begins.
   e. when a recession becomes a depression.

_____ 3. Stagflation is
   a. the persistent, simultaneous occurrence of transitional and structural inflation.
   b. the persistent, simultaneous occurrence of transitional and structural unemployment.
   c. the persistent, simultaneous occurrence of demand-pull and cost-push inflation.
   d. the persistent, simultaneous occurrence of unemployment and inflation.
   e. the difference between real GNP and potential real GNP.

_____ 4. Different policy may be required to address
   a. the different types of unemployment.
   b. the different types of inflation.
   c. the different phases of the business cycle.
   d. the different macroeconomic problems.
   e. all of the above.

_____ 5. The Phillips curve shows
  a. that an increase in unemployment will cause a decrease in inflation.
  b. the positive relationship between unemployment and the price level.
  c. the inverse relationship between the price level and the misery index.
  d. the economic cost of unemployment.
  e. stagflation.

_____ 6. Which of the following is *not* a type of unemployment?
  a. Transitional
  b. Structural
  c. Cost-push
  d. Cyclical
  e. None of the above

_____ 7. According to the cost-push theory of inflation, an increase in the general price level is most likely to be caused by
  a. a recession.
  b. an increase in total spending at a rate faster than an increase in the total supply of goods and services.
  c. a decrease in the competition among firms.
  d. strong labor union contracts.
  e. an increase in cyclical unemployment.

_____ 8. The inflation of the late 1970s that was blamed on OPEC is an example of
  a. demand-pull inflation.
  b. cost-push inflation.
  c. structural inflation.
  d. wage-push inflation.
  e. profit-push inflation.

_____ 9. The business cycle
  a. can be viewed in the context of shifting aggregate demand and aggregate supply curves.
  b. has four phases.
  c. is the periodic but irregular fluctuations in the level of macroeconomic activity.
  d. has an upward trend.
  e. is described by all of the above.

_____ 10. An increase in aggregate demand will
  a. be interpreted as a leftward shift in the aggregate demand curve.

b. cause an increase in the general level of prices and an increase in the national output and income levels.
c. cause a decrease in the general level of prices and a decrease in the national output and income levels.
d. cause the aggregate supply curve to shift to the right.
e. cause a decrease in the general price level.

____ 11. If we are faced with inflation, the monetarists would advocate which of the following policies?
a. An increase in the growth rate of the money supply
b. An increase in government spending and a decrease in taxes
c. A decrease in government spending and an increase in taxes
d. A decrease in growth rate of the money supply
e. None of the above because expectations would negate any policy move on the part of the government.

____ 12. According to Keynesian theory, a recession may be caused by
a. a decrease in investment spending.
b. an increase in government spending.
c. a decrease in taxes.
d. an increase in the total supply of goods and services.
e. an increase in the growth rate of the money supply.

____ 13. Which of the following is a macroeconomic problem?
a. Full employment
b. Price stability
c. Economic growth
d. Supply-side theory
e. None of the above

____ 14. Which of the following is most likely to cause an increase in productivity?
a. A decrease in the amounts of capital used with labor
b. The discovery of a new synthetic fuel to replace the use of fossil fuels
c. An increase in wages
d. A decrease in tax rates
e. None of the above

Discussion Questions

1. We know that monetary policy is rather effective in controlling demand-pull inflation. How effective is it in controlling cost-push inflation? *(KQ1)*

2. What causes each of the phases of the business cycle? *(KQ4)*
3. What are the political implications of each of the various schools of economic thought? *(KQ5)*
4. Why is Keynesian theory accused of being rather ineffective in addressing the problem of stagflation? *(KQ3, 5)*
5. Do you thing there are other macroeconomic goals that should be pursued? For instance, what about economic freedom, economic security, or an equitable distribution of income? Are these goals and others you think of easily measured (quantified)? If goals are not easily quantifiable, is there greater or less confusion in defining and implementing policy to realize them? Do the particular goals we pursue help define our macroeconomic problems? *(KQ1, 2, 3)*
6. Has the Phillips curve shifted to the right, or is it simply incorrect in assuming an inverse relationship between unemployment and the general price level? *(KQ3)*
7. One of the reasons for structural unemployment is that technological developments have rendered some jobs obsolete. For instance, some jobs that were once done by people are now done by machines. Give as many recent examples of this type of structural unemployment as you can. *(KQ2)*
8. Is there any connection between Herbert Hoover's "trickle-down" theory and the supply-side theory? *(KQ5)*
9. What could government do to reduce each type of unemployment? *(KQ2, 5)*

Answers

Problems and Applications

1. Demand-pull inflation occurs when planned expenditures (total spending) increases faster than total output. What needs to be done is to slow total spending down (to decrease it). Through fiscal policy, the federal government could decrease government spending and/or increase taxes. A decrease in government spending will lower total spending, while an increase in taxes will decrease personal consumption expenditures and gross private domestic spending. In terms of monetary policy, government should slow down the growth rate in the money supply.
2. They are related in that they can feed on each other. An increase in total demand greater than an increase in output will cause the

general price level to rise (demand-pull inflation). As prices rise, workers will demand higher wages. If they are able to receive higher wages (perhaps because of strong unions), production costs increase, which will push up prices (cost-push inflation). Moreover, an increase in workers' incomes may cause more demand-pull inflation, which may cause more cost-push inflation, and so on.

3. The economic cost of unemployment is the loss of potential output that can never be realized.
4. Transitional (frictional) unemployment may last a few days to a few weeks. Structural unemployment can persist for years. Cyclical unemployment generally lasts for a period of weeks to several months.
5. One of the differences is that those who are transitionally unemployed have salable skills while some of those who are structurally unemployed do not have salable skills (because their skills are no longer in demand).
6. Examples of changes include more and stronger unions (which limit membership to keep wages high) that could cause fewer employment opportunities; more and more women entering the labor force, thereby increasing the labor force participation rate; increases in technology that render jobs obsolete; an increase in the demand for certain types of labor in areas to which workers are unwilling to relocate, even when demand for their labor in their own area has decreased; and a decline in competition among businesses.
7. In terms of fiscal policy, increased government spending and/or a decrease in taxes will stimulate total spending, which causes greater employment. In terms of monetary policy, increasing the money supply will decrease the price of money (or interest rate), which will stimulate total spending by increasing investment.
8. By improving their skills through education and training programs, by using greater amounts of capital (machines), and by discovering new and less costly sources of energy and other scarce resources.
9. Keynesians: total spending
   Monetarists: money
   Supply-siders: total supply of goods and services
   Rational expectations theorists: expectations
10. a. The general price level increases, and national output and income increases.
    b. The general price level decreases, and national output and income decreases.

c. The general price level decreases, and national output and income increases.
d. The general price level increases, and national output and income decreases.
e. The change in the general price level is uncertain, but national output and income must increase.
f. The general price level must increase, but the change in national output and income is uncertain.
g. The change in the general price level is uncertain, but national output and income must decrease.
h. The general price level must decrease, but the change in national output and income is uncertain.

11. According to the Department of Commerce, a recession is a decline in macroeconomic activity that is at least six months long. If the decline is very severe with unemployment of 15 percent or more, then it is a depression.
12. If the business community experiences a structural change that results in a decrease in competition, structural inflation may result.

True-False

1. F: Demand-pull inflation is characterized by too many dollars chasing after too few goods and services.
2. F: The natural rate of unemployment is considered "normal" in that it will always occur.
3. T
4. F: One of the problems in dealing with inflation is to identify which type of inflation is at work.
5. F: Structural unemployment can persist for years.
6. T
7. F: Economic growth is one of our macroeconomic goals.
8. F: Price stability means acceptable rates of inflation.
9. F: Unemployment is a problem because it represents a loss of potential output that can never be realized and because it creates human hardship.
10. F: The Phillips curve expresses an inverse relationship between unemployment and inflation.
11. T 12. T

13. F: Economists disagree on what should be done to address the macroeconomic problems.
14. T
15. F: The monetarists emphasize money as the key variable affecting the business cycle.
16. T 17. T 18. T

Multiple Choice

1. b *(KQ2)* 2. c *(KQ4)* 3. d *(KQ3)*
4. e *(KQ1, 2, 4)* 5. a *(KQ3)* 6. c *(KQ2)*
7. d *(KQ1)* 8. b *(KQ1)* 9. e *(KQ4)*
10. b *(KQ5)* 11. d *(KQ5)* 12. a *(KQ5)*
13. e *(KQ1, 2, 3)* 14. b *(KQ5)*

CHAPTER 7

The Meaning and Creation of Money

Chapter Summary

Key Question 1: What is money?

Key Question 2: What determines the value of money?

Key Question 3: What are the three types of demand for money?

Key Question 4: What are our major forms of money?

Money takes different forms in different cultures, but all money serves several functions. Money is anything that is generally acceptable as a medium of exchange and that acts as a store of purchasing power. Another function of money is to act as a standard of value (or unit of account). For example, if product X costs $2 and product Y costs $1, then society values X twice as much as Y.

American money is fiat currency. Fiat currency has no real intrinsic value (after all, the dollar bill is only paper), and it cannot be redeemed for anything else (such as silver or gold). People accept this fiat currency as payment because they are confident that others will accept it now and in the future and that the government will keep the purchasing power of the dollar reasonably stable over time through appropriate fiscal and monetary policy.

The opportunity cost of holding money is the foregone interest rate that could have been earned or the foregone products that could have been purchased. But people do hold on to money because the benefits of doing so are at least equal to the opportunity cost. People demand money for transactions and for precautionary and speculative reasons. The demand for money is affected by economic variables including personal income, the general price level, expectations about changes in the general price level, the yields of various financial assets, and the interest rate.

The amount of money that exists in the economy at any one time depends on how we define the money stock. Economists use the terms money supply and money stock interchangeably. The narrowest definition is M1, followed by M2, M3, and then L.

Key Question 5:
What constitutes our banking system?

The American banking system can be divided into depository institutions and the Federal Reserve System (commonly known as simply the Fed). Depository institutions include commercial banks, savings and loan associations, mutual savings banks, and credit unions. Because of the Depository Institutions Deregulation and Monetary Control Act of 1980, all depository institutions are now under partial control of the Fed, and there is really no difference in the services offered by these institutions.

The Fed is run by a seven-member Board of Governors. The Board of Governors is aided in their policymaking decisions by the Federal Open Market Committee. The twelve Federal Reserve District Banks implement the policy set by the Fed.

The Fed serves many functions. However, the most important function of the Fed is to oversee monetary policy by altering the growth rate of M1 (or M2) primarily through the purchase or sale of government-issued bonds (known as open market operations), or by changing the discount rate or the reserve requirement ratio. First, however, the Fed must change excess reserves of banks by one or more of these methods before they can change the money stock. Excess reserves are equal to total reserves minus required reserves.

The Fed holds reserves of banks called reserve deposits. Banks hold reserve deposits at the Fed because it aids in accounting procedures (especially for the clearance of checks). A particular bank's vault cash plus their reserve deposits equals their total reserves. However, not necessarily all of their reserve deposits are required to be held on deposit at the Fed. The actual dollar amount of reserves required to be held on deposit at the Fed (known as required reserve, or the reserve requirement) is determined by the reserve requirement ratio (also known as the required reserve ratio). The reserve requirement is some percentage of a bank's demand deposit liabilities that must be kept on deposit at the Fed. Determined by the Fed, this percentage is often called the required reserve ratio (or the reserve requirement ratio). By subtracting required reserves from total reserves one obtains excess reserves.

Other functions of the Fed include (a) providing the economy with needed currency; (b) acting as a fiscal agent for the U.S. Treasury; (c) supervising and regulating depository institutions; (d) making loans to eligible banks as banks would to us (the interest rate charged by the Fed is called the discount rate); and (e) providing for the clearance of checks.

Key Question 6:
How do checks transfer money?

When checks are cleared by the Fed the total stock of money does not change. Whenever any person writes a check to another person, the demand deposit of the person who receives the check increases, while the deposit of the person writing the check decreases. The bank that pays the check loses reserve deposits while the bank that receives the check gains those reserve deposits. The money supply has not changed.

Key Question 7: How do banks create money?

A bank creates money when a loan is made because the borrower receives cash and/or a credit to their demand deposit (checking account), which is money. In exchange, the borrower signs a promissory note (which is not money but just a fancy IOU) to repay the loan. In this way, the money supply increases. Conversely, money is destroyed when a loan is repaid. In other words, there is less M1 (and M2) in the hands of the nonbanking public.

A bank cannot lend out more money than it has as excess reserves. In other words, the money-creating ability of a single bank is limited dollar for dollar with its excess reserves. Recall that excess reserves equal total reserves minus required reserves. If the Fed changed the reserve requirement ratio this will change required reserves and therefore excess reserves and the money-creating ability of banks. Therefore, the reserve requirement ratio (or, required reserve ratio) is a means whereby the Fed can control the supply of money.

Although a single bank is limited in its money-creating ability by its excess reserves, the entire banking system can create money by a multiple of its excess reserves. To calculate the potential change in the supply of money for the entire banking system, simply take the change in excess reserves and multiply by the reciprocal of the reserve requirement ratio, often referred to as the money multiplier.

Key Question 8: What causes the money stock to fluctuate?

Several important points should be noted. First, the potential change in the supply of money works in both an upward and a downward direction. Second, the potential change in the supply of money may not be met. Third, the money stock tends to fluctuate because of the unevenness in the granting and repayment of loans and changes in the public's willingness to hold money in the form of either currency or demand deposits.

Review Terms and Concepts

Specialization and trade
Comparative advantage
Production possibilities
Opportunity Cost
Monetary policy
Money

New Terms and Concepts

Liquidity
Transactions demand for money
Precautionary demand for money
Fiat money
Demand deposits
Time deposits
Depository institutions

Speculative demand for money
Asset demand for money
Money stock
M1
Checkable deposits
M2
M3
L
Full-bodied commodity money
Representative commodity money
Federal funds rate
Reserves
Reserve deposits
Target
Velocity *(V)*
Financial intermediary
Reserve requirement ratio (required reserve ratio)
Reserve requirement
Excess reserves

Completion

Money is anything that is generally acceptable as a
medium of exchange ________________________________ and that acts as a store of
purchasing power ______________________________. Another function of money is
standard of value (unit of account) that it acts as a ______________________________. Anything that
serves these three functions is money.

fiat Money in the United States is ________________ currency, which
less means its intrinsic value is ________________ (less/greater) than its
face value. However, people are still willing to use the American dollar
confidence because of their __________________ that its purchasing power will
stable remain reasonably __________________ through appropriate
fiscal, monetary ______________ and ______________ policy.

To say people demand money is to say they wish to
hold on to it ______________________________. People demand money for
three __________________reasons. One reason is to carry out anticipated
transactions purchases of goods and services. This is known as the ______________
demand for money. Second, people demand money in order to take

advantage of possible future opportunities, such as a decrease in the price
speculative — of bonds. This is known as the ________________ demand for money.
People also demand money to finance unexpected or emergency pur-
precautionary — chases. This is known as the ________________ demand for money.
All of these reasons added together will give us the total demand for money, or simply the demand for money. The demand for money is affected by economic variables.

The supply of money has different definitions. The broadest definition
money stock — of money supply is the __________________________. The narrowest
M1 — definition of money supply is ___________ (M1/L). Those economists
who view money primarily as a medium of exchange will use
M1 — ______________ (M1/M2); economists who view money as something
a broader definition of money — that is held will use ____________________________ (M1/a broader
definition of money).

depository — The American banking system can be divided into ________________
Federal Reserve — institutions and the ___________________________ System. The basic
policy making body of the Federal Reserve System is the
Board of Governors — ____________________________________ (Open Market Committee/
seven — Board of Governors). Each of the ______________________ (seven/
fourteen) Governors is appointed by the president and confirmed by the
fourteen- — Senate for _______________________ (seven-/fourteen-) year terms.
The Board of Governors is aided in implementing monetary policy by
Open Market Committee, twelve — the ___________________________________. The _____________
(fourteen/twelve) Federal Reserve District Banks implement the policy
outlined by the Board of Governors. The Federal Reserve System is
Fed — often referred to as simply the ___________.

	The most important function of the Fed is to oversee
monetary policy	______________________________. The Fed can alter the money supply
required	by changing ______________________ reserves. By changing required
excess	reserves, the Fed can change a bank's ____________________ reserves,
creating	which affects the money- ________________________ ability of banks.
made	A single bank can create money when a loan is __________________
	(made/repaid). A single bank cannot make loans by an amount greater
excess	than their __________________ (total/excess) reserves. So a single bank
	is limited in its money-creating ability dollar for dollar with
excess, total	__________________ reserves. Excess reserves equal ________________
required	(required/total) reserves minus ____________________ (required/total)
reserve requirement (or required reserve)	reserves. Required reserves are determined by the ___________________ ratio.
a multiple of	The entire banking system can create money by ___________________
	(an amount equal to/a multiple of) its excess reserves. This is because
are not	reserves lost by one bank _______________ (are/are not) lost to the entire
	banking system. To calculate the potential change in the money supply,
excess	we need to know what ___________________ reserves are and what the
required reserve	__________________________________ ratio is. Excess reserves are
multiplied	______________________ (divided/multiplied) by the reciprocal of the
reserve requirement	____ ratio to get the change
	in the money supply. The reciprocal of the required reserve ratio is also
multiplier	known as the money ____________________.
	The potential change in the supply of money for an entire banking
may not	system may not be met for two reasons. First, banks _________________

(may/may not) loan out all of their excess reserves. Second, there are

currency

________________ leakages as loans are made.

It is also important to realize that the multiple change in the money supply (given a change in excess reserves due to a change in required reserves) works in both an upward and downward direction. The supply

an increase

of money increases because of ___________ (an increase/a decrease) in

a decrease

excess reserves. The money supply decreases because of ___________ (an increase/a decrease) in excess reserves. So if the Fed is to change the

excess reserves

supply of money, they must first change ______________________.

Another important point is that the public's choice of holding money

will

either as currency or in the form of demand deposits ______________ (will/will not) affect the money-creating ability of banks (hence the

unevenness

supply of money). Also, the ______________________ (evenness/ unevenness) of the granting and repayment of loans can cause the money supply to fluctuate.

Problems and Applications

1. The transactions demand for money is affected by (a) personal income, (b) the general price level, (c) expectations about changes in the general price level, and (d) the interest rates. Exactly how do each of these economic variables affect the transactions demand for money?
2. Determine whether M1, M2, M3, or L, is being referred to by each of the following.
   a. Paper money, coins, and traveler's checks held by the public
   b. Savings accounts of the public
   c. Treasury bills held by the public
   d. Time deposits over $100,000
   e. Time deposits less than $100,000
   f. Certificates of deposit

3. a. What are total reserves equal to?
   b. What are required reserves (the reserve requirement) equal to?
   c. What are excess reserves equal to?
4. Assume Peabody National Bank has vault cash and reserve deposit totaling $100,000. Also assume demand deposit liabilities of the bank total $50,000 and that the reserve requirement ratio equals .20.
   a. What are the bank's total reserves?
   b. What is the bank's reserve requirement?
   c. What are the bank's excess reserves?
   d. How much money could this bank create (lend out)?
   e. What is the money multiplier equal to?
   f. What is the potential increase in the supply of money for the entire banking system?
   g. If the Fed reduced the reserve requirement ratio to .10, what would be the potential increase in the supply of money?
   h. Why may the potential increase in the supply of money not be met?
5. What motivated passage of the Depository Institutions Deregulation and Monetary Control Act of 1980?
6. Assume the Fed reduces required reserves for the banking system and this increases excess reserves. We know how to calculate the potential increase in the money stock. Why may this potential increase in the money stock not be met?

True-False

For each item, determine whether the statement is basically true or false. If the statement is false, rewrite it so it is a true statement.

_____ 1. Economists who view money as primarily a medium of exchange will use M1 as their measure of the money stock.

_____ 2. M1 is the public's holding of currency.

_____ 3. M2 equals M1 minus savings accounts, small time deposits, certificates of deposits, and money market accounts.

_____ 4. Money is destroyed when a loan is repaid.

_____ 5. Money is a medium of exchange and a store of purchasing power.

_____ 6. Money has value because it is backed by gold.

_____ 7. Monetary policy is under the control of Congress.

_____ 8. When checks are written and cleared, the supply of money remains the same.

_____ 9. There are twelve members of the Board of Governors appointed for fourteen-year terms.

_____ 10. All reserve deposits are required reserves.

_____ 11. American money is fiat currency.

_____ 12. Demand deposits are time deposits.

_____ 13. M3 is more liquid than M1.

_____ 14. People demand money for transactions and for precautionary and speculative reasons.

_____ 15. Liquidity is the ease with which assets can be converted into another form, especially money.

_____ 16. The required reserve ratio (or reserve requirement ratio) determines reserve requirements.

_____ 17. The asset demand for money is the combined transactions and speculative reasons for holding money.

_____ 18. Velocity is the rate of turnover or circulation of the money stock (M) relative to GNP; thus V = GNP/M.

Multiple Choice *Choose the best answer for each item.*

_____ 1. When a check is written against Bank A and deposited in Bank B, the reserves of Bank A

a. decrease and the reserves of Bank B increase.
b. decrease and the reserves of Bank B decrease.
c. increase and the reserves of Bank B increase.
d. increase and the reserves of Bank B decrease.
e. do none of the above.

_____ 2. The supply of money fluctuates because of

a. the unevenness of the granting and repayments of loans.
b. changes in excess reserves.
c. changes in the amount of currency the public wishes to hold.
d. all of the above.
e. none of the above.

_____ 3. The maximum amount of money a single bank can create is

a. equal to its total reserves.
b. limited dollar for dollar to its excess reserves.
c. equal to required reserves.
d. equal to the required reserve ratio.
e. zero because only the Treasury Department can create money.

_____ 4. Which of the following is true about the functions of money?
   a. Its intrinsic value must equal to its face value for money to be generally acceptable.
   b. M2 must be more liquid than M1 for money to act as a store of purchasing power.
   c. It must act as a standard of value in a barter economy.
   d. It must be generally acceptable as a medium of exchange and act as a store of purchasing power and a standard of value.
   e. All of the above are true about the functions of money.

_____ 5. In a barter economy,
   a. money is not used.
   b. more time would be required to find trading partners with a coincidence of wants.
   c. less specialization and trade based on comparative advantage would take place.
   d. production possibilities are lower.
   e. all of the above are true.

_____ 6. M1 includes
   a. M2 plus savings accounts and small time deposits.
   b. excess reserves.
   c. reserve deposits.
   d. demand deposits.
   e. M3.

_____ 7. Suppose Hutton Bank and Trust has vault cash and reserve deposits totaling $400,000 and demand deposit liabilities of $300,000. If the required reserve ratio is .20, what is the maximum amount of money the banking system could create?
   a. $340,000
   b. $60,000
   c. $1,700,000
   d. $40,000
   e. $1,000,000

_____ 8. The reserve requirement ratio is
   a. the same as excess reserves.
   b. the same as reserve deposits.
   c. total reserves minus required reserves.
   d. a percentage of a bank's demand deposit liabilities that must be kept on deposit at the Fed.
   e. a percentage of a bank's reserve deposits that must be kept on deposit at the Fed.

_____ 9. A single bank creates money
   a. when its total reserves are equal to required reserves.
   b. when a loan is made.
   c. by an amount greater than the entire banking system.
   d. when a loan is repaid.
   e. in none of the above ways.

_____ 10. A single bank is limited in its money-creating ability by an amount equal to
   a. its total reserves.
   b. its required reserves.
   c. its excess reserves.
   d. the required reserve ratio.
   e. its demand deposits.

_____ 11. The entire banking system can expand the money stock by an amount equal to
   a. the banking system's excess reserves.
   b. a multiple of the banking system's required reserves.
   c. a multiple of the banking system's excess reserves.
   d. a multiple of the banking system's demand deposits.
   e. the banking system's total reserves.

_____ 12. The potential increase in the supply of money may not be met because
   a. of restrictions imposed on the banking system by the Fed.
   b. of currency leakages as loans are made.
   c. banks may not wish to loan out all of their excess reserves.
   d. of all of the above.
   e. of both b and c above.

_____ 13. Velocity is
   a. a target the Fed manages in an attempt to control the money supply
   b. equal to M/GNP
   c. equal to (GNP) (M)
   d. equal to GNP/M
   e. defined by none of the above.

_____ 14. Which of the following statements about money is true?
   a. The transactions demand for money is a desire to hold money in anticipation of future profits.
   b. The precautionary demand for money is the combined transactions and speculative demand for money.

c. The speculative demand for money is a desire to hold money to carry out anticipated purchases of goods and services.
d. Money has value because people are confident it will remain relatively stable over time.
e. Money has value because its backed by gold.

Discussion Questions

1. What happens to the value of money as it becomes more plentiful? *(KQ2)*
2. What are the advantages of having paper money and coins whose intrinsic value is less than their stated (face) value? *(KQ1)*
3. What do you think would happen to the precautionary demand for money if people expected an extremely bad winter storm, or flood, or possibly a war? *(KQ3)*
4. How could a change in the interest rate affect the speculative demand for money? *(KQ3)*
5. We know what the functions of money are and it is these functions that help to define what we mean by money. But we also know that money increases our production possibilities by enabling us to escape the inefficiencies of a barter system. Is this a function of money, or is it just a consequence of the use of money? *(KQ1)*

Answers

Problems and Applications

1. a. An increase (decrease) in personal income increases (decreases) the transactions demand for money. With greater (less) income, people will spend more (less). Therefore, they need to hold on to more (less) money for transactions purposes.
   b. If the general price level increases (decreases), the transactions demand for money increases (decreases) because it takes more (less) money to carry out any given level of transactions.
   c. If people expect prices to rise, they will demand more money for transactions purposes in this time period so they can buy more products now rather than waiting for their prices to rise. If people expect prices to fall, they will demand less for transactions purposes in this time period because they will buy fewer products in anticipation of lower prices in the future.

d. As the interest rate rises (falls), the opportunity cost of holding money rises (falls), and people will demand less (more) money for transactions purposes (and all other purposes) in order to economize.

2. a. M1
   b. M2
   c. L
   d. M3
   e. M2
   f. M2
3. a. The cash a bank has in its vault plus its reserve deposits at the Fed
   b. Some percentage of a bank's demand deposit liabilities . The percentage, determined by the Fed is called the reserve requirement ratio (also known as the required reserve ratio). (Required reserves are equal to the reserve requirement ratio multiplied by a bank's demand deposit liabilities.)
   c. Total reserves minus required reserves
4. a. $100,000
   b. Reserve requirement = reserve requirement ratio × demand deposit liabilities. (.20) × ($50,000) = $10,000
   c. Excess reserves equal total reserves minus required reserves. $100,000 - $10,000 = $90,000
   d. $90,000
   e. The money multiplier = 1/required reserve ratio. 1/.20 = 5
   f. The potential increase in the supply of money = excess reserves × money multiplier. ($90,000) × (5) = $450,000
   g. First, required reserves would now equal $5,000. So excess reserves now equal $95,000. The money multiplier now equals 10. The potential increase in the money supply now equals $950,000.
   h. First, banks may not loan out all of their excess reserves. Second, some of the loans made may be held by the public as idle currency.
5. The purpose of the act is to increase competition among depository institutions and to increase the control the Fed has over their money-creating ability (hence, to increase the Fed's control of the supply of money). By forcing all banks to be members of the Federal Reserve System, the Fed increased its control over bank's excess reserves because of the reserve requirement.

6. Although the Fed may successfully increase excess reserves of banks, there is no guarantee that banks will loan out all of there additional excess reserves (and loans have to be made to increase the supply of money). In addition, when a loan is made, some of it may be held as idle cash balances, representing money which does not work its way back into the banking system and therefore, cannot be reloaned. To the extent that bank loans end up as currency, the ability of banks to expand loans and increase the supply of money is reduced.

True-False

1. T
2. F: M1 is the public's holding of currency, demand deposits, traveler's checks, and NOW and ATS accounts.
3. F: M2 equals M1 plus savings accounts, small time deposits, certificates of deposit, and money market accounts.
4. T 5. T
6. F: Money has value because it is backed by the public's confidence that it will remain generally acceptable as a medium of exchange and its purchasing power will remain reasonable stable over time through appropriate government fiscal and monetary policy.
7. F: Monetary policy is not under the direct control of Congress but is controlled by the Board of Governors of the Federal Reserve System.
8. T
9. F: There are seven members of the Board of Governors appointed for fourteen-year terms.
10. F: Not all reserve deposits are required reserves.
11. T
12. F: Demand deposits are checking accounts.
13. F: M3 is less liquid than M1.
14. T 15. T 16. T
17. F: The asset demand for money is the combined precautionary and speculative reasons for holding money.
18. T

Multiple Choice

1. a *(KQ6)*	2. d *(KQ8)*	3. b *(KQ7)*
4. d *(KQ1)*	5. e *(KQ1)*	6. d *(KQ4)*
7. c *(KQ7)*	8. d *(KQ7)*	9. b *(KQ7)*
10. c *(KQ7)*	11. c *(KQ7)*	12. e *(KQ8)*
13. d *(KQ5)*	14. d *(KQ2, 3)*	

CHAPTER 8

The Federal Reserve and the Money Stock

Chapter Summary

This chapter describes the tools the Fed uses to change excess reserves and control the money stock (supply). These tools are the reserve requirement, the discount rate (and the associated loans the Fed makes to banks), and open market operations.

Key Question 1: What are the Federal Reserve's three quantitative controls over the money stock, and how do they work?

Changing the reserve requirement ratio has a twofold impact on the supply of money: it changes excess reserves and it changes the money multiplier. Therefore, changing the reserve requirement ratio can potentially have a very powerful impact on the supply of money. This method of changing the money supply is the one that is least used because it may increase or decrease the supply of money too much.

The Fed is considered a banker's bank because commercial banks can receive loans from the Fed. The interest rate the Fed charges commercial banks is called the discount rate. If the discount rate is reduced, banks may be encouraged to borrow from the Fed. When the Fed grants loans to banks, money is eventually created when excess reserves of commercial banks are loaned out. When the Fed grants a loan to a bank, it writes a check drawn against itself in exchange for the bank's IOU, which increases the bank's reserve deposits as well as its excess reserves. By increasing excess reserves of banks, a multiple increase in the money supply occurs when these excess reserves are loaned out. If the Fed's loans don't increase excess reserves, but only enable banks to meet their required reserves, then at least the banks will not have to restrict loans, which would cause a contraction in the money supply. An increase in the discount rate will discourage banks from borrowing from the Fed and may help decrease the money supply. The Fed may also refuse to give loans, which may force a contraction in the money supply. (However, banks could receive loans from other banks, but a federal funds rate would have to be paid for such loans). In practice, a change in the discount rate and the number of loans the Fed makes is not that important in the money-creating process. The discount rate is basically used as a signal of what the Fed is planning to do in the future. But, in that respect, the discount rate can alter expectations.

Open market operations are used most often to change the money supply, and they are considered the Fed's most important tool because they allow for the greatest amount of fine-tuning and reversibility. The Fed buys government securities (bills, notes, or bonds) to increase the money supply and sells government securities to decrease the money supply. In either case, the Fed can buy from or sell to the public or commercial banks. Buying from or selling to commercial banks will have a greater effect on the money supply than dealing with the public because required reserves are unaffected when dealing with commercial banks.

By attempting to increase the money supply, or at least increase the rate of growth in the money stock, the Fed is pursuing an expansionary, or loose, monetary policy. To increase the money supply, the Fed must first increase excess reserves of banks. To increase excess reserves the Fed may (a) decrease the reserve requirement (by decreasing the required reserve ratio); (b) increase their loans to commercial banks (by decreasing the discount rate); and (c) buy government securities on the open market. By attempting to decrease the money supply, or at least decrease the growth rate in the money supply, the Fed is undertaking a contractionary, or tight, monetary policy. To decrease the money stock the Fed must decrease excess reserves of banks. To decrease excess reserves, the Fed must undertake actions opposite to those prescribed above.

It should be remembered that there are many factors over which the Fed has no control that may alter the money supply. The Fed cannot force banks to loan out additional excess reserves even after the Fed has increased them. And even if banks loan out all of their additional excess reserves, it takes time for the money expansion process to occur. Also, the predicted increase in the money stock will be less than precise, because no one knows for sure how much of these additional loans will be held as currency (idle cash balances). Moreover, the public's willingness to hold money in the form of currency versus demand deposits will affect the money supply. Similarly, the U.S. Treasury holds money in both commercial banks and at the Fed. If the Treasury shifts funds between these two holdings, the money supply will be altered. All of these factors are out of the hands of the Fed. Therefore, the Fed may set money growth targets, but many factors over which it has no control may alter the actual growth rate of money.

Key Question 2:
How does monetary policy affect the rate of inflation?

Inflation and deflation can also be explained in monetary terms. Inflation erodes the value of the dollar, and deflation increases the value of the dollar. The value of the dollar depends on the supply of dollars relative to the supply of goods and services in the economy. If the supply of dollars increases relative to the supply of goods and services, then prices rise and the value of the dollar decreases. Alternatively, an increase in the money supply may cause people to possess more dollars than they wish to hold (demand). Therefore, people will spend more, driving prices up and deflating the dollar. Basically, the dollar is no different than any other commodity. As it becomes more plentiful, its value decreases. Conversely, as the dollar becomes less plentiful, its value increases (deflation).

The equation of exchange $MV = PQ$ states that the dollar value of people's expenditures *(MV)* must equal the dollar value of what they produce *(PQ)*. In this respect, the equation of exchange is a truism (or an identity in mathematical terms). However, the equation also shows the relationship between the money supply (the money stock), velocity, the general price level, and the total output of goods and services. Changes in the money supply *(M)* or velocity *(V)* on the left side of the equation will be reflected in an equal change in prices *(P)*, output *(Q)*, or both, on the right side. Over short run, the extend to which prices or production levels are changed by an increase in the money supply depends on how close the economy is to full employment. Over the long run, however, we are certain that increases in the money supply are reflected by increases in prices.

Key Question 3:
What is the effect of a change in the money stock on aggregate demand and supply?

The same type of analysis can be undertaken in the context of aggregate demand and aggregate supply curves. If we are at or near full employment, the aggregate supply curve is vertical, and increases in the money supply will be reflected as rightward shifts in the aggregate demand curve. This causes prices to rise, but national output and employment will remain constant. (In other words, GNP increases, but real GNP remains constant.) If we are below full employment, then the aggregate supply curve slopes upward, and increases in the money supply will result in increases in prices and production levels. These are the same predictions that can be made with the equation of exchange. However, with the equation of exchange, one must consider what happens to velocity. Because the velocity of money tends to vary significantly over the short run, the Fed may need to change the money supply to prevent undesirable changes in prices and national output.

Key Question 4:
What are the politics of monetary policy?

Although monetary policy is intended to help smooth out fluctuations in the business cycle, it is also formulated in a political environment. For example, the Fed may come under strong political pressure to accommodate deficit spending by increasing the money supply in order to keep interest rates and unemployment down. In the long run, this accommodation will cause inflation, and Congress and the Fed probably share the blame. Given the tradeoff between unemployment and inflation, the Fed must contend with competing economic goals. Which goal should take precedence is a question that must be resolved politically. But, we will all have to live with the long-run effects of whatever choice is made.

Review Terms and Concepts

Deficits
Money
Monetary policy
Excess reserves
Checkable deposits
Financial intermediary
Required reserves
Aggregate demand
Aggregate supply
Cost-push inflation
Targets

New Terms and Concepts

Depository institutions
Reserve requirements
Discount rate
Federal funds rate
Open market operations
Equation of exchange ($MV = PQ$)
Velocity of money (V)

Completion

monetary

money supply

excess

The Fed's primary function is to oversee ________________ policy. In other words, the Fed attempts to control the ________________. In order to change the money supply, the Fed must first change ________________ (excess/required) reserves. There are three basic actions the Fed can take to alter excess reserves. These include changing the reserve requirements, changing the amount of loans made to banks, and using open market operations. The reserve requirement is some percentage of demand deposit liabilities that must be kept on deposit at the Fed. That percentage is determined by the Fed and is called the

required	reserve requirement ratio—also known as the ________________
	(excess/required) reserve ratio. The discount rate is the interest rate
member banks	charged ________________________ (member banks/the Fed) to bor-
the Fed	row from ________________ (member banks/the Fed). Open market
buying and selling	operations are the ____________________ of government securities
the Fed	on the open market by __________________ (member banks/the Fed).
	If the Fed wishes the increase the money supply, or at least keep the
decrease	money supply from contracting, they may want to ________________
decreasing	(increase/decrease) reserve requirements by ____________________
	(increasing/decreasing) the required reserve ratio.
	Finally, a change in the required reserve ration has a twofold impact.
required	First, it changes ________________ (total/required) reserves. Changing
excess	required reserves changes ______________ reserves. This is because
total, required	excess reserves equal ____________ reserves minus ____________
	reserves. Second, a change in the required reserve ratio affects the money
reciprocal	multiplier because the money multiplier equals the ________________
	of the required reserve ratio. Because of this very powerful potential
	change in the supply of money (which may cause the supply of money
	to increase of decrease too much), changing the required reserves of
	banks (by changing the required reserve ratio) is the tool which is
least	______________ (least/most) used by the Fed. Or if the Fed wishes
increase	to increase the money supply, they may want to ________________
	(increase/decrease) loans to member banks. To entice banks to borrow,
decrease	the Fed will ________________ (increase/decrease) the discount rate.
	Finally, the Fed may wish to increase excess reserves (and the money
	supply) by using open market operations. This means the Open Market

buy Committee will ____________ (buy/sell) government securities on the
open market.

To decrease the money supply, or at least keep the money supply form
excess increasing, the Fed must first decrease ______________ reserves. This
increasing can be accomplished by __________________ (increasing/decreasing)
selling reserve requirements and the discount rate and by __________________
(buying/selling) government securities on the open market.

open market operations The action used most often by the Fed is ______________________,
which allow for greatest amount of fine-tuning and reversibility. Chang-
powerful ing reserve requirements can have a very __________________ (weak/
powerful) impact on the money supply. In other words, changing re-
much serves may cause the money supply to change too ________________
(little/much). Therefore, changing reserve requirements is the tool
least ________________ (most/least) used. Changing the discount rate
does not __________________ (does/does not) affect significantly the money-
creating ability of banks. But the discount rate is watched as an indication of what the Fed may do in the future. In this way, the discount rate
expectations may affect ______________________.

Whenever it takes action to increase the money supply, the Fed is
loose undertaking __________________ (loose/tight) monetary policy, also
expansionary known as ________________________ (expansionary/contractionary)
monetary policy. On the other hand, contractionary or tight monetary
decrease policy is associated with the Fed's attempt to __________________
(increase/decrease) the money supply.

The Fed has control over the money supply. This control is
less than precise ________________________________ (perfect/less than precise)

because there are factors over which the Fed has no control that affect the money supply. This means the Fed may need to undertake loose or tight monetary policy just to keep the money supply growing at a reasonable stable rate.

Increases in the supply of money will cause inflation if the increase in
greater — the supply of dollars in ____________________ (greater/less) than the
decreases — increase in the supply of goods and services. Inflation ______________
(increases/decreases) the value of the dollar. The equation of exchange shows the relationship among money, velocity, the general price level, and the total output of goods and services. The equation of exchange can
$MV = PQ$ — be written as ____________________. If velocity is constant (or nearly constant), and if we are at full employment (meaning quantity is constant because we are on our production possibilities curve), then an increase in
increase — the money supply will cause the general price level to ______________
(increase/decrease). In this case, it is clear that too many dollars are chas-
demand-pull — ing too few goods and services, a situation known as ______________
inflation. On the other hand, if velocity is constant (or nearly so), and if we are below full employment (inside our production possibilities curve), an increase in the money supply will cause the general price level and/or
increase — the total output of goods and services to ____________________
(increase/decrease). Conversely, if velocity is reasonably stable and we experience a decrease in the money supply, then either the general price level must drop, or the total output level must decrease, or both.

The relationship among the variables in the equation of exchange can be viewed in the context of aggregate demand and aggregate supply
aggregate supply — curves. If we are at full employment the ________________________

(aggregate demand/aggregate supply) curve is vertical. An increase in the money supply would cause the ________________ (aggregate demand/aggregate supply) curve to shift to the ________________ (right/left). This results in ________________ (an increase/a decrease) in the general price level, and total output ________________ (increases/decreases/remains the same). If we are below full employment, the aggregate supply curve slopes ________________ (upward/downward). Therefore, an increase in the money supply will result in ________________ (an increase/a decrease) in the general price level, and the national output level will ________________ (increase/decrease/remain the same).

aggregate demand
right
an increase
remains the same
upward
an increase
increase

Monetary policy is less than precise, as we have seen. It also may create long-run problems of ________________ (higher/lower) rates of inflation if it is used to accommodate deficit spending. This fact reminds us that there are tradeoffs to short-run and long-run objectives.

higher

Problems and Applications

1. Assume a bank is just meeting reserve requirements of 20 percent when the Open Market Committee purchases $1,000 worth of government securities from the bank.
   a. How would this transaction affect the balance sheet for the bank?
   b. How would this transaction affect the balance sheet for the Fed?
   c. What happens to the bank's required reserves as a result of the open market transaction?
   d. What happens to the bank's total reserves as a result of the open market transaction?
   e. What happens to the bank's excess reserves as a result of the open market transaction?
   f. By how much could this bank increase the money supply?
   g. By how much could the entire banking system increase the money supply?

2. Why do open market operations affect excess reserves more when buying from or selling to commercial banks rather than dealing with the public? (*Hint:* Excess reserves = total reserves – required reserves.)
3. Indicate whether each of the following actions would increase or decrease the money supply.
   a. Fed purchases of bonds from the public
   b. Fed purchases of bonds from commercial banks
   c. decreasing the discount rate
   d. decreasing the reserve requirement
   e. Fed sales of government securities to commercial banks
   f. Fed sales of government securities to the public
   g. increasing the discount rate
   h. increasing the reserve requirement
4. Suppose people decide to hold more money as currency and less money in their checking accounts.
   a. What affect will this have on the money supply over time?
   b. What could the Fed do to correct for this situation?
   c. Based on your answers above, does the Fed always use its powers to increase or decrease the money supply?
5. If people wish to hold on to more or less money, what happens to velocity?
6. If the interest rate changes, what happens to the amount of money people demand?
7. How do changes in the money supply affect the interest rate (at least in the short run)?
8. Based on your answers to questions 4–6 above, what is the relationship between changes in the money supply and velocity? What impact does this relationship have on the effectiveness of monetary policy?
9. Use aggregate demand and aggregate supply curves to determine what happens to the general level of prices and national output under the following conditions.
   a. We are at full employment and there is an increase in the money supply.
   b. We are below full employment and there is an increase in the money supply.

True-False

For each item, determine whether the statement is basically true or false. If the statement is false, rewrite it so it is a true statement.

____ 1. Changing the reserve requirement has such a powerful impact on the money supply that it is the tool of monetary policy used most often.

____ 2. Borrowing from the Fed is considered a privilege, not a right.

____ 3. Open market operations by themselves will not alter the money supply but will only change banks' excess reserves.

____ 4. The interest rate that banks charge other banks is called the discount rate.

____ 5. The Open Market Committee buys and sells private securities on the New York Stock Exchange.

____ 6. If the Fed wishes to increases the money supply, it must first increase excess reserves.

____ 7. An increase in excess reserves, no matter how large, will not necessarily increase the money supply, but a large enough decrease in excess reserves will force a contraction in the money supply.

____ 8. In practice, the Fed may take actions not necessarily to increase the money supply, but to prevent it from otherwise decreasing.

____ 9. The Fed has very precise control over the money supply.

____ 10. The equation of exchange is $MP = VQ$.

____ 11. The equation of exchange shows that the total dollar value of expenditures in an economy must equal the total dollar value of what is produced in an economy.

____ 12. If we are at full employment and the money supply increases, then the general price level increases, but national output does not change.

____ 13. The Fed should take the blame for inflation.

____ 14. Fiscal and monetary policy are always coordinated to smooth out the business cycle.

____ 15. There is no one clearly defined cause of inflation.

____ 16. Over the long run, the interest rate will most likely decrease with relatively large increases in the money supply.

____ 17. Contractionary monetary policy is considered more effective than expansionary monetary policy.

____ 18. The federal funds rate is the interest rate charged one financial institution to borrow from another.

Multiple Choice *Choose the one best answer for each item.*

___ 1. Which of the following variables that affect the money supply is not under the Fed's control?
  a. The amount of loans made with excess reserves
  b. The amount of time it takes for a banking system to expand the money supply
  c. The percent of loans made that are held by the public as idle cash balances
  d. The public's willingness to hold money either as currency or as demand deposits
  e. All of the above

___ 2. If the supply of money increases faster than the total supply of goods and services, then
  a. the value of the dollar will decrease.
  b. the general price level will rise.
  c. we will have too many dollars chasing too few goods and services.
  d. we will experience demand-pull inflation.
  e. all of the above will occur.

___ 3. The equation of exchange shows that
  a. $MV = PQ$.
  b. $MP = VQ$.
  c. if we are at full employment and the money supply increases, the general price level and national output level will increase.
  d. $MQ = VP$.
  e. the velocity of money always moves in the same direction as the money supply.

___ 4. If the public decides to hold more money as currency and less money in demand deposits, this could cause
  a. an increase in the money supply.
  b. banks' excess reserves to increase.
  c. a decrease in the money supply.
  d. reserve requirements to increase.
  e. any of the above to occur.

___ 5. The "politics of monetary policy" refers to
  a. the fact that fiscal policy may run counter to monetary policy.
  b. political pressures from Congress to accommodate deficit spending.
  c. the political problems of addressing competing economic objectives.

d. problems of choosing short-run versus long-run objectives.
e. all of the above.

____ 6. When Congress is running a deficit and the Fed accommodates this deficit spending, we can conclude that
a. deficit spending will push interest rates up, and the Fed will increase the money supply to keep interest rates down.
b. deficit spending will push interest rates down, and the Fed will decrease the money supply to keep the interest rates down.
c. the general price level will decrease.
d. the national output level will decrease.
e. none of the above will occur.

____ 7. A high inflation rate is most likely caused by
a. deficit spending accommodated by expansionary monetary policy.
b. deficit spending accommodated by contractionary monetary policy.
c. fiscal policy alone.
d. monetary policy alone.
e. none of the above.

____ 8. If the Open Market Committee wants to increase the money supply by the greatest possible amount, then they should
a. buy government securities from commercial banks.
b. buy government securities from the public.
c. sell government securities to commercial banks.
d. sell government securities to the public.
e. buy government securities from the public, but sell to commercial banks.

____ 9. Loose monetary policy is characterized by the Fed
a. decreasing the discount rate, decreasing reserve requirements, and selling government securities.
b. decreasing the discount rate, decreasing reserve requirements, and buying government securities.
c. increasing the discount rate, increasing reserve requirements, and buying government securities.
d. decreasing the discount rate, increasing reserve requirements, and selling government securities.
e. doing none of the above.

____ 10. The interest rate the Fed charges on loans to member banks is called
a. the interest rate.
b. liquidity.

c. the discount rate.
d. the yield.
e. none of the above.

____ 11. If the Open Market Committee purchases government securities from commercial banks, then
a. the reserve deposits of banks will be increased.
b. the liabilities of banks will not be affected by this transaction.
c. the Fed will have to adjust both their assets and liabilities.
d. banks' excess reserves will increase.
e. all of the above will result.

____ 12. Which of the following instruments of monetary policy does the Fed use most often and consider most important?
a. Refusing to grant loans to member banks
b. Changing the discount rate
c. Changing reserve requirements
d. Open market operations
e. All of the above are equally important to the Fed.

____ 13. Which of the following instruments of monetary policy is the most powerful in changing excess reserves of banks?
a. Open market operations with the public as opposed to dealing with banks
b. The granting of loans to member banks
c. Changing reserve requirements
d. Decreasing the discount rate
e. Increasing the discount rate

____ 14. An increase in the discount rate
a. means a decrease in the interest rate banks must pay for loans from the Fed.
b. is a form of loose monetary policy.
c. will encourage loans from the Fed.
d. is not a very powerful instrument of monetary policy.
e. is characterized by all of the above.

____ 15. A decrease in the money supply will most likely cause
a. inflation.
b. a decrease in the value of the dollar.
c. a decrease in the interest rate and an increase in the velocity of money.
d. an increase in the interest rate and an increase in the velocity of money.
e. the discount rate to drop.

_____ 16. Tight monetary policy is characterized by the Fed
   a. selling government securities.
   b. decreasing the discount rate.
   c. buying government securities.
   d. decreasing reserve requirements.
   e. doing none of the above.

_____ 17. If the Fed undertakes a loose monetary policy when the economy is below full employment, then
   a. aggregate demand increases.
   b. the aggregate supply curve is sloping upward.
   c. the general price level will rise.
   d. the national output level will rise.
   e. all of the above will occur.

Discussion Questions

1. Do you think the Fed is more effective in controlling demand-pull inflation or cost-push inflation? *(KQ2)*
2. Is the Fed more effective in using an expansionary or a contractionary monetary policy? *(KQ1, 2, 3, 4)*
3. Given the relationship between changes in the money supply and velocity, does this mean monetary policy is rather ineffective in controlling the general price level and the national output level? (*Hint*: Think in terms of the equation of exchange.) *(KQ2)*
4. When the Fed buys bonds on the open market, what effect will this have on the price of those bonds? (*Hint*: Think in terms of demand for and supply of bonds.) When the price of bonds goes up, what happens to the interest rate on those bonds? (*Hint*: The interest rate on a bond—or the interest income on a bond—is equal to the yield, which is fixed, divided by the price of the bond.) Given your answers, what affect will the Fed's purchase of bonds have on the interest rate? How is this related to the fact that an increase in the money supply will cause a decrease in the interest rate? *(KQ1)*
5. Over the short run, an increase in the money supply will cause a decrease in the interest rate. How can it be possible for an increase in the money supply to cause an increase in the interest rate over the long run? (*Hint*: An increase in the money supply causes increases in the general price level and a devaluation of the dollar over the long run.) *(KQ2, 3)*
6. Why are there limits to the amount that velocity can change? *(KQ2)*

Answers

Problems and Applications

1. a. This transaction would increase the bank's reserve deposit at the Fed by $1,000. It would also decrease the bank's securities by $1,000. These are both entries on the assets side of the bank's balance sheet.
   b. The assets side of the Fed's balance sheet would increase by $1,000. On the liabilities side of the balance sheet, reserve deposits would increase by $1,000.
   c. Nothing happens because the demand deposit liabilities of the bank were unaffected by this transaction.
   d. Total reserves increase by $1,000 (because reserve deposits increased by $1,000, and total reserves equal vault cash plus reserve deposits).
   e. They increase by $1,000.
   f. $1,000
   g. $5,000
2. If the Fed buys from a bank, total reserves increase by an amount equal to the sale of the security and required reserves of the bank are unaffected. Therefore, excess reserves increase equal to the amount of the sale of the security. But, if the bank buys from the public, excess reserves increase by an amount less than the sale of the security because there is also an increase in the bank's required reserves (equal to the required reserve ratio times the sale of the security). Buying from a commercial bank will therefore have a greater potential expansionary effect on the money supply than buying from the public.

   Conversely, selling to commercial banks will decrease excess reserves equal to the amount of the sale of the security, and selling to the public will decrease excess reserves by an amount less than the sale of the security. Therefore, selling to banks will have a greater contractionary effect on the money supply than selling to the public.
3. a. increase the money supply
   b. increase the money supply
   c. increase the money supply
   d. increase the money supply
   e. decrease the money supply
   f. decrease the money supply
   g. decrease the money supply
   h. decrease the money supply
4. a. The money supply will contract over time because excess reserves will contract over time, forcing banks to call in loans at a greater rate than new loans will be granted. Excess reserves decrease because banks lose reserves as people withdraw

money from their checking accounts. Of course, required reserves will decrease (because the banks have fewer demand deposit liabilities) but not as much as total reserves will decrease.

b. The Fed should take action to increase excess reserves and expand the money supply. The Fed could decrease the reserve requirement, increase loans to member banks by lowering the discount rate, or buy government securities on the open market. (Open market operations are used most often.)

c. The Fed does not necessarily use its powers to decrease (or increase) the money supply, but may use its powers to prevent the money supply from decreasing (or increasing). In the above case, the Fed should buy on the open market to prevent the money supply from contracting—not necessarily to increase the money supply.

5. If people hold on to more (less) money, then the average number of times each dollars is used decreases (increases); in other words, velocity decreases (increases). So with an increase in the amount of money people wish to hold, velocity decreases, and vice versa.

6. As the interest rises (drops), the opportunity cost of holding money rises (drops). Therefore, people will hold on to less (more) money (for all purpose).

7. An increase in the amount of money in an economy means banks have more money to lend. To entice people to borrow more, banks will lower the interest rate. So an increase in the money supply will cause a decrease in the interest rate. Conversely, a decrease in the amount of money in an economy means banks have less money to lend. Therefore, given some demand for loans, banks are able to increase the interest rate. So a decrease in the money supply will cause an increase in the interest rate.

8. An increase in the money supply causes a decrease in the interest rate, which causes people to hold more money. Therefore, velocity decreases. A decrease in the money supply causes an increase in the interest rate, which causes people to hold less money. Therefore, velocity increases. In short, an increase (decrease) in the money supply causes a decrease (increase) in velocity. This relationship has a tendency to render monetary policy less effective. In terms of the equation of exchange, $MV = PQ$, any change in M accompanied by an opposite change in V will have a smaller effect on P or Q.

9. a. The general price level increases, but national output remains unchanged.
   b. The general price level increases, and national output also increases.

True-False

1. F: Changing the reserve requirement has such a powerful impact on the money supply that it is the tool of monetary policy used least often.
2. T 3. T
4. F: The interest rate that the Fed charges on loans to member banks is called the discount rate.
5. F: The Open Market Committee buys and sells government securities on the open market.
6. T 7. T 8. T
9. F: The Fed has imprecise control over the money supply.
10. F: The equation of exchange is $MV = PQ$.
11. T 12. T
13. F: The Fed and Congress should take the blame for inflation.
14. F: Fiscal and monetary policy are not always coordinated to smooth out the business cycle.
15. T
16. F: Over the long run, the interest rate will most likely increase with relatively large increases in the money supply.
17. T 18. T

Multiple Choice

1. e *(KQ1)*	2. e *(KQ2)*	3. a *(KQ2)*
4. c *(KQ1)*	5. e *(KQ4)*	6. a *(KQ4)*
7. a *(KQ4)*	8. a *(KQ1)*	9. b *(KQ1)*
10. c *(KQ1)*	11. e *(KQ1)*	12. d *(KQ1)*
13. c *(KQ1)*	14. d *(KQ1)*	15. d *(KQ2)*
16. a *(KQ1)*	17. e *(KQ3)*	

CHAPTER 9

The Costs and Benefits of Inflation

Chapter Summary

The extent of the costs and benefits of inflation depends on whether or not the inflation is anticipated and on the rate of inflation. Anticipated inflation is not usually a major problem. This is because people can make adjustments to avoid the costs associated with it. However, unanticipated inflation is a major problem. The major costs of unanticipated inflation are that it redistributes income and it reallocates resources. And the greater the rates of unanticipated inflation, the greater the costs.

Key Question 1: What are the costs of inflation?

Those who stand to lose from unanticipated inflation include (1) holders of currency and savers of money, (2) creditors or lenders, (3) buyers of relatively long-term assets with fixed interest rates or rates of return, (4) businesses and workers tied to long-term price and wage agreements, and (5) taxpayers.

Key Question 2: What are the benefits of inflation?

Generally, whenever someone stands to lose from inflation, there are those who stand to gain from it. (The obvious exception is when inflation contributes to a downturn in total production, in which case everyone loses.) Those who gain from inflation are those who are able to anticipate it and make adjustments to benefit from it. For instance, consumers could buy more (and save less) now rather than wait for prices to increase. Businesses could produce at today's costs and sell at tomorrow's higher prices and could also benefit from the fact that product prices increase before wages increase. There are gains to debtors also if they can get loans at fixed interest rates. Workers may benefit (or at least lose less) if they receive cost-of-living adjustments (COLAs).

Finally, politicians and government employees stand to gain from inflation. If the government is able to increase the money supply and spend that money on various programs, there are benefits to the politicians who promote the programs, the government workers who staff them, and the people who use them. In this way, creating money can redistribute resources from private to public uses. But increasing the money supply may cause inflation, and those who hold dollar assets and all those who must pay higher prices for private goods and services will bear the costs.

How does government create this money? The Federal Reserve could increase the money supply directly, but more often the federal government first runs a deficit that must be financed by borrowing. The federal government borrows by selling government securities on the open market. But deficit spending has a tendency to increase interest rates and unemployment. So the federal government may then put strong political pressure on the Federal Reserve's Board of Governors to keep interest rates and unemployment down by increasing the money supply. Quite often, the Federal Reserve will succumb to the pressure and accommodate the deficit spending by ordering the Open Market Committee to buy government securities. This increases the money supply and pushes interest rates and unemployment down. Over the long run, however, increases in the money supply cause inflation.

Key Question 3: Should inflation be slowed down or even eliminated?

Inflation can be viewed as taxation is disguise. In as much as politicians promote government programs without the tax revenues to pay for them, they may be misleading the electorate by not pointing out the real cost of deficit spending—higher taxes or higher inflation (or both) over time.

Considering both the short-term and long-term costs of inflation, we could view monetary stability as a public good to be provided by government. Whether the government should provide this good is something the electorate must decide. In this decision the electorate must, of course, weigh these costs against any benefits. However, the effects of any decision, or of indecision, can be predicted by economic theory.

Review Terms and Concepts

Barter
Inflation
Deficit
Stagflation
Demand-pull inflation
Cost-push inflation
Structural inflation
Public good or service
Macroeconomic policy
Monetary policy
Fiscal policy

New Terms and Concepts

Real interest rate
Real income
Fisher effect
Bracket creep
Inflation premium
Hyperinflation
Variable-rate or adjustable-rate mortgage
Cost-of-living adjustment (COLA)
Variable-rate mortgage

Completion

increase
is
anticipated, rate (degree)
is not
can
uneven
hyperinflation
is
greater
redistribute
decrease

Inflation is the ______________ (increase/decrease) in the general level of prices. Whenever some individuals lose from inflation, there usually __________ (is/is not) an opportunity for others to gain. The extent of the costs and benefits of inflation depends on whether or not the inflation is __________ and on the ____________ of inflation.

Anticipated inflation ____________ (is/is not) usually a problem because people ____________ (can/cannot) make various adjustments to prevent the redistributional effects on income. However, anticipated inflation can cause _________________ (smooth/uneven) production levels. In addition, periods of high anticipated inflation could lead to ___________________.

Generally, unanticipated inflation ____________ (is/is not) what creates the problems we think of as the costs of inflation. The greater the unexpected inflation, the ____________ (greater/smaller) the costs. The general cost of inflation is that it tends to _________________ income. Real income is the purchasing power of one's money income. Inflation can mean that some people's real income drops while others' real income rises. For those with fixed money incomes, inflation causes the purchasing power of their income to ____________ (increase/decrease). Or, if money income increases less than inflation, then real income will drop.

On the other hand, if money income increases at a faster rate than infla-
rise — tion, then people's real income will ______________ (rise/fall). The
government also redistributes income and resources by running a deficit.
private — A deficit redistributes resources away from the ________________
public — (private/public) sector to the ________________ (private/public) sector.

Creditors (lenders) lose from unanticipated inflation because they are
less — repaid with ____________ (more/less) valuable dollars. They also lose
decreases — because their real income (or rate of return) from lending ____________
(increases/decreases). Creditors can protect themselves against unanticipated inflation by adding an inflationary premium to the interest rate
they charge. This has been done in many mortgage markets around the
variable-rate — country. This type of home mortgage is known as a ________________
mortgage.

Bond buyers are hurt in much the same way as other savers. That is,
decreases — unanticipated inflation ________________ (increases/decreases) the purchasing power of their principle investment and their interest income
(real rate of interest).

Another group who loses from unanticipated inflation are holders of
currency, demand deposits, and savings accounts. This is because the pur-
decreases — chasing power of the money being held _______________ (decreases/
increases) and because the real interest rate (or real rate of return) from
decreases — savings _______________ (decreases/increases). The real interest rate is
equal to the interest rate at which one saves minus the inflation rate. If
the interest rate at which one saves is fixed and inflation increases, then
decreases — the real interest rate from savings _____________ (decreases/increases).

Answers	
	If the inflation rate is equal to the interest rate at which one saves, the
zero	real interest rate is ______________ (negative/zero/positive).
	Many businesses and workers lose from unanticipated inflation be-
long-term	cause they make _________________ (long-term/short-term) contracts
fixed	at ___________ (fixed/variable) prices and wages. In other words, their
decrease	profits or real income _______________ (increase/decrease) with unan-
	ticipated inflation. In the same way, those who depend on pensions and
lose	Social Security payments _____________ (gain/lose).
	Finally, taxpayers lose from unanticipated inflation due to
bracket creep	_________________________________ in the absence of tax
indexing	______________.
	Basically, those who benefit from inflation are those who are able to
can	anticipate it. If inflation can be anticipated, then people _____________
	(can/cannot) make adjustments to benefit from it. If consumers anticipate
now	inflation, they are likely to buy more ___________ (now/later) and save
less	___________ (more/less) now. By doing so, consumers can avoid
later	paying higher prices ___________ (now/later). Businesses may benefit
more	if they produce ___________ (more/less) now at today's costs and sell
higher	later at tomorrow's ____________ (lower/higher) prices. Debtors stand
fixed-	to gain if they can get loans at ______________ (fixed-/variable-) inter-
	est rates. This is because the real cost of borrowing (or the real interest
decreases	rate) _________________ (increases/decreases) with inflation. There
	are temporary benefits to businesses because product prices increase
before	_______________ (before/after) wages increase. Workers also may
	benefit if they receive cost–of–living adjustments (COLAs).

Finally, there are gains to politicians and government employees. An

increase _______________ (increase/decrease) in the money supply for funding government programs benefits the politicians who promote the programs, the workers who staff them, and those people who benefit directly from

inflation them. But increases in the money supply may cause ___________, and we know that this imposes some costs.

The Federal Reserve could increase the money supply directly, but what usually happens is that the federal government first runs a

deficit _______________ (surplus/deficit), which must be financed by

borrowing _______________________. The federal government borrows by

selling ________________ (buying/selling) government securities on the open

increase market, which has a tendency to ________________ (increase/decrease) interest rate. The Federal Reserve may then come under heavy political

decrease pressure to _________________ (increase/decrease) these interest rates and the accompanying unemployment. If the Federal Reserve Board of Governors succumbs to this pressure to accommodate deficit spending

buy they will order the Open Market Committee to ___________ (buy/sell) government securities on the open market. This has a tendency to

decrease _________________ (increase/decrease) interest rates and the unemploy-

increase ment rate. So deficit spending has a tendency to ________________ (increase/decrease) interest rates, but accommodative monetary policy

increases that _______________ (increases/decreases) the money supply has a ten-

down dency to push interest rates ____________ (up/down). Whether interest rates are greater, the same, or less than before depends on the magnitude of the deficit and the increase in the money supply. But as the money

increases supply increases over time, inflation _______________________

(increases/decreases). So deficit spending accommodated by monetary
inflation — policy causes ___________.

The inflation caused by deficit spending and accommodative monetary
policy can be viewed as taxation without representation. Like taxation, in-
unable — flation means that people are ___________ (able/unable) to buy as
is — much. In this way, inflation __________ (is/is not) taxation in disguise.
In as much as politicians promote deficit spending for programs without
the tax revenues to pay for them, they may be misleading the public by
inflation — not pointing out the real cost of doing so, which is _______________.
The government may also promote increases in the money supply that
inflation, decrease — cause ________________________ in order to _________________
(increase/decrease) the real value of the federal debt (caused by deficit
increased — spending). Taxes in the future may also have to be ________________
(increased/decreased) to pay the higher interest expense on a greater
increase — federal debt. Moreover, the interest rate on the debt may ___________
(increase/decrease) with increases in the money supply because greater
increase — inflation causes interest rates to ______________ (increase/decrease).

Because monetary stability helps prevent inflation, it could be viewed
public — as a _______________ (private/public) good. Whether the government
should provide for monetary stability is something the electorate must
decide. However, the effects of any decision, and of indecision,
can — __________ (can/cannot) be predicted by economic theory.

Problems and Applications

1. Assume people anticipate greater rates of inflation.
   a. What would happen to the level of saving and the level of consumption spending?

b. Based on your answer above, use demand and supply analysis to determine what would happen to prices and the output level of consumer products.
c. Are the higher prices for consumer products a result of demand-pull inflation?
d. Can we say that expectations with respect to higher prices (higher inflation) are self-fulfilling? How so?
e. Can self-fulfilling expectations about inflation result in hyper-inflation? How so?
f. Based on your answer to 1b above, what happens to the amount of our scarce resources devoted to consumer products?
g. Assume we are at full employment. In terms of the production possibilities model (see Chapter 2), if more consumer products are being produced, what happens to the amount of capital products produced?
h. Based on your answer to 1g above, what happens to the rate of economic growth?
i. Can we conclude that anticipated greater rates of inflation result in lower rates of economic growth because saving decreases?
j. What happens to interest rates?
k. Does investment consist of business expenditures for capital products?
l. Based on your answer to 1j above, what would you expect to happen to the level of investment?
m. Based on your answer to 1l above, use demand and supply analysis to determine what would happen to the output level of capital products.
n. Based on your answer to 1l above, what happens to the amount of resources devoted to capital products?
o. If we are at full employment and smaller amounts of our resources are devoted to capital products, does this mean more of our resources can be devoted to consumer products? Is this what happens when people anticipate a greater rate of inflation?
p. Assume we are at full employment. In terms of the production possibilities model, if fewer capital products and more consumer products are being produced, what happens to the rate of economic growth?
q. Can we conclude that anticipated greater rates of inflation result in lower rates of economic growth because investment decreases?

r. Can we conclude that an economy requires saving for investment to occur?

s. Can we conclude that an economy which experiences greater levels of saving and investment will experience greater rates of economic growth?

t. Finally, can we generally conclude that anticipated greater rates of inflation result in lower rates of economic growth?

2. How can inflation lead to higher interest rates over time?
3. How can inflation contribute to the business cycle?
4. Why is inflation taxation is disguise?
5. What is bracket creep? How is this related to indexing?
6. How could hyperinflation lead to a barter economy?

True-False

For each item, determine whether the statement is basically true or false. If the statement if false, rewrite it so it is a true statement.

_____ 1. Higher rates of inflation will cause lower rates of economic growth.

_____ 2. Bracket creep corrects for indexing.

_____ 3. Taxpayers can gain from inflation because of bracket creep.

_____ 4. Inflation can cause interest rates to rise.

_____ 5. During inflationary periods, individual product prices may rise, fall, or remain the same, but on the average the general price level will rise.

_____ 6. It is usually correct to say that behind every relatively great inflationary surge there is a relatively great contraction in the money supply.

_____ 7. The extent of the costs and benefits of inflation depends on whether or not the inflation is anticipated and on the rate of inflation.

_____ 8. Anticipated inflation can lead to hyperinflation.

_____ 9. A barter economy can lead to hyperinflation.

_____ 10. Inflation benefits those on fixed incomes.

_____ 11. Real income is the purchasing power of one's income.

_____ 12. Variable-rate mortgages pass the risks associated with inflation from banks to home buyers.

_____ 13. If people's income increases faster than inflation, they are better off.

_____ 14. The federal government borrows by selling government securities on the open market, which has a tendency to decrease interest rates.

_____ 15. When the Federal Reserve accommodates deficit spending, this increases the money supply and has a tendency to decrease interest rates.

_____ 16. Over the long run, when Congress runs a deficit and the Fed increases the money supply, this causes inflation.

_____ 17. Monetary stability could be viewed as a private good.

_____ 18. An increase in the money supply can cause decreases in inflation but not increases in taxes.

_____ 19. It is unanticipated inflation that creates the redistribution of income and uneven production levels.

_____ 20. The Fisher effect states that the market rate of interest equals a real rate of interest (or, real rate of return) plus an inflationary premium.

Multiple Choice *Choose the one best answer for each item.*

_____ 1. Inflation can cause
   a. some people to benefit while other people lose.
   b. everyone to lose if inflation causes lower production levels.
   c. people's real income to decrease.
   d. uneven production levels.
   e. all of the above.

_____ 2. Which of the following is *not* a result of anticipated inflation?
   a. Interest rates will decline in the near future.
   b. Consumers will buy more goods and services now.
   c. Businesses will increase inventories now.
   d. People will save less now.
   e. It could result in even higher rates of inflation over time.

_____ 3. A COLA is
   a. a capital outlay adjustment.
   b. a means whereby businesses protect their real profits from declining.
   c. a means whereby workers protect their real incomes from declining.
   d. an inflationary premium added on to interest rates to protect a creditor's real interest rate (or rate of return from loans made) from falling.
   e. an adjustment made to the consumer price index to measure the real rate of inflation.

_____ 4. If businesses increase their inventories because of anticipated inflation, this is because they expect
  a. interest rates to fall in the future.
  b. wages to increase in the future.
  c. product prices to decrease in the future.
  d. all of the above.
  e. none of the above.

_____ 5. Variable-rate mortgages reflect
  a. consumers' attempts to protect themselves against the losses associated with inflation.
  b. creditors' attempts to protect themselves against the losses associated with inflation.
  c. the fact that mortgage rates vary from region to region.
  d. changes in the demand for and supply of housing.
  e. the differing risks associated with lending money to different people.

_____ 6. If inflation rises, this will cause
  a. COLAs to rise.
  b. variable-rate mortgages to rise.
  c. interest rates to rise.
  d. temporary benefits to businesses because product prices increase before wages increase.
  e. all of the above to occur.

_____ 7. Inflation can affect
  a. the distribution of income.
  b. the allocation of resources.
  c. production levels in the economy.
  d. future rates of inflation.
  e. all of the above.

_____ 8. Bracket creep
  a. occurs because of inflation, which causes interest rates to rise to higher brackets.
  b. occurs because of deflation, which causes consumption expenditures to fall.
  c. is an automatic increase in one's income by a percent equal to the inflation rate.
  d. occurs because of inflation when incomes increase and people are pushed into higher tax brackets.
  e. shows that taxpayers can gain from inflation.

_____ 9. Which of the following groups stand to gain from unanticipated inflation?
   a. Government
   b. Creditors who lend at fixed interest rates
   c. Holders of money
   d. Bond buyers
   e. Taxpayers

_____ 10. Deficit spending accommodated by monetary policy will cause
   a. an increase in the money supply.
   b. inflation over time.
   c. interest rates to rise.
   d. the federal debt to rise.
   e. all of the above to occur.

_____ 11. Inflation may benefit
   a. those who owe money at fixed rates of interest.
   b. those who lend money at fixed rates of interest.
   c. those who hold money.
   d. those who have fixed incomes.
   e. those businesses tied to long-term price and wage adjustments.

_____ 12. Inflation
   a. can be viewed as taxation in disguise.
   b. can be viewed as taxation without representation.
   c. benefits those on fixed income.
   d. benefits creditors who lend at fixed interest rates.
   e. can be viewed as both a and b above.

Discussion Questions

1. Is there a limit to how high the federal debt can become? *(KQ1, 2, 3)*
2. How could demand-pull and cost-push inflation lead to hyperinflation? *(KQ1)*
3. Will unanticipated rates of inflation result in lower rates of economic growth? *(KQ1)*
4. What would happen to interest rates if we experienced deflation? *(KQ1)*
5. How could deficit spending accommodated by monetary policy cause stagflation? *(KQ2, 3)*
6. If the inflation rate reached what may be considered a dangerously high level, do you think price and wage controls would help? What problems can you foresee? *(KQ1, 3)*

7. Besides inflation, what else can cause a decline in workers' real incomes? *(KQ1)*
8. Is the bracket creep another example of inflation as taxation in disguise? *(KQ1)*
9. Why does inflation reduce economic efficiency? *(KQ1)*
10. Will inflation impose costs or benefits on the elderly who receive Social Security? *(KQ1)*
11. Should college students who receive government guaranteed student loans at fixed rates of interest pay them off quickly, or would they be better off paying the minimum monthly payment? *(KQ2)*

Answers

Problems and Applications

1. a. With greater anticipated rates of inflation, the level of saving decreases and the level of consumption spending increases (to avoid paying higher prices in the future).

   b. If consumption spending increases, then the demand for consumer products increases. This results in higher prices for consumer products and a greater output level. See the graph below.

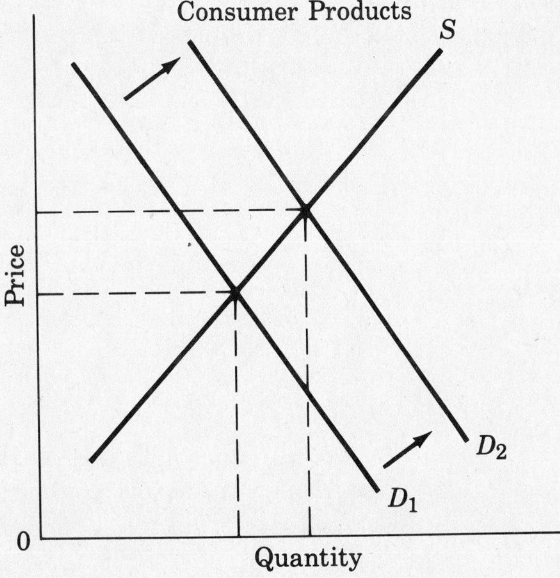

c. Yes.
d. Yes. When people expect higher prices, they rush out to buy more now rather than waiting for prices to rise. This means an increased demand for these products, which drives up prices.
e. Yes, although not necessarily. As people expect higher and higher prices, over time they will spend more and more out of their own self-interest, which causes prices to continually rise over time.
f. As the output level rises for consumer products, we will require greater amounts of our scarce resources to be devoted to consumer products. It simply takes more resources to produce more consumer products.
g. If we are at full employment, we are on the production possibilities curve. In order to get more consumer products, we have to give up some capital products. See the graph below.

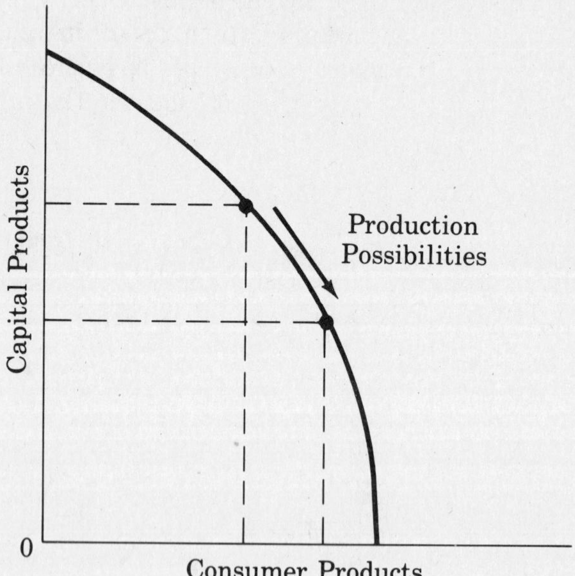

h. The rate of economic growth decreases. A greater amount of our resources devoted to consumer products and a smaller amount of our resources devoted to capital products results in smaller rightward shifts in the production possibilities curve over time.

i. Yes.
j. Interest rates rise with anticipated greater rates of inflation because creditors would add an inflationary premium to protect themselves against the devalued dollar when the loan is repaid. Also, an inflationary premium is added to ensure their desired rate of return.
k. Yes.
l. Investment would decrease because as interest rates rise, fewer funds would be borrowed to be invested in plant and equipment (capital products). Even if businesses don't have to borrow to finance expenditures on capital products, there would still be a decrease in investment, as many businesses would realize they could receive a greater rate of return by putting some of their money in an interest-bearing account at a bank.
m. If investment spending for capital products decreases, the demand for these products decreases. The result is a smaller output level of capital products produced. See the graph below.

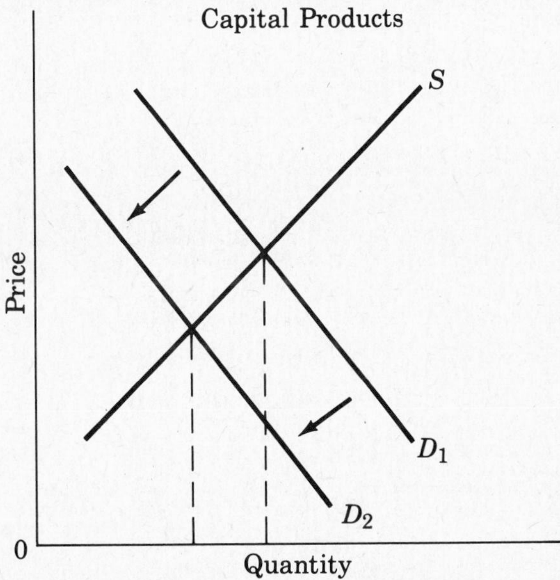

n. As the output level of capital products decreases, we will require smaller amounts of our scarce resources to be devoted to capital products. It simply takes fewer resources to produce fewer capital products.

o. Yes; see the graph above. Yes.
p. The rate of economic growth decreases. A smaller percent of our resources devoted to capital products and a greater percent of our resources devoted to consumer products means smaller rightward shifts in the production possibilities curve over time.
q. Yes.
r. Yes.
s. Yes.
t. Yes.

2. Creditors will add an inflationary premium to the interest rate they charge to protect themselves against the devalued dollar they are repaid and to ensure they receive their desired rate of return from the funds they lend. If the funds they lend are based on a fixed rate of interest, then an inflationary premium can be added on to the fixed rate of interest equal to the anticipated inflation rate. If the funds they lend are based on a variable rate of interest, then the inflationary premium fluctuates with inflation. In this way, we can see that as inflation increases, interest rates will increase.
3. If inflation is anticipated, business may increase their inventories now in order to produce at today's cost and sell at tomorrow's prices. This increases national output, employment, and income. But after the desired inventory level has been reached, businesses will cut back on production, causing employment and national income to drop.
4. Inflation erodes the purchasing power of one's income. Just as with taxation, people are unable to buy as much. And if the inflation was caused by deficit spending accommodated by expansionary monetary policy, then this distributes purchasing power from the public to the government without the approval of Congress.
5. Bracket creep results when increases in a person's income to keep up with inflation push the person into a higher tax bracket. Indexing is the adjustment of tax brackets to prevent bracket creep.
6. Hyperinflation could result in people ceasing to hold on to money as a medium of exchange or as a store of purchasing power, resulting in a moneyless economy or barter system.

True-False

1. T
2. F: Indexing corrects for bracket creep.
3. F: Taxpayers can lose from inflation because of bracket creep.
4. T 5. T
6. F: It is usually correct to say that behind every relatively great inflationary surge there is a relatively great expansion in the money supply.
7. T 8. T
9. F: Hyperinflation can lead to a barter economy.
10. F: Inflation hurts those on fixed incomes.
11. T 12. T 13. T
14. F: The federal government borrows by selling government securities on the open market, which has a tendency to increase interest rates.
15. T 16. T
17. F: Monetary stability could be viewed as a public good.
18. F: An increase in the money supply can cause increases in inflation and increases in taxes (because of bracket creep in the absence of indexing).
19. T 20. T

Multiple Choice

1. e *(KQ1, 2)*	2. a *(KQ1)*	3. c *(KQ2)*
4. b *(KQ2)*	5. b *(KQ2)*	6. e *(KQ2)*
7. e *(KQ1)*	8. d (KQ1)	9. a *(KQ2)*
10. e *(KQ1)*	11. a *(KQ2)*	12. e *(KQ3)*

CHAPTER 10

Unemployment and the Equilibrium Income Level: An Introduction

Chapter Summary

Key Question 1: What was the pre-Keynesian perspective on macroeconomics?

Not until Keynes wrote *The General Theory of Employment, Interest, and Money* in 1936 did we have a comprehensive theory of the macroeconomy. This work was really an attack on the classical theory of unemployment and other theories regarding causes of the business cycle. To understand the impact in the Keynesian revolution, we must first look at these earlier theories. The classical theory of unemployment was the most prominent of the earlier theories. The classical economists believed the economy would never be completely free from unemployment because of continuing adjustments in the labor market and because of obstructions in the labor market that may prevent the real wage rate from falling.

Other early theories of the business cycle include agricultural theories, the theory of general glut, and monetary theories. The agricultural theories blamed the business cycle on unfavorable growing seasons. The theory of general glut was naive in its contention that overproduction would necessarily cause unemployment and was quickly attacked by the notion of Say's law, which states that supply creates its own demand. Monetary theories of the business cycle blamed unemployment on the overextension of loans (or people's inability to repay loans and the resulting bank panics), which reduces the supply of money.

Key Question 2: What is the Keynesian perspective on macroeconomics?

Keynes rejected the classical labor market as a frame of reference. Instead, he concentrated on the interrelationship between the total output level and the total spending level in determining the level of economic activity. This interrelationship can be viewed in the context of the circular flow of income model.

Key Question 3: Why is equilibrium not necessarily at full employment?

An equilibrium income (output) level is established where the total dollar value of goods and services produced in the economy (which gives rise to an identical dollar income level) gives rise to a total dollar spending level that is just sufficient to clear that total output off the market. There are two ways to look at an equilibrium income level and how it may change. One way is to concentrate on total spending and total output. Another way is to concentrate on leakages and injections.

Total spending consists of consumption spending plus investment spending plus government spending plus exports minus imports. If total spending equals total output, then we have an equilibrium income level. If total spending is less than total output, then the level of economic activity will decline because some products will go unsold (in other words, business inventories, or unplanned investment, will rise). Businesses will therefore cut back their rate of production and lay off workers. With fewer workers employed, the nation's income drops, causing a further decline in total spending and another round of unsold products and so on until equilibrium income is established. Should prices fall in response to an increase in business inventories, a "wealth effect" may be created, which could correct for the decline in economic activity. But this adjustment process may take a relatively long time. In the meantime, businesses will decrease production and lay off workers.

If total spending is greater than total output, then the income level will rise because inventory levels will drop below a desired level. Businesses will therefore increase their rate of production, thereby increasing employment (if we are not already at full employment). With more workers employed, national income and total spending increases, causing another round of lower-than-desired levels of inventories and so on until a higher equilibrium income level is established.

Another way to understand equilibrium income level and how it may change is to concentrate on leakages and injections. Leakages represent money flowing out of the circular flow of income and include savings, taxes, and imports. Injections represent money flowing into the circular flow of income and include planned investment, government expenditures, and exports. If leakages equal injections, then an equilibrium income level will be observed. If leakages are greater than injections, then the level of economic activity will fall because total spending falls short of the total output level (inventories or unplanned investment are too high). If leakages are less than injections, then the income level will rise because total spending is more than sufficient to clear that total output off the market (inventories or unplanned investment are too low).

If we assume no government and no international trade, then leakages consist only of saving, and injections consist only of planned investment. Therefore, equilibrium exists where saving equals planned investment (in other words, where unplanned investment, which expresses change in inventories, is zero).

Classical economists believed saving would always equal planned investment. Their conception of interest rate determination guaranteed this equality. But Keynes objected to the classical conception of interest rate determination, contending that current saving is not always channeled into investment as quickly as the classical school supposed. If some saving is held as idle cash or bank balances, then the total funds available for investment may be less than actual saving, which would cause interest rates to rise and investment in decline. In this case, saving will be greater than planned investment and the income (output) level will drop. Conversely, if past accumulated money balances are lent out to supplement current saving, then the total funds available for investment will be greater than current saving, driving interest rates down. This would cause planned investment to exceed current saving, thus increasing the level of economic activity.

In short, Keynes concluded that there is no guaranteed equality between saving and planned investment over the short run, and this is why the level of economic activity changes. What, then, can government do to smooth out the business cycle?

Key Question 4: How does the government fit into the Keynesian paradigm?

When we bring government into our analysis, we see that equilibrium is defined where *total* leakages equal *total* injections. Total leakages become savings plus taxes, and total injections become planned investment plus government spending. Therefore, changes in taxes and/or government spending can help maintain a particular equilibrium income level, and sufficiently large enough changes can actually cause a higher or lower equilibrium income level, whether saving equals planned investment or not. For instance, if we are below full employment, then a sufficiently large enough decrease in taxes and/or an increase in government spending will cause total injections to exceed total leakages, causing the income level to rise toward full employment (whether saving equals planned investment or not). Therefore, the Keynesian prescription for unemployment is a budgetary deficit (or, at least a decrease in budgetary surplus). The overriding goal is to increase total spending so that it is more than sufficient to clear the current total output level off the market. This increase in total spending causes the income (output) level to rise toward full employment. Note, however, that an increase in government spending will tend to have a slightly greater effect on the national income level than would an equal decrease in taxes.

Review Terms and Concepts

Macroeconomic policy
Fiscal policy
Monetary policy
Circular flow of income
Keynesian school of thought
Equilibrium quantity
Real balances or real wealth effect
Classical school of thought
Demand
Supply
Equilibrium price

New Terms and Concepts

Real wage rate
Full employment
Say's law
Keynes's law
Circular flow of income
Leakage (outflow)
Injection (inflow)
Wealth effect
Investment
Planned investment
Unplanned investment
Equilibrium income level
Saving

Completion

total spending (aggregate demand)

The Keynesian school of thought emphasizes ____________________ as the key determinant of the level of macroeconomic activity. An in-

increase

crease in total spending causes national income to ______________

direct

(increase/decrease), and vice versa. So there is a ____________ (direct/ inverse) relationship between total spending and national income.

1936

The Keynesian revolution really began in __________ (1956/1936) when Keynes wrote *The General Theory of Employment, Interest, and*

was

Money. Keynes __________ (was/was not) the first to express effectively a general theory of the macroeconomy.

Other theories of unemployment and causes of the business cycle were

was

popular before Keynes. The classical theory __________ (was/was not) the most prominent. Classical economist believed the economy

could never

____________________ (could/could never) be completely free from

Answers	
continuing	unemployment because of ______________ (perfect/continuing)
	adjustments in the labor market. They also believed that obstructions in
falling	the labor market may prevent the real wage rate from ______________
	(falling/rising), which may cause some unemployment. One type of
unions	obstruction they mentioned was ______________.
	The agricultural theory of the business cycle put the blame for
unfavorable	economic fluctuations on ______________ (favorable/unfavorable)
overproduction	growing seasons. The theory of general glut held that ______________
	(underproduction/overproduction) was the problem. This theory was at-
Say's, supply	tacked by ______________ law, which states that ______________
demand	(demand/supply) creates its own ______________ (demand/supply).
monetary	The ______________ theories of the business cycle focused on the
	overextension of loans and peoples inability to repay loans. Overexten-
panics, decrease	sion may result in bank ______________ (loans/panics) that ______________
	(increase/decrease) the supply of money. In terms of the equation of
	exchange, if velocity of money is reasonably constant and the money
decreases	supply decreases, then the general price level ______________
decreases	(increases/decreases), or the total output level ______________
	(increases/decreases), or both. A decrease in total output causes unem-
increase	ployment to ______________ (increase/decrease). Keynes rejected
	these earlier theories and focused on the interrelationship between the
total spending, total output	______________ level and the ______________
	level in determining the level of national income. The interrelationship
can	______________ (can/cannot) be seen in the context of the circular flow of
	income model.

	An equilibrium income level exists when the total output level (which
	gives rise to an identical national income level) gives rise to a total spend-
just sufficient	ing level that is ____________ to clear that total output
may not	off the market. An equilibrium income level ________ (must/may
	not) result in a full-employment income (output) level. There are two
	ways to look at an equilibrium income level and how it may change. One
total spending	way is to concentrate on ____________ (total spending/
total output	injections) and ____________ (total output/injections).
leakages	Another way is to concentrate on __________ (total output/
injections	leakages) and ____________ (total output/injections).
outflow, inflow	Leakages are an ________ and injections are an ________
	in the circular flow of income.
	If total spending is equal to total output, then we are in
equilibrium	__________. If total spending is greater than total output,
increase	then the level of income will ________ (increase/decrease). If
	total spending is less than total output, then the level of economic activity
decrease	will ________ (increase/decrease).
equilibrium	If leakages equal injections, then we are in __________.
	If leakages are greater than injections, then national income will
decrease	________ (increase/decrease). If leakages are less than injec-
increase	tions, then national income will ________ (increase/decrease).
saving, taxes	In reality, total leakages include ________, ________,
imports, investment	and ________. Total injections include __________,
government expenditures, exports	________________, and ____________.
	If, however, we assume no international trade and no government, total
saving	leakages are __________ and total injections are

planned investment	______________________. Under these assumptions, then,
saving	the equilibrium income level exists when ______________ equals
planned investment	______________________.
always	Classical economists believed that saving would ______________
interest rate	(always/not) equal planned investment because the ______________
	would guarantee it. But Keynesians disagree that current saving will
	always find its way into investment as quickly as the classical econo-
	mists supposed. This is because some saving may be held as
idle cash or bank	______________________________ balances. If this occurs,
higher	then interest rates will be ______________ (higher/lower) and
saving	______________ (saving/planned investment) will exceed
planned investment	______________________ (saving/planned investment).
decreases	This means that national income ______________ (increases/decreases).
exceed	Conversely, it is possible for planned investment to ______________
	(exceed/be less than) current saving, causing national income to increase.
	Because saving and planned investment are not always equal, govern-
	ment expenditures and taxes may have to be adjusted either to maintain
	an equilibrium income level or to change it. If we are below full employ-
decrease	ment, the government should ______________ (increase/decrease)
increase	taxes, or ______________ (increase/decrease) government expendi-
increase	tures, or both. This will cause total spending to ______________
	(increase/decrease)and bring about a higher equilibrium income level.
	These actions mean that government is moving in the direction of a
deficit	budgetary ______________ (surplus/deficit). Deficits are recom-
below	mended by Keynesian policy if we are ______________ (at/below/
	above) full employment. However, government should run a budgetary

surplus

_________________ (surplus/deficit) to combat inflationary pressures in the economy.

Problems and Applications

1. We know that Keynesians view total spending as the key determinant of the level of economic activity. That is, if total spending increases, then the national income level increases, and vice versa.
   a. What are the components of total spending?
   b. Assuming no international trade, what effect will a change in taxes and government spending have on the components of total spending?
   c. What happens to the income level if total spending is greater than the total output level?
2. a. What are the components of total injections and total leakages?
   b. What are the components of total injections and total leakages assuming no international trade?
   c. Where does equilibrium income exist?
   d. Where does equilibrium income exist if we assume no international trade?
   e. What will happen to the income level if leakages exceed injections?
3. a. Assume we are at an equilibrium income level and there is no international trade. If $S = 20$, $I = 15$, and $T = 15$, what is G equal to?
   b. What is the budgetary surplus or deficit equal to?
   c. If this equilibrium income level is below full employment, what could government do with taxes and government spending to increase the income level?
4. The classical conception of interest rate determination guaranteed the equality between current saving and planned investment. That is, classical economists conceived of a positive relationship between saving and the interest rate and an inverse relationship between planned investment and the interest rate. This relationship can be expressed graphically as shown on the next page.

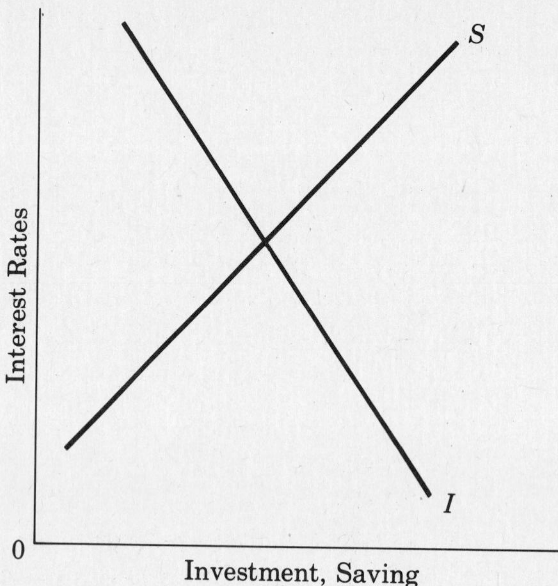

a. Where would the equilibrium interest rate exist?
b. If the interest rate is above equilibrium, what can we say about saving and planned investment? What would happen to the interest rate over time?
c. Keynes attacked the classical theory of interest rate determination by pointing out that current saving does not always flow into investment as quickly and smoothly as the classicalist assumed. Instead, some current saving may be held as idle cash or bank balances (which represents money that is neither spent nor loaned out to investors). Why would people accumulate idle cash or bank balances?
d. If people expected interest rates to rise, what would happen to their amount of idle cash or bank balances?
e. What effect would expectations of higher interest rates in the future have on the level of saving and planned investment?
f. What effect would expectations of higher interest rates in the future have on the national income level?
g. What effect would expectations of lower interest rates in the future have on saving and planned investment (hence the national income level)?
h. What can we conclude about saving and planned investment?

5. Why did the classical economists believe the economy would never be completely free from unemployment?

True-False

For each item, determine whether the statement is basically true or false. If the statement is false, rewrite it so it is a true statement.

_____ 1. The real wage is the wage rate after taxes.

_____ 2. Full employment was defined by classical economists as the equilibrium quantity of labor in the labor market.

_____ 3. Say's law states that demand creates its own supply.

_____ 4. Unplanned investment shows changes in inventories.

_____ 5. Savings represents a leakage (or outflow) from the circular flow of income.

_____ 6. Investment equals planned investment plus unplanned investment.

_____ 7. Inflation will cause the real wage rate to rise, with everything else held constant.

_____ 8. Keynes was the first economist to recommend budget deficits to correct for unemployment.

_____ 9. According to the classical school, the demand for labor is directly related to the real wage rate, and the supply of labor is inversely related to the real wage rate.

_____ 10. The theory of general glut was attacked by Say's law.

_____ 11. According to the monetary theories of the business cycle, widespread bank panics, which result from bad loans, would cause a decrease in the money supply and therefore an immediate decrease in prices.

_____ 12. An equilibrium national income level exists when total output gives rise to a level of total demand that is just sufficient to clear that total output off the market.

_____ 13. At an equilibrium income level, leakages exceed injections.

_____ 14. Unplanned investment will result in an increase in the income level.

_____ 15. The wealth effect means that if prices fall because of a recession, then the real value of assets increases, causing people to spend more and thereby helping to correct for the recession.

_____ 16. Total injections include planned investment, government spending, and exports.

____ 17. Government should increase taxes and/or decrease government spending to correct for unemployment.

____ 18. Government may have to run a deficit just to maintain an equilibrium income level because saving may exceed planned investment.

____ 19. Keynes's law states that demand creates its own supply.

Multiple Choice *Choose the one best answer for each item.*

____ 1. To correct for unemployment, it is best for government to
a. increase taxes.
b. run a budgetary deficit.
c. balance the budget.
d. decrease the supply of money.
e. decrease government spending.

____ 2. Leakages include
a. exports.
b. government spending.
c. taxes.
d. unplanned investment.
e. planned investment.

____ 3. If $I + G > S + T$, then
a. the income level will increase.
b. leakages are greater than injections.
c. investment must be greater than savings.
d. savings must be greater than investment.
e. the income level will decrease.

____ 4. If the general price level is rising faster than money incomes, then
a. the purchasing power of money is increasing.
b. the real wage rate is increasing.
c. this may cause greater employment.
d. leakages equal injections.
e. all of the above will be true.

____ 5. Which of the following statements most closely represents Keynes's objections to the classical theory of interest rate determination?
a. Keynes says saving always equals planned investment at the equilibrium interest rate.

b. Saving does not always flow into investment as smoothly and quickly as the classical economists assumed.
c. If the interest rate is below equilibrium, then there is a surplus of funds available for lending.
d. If the interest rate is above equilibrium, then planned investment will exceed saving.
e. all of the above.

____ 6. If $S = \$5$, $T = \$7$, planned $I = \$15$, and $G = \$3$, then
a. leakages are greater than injections.
b. the budgetary deficit equals $4.
c. we are at an equilibrium income level.
d. unemployment can be expected to increase in the near future.
e. unemployment can be expected to decrease in the near future.

____ 7. A budgetary deficit
a. can cause unemployment to decrease.
b. means taxes are greater than government spending.
c. should always be incurred.
d. was recommended by the classical economists.
e. is described in all of the above.

____ 8. Saving will *not* always equal planned investment because
a. idle cash balances may increase.
b. idle cash balances may decrease.
c. people may expect interest rates to increase.
d. people may expect interest rates to decrease.
e. of all of the above.

____ 9. A budgetary deficit
a. may only maintain an equilibrium income level if the deficit equals the amount by which saving exceeds planned investment.
b. may increase the national income level if the deficit exceeds the amount by which saving is greater than planned investment.
c. occurs when taxes are greater than government spending.
d. is a and b above.
e. is none of the above.

____ 10. Assuming government spending, total injections would equal
a. $I + G + T$.
b. $I + T$.
c. $G + I + S$.
d. $S + T$.
e. $I + G$.

____ 11. Assuming no international trade, total leakages equal
a. $S + I$.
b. $T + S$.
c. $I + G$.
d. $G + C$.
e. none of the above.

____ 12. An increase in government spending will have a greater impact than an equal decrease in taxes because
a. part of these lower tax liabilities will be saved.
b. people like government to run deficits.
c. in equilibrium the government's budget is always in balance.
d. planned investment never equals saving.
e. of none of the above.

____ 13. An equilibrium income level can result
a. in some unemployment.
b. from saving equal to planned investment if there is no government or international trade.
c. from $S + T = I + G$ if there is no international trade.
d. from $S = I$ if there is no government or international trade.
e. from all of the above.

____ 14. If total spending increases, then
a. inventories will rise, total output will drop, employment will drop, and national income will rise.
b. inventories will decline, total output will rise, employment will rise, and national output will rise.
c. this may have been due to an increase in saving.
d. it must have been due to leakages exceeding injections.
e. unplanned investment will rise.

____ 15. If people expect interest rates to rise in the future, this will cause
a. saving to exceed planned investment at the equilibrium interest rate.
b. planned investment to exceed saving at the equilibrium interest rate.
c. saving to equal planned investment at the equilibrium interest rate.
d. the equilibrium interest rate to drop.
e. people to hold fewer idle cash or bank balances.

____ 16. Which of the following statements is correct?
a. In equilibrium, total spending equals total output.
b. In equilibrium, leakages equal injections.

c. In equilibrium, unplanned investment, which shows changes in inventories, is zero.
d. Equilibrium can occur below full employment.
e. All of the above are correct.

Discussion Questions

1. How would Keynesian policy correct for inflation? *(KQ2, 4)*
2. Why was Keynes more concerned with the short run than the long run? *(KQ1, 2)*
3. How effective do you think Keynesian policy would be in combating stagflation? *(KQ4)*
4. Why must imports be subtracted from total spending? *(KQ2)*
5. We know from the equation of exchange that $MV = PQ$. Can we state the same idea as total spending equals consumption spending + investment spending + government spending + exports minus imports? *(KQ2)*
6. Assume saving equals planned investment and government spending equals tax revenues at an equilibrium below full employment. Could equal increases in government spending and taxes, which would maintain a balanced budget, create a higher equilibrium income level? *(KQ2, 3, 4)*

Answers

Problems and Applications

1. a. Total Spending (*TS*) consists of consumption spending on the part of households (*C*), plus investment spending on the part of firms (*I*), plus government spending (*G*), plus exports (*X*) minus imports (*M*). Exports minus imports equal net exports (*Xn*). Net exports can be positive or negative depending on our balance of payments. Therefore, $TS = C + I + G \pm Xn$.
   b. An increase (decrease) in *G* will increase (decrease) *TS* because *G* is a direct component of *TS*. An increase (decrease) in *T* will decrease (increase) *C* and *I* (hence *TS*).
   c. The income level rises until total spending equals the total output level.
2. a. Total injections equal planned investment (*I*), plus government spending (*G*), plus exports (*X*). Total leakages equal saving (*S*),

plus taxes (T), plus imports (M). Total injections = $I + G + X$; total leakages = $S + T + M$.

b. Total injections = $I + G$. Total leakages = $S + T$.

c. Equilibrium income exists when total injections equal total leakages.

d. Equilibrium income exists when $I + G = S + T$.

e. The income level drops until leakages and injections are equal.

3. a. For an equilibrium income level to exist, injections must equal leakages. That is, $I + G = S + T$. Therefore, G must equal \$20.

b. The budgetary deficit is \$5.

c. To increase the income level, the government could decrease taxes, or increase government spending, or both, moving in the direction of a deficit and causing injections to exceed leakages and total spending to increase.

4. a. The equilibrium interest rate exists at the intersection of the planned investment demand curve and the supply of current saving curve (that is, where the quantity of saving exactly equals the quantity of planned investment). As shown in the figure below, equilibrium exists at interest rate R_1 and where $S = I$.

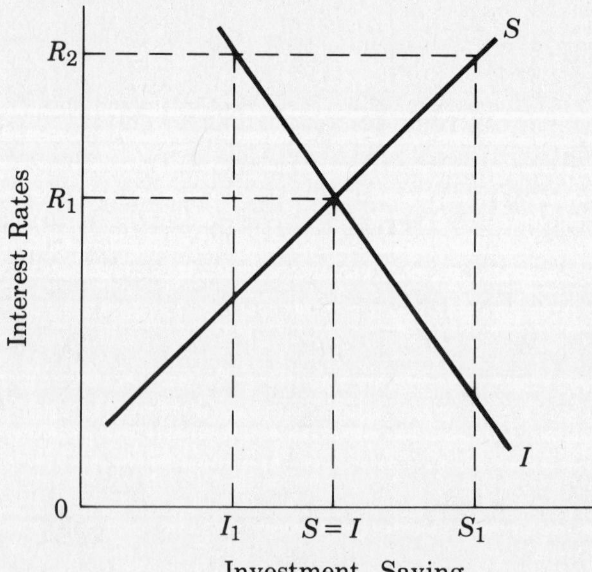

b. If the interest rate is above equilibrium, then saving will be greater than planned investment. In the figure above, R_2 is above equilibrium and S is greater than I. The interest rate will drop toward equilibrium because of the surplus of funds available for lending.

c. People need to hold some money for carrying out daily transactions, for emergency purchases, and for speculative purposes.

d. People would want to hold larger-than-usual money balances because if they lend their money out now, they will be stuck with a low interest rate in the future.

e. The effect would be an increase in accumulated money balances out of current saving. In other words, not all current saving will be channeled into investment. This means the real funds available for investment would be less than the supply of current saving at any interest rate. Graphically, this could be expressed as shown in the graph below, where the real funds available (F) curve is less than the supply of current saving curve. The interest rate becomes R_3, saving becomes S_2, while investment becomes I_1. We can see that the interest rate will be higher than otherwise, causing saving to exceed planned investment.

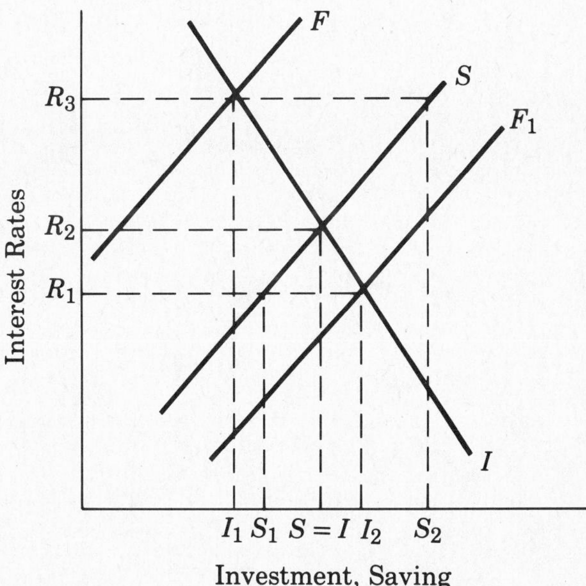

f. Because saving exceeds planned investment, the national income level would have a tendency to drop.

g. If people expected lower interest rates in the future, they would lend out all of their current saving *plus* accumulated idle cash balances. Therefore, the funds available for investment will exceed the current saving level at any interest rate. In the previous figure, this is represented by the curve F_1. The interest rate becomes R_1, saving becomes S_1, while investment becomes I_2. We can see that the interest rate will be lower than otherwise, causing planned investment to exceed saving. Therefore, the national income level will rise.

h. We can conclude there is no guaranteed equality between saving and planned investment. Do you know why?

5. Classical economists believed the economy would never be completely free from unemployment because of continuing adjustments in the labor market and because of obstructions in the labor market that may prevent the real wage rate from falling.

True-False

1. F: The real wage rate is the purchasing power of one's wage and is equal to the money wage rate divided by the general price level (measured by a price index).
2. T
3. F: Say's law states that supply creates its own demand.
4. T 5. T 6. T
7. F: Inflation will cause the real wage rate to fall, with everything else held constant.
8. F: Keynes was not the first economist to recommend budget deficits to correct for unemployment.
9. F: According to the classical school, the demand for labor is inversely related to the real wage rate, and the supply of labor is directly related to the real wage rate.
10. T 11. T 12. T
13. F: At an equilibrium income level, leakages equal injections.
14. F: Unplanned investment will result in a decrease in the income level.
15. T 16. T

17. F: Government should decrease taxes and/or increase government spending to correct for unemployment.

18. T

19. T

Multiple Choice

1. b *(KQ4)*	2. c *(KQ2)*	3. a *(KQ4)*
4. c *(KQ1)*	5. b *(KQ3)*	6. e *(KQ4)*
7. a *(KQ4)*	8. e *(KQ3)*	9. d *(KQ4)*
10. e *(KQ4)*	11. b *(KQ4)*	12. a *(KQ4)*
13. e *(KQ3)*	14. b *(KQ3)*	15. a *(KQ3)*
16. e *(KQ3)*		

CHAPTER 11

Unemployment and the Equilibrium Income Level: A More Complicated Model

Chapter Summary

Key Question 1: What is the planned investment and planned saving approach to income equilibrium?

As discussed in Chapter 10, there are two ways to view equilibrium national income level and how it may change. In terms of the leakages-injections approach, if leakages equal injections, then we are in equilibrium. If leakages exceed injections, then income will drop. If injections exceed leakages, then income will rise. In terms of the total spending-total output approach, if total spending equals total output, we are in equilibrium. If total spending exceeds output, then income will rise. If total spending is less than total output, then income will drop. This chapter develops a more sophisticated model of these two views of equilibrium income level and how it may change. Note, however, that the model assumes no government (and no international trade). Therefore, saving is the only leakage and planned investment is the only injection. Furthermore, total spending consists of only consumption spending and investment spending $(TS=C+I)$.

Investment spending depends on the interest rate, national income, expectations about future profitability, business taxes, and technology. National income is one of the most important variables affecting investment. We know investment tends to increase with increases in national income, and vice versa. However, to simplify our analysis, we have assumed an independent relationship between income and planned investment. That is, there will be the same amount of investment spending regardless of income level, and this results in a horizontal investment function. Let's assume the investment function is horizontal at $400 billion. How do we get this $400 billion? In other words, how did we derive the investment function?

To derive the investment function, we must be given a particular investment demand curve and a particular interest rate. Given this information, we can determine the level of investment. And if we assume the level of planned investment spending is independent of the income level, then we get the horizontal investment function of $400 billion. But if the interest rate changes or if the investment demand curve shifts, the investment function will also shift. A particular investment demand curve shows the inverse relationship between the interest rate and the amount of investment spending, holding expectations with regard to future profits, taxes, and technology constant. Therefore, a decrease (increase) in the interest rate will increase (decrease) the level of investment, and the investment function will shift up (down). On the other hand, if business expectations become more optimistic (pessimistic), or if taxes decrease (increase), or if technology increases (decreases), this will shift the investment demand curve to the right (left). A rightward (leftward) shift in the curve shows that more (less) investment will be undertaken at any given rate of interest. Therefore, a rightward (leftward) shift in the investment demand curve will cause the investment function to shift up (down).

Saving depends on the interest rate, the income level, taxes, job security, and expectations about future inflation rates and incomes. If we hold everything constant except income, then we are able to derive the positively sloped saving function, which shows the direct relationship between saving and national income. At very low income levels, there will be some dissaving, but as income increases so does the level of saving. To determine how much saving changes with a change in income (whether an increase or a decrease), we need to know what the *MPS* is. The *MPS* equals the slope of the saving function. A change in any of the variables other than income will cause the saving function to shift. An upward(downward) shift indicates more (less) saving at any income level.

When we bring the saving and investment functions together, we see that equilibrium exists where the two lines intersect, indicating saving (the leakage) equals planned investment (the injection). At any higher income level, saving exceeds planned investment by the amount that total spending falls short of the total output. This is the same amount by which inventories are above the desired level. This unplanned investment in inventories will cause income to drop until saving equals planned investment. At income levels below equilibrium, planned investment exceeds saving by the amount that total spending exceeds total output. This is the same amount by which inventories are below the desired level. Therefore, the income level will rise until saving equals planned investment. Note, however, that equilibrium does not necessarily imply full employment.

Key Question 2: What is the total spending approach to income equilibrium?

Equilibrium can also be viewed in terms of the total spending-total output approach. Because total spending determines the income (output) level, we need to consider what affects consumption spending and investment spending.

Consumption spending depends on the same variables as savings, because whatever is not saved is consumed out of a given income level (and vice versa). Nonetheless, consumption spending depends on the interest rate, taxes, income, personal wealth, and expectations about future inflation and incomes. If we hold all variables other than income constant, we are able to derive the positively sloped consumption function, which shows the direct relationship between consumption and national income. At very low income levels, consumption spending exceeds income. However, at higher income levels, consumption increases by a lesser amount than income. To determine how consumption changes with a change in income (whether an increase or a decrease), we need to know what the *MPC* is. The *MPC* equals the slope of the consumption function. Note that, in the absence of government, the saving function can be derived from the consumption function because whatever is not consumed is saved (and vice versa). Indeed, the vertical distance between the 45-degree line and the consumption function gives us saving at that income level. In the same way, given a change in income, whatever is not devoted to saving is devoted to consumption (and vice versa). Therefore, $MPS + MPC = 1$. A change in any of the variables other than income will shift the consumption function. An upward (downward) shift indicates greater (less) consumption at any income level.

To derive the total planned expenditures function (or the total spending function), all we need to do is add the investment function to the consumption function. This results in the total spending function lying parallel and above the consumption function equal to the amount of investment.

Equilibrium exists where the total spending function intersects the 45-degree line, indicating that total spending equals the income (output) level. At any higher income level, the total spending function lies below the 45-degree line, indicating that total spending falls short of clearing that total output off the market. (This is the same amount by which saving exceeds planned investment—the amount by which inventories are above the desired level). Therefore, income will drop back to equilibrium. At a lower income (output) level, the total spending function lies above the 45-degree line, indicating that total spending exceeds total output. (This the same amount by which planned investment exceeds saving—the amount by which inventories are below the desired level.) Therefore, income will rise to equilibrium. (Again, note that equilibrium does not necessarily imply full employment.)

Key Question 3: What effects do changes in planned total expenditures have on equilibrium income?

Once equilibrium is established, it will be sustained until there is a change in planned consumption spending (or a change in planned saving) or a change in planned investment spending. In other words, equilibrium changes when any of the functions change because this will give us a new point of intersection, both in terms of the leakages-injection approach or the total spending-total output approach. But any change in total spending results in a much larger change in income.

To calculate any change in income, take the change in total spending and multiply by the multiplier. The multiplier equals the reciprocal of the *MPS* (or 1 - *MPC)* and works in both an upward and a downward direction depending on the change in total spending. The multiplier effect helps explain the paradox of thrift. The theory states that if people attempt to save more, they will end up earning less in the aggregate, and saving no more (and possibly less) than before.

Review Terms and Concepts

Leakage
Injection
Saving
Investment
Planned investment
Unplanned investment
Equilibrium income level

New Terms and Concepts

Marginal efficiency of investment *(MEI)*
Investment function
Marginal propensity to save *(MPS)*
Saving function
Dissaving
Contractionary (expansionary) gap
Consumption function
Marginal propensity to consume *(MPC)*
Total expenditure function
Multiplier
Simplest multiplier *(m)*
Paradox of thrift
Potential GNP

Completion

The macroeconomic model developed in this chapter is a useful analysis of how the national income and employment levels are determined. To keep the model simple, however, we are ______________________ (omitting/including) government. Therefore, leakages include only

omitting

saving ________________________, and injections include only
planned investment ________________________________. Moreover, total spending
consumer spending consists only of ________________________________ and
planned investment ________________________________.

equilibrium If saving equals planned investment, then we are in ______________.
fall If saving exceeds planned investment, income will ____________
(rise/fall). If saving is less than planned investment, then income will
rise ____________ (rise/fall). On the other hand, if total spending equals
equilibrium total output, then we are in ____________________. If total spending
rise exceeds total output, then income will ___________ (rise/fall). If total
fall spending is less than total output, then income will ___________
(rise/fall).

Investment spending depends on many variables, of which national income is one of the most important. For the moment, let's hold all variables other than income constant to derive the investment function. In
increase reality, if income rises, this will have a tendency to ___________ (in-
crease/decrease) planned investment spending, and vice versa. But, to
independent simplify matters, we have assumed an _______________ (independent/
dependent) relationship between planned investment and income. This
assumption means that the investment function is represented by a
horizontal _______________ (horizontal/vertical) line. This horizontal invest-
will not ment function shows that planned investment spending _____________
(will/will not) vary with changes in income. For instance, planned investment spending will be $400 billion at each of the various possible income levels. But where did we get the horizontal investment function of $400 billion? It is derived from the interaction of a particular

interest rate	____________________________ and a particular
investment demand	____________________________. The investment demand curve
inverse	shows the ______________ (inverse/direct) relationship between the
	interest rate and the level of investment spending and is, therefore, a
negatively	____________________ (negatively/positively) sloped line or curve.
	That is, if the interest rate decreases, planned investment spending will
increase	______________ (decrease/increase), and vice versa. Furthermore, if
	the interest rate does not change but the investment demand curve
shifts	____________ (remains the same/shifts), then the result is a change in
	planned investment spending. If planned investment spending changes,
shifts	this ___________ (does not shift/shifts) the investment function. If
	planned investment increases, the investment function shifts
up	___________ (up/down), and vice versa. In other words, if the interest
	rate changes or if the investment demand curve shifts, then the invest-
shift	ment function will _____________. An upward shift indicates
more	_____________ (more/less) planned investment will be undertaken at
	each of the various income levels.
	Like investment spending, saving depends on many variables, of
	which national income is one of the most important. The relationship be-
	tween saving and income (holding all other variables constant) is ex-
function, positively	pressed by the saving _____________. This line is _____________
	(positively/negatively) sloped, showing that as income increases, planned
increases	saving _____________ (increases/decreases), and vice versa. However,
dissaving	at very low income levels, we may observe some _____________. The
MPS	slope of the saving function is equal to the ___________ (*MPS*/*MPC*),
saving	which shows us how much ___________ (saving/income) changes with

income	a change in ________________ (saving/income). A change in any of
	the variables (other than income) will cause the saving function to
shift, more	____________. An upward shift indicates ____________ (more/less)
	planned saving at any income level.
	By putting the saving function and investment function on the same
	graph, we can determine the equilibrium income level. Equilibrium ex-
intersect	ists where the two functions ________________ because, at that point,
equals	saving ____________ planned investment. The saving function lies
higher	above the investment function at ____________ (lower/higher) than
	equilibrium income levels. The amount by which saving exceeds planned
	investment represents the amount by which total spending
falls short of	______________________ (falls short of/exceeds) the total output
	level. In other words, this is the same amount by which inventories
rise	________________ (fall/rise). Therefore, the income level will
drop	________________ (drop/rise) until equilibrium is reached. The invest-
	ment function lies above the saving function at income levels
below	___________ (below/above) equilibrium. The amount by which
	planned investment exceeds saving represents the amount by which total
exceeds	spending ________________ (falls short of/exceeds) the total output
fall	level. This is the same amount by which inventories ____________
rise	(fall/rise). Therefore, the income level will ____________ (drop/rise)
	until equilibrium is reached. Any time saving does not equal planned in-
	vestment, the income level will change. If saving equals planned invest-
equilibrium	ment, then we are in __________________, and there is no tendency
	for income to change. However, an equilibrium income (output) level
	may not imply full employment.

C (planned consumption spending)
I (planned investment spending)

function, positively

increases

greater than

less than

consumption

income

MPC

MPC

shift, more

saving

consumed

saving function

Now consider the other approach to equilibrium, the total spending-total output approach. Given no government, total spending equals ______________________________ plus ______________________________. Like planned investment spending, planned consumption spending depends on many variables, and again, national income is one of the most important. By holding all variables other than income constant, we can derive the consumption ______________. This line is ______________ (negatively/positively) sloped, showing that as income increases, planned consumption spending ______________ (decreases/increases), and vice versa. At very low income levels, we may observe that consumption spending is ______________ (less than/greater than) income. But at higher income levels, planned consumption spending is ______________ (less than/greater than) income. To calculate how much ______________ (consumption/income) changes given a change in ______________ (consumption/income), we need to know the ___________ (*MPS*/*MPC*). The slope of the consumption function is equal to the ___________. A change in any of the variables (other than income) will cause the consumption function to ___________. An upward shift indicates ___________ (less/more) consumption at any income level.

Consumption is just the opposite of ______________. Therefore, at any given level (in the absence of government), whatever is not saved is ______________. This means we could have derived the consumption function from the ______________________, or vice versa. Indeed, the vertical distance between the 45-degree line and the

saving	consumption function equals ________________ at that income
	level. In the same way, given a change in income, whatever is not
saving	devoted to consumption must be devoted to ________________.
MPS	Therefore the *MPC* plus the ____________ equals 1.
	To derive the total planned expenditures function (or simply the total
consumption function	spending function), all we do is add the ______________________
investment function	and the ________________________ together. Equilibrium exists
45-degree line	where the total spending function intersects the ________________
	because total spending will be just sufficient to clear total output off the
	market. The total spending function lies above the 45-degree line at
lower	________________ (higher/lower) than equilibrium income levels. In
rise	such cases, the income level will ______________ (drop/rise) until
below	equilibrium is reached because inventories are ________________
	(above/below) their desired level. Alternatively stated, if the total spend-
	ing function lies above the 45-degree line, total spending is
more	____________ (less/more) than sufficient to clear total output off the
	market by the amount that inventories fall below their desired level. The
	total spending function lies below the 45-degree line at income levels
higher	________________ (higher/lower) than equilibrium. In such cases, the
drop	income level will ____________ (drop/rise) until equilibrium is reached
above	because inventories are ___________ (above/below) their desired level.
	Alternatively stated, if the total spending function lies below the 45-
less	degree line, total spending is ___________ (less/more) than sufficient
	to clear output off the market by the amount that inventories rise above
	their desired level.

just

In short, equilibrium exists where total spending is ____________ (more than/less than/just) sufficient to clear total output off the market, or where the total spending function and the 45-degree line

intersect

____________. Note however, that an equilibrium income level may not imply full employment.

Once equilibrium is established, it will be sustained until one of the functions changes, causing a new point of intersection (regardless of whether one views the change with respect to the leakages-injections approach or the total spending-total approach). However, any change in total spending results in a much larger change in income because of the

multiplier

____________. To calculate any change in income, multiply

total spending

the change in ____________ by the

multiplier

____________. The multiplier is equal to the reciprocal of the

MPS

____________ (*MPC*/*MPS*), or alternatively, the reciprocal of

1- *MPC*

____________ (1 - *MPC*/1 - *MPS*).

Problems and Applications

1. Assuming no government and therefore no tax payments, we know that at any given income level, whatever is not consumed is saved, and vice versa.
   a. Draw a consumption function and a saving function and show that one function implies the other. (In other words, show that, at various income levels, whatever is not consumed is saved and whatever is not saved is consumed.)
   b. What is the slope of the consumption function equal to?
   c. What is the slope of the saving function equal to?
   d. What does the *MPC* and the *MPS* tell us?
   e. Does the *MPC* + *MPS* = 1?
   f. If the consumption function shifts up (down) by some amount, does this mean the saving function will shift down (up) by the same amount?

   g. How would we interpret an upward (downward) shift in the consumption function, hence a downward (upward) shift in the saving function?

2. For each of the following, determine whether the consumption function shifts up (saving function shifts down), or whether the consumption functions shifts down (saving function shifts up), or whether there is simply movement along the consumption function (saving function).
   a. an increase in income
   b. an increase in the interest rate
   c. a decrease in personal wealth
   d. People expect prices to come down in the near future.
   e. People expect a severe recession in the near future, which threatens their job security.
   f. People expect their incomes to drop in the near future.
3. What could cause the consumption function to shift up and the saving function to shift down?
4. Assume government involvement to answer this question. What effect would a change in personal income taxes have on the consumption and saving functions?
5. Draw an investment demand curve and an investment function curve (assuming an independent relationship between the income level and planned investment). Then answer the following questions.
   a. If the interest rate decreases, what happens to the level of planned investment and the investment function?
   b. If the interest rate increases, what happens to the level of planned investment and the investment function?
   c. If technology increases, what happens to the level of planned investment and the investment function?
   d. If business taxes increase (decrease), what happens to the level of planned investment and the investment function?
   e. If businesses become more optimistic (pessimistic) about future profits, what happens to the level of planned investment and the investment function?
6. a. Using the leakages-injections approach, draw a saving function and an investment function on the same graph and indicate the equilibrium income level.

b. Using the total spending-total output approach, draw a total spending function and a 45-degree line on the same graph and indicate the equilibrium level.
c. Are the equilibrium income levels derived in both approaches the same?
d. For both approaches, express graphically an income level above equilibrium. Explain why this is not an equilibrium position. Also determine what will happen to the income level.
e. For both approaches, express graphically an income level below equilibrium. Explain why this is not an equilibrium position. Also determine what will happen to the income level.

7. Your answers to questions 2, 3, 4, and 6 above should indicate what may cause the saving, consumption, and investment functions to shift. Graph the leakages-injections and the total spending-total output approach and indicate an equilibrium income level. Now determine what happens to equilibrium in each of the following cases (assume no government involvement).
   a. The consumption function shifts up.
   b. The investment function shifts down.
8. Assume the economy is initially in equilibrium at the $600 income (output) level. For each of the following, calculate the multiplier and the new equilibrium income level.
   a. The *MPS* = .25, and planned consumption spending increases by $20.
   b. The *MPC* = .75, and planned saving increases by $30.
   c. The *MPS* = .20, and the investment function shifts up by $5.
   d. The *MPC* = .90, and the consumption function decreases by $5.

True-False

For each item, determine whether the statement is basically true or false. If the statement is false, rewrite it so it is a true statement.

_____ 1. In the Keynesian model, each interest rate is associated with a particular income level.

_____ 2. As income increases, consumption increases by a greater amount.

_____ 3. An upward shift in the consumption function usually implies a downward shift in the investment function.

_____ 4. The Great Depression was a result of a decline in total spending.

_____ 5. *MPC* + *MPS* = 1.

_____ 6. Dissaving is negative saving and results from households in the aggregate spending more than their incomes.

_____ 7. The saving function has a positive slope of 1 - *MPC*.

_____ 8. The paradox of thrift illustrates dissaving.

_____ 9. An increase in business taxes will shift the investment demand curve to the left, and therefore the investment function shifts down.

_____ 10. A change in the interest rate will cause the investment demand curve to shift.

_____ 11. An equilibrium income level means we are at full employment.

_____ 12. A saving function implies a consumption function, and vice versa.

_____ 13. In the absence of government, changes in the equilibrium income level can only result from changes in the consumption, saving, or investment functions.

_____ 14. The multiplier equals (1 - *MPC*).

_____ 15. Assuming no government, equilibrium exists where *C* + *I* intersects the 45-degree line.

_____ 16. The consumption function will shift down if, in the aggregate, personal wealth increases.

_____ 17. If the investment function shifts down, this means businesses plan to invest less at any income level.

_____ 18. If people expect higher rates of inflation (possibly because of another oil embargo), it is possible that the consumption function will shift up and the investment function will shift down by such an amount that there is no change in total spending and therefore no change in the equilibrium income level.

_____ 19. In the absence of government, if we know what causes the consumption and investment functions to shift, then we know what causes the income level to change, and therefore we know what causes the business cycle.

_____ 20. Any change in total spending times the multiplier equals the change in income.

_____ 21. If we assume an independent relationship between planned investment and national income, then the investment function is a vertical line.

_____ 22. A contractionary gap exists when actual *GNP* is less than the full employment *GNP*.

Multiple Choice *Choose the one best answer for each item.*

____ 1. To derive an investment function, we would require
   a. the saving function and the consumption function.
   b. the multiplier and the change in total spending.
   c. the interest rate and the investment demand curve.
   d. the demand for and the supply of investment.
   e. all of the above.

____ 2. The multiplier
   a. tells us how much income changes given a change in total spending.
   b. equals the reciprocal of (1 - *MPS*).
   c. tells us how much total spending changes given a change in income.
   d. measures the slope of the saving function.
   e. illustrates dissaving.

____ 3. In the absence of government, equilibrium is established where
   a. total spending results in negative unplanned investment.
   b. exports equal imports.
   c. saving equals planned investment.
   d. unplanned investment equals saving.
   e. the total planned expenditure function intersects the investment function.

____ 4. The *MPC* measures
   a. the slope of the saving function.
   b. the slope of the investment function.
   c. the change in consumption given a change in saving.
   d. the change in income given a change in planned consumption spending.
   e. the change in planned consumption spending given a change in income.

____ 5. Dissaving is illustrated by
   a. a negative *MPS*.
   b. the paradox of thrift.
   c. the intersection of the consumption function and the 45-degree line.
   d. the vertical distance by which the saving function lies below the *X*-axis.
   e. the vertical distance by which the saving function lies above the *X*-axis.

_____ 6. The consumption function
   a. shows the level of planned consumption spending at various income levels.
   b. lies above the 45-degree line at all income levels.
   c. intersects the 45-degree line where saving is zero.
   d. has a slope equal to the *MPS*.
   e. does both a and c above.

_____ 7. The investment function shifts up when
   a. the interest rate increases.
   b. business expectations regarding the profitability of future production become optimistic.
   c. the investment demand curve shifts to the left.
   d. business taxes are increased.
   e. income increases.

_____ 8. Which of the following may cause an increase in total spending and therefore an increase in the equilibrium income level?
   a. A leftward shift in the investment demand curve
   b. An increase in the interest rate
   c. Expectations of higher rates of inflation in the near future
   d. An increase in taxes
   e. An increase in *MPS*

_____ 9. The investment demand curve shows
   a. the inverse relationship between the interest rate and the level of planned investment.
   b. the inverse relationship between the interest rate and the level of unplanned investment.
   c. the direct relationship between planned investment and the income level.
   d. that as the interest rate decreases the level of planned investment decreases.
   e. that an upward shift in the investment function results in a multiple increase in the equilibrium income level.

_____ 10. Which of the following statements is true?
   a. The multiplier equals (1 - *MPC*).
   b. The vertical distance between the consumption function and the 45-degree line equals the vertical distance between the saving function and the *X*-axis.
   c. When the saving function shifts up, the income level increases.

d. A downward shift in the consumption function shows that households plan to spend more at each of the various income levels.
e. In reality, dissaving is impossible and has never occurred.

Answer questions 11-15 based on graphs (a) and (b) below.

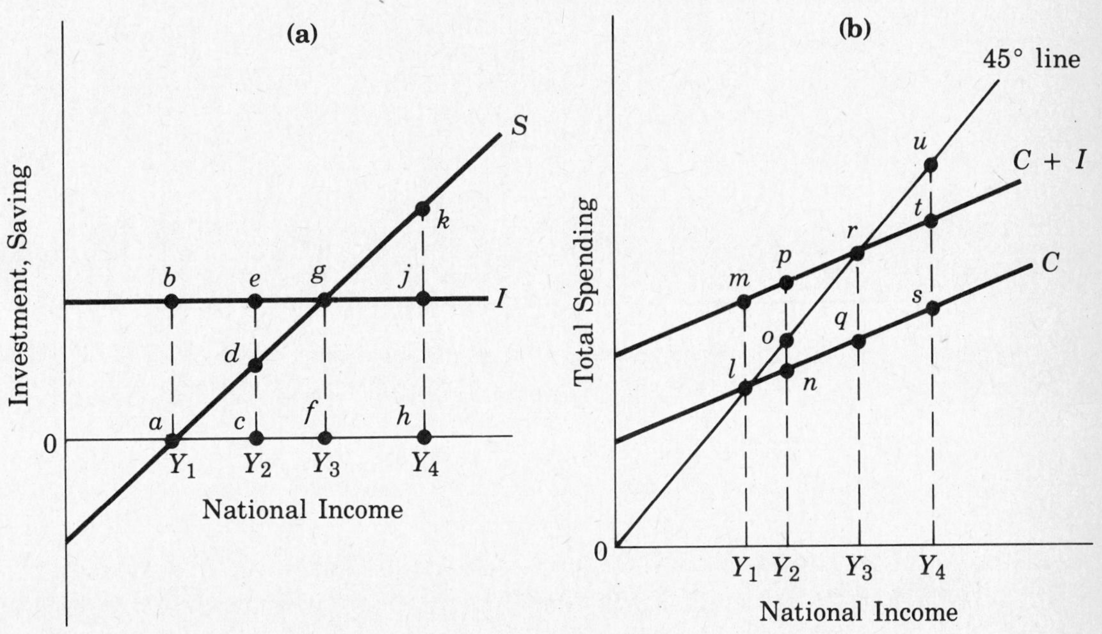

_____ 11. In graph (a), equilibrium exists at
a. Y_1.
b. Y_2.
c. Y_3.
d. Y_4.
e. none of the above.

_____ 12. In graph (b), equilibrium exists at
a. Y_1.
b. Y_2.
c. Y_3.
d. Y_4.
e. none of the above.

_____ 13. Compare graph (a) with graph (b). Which of the following statements is true?
a. Point *a* corresponds with point *l*.
b. At Y_2, *ce* equals *np*.
c. At Y_4, *jk* equals *tu*.
d. At Y_3, *fg* equals *qr*.
e. All of the above.

_____ 14. In graph (a), *jk* is equal to
a. the amount by which saving exceeds planned investment at Y_4.
b. the amount by which inventories are above their desired level at Y_4.
c. unplanned investment at Y_4.
d. *tu* in graph (b).
e. all of the above.

_____ 15. In graph (b), *op* is equal to
a. saving at Y_2.
b. the amount by which inventories are too high at Y_2.
c. the amount by which inventories are too low at Y_2.
d. planned investment at Y_2.
e. none of the above.

_____ 16. The paradox of thrift illustrates
a. dissaving.
b. that the multiplier effect works in the opposite direction as a change in total spending.
c. that saving, in the aggregate, may be a vice rather than a virtue.
d. that the *MPS* is constant.
e. none of the above.

_____ 17. An unplanned increase in inventories is expected to
a. decrease income.
b. decrease the absolute amount of saving.
c. decrease the absolute amount of consumption spending.
d. increase unemployment.
e. do all of the above.

_____ 18. To calculate any change in income given a change in total spending, it is necessary to
a. multiply the change in income by the change in total spending.
b. multiply the change in total spending by the reciprocal of the *MPS*.
c. add the change in total spending to the initial equilibrium income level.

d. find the point of intersection between the total spending function and total income.
e. find the point of intersection between the saving function and the consumption function.

_____ 19. The consumption function will shift down if
a. the saving function shifts down.
b. the income level decreases.
c. people expect their future incomes to be lower.
d. personal wealth increases.
e. people expect higher prices.

_____ 20. The saving function will shift up if
a. people expect a severe recession that threatens their job security.
b. the investment function shifts down.
c. interest rates decrease.
d. people expect higher rates of inflation.
e. none of the above happens.

_____ 21. An increase in the equilibrium income level can be caused by
a. an upward shift in the consumption function.
b. an upward shift in the investment function.
c. a downward shift in the saving function.
d. all of the above.
e. none of the above.

Discussion Questions

1. Factors other than those mentioned in the text may shift the consumption function (hence the saving function) and the investment function. For instance, the stock of liquid assets on hard, attitudes toward thrift, consumer indebtedness, and the stock of durable goods on hand may shift the consumption function. On the other hand, the stock of capital goods on hand and the acquisition, maintenance, and operating cost of equipment may shift the investment demand curve (hence the investment function). How do you think changes in these variables would affect the consumption and investment functions and therefore the equilibrium level? *(KQ3)*
2. Why is there a multiple change in the equilibrium income level given a change in total spending? Why does the multiplier get smaller as *MPS* increases? If we were to include government and international trade, how would this affect the multiplier? *(KQ3)*

3. As income increases, the percentage of higher income levels devoted to saving increases. For these higher income levels to be maintained (or to be equilibrium income levels), planned investment must continually rise as a percentage of income. In fact, this has happened in the last century due to continuing advances in technology. In other words, we have experienced continued economic growth (higher income levels over time) primarily due to increases in technology. Do you think this is likely to continue? Or will technological breakthroughs slow down or pick up over time? Can government do anything to promote increases in technology? *(KQ3)*

Answers

Problems and Applications

1. a. Compare the two graphs on page 193. At income Y_2 in graph (a), we see that households plan to spend all income on consumption. This means households plan to save zero dollars, and this is reflected in graph (b). So point *a* on the consumption function corresponds to point *a* on the saving function. At income Y_1 in graph (a), we see that consumption spending exceeds income by *db*, or C_1 - Y_1. This means dissaving is occurring, equal to *db, or* C_1 - Y_1. In graph (b), this dissaving is shown by *db*, or S_1 - O. So the vertical distance between the consumption function and the 45-degree line equals the vertical distance between the saving function and the *X*-axis. Likewise, at income Y_3 in graph (a), we see that consumption spending is less than income by *fe*, or Y_3 - C_3. This means some saving is occurring, equal to *fe*, or Y_3 - C_3. In graph (b), this saving is shown by *fe*, or S_3 - O. So as always, the vertical distance between the consumption function and the 45-degree line equals the vertical distance between the saving function and the *X*-axis. This is because when tax payments do not have to be considered, then whatever is not consumed must be saved, and whatever is not saved must be consumed, at any given income level.

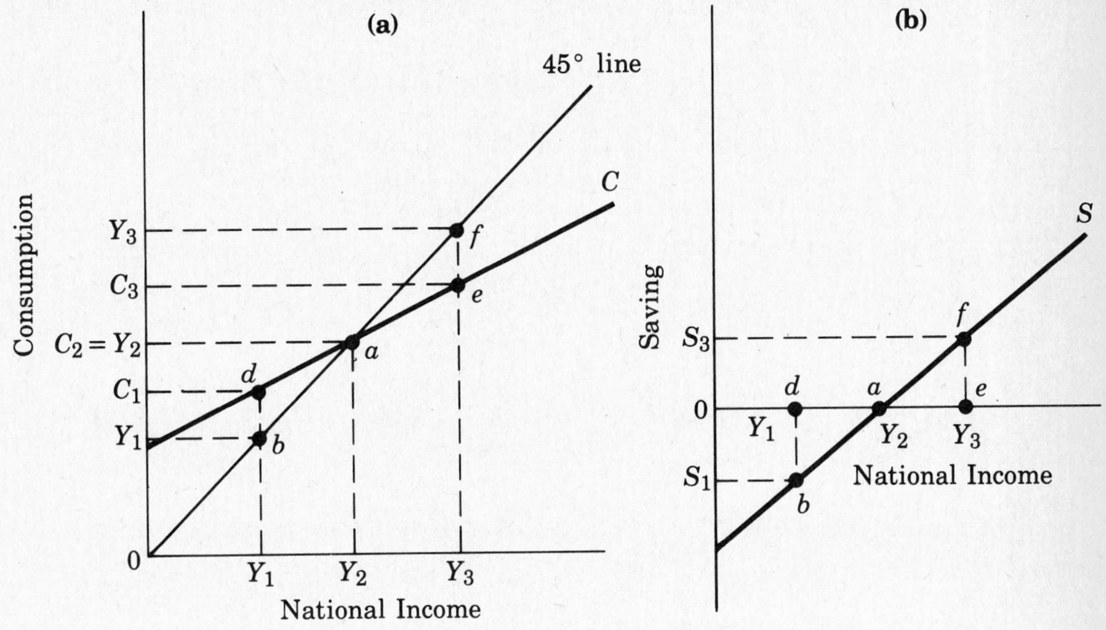

b. The slope is equal to the *MPC*.
c. The slope is equal to the *MPS*.
d. The *MPC* tells us what the change in planned consumption spending will be, given a change in income. The *MPS* tells us what the change in planned saving will be, given a change in income.
e. Yes. At any income level, whatever is not devoted to consumption must be devoted to saving, and vice versa.
f. Yes. The vertical distance between the consumption and the 45-degree line equals the vertical distance between the saving function and the X-axis. In other words, whatever is not consumed is saved, and vice versa.

g. An upward shift in the consumption function shows that households would plan to spend more on consumption, at any given income level. This means a downward shift in the saving function, showing households would plan to save less at any income level. The converse is true for a downward shift in the consumption function, hence an upward shift in the saving function.

2. a. There is movement along both the consumption and saving functions. In particular, an increase in consumption and an increase in saving would occur. (See the graph on page 193 as income increases from Y_2 to Y_3.)
   b. Consumption function shifts down; saving function shifts up.
   c. Consumption function shifts down; saving function shifts up.
   d. Consumption function shifts down; saving function shifts up.
   e. Consumption function shifts down; saving function shifts up.
   f. Consumption function shifts down; saving function shifts up.
3. Just the opposite of those factors listed for question 2 above.
4. An increase (decrease) in personal income taxes will cause the consumption function and the saving function to shift down (up). This is because at any national income (output) level, people would have less to consume or to save. This is the only variable that will cause the consumption and saving functions to shift in the same direction.
5. a. If the interest rate decreases, planned investment increases and therefore the investment function shifts up, showing that a greater amount of planned investment would be undertaken at any income level. In graph (a) on page 195, if the interest rate is initially R_2, the level of planned investment is I_2. Therefore, we get the investment function (I_2 in graph (b)). However, in graph (a), if the interest rate decreases to R_1, we see that planned investment increases to I_3. This causes the investment function to shift up to I_3 in graph (b).

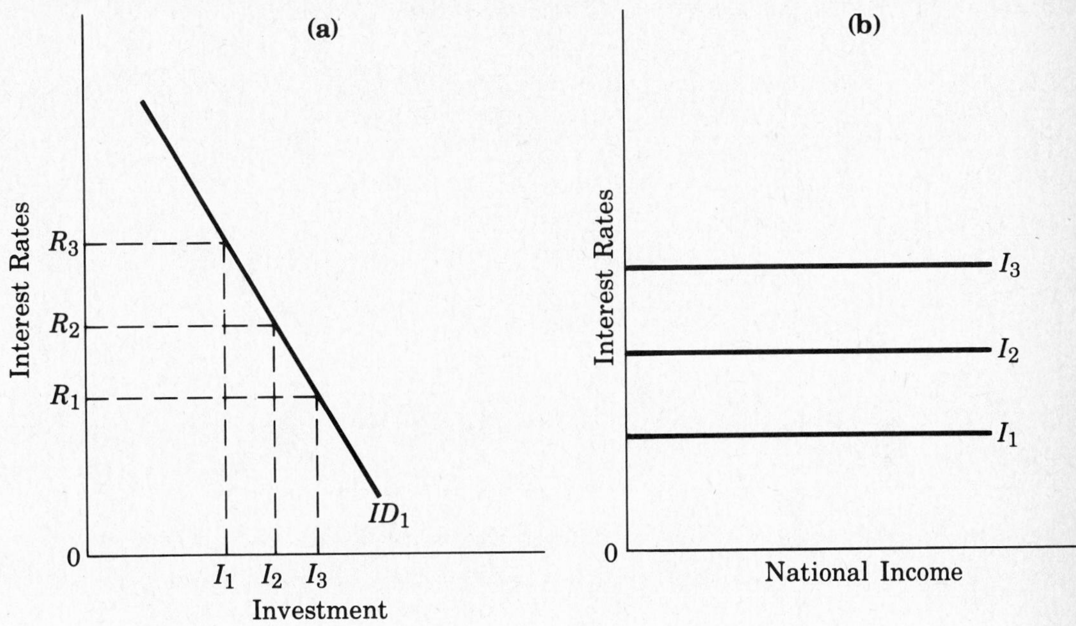

b. If the interest rate increases, planned investment decreases and therefore the investment function shifts down. See the graphs above. If the interest rate increases from R_2 to R_3, investment decreases from I_2 to I_1. Therefore, the investment function shifts down from I_2 to I_1.

c. An increase in technology will shift the investment demand curve to the right. Therefore, at any given (constant) interest rate, the level of planned investment will increase, causing an upward shift in the investment function. In the graph on page 196, the interest rate is unchanged at R_2. But because of the increase in technology, the investment demand curve shifts from ID_1 to ID_2. Therefore, planned investment increases from I_2 to I_3, and this causes the investment function to shift up from I_2 to I_3 in graph (b), above.

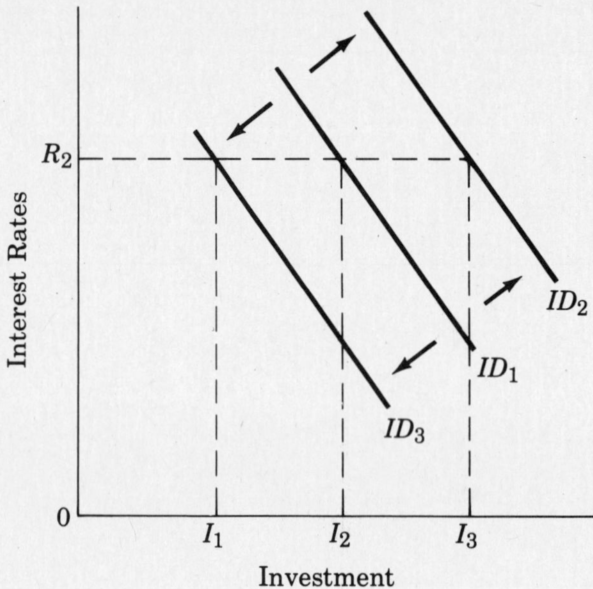

d. An increase in business taxes will shift the investment demand to the left. Therefore, at any given interest rate, the level of planned investment will decrease, causing a downward shift in the investment function. In the graph above, the interest rate is unchanged at R_2. But because of the increase in business taxes, the investment demand curve shifts from ID_1 to ID_3. Therefore, planned investment decreases from I_2 to I_1, and this causes the investment function to shift down from I_2 to I_1 in graph on page 195. A decrease in business taxes will cause the investment function to shift up.

e. If businesses become more optimistic (pessimistic) about future profits, the investment curve will shift to the right (left). Therefore, the investment function will shift up (down).

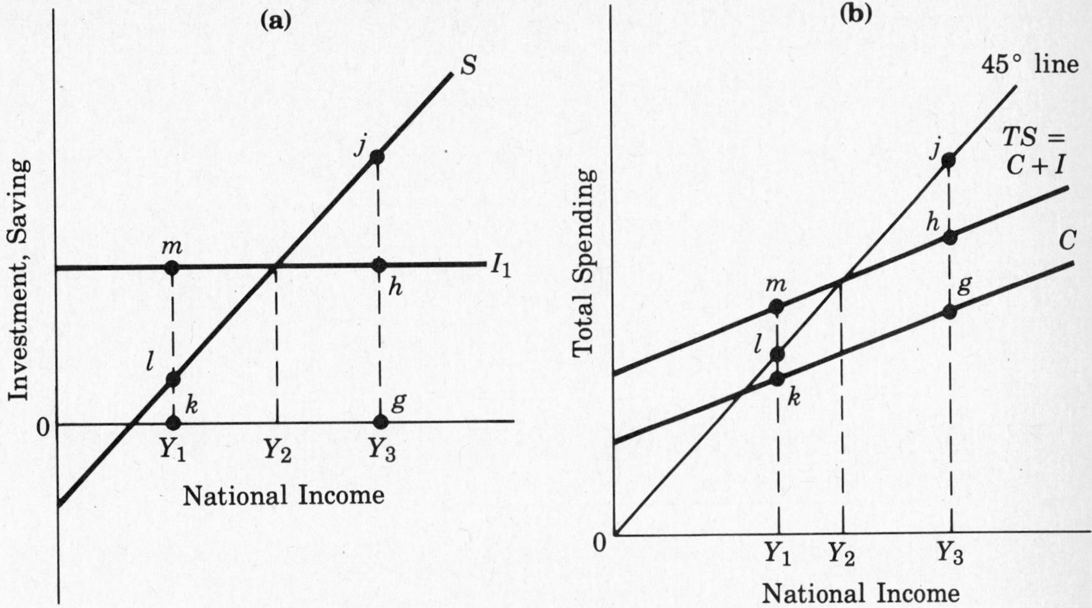

6. a. Equilibrium exists where saving equals planned investment because unplanned investment (which measures changes in inventories) is zero. Graphically, equilibrium exists where the two functions intersect. In graph (a), equilibrium exists at Y_2.
   b. Equilibrium exists where total spending is just sufficient to clear total output off the market (which implies that unplanned investment is zero). Graphically, equilibrium exists where the total spending function intersects the 45-degree line. In graph (b), equilibrium exists at Y_2.
   c. Yes. The leakages-injections approach and the total spending-total output approach are just two ways of looking at the same thing.
   d. In graph (a), Y_3 is above equilibrium. The same income level, Y_3, is also shown in graph (b) and is above equilibrium. This is not an equilibrium position because inventories are too high compared to the vertical distance *hj*. In other words, total spending falls short of clearing total output off the market by *hj*. Therefore, the income level will drop until equilibrium is established.
   e. In graph (a), Y_1 is below equilibrium. The same income level, Y_1, is also shown in graph (b) and is below equilibrium. This is not an equilibrium position because inventories are too low

equal to the vertical distance *lm*. In other words, total spending is greater than total output by *lm*. Therefore, the income level will increase until equilibrium is established.

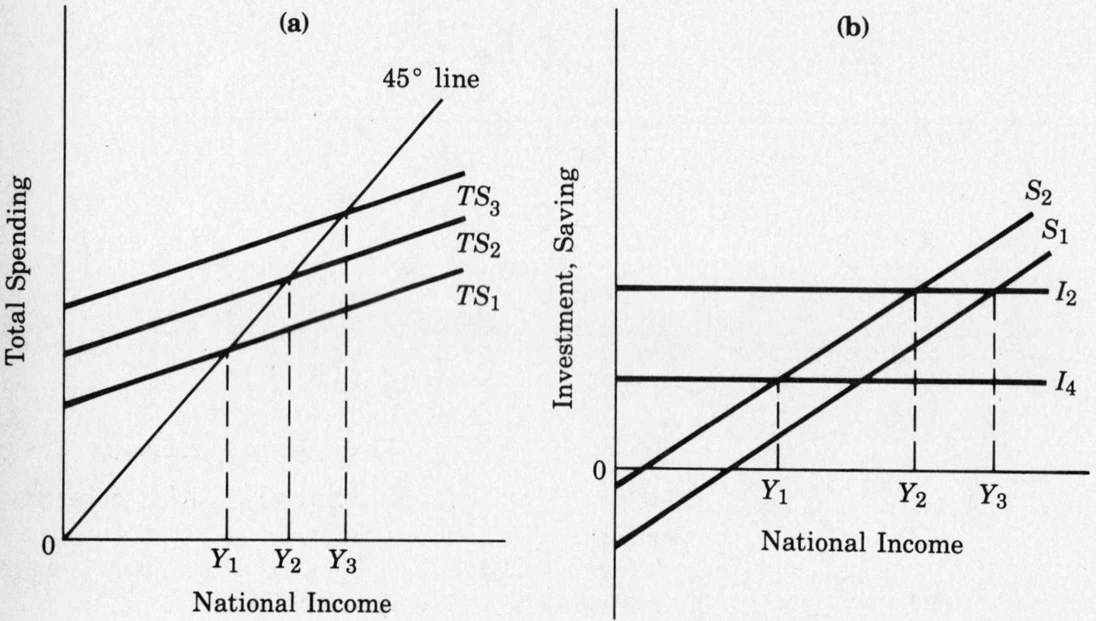

7. a. If the consumption function shifts up, the savings function shifts down. In graph (a), assume we start with the total spending function TS_2 and the equilibrium income level of Y_2. If the consumption function shifts up, this causes the total spending function to shift up to TS_3 (because consumption is a component of total spending), giving us the new equilibrium of Y_3. In graph (b), assume we start with the saving function S_2 and the investment function I_2, hence the equilibrium of Y_2. The saving function shifts down to S_1 because the consumption function shifted up. Therefore, we get the new equilibrium of Y_3.

   b. In graph (b), the investment function would shift down from I_2 to I_1, but the saving function remains at S_2. Therefore, income drops from Y_2 to Y_1. In graph (a), the total spending function would shift down from TS_2 to TS_1 (because investment is a component of total spending), causing income to drop from Y_2 to Y_1.

8. a. The multiplier (m) is equal to 1/*MPS* or 1/(1 - *MPC*). Any change in total spending times the multiplier equals the change in the equilibrium income level. So $m = 4$ and the new equilibrium income level is \$680.
   b. $m = 4$. The new equilibrium is \$480.
   c. $m = 5$. The new equilibrium is \$625.
   d. $m = 10$. The new equilibrium is \$550.

True-False

1. T
2. F: As income increases, consumption increases by a lesser amount.
3. F: An upward shift in the consumption function usually implies a downward shift in the saving function.
4. T   5. T   6. T   7. T
8. F: The paradox of thrift illustrates that as people attempt to save more, they will end up earning less in the aggregate and saving no more, or possibly less, than before.
9. T
10. F: A change in the interest rate will not cause the investment demand curve to shift.
11. F: An equilibrium income level does not necessarily mean we are at full employment.
12. T   13. T
14. F: The multiplier equals the reciprocal of (1 - *MPC*), or the reciprocal of the *MPS*.
15. T
16. F: The consumption function will shift down if, in the aggregate, personal wealth decreases.
17. T   18. T   19. T   20. T
21. F: If we assume an independent relationship between planned investment and national income, then the investment function is a horizontal line.
22. T

Multiple Choice

1. c *(KQ1)*	2. a *(KQ3)*	3. c *(KQ1, 2)*
4. e *(KQ2)*	5. d *(KQ2)*	6. e *(KQ2)*
7. b *(KQ3)*	8. c *(KQ3)*	9. a *(KQ1)*
10. b *(KQ2)*	11. c *(KQ1, 2)*	12. c *(KQ1, 2)*
13. e *(KQ1, 2)*	14. e *(KQ1, 2)*	15. c *(KQ1, 2)*
16. c *(KQ3)*	17. e *(KQ3)*	18. b *(KQ3)*
19. c *(KQ3)*	20. a *(KQ3)*	21. d *(KQ3)*

CHAPTER 12

Keynesian Fiscal Policy

Chapter Summary

We have seen where and why an equilibrium income level is established and how it may change according to Keynesian theory. We have also seen that equilibrium does not necessarily imply full employment. This chapter describes what government can do with fiscal policy to promote full employment and price stability. The chapter also looks at what Keynesian monetary policy can do to stabilize the economy.

Key Question 1: What can the government do to promote economic stability through fiscal policy?

Including government spending and taxes in our economic analysis modifies both the leakages-injections and total spending-total output models. Leakages (or outflows) now equal saving plus taxes. Because taxes increase as income rises, the slope of the leakages function is greater than the slope of the saving function. Injections (or inflows) now consist of planned investment plus planned government spending. By assuming an independent relationship between government spending and income, the addition of planned government spending to the investment function yields a higher horizontal injections function. But as always, the equilibrium income level is established where the two functions intersect (where leakages equal injections).

In terms of the total spending-total output model, personal income taxes cause the consumption function to have a lower slope. By adding the other injections of planned investment plus planned government spending to the consumption function, we get the total spending (or total planned expenditures) function. But as always, the equilibrium income level is established where the total spending function and the 45-degree line intersect (where total spending is just sufficient to clear total output off the market).

In either model, at income levels above equilibrium we have excessive outflows (leakages) that cause the income level to drop. At income levels below equilibrium, we have excessive inflows (injections) that cause the income level to rise. Moreover, changing government spending and taxes changes the equilibrium income level. Deficits (or smaller surpluses) increase the equilibrium income level and are incurred when government spending increased or when taxes are reduced. Surpluses (or smaller deficits) decrease the equilibrium income level and are incurred when government spending decreases or when taxes are increased.

Both models show that an increase in government spending (holding taxes constant) will increase income by a multiple of the increase in total spending (because of the multiplier), thereby reducing unemployment. However, the multiplier effect may be significantly smaller if there is a crowding-out effect. The crowding-out effect suggests that deficit spending financed by borrowing increases the interest rate and therefore crowds out some private investment. A decrease in government spending (holding taxes constant) has the opposite result and may be used to reduce inflationary pressures if total spending is above what is required to provide for full employment.

A decrease in taxes (holding government spending constant) increases national income. In the leakages/injections approach, a decrease in taxes causes the leakages curve to shift downward, but by not as much as the decrease in taxes because some of the lower tax liabilities will be saved. This downward shift causes the equilibrium income level to rise. In the total spending/total output approach, a decrease in taxes will increase consumption and shift upward the total spending function. The amount of the increase is determined by multiplying the decrease in taxes by the *MPC*. This upward shift causes the equilibrium income level to rise. An increase in taxes has the opposite result and may be used to reduce total spending if it is too high. However, an increase (decrease) in government spending will have a greater effect on national income than will an equal decrease (increase) in taxes.

Of course, government could increase government spending and decrease taxes at the same time in order to increase total spending and the income level. To decrease total spending and the income level, government could simultaneously decrease spending and increase taxes.

Not only can deficits and surpluses affect national income, but equal changes in government spending and taxes in the same direction can cause the very same change in income in the very same direction. This is because the balanced-budget multiplier is 1.

Key Question 2: How does deliberate fiscal policy compare with undiscretionary built-in, automatic fiscal stabilizers?

There are some problems in implementing proper fiscal policy to control for unemployment and inflation. One of the difficulties is proper timing. All too often, the effects of fiscal policy are felt too late because of recognition, action (or reaction), and impact lags. Tardy fiscal action may contribute to the business cycle rather than smooth it out. But automatic stabilizers, which do not require deliberate action on the part of Congress and the president, do not have these timing problems. The most important automatic stabilizers are income taxes and unemployment and welfare benefits. Because income taxes decrease (increase) and unemployment and welfare benefits rise (drop) when national income drops (rises) during a recessionary (inflationary) phase of the business cycle, the economy will automatically move in the direction of a deficit (surplus). Deficits tend to increase total spending when it is falling during recessionary phases, and surpluses tend to decrease total spending when it is rising during expansionary phases of the business cycle. In this way, automatic stabilizers help smooth out the ups and downs in the business cycle.

Key Question 3: Is deficit spending a problem?

Before Keynes, peacetime deficit spending was associated with fiscal irresponsibility because of the debt it created. A commonly held assumption was that the federal government was like an individual household—eventually, debt will have to be paid off. Keynesians question the validity of this assumption. As long as there are unemployed resources, then deficits can benefit future generations because of the higher incomes deficits create. And with higher incomes, tax revenues rise, enabling the government to pay at least the interest on the debt. But Keynesians agree that deficit spending at or near full employment means resources must be diverted away from the private sector. The opportunity cost of deficit spending, then, is the amount of private goods and services that must be foregone. Moreover, because the life of a government is unlimited, the debt that is owed the buyers of bonds (American citizens) never really comes due. Government debt can simply be refinanced by issuing new bonds to pay off that portion that does come due. The major constraint on the government's ability to expand its debt is citizens' willingness to buy bonds, which, in turn, depends on the stability of the government and people's propensity to save. In short, Keynesians believe that the benefits of deficit spending far outweigh the costs. In practice, however, deficits may be overused because of their political benefits.

Key Question 4: Why is monetary policy subordinate to fiscal policy for Keynesians?

Keynesians favor fiscal policy over monetary policy in controlling total spending and the business cycle. A change in the money stock changes the interest rate, which changes investment. In turn, a change in investment times the multiplier changes income.

Keynesians also reject the classical economists' notion that interest rates adjust until saving and investment are equal. Instead, Keynesians emphasize the demand for and supply of money in the determination of the interest rate. The total demand for money is determined by the transactions, precautionary, and speculative demand for money. The transactions demand for money is directly related to the national income level. The speculative demand for money is inversely related to interest rates. The horizontal portion of the total demand for money curve illustrates the liquidity trap. If we are in the liquidity trap during a severe recession, then an increase in the money stock will not decrease the interest rate. Therefore, investment will not increase, and the income level will remain depressed.

The liquidity trap was an explanation of the apparent ineffectiveness of monetary policy during the Great Depression. However, many Keynesians now agree that the demand for money curve never really flattens out. Therefore, monetary policy can help stimulate the economy, at least somewhat. The effectiveness of monetary policy depends on how flat (or steep) the demand for money curve is, how flat (or steep) the investment demand curve is, and the size of the multiplier. The size of the multiplier depends on the marginal propensity to consume and on income tax rates.

Review Terms and Concepts

Fiscal policy
Deficit
Surplus
Equilibrium income level
Full employment
Leakages
Injections
Saving
Investment
Planned investment
Unplanned investment
Multiplier
Consumption function
Saving function
Investment function
Total spending function
MPS
MPC
Monetary policy
Progressive income tax
Speculative demand for money
Total demand for money
Transactions demand for money

New Terms and Concepts

Lump-sum tax
Contractionary gap
Expansionary gap
Crowding-out effect
Balanced-budget multiplier
Recognition lag
Action (administrative) lag
Impact (operational) lag
Automatic fiscal stabilizer
National or public debt

Fiscal drag **Liquidity trap**
Political business cycle

Completion

When we add government to our analysis, leakages become saving plus
taxes, increase ________________. Because taxes collected ________________
(increase/decrease) as income increases, the slope of the leakages func-
greater tion is ________________ (greater/smaller) than the slope of the saving
function. The injections become planned investment plus planned
government ________________ spending. Government spending has been
independent assumed to be ________________ (dependent/independent)
with regard to the income level. Total spending now consists of planned
consumption, investment ________________ spending plus planned ________________
government spending plus planned ________________ spending.

Equilibrium exists in the leakages-injections approach where the two
intersect functions ________________ (just as before). In the total spending-total
output approach, equilibrium exists where the total spending function
intersects ________________ the 45-degree line (just as before). At income
contractionary levels above equilibrium, we get a (an) ________________ (expan-
sionary/contractionary) gap that causes the income level to drop. At in-
expansionary come levels below equilibrium, we get a (an) ________________
(expansionary/contractionary) gap that causes the income level to rise.

Deficits ________________ (Deficits/Surpluses) should be incurred to increase
income and reduce unemployment. This means government spending
increased should be ________________ (increased/decreased) and/or taxes should
decreased be ________________ (increased/decreased). However, deficit spending

increase	financed by borrowing may ____________________ (increase/decrease)
decrease	interest rates and therefore ____________________ (increase/decrease)
crowding-out effect	planned investment. This effect is known as the ____________________.
	Increases (decreases) in government spending have a greater multiple ef-
	fect on the income level than do equal decreases (increases) in taxes.
	This is because a decrease (increase) in taxes will affect both consump-
saving	tion and ____________________.
decrease	Surpluses should be incurred to ____________________ (increase/
inflation	decrease) national income and to reduce ________________________
	(unemployment/inflation). This means government spending should be
decreased	__________________ (increased/decreased) and/or taxes should be
increased	__________________ (increased/decreased). Once again, the reduction in
government spending	________________________________ (government spending/taxes) has a
	greater contractionary impact on income than do equal increases in
taxes	___________________ (government spending/taxes).
	Not only can deficits and surpluses affect income and the general level
	of prices, but equal changes in government spending and taxes in the
same	same direction may change income in the ___________________ (same/
the same	opposite) direction by ______________________ (a greater/the same/a
balanced budget multiplier	smaller) amount. This is known as the ____________________________
1	which is equal to ________________.
	There are some problems in implementing proper fiscal policy, one of
	which is proper timing. The effects of proper fiscal policy may be ex-
recognition, reaction	perienced too late because of ________________, ____________________,
impact	and _______________________ lags. These lags may contribute to
instability	________________________ (stability/instability) in the business cycle.

	However, automatic stabilizers may help smooth out the business cycle
decreases	by automatically incurring a deficit as the income level ____________
	(increases/decreases) and by automatically incurring a surplus as the
increases	income level ________________ (increases/decreases). Automatic sta-
do not	bilizers ______________ (do/do not) have any time lags associated
do not	with them because they _____________ (do/do not) require any
	deliberate action on the part of Congress and the president.
was not	Before Keynes, peacetime deficit spending _____________ (was/
	was not) considered desirable. However, Keynes and his followers have
	made strong arguments in favor of deficit spending. One of Keynes's
	greatest contributions to the whole issue of debt was to point out that, un-
forever	like households, government can incur debt ________________ (only
	once/forever). Government debt is simply refinanced by the federal
selling	government _______________ (buying/selling) more bonds to pay off
	that portion of the debt that comes due. But deficit spending at or near
decrease	full employment will ______________ (increase/decrease) the amount
	of resources devoted to the private sector. Therefore, we may have to
	give up some private goods and services. And in practice, deficits may be
overused	__________________ (underused/overused) because of their political
	benefits.
fiscal	Keynesians are more fond of _________________ (monetary/fiscal)
monetary	policy than they are of __________________ (monetary/fiscal) policy.
	They believe monetary policy may be totally ineffective in increasing in-
	vestment (hence total spending) during severe recessions because of the
liquidity	_________________ trap. Although the liquidity trap was used as an ex-
	planation for the continued low levels of income during the Great

Depression, most Keynesians now argue that the demand for money
can — curve never really flattens out. Therefore, monetary policy ___________
(can/cannot) help stimulate the economy, but the debate is over how
much. The effectiveness of monetary policy depends on how
flat (or steep) — __________________ the demand for money curve is, how
flat (or steep) — __________________ the investment demand curve is, and the
size — _____________ of the multiplier. The size of the multiplier in turn
MPC (or *MPS*) — depends on the __________________ and income tax
rates — _______________.

Problems and Applications

1. a. List the ways government can use fiscal policy to increase the income level and express these graphically.
   b. Why would government want to increase the income level?
   c. List the ways government can use fiscal policy to decrease the income level and express these graphically.
   d. Why would government want to decrease the income level?
2. Recall that changes in the reserve requirement, open market operations, and changes in the discount rate (and the consequent effect on Fed loans to banks) can all change the money stock.
   a. List the ways the Fed can use monetary policy to decrease the income level. Then express graphically the cause-effect chain relationship through which expansionary monetary policy increases the income level.
   b. Why would the Fed want to increase the income level?
   c. List the ways the Fed can use monetary policy to decrease the income level. Then express graphically the cause-effect chain relationship through which contractionary monetary policy decreases the income level.
   d. Why would the Fed want to decrease the income level?
   e. Assume the Fed increases the supply of money. What would happen to the effectiveness of monetary policy if the demand for money curve is flat, the investment demand curve is steep, the *MPC* is low, the income tax rates are high?
3. Express graphically the crowding-out effect.

4. Assume in a no-government economy that we are initially in equilibrium at $400. Also assume the *MPS* = .25 and there is no crowding-out effect.
   a. Now assume government enters the picture and increases government expenditures by $20. What will the new equilibrium income level be?
   b. What will happen to the equilibrium income level if government increases taxes by $20 to balance the budget?
   c. What can we conclude about the balanced-budget multiplier?
   d. Work through the entire process again, but this time assume the *MPS* = .10. Does this balanced-budget multiplier still equal 1? Will the balanced-budget multiplier always equal 1 no matter what the *MPC* or *MPS* is?
5. a. Why do taxes increase as income decreases?
   b. Why do taxes increase the slope of the leakages function and therefore decrease the slope of the consumption function?

True-False

For each item, determine whether the statement is basically true or false. If the statement is false, rewrite it so it is a true statement.

_____ 1. The balanced budget multiplier exists because decreases (increases) in government spending have a greater impact on the income level than equal increases (decreases) in taxes.

_____ 2. The liquidity trap refers to the vertical portion of the demand for money curve.

_____ 3. To calculate the change in total spending given a change in taxes, one must multiply the change in taxes by the *MPS*.

_____ 4. Increases in government spending have a greater impact on income than do equal decreases in taxes because part of the lower tax liabilities are saved.

_____ 5. According to the balanced-budget multiplier, an increase in government spending of $50 and an increase in taxes of $50 will increase income by $50.

_____ 6. The federal debt can be run forever by simply refinancing that portion which comes due by selling additional government bonds.

_____ 7. Changes in government spending and/or taxes have a multiplier effect on national income.

_____ 8. Government budgetary deficits should be continuously incurred.

_____ 9. The impact lag is the delay in getting Congress to take appropriate fiscal action.

_____ 10. Automatic stabilizers are fiscal actions that automatically require special action on the part of the administration or Congress.

_____ 11. When government and taxes are added, the condition for equilibrium is $C + I + G =$ total output.

_____ 12. Expansionary monetary policy should be used to combat inflation.

_____ 13. When taxes are increased, the equilibrium income level increases.

_____ 14. Deficits should be incurred during recession periods and surpluses should be incurred during inflation periods.

_____ 15. Government can increase total spending by increasing government spending, decreasing taxes, or both.

_____ 16. When we add government to the macroeconomic model, the leakages become $S + T$ and the injections become $I + G$.

_____ 17. In order to correct for fiscal drag government should increase spending, reduce taxes, or both.

Multiple Choice *Choose the one best answer for each item.*

_____ 1. When government is included in determining an equilibrium income level, then
   a. the equilibrium income level will always be higher.
   b. leakages become planned investment plus planned government spending.
   c. total spending consists of $C + I + G$.
   d. saving no longer equals planned investment.
   e. injections become planned saving plus taxes.

_____ 2. When government is added to the economy, the condition for equilibrium is
   a. that unplanned investment must be equal to saving.
   b. $S + T = I + G$.
   c. that there be no crowding-out effect.
   d. that the budget must be in balance.
   e. $C + I + G = S + T$.

_____ 3. Suppose we are in the midst of a severe recession. Which of the following policies would Keynesians recommend?
   a. An increase in corporate income taxes to balance the budget
   b. An increase in government spending

c. A decrease in government spending
d. A movement toward a surplus
e. A movement toward a deficit

_____ 4. Recognition, reaction, and impact lags
a. are problems with automatic stabilizers.
b. decrease the multiplier.
c. can contribute to the business cycle.
d. are never really a problem in implementing fiscal policy.
e. refer to the time it takes for consumers and businesses to respond to changes in the income level.

_____ 5. In Keynesian theory, interest rates are determined by
a. government price controls.
b. the adjustment process that occurs as saving and investment are brought into equality.
c. deficit spending.
d. fiscal policy.
e. the demand for and supply of money.

_____ 6. An increase in government spending (holding taxes constant) can be expected to
a. decrease interest rates.
b. shift downward the consumption and saving functions.
c. increase the income level equal to the increase in government spending.
d. increase the income level by a multiple of the increase in government spending.
e. increase the surplus (or at least decrease the deficit).

_____ 7. If we were to experience acute inflation, Keynesians would prescribe
a. a balanced budget.
b. an increase in government spending and/or a decrease in taxes, and an expansionary monetary policy.
c. a surplus and a contractionary monetary policy.
d. a larger crowding-out effect.
e. none of the above.

_____ 8. When taxes are considered in determining the equilibrium income level,
a. they have no effect on the equilibrium income level.
b. the total leakages function of $S + T$ becomes steeper than the saving function.
c. the slope of the consumption function increases.

d. the multiplier becomes larger.
e. b and c above.

_____ 9. The crowding-out effect
a. suggests that deficit spending financed by borrowing increases interest rates and thereby reduces private investment.
b. means the multiplier effect of a change in total spending increases.
c. makes monetary policy less effective.
d. applies only in the liquidity trap.
e. suggests that increases in government spending have a greater impact on the income level than do equal decreases in taxes.

_____ 10. If deficits are automatically incurred as the national income drops below some level and surpluses are automatically incurred as the national income rises above some level, then
a. the business cycle is intensified.
b. automatic stabilizers are in effect.
c. the liquidity trap is in effect.
d. a contractionary gap will be realized if the income level is below the equilibrium level.
e. an expansionary gap will be realized if the income level is above the equilibrium level.

_____ 11. Which of the following cases would make monetary policy most *ineffective?*
a. A steep demand for money curve, a steep investment demand curve, and a large *MPC*
b. A flat demand for money curve, a steep investment demand curve, and a large *MPC*
c. A flat demand for money curve, a flat investment demand curve, and a large *MPC*
d. A flat demand for money curve, a steep investment demand curve, and a small *MPC*
e. A steep demand for money curve, a steep investment demand curve, and a small *MPC*

_____ 12. Which of the following describes an expansionary monetary policy?
a. An increase in the supply of money causes an increase in investment, which causes a reduction in the interest rate and therefore an increase in total spending.
b. An increase in the supply of money causes a decrease in the interest rate, which causes an increase in investment and therefore total spending.

c. An increase in the income level causes an increase in the transactions demand for money, which causes interest rates to rise and therefore a decrease in investment and total spending.
d. A decrease in taxes and an increase in government spending
e. An increase in taxes and a decrease in government spending

_____ 13. The effect of government deficits on the equilibrium income level is basically the same as
a. increases in the investment function.
b. decreases in saving.
c. an upward shift of the consumption function.
d. a decrease in interest rates.
e. all of the above.

_____ 14. If the *MPC* = .75, the economy is initially at equilibrium at the $470 income level, and taxes decrease by $20, then the new equilibrium income level will be
a. $530.
b. $510.
c. $550.
d. $450.
e. $490.

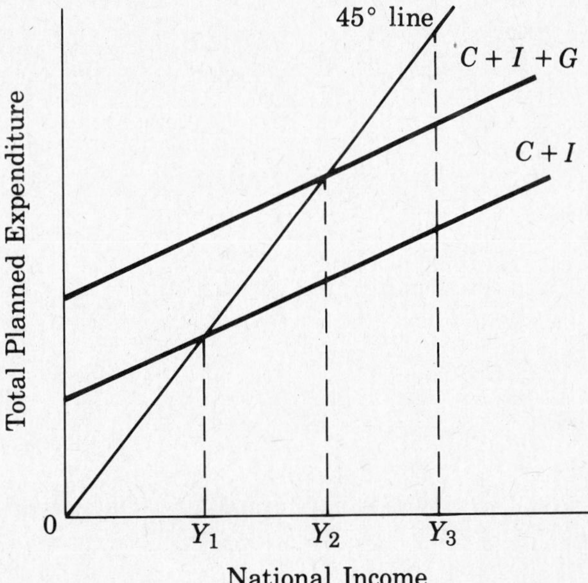

_____ 15. Based on the preceding graph, which of the following statements is correct?

a. Equilibrium is at Y_1.
b. If the full employment income level is Y_3, government should increase government spending and/or decrease taxes.
c. If the full employment income level is Y_3, government should decrease government spending and/or increase taxes.
d. If the full employment income level is Y_1, government should increase government spending and/or decrease taxes.
e. Equilibrium is at Y_3.

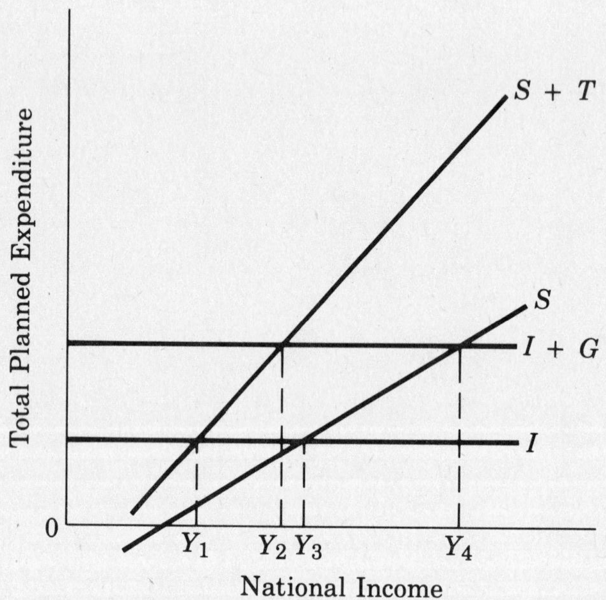

_____ 16. Based on the preceding graph, which of the following statements is true.

a. The introduction of government has increased the income level.
b. The government must be running a deficit.
c. With government included, the equilibrium income level is Y_4.
d. If the full employment income level is Y_4, the government should increase government spending and/or decrease taxes.
e. $(Y_3 - Y_2)$ represents a contractionary gap.

Discussion Questions

1. Recall from Chapter 11 that the investment demand curve shifts if there are changes in expectations about the profitability of future production. We also know that business expectations are heavily influenced by current profits. If we are in a recession, what happens to expectations and the investment demand curve? What effect does this have on the effectiveness of monetary policy? *(KQ4)*
2. In this chapter we have assumed a lump-sum tax on personal income. However, we know that personal income tax revenues are collected by way of the progressive personal income tax. This increases the slope of the leakages function and decreases the multiplier. How would the addition of progressive business income taxes affect the slope of the leakages function and the multiplier? *(KQ1, 2)*
3. How could an expansionary gap or a contractionary gap be quantified? (*Hint:* Any change in income is derived by multiplying the change in total spending by the multiplier.) *(KQ1)*
4. Why do Keynesians argue that deficit spending financed by borrowing, which decreases the money supply, will not cause a crowding-out effect during a very severe recession? (*Hint:* Consider the liquidity trap.) *(KQ4)*
5. What could Keynesian policy do to combat unemployment and inflation at the same time? *(KQ3, 4)*
6. Suppose expansionary monetary policy is successful in increasing the income level. What effect do you think this may have on the demand for money? The interest rate? The level of investment? The total spending level? The income level? If there is a "feed-back" effect, does it reinforce or counteract expansionary policy? *(KQ4)*

Answers

Problems and Applications

1. a. Because government expenditures are a direct component of total spending, an increase in government expenditures will increase total spending. A reduction in personal income taxes will increase consumption spending and savings (hence total spending). Obviously, both an increase in government spending and a decrease in taxes will increase total spending. An increase in total spending times the multiplier will increase the income level by a multiple of the increase in total spending. An increase in government expenditures from G_1 *to* G_2 is expressed graphically in graphs (a) and (b). A decrease in taxes is

expressed graphically in graphs (c) and (d). Note in graph (c) that a decrease in taxes will shift the leakages ($S + T$) down by the *MPC* times the decrease in taxes. On the other hand, a decrease in taxes will increase the total spending function in graph (d) by the *MPC* times the decrease in taxes. (Graphs (a) through (d) appear below and on page 217).

b. To reduce unemployment.

c. For reasons opposite to those described in 1a above, government should decrease government spending, increase taxes, or both. Graphically, the result is just the opposite of what is shown in graphs (a)-(d).

d. If the income level is above what is necessary to provide for full employment, then there will be inflationary pressures present in the economy. A reduction in total spending will reduce the rate of inflation.

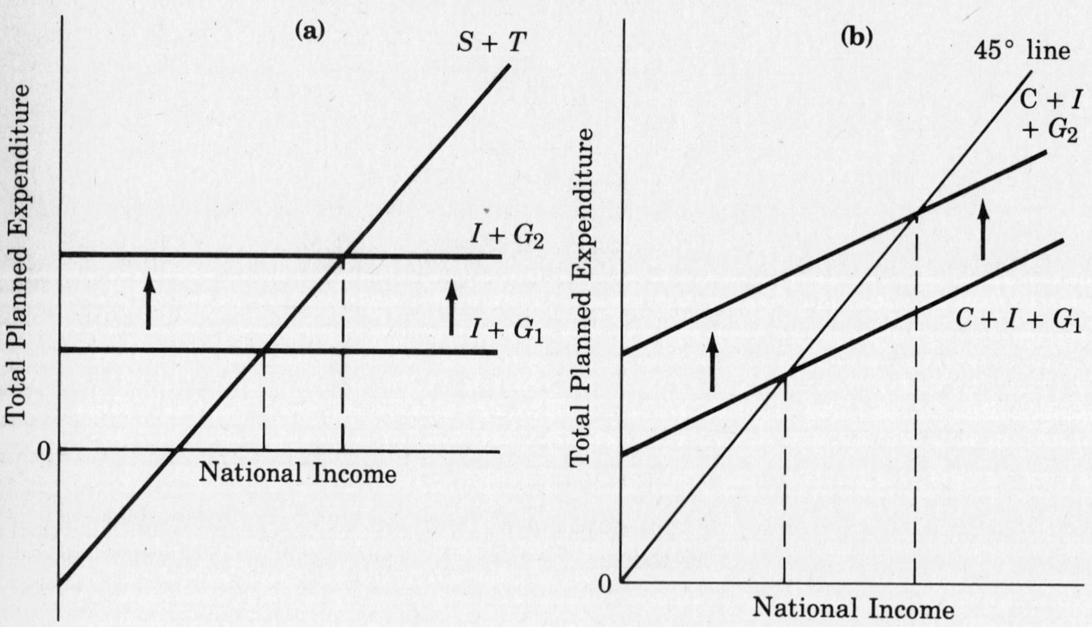

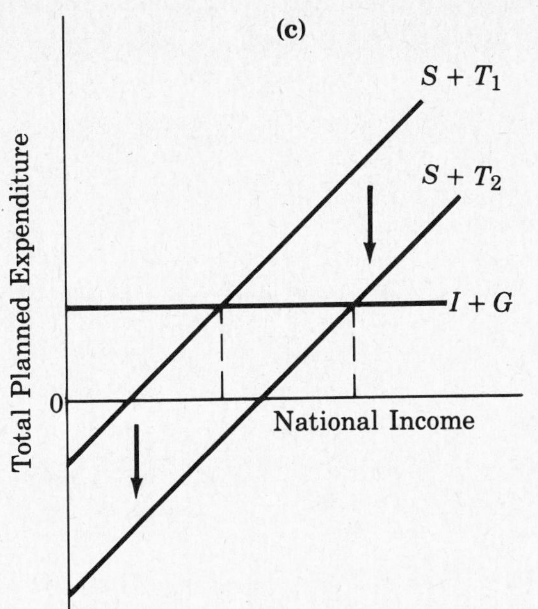

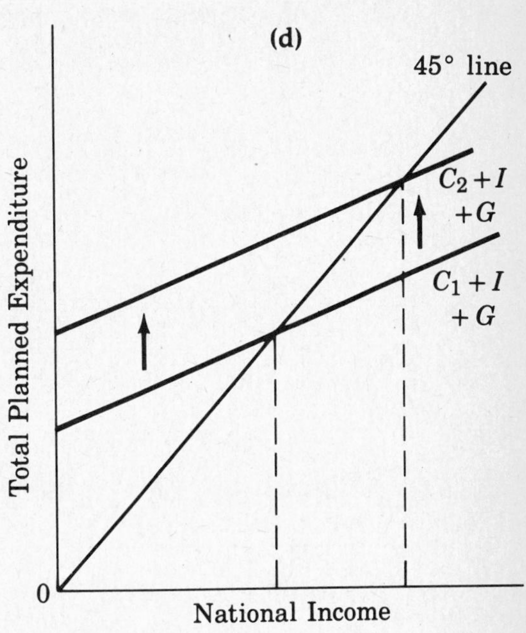

2. a. The Fed could (1) decrease the reserve requirement, (2) buy bonds on the open market, and/or (3) decrease the discount rate to encourage loans. This will increase excess reserves, and that increase time the money multiplier (reciprocal of the required reserve ratio) will cause a multiple increase in the supply of money. An increase in the supply of money (expansionary monetary policy) will decrease the interest rate, which increases planned investment. An increase in planned investment times the Keynesian multiplier (reciprocal of the *MPS)* will cause a multiple increase in national income. This cause-effect chain relationship is expressed graphically in the graphs below.
   b. To reduce unemployment.
   c. The Fed could (1) increase the reserve requirement, (2) sell bonds on the open market, and/or (3) increase the discount rate to discourage loans (or simply refuse to grant loans to banks). This will cause results opposite to those described in 2a above. Graphically, the cause-effect chain relationship is just the opposite as that illustrated in the graphs on the next page.

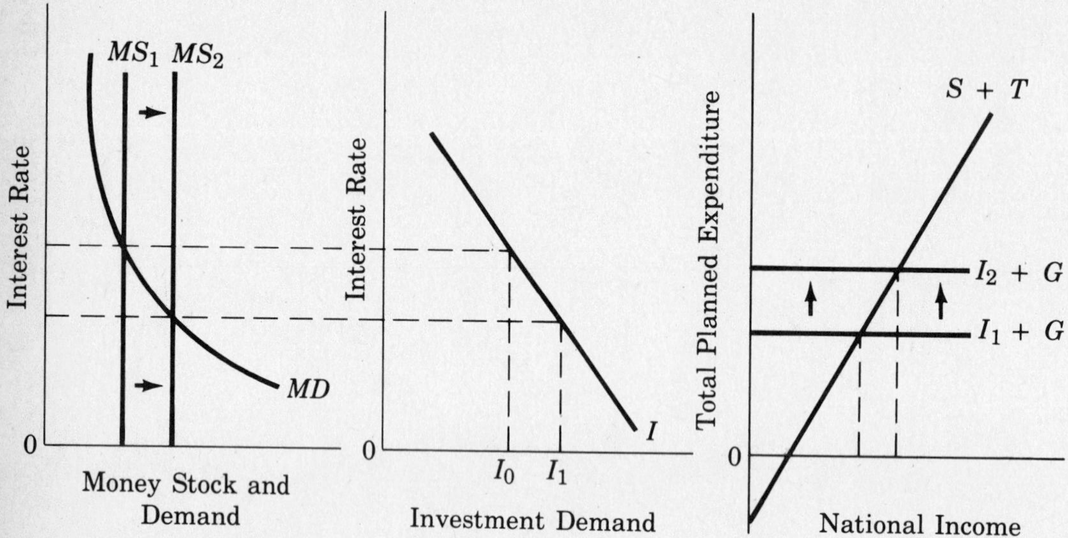

d. To combat inflationary pressures.
e. Monetary policy would be less effective in increasing national income. A flat demand for money curve will mean a lower reduction in the interest rate. A steep investment demand curve will mean less of an increase in planned investment. The lower the *MPC*, the smaller the multiplier, hence the smaller the increase in income. High tax rates also mean more leakages as income increases, resulting in a reduced multiple increase in income.

3. The crowding-out effect means government deficits financed by borrowing increase the interest rate (because of the reduction in the supply of money in the hands of the public after they purchase government bonds). This reduces investment spending that will partially (if not totally) offset the increase in government spending. The crowding-out effect is expressed in the graphs on the next page.

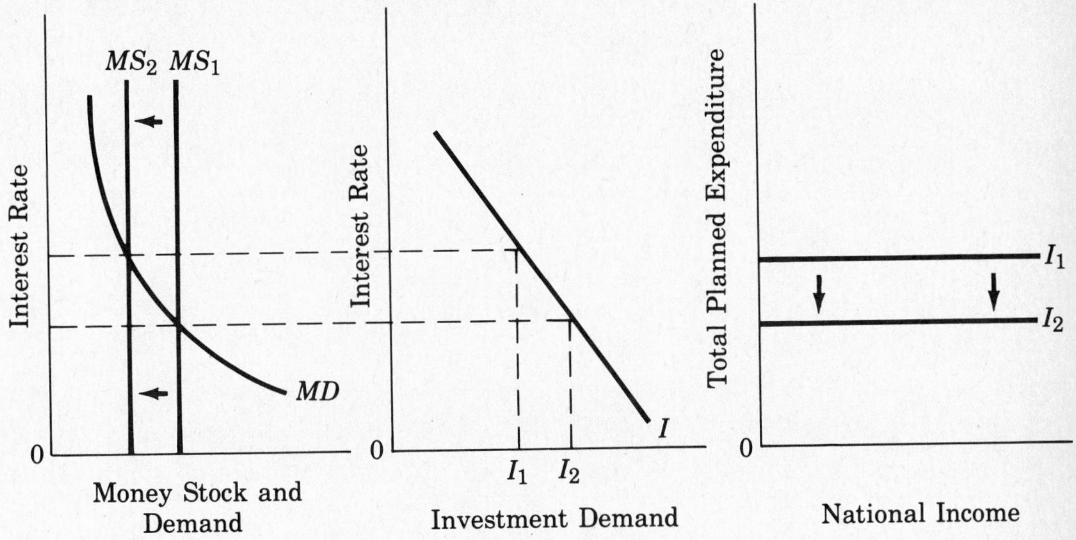

4. a. Any increase in total spending (regardless of which component increases) times the multiplier equals the increase in income. The increase in total spending equals \$20. The multiplier equals 4. Therefore, the new equilibrium income level will be \$480.

   b. An increase in taxes will cause a decrease in consumption and a decrease in saving because disposable income decreases. The decrease in consumption given any decrease in income is given by the *MPC*. Because the *MPS* = .25, the *MPC* = .75. Therefore, consumption decreases by (.75)(\$20), or \$15. The decrease in total spending of \$15 times the multiplier of 4 decreases income by \$60. So the new equilibrium income level is \$420.

   c. The balanced-budget multiplier equals 1 because the simultaneous increase in government spending of \$20 and the increase in taxes of \$20 would increase income by \$20.

   d. Yes. The balanced-budget multiplier always equals 1 regardless of the *MPS* and the *MPC*.

5. a. Taxes increase as income increases because of the progressive income tax and because as national income increases, more people are employed to collect taxes from.

b. Taxes increase the slope of the leakages function because taxes increase as income increases. Because taxes reduce consumption, the consumption function still slopes upward, but less than it would before taxes.

True-False

1. T
2. F: The liquidity trap refers to the horizontal portion of the demand for money curve.
3. F: To calculate the change in total spending given a change in taxes, one must multiply the change in taxes by the *MPC*.
4. T 5. T 6. T 7. T
8. F: Government budgetary deficits should be incurred only when the economy is below full employment.
9. F: The impact lag is the delay in realizing the effects of fiscal action.
10. F: Automatic stabilizers are fiscal actions that do not require special action on the part of the administration or Congress.
11. T
12. F: Expansionary monetary policy should be used to combat unemployment.
13. F: When taxes are increased, the equilibrium income level decreases.
14. T 15. T 16. T 17. T

Multiple Choice

1. c *(KQ1)* 2. b *(KQ1)* 3. e *(KQ1)*
4. c *(KQ2)* 5. e *(KQ4)* 6. d *(KQ1)*
7. c *(KQ1)* 8. b *(KQ1)* 9. a *(KQ1)*
10. b *(KQ2)* 11. d *(KQ4)* 12. b *(KQ4)*
13. e *(KQ1)* 14. a *(KQ1)* 15. b *(KQ1)*
16. d *(KQ1)*

CHAPTER 13

Aggregate Supply and Demand

Chapter Summary

In this chapter, we focus on the effect of changes in total spending (and hence national income) on the general level of prices. So far, we have assumed that changes in fiscal and monetary policies have no effect on prices, but make themselves felt only as much larger changes in national income (output) because of the multiplier. This chapter shows that the much larger changes in national income, due to changes in total spending and the multiplier, are not as great as previously assumed. Instead, they are partially absorbed as changes in prices.

Aggregate demand shows the inverse relationship between the price level and the total spending level. For instance, total spending increases as the price level decreases. Interest rates decrease along with the price level, causing planned investment to increase. People's real wealth also increases, causing consumption spending to increase. With both planned investment spending and planned consumption spending increasing, total spending must rise. Conversely, as the general level of prices rises, total spending drops. This inverse relationship is reflected in the downward slope of the aggregate demand curve.

Key Question 1: What is the nature and slope of the aggregate demand function?

Although the relationship between aggregate demand and total spending is well accepted, the strength of the relationship is controversial. This dispute centers around what the slope of the aggregate demand curve is. If it is flat, the relationship is strong. That is, total spending is very responsive to a change in prices. The slope of the aggregate demand curve depends on four factors: (1) how interest rates change in response to changes in the real money stock (slope of the demand for money curve); (2) how investment spending changes in response to changes in the interest rate (slope of the investment demand curve); (3) how consumption spending changes in response to changes in people's real wealth (strength of the wealth effect); and (4) how much the transactions demand for money changes with a change in national income (strength of the feedback effect). Most economists agree that the aggregate demand curve is flatter in the long run than in the short run. Over time, that is, people become better able to respond to changes in price level.

Aggregate demand can shift with changes in the factors that influence total spending. That is, if the consumption and/or investment functions shift up, then the aggregate demand shifts to the right. Also, expansionary fiscal and/or monetary policies can shift the aggregate demand curve to the right. Conversely, downward shifts of the consumption and/or investment functions cause leftward shifts of aggregate demand. Also, contractionary fiscal and/or monetary policies shift the aggregate demand curve to the left. However, economists disagree about the effectiveness of expansionary fiscal policy in shifting the aggregate demand curve to the right because it may crowd out private investment and consumption. Likewise, expansionary monetary policy may be ineffective in increasing the supply of money and therefore the aggregate demand curve because people may hold larger money balances (and for various other reasons discussed in Chapter 11 of this book).

Key Question 2: What is the nature and slope of the short-run and long-run aggregate supply functions?

Aggregate supply is a positively sloped curve expressing the positive relationship (at least in the short run) between the price level and the total output level produced during a given period. For instance, an increase in the level of prices provides an incentive for producers to increase the total output level and for workers to work harder and longer hours because of "money illusion." How much output expands as the price level increases depends on the slope of the aggregate supply curve. This in turn depends on (1) the availability of unemployed resources, (2) the ease with which unemployed resources can be put into use when prices rise, (3) the extent of money illusion, and (4) the extent to which labor contracts fix wages in current dollar terms. Furthermore, the slope of the aggregate supply curve becomes nearly flat during a recession and is much steeper during normal times. It is vertical, or nearly so, at and beyond full employment.

As the price level increases, the money illusion eventually fades. Because people adjust to the higher price level, the aggregate supply curve shifts backward. But by how much is unclear. The result over the long run is the same as if the economy moved up the vertical portion of the aggregate supply curve. That is, output (income) remains the same, but prices have increased.

The aggregate supply curve shifts because of the availability of resources or people's incentives to work—the lower the availability of resources (the greater their prices), and the lower the incentive to work, the farther the leftward shift. Other factors that cause the aggregate supply curve to shift include changes in technology and productivity, expectations about future inflation, and institutional factors such as government regulations.

Key Question 3: What is the aggregate demand and supply approach to equilibrium income?

By considering both aggregate demand and aggregate supply, we can simultaneously determine the equilibrium national income level and the equilibrium price level. For example, if the price level is above equilibrium, unwanted inventories will cause producers to competitively bid down the price level until equilibrium is reached.

By combining the aggregate demand and aggregate supply curves, we can predict how changes in aggregate demand and/or aggregate supply will affect the price level and the national income level. We also find that expansionary fiscal and monetary policies may stimulate national income in the short run. Because the price level rises, however, over time the aggregate supply curve shifts back, rendering these policies less effective in the long run. If the long-run aggregate supply curve is vertical, the end result will be a return to the original income level, but with higher prices. Indeed, some critics say, expansionary fiscal and monetary policies may create a business cycle of their own.

In the Keynesian analysis we looked at, prices have been assumed to stay constant. That is, we assumed that the aggregate supply curve is horizontal. Therefore, changes in total spending have been reflected in much larger changes in the income level alone. But in fact the aggregate supply curve does slope upward, and so part of a change in total spending is reflected in changes in prices. Therefore, the multiplier effect is weaker, and fiscal and monetary policies are not quite as effective as we have assumed.

Review Terms and Concepts

Aggregate demand
Aggregate supply
Expansionary fiscal policy
Contractionary fiscal policy
Expansionary monetary policy
Contractionary monetary policy
Crowding-out effect

New Terms and Concepts

Aggregate demand
Real balances or real wealth effect
Money illusion
Short-run aggregate supply
Natural rate of unemployment
Long-run aggregate supply
Econometrics
Econometric model
Linear regression

Completion

inverse	Aggregate demand shows the ________________ (positive/inverse)
total spending	relationship between the price level and the ________________
	(total spending/total output) level. In other words, a decrease in the price
increase	level causes total spending to ________________ (decrease/increase).
decrease	If the price level increases, total spending will ________________
	(decrease/increase). Therefore, the aggregate demand curve has a
negative	________________ (positive/negative) slope. This relationship reflects
interest rates	the effects of changes in the price level on ________________ and
real wealth	people's ________________. If the price level decreases, this causes
increase	the real money stock to ________________ (decrease/increase), which
decrease	causes the interest rate to ________________ (decrease/increase). This
increase	in turn causes planned investment to ________________ (decrease/
	increase). On the other hand, a decrease in the level of prices will cause
increase	the value of dollar assets held to ________________ (decrease/increase).
	This creates a wealth effect. That is, people feel wealthier and therefore
increase	________________ (decrease/increase) their planned consumption spend-
	ing. With an increase in planned investment and an increase in planned
increase	consumption, total spending ________________ (decreases/increases).
	So with a reduction in the level of prices, total spending increases. Like-
	wise, an increase causes total spending to decrease. This inverse relation-
negative	ship explains why the aggregate demand curve has a ________________
	(positive/negative) slope.
	Although economists agree that there is an inverse relationship
	between the price level and total spending, they differ as to the strength
slope	of that relationship. This dispute depends on the ________________

	(direction/slope) of the aggregate demand curve. If the slope is flat, the
strong	relationship is ______________ (strong/weak). That is, total spending
is	__________ (is/is not) very responsive to a change in prices. The slope
	of the aggregate demand curve depends on many factors. However, most
flatter	economists agree that the aggregate demand curve is _______________
	(flatter/steeper) in the long run than in the short run. That is, with more
better	time, people are ___________________ (less/better) able to respond to
	changes in the price level.
	The aggregate demand curve shifts if there are shifts in the
total spending	____________________ (total spending/total output) function. That is,
	whatever causes the total spending function to shift can cause the ag-
	gregate demand curve to shift. Shifts in aggregate demand can come
fiscal, monetary	from changes in __________________ and/or ____________________
	policies, as well as from shifts in the consumption and investment func-
disagreement	tions. Because there is __________________ (agreement/disagreement)
	about the effectiveness of fiscal and monetary policies, there is
disagreement	______________________ (agreement/disagreement) about how much
	these policies can shift the aggregate demand curve.
positively	Aggregate supply is ___________________ (positively/negatively)
positive	sloped. This is because there is a _______________ (positive/inverse)
	relationship (at least in the short run) between the price level and the total
produced	output level that will be __________________ (consumed/produced) in
	the economy during a given time period. As the level of prices increases,
increases	the total output level __________________ (increases/decreases). The
money illusion	total output level increases because of _____________________,
	which provides an incentive for producers to produce more and for

workers to work more. Just how much output expands as the price level
increases depends on many factors. The more output responds to an in-
smaller (flatter) crease in the level of prices, the ______________ (greater
(steeper)/smaller (flatter)) the slope of the aggregate supply curve.

However, the slope of the aggregate supply curve changes over the
business cycle course of the ______________. It is nearly flat during
recession a severe ______________ and much steeper during normal
vertical times. When we are at full employment it is ______________
(horizontal/vertical). Furthermore, if the price level continues to increase
does not in the long run, the money illusion ______________ (does/does not)
persist. Instead, people adjust to the higher price level so that the ag-
left gregate supply curve shifts to the ______________ (right/left). But the
extent of the shift is unclear. The result is the same as if the economy
moved up the vertical portion of the aggregate supply curve. That is, out-
remains the same put ______________ (increases/remains the same/decreases)
increase and prices ______________ (increase/remain the same/decrease).

The aggregate supply curve shifts because of the availability of
resources and people's incentives to work. If resources become more
readily available and there are greater incentives to work, then the ag-
right gregate supply curve will shift to the ______________ (left/right).

By bringing aggregate demand and aggregate supply together, we can
national income determine the equilibrium ______________ level
price and the equilibrium ______________ level. At any price level except
undesired equilibrium, there will be ______________ (desired/undesired)
above inventory levels. They will be too high at price levels ______________
below (above/below) equilibrium and too low at price levels ______________

(above/below) equilibrium. Therefore the price level adjusts until equilibrium is obtained.

When aggregate demand and aggregate supply are brought together we can also predict changes in the price and national income levels, given changes in aggregate demand and/or aggregate supply. In this way we can predict the effects of fiscal and monetary policy changes on prices and national income. We find that expansionary fiscal and monetary
can — policy changes _______________ (can/cannot) stimulate national in-
rise — come in the short run. However, in the process, prices _______________
(rise/fall), and over the long run this causes the aggregate supply curve to
left — shift to the _______________ (right/left), which renders these policies
less — _______________ (more/less) effective in the long run. If the aggregate
supply curve is vertical in the long run, the end result will be a return to
higher — the original income level, but with _______________ (higher/lower)
prices.

The Keynesian analysis we examined has assumed prices
are constant — ____________________ (can vary/are constant). That is, the aggregate
horizontal — supply curve has been assumed to be ____________________ (upward
sloping/horizontal). Therefore, changes in total spending have been reflected in much larger changes in the income level alone. But because the aggregate supply curve has a positive slope, part of a change in total
prices — spending is reflected in changes in _______________. Therefore, the
multiplier effect is weaker, and fiscal and monetary policies are
not quite as effective as — ____________________________________ (not quite a effective as/more
effective than) we have assumed.

Problems and Applications

1. a. Explain why an increase in the price level would cause a decrease in planned investment spending (hence total spending), which ultimately means a much larger decrease in national income because of the multiplier.
   b. Is this why the aggregate demand curve is negatively sloped?
   c. What could cause this increase in the price level?
   d. Explain why an increase in the price level would cause a decrease in planned consumption spending (hence total spending), which ultimately means a multiple decrease in national income.
   e. Is this why the aggregate demand curve is negatively sloped?
   f. Graph an aggregate demand curve.
2. For each of the following situations, determine whether the slope of the aggregate demand curve would be steeper or flatter than otherwise.
   a. The demand for money curve is flat (i.e., interest rates are not very responsive to a change in the real money stock).
   b. The investment demand curve is flat (i.e., investment spending is very responsive to a change in interest rates).
   c. There is a strong wealth effect (i.e., people's consumption spending is very responsive to a change in their real wealth).
   d. There is a strong feedback effect (i.e., the transactions demand for money changes dramatically given a change in income).
3. For each of the following situations, determine whether the aggregate demand curve would shift to the right or to the left. *Hint:* Whatever causes the total spending function to shift up (down) will cause the aggregate demand curve to shift to the right (left).
   a. The consumption function increases.
   b. The investment function decreases.
   c. People decide to save less.
   d. The government engages in deficit spending.
   e. The government pursues an expansionary monetary policy.
   f. Business taxes increase.
   g. Business expectations become more optimistic.
   h. Personal income taxes increase.
4. a. Explain why an increase in the price level will increase the total output level.
   b. Is this why the aggregate supply curve has a positive slope?
   c. What could cause this increase in the price level?
   d. Graph an aggregate supply curve on the same graph as in question 1f above.

5. For each of the following situations, determine whether the slope of the aggregate supply curve would be steeper or flatter than otherwise.
   a. We are in a deep depression, with millions of workers seeking employment.
   b. We are fully employing all of our resources.
   c. People are easily fooled by money illusion.
   d. Workers' wages are fixed and tied to long-term contracts.
6. For each of the following situations, determine whether aggregate supply would shift to the right or to the left.
   a. The OPEC nations impose another oil embargo.
   b. Personal income taxes become much more progressive.
   c. A cheap synthetic fuel is discovered.
   d. Invasion by a foreign power seems inevitable.
   e. Workers are no longer fooled by money illusion. They realize that even the sizable increases in their wages are not sufficient to keep up with inflation. Therefore, they unionize, or call on their current unions, to demand yet higher wages. Furthermore, businesses adjust their prices upward because they are no longer fooled by money illusion.
7. On the same graph you used to draw aggregate demand and aggregate supply curves in answering questions 1f and 4d above, determine the equilibrium price and national income level. (Do you know why equilibrium exists there?)
8. We can identify the equilibrium price and national income level, and we know that if the price level is above equilibrium, an undesirably high level of inventories will cause it to drop; conversely an undesirably low level of inventories will cause the price level to rise, if it is below equilibrium. We also know why aggregate demand and aggregate supply curves may shift, and that this will yield new equilibrium price and national income levels. Furthermore, we know the slope of the aggregate demand curve becomes flatter over the long run. But the aggregate supply curve may shift to the left over time as people adjust to higher prices (workers may demand higher wages or producers higher prices) — in essence causing the aggregate supply curve to become vertical (or nearly so). To test your understanding of these principles, discuss the effects of expansionary fiscal and monetary policies on our aggregate demand-aggregate supply model in the short run and the long run.

(In so doing, you will also be able to evaluate the effectiveness of expansionary policies.)

9. Why do expansionary fiscal and monetary policies actually produce a much smaller increase in income because of the multiplier than we assumed earlier?

True-False

For each item, determine whether the statement is basically true or false. If the statement is false, rewrite it so it is a true statement.

_____ 1. Aggregate demand-aggregate supply analysis shows that contractionary fiscal and monetary policies are successful in curbing stagflation.

_____ 2. Aggregate demand is negatively sloped because of the wealth effect and the effect of changes in the price level on interest rates.

_____ 3. Anything that shifts the total spending function causes a shift in the aggregate demand curve.

_____ 4. The slope of the aggregate demand curve is steeper in the long run.

_____ 5. The money illusion means people do not consider the real purchasing power of price changes.

_____ 6. The wealth effect means people will spend more as prices decrease because the purchasing power of their dollar assets rises.

_____ 7. Aggregate demand-aggregate supply analysis shows that the multiplier effect of a change in total spending is larger than we have assumed in previous chapters.

_____ 8. The aggregate supply curve slopes upward because money illusion creates incentives to produce and work more.

_____ 9. The aggregate supply curve may be vertical in the long run.

_____ 10. The slope of the aggregate supply curve depends on the extent of the money illusion, among other things.

_____ 11. A leftward shift in the aggregate supply curve could be caused by contractionary fiscal and monetary policies.

_____ 12. The aggregate supply curve may shift back to the left as people no longer operate under the money illusion in the long run.

_____ 13. An increase in aggregate supply would increase prices and increase income.

_____ 14. In the long run the expansionary policies of government may have a zero multiplier effect.

____ 15. Expansionary fiscal policy will be more effective in increasing aggregate demand if there is no crowding-out effect.

Multiple Choice

Choose the one best answer for each item.

____ 1. Which of the following statements is true with respect to a rightward shift in the aggregate demand curve?
   a. It must have been due to a decrease in the total spending function.
   b. Expansionary fiscal policy will shift it farther if there is no crowding-out effect.
   c. Expansionary monetary policy will shift it farther if people hold larger money balances.
   d. Expansionary monetary policy will shift it farther if the investment demand curve shifts to the left.
   e. It will cause the income level to rise, but prices will come down.

____ 2. Aggregate supply is defined as
   a. the inverse relationship between the price of a product and the quantity demanded during a given period of time.
   b. the direct relationship between the price of a product and the quantity produced during a given period of time.
   c. the inverse relationship between the general price level and the total quantity of goods and services produced in the economy during a given period of time.
   d. the direct relationship between the general price level and the total quantity of goods and services consumed in the economy during a given period of time.
   e. none of the above.

____ 3. In the long run, aggregate demand-aggregate supply analysis shows
   a. people are no longer fooled by money illusion.
   b. the aggregate supply curve shifts back to the left.
   c. the aggregate supply curve may be vertical
   d. expansionary fiscal and monetary policy may result in the same income level but a higher price level.
   e. all of the above.

____ 4. An increase in the price level results in
   a. the real stock of money increasing.
   b. the real stock of money decreasing.
   c. the real stock of money remaining unchanged.

d. a wealth effect causing increased consumption.
e. an increase in the total spending level.

_____ 5. If people come to realize that changes in dollar prices do not necessarily reflect real prices, then
a. we are in equilibrium.
b. people are no longer operating under money illusion.
c. aggregate demand equals aggregate supply.
d. prices will drop.
e. income will rise.

_____ 6. Which of the following statements is true?
a. The aggregate demand curve is flatter in the long run than in the short run.
b. The wealth effect explains why the aggregate supply curve slopes upward.
c. Expansionary fiscal and monetary policies can increase employment and decrease the price level.
d. An increase in the price level has substantially the same effect on investment spending as expansionary monetary policy.
e. In the long run the aggregate supply curve is horizontal.

Answer questions 7 through 9 based on the following graph.

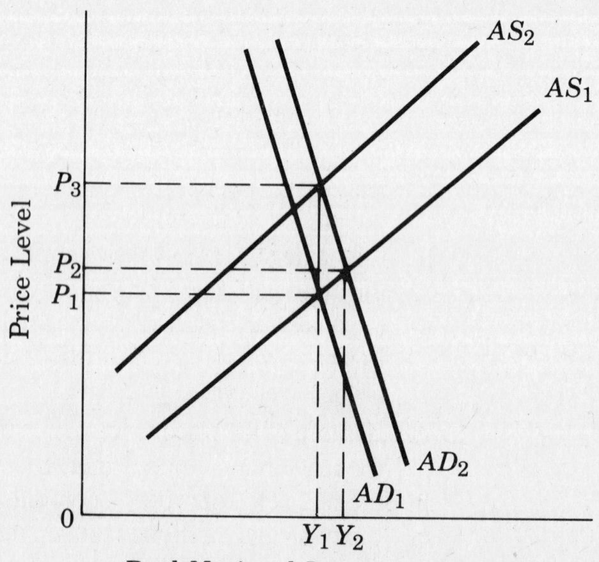

_____ 7. Which of the following statements is true?
   a. Given AD_1 and AS_1, equilibrium exists at Y_1 and P_1.
   b. Given AD_2 and AS_2, equilibrium exists at Y_1 and P_3.
   c. Movement from AD_1 to AD_2 may have been caused by expansionary fiscal and monetary policies.
   d. Movement from AS_1 to AS_2 may have been caused by a decrease in incentives to work.
   e. all of the above

_____ 8. If we are initially given AD_1 as AS_1, and if government undertakes expansionary fiscal and monetary policy, the result may be
   a. movement from AD_1 to AD_2.
   b. a rise in the income level to Y_2 and a rise in the price level to P_2 in the short run.
   c. movement from AS_1 to AS_2 as people adjust to higher prices over time.
   d. the same income level, Y_1, but a rise in the general level of prices from P_1 to P_3 in the long run.
   e. all of the above

_____ 9. Expansionary fiscal and monetary policy will be more effective in increasing aggregate demand if
   a. the investment demand curve shifts to the left.
   b. people hold larger money balances.
   c. there is no crowding-out effect.
   d. the demand for money curve is flat.
   e. the investment demand curve is flat.

Discussion Questions

1. Assume we are in the short run and aggregate supply slopes upward. We know that expansionary fiscal and monetary policies shift aggregate demand to the right (by shifting the total spending function up). But there is some disagreement over how much these policies shift the aggregate demand curve to the right (i.e., how much the total spending function shifts up). Try to list all the factors that would tend to render expansionary fiscal and expansionary monetary policy effective, and all those that would render these policies ineffective. Of course, economists disagree about some of these factors, and what government can do about them. But making the list will help you understand why controversy exists over the effectiveness of expansionary fiscal and monetary policies. Furthermore, you will have discovered some of the most pressing

macroeconomic issues of the day and why the different schools of thought disagree. *(KQ1, 2, 3)*

2. Why do some people believe that macroeconomic stabilization policy can actually contribute to the business cycle rather than stabilize it? *(KQ3)*

Answers

Problems and Applications

1. a. An increase in the price level means a decrease in the purchasing power of money. Because the amount of money in existence will no longer cover as many transactions, the real money stock has declined. This has the same effect as a decrease in the money stock: interest rates are driven up and planned investment spending decreases, which translates into a much larger decrease in national income because of the multiplier.
   b. Yes, combined with the wealth effect, which affects consumption spending.
   c. A decrease (or leftward shift) in aggregate supply. In other words, whatever could cause a decrease in aggregate supply.
   d. With an increase in the price level, the purchasing power of dollar assets held will decrease. This makes people feel less wealthy. As a result they will spend less on consumption (save more), which translates into a multiple decrease in national income. Thus there is kind of a negative wealth effect.
   e. Yes, combined with the effect a change in prices has on interest rates, which affects investment spending.

f.

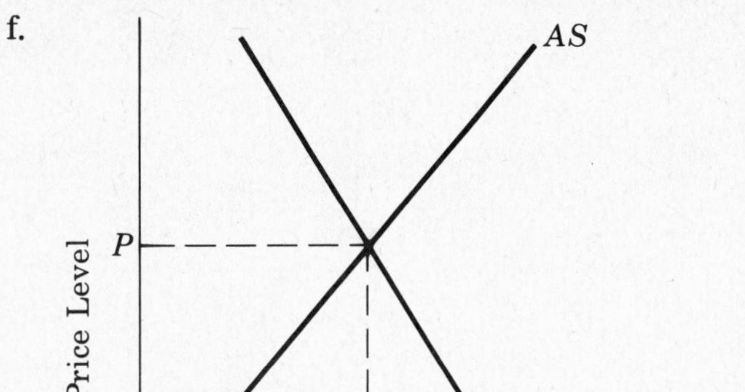

2. a. steeper
   b. flatter
   c. flatter
   d. steeper
3. a. This shifts the total spending function up, so it shifts aggregate demand to the right.
   b. This shifts the total spending down, so it shifts aggregate demand to the left.
   c. This shifts the consumption function (hence total spending function) up, so aggregate demand shifts to the right.
   d. This shifts the total spending function (hence total spending function) up, so aggregate demand shifts to the right.
   e. This shifts the investment function (hence total spending function) up, so aggregate demand shifts to the right.
   f. This shifts the investment demand curve to the left, so the investment function (hence total spending function) shifts down and aggregate demand shifts to the left.
   g. This shifts the investment demand curve to the right, so the investment function (hence total spending function) shifts up and aggregate demand shifts to the right.
   h. This shifts the consumption function (hence total spending function) down, so aggregate demand shifts to the left.

4. a. Because of the incentives the money illusion produces. This causes producers to produce more and workers to work more and longer hours.
   b. Yes.
   c. An increase (or rightward shift) in aggregate demand. In other words, whatever could cause an increase in aggregate demand.
   d. See the graph to answer 1f.
5. a. flatter
   b. steeper (indeed it may be vertical)
   c. flatter
   d. flatter
6. a. Aggregate supply shifts to the left.
   b. Aggregate supply shifts to the left.
   c. Aggregate supply shifts to the right.
   d. Aggregate supply shifts to the right.
   e. Obviously, because workers and producers are no longer fooled by money illusion, we are in the long run. The behavior described will shift aggregate supply to the left.
7. See the graph to answer 1f. Equilibrium exists at *P* and *Y*, where the two curves intersect.
8. Given any expansionary fiscal and/or monetary policy, in the short run aggregate demand shifts to the right, causing both income and prices to increase. In the long run, people are no longer fooled by money illusion and make adjustments (see question 6e or Problems and Applications and the accompanying answer above). These adjustments shift aggregate supply to the left (by how much is debatable). This may result in the same original output level (if aggregate supply is vertical in the long run—that is, if aggregate supply shifts that far back), but higher prices. See the graph on page 237, where we start with AD_1 and AS_1, thus P_1 and Y_1. Aggregate demand increases to AD_2, hence income increases to Y_2, and prices increase to P_2, in the short run. But, in the long run, aggregate supply shifts back to, say, AS_2. This causes income to drop back to its original level, Y_1, but prices are higher than before, at P_3. (Note that income first increases and later drops. Is this why some economists say that expansionary fiscal and monetary policy can create a business cycle of its own?)
9. Because part of the increase in total spending is absorbed in higher prices rather than entirely reflected in much larger increases in income because of the multiplier.

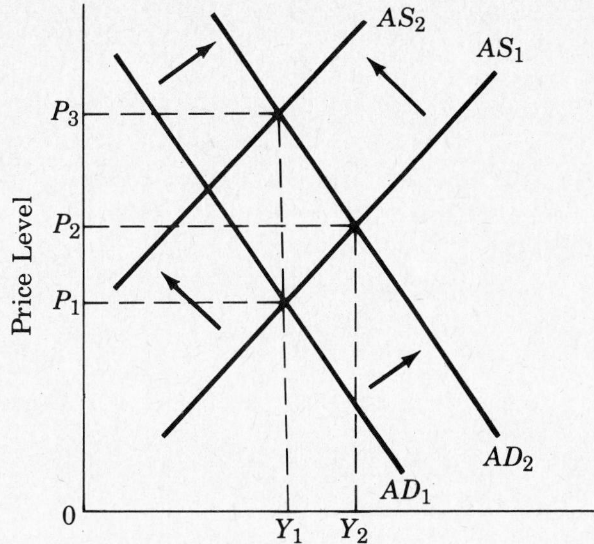

True-False

1. F: Aggregate demand-aggregate supply analysis shows that contractionary fiscal and monetary policies are not successful in curbing stagflation.
2. T 3. T
4. F: The slope of the aggregate demand is flatter in the long run.
5. T 6. T
7. F: Aggregate demand-aggregate supply analysis shows that the multiplier effect of a change in total spending is smaller than we have assumed in previous chapters because part of the effect is absorbed as price changes.
8. T 9. T 10. T
11. F: A leftward shift in the aggregate supply curve could be caused by disincentives to work and lower availability of resources.
12. T
13. F: An increase in aggregate supply would decrease prices and increase income.
14. T 15. T

Multiple Choice

1. b *(KQ1)*	2. e *(KQ2)*	3. e *(KQ3)*
4. b *(KQ1)*	5. b *(KQ1)*	6. a *(KQ1)*
7. e *(KQ3)*	8. e *(KQ3)*	9. c *(KQ3)*

CHAPTER 14

The Monetarist View of Unemployment and Inflation

Chapter Summary

Key Question 1: What are the basic doctrines of monetarism?

Key Question 2: How do monetarists explain unemployment?

Key Question 3: What is the basic cause of inflation?

The monetarist school of thought is the most widely accepted alternative to Keynesian analysis. Monetarism is based on the quantity theory of money and monetarists believe money is the single most important variable affecting the economy. They point out that the primary cause of short-run fluctuations in unemployment and inflation is changes in the growth rate of the money stock. The Fed, they say, increases the growth rate too much at some times and too little at other times. The monetarists would therefore advocate steady growth in the money stock at an annual rate equal to the potential annual growth rate in real GNP—somewhere around 4 percent.

According to monetarists, unemployment is determined by conditions in the labor market. The economy tends to settle at the long-run or natural rate of unemployment. In the short run, unanticipated changes in money and prices can cause unemployment to rise or fall. The Phillips curve embodies this short-run relationship. The historical evidence indicates that the long-run Phillips curve is vertical (that is, it doesn't exist).

The monetarists also argue that an excessive rate of growth of the money stock causes inflation. The rate of growth of the money stock is excessive if it exceeds the rate of growth of real output (real GNP).

Monetarists' arguments may be most easily understood in terms of aggregate demand-aggregate supply analysis. In a period of high unemployment, Keynesian prescriptions would call for expansionary fiscal and monetary policies to increase aggregate demand, hence income and employment. Monetarists, on the other hand, say that increases in aggregate demand are due *only* to increases in the money supply (stock). They argue that expansionary fiscal policy is not effective, even in the short run, because of the crowding-out effect. It is not deficits, they say, that increase income, but the increases in the money supply to finance these deficits. Furthermore, over the long run, they argue deficits reduce economic growth by diverting resources away from the private sector (crowding out). According to monetarists, because resources are used less efficiently by government than they would be by the private sector, the nation's capital stock—stock of plant and equipment—grows more slowly and therefore economic growth is lower.

Key Question 4: What are the effects of an increase in the stock of money?

Aggregate demand increases when the money supply increases because then people have more money than they wish to hold. Therefore, consumption spending increases. Increases in the money stock also decrease interest rates (as people buy more bonds), which increases planned investment. This increase in total spending pushes prices up. Prices are competitively bid up because of demand-pull inflation—too many dollars chasing too few goods and services. The monetarists point out that the inflation rate will rise faster than the rate of growth in the money supply because velocity increases as people spend more money. As prices rise, real wage rates drop, causing employment (hence output and income) to rise. So in terms of aggregate demand-aggregate supply analysis, an increase in the money supply increases the total spending function, which shifts aggregate demand to the right. The result is a higher income level (lower unemployment rate) *and* higher inflation.

According to the monetarists the higher income (lower unemployment rate) will not persist beyond the short run. Over time, as people begin to anticipate a rise in inflation, they will adjust by demanding higher money wages. Once money wages rise, real wages rise, and the unemployment rate rises back to its original level—which is the natural rate of unemployment. But workers' successful demands for higher money wages will cause some cost-push inflation, which adds to the already high inflation rate (that is, it further raises the general level of prices). In other words, as people adjust to higher expected rates of inflation, the aggregate supply curve shifts back, and we are left with the same income level as before (the same original natural rate of unemployment), but an even higher inflation rate. The monetarists say that unemployment cannot be reduced below the natural rate in the long run until the removal of obstacles in the labor market that keep the real wage rate artificially high. Such obstacles include minimum wage legislation, union contracts, and restrictions on labor mobility—for instance, lack of information as to where jobs exist.

Thus expansionary monetary policy may relieve unemployment in the short run, but at the cost of higher rates of unanticipated inflation (which creates problems in and of itself). In the long run attempts to relieve unemployment with expansionary monetary policy will be fruitless. Unemployment will persist, say the monetarists, until the obstacles in the labor market are removed. It is not possible, in the long run, to trade off unemployment against inflation. Therefore, to the monetarist, the Phillips curve is vertical in the long run at the natural rate of unemployment. The monetarists also point out that high inflation rates, caused by excessive increases in the money stock, contribute to high interest rates, which may eventually impede economic growth. There is some evidence to support all of these propositions.

Key Question 5: What effect does inflation have on interest rates?

Key Question 6: What macroeconomic policy do monetarists propose?

In sum, the monetarists believe discretionary fiscal policy is ineffective in stabilizing the business cycle and actually causes lower rates of economic growth. In the long run, they say, discretionary monetary policy contributes to inflation, higher rates of interest, and therefore lower rates of economic growth. They advocate a constant growth rate in the money stock year after year to avoid unanticipated inflation and the problems it creates. They would address the unemployment problem by attacking the obstacles in the labor market.

Key Question 7: What are the problems with monetarism?

Opponents of the monetarists point out that it is difficult to decide which measure of the money stock should be controlled. Moreover, critics argue, changes in money stock should be controlled. Moreover, critics argue, changes in money stock growth rates may be necessary to offset changes in velocity. Otherwise inflation or unemployment may result. Finally, it is not clear that the Fed would be capable of controlling the growth rate of the money supply as closely as monetarism would require.

Review Terms and Concepts

Keynesian school of thought
Monetarist school of thought
Fiscal policy
Monetary policy
Full employment
Frictional unemployment
Structural unemployment
Cyclical unemployment
Natural rate of unemployment
Real wage
Inflation
Demand-pull inflation
Cost-push inflation
Crowding-out effects
Money illusion
Equation of exchange

New Terms and Concepts

Quantity theory
Velocity
Monetarism
Phillips curve
Cambridge equation
Demand for money
Fisher effect

Completion

The monetarists offer the most widely accepted alternative to Keynesian
money — analysis. They believe ________________ (total spending/money) is the
single most important variable affecting the economy. They believe that
should not — the money stock __________________ (should/should not) be increased
should not — during recession and ___________________ (should/should not) be
decreased during inflationary periods. This is because they believe these
contribute to — policies ___________________________ (smooth out/contribute to) the
fluctuations in the business cycle. Instead, they believe the money supply
increased — should be ______________________ (increased/decreased) by a
constant — ___________________ (variable/constant) rate year after year.

If we are in a recession and are experiencing some unemployment,
an increase — then ___________________ (an increase/a decrease) in the money stock
short — will increase income in the _______________ (long/short) run, but at the
inflation — cost of some ___________________ (inflation/deflation). This inflation
unanticipated — would be _______________________ (anticipated/unanticipated) by the
decrease — public. This inflation causes the real wage rate to __________________
an increase — (increase/decrease), which causes ____________________ (an increase/
a decrease) in employment. With more workers employed, our output
(income) level rises. This is why short-run expansionary monetary policy
increases income — at least in the short run. This reduction in unemployment, which costs us some unanticipated inflation, is represented by a
movement along — ___________________________ (shift of/movement along) the Phillips
curve. In terms of aggregate demand-aggregate supply analysis, an
increase in the money supply causes aggregate demand to shift to the
right — _______________ (right/left). This causes the income (employment)

rise, rise	level to ____________ (rise/fall) and the price level to ____________
	(fall/rise). This is just another way of looking at what we have already
	concluded.
	In the long run, people will make adjustments to this inflation. Realiz-
decreasing	ing that their real wages have been ________________ (increasing/
	decreasing) with this unanticipated inflation, they will come to anticipate
higher	inflation and therefore demand ________________ (lower/higher)
increase	money wages. Consequently the real wage rate will ______________
fewer	(increase/decrease) and businesses will hire ______________
unemployment	(more/fewer) workers. This creates some ____________________
	(employment/unemployment). Indeed the employment (income) level
	will drop back to its original level, known as the natural
rate of unemployment	________________________________. But the inflation rate
higher	will be ______________ (higher/lower) than before the expansionary
	monetary policy was implemented.
an increase	Initially an increase in the money supply results in ______________
	(an increase/a decrease) in total spending. The total spending level in-
	creases, because with more money in the economy, people have
more	______________ (more/less) money than they wish to hold. There-
increase	fore, they ______________ (increase/decrease) their consumption
up	spending, driving prices ____________ (up/down). Also, an increase in
decrease	the money supply will ______________ (increase/decrease) the inter-
increase	est rate. This causes investment spending to ______________ (in-
	crease/decrease). The increase in consumption spending and investment
demand-pull	spending creates ______________ (cost-push/demand-pull) inflation,

many — which can be viewed as too ____________ (many/few) dollars chasing
few — too ____________ (many/few) goods and services.

Demand-pull inflation is only one of the reasons why the inflation rate is higher in the long run under an expansionary monetary policy. Another reason can be traced to costs of production. People's demand for
higher — __________________ (higher/lower) money wages creates some
cost-push — ____________________ inflation. It is because of these higher money
rise — wages that real wages ________________ (rise/fall) and the unemploy-
falls — ment level ________________ (rises/falls) back to its natural rate.

These long-run adjustments back to the natural rate of unemployment accompanied by a higher inflation rate may be considered in terms of the Phillips curve and aggregate demand-aggregate supply analysis. When people demand higher money wages, the Phillips curve shifts
out — ___________(out/in). This illustrates that the same unemployment rate
higher — (the natural rate) will be associated with a ________________ (higher/
lower) inflation rate than before. Because people demand higher money
left — wages, the aggregate supply curve shifts to the ________________
(right/left). This results in the same income level (unemployment rate)
higher — but a ________________ (higher/lower) inflation rate than before.

decrease — In sum, expansionary monetary policy will ____________________
short — (increase/decrease) unemployment in the _____________ (short/long)
rise — run but the inflation rate will ________________ (fall/rise). In the long
the same — run, we are left with ________________ (a different/the same) natural
higher — unemployment rate but an even ________________ (higher/lower) infla-
tion rate. In the long run, according to the monetarists, there is nothing we can do to reduce the natural rate of unemployment unless the

obstacles __________ (obstacles/money wages) in the labor market are
high removed. These obstacles keep the real wage artificially __________
(high/low). Therefore, in the long run, the Phillips curve is
vertical __________ (horizontal/vertical) at the natural rate of unemploy-
vertical ment. Furthermore, the aggregate supply curve is __________
(upward sloping/vertical) in the long run, showing that changes in aggregate demand do not affect the employment (income) level but only
change the inflation rate.

So far, we have considered only expansionary monetary policy. Ac-
is not cording to the monetarists, expansionary fiscal policy __________
or (is/is not) effective in the short run __________ (and/or) the long run.
crowding-out This is because of the __________ (multiplier/crowding-
decreases out) effect. Indeed, in the long run, deficit spending __________
(increases/decreases) economic growth, according to the monetarists.

The monetarists conclude that attempts to reduce unemployment only
increase inflation and retard economic growth. They also conclude that
up higher inflation rates push interest rates __________ (up/down). This
is because the market rate of interest equals the real rate of interest
plus __________ (plus/minus) the inflation rate.

reject The monetarists __________ (accept/reject) discretionary
increasing fiscal and monetary policies. Instead, they advocate __________
constant (increasing/decreasing) the money supply by a __________
(variable/constant) rate year after year, a rate equal to the potential an-
real GNP nual growth rate in __________ (money GNP/real GNP).

Several criticisms of the monetarist school of thought have been ad-
definition vanced. First there is the problem of which __________ of the

money supply should be controlled. Secondly, there may be changes in

velocity

_______________ that could destabilize the economy unless the money supply is changed in the opposite direction. Finally, there is some debate over whether the fed could control the money supply as much as monetarism would require.

Problems and Applications

1. a. Assume we are in the short run. Therefore, the aggregate supply curve slopes upward. Draw aggregate demand and aggregate supply curves on the same graph and determine the equilibrium price and income levels.
   b. Assume this income level entails some unemployment. What would Keynesians prescribe to reduce this unemployment?
   c. According to the monetarists, would expansionary fiscal policy be effective in eliminating unemployment in the short run? Why or why not? What about the long run?
   d. According to monetarists, would expansionary monetary policy be effective in eliminating unemployment in the short run? Why or why not?
   e. Given your answer above, what happens to prices and real wages under expansionary monetary policies?
   f. How does expansionary monetary policy affect aggregate demand in the short run? Illustrate this effect on the same graph as before.
   g. Given the above change in the aggregate demand, what happens to the price and income levels? Show these effects on the same graph as before.
   h. Given your answer above, what type of inflation is this?
   i. We know the Phillips curve shows the tradeoff between unemployment and inflation. Graph a Phillips curve and express the effects of expansionary monetary policy on the inflation and unemployment rates in the short run.
   j. Given your answer above, was this inflation rate anticipated or unanticipated by people in the aggregate?
   k. What would you expect people to do in the long run because of unanticipated inflation?
   l. In the long run how would adjustments to anticipated inflation affect the economy? In other words, what would happen to

aggregate supply and the Phillips curve? Show these effects on the same graph as before.

m. Given your answer above, is this why the monetarists believe aggregate supply is vertical in the long run at the natural rate of unemployment (in other words, given any change in aggregate demand in the long run, we will experience changes in inflation but no change in the natural rate of unemployment)?

n. Given your answer to 1*l* above, is this why the monetarists believe the Phillips curve is vertical in the long run (in other words, there is no tradeoff between unemployment and inflation in the long run)?

o. In sum, according to the monetarists, is discretionary (deliberate) fiscal and monetary policy effective in controlling unemployment in the long run?

2. The monetarists argue that discretionary fiscal policy is ineffective because of the crowding-out effect and that monetary policy is effective only in the short run—but at the cost of unanticipated inflation. In the long run, monetary policy only causes greater inflation rates. What would the monetarists do to stabilize the business cycle and why?
3. The monetarists point out that increases in the money stock increase inflation rates more than the rate of increase in the money supply. How could this be?
4. What is the natural rate of unemployment?
5. a. If the market interest rate is 10 percent and the inflation rate is 5 percent, what is the real interest rate?
   b. If the market interest rate is 7 percent and the inflation rate is 5 percent, what is the real interest rate?
   c. If the market interest rate is 18 percent and the real interest rate if 8 percent, what is the inflation rate?
   d. If the inflation rate rises, will this cause the market interest rate to fall?

True-False

For each item, determine whether the statement is basically true or false. If the statement is false, rewrite it so it is a true statement.

____ 1. According to the monetarists, deficit spending reduces the federal debt.

____ 2. There is no historical evidence to support the monetarists' positions.

_____ 3. To the monetarists, money is the most important variable affecting the macroeconomy.

_____ 4. The real wage rate is equal to the money wage rate divided by a price index (which is a measure of the level of prices).

_____ 5. The natural rate of unemployment is determined by frictional unemployment and structural focus in the economy, such as unions and the minimum wage.

_____ 6. If inflation decreases, unemployment decreases because the real wage decreases.

_____ 7. Keynesian policy is primarily concerned with shifting the Phillips curve inward.

_____ 8. According to the monetarists, expansionary fiscal policy creates lower rates of economic growth over time.

_____ 9. Critics of the monetarists point out that because velocity may change, the money stock should change in the same direction to stabilize prices and unemployment.

_____ 10. A decrease in the price level will cause real wages to increase temporarily, causing some short-run unemployment. As competition for jobs increases, however, real wages will fall, correcting for the unemployment.

_____ 11. The Keynesian school of thought advocates governmental intervention whereas the monetarist school does not.

_____ 12. The monetarists advocate that the money supply should be constant year after year.

_____ 13. The monetarists say that the inflation rate will increase at the same rate as the increase in the money supply.

_____ 14. There are three ways to look at the effect of changes in monetary policy—the effects on real wages, the effects on the Phillips curve, and the effects on the price and income levels in terms of aggregate demand-aggregate supply analysis.

_____ 15. The demand for money depends in part on the inflation rate.

_____ 16. The market rate of interest equals the real rate of interest plus the inflation rate.

_____ 17. If government increases taxes, this crowds out consumption and investment spending.

_____ 18. If the money wage rises, the real wage rises.

_____ 19. If the inflation rate if 5 percent and the market interest rate if 11 percent, then the real rate of interest is 16 percent.

_____ 20. The monetarists advocate a steady growth rate in the money supply, which they argue will avoid the problems associated with unanticipated inflation and reduce interest rates over time.

_____ 21. One of the criticisms of the monetarist school of thought is that the Fed may be unable to control the money supply as closely as monetarist policy would require.

_____ 22. In the Cambridge equation, *k* represents the fraction of income people wish to hold in the form of money.

_____ 23. The monetarists argue that velocity is quite stable.

Multiple Choice

Choose the one best answer for each item.

_____ 1. From the monetarist point of view, which of the following is the primary cause of changes in the level of economic activity?
   a. Expections
   b. Money
   c. Total spending
   d. The total supply of goods and services
   e. Interest rates

_____ 2. Which of the following policies would the monetarists be most likely to recommend for solving unemployment in the long run?
   a. Expansionary fiscal policy
   b. Expansionary monetary policy
   c. Reduction in tax rates to shift aggregate supply to the right
   d. Increase in the minimum wage
   e. Abolition of the minimum wage

_____ 3. According to the monetarists, in the short run, expansionary fiscal policy is most likely to
   a. decrease real wages.
   b. increase income.
   c. increase inflation.
   d. create movement along the short-run Phillips curve.
   e. none of the above.

_____ 4. According to the monetarists, inflation will cause
   a. some relief for the unemployed in the short run.
   b. a reduction in interest rates over the long run.
   c. increased rates of economic growth over the long run.
   d. people to accept lower money wages over the long run.
   e. all of the above.

_____ 5. According to the monetarists, in the long run, an excess supply of money will cause
a. the demand for money to fall.
b. lower inflation rates.
c. lower wages and other resource prices to fall.
d. market interest rates to fall.
e. no change in real national income.

_____ 6. In the short run, inflation may cause
a. an increase in output and income because of the wealth effect.
b. an increase in output and income because of money illusion.
c. the aggregate supply curve to shift to the left.
d. the aggregate supply curve to shift to the right.
e. the real wage to increase.

_____ 7. According to the monetarists
a. aggregate supply is horizontal in the long run.
b. real wages are artificially held below equilibrium, causing unemployment.
c. the Phillips curve is vertical in the long run.
d. the money supply should be held constant.
e. the short-term Phillips curve shifts inward as people come to anticipate inflation.

_____ 8. If people expect inflation
a. the demand for loanable funds will increase.
b. the supply of loanable funds will decrease.
c. the market rate of interest will rise.
d. they will demand higher money wages.
e. all of the above will occur.

_____ 9. According to the monetarists, in the short tun, if the money supply decreases
a. inflation will decrease.
b. real wages will rise.
c. unemployment will rise.
d. there will be movement down along the Phillips curve.
e. all of the above will occur.

_____ 10. According to the monetarists, over the long run, if the money supply decreases
a. inflation will rise.
b. the real wage will decrease because of the increased competition for jobs.
c. the natural rate of unemployment will rise.

d. the short-run Phillips curve shifts outward.
e. all of the above will occur.

Answer the next question based on the following graph.

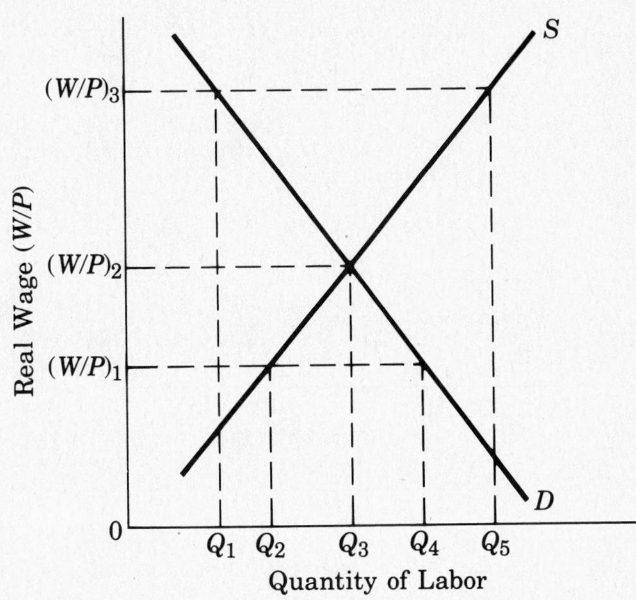

_____ 11. According to the monetarists, which of the following statements is true?
a. Equilibrium exists at $(W/P)_1$ and Q_3.
b. According to the monetarists, because of obstacles in the labor market the real wage is $(W/P)_1$ and the natural rate of unemployment is $(Q_3 - Q_2)$.
c. At $(W/P)_3$ there are more people willing and able to work than can find employment.
d. As the price level increases, (W/P) increases.
e. Over the long run, if there were no obstacles in the labor market, supply would shift to the left.

_____ 12. The natural rate of unemployment consists of
a. cyclical unemployment.
b. structural unemployment.
c. frictional unemployment.
d. b and c above.
e. a and b above.

_____ 13. According to the monetarists, which of the following statements is true?

a. In the long run an increase in the money supply by some percentage will result in a greater percentage decrease in prices.
b. In the long run an increase in the money supply by some percentage will result in the same percentage increase in prices.
c. The money supply should be decreased year after year by a constant rate equal to the potential annual growth rate in real GNP.
d. The money supply should be increased year after year by a constant rate equal to the potential annual growth rate in real GNP.
e. b and d above

_____ 14. According to the monetarists, expansionary monetary policy will

a. not be effective in reducing unemployment in either the short run or the long run because of the crowding-out effect.
b. increase aggregate demand in the short run but decrease aggregate supply in the long run.
c. decrease interest rates in the short run but increase interest rates in the long run.
d. a and c above.
e. b and c above.

_____ 15. Which of the following statements is true?

a. The Phillips curve shows a direct (positive) relationship between inflation and unemployment.
b. The monetarists argue that velocity is quite unstable in the short run.
c. The Cambridge equation can be interpreted as the demand for money.
d. The quantity theory of money indicates that an increase in the stock of money will, in the long run holding all other things the same, result in a much larger increase in the price level.
e. Velocity is equal to k (the fraction of income people wish to hold as money).

_____ 16. The Fisher effect indicates that

a. the money supply should be increased during recessions and decreased during economic expansion.
b. as inflation rises market interest rates rise.
c. as market interest rates rise inflation rises.
d. as market interest rates fall inflation rises.
e. the real interest minus anticipated inflation equals the nominal interest rate.

Discussion Questions

1. Why has Keynesian policy apparently been effective for many years, but has recently become less effective? What problems have developed in the last several years that Keynesian economics is less well equipped to handle? *(KQ2, 7)*
2. According to the monetarists, what could be done to reduce the natural rate of unemployment? Given political realities, how successful would a monetarist President be in removing obstacles in the labor market? What would be required to be politically successful? What would be the political ramifications? If monetarists abolished the minimum wage, how would they address the issue of poverty? What would happen to the distribution of income if obstacles in the labor market were removed? *(KQ2)*
3. How do the political implications of Keynesian analysis differ from those of the monetarists? *(KQ6, 7)*
4. Why does unanticipated inflation create problems? (*KQ5*. See also Chapter 9.)
5. How would deliberate changes in the money supply (discretionary monetary policy) create a business cycle of its own? (*KQ7*. See also Chapter 12.)
6. We have seen that the monetarists reject government spending and taxation policies as effective tools in correcting for macroeconomic instability, because of the crowding-out effect. But macroeconomic instability is only one type of market failure. Would the monetarists also reject government spending and taxation policies in providing for public goods and services? Would they provide as many? Would they reject government taxes and subsidies to correct for external cost and benefits? Would they be as actively involved in correcting for these problems? Current tax policy redistributes income by way of the progressive income tax and the revenues they provide for welfare assistance. Do you think the monetarists would change the tax system? The welfare system? Who would stand to gain and lose? What do you think would happen to the percentage of our population below the poverty line – would it rise or fall? Why? *(KQ1-7)*

Answers

Problems and Applications

1. a. See the graph on page 254. The original aggregate demand and aggregate supply curves are AD_1 and AS_1. The equilibrium price level is P_1 and the equilibrium income level is Y_1.

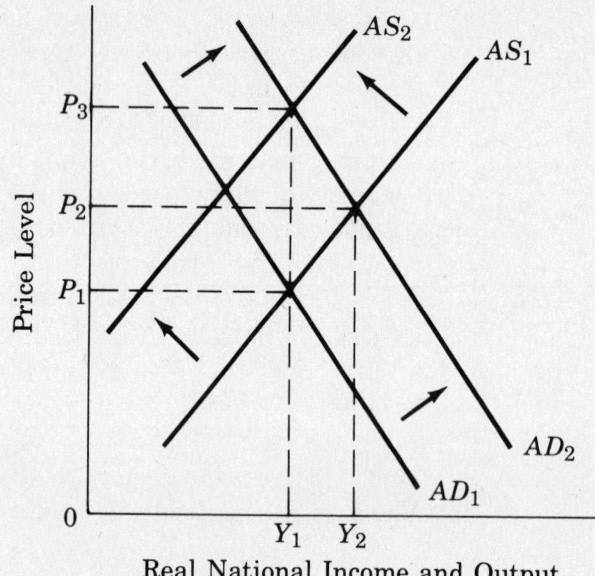

b. Keynesians would prescribe expansionary fiscal and monetary policy.

c. Expansionary fiscal policy would not be effective in the short run because of the crowding-out effect. In the long run, such policy will only divert resources away from private investment in plant and equipment. If fewer resources are devoted to the production of plant and equipment, economic growth will slow (see production possibilities in Chapter 2). According to the monetarists, fiscal policy is ineffective in both the short run and the long run.

d. According to the monetarists, expansionary monetary policy would be effective in eliminating some unemployment in the short run. Because people have more money than they wish to hold, consumption spending increases. Furthermore, increases in the money supply reduce interest rates, and this increases investment spending. Because consumption and investment spending increases, total spending increases. This causes a much larger multiple increase in output and income in the short run because of the multiplier, and hence an increase in employment (the unemployment rate decreases).

e. The price level is competitively bid up as total spending increases. (In terms of aggregate supply analysis, the increase in prices creates a money illusion that increases output and income.) Real wages (which equal money wages divided by the price level) decrease, causing increased employment—as we have already noted.
f. Because expansionary monetary policy increases total spending, it increases aggregate demand, shifting the curve to the right. In the preceding graph, aggregate demand shifts from AD_1 to AD_2.
g. In the preceding graph we see the price level rises from P_1 to P_2 and income rises from Y_1 to Y_2. This is just another way of looking at what we already concluded.
h. Demand-pull inflation.
i. See the following graph. Assume we start with Phillips curve A_1. The reduction in the unemployment rate from U_2 to U_1 results in a higher inflation rate (P_1 to P_2). This is yet another way of looking at the short-run effects of expansionary monetary policy.

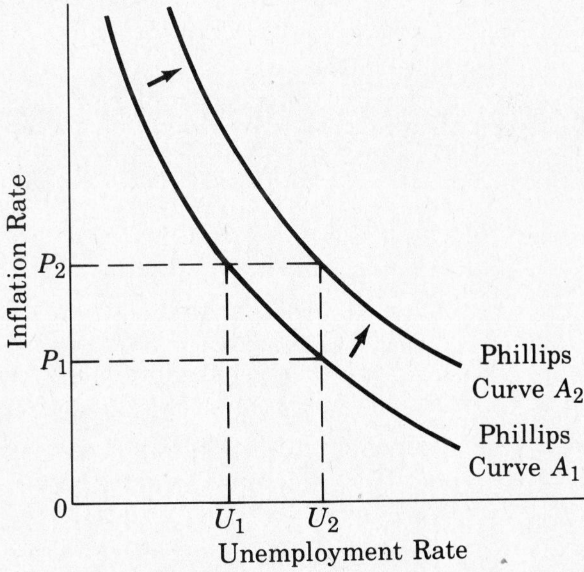

j. Unanticipated.
k. People will realize their real wages (the purchasing power of their money wages) are declining with inflation. They will come to anticipate inflation and will try to protect themselves against a decline in real wages by demanding higher money wages.
l. Long-run adjustments to anticipated inflation will cause more inflation as workers demand higher money wages. But this time it is cost-push inflation. The result is a leftward shift in the aggregate supply curve, from AS_1 to AS_2 in the graph accompanying answer 1a. The income (hence employment) level declines from Y_2 back to the original income (employment) level of Y_1, but now the inflation rate has increased to P_3, as opposed to the original inflation rate of P_1. (Note that employment drops as money wages rise because real wages rise.) In terms of the Phillips curve, because workers demand higher money wages, a higher inflation rate will be associated with any given unemployment (employment) rate. Therefore, the curve shifts outward to A_2. The result is a higher inflation rate (of P_2) associated with the original unemployment rate (U_1). (Unemployment rises back to U_1 because as money wages rose, real wages rose.)
m. Yes.
n. Yes.
o. No.

2. They would increase the growth rate in the money stock by a constant rate year after year – a rate equal to the potential annual growth rate in real GNP (somewhere around 4 percent). This, they say, will eliminate any unanticipated inflation (which redistributes income). Therefore, the risks of holding wealth in assets will decrease, decreasing interest rates and increasing economic growth. Furthermore, this steady growth of the money stock will eliminate some causes of the business cycle associated with changes in monetary policy. (Note that changes in the money stock affect the price level, which affects real wages, which in turn affects unemployment.)
3. Increases in the rate of growth in the money supply cause velocity to increase. To see this, look at the equation of exchange (MV–PQ). In the long run, the aggregate supply is vertical at full employment (the natural rate of unemployment) and therefore Q is constant. If M (the money stock) increases, people will have more money than

they wish to hold. Therefore they will spend more money. This is the same as saying that *V*, velocity (the turnover rate of money), increases. So if *M* increases by some percentage (representing the rate of growth in the money supply) and *V* increases also, then *P* (the price level) must rise because of the changes in both *M* and *V*. Hence, the inflation rate (the increase in the price level) will be greater than the increase in the growth rate of money.

4. The natural rate of unemployment consists of frictional and structural unemployment.
5. a. 5 percent.
   b. 2 percent.
   c. 10 percent.
   d. No, increases (decreases) in the inflation rate cause interest rates to rise (drop) accordingly.

True-False

1. F: According to the monetarists, deficit spending reduces planned investment spending because of the crowding-out effect and increases the federal debt.
2. F: There is historical evidence to support the monetarists' position.
3. T   4. T   5. T
6. F: If inflation decreases, unemployment increases because the real wage increases.
7. F: Keynesian policy is primarily concerned with finding a suitable tradeoff between unemployment and inflation.
8. T
9. F: Critics of the monetarists argue that if velocity changes, the money stock should change in the opposite direction to stabilize prices and unemployment.
10. T   11. T
12. F: The monetarists advocate a constant rate of increase in the money stock year after year.
13. F: The monetarists say that the inflation rate will increase more than the increase in the money supply.
14. T   15. T   16. T   17. T   18. T

19. F: If the inflation rate if 5 percent and the market interest rate is 11 percent, the real rate of interest is 6 percent.

20. T 21. T 22. T 23. T

Multiple Choice

1. b *(KQ1, 2, 3)* 2. e *(KQ2, 6)* 3. e *(KQ1, 2, 3)*
4. a *(KQ2)* 5. e *(KQ4)* 6. b *(KQ1, 3, 4)*
7. c *(KQ2)* 8. e *(KQ3, 4)* 9. e *(KQ1, 4)*
10. b *(KQ4)* 11. c *(KQ2)* 12. d *(KQ2)*
13. e *(KQ4)* 14. e *(KQ1, 6)* 15. c *(KQ1)*
16. b *(KQ5)*

Chapter 15

Supply-Side Economics

Chapter Summary

The supply-side school of thought is an alternative to Keynesian analysis that grew out of Keynesians' apparent failure to control stagflation during the 1970s. Supply-side economics emphasizes aggregate supply (total supply, or GNP) management over aggregate demand (total spending) management. Although there are many determinants of aggregate supply, the most basic proposition of the supply-siders is that high tax rates are a major cause of stagflation and lagging economic growth. To attack these problems they would reduce marginal tax rates. This, they say, will provide greater incentives to work, save, and invest, thereby reducing unemployment and inflation and increasing economic growth over time.

Key Question 1: What are the basic propositions of supply-side economics?

Supply-side theory rests on three major propositions. First, if a relatively large percentage of additional income earned from working harder or longer is taxed away, many people may be discouraged from working as much as they otherwise would. Therefore, a reduction in marginal tax rates should encourage more people to enter the labor force and to work longer hours. This would increase the supply of labor. A reduction in marginal tax rates on business income should increase the demand for labor by increasing the after-tax return on labor expenditures. Together these effects in the labor market should result in greater employment and therefore greater national output (income) over time. With more people working, and therefore greater tax revenues collected, deficits created by tax cuts should decline over time. If deficits are lower and more goods and services are produced in the economy, inflation should be reduced.Higher incomes will stimulate saving, thereby increasing the quantity of lendable funds. This effect, along with lower inflation, should drive down interest rates, increasing investment. With greater investment over time, the economy should grow faster.

Second, high marginal tax rates discourage people from investing in education and improving their work-related skills because taxes will take a relatively large percent of the additional income that could be earned. High tax rates may also encourage businesses to invest abroad, reducing our capital stock and economic growth. Therefore, tax cuts should increase productivity and national income over time.

The third basic proposition of the supply-siders is that high marginal tax rates encourage people to work in the underground economy, to barter and trade for cash, and to use productive resources in search of ways to avoid paying taxes. Tax cuts should discourage this type of activity, increasing not only the amount of income people report (and therefore tax revenues collected), but also the nation's total income.

The effects of a reduction in tax rates can be described in terms of aggregate demand-aggregate supply analysis. Tax cuts would increase aggregate demand and the national income and price levels. Over time, however, according to Keynesians and monetarists, as people adjust to higher inflation, aggregate supply is expected to shift back, increasing the inflation rate further and reducing, if not entirely offsetting, the increase in income. Supply-siders argue that tax cuts will increase aggregate supply as well as aggregate demand, because of greater incentives to work, save, and invest. The increase in aggregate supply will offset any inflationary pressures associated with an increase in aggregate demand. This means a tax reduction is not as inflationary as Keynesians theory might suggest. Hence, there is no need for adjustments, and the aggregate supply curve does not shift back. Furthermore, if the tax rate reduction is perceived as permanent, the long-run aggregate supply curve (which is vertical) shifts outward. In the end, the actual price and income levels will depend on how much aggregate demand and aggregate supply shift outward and how much the money stock is increased when tax rates are lowered. In any case, the national income level rises, and supply-siders attribute the rise to the increase in aggregate supply—not to the increase in aggregate demand (as Keynesians would argue) or to the increase in the money stock (as monetarists would argue).

Key Question 2: What are the basic criticisms of supply-side economics?

Three fundamental arguments have been raised against supply-side theory. In essence, they all question whether aggregate supply increases with lower marginal tax rates. The first and most serious objection is that lower tax rates may not cause people to work longer hours. As tax rates are lowered, and take-home pay increases, people may choose to have more leisure time rather than to work more and have more income. The effect of a tax cut on the number of hours worked depends on whether tax rates are initially high or low. If tax rates are high, a reduction would probably increase the number of hours worked, because the opportunity cost of leisure and the effect on the relative price of goods and services would be relatively great. The precise definition of "high" tax rates and the effect of a tax cut on the number of hours worked are empirical questions for which the evidence is inconclusive. Unfortunately, the effect of tax cuts on saving and investment is also uncertain.

Critics also question whether tax revenues will rise with tax cuts. The outcome of a tax cut depends on three factors: the responsiveness of workers, savers, and investors; the nation's present location on the Laffer curve; and the size of the tax cut.

Finally, critics argue that cuts in marginal tax rates increase deficit spending, eventually causing greater inflation.

Key Question 3: What variables determine the actual impact of supply-side policies?

The actual consequences of supply-side policy depends on: (a) the responsiveness of people to a change in tax rates; (b) the effect of a change in tax rates on tax revenues collected; and (c) the relative impact of a change in tax rates on aggregate supply and demand and therefore inflation. Nonetheless, supply-side economics do not believe government can fine-tune the economy. They do not recommend tax cuts as a quick fix. Instead, a reduction in marginal tax rates should gradually solve stagflation and lagging economic growth by stimulating investment in human skills and plant and equipment. Moreover, they argue, the full effects of tax reductions will not be felt unless tax rates are held down for some time. Because supply-side policies take time to work, they may not be implemented by politicians. Indeed, in the short run, tax cuts can be politically disasterous. Because of this conflict between the needs of the economy and political realities, some supply-side economists have recommended the establishment of constitutional checks on the government's spending and taxing powers.

Review Terms and Concepts

Stagflation
Marginal tax rate
Progressive income tax
Keynesian school of thought
Monetarist school of thought
Supply-side school of thought
Fiscal policy
Inflation
Economic growth
Aggregate demand
Aggregate supply
Deficits

New Terms and Concepts

Supply-side economics
Laffer curve
Income demand
Opportunity cost of leisure
Flat tax

Completion

The supply-side school of thought grew out of Keynesians' apparent lack
stagflation — of success in controlling ________ (inflation/stagflation)
high — during the 1970s. The supply-siders believe ________ (high/low)
marginal tax rates are a major cause of stagflation and lagging economic
a reduction — growth. Therefore they advocate ________ (an increase/
a reduction) in marginal tax rates. This, they say, will provide
greater — ________ (greater/less) incentives to work, save, and invest.
Supply-side economists emphasize the effect of tax rates on the
supply of — ________ (demand for/supply of) goods and services
produced.

Supply-side theory rests on three major propositions. First, beyond
less — some point, people will work ________ (more/less) as their
income is taxed at higher rates. Therefore, if tax rates are reduced,
more — ________ (more/fewer) people will be encouraged to enter the
longer — labor force and work ________ (longer/shorter) hours. This
supply of — should increase the ________ (supply of/demand for) labor.
encourage — Lower tax rates on businesses should ________ (encourage/
more — discourage) businesses to hire ________ (more/fewer) workers at
demand for — any given wage rate. This would cause the ________ (supply
of/demand for) labor to increase. These combined effects on the labor
increase — market would ________ (increase/decrease) the level of

increase — employment and, in turn, ______________ (increase/decrease) national
output (income) over time. Greater employment should cause tax
rise — revenues collected by government to ____________ (rise/fall). This
means deficits caused by reduced marginal tax rates should
decrease — _______________ (increase/ decrease) over time. (Keynesians predict
increase — tax cuts would ______________ (increase/decrease) deficit spending.)
Lower deficits and increased national output of goods and services
decrease — should _______________ (increase/ decrease) inflation. The rise in in-
increase — comes caused by tax cuts should _______________ (increase/decrease)
saving and therefore the quantity of lendable funds. If the inflation rate is
lower and the quantity of lendable funds is greater, then interest rates
come down — should _______________ (come down/go up). This would cause invest-
increase — ment to _________________ (increase/decrease). With greater invest-
faster — ment over time, the economy would experience _______________
(faster/slower) rates of economic growth.

The second basic proposition of supply-side economists is that a tax
encourage — cut would _______________ (encourage/discourage) people to invest in
more education and improve their work-related skills. It may also en-
domestically — courage businesses to invest more ______________________ (domesti-
more — cally/abroad). The end result will be a _______________ (more/less)
greater — productive economy with _______________ (smaller/greater) national
income over time.

The third basic proposition of the supply-side economists is that tax
discourage — cuts should _________________ (encourage/discourage) black market,
discourage — or underground, activity. Lower tax rates should also _________________
(encourage/discourage) barter and trade for cash, and the use of

Answers	Text
	productive resources in search of tax loopholes. Therefore, tax cuts
increase	would ______________ (increase/decrease) the amount of income
	people report to the Internal Revenue Service and the amount of tax
	revenues collected. Furthermore, because fewer productive resources are
	used in search of tax loopholes, the nation's total income should
rise	____________ (rise/fall).
can	The effects of tax rate reductions ____________________ (can/
	cannot) be described in terms of aggregate demand-aggregate supply
	analysis. Whereas Keynesians believe reduced tax rates will
increase aggregate demand	________________ (increase aggregate demand/increase both ag-
	gregate demand and aggregate supply) the supply-siders believe reduced
increase both aggregate demand and aggregate supply	tax rates will ______________________________________
	(increase aggregate supply/increase both aggregate demand and ag-
	gregate supply). The supply-side economists also believe the long-run
aggregate supply	______________________ (aggregate demand/aggregate supply) curve
outward	will shift ___________________ (inward/outward) with tax cuts. This
less	means the inflation rate will increase ______________ (more/less) than
	Keynesian theory suggests. Furthermore, supply-side economists, as op-
increase	posed to Keynesians, argue the ______________ (increase/decrease) in
aggregate supply	national income is caused by an increase in ______________________
	(aggregate demand/aggregate supply).
	There are three chief objections to supply-side theory. In essence, they
	all stem from a belief that tax cuts are ineffective in increasing
aggregate supply	______________________________ (aggregate demand/aggregate
	supply). The first and most serious criticism is that lower tax rates
may not	______________ (will/may not) cause people to work longer hours.

	The effect of a tax cut on the number of hours worked depends on
high	whether tax rates are high or low. If tax rates are ________
	(high/low), a tax cut would most likely increase the number of hours
	worked because the opportunity cost of leisure and the effect on the rela-
greater	tive price of goods and services is ________ (greater/smaller)
	than otherwise. The effect of tax cuts on the number of hours worked is
inconclusive	an empirical question, and the evidence is ________
	(inconclusive/certain). The effect of tax cuts on saving and investments
also inconclusive	is ________ (also inconclusive/more certain).
aggregate supply	Therefore, critics argue, the ________ (aggregate
outward	demand/aggregate supply) curve may not shift ________
	(inward/outward) with tax cuts.
	Second, critics argue that tax cuts will cause tax revenues to
fall	________ (rise/fall). The outcome of a tax cut depends on
	three factors: the responsiveness of workers, savers, and investors; the
present	nation's ________ (future/present) location on the
Laffer	________ (Laffer/production possibilities) curve; and the
size	________ (direction/size) of the tax cut.
greater	Finally, critics argue that tax cuts will cause ________
increase	(greater/less) inflation because deficits will ________
	(increase/decrease) with tax cuts. Once again, this would occur if the
aggregate supply	________ (aggregate demand/aggregate supply)
	curve does not shift outward.
	Supply-side economists believe tax cuts are effective in the
long run	________ (short run/long run). They maintain that tax cuts
reduced	should not only be ________ (increased/reduced) but should

down — be held ________________ (up/down) for quite some time for the positive

unlikely — effects to be felt. However, politicians are ________________ (likely/unlikely) to wait for the results. Instead, they will probably continue as they have in the past. Therefore, some supply-side economists have suggested a constitutional amendment limiting government's spending and taxing powers.

Problems and Applications

1. a. Assume we are in the short run, and so the aggregate supply curve slopes upward. Draw aggregate demand and aggregate supply curves on the same graph, and determine the equilibrium price and income levels.
   b. According to Keynesians and monetarists, what happens to aggregate demand, aggregate supply, and the price and national income levels given a reduction in tax rates? What would they expect to happen over time?
   c. According to supply-side economists, what happens to aggregate demand, aggregate supply, and the price and national income levels given a reduction in tax rates? What would they expect to happen over time?
2. a. Graph an individual's labor-leisure tradeoff (or production possibilities) curve, putting leisure time on the x axis and take-home pay on the y axis. Choose a point on that curve representing the individual's choice between work (take-home pay) and leisure time. Label that point a. Indicate the amount of leisure time as L_1, and the amount of take-home pay as Y_1.
   b. What happens to the slope of the individual's production possibilities curve if personal income tax rates are reduced? Express this graphically.
   c. According to supply-side economics, what would happen to the number of hours worked (and therefore leisure time) if personal income taxes are reduced? Express this graphically.
   d. Given your answer to 2c above, what would critics of supply-side theory argue? What would the critics say happens to aggregate supply given a tax rate cut?
3. a. Graph a Laffer curve and indicate a tax rate that maximizes tax revenues. What happens to tax revenues if tax rates are

increased above this level? Why? What happens to tax revenues if tax rates are decreased below this level? Why?

b. What three factors determine whether tax revenues rise or fall given a tax rate cut?

c. According to supply-side economics, on which portion of the Laffer curve are the United States' marginal tax rates? What effect would tax rate cuts have on deficit spending?

d. According to critics of supply-side theory, on which portion of the Laffer curve are the United States' marginal tax rates? What effect would tax rate cuts have on deficit spending and the inflation rate?

4. Besides reducing tax rates, what else would supply-side policy recommend to reduce deficits and therefore any potential crowding-out of private investment?

True-False

For each item, determine whether the statement is basically true or false. If the statement is false, rewrite it so it is a true statement.

_____ 1. Supply-side economists emphasize changes in aggregate demand as the key determinant of the level of economic activity.

_____ 2. Supply-side economists believe lower marginal tax rates will increase the supply of and the demand for labor.

_____ 3. Supply-side economists believe the United States economy is on the upper portion of the Laffer curve.

_____ 4. Supply-side economists attribute the long-run increase in national income due to a tax rate cut to an increase in aggregate supply.

_____ 5. According to supply-side economists, lower tax rates will increase inflation.

_____ 6. Critics of supply-side theory argue lower marginal tax rates will increase aggregate supply.

_____ 7. Critics of supply-side theory argue the relationship between tax rates and incentives to work, save, and invest is small and of uncertain direction.

_____ 8. Supply-side theory argues lower marginal tax rates increase the amount of resources used in search of tax loopholes.

_____ 9. According to supply-side theory, a reduction in tax rates will decrease interest rates and deficits.

_____ 10. According to supply-side theory, a reduction in tax rates will increase aggregate demand and increase aggregate supply.

_____ 11. According to critics of supply-side theory, a reduction in tax rates will shift the long-run aggregate supply curve outward.

_____ 12. Supply-side theory is predicted to control stagflation and stimulate economic growth.

_____ 13. Critics of supply-side theory argue the nation is on the lower portion of the Laffer curve.

_____ 14. Supply-side theory is expected to correct for stagflation and lagging economic growth relatively quickly.

_____ 15. Most economics adhere to supply-side theory.

_____ 16. Critics of supply-side theory argue it is very possible that tax rate cuts may enable people to work less and enjoy higher take-home pay simultaneously.

_____ 17. A decrease in tax rates will increase the slope of an individual's labor-leisure tradeoff (production possibilities) curve.

_____ 18. Supply-side economists say that tax rate reductions are likely to lead to deflation because aggregate supply will probably increase more than aggregate demand.

_____ 19. Supply-siders recommend increasing the money supply along with tax rate reductions to prevent deflation.

Multiple Choice

Choose the one best answer for each item.

_____ 1. Supply-side economists recommend
   a. increasing tax rates to correct for deficits.
   b. decreasing tax rates to correct for inflation.
   c. increasing tax rates to correct for lagging economic growth.
   d. decreasing the money supply if tax rates are reduced to prevent inflation.
   e. a constant increase in the money supply equal to the increase in real GNP.

_____ 2. Which of the following statements is true about supply-side theory?
   a. No administration has attempted to base its policy on the theory.
   b. Its primary purpose is to increase aggregate demand.
   c. The debate between critics and supply-side economists will have to be resolved empirically.

d. Its ultimate goal is to increase governmental influence in the economy.
e. It seeks a favorable tradeoff between unemployment and inflation.

_____ 3. According to supply-side economics, over the long run
a. the aggregate demand curve is vertical and shifts outward.
b. deficits can be reduced only if tax rates are increased and the "fat," "waste," and "inefficient government programs" are eliminated.
c. tax rates must be held down for sustained high levels of investment to correct for stagflation and provide for greater rates of economic growth.
d. the aggregate supply curve is vertical and shifts inward.
e. aggregate demand must be increased to correct for unemployment

_____ 4. Critics of supply-side economics argue
a. workers are discouraged from entering the labor force and working longer hours because of high tax rates.
b. the long-run aggregate supply curve is vertical and shifts outward with tax rate increases.
c. the total output of goods and services has little effect on the inflation rate.
d. aggregate supply can never shift outward.
e. in the short run, reduced tax rates cause spending to increase more rapidly than output, resulting in an increase in velocity and therefore higher inflation.

_____ 5. According to supply-side economists, reduced tax rates will cause
a. the demand for and supply of labor to increase and therefore employment to increase.
b. saving to increase, and interest rates to decrease, and therefore investment to increase.
c. total output of goods and services to increase and therefore inflation to decrease.
d. employment to increase and therefore deficits to decrease.
e. all of the above to occur.

_____ 6. Supply-side economists recommend
a. longer terms for the President and Congress.
b. constitutional checks on government spending and taxing powers.

c. avoiding future deficits by authorizing tax cuts to take effect in the future.
d. reducing tax rates to reduce deficits.
e. all of the above.

_____ 7. Critics of supply-side economics argue reduced tax rates
a. may not increase tax collections.
b. are not inflationary as Keynesian theory suggests.
c. cause the short-run supply curve to be vertical.
d. shift aggregate supply to the right.
e. encourage people to work in the underground economy.

_____ 8. Which of the following are true about the criticism of supply-side theory?
a. They all question whether the short-run aggregate supply curve shifts outward with lower tax rates.
b. Lower tax rates may not increase tax collections.
c. Lower tax rates may not decrease deficits.
d. The effects of supply-side policy may take too long.
e. All of the above are true.

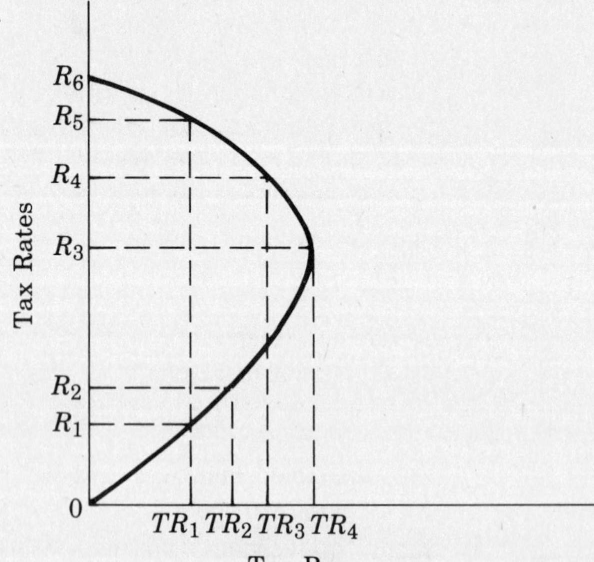

_____ 9. Based on the preceding graph of the Laffer curve, which of the following statements are false?
   a. Tax revenues are maximized at R_3.
   b. The portion from R_3 to R_6 is the range in which supply-side economists believe the United States' tax rate system is located.
   c. A decrease in tax rates from R_5 to R_1 increases tax revenues.
   d. A decrease in tax rates from R_3 to R_2 decreases tax revenues.
   e. An increase in tax rates from R_3 to R_4 decreases tax revenues.

_____ 10. Which of the following statements is true?
   a. Most economists do not accept the general shape of the Laffer curve but instead insist that increases in tax rates always increase tax revenues.
   b. Keynesians argue an increase in national income due to a tax rate cut is caused by an increase in total spending, not total output.
   c. A decrease in tax rates will always cause saving and investment to increase.
   d. High tax rates may encourage people to find ways to escape paying taxes or move productive activity underground.
   e. Both b and d are true.

_____ 11. According to supply-side economists, reduced tax rates
   a. if perceived as permanent will shift the long-run aggregate supply curve inward.
   b. may be desirable even if they do not correct from stagflation, assuming stagflation does not get worse.
   c. will cause some private investment to be crowded out.
   d. may require the money supply to be reduced.
   e. both a and c.

_____ 12. According to supply-side economists
   a. tax rate reductions are not a quick-fix scheme.
   b. deficit spending will not crowd out private investment.
   c. the slope of the work-leisure tradeoff curve decreases as tax rates decrease.
   d. politicians should find it in their self-interest to implement supply-side policy.
   e. the income demand curve is not applicable to a tax rate cut.

_____ 13. Reduced tax rates would result in lower production if
   a. saving and investment increased.
   b. aggregate supply increased more than aggregate demand.

c. people decided on more leisure time because they were satisfied with their take-home pay.
d. people decided to work more because taxes were still too high.
e. Both a and c occurred.

Discussion Questions

1. The supply-side economists, like the classical economists, rely on microeconomic, or market, solutions to macroeconomic problems. However, market solutions take time. Keynes responded to the classical school by observing, "In the long run we are all dead." If Keynes were alive today, would he respond to the supply-side economists in the same way, or would he be more willing to downplay short-run policy in favor of long-run policy? *(KQ2, 3)*
2. According to supply-side economists, could tax rates be reduced so low that people would actually work less, or will they always work more? *(KQ2)*
3. Did you consider future tax rates in your decision to attend college? *(KQ2)*
4. How would Keynesians and monetarists correct for stagflation? *(KQ1, 2, 3.* See also Chapters 12 and 14.)
5. The first-term Reagan administration based its economic recovery strategy on supply-side policy. How is the second term different from the first? What were the successes and failures of Reagan's economic recovery strategy? *(KQ1, 2, 3)*
6. Why do some supply-side economists favor a balanced budget amendment to the Constitution? *(KQ3)*
7. Do supply-side economists argue a tax rate increase will only compound the deficit problem? *(KQ1, 2, 3)*
8. Why do many supply-side economists favor a flat tax? What do you think the implications of such a tax would be? *(KQ1)*
9. Would the supply-side economists favor longer terms for the Presidency and Congress? *(KQ3)*
10. Is there any relationship between Herbert Hoover's "trickledown" theory and supply-side theory? *(KQ1)*

Answers

Problems and Applications

1. a. On the following graph, the original aggregate demand and aggregate supply curves are AD_1 and AS_{sr1}. The equilibrium price level is P_1, and the equilibrium income level is Y_1.

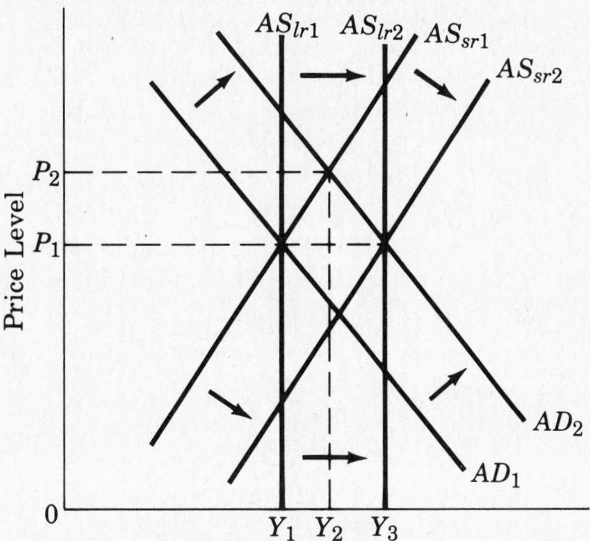

b. Both Keynesians and monetarists agree aggregate supply remains unchanged but aggregate demand increases in the short run. However, Keynesians argue the increase in aggregate demand is due to deficit spending because of the tax cut, whereas the monetarists argue the increase in aggregate demand is due to an increase in the money supply which would occur to finance the deficit spending. In the preceding graph aggregate demand shifts from AD_1 to AD_2. The price level rises from P_1 to P_2, and national income rises from Y_1 to Y_2. Over time, as people make adjustments to higher inflation, the aggregate supply curve shifts back, offsetting part or all of the increase in national income and contributing to greater inflation. Keynesians argue that although the increase in national income is partly offset, there is still a net increase. The monetarists, on the other hand, argue aggregate supply shifts so far back it entirely offsets any increase in national income, leaving us with the initial level.

c. A reduction in tax rates would increase aggregate demand. However, supply-side economists would argue that in the short run, because people have a greater incentive to work, save,and invest, this also increases aggregate supply. In the preceding graph the aggregate demand curve increases from AD_1 to AD_2, but at the same time aggregate supply increases from AS_{sr1} to AS_{sr2}. Given the shifts shown, the price level remains at P_1, but the income level rises from Y_1 to Y_3. However, the actual price and income levels depend on how much aggregate demand and aggregate supply increases. Supply-side economists believe tax reductions are not nearly as inflationary as Keynesian theory suggests. Indeed the price level may drop if aggregate supply increases more than aggregate demand. In that case, they recommend an increase in the money supply (to increase *AD*) to prevent deflation.

Over time, if the tax reduction is perceived as permanent, there are greater incentives to work, save, and invest. This adds to the nation's capital stock, accelerating economic growth. The long-run aggregate supply curve (which is vertical) shifts outward. In the graph, AS_{lr1} moves to AS_{lr2}. This outward shift means some or all of the income effect of the tax rate cut can be permanent. It also means that the money stock can be expanded more than Keynesians theory suggests.

2. a. See the following graph.

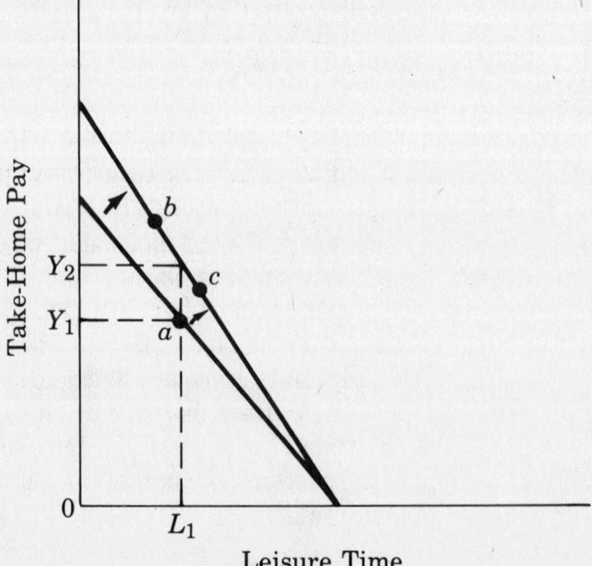

b. The slope becomes greater. That is, it pivots out from above, indicating greater take-home pay could be earned for the same amount of leisure time. For instance, the same leisure time (therefore, the same amount of work), L_1, now yields a greater take-home pay of Y_2.

c. Supply-side economists argue individuals will work longer hours (take less leisure time) if tax rates are reduced. Graphically, the individual will move to a point such as *b* indicating leisure time (and therefore more work) and more income (take-home pay).

d. Critics would argue it is equally likely an individual will decide on more leisure time (not less), given a tax rate cut. With a tax rate cut, the individual could have more of both leisure time and take-home pay, as represented at point *c* in the graph. If a tax rate cut encourages people to work less, aggregate supply would not shift to the right. (Could it possibly shift to the left?)

3. a. See the graph below. A tax rate of R_2 will maximize tax revenues at TR_2. At higher tax rates, tax revenues will fall, because many people will make the effort to avoid taxes. For instance, an increase to R_3 will cause tax revenues to fall to TR_1. Tax revenues fall when tax rates are reduced below R_2. Alternatively, an increase in tax rates below R_2 will increase tax revenues because at relatively low rates people have little incentive to avoid paying taxes.

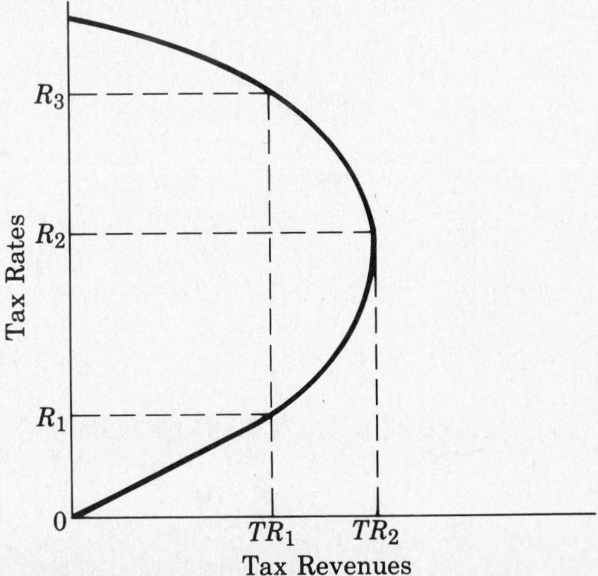

b. The three factors are our present location on the Laffer curve (whether we are on the upper or lower portion); how much people respond to a change in the tax rate; and the size of the tax cut (for instance, a tax cut from R_3 to R_1 does not change tax revenues collected).
c. According to supply-side economists, marginal tax rates in the United States are so high we are on the upper portion of the Laffer curve. Therefore, a reduction in tax rates will stimulate production (by increasing incentives to work, save, and invest), and employment and tax revenues collected will rise. As a result, deficit spending will decline.
d. According to critics of supply-side theory, we are on the lower portion of the Laffer curve. After all, why would politicians push tax rates into the upper portion in the first place? No one has anything to gain from being there. If tax rates are reduced, tax revenues will fall and deficit spending will increase. Increases in deficit spending eventually cause greater inflation.

4. They would recommend eliminating "fat," "waste," and "counterproductive programs" from the federal budget. They would also authorize tax cuts to take effect in the future, thus encouraging current business investment to take advantage of lower tax rates on future income.

True-False

1. F: Supply-side economists emphasize the effect lower marginal tax rates have on incentives to work, save, and invest.
2. T 3. T 4. T
5. F: According to supply-side economists lower tax rates will decrease inflation.
6. F: Critics of supply-side theory argue lower marginal tax rates will increase inflation.
7. T
8. Supply-side theory argues lower marginal tax rates decrease the amount of resources used in search of tax loopholes.
9. T 10. T
11. F: Supply-side theory predicts a reduction in tax rates will shift the long-run aggregate supply curve outward.

12. T 13. T
14. F: Supply-side theory is expected to correct for stagflation and lagging economic growth over a period of time.
15. F: Supply-side theory is adhered to by a minority of economists.
16. T 17. T 18. T 19. T

Multiple Choice

1. b *(KQ1)* 2. c *(KQ3)* 3. c *(KQ1)*
4. e *(KQ2)* 5. e *(KQ1)* 6. e *(KQ1, 3)*
7. a *(KQ2)* 8. e *(KQ2)* 9. c *(KQ2)*
10. e *(KQ2)* 11. b *(KQ1)* 12. a *(KQ1)*
13. c *(KQ3)*

CHAPTER 16

Rational Expectations

Chapter Summary

The rational expectations theory is another alternative to Keynesian analysis that emerged from Keynesians' apparent lack of success in controlling the macroeconomy during the 1970s. It emphasizes the role expectations play in people's reactions to fiscal and monetary policies. In its extreme, the rational expectations model argues people acquire some rationally determined amount of information about the expected effects of fiscal and monetary policies based on past experience. Then, acting in their own self-interest, they behave so as to negate those policies – not only in the long run, but in the short run as well. In other words, government policy is entirely ineffective in controlling the macroeconomy over both the short and long run.

Key Question 1: How does Keynesian theory handle expectations?

Keynesian analysis recognizes that changes in expectations will shift the investment demand curve (and therefore the investment function), the consumption function, and the demand for money curve. But Keynesians argue that changes in fiscal and monetary policies do not significantly alter expectations, and therefore these curves, in the short run. In the long run, they admit, these curves may shift adversely, but fiscal and monetary policies are still effective in altering the national income and price levels.

Key Question 2: What do the rational expectationists believe?

Economists of the rational expectations school disagree. They believe changing fiscal and monetary policies will alter expectations instantaneously. For instance, assume an expansionary fiscal policy is pursued. According to rational expectations theorists, people have come to associate deficit spending with higher interest rates (because of the increased demand for lendable funds to finance these deficits). Therefore they will sell bonds immediately in order to get a higher interest rate in the future. This means the demand for money curve has shifted to the right (people simply want to hold on to more money now to invest at higher interest rates in the future). Because the demand for money increases very quickly, interest rates rise very quickly (if not instantaneously). Any time lag between the adoption of expansionary fiscal policy and the resulting increase in the interest rate is reduced (if not eliminated altogether) by the impact of people's expectations. A similar argument could be made about the expected higher interest rates given expansionary monetary policy.

Because interest rates rise, the level of investment falls. According to rational expectations economists, the decline in investment can be great enough to offset entirely any effect expansionary fiscal policy has on aggregate demand. In such a case, national income and employment are unaffected – even in the short run. In sum, there can be an instantaneous and total crowding-out effect because of the rightward shift in the demand for money curve due to expectations associated with expansionary fiscal policy.

Expansionary monetary policy is also ineffective, according to the rational expectations school. Because people have come to expect higher inflation rates with increases in the money stock, they will buy more now (increasing the investment and consumption functions), rather than waiting for prices to rise. This increases aggregate demand, causing higher prices. So any lag between the adoption of monetary policy and the resulting inflation is reduced (if not eliminated altogether) by the impact of people's expectations. A similar argument can be made about the expected higher rates of inflation given expansionary fiscal policy. The reader may conclude that this should enforce the effect expansionary fiscal and monetary policies have on the national income and employment levels. This would be an incorrect conclusion from the rational expectationists perspective, because aggregate supply simultaneously shifts back as workers demand higher wages to protect their future purchasing power.

Key Question 3: How do the monetarists handle expectations?

Rational expectations theorists and monetarists agree that aggregate demand may increase in the short run and cause the price level to rise. They also agree that aggregate supply shifts back when people are no longer fooled into thinking increases in their money wages are increases in their real wages (money illusion), thus eliminating any increase in national income and employment. However, they disagree about how long it takes for people to adjust to inflation. That is, they disagree about how quickly the aggregate supply curve shifts back the Phillips curve shifts outward. The monetarists believe people are fooled by money illusion in the short run, but not over the long run. So, to the monetarists, the short-run aggregate supply curve is positively sloped and the short-run Phillips curve is negatively sloped. However, both are vertical in the long run. Therefore, according to the monetarists, expansionary monetary policy is effective in the short run but not over the long run. Recall, the monetarists believe expansionary fiscal policy is ineffective even in the short run because it causes a higher interest rate, which crowds out private investment. But according to the rational expectations theorists, because people adjust almost immediately (if not instantaneously) to higher prices and interest rates, the aggregate supply curve shifts back, and the Phillips curve shifts outward, almost immediately. In other words, they argue, both the aggregate supply curve and the Phillips curve are vertical in the short run. This means expansionary fiscal and monetary policies are not effective in the short run.

Key Question 4: What are criticisms of rational expectations theory?

Several criticisms of the rational expectations school of thought have been made. Most of them pertain to the extreme nature of the assumptions underlying the theory. First, rational expectations theorists underestimate the cost or delay in gathering information on which to base expectations. Because of miscalculations and time lags, at lease some short-run effects of fiscal and monetary policies are felt. Second, people may have an incentive to be rationally ignorant of government economic policy because of its complexity. Third, critics argue that short-run fiscal and monetary policies alter the composition of national output and therefore must have some long-run affects. Finally, prices and wages are not perfectly flexible. Therefore, at least in the short run, fiscal and monetary policies must influence the national income and employment levels.

Review Terms and Concepts

Keynesian school of thought
Monetarist school of thought
Supply-side school of thought
Rational expectations school of thought
Expansionary fiscal policy
Contractionary fiscal policy
Expansionary monetary policy
Contractionary monetary policy
Aggregate demand
Aggregate supply
Phillips curve
Money illusion
Real wage
Money wage
Deficit
Investment demand curve
Investment function
Consumption function
Demand for money curve
Supply of money curve
Crowding-out effect

New Terms and Concepts

Efficient market hypothesis
Rational expectations theory
Adaptive expectations theory
Share economy
Policy neutrality or policy effectiveness theorem
Rational ignorance

Completion

expectations	The rational expectations theory emphasizes the role ________________
	(total spending/expectations) play(s) in people's reactions to fiscal and
1970s	monetary policies. This school of thought began in the ____________
Keynesian	(1940s/1970s). It is another alternative to ____________________
	(classical/Keynesian) analysis. In its extreme form it sees fiscal and
totally ineffective	monetary policies ____________________________ (very effective/
short and long	totally ineffective) over the ____________________ (short/long/short
rationally	and long) run. This is because people acquire some ________________
past	(rationally/irrationally) determined information based on ____________
	(present/past) experience with fiscal and monetary policies and act in
negate	their own self-interest in such a manner as to ______________ (enforce/
	negate) those policies.
does not ignore	Keynesian analysis ________________________ (ignores/does not
	ignore) the role of expectations. Keynesians, like all other economists,
will	agree that changes in expectation ____________ (will/will not) shift the
	investment demand curve, the demand for money curve, and the con-
	sumption function. However, in the short run, Keynesians believe that
do not	changes in fiscal and monetary policies _____________ (do/do not) have
	considerable effect on expectations. Therefore, these curves are likely to
little, if at all	shift _________________________ (considerably/little, if at all). In the
	long run, Keynesians believe changes in fiscal and monetary policies
may	________________ (may/will not) shift these curves adversely as expec-
	tations change. This means fiscal and monetary policies are
less effective	____________________ (less effective/totally ineffective) in altering

national income and employment and therefore the price level in the long run.

disagree — The rational expectations theorists ________ (agree/disagree). In the short run they believe changes in fiscal and monetary

do — policies ________ (do/do not) affect expectations and therefore the investment demand curve, the demand for money curve, and the consumption function. They believe changes in fiscal and monetary policies

almost immediately — cause changes in expectations ________ (over time/almost immediately).

For instance, if expansionary fiscal policy has led to higher interest

will — rates in the past, people ________ (will/will not) come to expect them whenever deficits are incurred. Therefore, if expansionary fiscal

sell — policy is pursued, people will want to ________ (sell/buy) bonds immediately. This drives their prices down and interest rates

up — ________ (down/up). Alternatively, this will cause

an increase — ________ (an increase/a decrease) in the demand for money. Therefore, interest rates rise. Thus, the expectation of higher in-

almost immediately — terest rates leads ________ (over time/almost immediately) to higher interest rates. According to rational expectations theorists, this is just one example of the fact that any expectations about

almost immediately — the effects of macroeconomic policy will be felt ________ (over time/almost immediately).

less — Higher interest rates will cause ________ (less/more) invest-

decreases — ment. If investment spending ________ (decreases/increases), this at least partially offsets the increase in aggregate demand due to deficit spending. According to rational expectations theorists, this

totally — crowding-out effect may ____________________ (only partially/totally)
offset any increase in aggregate demand. Therefore aggregate demand
remain unchanged — would ______________________________ (increase/decrease/remain
unchanged). In turn, national income and employment would be unaffected. In sum, this means people's expectations about the effects of
ineffective — deficit spending render expansionary fiscal policy __________________
(effective/ineffective). Furthermore, because expectations respond so
quickly, expansionary fiscal policy is totally ineffective in the
short run — __________________ (short run/long run). The same argument holds for
expansionary monetary policy. The result for contractionary fiscal and
the same — monetary policies is __________________ (different/the same). That is,
according to rational expectations theorists, any macroeconomic policy is
totally ineffective, even in the short run.

Rational expectations theorists' predictions about the effectiveness of
aggregate supply — expansionary fiscal and monetary policies mean ____________________
(aggregate demand/aggregate supply) is vertical, even in the
short run — __________________ (short run/long run). Rational expectations theorists
vertical — also argue the Phillips curve is ______________________ (horizontal/
are not — vertical) in the short run. This is because people __________________
(are/are not) fooled by money illusion (thinking increases in their money
wages are increases in their real wages), even in the short run. This is
unlike — ______________________ (like/unlike) the monetarists' arguments. The
are — monetarists argue people __________________ (are/are not) fooled by
money illusion in the short run. Therefore, the aggregate supply curve is
upward sloping — ______________________ (upward sloping/vertical) in the short run.
However, over time, as people are no longer fooled by money illusion,

inward	the aggregate supply curve shifts ________________ (inward/out-
	ward), eliminating any long-run increase in national income. Also over
outward	time, the Phillips curve shifts ________________ (inward/outward).
	The rational expectations theorists agree with the monetarists that
faster	these shifts take place, but argue that they occur much ______________
	(slower/faster). Indeed, they argue, these shifts occur as quickly as ag-
	gregate demand increases. So, for the monetarists, the aggregate supply
long run	and Phillips curves are vertical only in the ____________________
	(short run/long run). This means monetary policy is effective in the
short run, long run	________________ (short run/long run) but not the ________________
	(short run/long run). The rational expectations theorists argue the ag-
	gregate supply and Phillips curves are vertical even in the
short run	________________ (short run/long run). This means fiscal and monetary
both the short run and the long run	policy is ineffective in ____________________________ (the short run/
	the long run/both the short run and the long run).
	Several criticisms of rational expectations theory focus on the
assumptions	________________ (assumptions/expectations) that underlie it. Critics
is	contend that information ____________ (is/is not) costly to acquire and
remain ignorant of	that citizens have an incentive to ______________________________
	(gather information on/remain ignorant of) government policy. Critics
	also argue that in the short run, fiscal and monetary policies
do	____________ (do/do not) alter the composition of national output and
must	therefore ________________ (must/must not) have long-run effects.
are not	Finally, critics point out that prices and wages ________________
	(are/are not) perfectly flexible.

Problems and Applications

1. a. Graph an investment demand curve, a consumption function, and demand for and supply of money curves.
   b. According to Keynesians, how would expansionary fiscal and monetary policies affect the investment demand curve, the consumption function, and the demand for money curve in the short run? What happens to these curves in the long run?
   c. According to rational expectations theory, how would expansionary fiscal and monetary policies affect the investment demand curve, the consumption function, and the demand for money curve in the short run?
2. a. Assume we are in the short run. Draw aggregate demand and aggregate supply curves on the same graph and determine the equilibrium national income and price levels.
   b. Assume expansionary fiscal and monetary policies are pursued. According to Keynesians, what affect will this have on the aggregate demand-aggregate supply model in the short run? What happens over the long run?
   c. According to the monetarists, what affect will this have on the aggregate demand-supply model in the short run? What happens over the long run?
   d. According to rational expectations theorists, what effect will this have on the aggregate demand-aggregate supply model in the short run? What happens over the long run?
3. What are the similarities and differences between the monetarists' conception of the aggregate supply and Phillips curves in the short run and over the long run? What are the implications for the effectiveness of fiscal and monetary policies in increasing national income?
4. What are the assumptions of rational expectations theory? How do critics respond to these assumptions?

True-False

For each item, determine whether the statement is basically true or false. If the statement is false, rewrite it so it is a true statement.

_____ 1. According to rational expectations theory, people react to fiscal and monetary policies over time.

_____ 2. According to rational expectations theory, the cost of gathering information may be quite high.

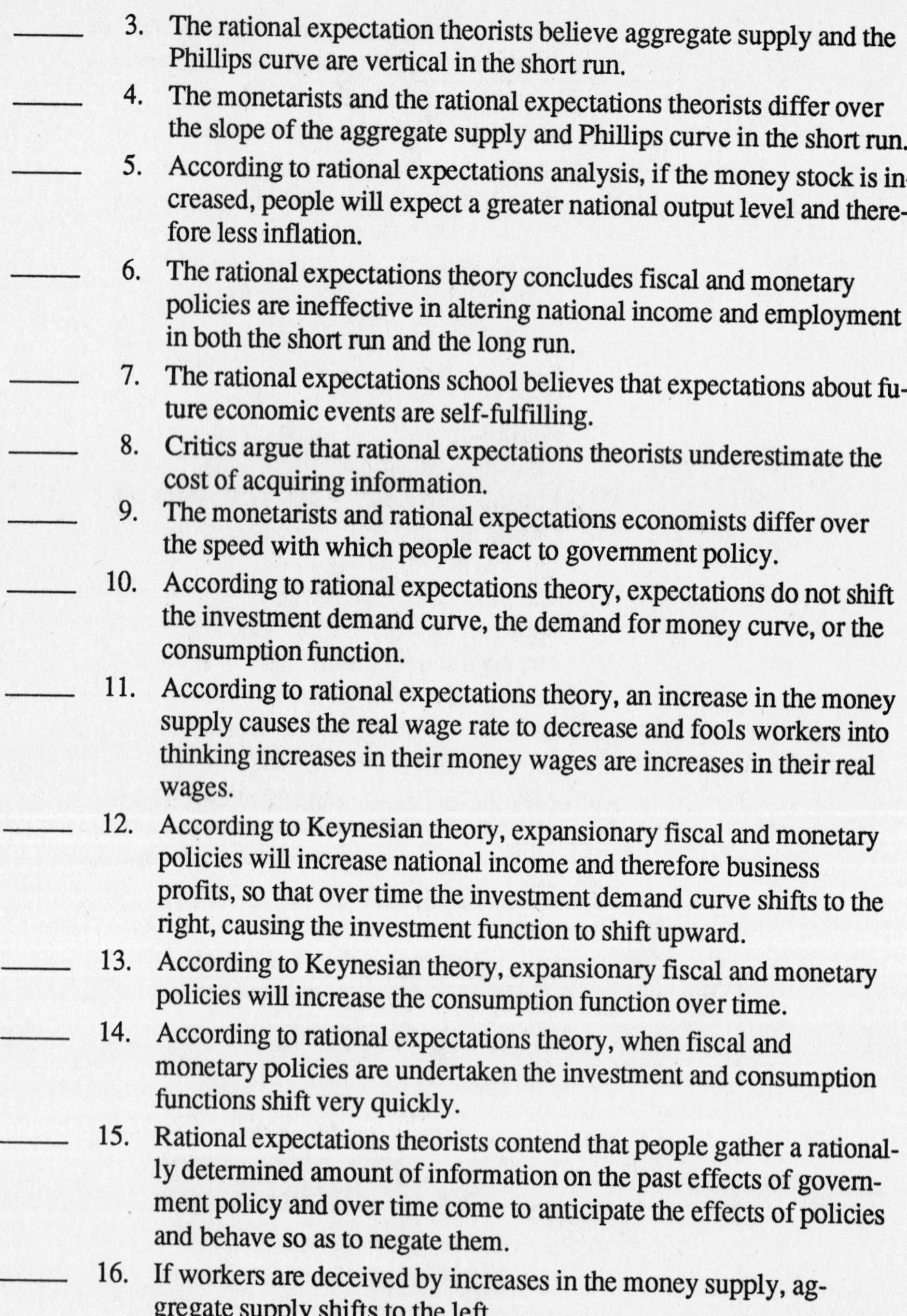

______ 3. The rational expectation theorists believe aggregate supply and the Phillips curve are vertical in the short run.

______ 4. The monetarists and the rational expectations theorists differ over the slope of the aggregate supply and Phillips curve in the short run.

______ 5. According to rational expectations analysis, if the money stock is increased, people will expect a greater national output level and therefore less inflation.

______ 6. The rational expectations theory concludes fiscal and monetary policies are ineffective in altering national income and employment in both the short run and the long run.

______ 7. The rational expectations school believes that expectations about future economic events are self-fulfilling.

______ 8. Critics argue that rational expectations theorists underestimate the cost of acquiring information.

______ 9. The monetarists and rational expectations economists differ over the speed with which people react to government policy.

______ 10. According to rational expectations theory, expectations do not shift the investment demand curve, the demand for money curve, or the consumption function.

______ 11. According to rational expectations theory, an increase in the money supply causes the real wage rate to decrease and fools workers into thinking increases in their money wages are increases in their real wages.

______ 12. According to Keynesian theory, expansionary fiscal and monetary policies will increase national income and therefore business profits, so that over time the investment demand curve shifts to the right, causing the investment function to shift upward.

______ 13. According to Keynesian theory, expansionary fiscal and monetary policies will increase the consumption function over time.

______ 14. According to rational expectations theory, when fiscal and monetary policies are undertaken the investment and consumption functions shift very quickly.

______ 15. Rational expectations theorists contend that people gather a rationally determined amount of information on the past effects of government policy and over time come to anticipate the effects of policies and behave so as to negate them.

______ 16. If workers are deceived by increases in the money supply, aggregate supply shifts to the left.

_____ 17. The rational expectations theory incorporates past, present, and future information in formulating expectations, whereas the adaptive expections theory incorporates only past and present information.

Multiple Choice

Choose the one best answer for each item.

_____ 1. Keynesian analysis assumes fiscal and monetary policy will shift
   a. the consumption function.
   b. the investment function.
   c. the demand for money curve.
   d. all of the above.
   e. none of the above.

_____ 2. Rational expectations theory assumes
   a. the Phillips curve is horizontal in the long run.
   b. there are no costs of acquiring information.
   c. the investment demand curve will not shift in the short run, given any change in fiscal and monetary policy.
   d. price and wages are fixed in the short run.
   e. all of the above.

_____ 3. Rational expectations theory argues
   a. an increase in the money supply will be effective in increasing national income.
   b. an increase in deficit spending will be effective in increasing national income.
   c. fiscal policy is more effective than monetary policy in increasing national income.
   d. a and b above.
   e. none of the above.

_____ 4. If workers are fooled by money illusion
   a. aggregate demand shifts inward.
   b. aggregate supply shifts inward.
   c. we must be in the long run.
   d. employment will rise.
   e. their real wages have not risen but their money wages have fallen.

_____ 5. Rational expectations theorists believe
   a. workers are fooled by money illusion only in the short run.
   b. aggregate supply increases with increases in aggregate demand.
   c. the short-run Phillips curve is negatively sloped.

d. increases in aggregate demand cause simultaneous decreases in aggregate supply.
e. the short-run aggregate demand curve is vertical.

_____ 6. Which of the following belief(s) is (are) common to both the monetarists and the rational expectations theorists?
a. Expansionary fiscal policy increases aggregate demand.
b. Aggregate supply shifts back when workers are no longer fooled by money illusion.
c. Aggregate supply is vertical in the short run.
d. The Phillips curve is vertical in the short run.
e. All of the above.

_____ 7. According to rational expectations theory, deficit spending will
a. shift the consumption function up.
b. shift the investment function up.
c. increase the demand for money and therefore increase the interest rate.
d. cause some inflation.
e. cause all of the above to occur.

_____ 8. Which of the following statements is false?
a. Both the monetarists and the rational expectations theorists argue the aggregate supply curve shifts back, eliminating any increase in national income caused by an increase in aggregate demand.
b. The monetarists and rational expectations theorists agree on the speed with which people adjust to changes in government policy.
c. The monetarists argue the short-run aggregate supply curve is positively sloped and the short-run Phillips curve is negatively sloped.
d. The monetarists believe fiscal policy is ineffective even in the short run.
e. The rational expectations theorists argue the aggregate supply and Phillips curves are vertical in the short run.

_____ 9. According to the rational expectations theorists
a. the only effect of fiscal and monetary policies is to increase the inflation rate.
b. there is some cost in obtaining information to base expectations on.
c. prices and wages are inflexible downward.

d. the transactions cost of reacting to government policy may be quite high.
e. all of the above are true.

_____ 10. Critics of the rational expectations theory argue
a. prices and wages are not perfectly flexible.
b. there are time lags in responses to government policy.
c. expectations about certain government policies may lead people to different conclusions and therefore actions.
d. government policy can alter that composition of output and therefore effects must be felt in the long run.
e. all of the above are true.

_____ 11. According to rational expectations theory, an increase in the money stock will cause
a. real wages to drop.
b. greater employment in the short run.
c. money wages to drop.
d. workers to demand higher money wages almost instantaneously.
e. prices to fall.

Discussion Questions

1. Do you think it is possible for rational people to receive the same amount of information about past consequences associated with government policy and then come to different conclusions about the causes of those consequences? *(KQ1, 2, 4)*
2. Rational expectations theory concludes governmental policy is unsuccessful in stabilizing the macroeconomy. Any attempt to do so only creates higher interest rates and greater inflation because of expectations macroeconomic policy generates. According to rational expectations theory, would government policy designed to correct for microeconomic market failure also be sterile? For instance, would expectations generated by governmental attempts to correct for externalities or an inequitable distribution of income render those attempts unsuccessful? Are such attempts unsuccessful? *(KQ4.* See also Chapter 4.)
3. "Expansionary fiscal and monetary policies increase national output. The increase in the total supply of goods and services puts downward pressure on the inflation rate. Therefore, we should expect the rate of inflation to decline." How would rational expectations theorists respond? *(KQ1, 2, 4)*

Answers

Problems and Applications

1. a. See the graph on page 291. The initial investment demand curve is ID_1, the initial consumption function is C_1, and the initial money demand curve is MD_1.
   b. See the graph on page 291. According to Keynesians, expansionary fiscal and monetary policies do not affect expectations much, if at all, in the short run. Therefore these curves do not shift in the short run. However, over the long run as people come to expect higher inflation rates, the investment demand curve may shift to the right, from ID_1 to ID_2 in part (a), as businesses attempt to increase their purchases of plant and equipment to avoid higher prices in the future. Likewise, consumers may increase their purchases to avoid higher prices in the future, shifting the consumption function up, from C_1 to C_2 in part (b). The demand for money curve is likely to increase from MD_1 to MD_2 in part (c) as people sell bonds. People would want to increase their cash holdings now in order to receive a greater interest rate in the future.
   c. See the graph on page 291. The rational expectations theorists belive expansionary fiscal and monetary policies affect expectations almost immediately (or instantaneously). The expected higher rates of inflation associated with such policies will very quickly cause the investment demand curve to shift to the right, causing the investment function to shift up. The consumption function also increases almost instantaneously as people attempt to buy before prices rise. Such reactions actually cause prices to rise. The expected higher interest rates associated with expansionary fiscal and monetary policies will very quickly cause the demand for money curve to shift to the right, increasing the interest rate. Any time lag between the adoption of expansionary fiscal and monetary policies and the resulting higher prices and interest rates is reduced (if not eliminated altogether) by the impact of people's expectations. (However, higher expected interest rates may dampen, if not offset, the tendency for consumption and investment functions to shift up. The outcome on aggregate demand is uncertain.)

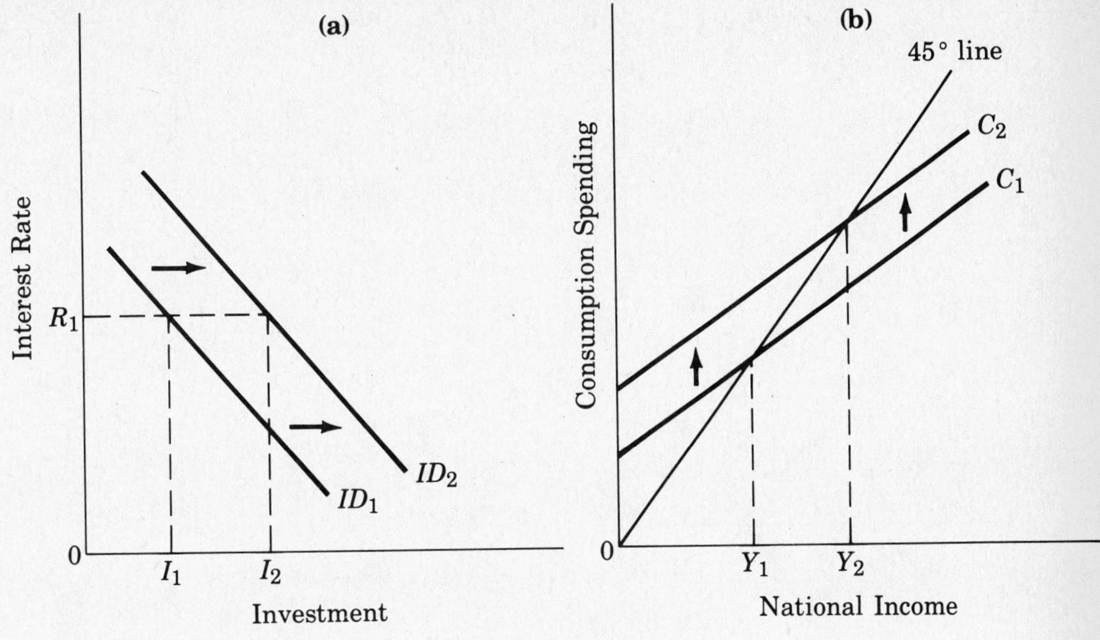
(a)
Interest Rate
R_1
0
I_1
I_2
Investment
ID_1
ID_2
(b)
45° line
Consumption Spending
C_2
C_1
0
Y_1
Y_2
National Income

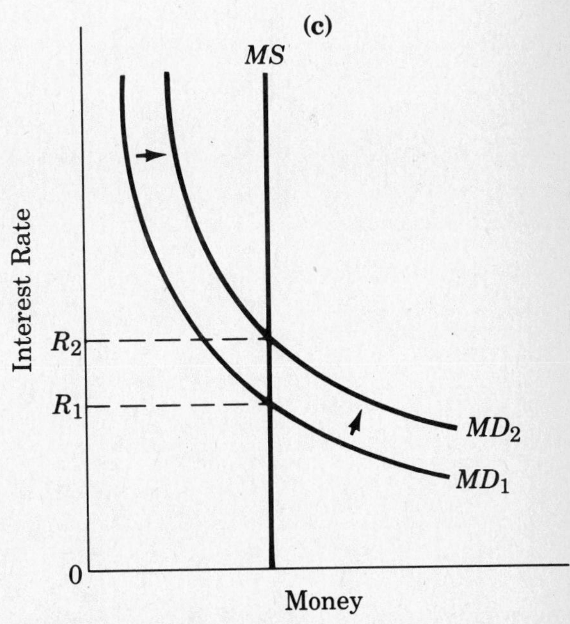
(c)
MS
Interest Rate
R_2
R_1
0
Money
MD_2
MD_1

2. a. See the following graph. The original aggregate demand curve, in part (a), is AD_1. The original short-run aggregate supply curve is AS_{sr1}. The equilibrium national income and price levels are Y_1 and P_1.

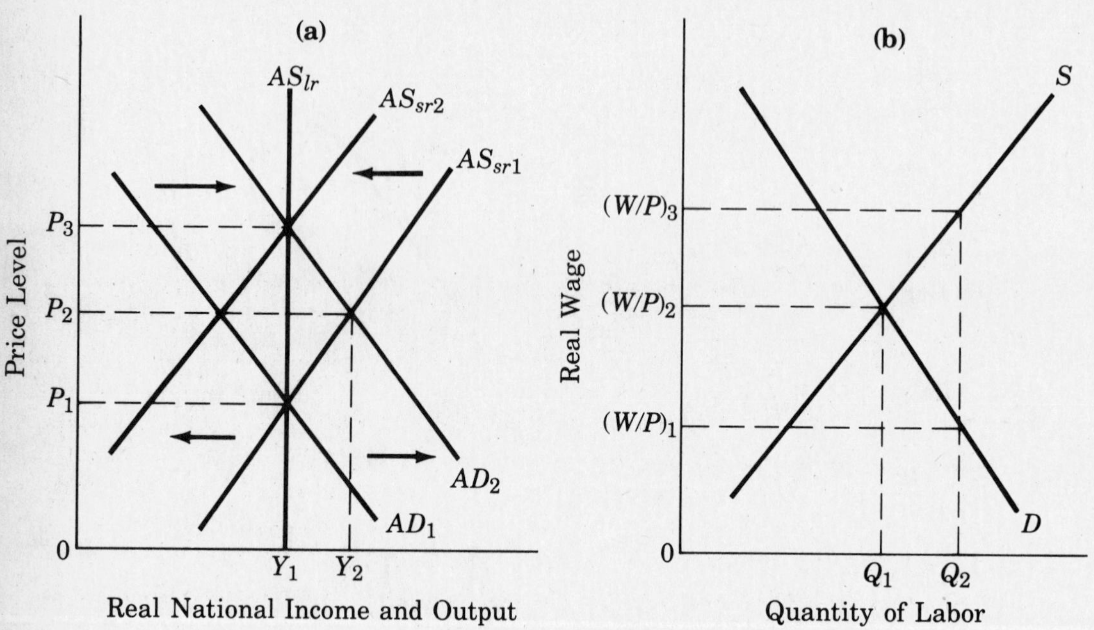

b. See the preceding graph. In the short run, aggregate supply does not change because expectations are unaffected. However, aggregate demand would increase from AD_1 to AD_2 in part (a), increasing the national income and price levels to Y_2 and P_2. Over time, the investment demand curve may increase and therefore shift the investment function up. The consumption function may also increase because of the expectations of higher inflation rates. This would have a tendency to increase aggregate demand. But at the same time interest rates are rising, because the demand for money is rising. As interest rates rise, the investment and consumption functions would shift down. This would have a tendency to decrease aggregate demand.

Assume these two tendencies cancel each other out, leaving aggregate demand unaffected in the long run. Aggregate supply will shift back to the left in the long run. This is because people are no longer fooled by money illusion and adjust to the higher price level by demanding higher money wages. Aggregate supply would not shift back as far as AS_{sr2} because Keynesians believe expansionary fiscal and monetary policies are effective in the long run. In other words, there is some net increase in national income.

c. See graph (a). Monetarists believe expansionary fiscal policy is ineffective in both the short run and the long run because of the crowding-out effect. However, in the short run, monetarists believe expansionary monetary policy can increase aggregate demand and therefore national income and employment. In terms of the effect on the labor market shown in part (b), because the price level also rises with an increase in aggregate demand, employers will hire more workers, Q_2 rather than Q_1, as the real wage decreases, from $(W/P)_2$ to $(W/P)_1$. As long as workers are fooled into thinking the rise in their money wages is an increase in real wages, from $(W/P)_2$ to $(W/P)_3$, the quantity of labor supplied will also rise, from Q_1 to Q_2. Therefore, national output and income rise. Over the long run, however, when workers are no longer fooled by money illusion (inflation), equilibrium will be re-established in the labor market. That is, workers will demand higher money wages, increasing real wages. The quantity of labor employed will decrease, as will the national output and income levels. In terms of graph (a), the aggregate supply curve shifts back to AS_{sr2}. So, in the long run, the initial national income level is re-established but the price level is higher than before. Therefore the long-run aggregate supply curve is vertical, as shown by AS_{lr}.

d. See graph (a). The rational expectations theorists believe expansionary fiscal and monetary policies are ineffective in increasing national income in both the short run and the long run. Expectations of higher interest rates and inflation cause instantaneous shifts in the investment demand curve, the demand for money curve, and the consumption function. (See answer 1c, above.) Any net increase in aggregate demand due to increases in the investment and consumption functions will be simultaneously offset by leftward shifts in the aggregate supply curve. This is because workers are not fooled by inflation (money illusion) – not even in the short run. In graph (b), this means the real wage remains at $(W/P)_2$ and therefore employment, output, and income are unaffected. So, any increase in aggregate demand is simultaneously offset by decreases in aggregate supply as workers instantaneously adjust to inflation. Therefore, the aggregate supply curve is vertical at AS_{lr} – even in the short run. We can therefore conclude any attempts by government to eliminate unemployment through expansionary macroeconomic policy will only result in inflation – even in the short run.

3.

	Monetarists	
	Short Run	Long Run
Aggregate supply	positively sloped	vertical
Phillips curve	negatively sloped	vertical
Effectiveness of fiscal and monetary policies in increasing national income	Fiscal policy is ineffective. Monetary policy is effective.	Both fiscal and monetary policies are ineffective.

	Rational Expectations Theory	
	Short Run	Long Run
Aggregate supply	vertical	vertical
Phillips curve	vertical	vertical
Effectiveness of fiscal and monetary policies in increasing national income	Both fiscal and monetary policies are ineffective.	Both fiscal and monetary policies are ineffective.

4. Rational expectations theory assumes that (1) no cost is involved in gathering information about the nature and structure of the economy and the consequences of fiscal and monetary policies; (2) prices and wages are perfectly flexible, both upward and downward; (3) transactions based on expectations of government policy changes and their consequences are costless. Critics argue that there is at least an opportunity cost with respect to time spent gathering information and making transactions based on expectations (which may be quite costly). Furthermore, prices and wages are not perfectly flexible.

True-False

1. F: According to the rational expectations theory, people react to fiscal and monetary policies almost instantaneously, if not instantaneously.
2. F: According to the rational expectations theory, the cost of gathering information is zero.
3. T
4. T
5. F: According to rational expectations analysis, if the money stock is increased people will expect greater inflation.
6. T
7. T
8. T
9. T
10. F: According to the rational expectations theory, expectations shift the investment demand curve, the demand for money curve, and the consumption function.
11. F: According to the rational expectations theory, an increase in the money supply does not have any effect on the real wage because workers are not fooled by inflation but demand higher money wages immediately.
12. T
13. T
14. T
15. T
16. F: If workers are deceived by increases in the money supply, aggregate supply does not shift but the real wage increases.
17. T

Multiple Choice

1. e *(KQ1)*
2. b *(KQ2)*
3. e *(KQ2)*
4. d *(KQ2, 3)*
5. d *(KQ2, 3)*
6. b *(KQ2, 3)*
7. e *(KQ2)*
8. b *(KQ3)*
9. a *(KQ2)*
10. e *(KQ4)*
11. d *(KQ2)*

CHAPTER 17

Principles of Rational Behavior

Chapter Summary

This chapter begins a detailed examination of microeconomics, the study of scarcity, choice, and cost in terms of individual markets. A market exists when there are both buyers (demanders) and sellers (suppliers) of an item. If the item is a good or service, then it's a product market. If the item is a resource, then it's a resource market. In the product market, buyers (households or consumers) attempt to maximize their consumption of goods and services, given their budget constraints. Sellers (businesses) attempt to minimize their costs of production, given their production targets. In the resource market, buyers of resources (businesses) attempt to minimize the cost of acquiring the resources needed to produce a given output. Sellers of these resources (households or resources owners) attempt to maximize the revenue from the use of their resources, given the resources they have control over. The interaction between what buyers want and what sellers want, given their constraints, determines the equilibrium price and quantity in any market. However, in economics, market behavior is presumed to stem from individual behavior (as opposed to group behavior). So, to understand market behavior we must first understand individual behavior. In the process, one must keep in mind that all individual behavior is constrained in one form or another (because individuals are unable to have all they would like all the time). Therefore, choices must be made, and costs are always incurred in making those choices.

Key Question 1: How do economists define rational behavior?

Economists assume that individuals behave rationally. In general, this means individuals are aware of their constraints and therefore make choices that maximize their utility (satisfaction). Rational behavior rests on three assumptions. First, the individual has a preference and can identify, within limits, what he or she wants. Second, the individual can consistently order his or her wants from most to least preferred. Third, the individual will choose from these ordered preferences so as to maximize his or her satisfaction.

These assumptions imply many things. To begin with, an individual has an array of choices to select from. However, they are constrained choices — choices that are limited by external forces. This can be expressed in terms of an individual's production possibilities (or trade-off) curve. One choice could be put on one axis and another on the other axis. Any point outside the curve is unobtainable. Any point inside the curve means the individual is not maximizing his or her utility because more of one choice could be received without having to give up any of the other. (Because we have assumed rational behavior, we have assumed this possibility away.) Any point on the curve means the individual is maximizing his or her utility, given a constraint or group of constraints. Exactly which point is chosen on the curve depends on the individual's preferences. Change in the individual's environment or physical or mental capabilities that relaxes a constraint will cause the individual's production possibilities curve to expand outward. This will enable the individual to have more of both choices.

Key Question 2: What is the relationship between cost and choice?

Whenever a particular preference is chosen (that is, when a choice is made) a cost (real, or opportunity, cost) is involved. Cost is defined as the highest-valued alternative not taken. Notice that cost is not defined in terms of money. Money is only a means of measuring cost, and not all costs can be measured in terms of money. Whenever economists use the term *cost*, they mean real, or opportunity, cost.

Rational behavior also implies that whenever choices are selected, the benefits exceed their costs. Furthermore, people will select those choices whose benefits to cost ratios exceed the benefits to cost ratios of the most favored opportunities not taken. If costs change, then behavior changes. In other words, if costs change, then another choice will yield greater utility.

Key Question 3: How are choices affected by time and risk?

Adjustments for time and risk on benefits and costs may have to be made to enable individuals to maximize their satisfaction. If costs and benefits are not necessarily incurred or received immediately, then rational decisions may require discounting future costs and benefits to arrive at their present value. Also, if there is any uncertainty about whether future benefits or cost will actually be received or paid, further adjustments must be made.

Key Question 4: What are the limits, to rational behavior?

If people behave rationally, they are maximizing their utility (satisfaction), given their constraints. However, rational behavior does not mean that people never make mistakes or that they always behave selfishly. Nor does it require perfect information. Furthermore, among people's physical and mental constraints are often forces of habit or hang-ups. These psychological quirks may make the choice process more difficult and contribute to mistakes, but it does not prevent people from behaving rationally. Also, what is considered rational behavior rests with the individual, not some observer or social critic. In other words, what seems rational to one person may not seem very rational to someone else because of differences in value judgments. Nonetheless, some behavior is irrational: behavior that is inconsistent or clearly not in the individual's best interests, and the individual recognizes it as such at the time of the behavior. The existence of such behavior adds an element of imprecision to economic predictions, but does not contradict them.

Review Terms and Concepts

Scarcity
Cost (opportunity cost)
Production possibilities curve
Microeconomics

New Terms and Concepts

Utility
Rational behavior
Money cost
Real cost
Cost-benefit analysis
Present value
Irrational behavior
Discounting

Completion

individual markets — Microeconomics is the study of ______________________ (individual markets/the overall economy). For a market to exist there

demanders — must be both ______________________ (demanders/scarcity) and

suppliers — ____________________ (suppliers/cost). The interaction between buyers and sellers determines the equilibrium price and quantity in a market. The behavior of demand and supply in a market stems from

individual — ______________________ (individual/group) behavior. So, to understand

individual behavior — market behavior we must first understand ______________________ (how prices are determined/individual behavior).

constrained — All individual behavior is ____________________ (unconstrained/
external — constrained). Individuals are constrained by ____________________
(internal/external) forces. That is, because we are faced with
scarcity — ____________________ (abundance/scarcity) our behavior is
constrained — ____________________ (unconstrained/constrained). There
are — __________ (are/are not) other constraints. Because we are unable to
choices — have all we would like all the time we must make ________________
(opportunity costs/choices). Whenever a choice is made
an opportunity cost — ________________________ (a money cost/an opportunity cost) is
incurred. So, the study of microeconomics is ultimately the study of how
people (whether they be demanders of suppliers of an item) behave under
constrained — ______________________ (unconstrained/constrained) conditions.

rationally — In economics, we assume people behave ____________________
(like others/rationally). In general, this means that people
attempt to maximize — ____________________________ (always maximize/attempt to
utility — maximize) their ___________________ (utility/leisure). So, market
equilibrium prices and quantities are determined by everyone (demanders
and suppliers) attempting to maximize satisfaction.

Rational behavior rests on three assumptions. First, the individual
can — ___________ (can/cannot) identify, within limits, what he or she wants.
consistently — Second, the individual will ____________________ (inconsistently/
consistently) order his or her wants from most to least preferred. Third,
the individual will choose from those ordered preferences so as to
maximize — ____________________ (minimize/maximize) his or her satisfaction.
These assumptions imply many things.

	Although an individual has many choices to choose from, they are
constrained, can	__________________ (constrained/unlimited) choices. This ________
	(can/cannot) be expressed in terms of an individual's production pos-
	sibilities curve. The curve represents many different combinations of two
	choices that can be made. Any point outside the curve represents a com-
is unobtainable	bination that __________________ (maximizes utility/is unobtainable).
	A point inside the curve represents a combination of choices that
does not	__________________ (does/does not) maximize the individual's
	utility. Any point chosen on the curve means the individual is
maximizing	__________________ (maximizing/not maximizing) his or her satisfac-
	tion. The actual point chosen on the curve depends on the individual's
preferences	_____________________ (preferences/rationality). If the individual's
	environment or physical or mental capabilities change to relax a con-
outward	straint, then the individual's curve will shift __________________
	(inward/outward).
an opportunity	Whenever a particular preference is chosen ____________________
	(an opportunity/a money) cost is always incurred. The cost is the
highest, not taken	____________ (lowest/highest) valued alternative ________________
	(taken/not taken). The highest valued alternative not taken represents the
	actual benefits that would have been received by doing something else
forgone	but had to be __________________ (incurred/forgone) in order to make
not always	the choice actually selected. Note, money is __________________
	(always/not always) an effective measure of cost; it is only a means of
	measuring cost. Whenever economists use the term *cost* they mean
real or opportunity	__________________________ (real or opportunity/money) cost.

	Rational behavior also implies that whenever choices are selected the
are greater than	benefits ____________________ (are less than/are greater than)
	their costs. If costs change (that is, the benefits of the most favored op-
another	portunities not taken change) then ________________ (the same/
	another) choice will yield greater utility.
may have to be	Adjustment for time and risk on benefits and costs ____________
	(may have to be/are never) made to enable individuals to maximize their
	satisfaction. If costs and benefits are not necessarily incurred or received
discounting	immediately, then rational decision may require ________________
	(choosing/discounting) future costs and benefits to arrive at their
present value	________________ (equilibrium/present value). If there is some risk
	or uncertainty about whether future benefits or costs will actually be
must be made	received or paid, adjustments ____________________ (must be
	made/cannot be made).
	Economists' use of the term *rational behavior* does not mean that
make mistakes	people never __________________________ (maximize
	their satisfaction/make mistakes) or that they always behave
selfishly, is	__________________ (rationally/selfishly). Altruism __________
	(is/is not) rational behavior. Nor does rational behavior require
perfect	________________ (imperfect/perfect) information. Also, what is
	considered rational behavior is a judgment that is made by
the individual	___________________ (social critics/the individual). Even illegal
	behavior may be rational to the criminal. Nonetheless, some behavior is
	irrational. The fact the some individual behavior is irrational renders the
less precise	predictions made by economic theory _______________ (inopera-
does not	tive/less precise), but it ________ (does/does not) contradict them.

Problems and Applications

1. List and explain the cause-effect relationship of the following terms: opportunity cost, choice, scarcity.
2. Why are the choices we must make constrained choices?
3. a. Draw a theoretical production possibilities (or tradeoff) curve for an individual who has only two choices: to purchase clothes (put on *Y*-axis) or to purchase entertainment (put on *X*-axis).
   b. What are some constraints in this instance?
   c. Label a point outside the curve point *a*. What does point *a* represent?
   d. Label a point inside the curve point *b*. What does point *b* represent?
   e. Label a point on the curve point *d*. What does point *d* represent?
   f. What is the cost of choosing more clothes? More entertainment?
   g. What must be required for point *d* to be a rational choice?
   h. What would an outward shift in this individual's production possibilities (or tradeoff) curve mean? What could cause this outward shift?

True-False

For each item, determine whether the statement is basically true or false. If the statement is false, rewrite it so it is a true statement.

_____ 1. Illegal behavior is never rational behavior.

_____ 2. Cost can always be measured in monetary terms.

_____ 3. Present value is the value of future costs or benefits in terms of current dollars.

_____ 4. Irrational behavior is inconsistent behavior, or behavior that is clearly not in the individual's best interests, and the individual realizes this at the time of the behavior.

_____ 5. All of our choices are constrained choices.

_____ 6. When economists cause the term *cost* they are really referring to real, or opportunity, cost.

_____ 7. Cost-benefit analysis is useful only when costs and benefits need to be adjusted for time or risk.

_____ 8. Economists assume that individuals behave in such a manner as to maximize their satisfaction.

_____ 9. Constrained choices can be illustrated by an individual's production possibilities (or tradeoff) curve.

_____ 10. An opportunity cost is the highest valued alternative not taken.

_____ 11. Any point on an individual's production possibilities (or tradeoff) curve between two choices will maximize his or her satisfaction.

_____ 12. People who are rational behave alike.

_____ 13. To understand microeconomic market behavior we must first understand individual behavior.

_____ 14. A point outside an individual's production possibilities (or tradeoff) curve represents irrational behavior.

_____ 15. Rational behavior means that people behave selfishly.

Multiple Choice

Choose the one best answer for each item.

_____ 1. Which of the following statements most closely represents the notion of opportunity cost?
   a. "A bird in the hand is better than two in the bush."
   b. "There is no such thing as a free lunch."
   c. "What goes up must come down."
   d. "What goes around comes around."
   e. "A stitch in time saves nine."

_____ 2. Which of the following would *not* be a constraint on an individual's choices?
   a. Institutions
   b. Preferences
   c. The cost of acquiring that choice
   d. Physical ability
   e. Intellectual ability

_____ 3. Present value is
   a. helpful in considering the costs and benefits of past choices.
   b. helpful in considering the costs and benefits of future choices.
   c. used to adjust future costs and benefits so they can be compared with costs and benefits realized today.
   d. used to compare future benefits with costs realized today.
   e. all of the above.

_____ 4. If people behave rationally, they
   a. never make mistakes.
   b. make choices whose costs exceed their benefits.
   c. behave in accordance with generally accepted standards of conduct.

d. never behave habitually.
e. do none of the above.

_____ 5. Irrational behavior
a. is illegal behavior.
b. is immoral behavior.
c. contradicts microeconomic predictions.
d. is behavior that is not in the best interests of the individual, and the individual is aware of it at the time.
e. is all of the above.

_____ 6. Microeconomics
a. is the study of individual markets.
b. is the study of individual behavior.
c. assumes that people are rational.
d. assumes that people attempt to maximize their satisfaction.
e. is described by all of the above.

_____ 7. Those choices that are undertaken are those whose
a. benefits exceed their costs.
b. costs exceed their benefits.
c. benefit-to-cost ratios are the greatest.
d. cost-to-benefit ratios are the greatest.
e. opportunity costs are lowest.

_____ 8. If a constraint facing an individual's choices disappears, this can be represented by
a. a point on the individual's production possibilities curve.
b. a movement from one point to another on the individual's production possibilities curve.
c. a point inside the individual's production possibilities curve.
d. an inward shift of the individual's production possibilities curve.
e. an outward shift of the individual's production possibilities curve.

_____ 9. Which of the following statements is true?
a. Costs are always incurred immediately.
b. Benefits are always incurred immediately.
c. Uncertainty about costs and benefits makes rational decisions impossible.
d. Other people can determine whether your behavior is rational.
e. None of the above are true.

_____ 10. Discounting is
a. whenever a product is put on sale at a lower-than-usual price.

b. the use of coupons to purchase a product.
c. adjusting costs or benefits to arrive at their present value.
d. minimizing opportunity costs.
e. changing money cost into real cost.

_____ 11. A synonym for utility is
a. pain.
b. satisfaction.
c. electricity.
d. discounting.
e. rationality.

Discussion Questions

1. It has been said, "If you can't do the time, don't do the crime." What is the real cost of time spent in prison? Would the cost of a one-year sentence in prison be the same for everyone? Are judges capable of measuring these costs accurately? Do you think this is why judges sentence some people to longer periods of time in prison than others, all other things the same? If so, is this just? In light of this, who's likely to spend a longer time in jail — a poor person or a rich person? *(KQ2)*
2. What, in your opinion, are the present benefits and costs of attending college? What adjustments for time and risk on benefits and costs did you make in your decision to attend college? *(KQ2)*
3. How many costs have you incurred in choosing alternatives in the last twenty-four hours that were not measured in monetary terms? *(KQ2)*

Answers

Problems and Applications

1. Scarcity → choice → opportunity cost. Because we are faced with scarcity we must make choices. Whenever a choice is made an opportunity cost is incurred.
2. Choices are constrained because of scarcity. In other words, our choices are constrained because we are unable to have all we would like all the time.
3. a. The curve C_3E_3 is the individual's production possibilities curve. (See graph on page 306.)

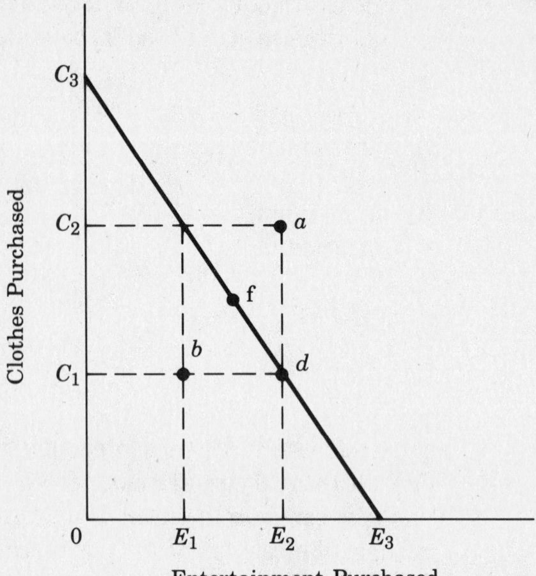

b. Constraints include the individual's income, the price of clothing, and the price of entertainment.

c. Point *a* represents a combination of clothes and entertainment (C_2 and E_2) that is unobtainable, given this individual's constraints. For example, if the individual wanted C_2 clothes, he or she could have only E_1 entertainment. Likewise, to get E_2 entertainment means that he or she could have only C_1 clothes.

d. Point *b* means the individual is not maximizing his or her satisfaction, given his or her constraints. (We have assumed the individual has only two choices — saving is not among them.) For instance, more clothing, C_2 rather than C_1, could be obtained without sacrificing any entertainment. Likewise, more entertainment, E_2 rather than E_1, could be obtained without sacrificing any clothes. Indeed, more of both could be obtained, shown by point *f*. Surely, having more of one without having to sacrifice the other, or having more of both choices, would increase the individual's satisfaction.

e. Point *d* represents one among many different combinations of clothes and entertainment the individual can choose that may maximize his or her satisfaction. Point *f* is just another combination that may maximize his or her satisfaction. *Note:* Point *f may* maximize satisfaction. The actual combination (point on the curve) chosen depends on the individual's preferences for clothing and entertainment.

f. The cost of choosing more clothes is the benefits that would have been received from entertainment but had to be forgone. The cost of choosing more entertainment is the benefits that would have been received from clothes but had to be forgone.

g. The benefits must exceed the costs by a greater amount than any other combination of entertainment and clothing that can be obtained.

h. An outward shift in the curve means that one or more of the individual's constraints have disappeared and the individual is able to obtain more of both choices (which may be shown by point *a*, given a large enough outward shift). An outward shift means, ultimately, that the individual can obtain more satisfaction. An outward shift in this example may be caused by an increase in the individual's income or a decrease in the price of clothes or in the price of entertainment.

True-False

1. F: Illegal behavior may be rational behavior.
2. F: Cost cannot always be measured in monetary terms.
3. T 4. T 5. T 6. T
7. F: Cost-benefit analysis is always useful in deciding whether a course of action should be undertaken to maximize satisfaction.
8. T 9. T 10. T
11. F: Only one point on an individual's production possibilities (or tradeoff) curve between two choices will maximize his or her satisfaction, and the exact location of that point depends on the individual's preferences between those two choices.
12. F: People who are rational may behave quite differently because they have different preferences.
13. T
14. F: A point outside an individual's production possibilities (or tradeoff) curve represents a combination between choices that is unobtainable.
15. F: Rational behavior does not necessarily mean that people behave selfishly.

Multiple Choice

1. b *(KQ2)*	2. b *(KQ1, 2)*	3. c *(KQ3)*
4. e *(KQ1, 4)*	5. d *(KQ5)*	6. e *(KQ1)*
7. c *(KQ2)*	8. e *(KQ2)*	9. e *(KQ3, 4)*
10. c *(KQ3)*	11. b *(KQ1)*	

CHAPTER 18

Consumer Choice and Demand

Chapter Summary

In this chapter, we extend the discussion of rational behavior to a derivation of the law of demand. We also look at the elasticity of demand and the nonprice determinants of demand.

Key Question 1: What is the basis of economists' predictions about the actions of consumers?

Rational behavior, as we have seen, means that an individual attempts to maximize his or her satisfaction. That is, he or she will choose those alternatives whose benefit-to-cost ratios are the greatest. Rational behavior also means that people prefer more to less. These statements imply that an individual will use his or her entire income in consumption or in saving, or in some combination of the two, to maximize his or her satisfaction. These statements also imply that the individual will use some method of comparing the value (benefits) of various goods and services. The amount of extra satisfaction (benefit) received from any one unit of a product depends on the amount that has already been consumed. Marginal utility measures the extra satisfaction from an additional unit consumed. According to the law of diminishing marginal utility, as more of a good or service is consumed, its marginal utility, relative to the marginal utility of other goods and services, diminishes.

We now need to look more closely at the cost side of a rational decision. Price is the cost of acquiring a unit of a good or service. It is not always stated in monetary terms. Nor is price necessarily equal to costs of production. In other words, what the buyer gives up to obtain the good or service does not have to match what the seller or producer gives up to provide the good or service.

Key Question 2: How do consumers maximize utility?

The combination of goods and services that maximizes an individual's satisfaction occurs when $MU_a/P_a = MU_b/P_b = \ldots MU_n/P_n$. In other words, the individual will maximize his or her satisfaction when the extra satisfaction per last dollar spent on all goods and services is the same. If this occurs, the consumer is in equilibrium. In reality, a consumer may never reach equilibrium (the maximum satisfaction possible given the individual's constraints). However, rational behavior attempts to reach equilibrium.

Key Question 3: What is the relationship between diminishing marginal utility and the law of demand?

If the price of a product decreases, then the ratio of its marginal utility to its price will increase, relative to that of all other products. That is, the extra satisfaction per last dollar spent on that product will now be greater than that for all other products. Therefore, the consumer is no longer in equilibrium and should purchase more of the product. In so doing, the marginal utility of that product will decrease. Therefore, the ratio of its marginal utility to its price (*MU/P*) will decrease. The consumer should continue to purchase the product until the ratio of its marginal utility to its price is just equal to that for all other products. Because consumers behave rationally in this manner, we can conclude that a reduction in price will cause an increase in the quantity demanded. If the price rises, similar logic shows that the quantity demanded will fall. This inverse relationship between the price and the quantity demanded gives rise to the law of demand, which is expressed graphically as a downward-sloping line (or curve).

In sum, because an individual behaves rationally, and because an individual can substitute relatively cheap products for more expensive ones, the demand curve slopes downward. Alternatively, the demand curve can be said to slope downward because of the law of diminishing marginal utility. That is, the only way a consumer can be enticed to buy more of a product (where the marginal utility of each additional unit consumed decreases) is if its price is reduced. In other words, if each additional unit yields smaller extra satisfaction, then a consumer is not going to be willing to pay as much for it. Therefore, its price must fall. Note that the law of demand can be applied to anything a consumer values, whether or not its price can be stated in dollars and cents.

Key Question 4: What is the relationship between individual demand curves and market demand curve?

To arrive at market demand, simply horizontally sum all individuals' demand curves in the market. The greater the number of consumers, the more the demand curve flattens out and extends to the right.

Key Question 5: What is the purpose of the elasticity of demand?

Price elasticity of demand takes a closer look at the law of demand. The law of demand simply states that there is an inverse relationship between price and the quantity demanded. Price elasticity of demand measures the responsiveness of the quantity demanded to a change in price. If a product has an elastic demand, then consumers are relatively responsive (sensitive) to a change in the price of that product. If a product has an inelastic demand, then consumers are relatively unresponsive (insensitive) to a change in the price of that product.

There are two way to determine the elasticity of a product. One way is to calculate the effect of a change in price on total consumer expenditures (which equals producers' total revenue). Another way is to develop mathematical values for various levels of elasticity.

In terms of total consumer expenditures (total revenue), demand is elastic if there is an inverse relationship between price and total consumer expenditures (total revenue). Whatever price does, total consumer expenditures (total revenue) does the opposite. Demand is inelastic if there is a positive (direct) relationship between price and total consumer expenditures (total revenue). Whatever price does, total consumer expenditures (total revenue) does the same. Demand is unitary elastic if there is no relationship between price and total consumer expenditures (total revenue). In that case, price can increase or decrease and there is no change in total consumer expenditures (total revenue).

The advantage of mathematically determining elasticity, as opposed to the total consumer expenditures (total revenue) test, is that mathematical values enable us to distinguish degrees of elasticity and inelasticity. The mathematical value for the degree of elasticity or inelasticity is the elasticity coefficient of demand (E_d). It is the ratio of the percentage change in the quantity demanded to the percentage change in price. The mathematical process of determining the degree of elasticity and inelasticity also shows that the elasticity coefficient will be different at different points on the curve. For a linear demand curve, the inelastic range is at the bottom. Somewhere in the center it is unitary elastic, and the elastic range is at the top of the demand curve. When an elasticity coefficient is calculated, be sure to take its absolute value (drop the negative sign). If the coefficient is greater than 1, demand is elastic. If it is less than 1, demand is inelastic. If it is equal to 1, demand is unitary elastic.

Small differences in elasticity coefficients of demand may not be very meaningful, because the data on which the coefficients are calculated are often less than precise. For instance, a reduction in price may lead to a much larger increase in the quantity demanded than would otherwise occur because of a change in one or more of the nonprice determinants of demand. Further, elasticity measures are not measurements of a demand curve's slope. Be careful not to judge the elasticity of demand by looking at a demand curve's slope. Finally, two parallel demand curves do not have the same elasticity coefficients.

Key Question 6: What determines the size of the elasticity of demand?

Factors that determine the elasticity of demand (consumer responsiveness to a price change) include the number of substitutes, the number of competitors, and the amount of time under consideration. In general, the greater the number of substitutes, competitors, and amount of time under consideration, the greater the elasticity of demand.

Key Question 7: Why does demand change?

There are other determinants of demand besides price. These include consumer incomes, the prices of other goods and services, the number of consumers, expectations concerning future prices and incomes, and consumer tastes and preferences. There may be others, but these seem to be the most important for most products. These nonprice determinants of demand determine the position of the demand curve. If any of these variables change, so will the position of the demand curve. If demand increases (decreases) because of a change in one or more of these variables, then the demand curve will shift outward to the right (inward to the left). This means that consumers will buy more (less) at any specific price or, alternatively, that they are willing to pay a higher (they will only pay a lower) price to receive the same quantity.

Key Question 8: Will irrational behavior lead to a violation of the law of demand?

So far, we have been concerned with rational behavior. As long as some people behave rationally, then irrational behavior does not contradict the law of demand, although it will reduce the elasticity of demand.

Review Terms and Concepts

Scarcity
Cost (opportunity cost)
Rational behavior
Irrational behavior
Cost-benefit analysis
Utility
Demand
Supply
Inverse relationship
Positive (direct) relationship
Quantity demanded
Util

New Terms and Concepts

Marginal utility
Consumer equilibrium
Law of diminishing marginal utility
Law of demand
Price
Market demand
Price elasticity of demand
Elastic demand
Inelastic demand
Unitary elastic demand
Elasticity coefficient of demand
Perfectly elastic demand
Normal good or service
Luxury good or service
Inferior good or service
Indifference curve
Budget line

Completion

maximize	Rational behavior means an individual attempts to ________________
	(minimize/maximize) his or her satisfaction by choosing those alterna-
benefit, cost	tives whose ________________ (cost/benefit)-to-________________
greatest	(cost/benefit) ratios are ________________ (greatest/smallest). The
	individual must use some method of measuring the value (benefits) of
marginal utility	various goods or services. The method used is ________________
	(marginal utility/price). Marginal utility measures the extra
satisfaction	________________ (satisfaction/cost) from the consumption of
	an additional unit of a good or service. According to the law of diminish-
	ing marginal utility, as more of a good or service is consumed, its mar-
	ginal utility, relative to the marginal utility of other goods and services,
decreases	________________ (increases/decreases).
Price	A rational decision also requires some measure of cost. ____________
	(Price/Demand) is the cost of acquiring a unit of a good or service. It is
not always	________________ (always/not always) stated in dollars and cents.
not necessarily	Price is ________________ (necessarily/not necessarily) equal
	to the costs of production.
	The combination of goods and services that maximizes an individual's
	satisfaction occurs when $MU_a/P_a = MU_b/P_b = \ldots MU_n/P_n$. In other words,
	the individual will maximize his or her satisfaction when the
extra satisfaction per last dollar	________________________________ (satisfaction
the same	per dollar/extra satisfaction per last dollar) spent is ________________
	(equal to one/the same) for all goods and services. If this occurs, the con-
in equilibrium	sumer is ________________ (in equilibrium/irrational). In reality,

may never	a consumer ____________ (will/may never) reach equilibrium but
attempt to	rational consumers ____________ (may not/attempt to).
can	We ____________ (can/cannot) derive the law of demand from
	rational behavior. For instance, if the price of a product decreases, then
increase	the ratio of its marginal utility to its price will ____________
	(increase/decrease), relative to that of all other products. That is, the
	extra satisfaction per last dollar spent on that product will now be
greater	____________ (smaller/greater) than that for all other products.
more	Therefore, the consumer should purchase ____________ (more/less) of
	this product. In so doing, the marginal utility of that product will
decrease	____________ (increase/decrease). Therefore, the ratio of its
decrease	marginal utility to its price (MU/P) will ____________ (increase/
	decrease). The consumer should continue to purchase the product until
just equal to	the ratio of its marginal utility to its price is ____________
	(greater than/just equal to/smaller than) that for all other products. Be-
	cause consumers behave rationally in this manner we can conclude that a
an increase	price reduction will cause ____________ (an increase/a
	decrease) in the quantity demanded. If the price rises, similar logic shows
fall	the quantity demanded will ____________ (rise/fall). Note, this
inverse	____________ (direct / inverse) relationship between the price
demand	and the quantity demanded gives rise to the law of ____________
a downward	(rational behavior/demand). This law is expressed as ____________
	(a downward/an upward)-sloping line (or curve). The law of demand can
to anything	be applied ____________ (to anything/only to goods and ser-
whether or not	vices) the consumer values, ____________ (only if/whether
	or not) its price can be stated in dollars and cents.

horizontally	To derive the market demand curve one must ________________
all	(vertically/horizontally) sum ____________ (a few/all) individuals'
	demand curves in the market.
	Price elasticity of demand takes a closer look at the law of demand be-
the quantity demanded	cause it measures the responsiveness of ____________________
price	(price/the quantity demanded) to a change in ________________
	(price/quantity demanded). If demand is elastic, this means that con-
responsive	sumers are relatively __________________ (responsive/unresponsive)
price	to a change in ____________________ (price/the quantity demanded).
	If demand is inelastic, this means that consumers are relatively
insensitive	__________________ (sensitive/insensitive) to a change in price.
	There are two ways to determine the elasticity of a product. It can be
	determined by the total consumer expenditures (total revenue) test or
	mathematically. In terms of the total consumer expenditures (total
an inverse	revenue) test, demand is elastic if there is __________________ (an
	inverse/a positive) relationship between price and total consumer expen-
inelastic	ditures (total revenue). Demand is ____________________ (elastic/
	inelastic) if there is a positive (direct) relationship between price and
	total consumer expenditures (total revenue). Demand is unitary elastic if
no	there is ______________ (an inverse/no/a direct) relationship between
	price and total consumer expenditures (total revenue). Mathematically
makes it possible	determining the value of elasticity ________________________
	(makes it possible/does not enable one) to distinguish the degrees of
	elasticity. The mathematical value for the degree of elasticity is the
elasticity coefficient	________________________________ (price elasticity/elasticity
percentage change	coefficient) of demand. It is the ratio of the ____________________

(change/percentage change) in the ______________________ (price/quantity demanded) to the ______________________ (change/percentage change) in ________________ (price/quantity demanded). The elasticity coefficient of demand will be ________________ (the same/different) at different points along a straight-line demand curve. The inelastic range is at the ________________ (bottom/top) of the demand curve. Somewhere in the middle it is ________________ (elastic/unitary elastic/inelastic). The elastic range is at the __________ (bottom/top). When a coefficient is calculated, be sure to __________ (keep/drop) the negative sign. If the coefficient is greater than 1, demand is ________________ (elastic/unitary elastic/inelastic). If the coefficient is equal to 1, demand is ______________________ (elastic/unitary elastic/inelastic). If the coefficient is less than 1, demand is ________________ (elastic/unitary elastic/inelastic).

When using elasticity of demand coefficients, one should realize that ______________ (small/large) differences may not be very meaningful. Also, elasticity measurements ____________ (are/are not) measurements of a demand curve's slope. Furthermore, two parallel demand curves ________________ (have/do not have) the same elasticity coefficients.

There are three major factors that determine whether a product has an elastic or inelastic demand. A product that has an elastic demand is likely to have ______________ (many/few) substitutes. There are also likely to be ______________ (many/few) competitors and a relatively ____________ (short/long) time period under consideration.

quantity demanded
percentage change
price
different
bottom
unitary elastic
top
drop
elastic
unitary elastic
inelastic
small
are not
do not have
many
many
long

are — There ______________ (are/are not) other determinants of demand be-
determine — sides price. The nonprice determinants of demand ______________
(determine/do not determine) the position of the demand curve. If any of
so will — these variables change, ______________ (so will/it won't change)
the position of the demand curve. If the demand curve shifts outward to
increased — the right, then demand has ______________ (increased/
more — decreased). This means that consumers will buy ______________
(less/more) at any specific price. It can also mean that they are willing to
higher — pay a ______________ (higher/lower) price to receive the same
quantity.

does not contradict — If some consumers behave irrationally, this ______________
(contradicts/does not contradict) the law of demand. However, it will
decrease — ______________ (increase/decrease) the elasticity of demand.

Problems and Applications

1. What is a synonym for marginal utility?
2. What is a util?
3. Assume that a consumer is spending his or her entire income on the consumption of good X and good Y.
   a. What should the consumer do to maximize his or her satisfaction between the consumption of X and Y if MU_x/P_x is greater than MU_y/P_y? Explain why.
   b. If the consumer was initially in equilibrium, what change in the price of X and/or the price of Y could cause MU_x/P_x to be greater than MU_y/P_y?
   c. Given your answers to b and c, if the price of X decreases and/or the price of Y increases, does the quantity demanded of X and/or Y change in the direction the law of demand predicts? Graph a demand curve for X and Y and express the effect a change in the price of X and Y would have on the quantity demanded of X and Y.

d. What should the consumer do to maximize his or her satisfaction between the consumption of X and Y if MU_x/P_x is less than MU_y/P_y?
e. If the consumer was initially in equilibrium, what change in the price of X and/or the price of Y could cause MU_x/P_x to be less than MU_y/P_y?
f. Given your answers to d and e, if the price of Y decreases and/or the price of X increases, does the quantity demanded of Y and/or X change in the direction the law of demand predicts? Graph a demand curve for X and Y and express the effect the change in the price of X and Y would have on the quantity demanded of X and Y.

4. Given a linear (straight-line) demand curve, price elasticity of demand changes along that curve. Determine whether each of the following portions of the curve is elastic, unitary elastic, or inelastic.
   a. upper portion
   b. somewhere in the middle
   c. lower portion
5. For each of the following elasticity coefficients of demand, indicate whether demand is elastic, unitary elastic, or inelastic. (*Note:* These are absolute values. The negative sign has been dropped.) Interpret what the percentage change in the quantity demanded would be for every one percentage change in price.
   a. $E_d = 2$
   b. $E_d = 1.05$
   c. $E_d = 0.35$
   d. $E_d = 1$
6. a. If price increases by some percentage and quantity demanded decreases by a larger percentage, is demand elastic, unitary elastic, or inelastic? Why?
   b. What is total consumer expenditures (total revenue) equal to?
   c. If price increases by some percentage and quantity demanded decreases by a greater percentage, what happens to total consumer expenditures (total revenue)?
   d. Given your answers to a through c, is this why we generally say that an increase in price accompanied by a decrease in total consumer expenditures (total revenue) means demand is elastic?
   e. Is demand elastic, unitary elastic, or inelastic if price decreases and total consumer expenditures (total revenue) rise? Explain why demand must be elastic, unitary elastic, or inelastic.

   f. Is demand elastic, unitary elastic or inelastic if price decreases (increases) and total consumer expenditures fall (rise)? Explain why demand must be elastic, unitary elastic, or inelastic.

7. For each of the following situations, determine whether demand is elastic, unitary elastic, or inelastic.
   a. Price increases and total consumer expenditures (total revenue) rise.
   b. Price increases and total consumer expenditures (total revenue) falls.
   c. Price decreases and total consumer expenditures (total revenue) rises.
   d. Price decreases and total consumer expenditures (total revenue) falls.
   e. Price increases and total consumer expenditures (total revenue) remains the same.
8. What is the advantage of mathematically determining the price elasticity of demand as opposed to the total consumer expenditures (total revenue) test?
9. For each of the following situations, determine whether there would be a tendency for a product to have an elastic or inelastic demand.
   a. There are a large number of substitutes.
   b. There are a large number of competitors.
   c. There is a relatively long time period under consideration.
   d. There is a relatively short time period under consideration.
   e. There are a small number of substitutes.
   f. There are a small number of competitors.
10. Graphically express an increase and decrease in demand.
11. Determine whether each of the following situations can be interpreted as an increase or a decrease in demand.
    a. Consumers are willing to buy more at any given price.
    b. Consumers are willing to pay a higher price to receive any given quantity.
    c. Consumers are willing to buy less at any given price.
    d. Consumers are not willing to pay as much for any given quantity.
12. For each of the following situations, determine whether demand would increase or decrease.
    a. Consumer incomes increase and the product is a normal good.
    b. The price of a substitute product increases.
    c. The number of consumers in the market decreases.

d. Consumers expect the price of the product to fall in the near future.
e. Consumer tastes for this product increase.
f. Consumer incomes fall and the product is an inferior good.
g. The price of a complementary product increases.
h. Consumers expect their incomes to fall.

13. If price decreases and demand decreases simultaneously, what happens to the quantity demanded?
14. Given an indifference map (a set of indifference curves) and a budget line, where does consumer equilibrium exist?

True-False

For each item, determine whether the statement is basically true or false. If the statement is false, rewrite it so it is a true statement.

_____ 1. In the real word, we can predict precisely how much quantity demanded will change, given a change in price.

_____ 2. We can derive the law of demand from indifference curves and budget line analysis.

_____ 3. Marginal utility is associated with the extra satisfaction of all units consumed.

_____ 4. The law of demand states that there is an inverse relationship between price and quantity demanded.

_____ 5. Comparing the ratios of different products' marginal utilities to their prices enables us to compare products of unlike nature whose prices may be vastly different (such as candy bars and Cadillacs).

_____ 6. A consumer should not alter his or her consumption patterns once they have reached equilibrium.

_____ 7. If a consumer purchases less of a product, then that product's marginal utility will increase.

_____ 8. The law of diminishing marginal utility explains why the demand curve is upward-sloping.

_____ 9. Price elasticity of demand is a measurement of the slope of a demand curve.

_____ 10. An inelastic product has an elasticity coefficient greater than 1.

_____ 11. If $E_d = 1.2$, then a 10 percent change in price will result in a 12 percent change in quantity demand.

_____ 12. If the price of a product falls and people buy less of it, then most likely there was change in one of the nonprice determinants of demand.

_____ 13. If the price of X increases and the demand for Y decreases, then X and Y are complementary products.

_____ 14. If a consumer's income increases, his or her indifference curves shift outward.

_____ 15. A consumer is in equilibrium where the budget line intersects an indifference curve.

Multiple Choice *Choose the one best answer for each item.*

_____ 1. A perfectly elastic demand curve
   a. is impossible.
   b. is expressed graphically as a downward-sloping line.
   c. means price changes will not alter the quantity demanded.
   d. is expressed graphically as a horizontal line.
   e. is expressed graphically as a vertical line.

_____ 2. An inferior good is
   a. an inexpensive luxury good.
   b. a good whose demand curve increases with a decrease in income.
   c. a good whose demand curve increases with an increase in income.
   d. a good whose demand curve increases with an increase in the price of a substitute.
   e. a good whose demand curve increases with an increase in the price of a complement.

_____ 3. Which of the following are most likely complements?
   a. Cigarettes and gasoline
   b. Toothpaste and hairspray
   c. Bacon and eggs
   d. Beef and pork
   e. All of the above

_____ 4. Irrational behavior on the part of some but not all consumers
   a. results in an upward-sloping demand curve.
   b. results in an inferior good.
   c. results in a more elastic demand curve.

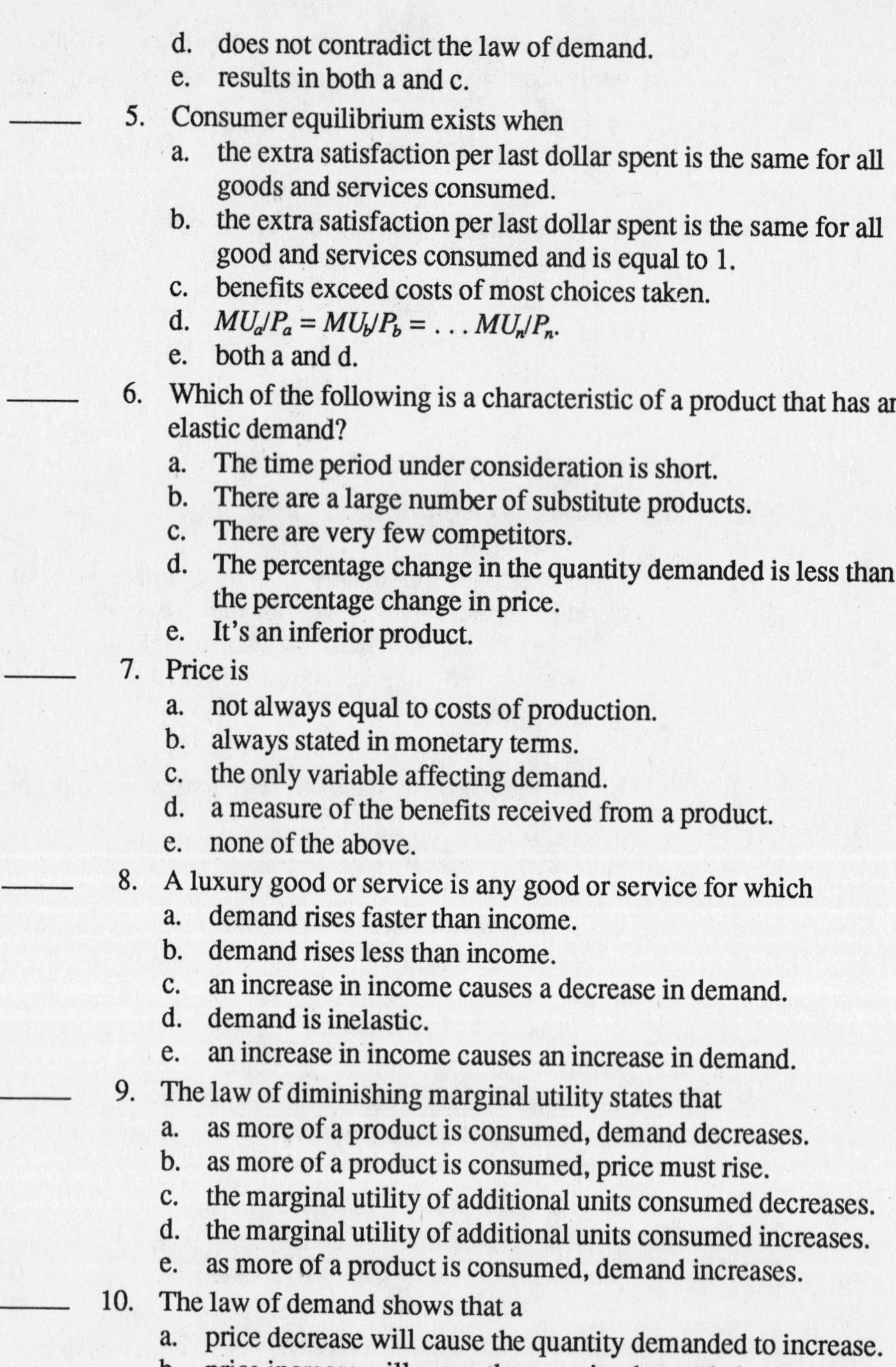

d. does not contradict the law of demand.
e. results in both a and c.

_____ 5. Consumer equilibrium exists when
a. the extra satisfaction per last dollar spent is the same for all goods and services consumed.
b. the extra satisfaction per last dollar spent is the same for all good and services consumed and is equal to 1.
c. benefits exceed costs of most choices taken.
d. $MU_a/P_a = MU_b/P_b = \ldots MU_n/P_n$.
e. both a and d.

_____ 6. Which of the following is a characteristic of a product that has an elastic demand?
a. The time period under consideration is short.
b. There are a large number of substitute products.
c. There are very few competitors.
d. The percentage change in the quantity demanded is less than the percentage change in price.
e. It's an inferior product.

_____ 7. Price is
a. not always equal to costs of production.
b. always stated in monetary terms.
c. the only variable affecting demand.
d. a measure of the benefits received from a product.
e. none of the above.

_____ 8. A luxury good or service is any good or service for which
a. demand rises faster than income.
b. demand rises less than income.
c. an increase in income causes a decrease in demand.
d. demand is inelastic.
e. an increase in income causes an increase in demand.

_____ 9. The law of diminishing marginal utility states that
a. as more of a product is consumed, demand decreases.
b. as more of a product is consumed, price must rise.
c. the marginal utility of additional units consumed decreases.
d. the marginal utility of additional units consumed increases.
e. as more of a product is consumed, demand increases.

_____ 10. The law of demand shows that a
a. price decrease will cause the quantity demanded to increase.
b. price increase will cause the quantity demanded to increase.
c. price increase will cause the demand to increase.

d. price decrease will cause the demand to increase.
e. demand curve is upward sloping.

_____ 11. An elastic demand for a product means that
a. producers are relatively responsive to a price change.
b. the percentage change in the quantity demanded is greater than the percentage change in price.
c. the percentage change in price is greater than the percentage change in the quantity demanded.
d. consumers are relatively unresponsive to change in the price of the product.
e. the slope of the demand curve is relatively steep.

_____ 12. In which of the following cases would demand be elastic?
a. Price falls and total revenue falls.
b. Price rises and total revenue falls.
c. Price rises and total revenue remains the same.
d. The elasticity of demand coefficient is greater than 1.
e. Both b and d.

_____ 13. The elasticity of demand coefficient is
a. calculated by dividing the percentage change in the price by the percentage change in the quantity demanded.
b. calculated by multiplying the percentage change in the price by the percentage change in the quantity demanded.
c. greater than 1 for an inelastic demand.
d. a more precise measure of consumer responsiveness to price changes than the total consumer expenditures (total revenue) test.
e. the ratio of the change in the quantity demanded to the change in price.

_____ 14. An increase in demand could be caused by
a. an increase in the number of consumers.
b. an increase in people's desire for the product.
c. a decrease in the price of a complementary product.
d. an increase in the price of a substitute product.
e. all of the above.

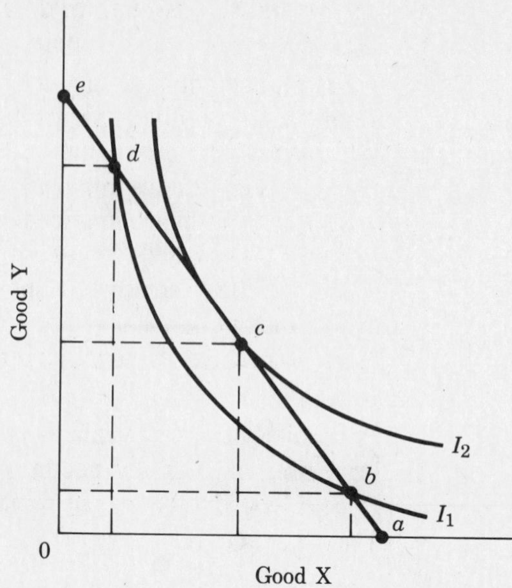

_____ 15. Based on the preceding graph, which of the following statements is true?

a. The budget line is I_2.
b. I_1 is a greater level of utility than I_2.
c. At point *d* the $MU_x/P_x > MU_y/P_y$.
d. If the price of X decreases, then the budget line will pivot in from below.
e. If the consumers' income increases, the budget line will shift inward.

Discussion Questions

1. Why may rational consumers be unable to reach equilibrium in their consumption patterns? *(KQ1, 8.* See also Chapter 17.)
2. List some goods and services you think are inferior. *(KQ7)*
3. Does the law of demand's predictive power increase when larger numbers of consumers are considered? *(KQ8)*
4. Do all the factors that contribute to inelasticity have to be present for a product to have an inelastic demand, or does just one of them have to be strong enough to overwhelm any tendencies for its demand to be elastic? *(KQ6)*

5. What are some other variables that can shift the demand curve for a product? *(KQ7)*
6. If a product is considered a necessity would it most likely have an elastic or an inelastic demand? What about a good or service that is considered a luxury? *(KQ6)*
7. Considering the factors that determine whether a product is elastic or inelastic, what do you think is the price elasticity of demand for medical care, gasoline, food, rental housing, giving to charity? *(KQ6)*
8. What effect do you think a successful advertising campaign would have on the price elasticity of demand? *(KQ6)*

Answers

Problems and Applications

1. Extra satisfaction.
2. A theoretical measure of one unit of utility (satisfaction).
3. a. The consumer should purchase more of X and less of Y because the extra satisfaction per last dollar spent on good X is greater than that for good Y. In so doing, the marginal utility of X will decrease, while the marginal utility of Y increases. The consumer should continue purchasing more of X and less of Y until the extra satisfaction per last dollar spent on good X is just equal to that for good Y ($MU_x/P_x = MU_y/P_y$).

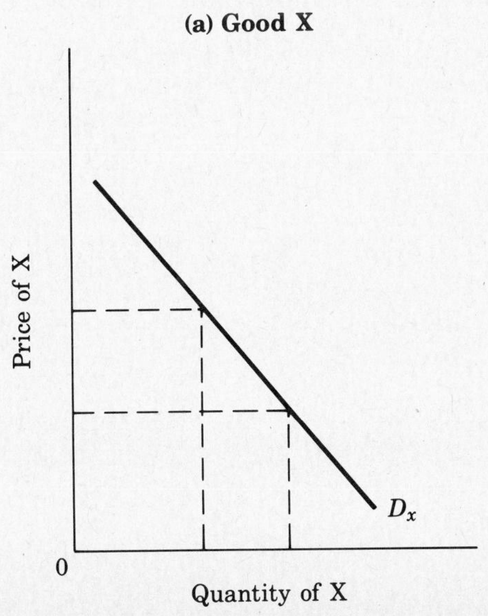

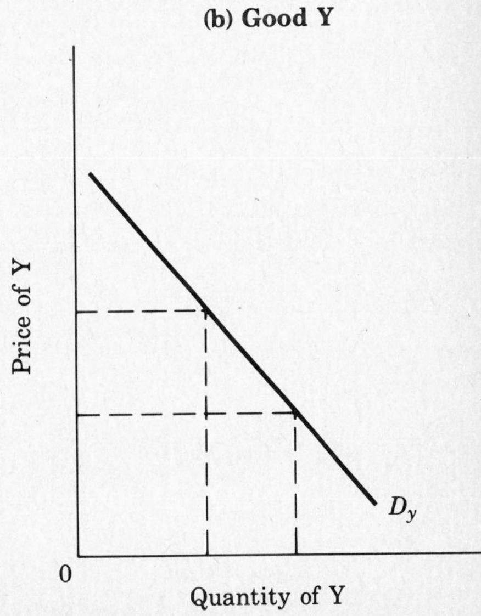

b. A decrease in the price of X and/or an increase in the price of Y.
c. Yes. A decrease in the price of X causes an increase in the quantity demanded of X and an increase in the price of Y causes a decrease in the quantity demanded of Y.
d. The consumer should purchase more of Y and less of X because the extra satisfaction per last dollar spent on good Y is greater than that for good X. In so doing, the marginal utility of Y will decrease while the marginal utility of X increases. The consumer should continue purchasing more of Y and less of X until the extra satisfaction per last dollar spent on good Y is just equal to that for good X ($MU_x/P_x = MU_y/P_y$).
e. A decrease in the price of Y and/or an increase in the price of X.
f. Yes. A decrease in the price of Y causes an increase in quantity demanded of Y, and an increase in the price of X causes a decrease in the quantity demanded of X. (See the preceding graph.)

4. a. Elastic
   b. Unitary elastic
   c. Inelastic

5. a. Elastic. For every one percentage change in price there will occur a two percentage change in the quantity demanded.
   b. Elastic. For every one percentage change in price there will occur a 1.05 percentage change in the quantity demanded.
   c. Inelastic. For every one percentage change in price there will occur a .35 percentage change in the quantity demanded.
   d. Unitary elastic. For every one percentage change in price there will occur a one percentage change in the quantity demanded.

6. a. Elastic. Because the percentage change in the quantity demanded was greater than the percentage change in price, the elasticity coefficient will be greater than 1. In other words, consumers are relatively responsive (sensitive) to a change in the price.
   b. Total consumer expenditures (*TCE*) is equal to the price of the product multiplied by the quantity bought (sold): $TCE = P \times Q$ or $TR = P \times Q$.
   c. Because $TCE = P \times Q$ (or $TR = P \times Q$) a given percentage increase in price accompanied by a larger percentage decrease in quantity will cause the product of price and quantity — *TCE* (or *TR*) — to decrease.

d. Yes, because if price increases by some percentage and total consumer expenditures (total revenue) falls, then the percentage decrease in the quantity demanded must have been greater than the percentage increase in price. Therefore, demand is elastic.

e. Demand is elastic. We know $TCE = P \times Q$ $(TR = P \times Q)$. If *TCE* (or *TR*) rises with some percentage decrease in *P*, then the percentage increase in *Q* must be larger than the percentage decrease in *P*. If the percentage increase in *Q* is greater than the percentage decrease in *P*, then consumers are relatively responsive to a change in the price and demand is elastic (and the elasticity of demand coefficient is greater than 1).

f. Demand is inelastic. Let's explain why demand must be inelastic if price decreases and total consumer expenditures (total revenue) falls. (Similar logic will explain why demand must be inelastic if price increases and total consumer expenditures [total revenue] rises.) We know $TCE = P \times Q$ $(TR = P \times Q)$. If *TCE* (or *TR*) falls with some percentage decrease in *P*, then the percentage increase in *Q* must be smaller than the percentage decrease in *P*. If the percentage increase in *Q* is less than the percentage decrease in *P*, then consumers are relatively unresponsive (insensitive) to a change in the price, and demand is inelastic (and the elasticity of demand coefficient is less than 1.)

7. a. Inelastic
   b. Elastic
   c. Elastic
   d. Inelastic
   e. Unitary elastic
8. Mathematically determining the price elasticity of demand enables us to determine the degree of elasticity or inelasticity.
9. a. Elastic
   b. Elastic
   c. Elastic
   d. Inelastic
   e. Inelastic
   f. Inelastic
10. The original demand curve is D_1. An increase in demand is graphically expressed as a rightward shift, such as from D_1 to D_2. A decrease in demand is graphically expressed as a leftward shift, such as from D_1 to D_3. (See graph on page 328.)

Graph for Answer 10.

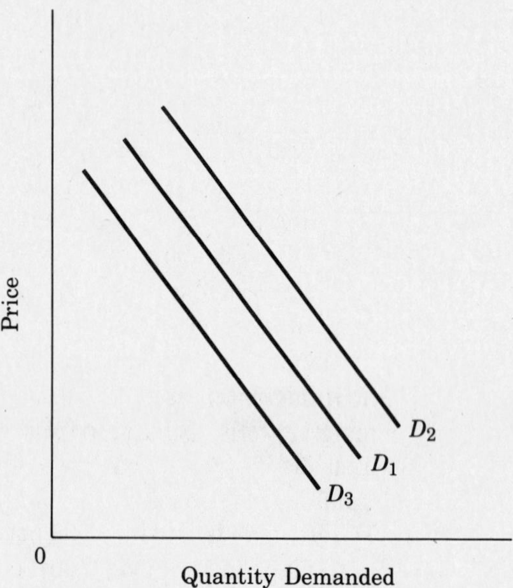

11. a. Increase in demand
    b. Increase in demand
    c. Decrease in demand
    d. Decrease in demand
12. a. Demand would increase.
    b. Demand would increase.
    c. Demand would decrease.
    d. Demand would decrease.
    e. Demand would increase.
    f. Demand would increase.
    g. Demand would decrease.
    h. Demand would decrease.
13. If price decreases we know from the law of demand that the quantity demanded will increase. But if demand is decreasing at the same time, this will partially — or totally — offset the increase in the quantity demanded. It's even possible the quantity demanded would decrease. The actual outcome on the quantity demanded depends on how much price and demand decrease.
14. Consumer equilibrium exists where the budget line is just tangent to an indifference curve.

True-False

1. F: In the real world we cannot predict precisely how much quantity demanded will change, given a change in price, but we can predict the direction of change in the quantity demanded, given a change in price.
2. T
3. F: Marginal utility is associated with the extra satisfaction of the last unit consumed but depends on the number of units already consumed.
4. T 5. T 6. T 7. T
8. F: The law of diminishing marginal utility explains why the demand curve is downward-sloping.
9. F: Price elasticity of demand is not a measurement of the slope of a demand curve but instead a measurement of the responsiveness of consumers to a price change.
10. F: An inelastic product has an elasticity coefficient less than 1.
11. T 12. T 13. T
14. F: If a consumer's income increases, his or her budget line shifts outward.
15. F: A consumer is in equilibrium where the budget line is just tangent to an indifference curve.

Multiple Choice

1. d *(KQ6)* 2. b *(KQ7)* 3. c *(KQ7)*
4. d *(KQ8)* 5. e *(KQ2)* 6. b *(KQ6)*
7. a *(KQ3)* 8. a *(KQ7)* 9. c *(KQ2)*
10. a *(KQ3)* 11. b *(KQ5)* 12. e *(KQ6)*
13. d *(KQ5)* 14. e *(KQ7)* 15. c (See appendix)

CHAPTER 19

Business Organizations

Chapter Summary

This chapter investigates the three major types of business organization and the advantages and disadvantages of each. It also takes a closer look at what is meant by profits and briefly evaluates the influence of big business.

Key Question 1: What are the three types of business organizations?

The three major categories of business organization are the sole proprietorship, the partnership, and the corporation. The fewest number of firms are partnerships. There are about twice as many corporations as partnerships, but most businesses in the United States are sole proprietorships. However, corporations dominate sales in the United States because of the advantages of this type of business organization.

A sole proprietorship's major advantage is the owner's flexibility in terms of production plans, financing, and the disbursement of profits. The disadvantages stem directly from the fact that sole proprietorships are owned by one individual. The size of the firm is limited by the individual's ability to raise money. The owner does not benefit from the advice and encouragement of co-owners and must assume all of the risks of failure. Furthermore, because the owner is fully liable for all the firm's debts, if the business fails the owner's personal property can be sold to pay off business debts. The firm also ceases to exist with the death of the proprietor.

A partnership has the advantage of greater access to financial capital, enabling it to grow and take advantage of economies of scale. Also, profits and losses are shared in a manner prescribed by the articles of partnership, a legal agreement drawn up at the start of the business. Disadvantages include complete and full responsibility on the part of all partners for the partnership's debts. Furthermore, the partnership ceases to exist when a partner dies or withdraws from the business or when a new partner joins the firm. This can make long-term operation of the business difficult.

A corporation is conducted in its own name, not in the name of its owners. The major advantage of a corporation is its limited liability. In the event of bankruptcy, the owners lose only the money they invested, not their personal property. This reduces the risk of investment and increases the corporation's ability to raise financial capital. Other advantages are that the life of the corporation is independent of the life of its owners; ownership rights are easily transferred from seller to buyer; and there is a separation of ownership and management so owners need not devote time to the business in order to reap the rewards of ownership. Disadvantages include the cost of acquiring a chapter; having to report to the chartering agency; having to report to the Securities and Exchange Commission (if enough shares have been issued to the general public); higher interest rates that may have to be paid to secure loans (or owners may be asked to sign for loans in their own names); and the fact that corporate income is taxed twice.

Key Question 2: How do firms raise financial capital?

Firms raise money either from personal savings, business savings (retained earnings), loans from banks, credit unions, friends or relatives, trade credit, or from the sale of stocks and bonds (limited to corporations).

A fundamental difference between selling bonds and selling stock to raise financial capital is that selling bonds is a form of borrowing, whereas selling stock is selling ownership rights to the corporation.

Bonds are considered a relatively safe investment. Selling them enables corporations to obtain financial capital at low interest rates — a major advantage. However, the corporation's fixed interest payments on bonds is a major disadvantage because it limits the firm's control over the use of its revenue.

Corporations usually sell either preferred or common stock. Preferred stock entitles the purchaser to fixed dividends, as long as the corporation makes a profit. If the company earns very large profits, the preferred stockholders continue to receive the same fixed payments — nothing more. Cumulative preferred stock enables stockholders to receive dividends not paid during unprofitable years later on, when the firm becomes profitable again. Convertible preferred stock gives owners the right to convert their preferred stock into common stock. Common stock entitles investors to a share of any profits remaining after all other obligations have been met. Common stockholders can exercise their control over management by electing all or a majority of the company's directors but usually do not. Instead, if they are unhappy with the company they usually sell their stock and invest elsewhere. Because dividends do not have to be paid on common stock, firms have greater flexibility over the disposal of their after-tax profits.

From the investor's point of view, common stock carries the greatest risk of the three types of securities (bonds are the least risky), but also the greatest potential for gain (bonds carry the least potential for gain).

Key Question 3: How do economists calculate profits?

All firms attempt to maximize profits. However, one must distinguish between book profit and economic profit. Economic profit is the amount left after all costs, including the opportunity cost of capital and the risk of losing money, have been deducted from company revenues.

Key Question 4: Is "big business" too big?

The corporate form of business organization dominates the U.S. economy, producing around 88 percent of our national's total output. One should not necessarily conclude, however, that this means consumers must accept higher prices, lower-quality products, or restricted production. Indeed, big business may be more efficient than the other types of business organization. The controversy surrounding big business is not likely to be resolved until we learn more about how the market and political systems operate.

Review Terms and Concepts

Economies of scale
Positive relationship
Inverse relationship

New Terms and Concepts

Proprietorship
Partnership
Corporation
Bond
Preferred stock
Common stock
Book profit
Cumulative preferred stock
Financial cost
Economic profit
Opportunity cost of capital
Risk cost
Economic losses
Articles of partnership
Trade Credit
Effective interest rate
Convertible preferred stock

Completion

The sole proprietorship is a business venture owned and managed by

one ____________________ (one/two or more) individual(s). It accounts for

greatest the ____________________ (greatest/fewest) number of firms in the

United States. The major advantage of a sole proprietorship is the
freedom ____________________ (limited liability/freedom) of the owner. In other
a lot of words, the individual owner has ____________________ (a lot of/very
little) flexibility in terms of production plans, the financing of the business, and the disbursement of profits. However, the disadvantages stem directly from the fact the sole proprietorship is owned by one individual.
limited The size of the firm is ____________________ (limited/unlimited) by the
does not benefit individual's ability to raise money. The owner ____________________
(benefits/does not benefit) from the advice and encouragement of co-
all owners and must assume ____________ (all/some) of the risks of failure.
fully The owner is ________________________ (fully/partially) liable for
all ____________ (all/some) of the firm's debts. If the business fails, the
can owner's personal property ____________________ (can/cannot) be sold
ceases to pay off business debts. The firm ____________________ (continues/
ceases) to exist with the death of the proprietor.

The partnership is a business venture owned and managed by
two or more individuals ____ (a corporation/two or
fewest more individuals). Partnerships account for the ____________________
smallest (greatest/fewest) number of firms and the ______________________
(greatest/smallest) amount of sales receipts (total output) of all firms in the United States. One of the advantages of a partnership is
greater access to financial capital ____ (limited
liability/greater access to financial capital). This enables the firm to grow
economies and take advantage of ____________________ (diseconomies/economies)
of scale. Also, profits and losses are shared in a manner prescribed by the
partnership articles of ______________________ (confederation/partnership), a legal

agreement drawn up at the start of the business. Disadvantages of partner-
all — ships include complete and full responsibility on the part of __________
(all/some) partners for the partnership's debts. The partnership
ceases — ____________________ (ceases/does not cease) to exist when a partner
dies or withdraws from the business. This makes long-term operation of
difficult — the business ____________________ (easier/difficult).

greatest — Corporations account for the ______________________ (greatest/
smallest) percentage of total receipts (output) in the United States and are
their own name — operated in ____________________________________(their
own name/ the name of their owners). The major advantage of a corpora-
limited liability — tion is its ______________________ (size/limited liability). This
reduces — __________________ (increases/reduces) the risk of investment and
increases — __________________ (increases/decreases) the corporation's ability to
raise financial capital. However, because of the corporation's limited
higher — liability, it will probably have to pay a ____________________ (higher/
lower) interest rate to secure loans from creditors. There are other
advantages of incorporating. One is that the life of the company is
independent — __________________ (dependent/independent) of the life of its
are — owners. Ownership rights __________________ (are/are not) easily
is — transferred, and there __________ (is/is not) a separation of ownership
and management. The disadvantages associated with the corporation are
sometimes — __________________ (never/sometimes) greater than the advantages.
is some — There ______________________ (is some/is not any) cost involved in
have — acquiring a charter. Corporations __________________ (have/do not
have) to report to the chartering agency. Also, higher interest rates may

have to be paid to secure loans. Finally, corporate income is taxed
twice | ____________________ (twice/three times).

Firms raise financial capital in many different ways. The method
the sale of stocks and bonds | limited to corporations is ____
(trade credit/the sale of stocks and bonds). When a corporation sells
borrowing | bonds it is really __________________________ (borrowing/selling
long-term | ownership rights). Bonds are __________________________ (long-term/
short-term) debt obligations of a corporation. When an investor is
considering the purchase of a bond he or she must consider the
effective interest rate | ____ (past interest
an inverse | rate/effective interest rate). There is ____________________ (a positive/
an inverse) relationship between the price of a bond and the market interest rate. The effective interest rate equals the stated interest payment
divided | ______________________ (multiplied/divided) by the market price of
safe | the bond. Purchasing bonds is considered a relatively ______________
(risky/safe) investment. Therefore, the potential for gain is relatively
low | _______________ (high/low). A disadvantage of selling bonds to raise
reduce | financial capital is that their fixed interest payments _______________
(increase/reduce) the firm's control over the use of its revenues.

Corporations also sell preferred and common stock. The type of stock
preferred | that pays a fixed dividend is ____________________ (preferred/common)
Common | stock. __________________________ (Preferred/Common) stockholders
are paid after all other debt obligations have been met. Generally,
common | ____________________ (preferred/common) stock is considered a riskier
investment but has the greatest potential for gain. There is also cumulative preferred stock, which enables stockholders to receive dividends that

were not	_______________ (were not/are to be) paid in
unprofitable	_______________ (unprofitable/future) years. Convertible
preferred	preferred stock enables stockholders to convert _______________
common	(preferred/common) stock into _______________ (preferred/ common) stock.
profits	All firms attempt to maximize their _______________ (profits/
is	size). There _______________ (is/is not) a difference between book
Book	profit and economic profit. _______________ (Book/Economic)
economic	profit is greater than _______________ (book/economic) profit.
subtract	This is because we must _______________ (add/subtract) the opportunity cost of capital and risk cost from book profit to arrive at economic profit.
cannot	Economically, we _______________ (can/cannot) conclude that big business is necessarily detrimental to consumer welfare.

Problems and Applications

1. a. Which type of business organization is the most common in the United States? Second most common? Third?
   b. Which type of business organization has the greatest number of sales in the United States? Which has the second greatest number? Third?
   c. Which form of business organization(s) is (are) characterized by limited liability?
   d. Which form of business organization allows the greatest control over managing the business?
   e. Which form of business organization has the greatest opportunity for raising financial capital?
   f. In which form of business organization(s) are the owners not necessarily required to take an active role in management decisions?
   g. In which form of business organization(s) are the rights of ownership and the responsibilities of management clearly separated?

h. The sale of stocks and bonds is limited to which form of business organization?

2. How are corporate profits taxed twice?
3. For each of the following, determine the effective interest rate on the bond.
   a. The stated interest payment is $7, and the market price of the bond is $100.
   b. The stated interest payment is $12, and the market price of the bond is $114.
   c. The stated interest payment is $13, and the market price of the bond is $94.
4. What is the relationship between the price of bonds and market interest rate?
5. a. What is the order of payment to owners of bonds, preferred stock, and common stock? From the investor's point of view, how is this related to the riskiness of each type of investment and the potential for gain?
   b. From the corporation's point of view, what are the major advantages and disadvantages of selling bonds, preferred stock, and common stock?
6. Assume that a firm buys a new office building that costs $1 million. However, this purchase reduces its tax liability by $100,000. What is the financial cost of the new office building?
7. What effect would legislation reducing the number of years over which an asset (such as a piece of equipment) can be depreciated have on a firm's total funds available for reinvestment?

True-False

For each item, determine whether the statement is basically true or false. If the statement is false, rewrite it so it is a true statement.

_____ 1. Most firms are corporations.

_____ 2. The major advantage of sole proprietorships is their limited liability.

_____ 3. The opportunity cost of capital is the return that could have been realized on the best alternative investment not taken.

_____ 4. Because corporations are characterized by limited liability they may have to pay a higher interest rate to secure funds from creditors.

_____ 5. The sale of stocks and bonds is limited to corporations.

_____ 6. From the investor's point of view, common stock is the safest investment, followed by preferred stock and then bonds.

_____ 7. Common stockholders usually exercise their control over management by electing all or a majority of the company's directors.

_____ 8. Economic profit is usually greater than book profit.

_____ 9. Dividends do not have to be paid on preferred stock if the firm is losing money.

_____ 10. Cumulative preferred stock can earn dividends even in unprofitable years, but they are not paid until the firm becomes profitable again.

_____ 11. Economic profit is the amount left after all costs, including the opportunity cost of capital and the risk of losing money, have been deducted from company revenues.

_____ 12. Risk cost is the cost of purchasing a risky security.

_____ 13. Income earned by sole proprietors and partners is taxed as ordinary income by the IRS.

_____ 14. Corporations dominate the U.S. economy because of the ease with which this form of business organization is able to raise financial capital.

Multiple Choice *Choose the one best answer for each item.*

_____ 1. The effective interest rate
   a. is applicable to the decision to purchase common stock.
   b. is equal to the dividend payment divided by the market price of the preferred stock.
   c. is equal to the stated interest payment divided by the market price of the bond.
   d. shows there is a positive relationship between the price of a bond and the interest rate.
   e. is the stated interest payment on a bond.

_____ 2. Trade credit
   a. is a discount for purchasing a large volume.
   b. is credit extended to firms based on a fixed interest rate.
   c. is a loan received from a trade union.
   d. is credit extended when materials and supplies are purchased and immediate payment is not required.
   e. is profit earned by a firm that is not distributed in the form of dividends.

_____ 3. Convertible stock is
   a. common stock that can be easily converted into cash.
   b. preferred stock that can be easily converted into common stock.
   c. preferred stock that can be easily converted into cash.
   d. preferred stock that can be easily converted into bonds.
   e. stock that enables the investor to receive dividends not paid in unprofitable years later, when the corporation becomes profitable again.

_____ 4. Big corporations
   a. are necessarily more efficient.
   b. always increase the price of the product and produce a lower quality product.
   c. are not competitive.
   d. dictate what consumers want and get.
   e. are described by none of the above.

_____ 5. In the event of a corporation's bankruptcy, which of the following would be paid last?
   a. Owners of bonds
   b. Owners of preferred stock
   c. Owners of cumulative preferred stock
   d. Owners of convertible preferred stock
   e. Owners of common stock

_____ 6. Which of the following is an advantage of corporations as opposed to other business organizations?
   a. They have easier access to financial capital.
   b. The owners must devote time to the operation of the business to reap the benefits of ownership.
   c. The life of the firm is dependent upon the life of the owners.
   d. Owners must cooperate and trust each other.
   e. All of the above.

_____ 7. Which of the following statements about the corporation is true?
   a. The rights of ownership and the responsibilities of management are clearly separated.
   b. The creation of the corporation does not require any fees.
   c. Personal property may be used to retire business debt.
   d. Income is treated as ordinary income by the IRS
   e. When the owners dies the business folds.

_____ 8. Which of the following is a difference between bonds and stocks?
   a. Bonds are short-term debt obligations, whereas stocks are long-term debt obligations.

b. Stocks are less risky than bonds.
c. Owners of bonds are entitled to repayment of their funds, but owners of stocks are not.
d. When a bond is sold, money is created, but when a stock is sold, money is destroyed.
e. All of the above.

____ 9. From the investor's point of view, the degree of riskiness, and therefore the potential for gain, from least to greatest is
a. bonds, preferred stock, common stock.
b. preferred stock, common stock, bonds.
c. common stock, preferred stock, bonds.
d. common stock, bonds, preferred stock.
e. bonds, common stock, preferred stock.

____ 10. Critics of big business argue that big business is "bad" because it has the ability to
a. convince consumers what is "best" for them and therefore what they should buy.
b. bribe political officials.
c. spend large amounts on political campaigns.
d. overthrow governments.
e. do all of the above.

____ 11. In which types of business organizations is the owners' personal property subject to confiscation by the court in the event of bankruptcy?
a. Corporations and sole proprietorships
b. Partnerships and sole proprietorships
c. Partnerships and corporations
d. Churches and other nonprofit organizations
e. None of the above

____ 12. Competition is based on
a. the size of firms in the industry.
b. the number of firms in the industry.
c. the legal form of firms in the industry.
d. the amount of advertising in the industry.
e. none of the above.

____ 13. Economic profit is equal to
a. book profit.
b. total revenue minus all costs including the opportunity cost of capital and a risk cost.
c. book profit minus economic losses.

d. the opportunity cost of capital plus risk cost.
e. none of the above.

Discussion Questions

1. In which form of business organization should a person who does not care to become involved in the firm's day-to-day operations invest? *(KQ1)*
2. Can competition in an industry be judged by the number or size of firms in the industry? *(KQ4)*
3. Can you think of any reasons why a sole proprietor may wish to remain in business even if he or she is not earning as much income as could be made elsewhere? *(KQ1)*
4. What do you see as the pros and cons of big business? Do you think the government can or should correct for any of these problems? *(KQ4)*

Answers

Problems and Applications

1. a. The greatest number of firms are sole proprietorships, followed by corporations. The fewest number of firms are partnerships.
   b. The greatest number of sales are made by corporations, followed by sole proprietorships. Partnerships make the fewest sales.
   c. corporation
   d. sole proprietorship
   e. corporation
   f. partnership and the corporation
   g. corporation
   h. corporation
2. Corporate profits are taxed first as the income of the corporation and later, if dividends are distributed to owners, as the personal income of the owners.
3. a. 7 percent
   b. 10.5 percent
   c. 13.8 percent
4. The relationship is inverse.
5. a. Bondholders are entitled to repayment of funds invested in the corporation and are paid even when the corporation is losing

money. Therefore, bonds are the least risky investment, and the potential for gain is the lowest. Preferred stock entitles owners to a fixed dividend, but only when the firm is earning a profit and after the interest on the corporation's bonds have been paid. Common stock is the riskiest investment because it represents residual claim to ownership. Dividends are paid only after all other debts of the corporation have been paid. Furthermore, dividends are not fixed. They can vary from nothing to a very high return, depending on the firm's profitability and plans for reinvestment of its profits. However, common stockholders stand to gain the most. In sum, risk and the potential for gain are directly (positively) related.

b. Bonds have the advantage of being easily sold (because they are such a safe investment), but the disadvantage is that their fixed interest payments reduce the firm's discretion over how to use its revenues. Preferred stocks have the advantage of being a means of raising funds that need not be repaid. The disadvantage of preferred stock is that part of the firm's aftertax profits are committed to dividends and cannot be reinvested. Common stocks have the advantage of maximum flexibility in the disposal of after-tax profits but the disadvantage of being relatively more difficult to sell.

6. Financial cost is the expense minus the reduction in taxes the company realizes because of the expenditure. Therefore, the financial cost of the new office building is $900,000.
7. Legislation that reduces the number of years over which an asset can be depreciated raises the depreciation expense, reducing the firm's profits on paper but increasing the total funds (after-tax profits plus depreciation) available for reinvestment.

True-False

1. F: Most firms are sole proprietorships.
2. F: The major advantage of sole proprietorships is the owner's flexibility to do within the bounds of the law and the forces of competition what he or she wants.
3. T
4. T
5. T
6. F: From the investor's point of view, bonds are the safest investment, followed by preferred stock and then common stock.

7. F: Common stockholders usually do not exercise their control over management by electing all or a majority of the company's directors, but instead, if they are unhappy with the company they will sell their stock and invest elsewhere.
8. F: Book profit is usually greater than economic profit.
9. T
10. T
11. T
12. F: Risk cost is the loss that can be anticipated because of the failure of a certain percentage of a firm's ventures.
13. T
14. T

Multiple Choice

1. c *(KQ2)*
2. d *(KQ2)*
3. b *(KQ2)*
4. e *(KQ4)*
5. e *(KQ2)*
6. a *(KQ1)*
7. a *(KQ1)*
8. c *(KQ2)*
9. a *(KQ2)*
10. e *(KQ4)*
11. b *(KQ1)*
12. e *(KQ4)*
13. b *(KQ3)*

CHAPTER 20

Cost and Producer Choice

Chapter Summary

Key Question 1: What is the difference between an explicit and an implicit cost?

Key Question 2: What is marginal cost?

In Chapters 17 and 18, we looked at rational consumer behavior. This chapter looks at rational behavior from the producer's point of view. Like all rational behavior, rational production decisions require careful calculation of both costs and benefits. Not all costs are obvious, however. Obvious out-of-pocket costs are called explicit costs. Costs that measure the foregone opportunity to acquire or do something are called implicit costs. Although implicit costs may not be recognized, they are often larger than explicit costs. Explicit and implicit costs combine to form total costs. When evaluating the total costs of a decision, sunk costs (costs that have already been incurred because of past decisions) should be ignored because they cannot be altered by current decisions.

The rational person must also consider the marginal, or additional, cost incurred by producing one additional unit of a good, service, or activity. Marginal cost may be constant or rising as the level of output (production) expands. It can increase as output increases for two reasons: because the producer's opportunity cost of time increases and/or because of the law of diminishing marginal returns.

The law of diminishing marginal returns states that when at least one resource is fixed (cannot be varied) and greater amounts of a variable resource (for example, labor) are added to the production process, then at some point the additions to the output level begin to diminish. The law of diminishing marginal returns applies to any production process, although the output level at which it becomes operative depends on what is being produced and the methods of production used.

Once diminishing marginal returns set in, the marginal product of the variable resource added starts decreasing. In other words, once diminishing marginal returns set in, the extra output associated with each additional unit of the variable resource added declines. If each unit of a variable resource added to the production process adds less to the output level than the unit added before it, then successively larger additions of the variable resource will be required to produce constant increases in the output level. In other words, if each additional unit of output now requires more resources to be produced — if diminishing marginal returns have set in — then marginal cost rises. If marginal cost is rising as output expands, it is expressed graphically as an upward-sloping curve.

Key Question 3: How is the difference between total benefits and total costs maximized?

We can combine the producer's marginal cost curve with the consumer's marginal benefit (demand) curve and determine the quantity of the good, service, or activity that maximizes welfare. The quantity that maximizes welfare occurs where the two curves intersect, because at this point the marginal benefits of the last unit consumed just equal the marginal cost of producing that last unit. Any quantity below this level shows that the marginal benefits of consuming this good, service, or activity exceed the marginal cost of producing this good, service, or activity. Therefore, people's welfare would be increased through increased production and consumption. On the other hand, any quantity above the point of intersection between the marginal cost and demand curves shows that marginal cost of production exceeds marginal benefits of consumption and therefore people could gain from less production and consumption.

Key Question 4: How are profits maximized?

Rational production decisions also require careful calculation of benefits. Most business people measure the benefits of production from the revenues that are generated. Marginal revenue measures the additional revenue (extra benefit) a firm acquires by selling an additional unit of output. We have seen that marginal cost measures the extra cost of producing an additional unit of output. Therefore, the rational producer will produce that quantity of output where marginal revenue (the extra benefit) is just equal to marginal cost (the extra costs). By producing where marginal revenue equals marginal cost, a business will maximize its profits. This is because at any output level below this point marginal revenue exceeds marginal cost, and an increase in the output level will cause revenues to rise more than costs and therefore profits to rise. On the other hand, it the producer increases the output level above the point where marginal revenue equals marginal cost, then marginal cost exceeds marginal revenue. Therefore the firm will be adding more to costs than to revenues, and profits will fall.

The upward-sloping portion of a firm's marginal cost curve is the firm's supply curve. This can be most readily seen if we assume that the firm can

Key Question 5: What is the relationship between individual supply curves and the market supply curve?

sell all it wishes at a particular price. In such a case, the marginal revenue curve becomes a horizontal line at that price. Where the marginal revenue and marginal cost curves intersect they are equal and indicate the profit-maximizing output level. If price rises, so does the horizontal marginal revenue curve (because price equals marginal revenue) and the new point of intersection between the marginal revenue and marginal cost curves indicates the new profit-maximizing output level. (Both profits and the output level will be greater.) In this way, by reading off of the upward-sloping portion of the firm's marginal cost curve we can determine how much the firm should produce at any price. Hence, the upward-sloping portion of the firm's marginal cost curve is the firm's supply curve.

Quite often we are not interested just in one firm's supply curve but in the market supply curve as well. Because the market supply curve is the amount all producers are willing to produce at various prices, we can obtain it by adding together (horizontally summing) the upward-sloping portions of all firms' marginal cost curves in the market. When we do, we find that the market supply curve lies farther from the origin and is flatter than individual producers' supply curves.

Review Terms and Concepts

Rational behavior
Opportunity cost
Cost-benefit analysis
Supply
Market supply
Price
Marginal utility
Law of diminishing marginal utility
Demand
Market demand

New Terms and Concepts

Explicit cost
Implicit cost
Sunk cost
Marginal cost
Law of diminishing marginal returns
Marginal product
Marginal revenue
Fixed resource
Variable resource

Completion

the same

Rational behavior is basically ________________ (different/the same) for consumers and producers. Each must weigh the benefits and costs

	of a decision. However, one difference between them is that consumers
utility	attempt to maximize their ________________ (utility/employment),
profits	whereas producers attempt to maximize their ________________
	(revenues/profits). Producers maximize their profits by maximizing the
total revenue	difference between ____________________ (total revenue/marginal
total cost	revenue) and ________________ (total cost/marginal cost). They do
marginal revenue	this by equating ______________________ (total revenue/marginal
marginal cost	revenue) with ____________________ (total cost/marginal cost).
	Any rational decision requires careful calculation of both costs and
are not	benefits. All costs ________________ (are/are not) obvious. Costs that
explicit	are obvious are called ________________ (explicit/implicit) costs.
	Those costs that measure the foregone opportunity to acquire or do some-
implicit	thing are called ________________ (explicit/implicit) costs. When
total	explicit and implicit costs are added together, we get ____________
	(marginal/total) costs. When evaluating the total costs of a decision, sunk
should not	costs ____________________ (should/should not) be considered. A
	rational person should not only consider the total costs of a decision but
marginal	also the ______________ (marginal/sunk) costs. A cost that measures
	the additional cost incurred by producing one additional unit of a good,
marginal	service, or activity is ________________ (marginal/total) cost.
	Marginal cost may be constant or rising. Marginal cost can increase as
producer's	output increases either because the ________________ (consumer's/
increases	producer's) opportunity cost of time________________ (increases/
returns	decreases) or because of the law of diminishing marginal __________
	(returns/utility).

	The law of diminishing marginal returns states that when at least one
	resource is fixed and greater amounts of a variable resource (such as
added to	labor) are ______________ (added to/subtracted from) the production
	process, then at some point the additions to the output level begin to
decrease	______________ (increase/decrease). The law of diminishing marginal
all	returns applies to ________________ (many but not all/all) production
	processes.
	Once diminishing marginal returns set in, then the extra output as-
	sociated with each additional unit of the variable resource added
decreases	________________ (increases/decreases). This is the same as saying the
decreasing	marginal product of the variable resource is ________________
	(increasing/decreasing). If each unit of the variable resource added to the
	production process adds less to the output level than the unit added
larger	before it, then successively ______________ (smaller/larger) additions
	of the variable resource will be required to produce constant increases in
	the output level. If this happens, then we can say that each additional unit
more	of output now requires ________________ (more/fewer) resources to be
	produced. If each additional unit of output requires more resources to be
rising	produced, then marginal cost must be ____________________ (falling/
	remaining the same/rising). If marginal cost is rising, then the marginal
positive	cost curve will have a __________________ (negative/positive) slope.
	In sum, at the output level at which the law of diminishing marginal
	returns becomes operative, the marginal product of the variable resource
decline	added begins to ______________ (rise/decline) and this causes mar-
rise	ginal cost to begin to ______________ (rise/fall).

can — We ______________ (can/cannot) combine the producer's marginal cost curve with the consumer's marginal benefits (demand) curve and determine the quantity of the good, service, or activity that maximizes welfare. That quantity that maximizes welfare occurs when the demand

intersects — curve ______________ (lies above/intersects/lies below) the marginal cost curve. If the demand curve lies above the marginal cost curve, then

exceed — marginal benefits ____________________ (exceed/equal/are less than)

more — marginal cost and therefore welfare could be increased if ____________ (more/less) was produced and consumed. This occurs at a quantity

below — demanded and supplied ______________ (below/above) the optimal. If the demand curve lies below the marginal cost curve, then the quantity

above — demanded and supplied is ________________ (above/below) that which maximizes welfare. This is because marginal benefits are

less than — ____________________ (greater than/less than) marginal cost, and

less — welfare could be increased if ________________ (more/less) was produced and consumed.

Any rational production decision requires careful calculation of both costs and benefits. The measure of extra (or additional) costs is

marginal cost — ________________________ (marginal cost/marginal revenue).

Marginal revenue — ________________________ (Marginal revenue/Total revenue) is a business person's measure of the extra revenues (benefits) from the sale of an additional unit of output. A rational producer will continue to

marginal revenue — produce until ____________________ (marginal revenue/total revenue)

marginal cost — is just equal to ______________________ (marginal cost/total cost) because this maximizes profits. If marginal revenue exceeds marginal

below — cost, then the output level is ______________ (above/below) the

	profit-maximizing level. If the firm increased its output level, it would be
revenues	adding more to ____________________ (costs/revenues) than to
costs	________________ (costs/revenues). If marginal cost exceeds marginal
costs	revenue, then the firm is adding more to __________________ (costs/
revenues	revenues) than to ____________________ (costs/revenues), and the out-
above	put level is ______________ (above/below) the profit-maximizing level.
upward	The firm's supply curve is the __________________ (downward/
marginal cost	upward) -sloping portion of its _______________________ (marginal
	cost/total profit) curve. This is because if price equals marginal revenues,
marginal cost	then at any price we can read off of the _______________________
	(marginal cost/marginal revenue) curve and determine the quantity the
	firm would produce. If the price rises, then the quantity produced and
rise	made available in the market will ______________ (rise/fall). If the
	price falls, then the quantity produced and made available in the market
fall	will _____________ (rise/fall).
	To determine the market supply curve we would have to
horizontally	_________________________ (vertically/horizontally) sum all firms'
is	upward-sloping marginal cost curves. This process _______________
	(is/is not) similar to the way in which we derived the market demand
farther from	curve. We find that the market supply curve lies __________________
flatter	(closer to/farther from) the origin and is __________________ (steeper/
	flatter) than individual producers' supply curves.

Problems and Applications

1. Many people search out and purchase "bargains" at garage and yard sales. What are some implicit costs associated with this type of shopping?
2. Why might a carnival or amusement park remain open on a rainy day when very few customers are expected?

3. If marginal cost is constant at $100 over some relevant range of output, how would the marginal cost curve look graphically over this range of output?
4. a. Fill in the marginal product of each worker and marginal cost columns based on the information given in the following production schedule.

Number of Workers	Total Product (Output) of All Workers	Marginal Product of Each Worker	Total Cost	Marginal Cost
1	1.0		$ 30	
2	2.5		$ 50	
3	3.9		$ 90	
4	5.2		$150	
5	6.4		$230	

   b. Graphically express marginal cost for this production process. At which output level does marginal cost begin to rise? How is this related to the marginal product of workers and the law of diminishing marginal returns?
   c. Assume this firm can sell all it wants at a price of $60. What is the marginal revenue from any additional unit sold for this firm? Graph this firm's marginal revenue curve on the same graph you used for the marginal cost curve earlier.
   d. What output level should this firm produce to maximize profits? Explain.
   e. The profit from the production and sale of any output level equals total revenue minus total cost. We are given the total cost of producing the various output levels shown. Total revenue equals the price for which the output level is sold multiplied by the quantity sold. Assume the firm can sell as much as it wants at a price of $60. Calculate the profit at each of the various output levels shown. At which output level are profits maximized? Why are this output level and the answer to question 4d the same? Graph total profit against the quantity produced.
5. For each of the following situations, determine whether a producer should increase, decrease, or keep its production (output) level the same to maximize profits.
   a. Marginal revenue exceeds marginal cost.
   b. Marginal revenue equals marginal cost.
   c. Marginal cost exceeds marginal revenue.

6. a. Does a demand curve for any good, service, or activity measure the marginal benefits from the consumption of that good, service, or activity at various quantities? What is the relationship between the price of that good, service, or activity and the quantity demanded? Graph this relationship.
   b. Graph a marginal cost curve for any good, service, or activity on the same graph you used to answer question 6a.
   c. If marginal benefits exceed marginal cost, is welfare being maximized or should consumption and production be increased or decreased? On the graph you have used to draw the demand and marginal cost curves indicate a quantity that expresses the situation.
   d. If marginal cost exceeds marginal benefits, is welfare being maximized or should consumption and production be increased or decreased? On the graph you have used to draw the demand and marginal cost curves indicate a quantity that expresses the situation.
   e. If marginal cost equals marginal benefits, is welfare being maximized or should consumption and production be increased or decreased? On the graph you have used to draw the demand and marginal cost curves indicate a quantity that expresses the situation.
7. Which portion of a firm's marginal cost curve is its supply curve?
8. How is a market supply curve derived? How is it distinguished from individual producers' supply curves?

True-False

For each item, determine whether the statement is basically true or false. If the statement is false, rewrite it so it is a true statement.

_____ 1. Marginal cost begins to rise when the law of diminishing returns sets in, causing the marginal product of the variable resource added to the production process to decline.

_____ 2. The law of diminishing marginal returns applies to every production process.

_____ 3. If the demand curve for a good, service, or activity lies above its marginal cost curve, then marginal benefits exceed marginal cost.

_____ 4. Implicit costs are more easily recognized than explicit costs.

_____ 5. Sunk costs are costs that begin to rise after the law of diminishing marginal returns sets in.

_____ 6. The marginal cost curve begins to slope upward when the marginal product of a variable resource added to the production process begins to decline.

_____ 7. If a firm can sell all it wishes at a constant price, marginal revenue decreases as more is sold.

_____ 8. If marginal revenue exceeds marginal cost, the firm should decrease its output level to maximize profits.

_____ 9. The market supply curve is steeper than an individual producer's supply curve and lies farther from the origin.

_____ 10. The upward-sloping portion of a firm's marginal cost curve is its demand curve.

_____ 11. Rational production decisions require careful calculations of both costs and benefits.

_____ 12. The marginal cost curve slopes upward because of the law of diminishing marginal returns.

_____ 13. If the marginal product of the variable resources is declining, then more resources will be required to produce constant increases in the output level, and this is why marginal costs are rising.

Multiple Choice *Choose the one best answer for each item.*

_____ 1. Sunk costs
a. should be ignored in current decisions.
b. increase as output increases.
c. decrease as output increases.
d. can be altered by current decisions.
e. are implicit costs.

_____ 2. The law of diminishing marginal returns states that when at least one resource is fixed and greater amounts of a variable resource are
a. added to the production process, then at some point the additions to the output level begin to rise.
b. added to the production process, then at some point the additions to the output level begin to fall.
c. taken away from the production process, then at some point the decreases in the output level begin to rise.
d. taken away from the production process, then at some point the decreases in the output level begin to fall.
e. none of the above.

_____ 3. If a firm can sell all it would like at a given price and that price falls, then

a. marginal revenue increases.
b. a higher output level should be produced to maximize profits.
c. the total profit curve will fall.
d. the marginal cost falls.
e. none of the above.

_____ 4. Just as the law of diminishing marginal utility explains why the demand curve slopes downward, the law of diminishing marginal returns explains

a. why the marginal cost curve slopes upward.
b. why an individual producer's supply curve slopes upward.
c. why the market supply curve slopes upward.
d. all of the above.
e. none of the above.

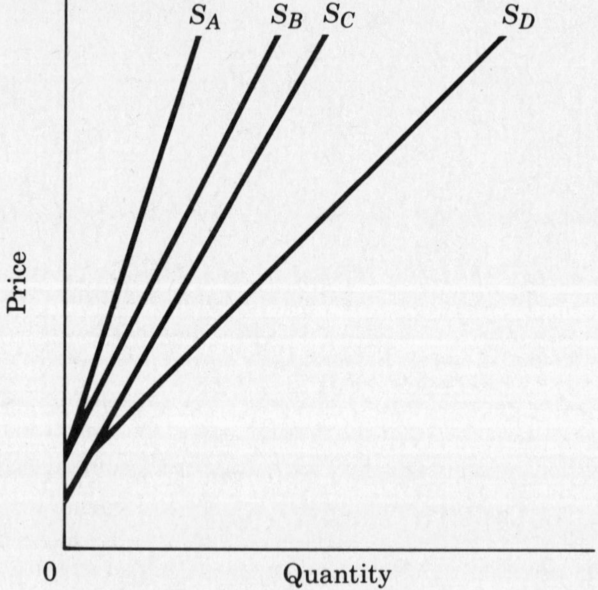

_____ 5. Based on the preceding graph, which of the following supply curves is most likely a market supply curve?

a. S_A
b. S_B
c. S_C

d. S_D
e. All of the above are equally likely to be market supply curves.

_____ 6. If marginal benefits exceed marginal cost for any good, service or activity, then
a. more should be produced and consumed.
b. less should be produced and consumed.
c. welfare is maximized.
d. the demand curve lies above the marginal cost curve.
e. both a and d.

_____ 7. A market supply curve is derived from individual producers' marginal curves by
a. vertically summing all firms' upward-sloping marginal cost curves.
b. horizontally summing all firms' upward-sloping marginal cost curves.
c. horizontally summing all firms' downward-sloping marginal cost curves.
d. vertically summing all firms' downward-sloping marginal cost curves.
e. any of the above methods.

_____ 8. Firms should attempt to
a. equate marginal revenue and marginal cost.
b. maximize their profits.
c. measure all benefits and costs of a decision.
d. include implicit costs and ignore sunk costs in their decisions.
e. do all of the above.

_____ 9. Marginal cost may vary with output because
a. of the law of diminishing marginal utility.
b. the opportunity cost of producers' time may increase.
c. the opportunity cost of consumers' time may increase.
d. of sunk costs.
e. of the law of increasing marginal returns.

_____ 10. The profit on any unit produced can be obtained by
a. subtracting total revenue from total cost.
b. subtracting total cost from total revenue.
c. adding marginal revenue and marginal cost.
d. subtracting marginal revenue from marginal cost.
e. subtracting marginal cost from marginal revenue.

_____ 11. "Bargains" may be more expensive than one realizes because
  a. of the opportunity cost of time.
  b. of the opportunity cost of transportation.
  c. the explicit costs of nonsale items may be marked down.
  d. the cost of acquiring information on sales items is free.
  e. of both a and b.

_____ 12. Any firm will maximize profits when
  a. marginal revenue equals marginal cost.
  b. marginal revenue exceeds marginal cost.
  c. marginal cost exceeds marginal revenue.
  d. total revenue equals total cost.
  e. sunk costs are zero.

_____ 13. Marginal cost may be decreasing due to
  a. diminishing marginal returns.
  b. diminishing marginal product of a variable resource.
  c. economics of specialization.
  d. increasing marginal revenue.
  e. none of the above.

Discussion Question

1. How is rational behavior on the part of producers similar to rational behavior on the part of consumers? How is it different? *(KQ1-5. See also Chapters 17 and 18.)*
2. Assume a college installed lights in its football stadium so that one game could be played live at night on television. Also assume that ticket sales are not affected by whether kickoff time is in the afternoon or in the evening. In later seasons would it be advisable for the kickoff times to be rescheduled for the evening so that more use may be gotten out of the lights? *(KQ1)*
3. Consider a competitive market for any good or service. Does the competitive interaction between demand and supply maximize people's welfare? That is, do marginal benefits just equal marginal costs? *(KQ3)*
4. Consider the production of any good or service. Which resources (inputs into the production process) are fixed resources and which are variable? What determines which are fixed and which are variable? *(KQ2)*

5. Do you think the point at which the law of diminishing returns begins to operate in the production process depends on how many resources are fixed? *(KQ2)*

Answers

Problems and Applications

1. Implicit costs include the time spent and gasoline used traveling from one garage sale to another. Also, there is no guarantee how long these used items may last. After all this is considered, the items purchased at garage sales may not be such bargains after all.
2. Because both the cost of a carnival traveling to and setting up in a particular town and the construction of an amusement park are sunk costs. In both cases these costs should be ignored in the decision to remain open on a rainy day. All that is required to justify remaining open is that revenues be sufficient to cover out-of-pocket costs. If revenues are more than sufficient, then they can be applied toward the retirement of sunk costs. If the carnival or park closes for the day, they will not earn any revenues.
3. The marginal cost curve would be expressed graphically as a horizontal line at $100.

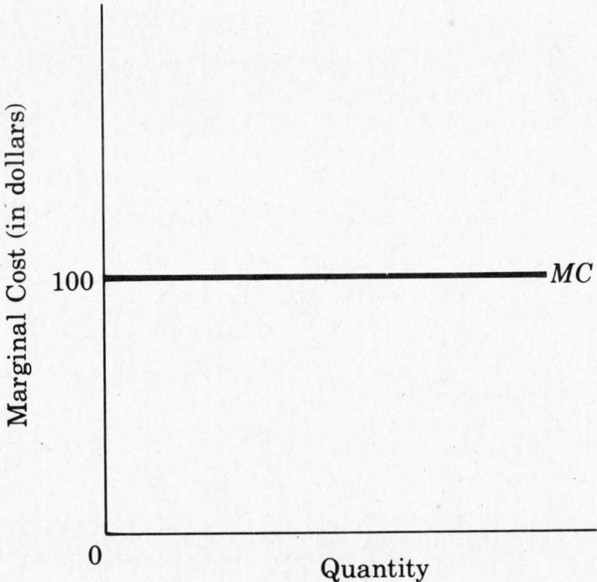

4. a.

Marginal Product of Each Worker	Marginal Cost
1.0	\$30
1.5	\$20
1.4	\$40
1.3	\$60
1.2	\$80

b. Marginal cost begins to rise with 2.5 units produced. This is the same output level at which each additional worker added has a diminishing marginal product. Therefore, the law of diminishing marginal returns sets in after the second worker. When diminishing marginal returns set in, then the marginal product of workers declines and marginal cost begins to rise.

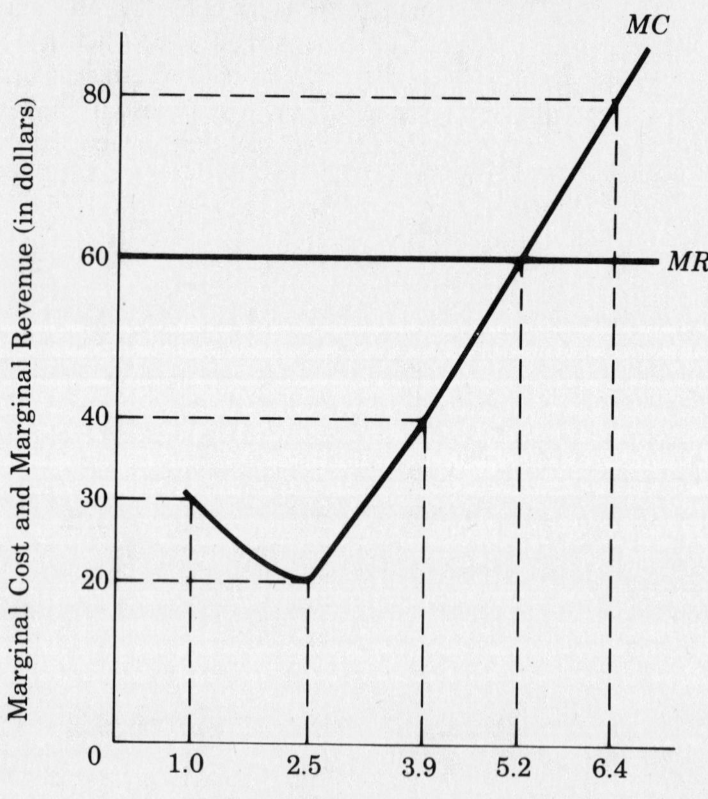

c. Marginal revenue equals $60 from any additional unit sold. This firm's marginal revenue curve would be a horizontal line at a price of $60, meaning that the extra revenue from the sale of any additional unit sold would equal $60.

d. This firm should produce 5.2 units to maximize profits, because that is the output level at which marginal revenue equals marginal cost. In terms of the graph, the marginal revenue and marginal cost curves intersect and are therefore equal at any output level of 5.2 units. At an output level below 5.2 units, marginal revenue exceeds marginal cost. An increase in the output level will cause revenues to rise more than costs and therefore profits to rise. On the other hand, and expansion of output beyond 5.2 units will cause costs to rise more than revenues (because marginal cost exceeds marginal revenue) and therefore profits to fall.

e.

Price	Total Product (Output) of All Workers	Total Revenue	Total Cost	Profits
$60	1.0	$ 60	$ 30	$ 30
$60	2.5	$150	$ 50	$100
$60	3.9	$234	$ 90	$144
$60	5.2	$312	$150	$162
$60	6.4	$384	$230	$154

Profits are maximized at the output level of 5.2. This is the same output that maximized profits when marginal revenue and marginal cost were equated. That is, when marginal revenue equals marginal cost, total revenue exceeds total cost by the greatest amount and profits are maximized. Marginal revenue measures the increase in total revenue and marginal cost measures the increase in total cost as output rises. If marginal revenue exceeds marginal cost (which occurs at an output level below 5.2), then an increase in the output level causes total revenue to rise more than total cost. Therefore, profits rise. On the other hand, if marginal cost exceeds marginal revenue (which occurs at an output level above 5.2), then an increase in the output level causes total costs to rise more than total revenue. Therefore profits fall. (See graph on the top of page 360.)

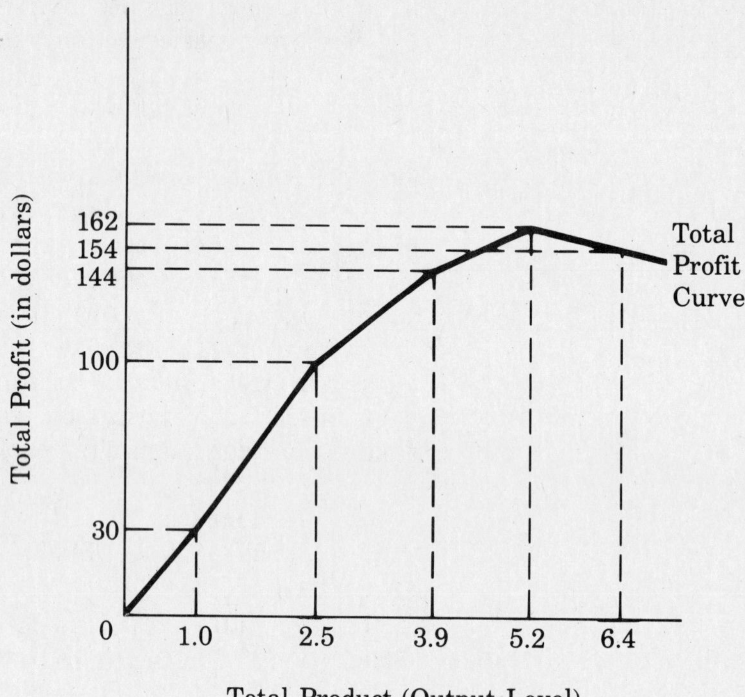

5. a. Increase
   b. Keep the same
   c. Decrease
6. a. Yes. The relationship between the price and quantity demanded is inverse.

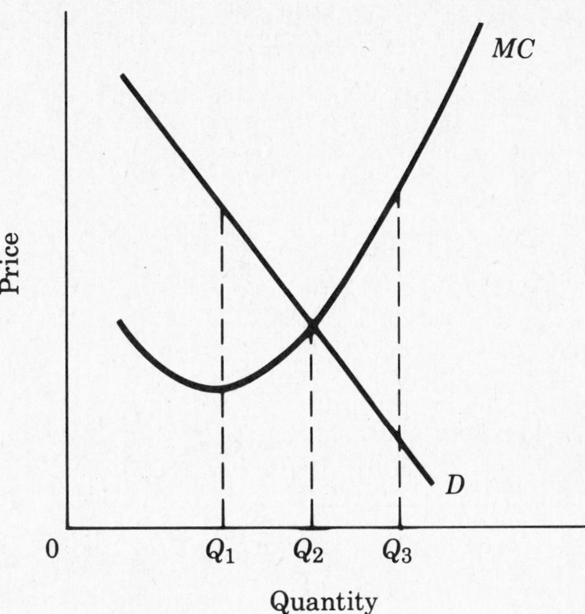

b. See the preceding graph.
c. Consumption and production should be increased to maximize welfare until marginal benefits equal marginal cost. In the preceding graph at Q_1, the demand (marginal benefits) curve lies above the marginal cost curve and therefore consumption and production should be increased until Q_2 is reached, where marginal benefits equal marginal cost.
d. Consumption and production should be decreased to maximize welfare until marginal benefits equal marginal cost. At Q_3 in the preceding graph the marginal cost curve lies above the demand (marginal benefits) curve and therefore consumption and production should be decreased until Q_2 is reached, where marginal cost equals marginal benefits.
e. Welfare is maximized when marginal benefits equal marginal cost. This occurs at Q_2 in the preceding graph.

7. The upward-sloping portion. Because by reading off of the marginal cost curve at any price we determine the profit-maximizing output level for the firm.

8. A market supply curve is derived by horizontally summing all individual firms' upward-sloping marginal cost curves. That is, the market supply curve is derived by adding together the quantities produced by all firms at various prices. The market supply curve can be distinguished from individual producers' supply curves because it lies farther from the origin and is flatter.

True-False

1. T 2. T 3. T
4. F: Explicit costs are more easily recognized than implicit costs.
5. F: Sunk costs are costs that have already been incurred by past decisions and cannot be altered by present decisions.
6. T
7. F: If a firm can sell all it would like at a constant price, marginal revenue is constant (and equal to that price) as more is sold.
8. F: If marginal revenue exceeds marginal cost, the firm should increase its output level to maximize profits.
9. F: The market supply curve is flatter than an individual producer's supply curve and lies farther from the origin.
10. F: The upward-sloping portion of a firm's marginal cost curve is its supply curve.
11. T 12. T 13. T

Multiple Choice

1. a *(KQ1)* 2. b *(KQ2)* 3. c *(KQ4)*
4. d *(KQ2, 4, 5)* 5. d *(KQ5)* 6. e *(KQ3)*
7. b *(KQ5)* 8. e *(KQ1, 3, 4)* 9. b *(KQ2)*
10. e *(KQ4)* 11. e *(KQ1)* 12. a *(KQ4)*
13. c *(KQ2)*

CHAPTER 21

Cost in the Short Run and the Long Run

Chapter Summary

Key Question 1: What are short-run costs?

Key Question 2: How are cost curves drawn for the short run?

Practically all firms, whether they are operating within a competitive or a monopolistic market environment, are faced with basically the same general cost structure in both the short and the long run. In the short run, because at least one resource is fixed, the firm will have some fixed costs (*FC*) that do not vary with the level of output. Those costs that do vary with the level of output (*VC*). Together, fixed and variable costs equal total costs (*TC*). Graphically, fixed costs are expressed as a horizontal line. The total cost curve begins at the same point as the fixed cost curve and slopes upward. The vertical distance between the two curves equals variable costs at any output level.

To determine a firm's profit-maximizing (loss-minimizing) production level and the actual level of profits (or losses) earned, we need four additional measures of cost: marginal cost (*MC*), average fixed cost (*AFC*), average variable cost (*AVC*), and average total cost (*ATC*). (The three average cost measures really measure the per unit cost of production at any output level.) Together, these four cost measures cover all costs associated with production, including risk cost and opportunity cost in the short run.

MC equals the change in total cost divided by the change in quantity produced. Alternatively, it equals the change in variable cost divided by the change in the quantity produced (because the difference between *TC* and *VC* is *FC*, and *FC* is constant as output changes). *MC* begins to rise when the law of diminishing returns sets in — when the marginal productivity of variable resources added to the production process begins to decline. Graphically, the curve takes on a U-shape, described in the last chapter.

AFC, at any output level, equals total *FC* divided by the quantity produced. Because *FC* is indeed fixed, *AFC* decreases as the quantity produced increases. This is why the *AFC* curve slopes downward (but never reaches zero).

AVC, at any output level, equals total *VC* divided by the quantity produced. Graphically, the *AVC* curve takes on a U-shape. At an output of one unit, *AVC* necessarily equals *MC*. At first, as output increases *MC* falls below *AVC*, pulling *AVC* down. After the law of diminishing returns sets in, *MC* begins to rise. However, because *MC* is still below *AVC*, *AVC* continues to fall. As the output level continues to increase, then at some production level they become equal and intersect on the graph. As output and *MC* continue to rise past this point of intersection, *MC* becomes greater than *AVC*, pulling *AVC* up. Therefore, the low point on the *AVC* curve is where the *MC* curve intersects the *AVC* curve .

ATC, at any output level, equals *TC* (*FC* plus *VC*) divided by the quantity produced. Graphically, the *ATC* curve is U-shaped for the same reason the *AVC* curve is U-shaped. When *MC* is below *ATC*, *MC* pulls *ATC* down. When *MC* equals *ATC*, they intersect on the graph. As *MC* continues to rise as the production level rises, it pulls *ATC* up. Therefore, just as with the *AVC* curve, the *MC* curve intersects the *ATC* curve at its low point.

Because $AFC = ATC - AVC$, the vertical distance between the *ATC* curve and the *AVC* curve equals *AFC* at any output level. Therefore, the *AFC* curve is usually not presented graphically when the *ATC* and *AVC* curves are present.

Key Question 3: What are the main characteristics of long-run costs?

In the long run, all resources are variable resources. Therefore, there are no fixed costs. Firms, for example, have the ability to alter their plant size. A short-run *ATC* curve represents only one possible scale of operation. As the plant size (scale of operation) changes, so do the firm's marginal and per unit costs. At first, larger plant sizes reduce *ATC* because of economies of scale. Economies of scale enable firms to produce more at lower average total costs and are basically a result of greater specialization of labor and management skills. However, as the scale of operation continues to increase, eventually diseconomies of scale set in, causing higher marginal and per unit average costs of production. Diseconomies of scale set in if people at the top of the business organization lose contact with or control over the people below them. This is reflected as an *ATC* curve that lies father to the right and above those *ATC* curves associated with smaller scales of operation.

Firms choose the scale of operation that minimizes *ATC* in producing an output level they can expect to sell profitably. If a higher level of output is expected to sell profitably, then in the long run, a larger scale of operation may be chosen. By assuming an infinite (or nearly infinite) number of different output levels and associated scales of operation that minimize *ATC*, we get the long-run average total cost curve (*LRAC*). The *LRAC* curve is really an envelope curve encompassing many different scales of operation and their associated short run *ATC* curves.

Like short-run *ATC* curves, the *LRAC* curve has an accompanying long-run marginal cost *(LRMC)* curve. If *LRAC* is falling, it is because *LRMC* is below *LRAC*, pulling it down. If *LRAC* is rising, it is because *LRMC* is above *LRAC*, pulling it up. On a graph, the *LRMC* curve intersects the *LRAC* curve at its minimum point. This is why the *LRAC* curve is U-shaped.

The downward-sloping portion of a firm's *LRAC* curve shows economies of scale, whereas the upward-sloping portion reflects diseconomies of scale. Not all firms experience the same degrees of economies and diseconomies of scale. The degree of economies and diseconomies of scale associated with the production of different goods and services helps explain the number and size of firms in different industries. For instance, some firms may experience extensive economies of scale over a large range of output. This would be expressed graphically as a long, downward-sloping *LRAC* curve. In such a case we would expect very few producers operating on a very large scale. If the economies of scale are great enough, the industry may be characterized by a natural monopoly (such as an electric utility company). In other words, given an industry's cost structure, one firm may be able to expand its scale of operation, lower its per-unit costs, and thereby underprice other firms that attempt to produce on a lower, higher-cost scale.

Key Question 4: What causes cost curves to shift?

In the short run, given a change in a firm's fixed or variable resource cost, we can predict the effect of changes in *FC* or *VC* on the production decision of a firm. We know that any firm will maximize profits (or minimize losses) by producing that quantity where marginal revenue equals *MC*. However, if a firm can sell all it likes at a constant price (*P*), then marginal revenue equals price. Therefore, the firm will produce where $MC = P$. If *MC* changes, then the output of the firm will change. If *MC* increases (decreases), then the *MC* curve shifts upward (downward), and the profit-maximizing output level falls (rises). Therefore, if *VC* increases (decreases), then the *MC* curve — as well as the *AVC* and *ATC* curves — shifts upward (downward) and less (more) will be produced by the firm. (A change in *VC* leaves *FC* and therefore *AFC* unaffected.) However, a change in *FC* has no effect on *MC* and therefore does not alter a firm's production decision — even though an increase (decrease) in *FC* will increase (decrease) *ATC* and therefore shift the curve upward (downward). (A change in *FC* leaves *VC* and therefore *AVC* unaffected.)

In the long run, all costs are variable costs. Therefore, a change in the price of any resource will affect a firm's production decision. However, long-run changes in the output level of firms affects the market price of the final product as well as consumer purchases. This complicates our predictions somewhat and will be investigated later.

Our entire discussion has assumed that costs were minimized at any output level. With the aid of isoquant and isocost analysis we can determine the least-cost combination of resources to employ in producing any output level in either the short or the long run.

Review Terms and Concepts

Risk cost
Opportunity cost
Marginal cost
Law of diminishing marginal returns
Marginal product
Economies of scale
Diseconomies of scale
Fixed resource
Variable resource
Marginal revenue

New Terms and Concepts

Short run
Fixed cost
Variable cost
Total cost
Cost structure
Average fixed cost
Average variable cost
Average total cost
Long run
Natural monopoly
Isoquant curve
Isocost curve

Completion

alike

Basically, all firms' cost structures are ______________ (alike/different) in both the short and the long run. In other words, in both the short and

the same

the long run, firms' cost curves look basically __________________ (the same/ different). In the short run, this is because firms are confronted

returns

with the law of diminishing marginal __________________

decline

(utility/returns). This causes marginal productivity to _______________

	(increase/decline). As this occurs — or soon thereafter — costs begin to
rise	_______________ (rise/fall). This is why most cost curves eventually
rise	_______________ (rise/fall).
	In analyzing any firm's cost structure we must distinguish between the
is not	short and the long run. The distinction between them ____________ (is/
	is not) made in terms of calendar time. Instead, the distinguish is made in
	terms of the amount resources used in the production process that are
fixed	_______________ (fixed/human). If we are referring to the short run, we
at least one	mean that __________________________ (at least one/more than one)
cannot	resource is fixed. The use of a fixed resource ________________ (can/
	cannot) be increased or decreased in the short run. In the long run,
all, variable	_________________ (most/all) resources are ___________________
	(fixed/variable) in the production process. Fixed resources give rise to
	fixed costs (*FC*). Variable resources give rise to variable costs (*VC*).
plus	Fixed costs _______________ (plus/minus) variable costs equal total
	costs (*TC*).
FC + VC	In the short run, costs of production consist of _________________
horizontal	(*FC + VC*/*FC - VC*). The *FC* curve is a _______________________
upward	(vertical/horizontal) line. The *TC* curve slopes__________________
	(upward/downward). The vertical distance between the *TC* and *FC*
VC	curves equals____________________ (*VC*/marginal cost or *MC*). *VC*
rises	_______________ (rises/falls) as output increases.
	In order to determine a firm's profit-maximizing output level and the
	actual level of profits earned, we need to consider marginal and average
	(per unit) costs of production.

divided

Marginal cost (*MC*) equals the change in *TC* ________________ (divided/multiplied) by the change in the quantity produced.

FC + *VC*

Alternatively, it's equal to the change in ________________ (*FC* + *VC*/ *TC* - *VC*) divided by the change in the quantity produced. *MC*

falls, rises

________________ (rises/falls) at first, then ________________ (rises/falls) as the output increases.

Average fixed cost (*AFC*), at any output level, equals *FC*

divided

________________ (multiplied/divided) by the quantity produced.

downward

The *AFC* curve slopes ________________ (upward/downward).

Average variable cost (*AVC*), at any output level, equals *VC* divided

the quantity produced

by ________________ (the quantity produced/*MC*).

downward

The *AVC* curve slopes ________________ (upward/downward)

upward

at first and then slopes ________________ (upward/downward) as output increases. The *AVC* curve is mathematically related to the

MC

____________ (*MC*/*FC*) curve. The *AVC* curve falls when the *MC* curve

below

lies ____________ (above/below) it. The *MC* curve intersects the *AVC*

at a minimum

curve when the *AVC* curve is ________________ (falling/at a minimum/rising). If the *MC* curve lies above the *AVC* curve,

rising

then *AVC* will be ________________ (falling/rising). Because of this relationship we can say that *AVC* rises due to

the law of diminishing returns

________________ (the law of diminishing returns/diseconomies of scale).

Average total cost (*ATC*), at any output level, equals *TC* divided by the

AFC + *AVC*

output level. It is also equal to ________________ (*AFC* + *AVC*/ *AFC* - *AVC*) at a given output level. The *ATC* curve is U-shaped for

the same

________________ (the same/a different) reason that (than) the

AVC curve is U-shaped. The low point on the *ATC* curve is where the
MC ______________ (*AFC/MC*) curve intersects it.

The vertical distance between the *ATC* and *AVC* curves, at any output
AFC level, equals ______________ (*MC/AFC*) at that output level. For this
AFC reason the ______________ (*MC/AFC*) curve is usually not presented
graphically when the *ATC* and *AVC* curves are present.

have In the long run, firms ______________ (do not have/have) the ability
to change the amount of all resources utilized in the production process.
includes This ____________________ (includes/does not include) the ability to
change their plant size (or scale of operation). A short-run curve repre-
only one sents ____________________ (many/only one) scale of operation. Each
a different scale of operation has ________________________ (the same/a different)
short-run *ATC* curve associated with it. At first, an increase in the scale
decrease of operation should ________________ (increase/decrease) *ATC*. If this
economies happens, the firm is experiencing ______________________ (economies/
diseconomies) of scale. This enables firms to produce more but at
lower ___________________ (lower/higher) per unit costs. Therefore, the long-
downward run average total cost curve (*LRAC*) must be sloping ________________
(downward/upward). The *LRAC* slopes downward when economies
of scale are present and when long-run marginal costs (*LRMC*) are
below ____________________ (above/below) *LRAC*. As the scale of operation
diseconomies increases we would eventually expect __________________________
(economies/diseconomies) of scale to set in. In other words, larger plant
sizes are expected to be associated with short-run *ATC* curves, which lie
right, above further to the ________________ (right/left) and ________________
(above/below) those *ATC* curves associated with smaller plant sizes.

	If diseconomies of scale set in, then the *LRMC* curve must lie
above	________________ (above/below) the *LRAC* curve, and the *LRAC*
upward	slopes ________________ (upward/downward). The *LRAC* curve can
	also be thought of as the envelope curve of many different short-run *ATC*
can	curves. At any given output level the firm ______________ (can/cannot)
	choose the appropriate scale of operation in the long run. Economies and
	diseconomies of scale and the associated shape of the *LRAC* curve
can	____________ (can/cannot) help explain the size and number of firms
	found in different industries.
	In the short run, assuming marginal revenue equals price, a firm will
MC	produce where price equals ______________ (*MC*/*ATC*) to maximize
	profits. Therefore, any change in *MC* will change production. A change
will	in *FC* ______________ (will/will not) shift the *ATC* curve. The *ATC*
same	curve will shift in the ______________ (same/opposite) direction as
will not	the change in *FC*. A change in *FC* ______________ (will/will not)
will not	shift the *MC* curve. Therefore, there ______________ (will/will not)
	be a change in the firm's production decision. change in *VC* will shift
both the *ATC* and *MC*	________________________ (the *ATC*/both the *ATC* and *MC*/*MC*)
same	curve(s) in the ______________ (same/opposite) direction as the
	change in *VC*. This will cause the firm to change its profit-maximizing
opposite	output level in the ______________ (same/opposite) direction as
	the change in *VC*.

Problems and Applications

1. What do economists mean when they say the cost structure of all firms is basically the same in both the short and long run?
2. a. Complete the following cost schedule.

Output Level	Fixed Cost (*FC*)	Variable Cost (*VC*)	Total Cost (*TC*)	Marginal Cost (*MC*)	Average Fixed Cost (*AFC*)	Average Variable Cost (*AVC*)	Average Total Cost (*ATC*)
1	$100	$ 20					
2	$100	$ 30					
3	$100	$ 60					
4	$100	$110					
5	$100	$180					
6	$100	$270					

b. Is this firm operating in the short run or the long run?

c. Graph fixed, variable, and total costs for this cost schedule. How are the total and fixed cost curves related to variable costs? What is the total cost when output is zero?

d. Consider the cost of producing five units. How much are fixed costs? Variable costs? How much are per unit total costs of producing five units? What are the total costs of producing five units?

e. We know what *AFC*, *AVC*, and *ATC* are equal to. With reference to this cost schedule, is it true that in producing any output level $FC = (AFC)(Q)$? $VC = (AVC)(Q)$? $TC = (ATC)(Q)$?

f. Graph *MC*, *AVC* and *ATC* curves for this cost schedule on the same diagram. At which output level does the law of diminishing returns set in, and how is this related to the *MC*, *AVC*, and *ATC* curves? What is the vertical distance between the *ATC* and *AVC* curves equal to?

g. Assume this firm can sell all it likes at a constant price equal to $70. How much should the firm produce to maximize its profits (minimize its losses)? What are the firm's profits (losses) equal to? (*Reminder:* Total profit equals total revenue minus total cost, where total revenue equals price times quantity sold.)

3. a. Graph marginal and average cost curves. Assume fixed costs increase. Would this change any of the cost curves? Which ones? Would this change the firm's production decision?

   b. Graph marginal and average cost curves. Assume variable costs increase. Would this change any of the cost curves? Which ones? Would this change the firm's production decision?

4. Use the graph on page 372, which assumes a firm has only three plant sizes (or scales of operation) from which to choose, to answer questions a through g.

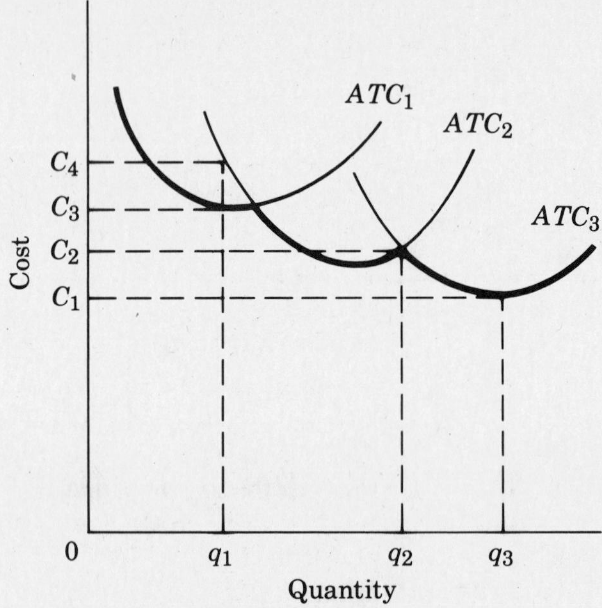

a. Is the firm in the short run or the long run if it has the ability to alter its scale of operation (plant size)?

b. Which plant size minimizes long-run average total cost (*LRAC*) of production? What output level is required to minimize *LRAC* and what are those costs equal to?

c. If the firm wishes to produce q_1, which plant size is the most appropriate?

d. If the firm wishes to produce q_2, which plant size is the most appropriate?

e. What is the firm's *LRAC* curve?

f. Do these short-run *ATC* curves illustrate economies or diseconomies of scale?

g. If this firm was able to alter its plant size indefinitely, what would happen to the firm's *LRAC* curve?

5. a. Graph a *LRAC* curve and indicate the portions that correspond to economies and diseconomies of scale.

   b. If economies of scale are extensive and diseconomies of scale set in only at a large output level, what would the *LRAC* curve look like? What can we say about the size and number of firms in this industry?

True-False

For each item, determine whether the statement is basically true or false. If the statement is false, rewrite it so it is a true statement.

_____ 1. $AFC = ATC - AVC$.

_____ 2. The law of diminishing returns explains why *AVC* and *ATC* curves eventually slope upward.

_____ 3. A fixed cost decreases as output increases.

_____ 4. The vertical distance between the *ATC* curve and the *AVC* curve equals fixed costs.

_____ 5. Total costs include fixed, variable, risk, and opportunity costs.

_____ 6. Average total cost at any output level measures the per unit total cost of producing at that output level.

_____ 7. Marginal cost equals total cost divided by the output level.

_____ 8. Diseconomies of scale are associated with the downward-sloping portion of the *LRAC* curve.

_____ 9. The *LRAC* curve envelopes many short-run *ATC* curves.

_____ 10. A natural monopoly is likely to exist in an industry with extensive economies of scale.

_____ 11. An increase in variable costs will increase a firm's output level.

_____ 12. When the isoquant and isocost curves are just tangent to each other, the firm is minimizing its cost of production in producing that output level.

_____ 13. The cost structure of a firm shows how various measures of cost vary with the production level.

_____ 14. Economies of scale are associated with the management losing control over the operations of the firm.

_____ 15. If marginal cost is falling, average total cost must be rising.

_____ 16. Economies of scale cause short-run *ATC* curves to shift up and lie farther to the right.

_____ 17. Total costs at any output level equal average total cost multiplied by that output level.

Multiple Choice

Choose the one best answer for each item.

_____ 1. If fixed costs increase

a. *AVC* decrease.

b. the *MC*, *AVC*, and *ATC* curves shifts up and the firm produces less.

c. the *ATC* curve shifts up and the firm's production decision remains the same.
d. marginal costs increase.
e. the *AFC* curve shifts downward.

_____ 2. To determine a firm's profit-maximizing (loss-minimizing) output level and the actual level of profits (or losses) we would require
a. marginal cost.
b. average fixed costs.
c. average variable costs.
d. average total costs.
e. all of the above.

_____ 3. The short-run *MC* curve intersects which of the following curves at its minimum point?
a. The *AFC* curve
b. The *AVC* curve
c. The *ATC* curve
d. The *LRAC* curve
e. Both b and c

_____ 4. Which of the following statements is true?
a. Average total cost equals variable plus fixed costs divided by the output level.
b. Marginal cost equals total costs divided by the output level.
c. Average variable cost equals the change in variable costs divided by the change in the output level.
d. Average fixed cost equals the change in fixed costs divided by the change in the output level.
e. All of the above are true statements.

Use the graph on page 375 to answer questions 5 and 6.

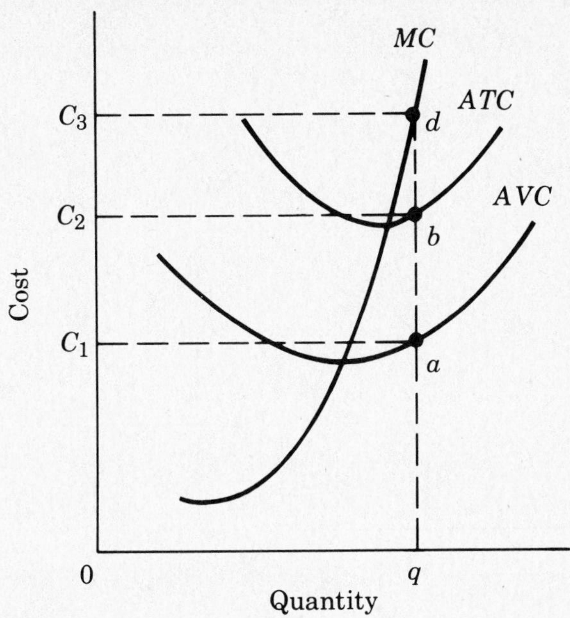

_____ 5. Assuming this firm is producing q units, which of the following statements is true?
   a. Total costs equal area OC_2bq.
   b. Average total costs equal OC_2.
   c. Average fixed costs equal ab.
   d. Marginal cost of the qth unit equals OC_3.
   e. All of the above.

_____ 6. Assuming this firm is producing q units, fixed costs equal area
   a. OC_1aq.
   b. C_1C_2ba.
   c. C_2C_3da.
   d. C_1C_3da.
   e. OC_2bq.

_____ 7. The vertical distance between the total cost curve and the fixed cost curve graphically measures
   a. marginal cost.
   b. average fixed cost.
   c. average variable cost.
   d. average total cost.
   e. none of the above.

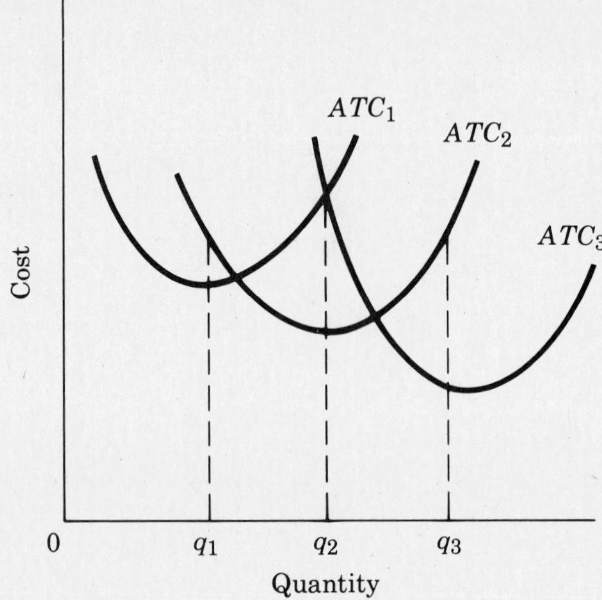

______ 8. Based on the preceding graph, which of the following statements is true?
   a. This diagram illustrates economies of scale.
   b. At output level q_1 the appropriate scale of operation is associated with ATC_2.
   c. At output level q_2 the appropriate scale of operation is associated with ATC_3.
   d. Given these three plant sizes, per unit total costs are minimized at output level q_3.
   e. Both a and d.

______ 9. If the economies of scale are extensive, this may illustrate by
   a. a long, downward-sloping portion of the *LRAC* curve.
   b. a long, upward-sloping portion of the *LRAC* curve.
   c. a short, downward-sloping portion of the *LRAC* curve followed by a long, upward-sloping portion.
   d. a short, downward-sloping portion of the *LRAC* curve followed by a short, upward-sloping portion.
   e. many firms in the industry of varying sizes.

_____ 10. Which of the following statements is true?
   a. All cost curves assume the most technically efficient use of resources.
   b. The point of tangency between the isocost and isoquant curves indicates the most technically efficient use of resources in producing a particular output level.
   c. An increase in a firm's production budget will cause the isocost curve to shift outward.
   d. An isoquant curve that lies farther from the origin indicates a greater output level.
   e. All of the above.

_____ 11. Which of the following is true?
   a. In the short run, all costs are fixed.
   b. In the long run, all resources are variable except plant size.
   c. All firms experience economies and diseconomies of scale to the same degree.
   d. The degree of economies and diseconomies of scale helps explain the shape of the *LRAC* curve and the size and number of firms found in different industries.
   e. The *MC* always intersects the *AFC*, *AVC*, and *ATC* curves at their minimum points.

Discussion Questions

1. Consider the varying degrees of economies and diseconomies of scale and the associated number and size of firms that should be found in industries under these varying circumstances. List as many real-world industries that fit these differing circumstances as you can. *(KQ3)*
2. Why might an industry consist of many relatively small and large firms competing with each other? *(KQ3)*
3. Consider the short-run production of any item. What would be some fixed costs and what would be some variable costs? What could cause these costs to change? What effect would these cost changes have on the output decisions of the firm? *(KQ1, 2, 3, 4)*
4. If the minimum wage were to increase, what effect would this have on costs and the firm's production decision? *(KQ4)*
5. What is required for a firm to be able to produce profitably on a larger scale of operation? *(KQ3)*

Answers

Problems and Applications

1. This means that practically all firms' production processes encounter diminishing returns in the short run and economies and diseconomies of scale in the long run — albeit to differing degrees. Therefore, in the short run, the *MC*, *AVC*, and *ATC* curves are U-shaped for all firms. That is, *MC* (and therefore the *MC* curve) rises when diminishing returns set in and therefore the *AVC* and *ATC* curves begin to rise soon thereafter In the long run, because almost all firms experience economies and diseconomies of scale, their *LRAC* curve are also U-shaped.

2. a.

Total Cost (*TC*)	Marginal Cost (*MC*)	Average Fixed Cost (*AFC*)	Average Variable Cost (*AVC*)	Average Total Cost (*ATC*)
$120	$20	$100	$20	$120
$130	$10	$ 50	$15	$ 65
$160	$30	$ 33.33	$20	$ 53.33
$210	$50	$ 25	$27.50	$ 52.50
$280	$70	$ 20	$36	$ 56
$370	$90	$ 16.66	$45	$ 61.66

b. This firm must be operating in the short run because there are some fixed costs, reflecting that there must be some fixed resources.

c. The vertical distance between the *TC* and *FC* curve equals *VC*. Alternatively, the vertical distance between the *TC* and *VC* curves equals *FC* (as must be mathematically true if $FC + VC = TC$). *TC* equals *FC* when output is zero because *VC* is zero.

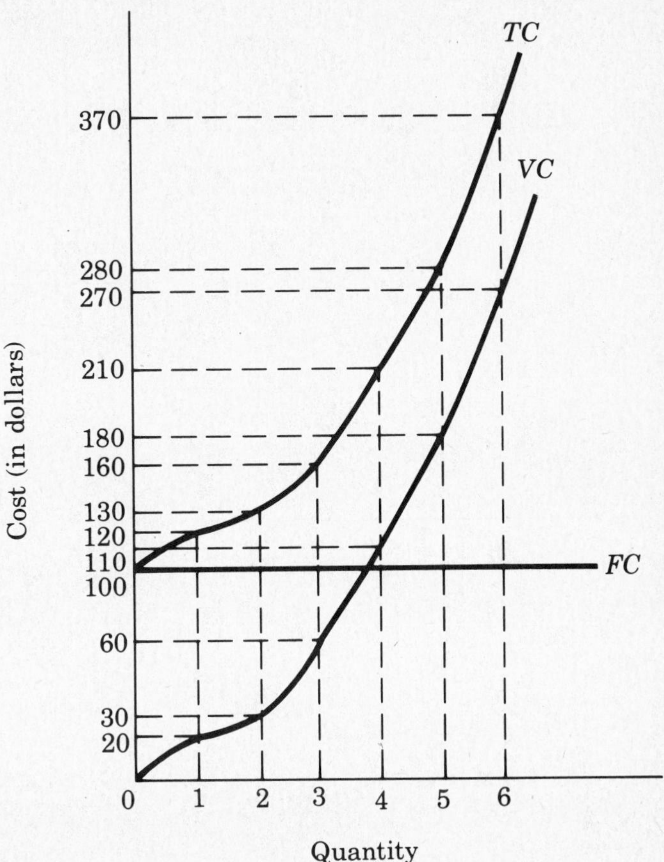

d. The *FC* of producing the five units equals \$20 (*AFC* = \$20). The *VC* of producing the five units equals \$36 (*AVC* = \$36). Therefore, the *ATC* of producing the five units equals \$56. (*Note:* Average cost measures measure per unit costs.) The *TC* of producing the five units equals (*ATC*)(*Q*) or *(\$56)(5)* or \$280.

e. Yes, this must be mathematically true. Also note that *TC* can be derived by adding *FC* and *VC*.

f. The law of diminishing returns sets in with the second unit produced. This causes the *MC* curve to begin to slope upward. As the *MC* curve rises, this eventually pulls the *AVC* and *ATC* curves upward. Note that the *MC* curve intersects the *AVC* and *ATC* curves at their minimum points, as is mathematically predicted. So we can say these cost curves are U-shaped because of diminishing returns. That is to say, marginal and per unit costs eventually rise because of diminishing returns.

The vertical distance between the *ATC* and *AVC* curves equals *AFC*. Therefore, there is no need to express *AFC* graphically because it only complicates the graph without adding any new information.

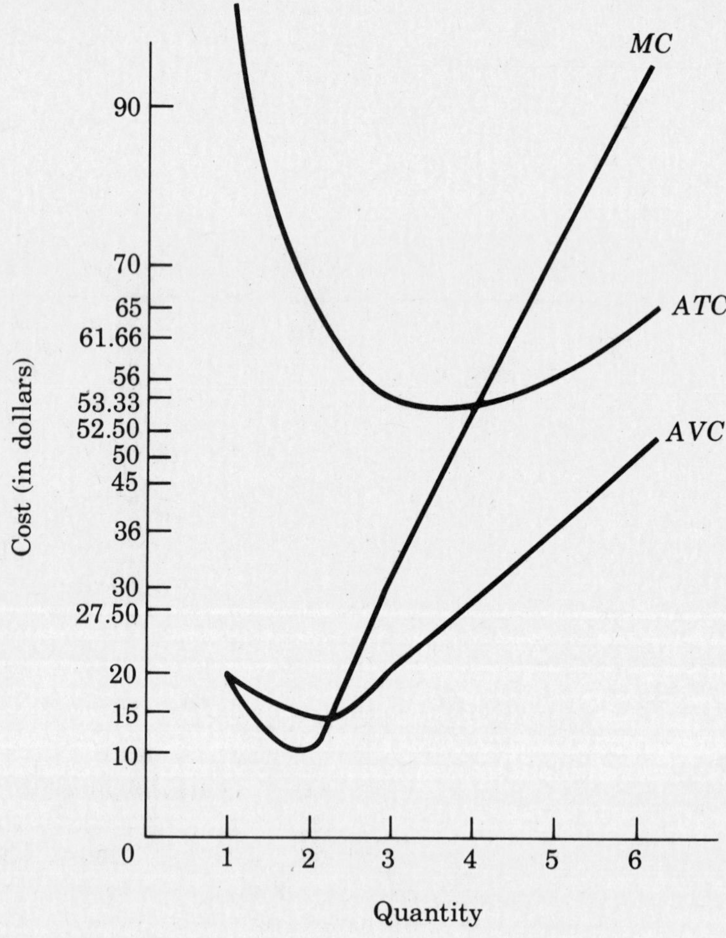

g. If this firm can sell all it likes at a constant price (*P*) equals to \$70, this means the firm's marginal revenue from any unit sold is \$70. A firm will maximize profits (minimize losses) by producing where marginal revenue equals *MC* — in this case, where *P* = *MC*. The firm will therefore produce five units. The profit level from producing five units is \$70.

3. a. If fixed costs increase, this increases total cost and shifts the *ATC* curve upward. In the graph the *ATC* curve shifts vertically upward from ATC_1 to ATC_2. The *AVC* and *MC* curves are unaffected by any change in fixed costs. Because a firm produces that output level where marginal revenue (which equals price if the firm can sell all it wants at a constant price) equals marginal cost and because marginal cost is unaffected (therefore the *MC* curve is unaffected), the firm's production decision would not change. In the graph, if the price (P_1) equals marginal revenue, then the output decision remains at q_1 even though the *ATC* curve shifted upward because of the increase in fixed costs.

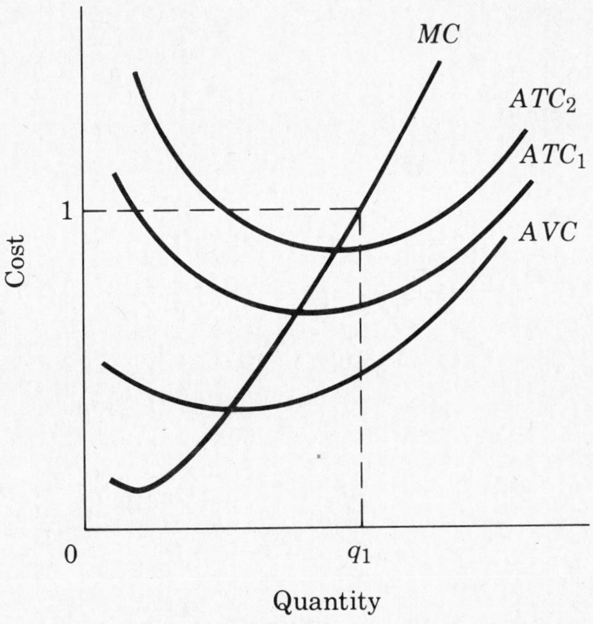

b. If variable costs increase, this increases total costs and marginal cost as well. Therefore, the *MC*, *AVC*, and *ATC* curves will all shift upward. (The vertical distance between the *ATC* and *AVC* curves will be the same because there has been no change in fixed costs and therefore average fixed costs.) Assuming the firm can sell all it wishes at P_1, the firm will cut back on its production level to q_2. This is because marginal revenue now equals marginal cost at a lower production level. In general, any time a change in costs affects the *MC* curve, the production decision of the firm will be changed.

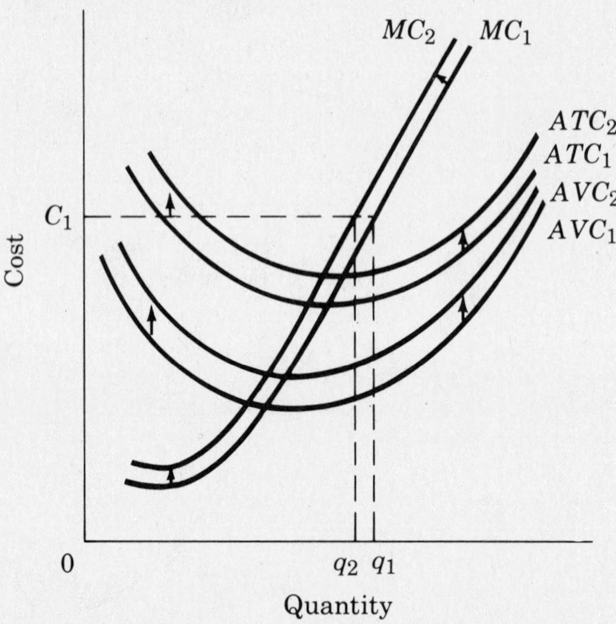

4. a. The firm is in the long run because all resources (including plant size) are variable resources.
   b. The plant size associated with the short-run *ATC* curve ATC_3 would minimize costs of production in the long run. However, an output level of q_3 would be required to minimize costs at C_1. Note that for costs to be minimized in the long run the firm must produce at the minimum of the *ATC* curve of the largest scale of operation. This occurs at q_3 and C_1.
   c. The plant size associated with the short-run *ATC* curve ATC_1 is the most appropriate because costs are minimized at C_3. The firm could use a larger plant size (such as that associated with the short-run *ATC* curve ATC_2) but per unit total costs would be greater (C_4 rather than C_3).
   d. The firm would be indifferent between the two plant sizes associated with the short-run *ATC* curves ATC_2 and ATC_3 because in either case *LRAC* would equal C_2.
   e. This firm's *LRAC* curve would envelope the lowest portions of all *ATC* curves considered together. This is shown by the darker-lined segments of these short-run *ATC* curves in the graph above.

f. Economies of scale, because the firm experiences lower *LRAC* as output expands..

g. The *LRAC* curve would become smooth (as opposed to the dark-lined portions in the graph on page 382). Furthermore, assuming diseconomies of scale would set in at some point, the curve would be U-shaped.

5. a. 

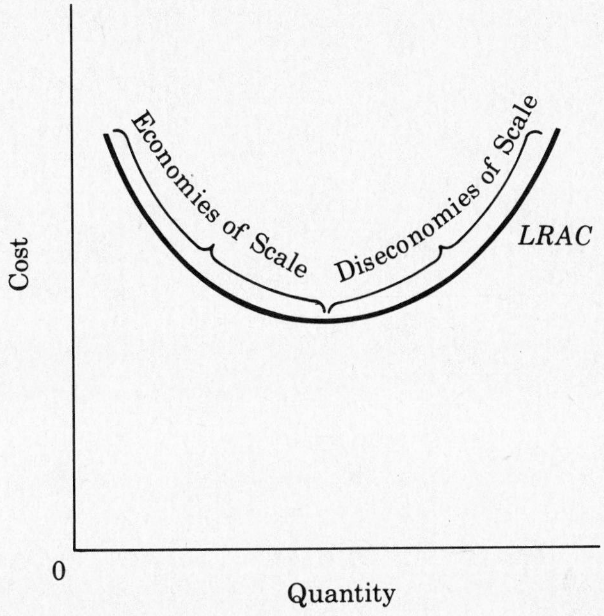

b. If economies of scale are extensive, the downward-sloping portion of the *LRAC* curve would be relatively long. The curve would turn at the output level in which diseconomies of scale set in. There would probably be relatively few, but relatively larger, firms in this industry. If the economies of scale are great enough, a natural monopoly may dominate production.

True-False

1. T   2. T

3. F: A fixed cost does not vary as output changes.

4. F: The vertical distance between the *ATC* curve and the *AVC* curve equals average fixed costs (*AFC*).
5. T
6. T
7. F: Marginal cost equals the change in total cost divided by the change in the output level.
8. F: Diseconomies of scale are associated with the upward-sloping portion of the *LRAC* curve.
9. T
10. T
11. F: An increase in variable costs will decrease a firm's output level.
12. T
13. T
14. F: Diseconomies of scale are associated with management losing control over the operation of the firm.
15. F: If marginal cost is falling, average total cost must be falling.
16. F: Economies of scale cause short-run *ATC* curves to shift down and lie father to the right.
17. T

Multiple Choice

1. c *(KQ1, 2, 4)*
2. e *(KQ1, 2)*
3. e *(KQ2)*
4. a *(KQ1, 2)*
5. e *(KQ1, 2)*
6. b *(KQ1, 2)*
7. e *(KQ1, 2)*
8. e *(KQ3)*
9. a *(KQ3)*
10. e (See Appendix)
11. d *(KQ1, 2, 3)*

CHAPTER 22

Perfect Competition

Chapter Summary

Key Question 1: How are market structures classified?

This chapter begins by outlining the basic characteristics of the four general market structures — perfect competition, pure monopoly, monopolistic competition, and oligopoly. These market structures differ in terms of the number of producers, the degree of control producers have over product price, whether the producer sells a homogenous or a differentiated product, and the freedom of entry into the market. There are very few, if any, real-world markets that conform perfectly to any one of these market structure definitions. However, most real-world markets closely approximate one of them. These theoretical market structures act as models that enable us to predict and explain pricing and production tendencies in the real world over both the short and the long run. These market models also enable us to evaluate the relative efficiency of various real-world markets in contributing to social welfare. This chapter focuses on the way in which individual firms react to consumer demand in perfectly competitive markets.

Key Question 2: What output will the perfect competitor produce?

Because the perfectly competitive firm is a price taker, marginal revenue from any unit sold is constant and equals market price. The firm's marginal revenue curve is a horizontal line at the market price. Furthermore, the firm's marginal revenue curve is also its demand curve, because it can sell all it likes at the market price. If the market price rises (falls), the demand and marginal revenue curve facing the firm rises (falls).

Key Question 3: How are profits maximized in the short run?

When the cost structure of the firm is considered along with its demand (marginal revenue) curve, we can determine the profit-maximizing (loss-minimizing) output level and the amount of profits (losses) earned. Like any firm, the perfectly competitive firm will maximize profits (minimize losses) by producing where marginal revenue equals marginal cost ($MR =$

MC). A firm should not attempt to produce where average total costs are at a minimum. The amount of profits (or losses) at the $MR = MC$ output level is determined by subtracting total cost from total revenue. Total cost equals average total cost multiplied by the output level. Total revenue equals price per unit multiplied by the output level. A perfectly competitive firm (like any firm) can earn economic profits or lose money in the short run.

Key Question 4: How are losses minimized in the short run?

Economic profits are earned when price exceeds average total costs. If price equals average total costs, economic profits are zero. When price falls below average total costs, losses are incurred. Although firms cannot suffer losses indefinitely, they should remain in operation in the short run as long as revenues cover total variable costs (out-of-pocket costs). That is, as long as price is above the minimum point in the average variable cost curve, the firm should remain in operation. In other words, as long as losses are less than total fixed costs the firm will minimize losses by remaining in operation. If the firm shuts down, losses will equal total fixed costs. This illustrates why fixed costs are sunk costs and should be ignored in the production decision. The relevant question if a firm is losing money is whether it can add more to its revenues than to its variable costs by remaining in operation. If it can, it should remain in operation. By doing so, it will lose less. Only if price falls below the minimum point on the average variable cost curve should the firm shut down, because total revenue will be insufficient to cover total variable costs. (Losses are greater than total fixed costs.)

Because the firm produces where price (equal to marginal revenue) equals marginal cost and remains in operation as long as price is above average variable costs, the marginal cost curve above the minimum point on the average variable cost curve is the firm's short-run supply curve. Also, because the marginal cost curve is rising (has an upward slope) at the point of intersection with the average variable cost curve (its minimum point) and continues to rise beyond this point, it follows that if the firm produces at all, it produces in the range of increasing marginal cost — and of diminishing marginal returns. Furthermore, because the market supply curve is the sum of all firms' marginal cost (supply) curves in the market, the market supply curve is upward-sloping because of the law of diminishing marginal returns.

Key Question 5: How does long-run equilibrium differ from short-run equilibrium?

In the long run, because of complete freedom of entry into and exit from the competitive market, any economic profits and losses will tend to disappear, leaving zero economic profits earned by firms. This is a profit level just sufficient to cover all costs of production, including opportunity and risk costs. In a competitive market, zero economic profits exist when price is just equal to minimum average total cost. So, a competitive firm will produce at the low point on its average total cost curve in the long run.

If economic profits are earned in the market, then over time investors move into the market, increasing the number of producers and therefore market supply. This depresses the market price and the economic profits earned by firms. Investors continue to move into the industry until all economic profits disappear. The result in the long run is a lower market equilibrium price and a greater market equilibrium quantity. The quantity demanded is greater because the market price has fallen. The quantity supplied is greater due to the greater number of sellers — even though each firm produces less.

If losses characterize the market, then over time the least efficient firms either voluntarily sell out and leave the market (there are no fixed costs in the long run) or they are driven out of the market by bankruptcy. This decreases the number of sellers and therefore market supply. The market price rises and the losses of existing firms decrease. This process continues until those firms left in the industry earn zero economic profit. The result in the long run is a higher market equilibrium price and a lower market equilibrium quantity. The quantity demanded is lower because the market price has risen. The quantity supplied is lower due to the smaller number of sellers — even though each remaining firm produces more.

In the long run, perfectly competitive firms will take advantage of any economies of scale, if they exist. This is because short-run economic profits can be earned by firms that produce on a larger, smaller-cost scale. Therefore, over time, we would expect all firms to be producing at the minimum of long-run average total costs.

Key Question 6: In what respect is perfect competition efficient?

Although the perfectly competitive market is very efficient, it is not perfectly efficient. First in a world of imperfect information, price does not always move smoothly toward equilibrium. This concept may be illustrated by a supply and demand cobweb. Second, some critics complain that the market system creates wasteful surpluses and shortages. However, this criticism is not valid, for we know that surpluses and shortages will not persist for long if free market forces are allowed to operate. Third, external costs, if left unchecked, may result in the overproduction of some products. Fourth, the efficiency of the competitive market system is based on a given distribution of property rights and therefore a given distribution of income. Some critics argue this distribution of income may not be fair, or "best." Finally, critics argue that most real-world markets are not perfectly competitive. However, the perfectly competitive market model was never meant to represent all or even most markets. It is merely one analytical tool used by economists when considering the consequences of changes in market conditions and government policy.

These shortcomings notwithstanding, the competitive market is very efficient. At market equilibrium, the marginal benefits from the consumption of the last unit produced equal the marginal cost of its production. (This means that producers produce up to the point where price equals marginal cost.) All quantities produced and consumed before the last unit result in marginal benefits exceeding marginal costs. A kind of surplus value accrues to consumers up to the last unit produced. Furthermore, firms are forced to produce at the minimum of average total costs in the long run and are forced to take advantage of all economies of scale over time. Also, firms can earn only zero economic profits in the long run. Thus, consumers get the product at its cheapest possible price.

Review Terms and Concepts

Pure competition
Opportunity cost
Risk cost
Sunk cost
Marginal revenue
Marginal cost
Total cost
Variable cost
Fixed cost
Average total cost
Average variable cost
Average fixed cost
Economic profits
Economic losses
Market demand
Market supply
Equilibrium price
Equilibrium quantity
Market equilibrium
Elastic demand
Inelastic demand
Perfectly elastic demand
External costs
External benefits

New Terms and Concepts

Price taker
Price searcher
Pure monopoly
Monopolistic competition
Oligopoly
Supply and demand cobweb
Homogenous product
Differentiated product

Completion

four

perfectly competitive

There are ______________ (four/six) basic market structures. The most competitive is the ______________________________ (oligopoly/ perfectly competitive). This market structure is characterized by such a

Answers	Text
large	__________ (large/small) number of buyers and sellers that all
price takers	buyers and sellers are __________ (price takers/price
homogenous	searchers). Producers sell a __________ (differentiated/
	homogenous) product. The perfectly competitive market, as opposed to
greatest	other markets, is also characterized by the __________
	(greatest/least) amount of freedom of entry into and exit from the market.
	Because the perfectly competitive producer is a price taker, the firm is
elastic	faced with a perfectly __________ (elastic/inelastic) demand
horizontal	curve at the market price. This __________ (horizontal/
marginal revenue	vertical) demand curve is also the firm's __________
	(marginal revenue/marginal cost) curve. When we add the firm's cost
can	structure to its demand (marginal revenue) curve we __________
	(can/cannot) determine the profit-maximizing (loss-minimizing) output
	level and the actual profits (losses) earned.
	For any firm to maximize its profits in the short run it should produce
marginal cost	where marginal revenue equals __________
	(marginal cost/average total cost). Because the perfectly competitive firm
	can sell all it likes at a constant market price, marginal revenue equals
market price	__________ (market price/marginal cost). There-
	fore, the perfectly competitive firm produces where price equals
marginal cost	__________ (marginal cost/average total cost).
economic profits	If price is above average total cost, then __________
	(economic profits/losses) are incurred. If price equals average total cost,
zero economic profits	then __________ (economic profits/
	losses/zero economic profits) are incurred. If price falls below the mini-
losses	mum of average total cost, then __________ (economic

profits/losses) are incurred. To minimize short-run losses the firm should
above — remain in operation as long as price is ________ (above/below)
the minimum of average variable costs. This is because total revenue
will — ________ (will/will not) cover variable costs of production and
some of the fixed costs. However, if price falls below the minimum of
shut down — average variable costs, the firm should ________ (remain
will not — in operation/shut down) because total revenue ________
(will/will not) be sufficient to cover variable costs of production. In other
words, if price falls below the minimum of average variable costs, the
greater — firm's losses will be ________ (greater/smaller) than its fixed
fixed — costs. If the firm shuts down, its losses will only equal ________
(fixed/variable) costs.

Because a firm remains in operation as long as price is above the mini-
variable — mum of average ________ (variable/total) costs, the
marginal cost — firm's ________ (marginal revenue/marginal cost)
variable — curve above the minimum point on the average ________
(variable/total) cost curve is the firm's short-run supply curve. Because
marginal costs are rising over this range of output, the firm always
beyond — produces an output level ________ (before/beyond)
that output level at which diminishing marginal returns set in. Furthermore, because the market supply curve is the sum of all firms'
marginal cost — ________ (marginal revenue/marginal cost) curves,
upward — the market supply curve is ________ (upward/downward)-
sloping because of the law of diminishing marginal returns.

In the long run, any economic profits earned or losses incurred by
disappear — firms will tend to ________ (increase/disappear). This is

because of the complete freedom of entry into and exit from the industry.

supply — As firms enter or exit the market, this changes market ______________ (demand/supply) and therefore the equilibrium price and quantity.

If economic profits are earned in the market, then in the long run inves-

into — tors will move ______________ (into/out of) the market. This

increases — ______________________ (increases/decreases) market supply. The

decreases — equilibrium price ______________________ (increases/ decreases) and

increases — the equilibrium quantity ______________________ (increases/decreases).

fall — As the market price falls, firms' economic profits ________________

zero economic profits — (rise/fall). This process continues until ________________________ (economic profits/ zero economic profits/losses) are incurred.

If losses are incurred in the market, then in the long run investors will

out of — move ______________________ (into/out of) the market. This

decreases — __________________ (increases/decreases market supply. The equi-

rises — librium price _______________ (rises/falls) and the equilibrium quantity

falls — _______________ (rises/falls). As the market price rises, firms'

fall — economic losses _______________ (rise/fall). This process continues

zero economic profits — until _________________ (economic profits/zero economic profits/losses) are incurred.

necessarily — In the long run, perfectly competitive firms will ______________ (necessarily/not necessarily) take advantage of any economies of scale. If a firm does not produce at the minimum of long-run average total costs,

underpriced — then it will be _________________ (underpriced/overpriced) and driven out of the market by firms that do produce on a larger, smaller-cost scale.

is not — The perfectly competitive market _________________ (is/is not) perfectly efficient. It is very efficient in that it produces where price equals marginal cost ______________ (marginal revenue/marginal cost). This means the marginal benefit from the last unit produced is just equal to its marginal cost. All quantities produced and consumed up to this point

surplus result in some ______________ (surplus/shortage) value. The perfectly competitive market is also very efficient because firms are forced to

minimum produce where average total costs are at a ______________

economies (minimum/maximum) and to take advantage of any ______________ (economies/diseconomies) of scale. All this, along with the fact that

zero economic profits are ______________ (positive/zero/negative) in the long run, means consumers get the product at the cheapest possible price.

Problems and Applications

1. a. List the characteristics of each market structure. How do these characteristics affect the firm's ability to control the price and the demand curve it faces?
   b. Fill in the following table.

	Number of Firms	Freedom of Entry	Type of Product
Perfect competition:			
Pure monopoly:			
Monopolistic competition:			
Oligopoly:			

   c. Consider the three diagrams (a), (b), and (c) in the graph on page 393, which represent possible demand curves facing a firm. Which diagram most likely represents a demand curve facing a
      i. perfectly competitive firm?
      ii. monopolistic firm?
      iii. monopolistically competitive firm?

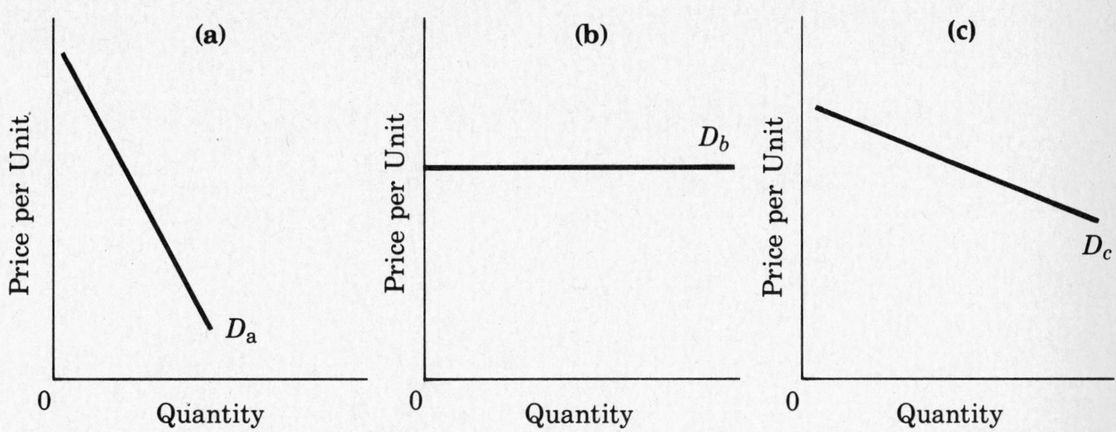

2. Answer the following questions based on diagrams (a) and (b) in the graph below. Diagram (a) represents a perfectly competitive market. Diagram (b) represents a perfectly competitive firm.

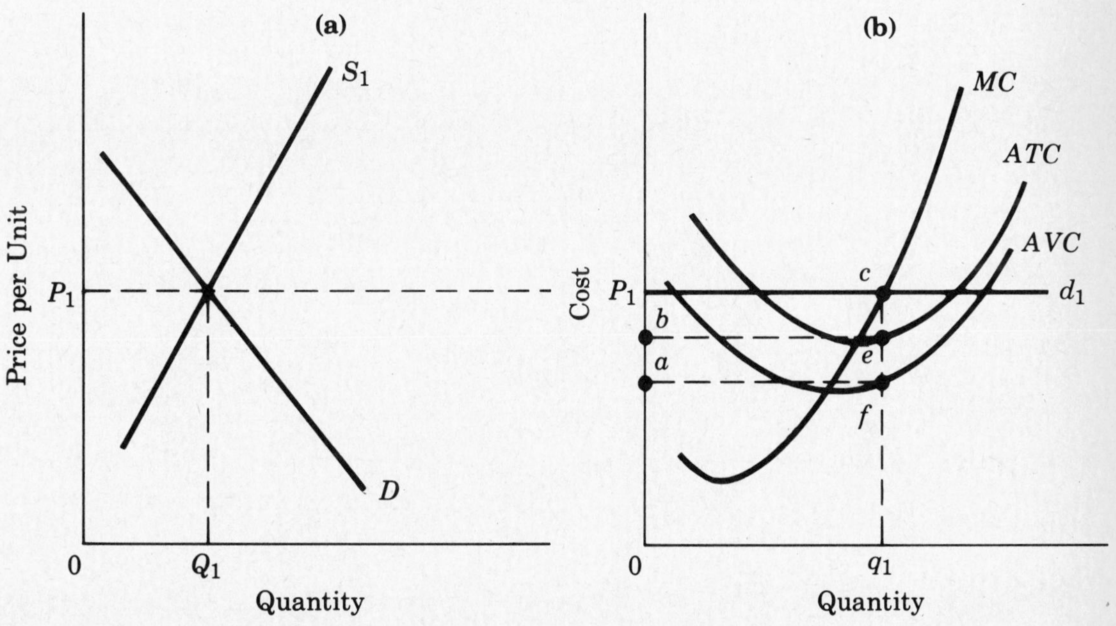

a. Why is the demand curve facing the perfectly competitive firm (shown as the horizontal line d_1) perfectly elastic (horizontal) at the market price, P_1? How is this related to the firm's marginal revenue?
b. If demand or supply changes in the market, what happens to the market price and therefore the demand curve facing the firm?
c. What is the profit-maximizing (or loss-minimizing) production rule for any firm? What output level should this firm produce to maximize profits (or minimize losses)?
d. At the profit-maximizing (loss-minimizing) output level, what is
   i. total revenue equal to mathematically and graphically?
   ii. total fixed costs equal to mathematically and graphically?
   iii. total variable costs equal to mathematically and graphically?
   iv. total costs equal to mathematically and graphically?
   v. the economic profit (or loss) equal to mathematically and graphically?
e. Given that short-run economic profits are earned, what is expected to happen in the long run to: (1) the number of investors in the market, (2) the market supply curve, (3) market price and quantity, (4) the demand (marginal revenue) curve facing the firm, (5) the production level of the firm, and (6) the profits of the firm? Graphically express these changes on a new graph so the original situation in the market and for the firm can be compared with the long-run effects.
f. Is if true that a perfectly competitive firm earns zero economic profits in the long run?
g. What can we conclude about economic profits if price exceeds average total costs? What can we conclude about economic profits if price equals minimum average total costs?

3. Answer the following questions based on diagrams (a) and (b) in the graph below. Diagram (a) represents a perfectly competitive market. Diagram (b) represents a perfectly competitive firm.

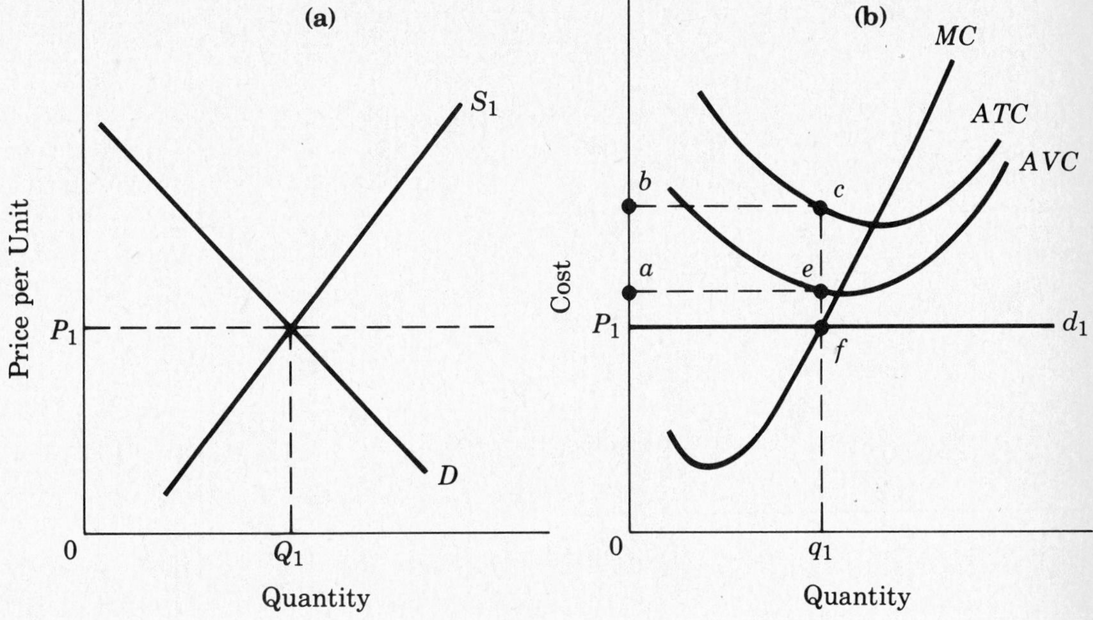

a. What output level should this firm produce to maximize profits (or minimize losses)?
b. At the profit-maximizing (loss-minimizing) output level, what graphical area equals
   i. total revenue?
   ii. total fixed costs?
   iii. total variable costs?
   iv. total costs?
   v. economic profit (or loss)?
c. Whenever a firm is losing money it must decide whether to remain in operation or shut down to minimize its losses. It should remain in operation to minimize its losses as long as total revenue covers total variable costs. Alternatively, it should remain in operation as long as losses are less than total fixed costs — because if the firm shuts down, its losses equal total fixed costs. Should this firm remain in operation or shut down to minimize its losses? Why or why not?
d. If price was above minimum average variable costs, should the firm shut down?

e. Given that losses are incurred, what is expected to happen in the long run to: (1) the number of investors in the market, (2) the market supply curve, (3) market price and quantity, (4) the demand (marginal revenue) curve facing the firm, (5) the production level of the firm, and (6) the losses of the firm? Graphically express these changes on a new graph so the original situation in the market and for the firm can be compared with the long-run effects.
f. Is if true that the perfectly competitive firm earns zero economic profits in the long run?
g. What can we conclude about losses when price equals minimum average total costs? What can we conclude about losses when price is below minimum average total costs? Assuming losses are incurred, what can we conclude about the decision to remain in operation or to shut down when price is above and when price is below minimum average variable costs?
h. Given you answer to 3g, what can we conclude is the firm's short-run supply curve?

4. Why are perfectly competitive firms expected to take advantage of any economies of scale? In the long run, which scale of operation (or plant size) would a firm choose on its long-run average total cost curve? Express this graphically.
5. a. Draw a market demand curve and a supply curve on the same graph. Let these market demand and supply curves represent a perfectly competitive market.
b. Which curve measures marginal benefits received from the consumption of any given quantity?
c. Which curve measure the marginal cost of producing any given quantity?
d. If marginal benefits (price) exceed marginal cost at some quantity, is that quantity below, at, or above equilibrium?
e. If marginal cost exceeds marginal benefits (price) at some quantity, is that quantity below, at, or above equilibrium?
f. What quantity is produced in a perfectly competitive market? What can we say about the marginal benefits (price) and marginal cost of this last unit produced and therefore the efficiency of a perfectly competitive market?
g. Indicate the area of surplus value (net gain received because marginal benefits exceed marginal cost from the production of this product).

True-False

For each item, determine whether the statement is basically true or false. If the statement is false, rewrite it so it is a true statement.

____ 1. Of all the market structures the pure monopoly has the strongest barriers to entry, while the perfectly competitive market has the weakest barriers to entry.

____ 2. The pure monopolist is faced with a perfectly elastic demand curve.

____ 3. A monopolistically competitive firm sells a homogenous (or standardized product.

____ 4. The critical characteristic of the oligopolistic market structure is that firms sell either differentiated or standardized products.

____ 5. The monopolistically competitive market structure is characterized by advertising and other forms of nonprice competition.

____ 6. Any firm should produce that output level that minimizes average total costs to maximize profits or minimize losses.

____ 7. A pure monopolist is a price searcher.

____ 8. If price is above minimum average variable costs and below minimum average total costs, the firm will be incurring losses but should remain in operation.

____ 9. If price is above minimum average total costs, a competitive firm is earning short-run economic profits.

____ 10. A market supply curve slopes upward because of diminishing marginal returns.

____ 11. A perfectly competitive firm's short-run supply curve is that portion of its marginal cost curve that lies above the minimum point on its average total cost curve.

____ 12. If a firm's losses are greater that its fixed costs, it should remain in operation to minimize short-run losses.

____ 13. If a firm is losing money but total revenue is sufficient to cover variable costs of production, it should remain in operation to minimize short-run losses.

____ 14. In the long run, a perfectly competitive firm can earn only zero economic profits because of the complete freedom of entry into and exit from the market.

____ 15. A perfectly competitive firm is expected to take advantage of all diseconomies of scale.

____ 16. If economic profits are earned in a perfectly competitive market, then we can expect market price and the production level of individual firms to rise.

_____ 17. If losses are incurred in a perfectly competitive market, then some firms will leave the market.

_____ 18. An output level below equilibrium means the marginal benefits from consumption exceed the marginal costs of production, and consumer welfare could be increases if more was produced and consumed.

_____ 19. A perfectly competitive market is very efficient because it produces where $P = MC$, and the marginal cost of production is the same for all producers.

_____ 20. A perfectly competitive market is very efficient because it produces at the minimum of average total costs in the long run.

Multiple Choice

Choose the one best answer for each item.

_____ 1. If zero economic profits are earned by a firm
   a. it will shut down.
   b. it is covering all costs of production, including opportunity and risk costs.
   c. it its covering variable and fixed costs of production.
   d. it is covering only variable costs of production.
   e. it is covering only fixed costs of production.

_____ 2. A perfectly competitive market is efficient because in the long run firms
   a. produce where $P = MC$.
   b. produce at minimum average total costs.
   c. produce at the minimum of long-run average total costs.
   d. will take advantage of any economies of scale.
   e. do all of the above.

_____ 3. If short-run economic profits are earned in a perfectly competitive market, then over the long run we would expect
   a. fewer firms in the market
   b. market price to rise.
   c. individual firms to produce less.
   d. economic profits to increase.
   e. all of the above.

Use the graph on page 399 based on a perfectly competitive firm to answer questions 4-9.

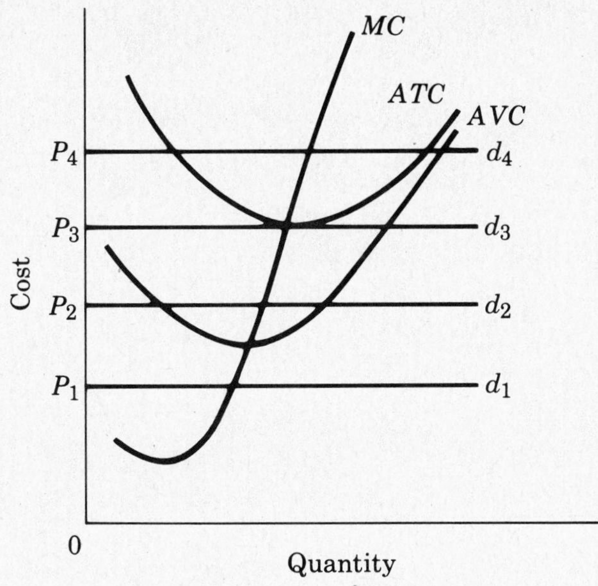

_____ 4. At which price is the firm earning economic profits?
   a. P_1
   b. P_2
   c. P_3
   d. P_4
   e. none of the above

_____ 5. At which price is the firm incurring losses but should remain in operation?
   a. P_1
   b. P_2
   c. P_3
   d. P_4
   e. P_1 and P_2

_____ 6. At which price is the firm incurring losses and should shut down?
   a. P_1
   b. P_2
   c. P_3
   d. P_4
   e. none of the above

_____ 7. At which price is the firm earning zero economic profits?
a. P_1
b. P_2
c. P_3
d. P_4
e. none of the above

_____ 8. At which price is the firm producing the greatest quantity when maximizing profits or minimizing losses?
a. P_1
b. P_2
c. P_3
d. P_4
e. none of the above

_____ 9. Which price would we expect to exist in the long run?
a. P_1
b. P_2
c. P_3
d. P_4
e. any of the above

_____ 10. The market supply curve is
a. the sum of all individual firms' marginal cost curves above minimum average total costs.
b. upward-sloping because of the law of diminishing marginal returns.
c. upward-sloping because of decreasing marginal costs of production.
d. a measure of the marginal cost of producing the last unit of any given quantity.
e. both b and d.

_____ 11. Which type of firm faces the market demand curve?
a. Perfectly competitive
b. Monopolistic
c. Oligopolistic
d. Monopolistically competitive
e. Both b and c

_____ 12. In which market structure do we find the greatest number of firms?
a. Perfect competition
b. Pure monopoly
c. Monopolistic competition

d. Oligopoly
e. None of the above

_____ 13. The supply and demand cobweb shows
a. market equilibrium is obtained instantaneously.
b. the presence of external costs may render a perfectly competitive firm rather inefficient.
c. price does not always move smoothly and quickly toward equilibrium.
d. real-world markets are not perfectly competitive.
e. all of the above.

_____ 14. In which of the following market structures does a firm *not* have any control over the price of its product?
a. Perfect competition
b. Pure monopoly
c. Monopolistic competition
d. Oligopoly
e. Firms in all of the above market structures have at least some control over the price of their product.

_____ 15. The presence of external costs
a. is not counted as part of the cost of production in a competitive market.
b. if accounted for in the market would cause the supply curve to shift to the left.
c. if unaccounted for in the market would result in marginal costs exceeding marginal benefits at the equilibrium quantity.
d. if unaccounted for in the market could result in some overproduction.
e. is described by all of the above.

Use the graph on page 402 based on a perfectly competitive firm to answer questions 16-17.

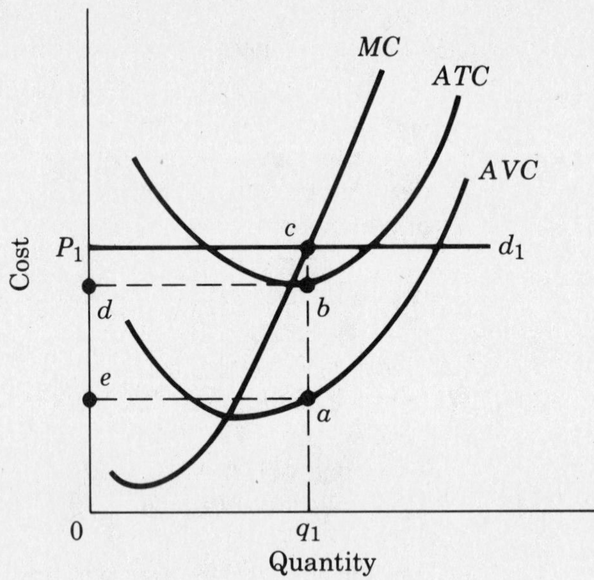

_____ 16. Which of the following statements is true?
   a. Total revenue equals $0P_1cq_1$.
   b. Total costs equal area $0eaq_1$.
   c. Variable costs equal area $0dbq_1$.
   d. Fixed costs equal area dP_1cb.
   e. Losses equal area *edba*.

_____ 17. Which of the following statements is true?
   a. In the long run we would expect the demand curve facing this firm to shift down.
   b. This firm is maximizing profits by producing q_1 units.
   c. Fixed costs equal area *edba*.
   d. Economic Profits equal area dP_1cb.
   e. All of the above are true statements.

_____ 18. A perfectly competitive firm's short-run supply curve is its
   a. *ATC* curve.
   b. *AVC* curve.
   c. *MC* curve above the minimum point on the *ATC* curve.
   d. *MC* curve above the minimum point on the *AVC* curve.
   e. marginal revenue curve.

_____ 19. Which of the following is *not* an argument made by critics of the market system?
  a. The presence of external costs may result in overproduction.
  b. The distribution of property rights and therefore income may be unfair.
  c. Firms have no control over the price of their product.
  d. Many markets are not competitive.
  e. The market system results in wasteful surpluses and shortages.

_____ 20. A perfectly competitive firm
  a. sells a homogenous product.
  b. is a price taker.
  c. enjoys complete freedom of entry into and exit from the industry.
  d. faces a perfectly elastic demand curve that is also its marginal revenue curve.
  e. is described by all of the above.

_____ 21. A competitive market produces where
  a. price exceeds marginal cost.
  b. marginal benefits exceed marginal cost.
  c. marginal cost exceeds marginal benefits.
  d. marginal cost equals marginal benefits.
  e. none of the above occurs.

_____ 22. If losses are incurred in a perfectly competitive market, then
  a. when the firm shuts down its losses equal its fixed costs.
  b. in the long run we would expect market supply to decrease.
  c. in the long run we would expect individual firms remaining in the market to produce more.
  d. in the long run we would expect those losses to disappear.
  e. all of the above can be expected to happen.

Discussion Questions

1. What are some real-world industries that closely approximate each of the four basic market categories? Which market model do you think represents the greatest number of real-world industries? *(KQ1)*
2. What are some real-world industries that are oligopolistic and sell differentiated products? Homogenous products? *(KQ1)*
3. What determines the degree of price elasticity of demand facing a monopolistically competitive firm? What could a monopolistically

competitive firm do to make the demand curve it is facing more inelastic and therefore experience greater control over its price? *(KQ1)*

4. What can we expect to happen to the prices and employment of resources in an industry (market) that is earning economic profits? Economic losses? What effect would this have on the cost structure of firms in the industry? *(KQ5)*
5. A market that earns economic profits will experience a decline in equilibrium price and an increase in equilibrium quantity (an increase in both the quantity demanded and the quantity supplied). However, as price falls, individual firms produce less. How can the quantity supplied increase in the market if individual firms are producing less? *(KQ5)*
6. What effect would the presence of external benefits have on the efficiency of a perfectly competitive market? *(KQ6)*

Answers

Problems and Applications

1. a. Perfect competition is characterized by a large number of producers and consumers who are price takers, producers who sell a homogenous product, and producers who enjoy complete freedom of entry into and exit from the market. Because the perfectly competitive producer is a price taker (the firm can sell as much as it wishes at the going market price), it faces a perfectly elastic demand curve. This is expressed graphically as a horizontal demand curve at the going market price.

   A pure monopoly market structure is characterized by a single seller of a product for which there are no close substitutes. The seller is therefore a price searcher and creates very strong barriers to entry, which prevent competitors from entering the market. Because a pure monopoly is the only seller of a product, this firm faces the market demand curve (which is downward-sloping). Furthermore, because there are no close substitutes for the monopoly's product, the market demand curve it faces is inelastic.

   Monopolistic competition is characterized by a number of competitors who have relatively little control over the price of their product, producers who sell slightly differentiated products, and relatively easy entry into the industry. Because monopolistically competitive firms sell differentiated products, advertising and other forms of nonprice competition are prevalent. Also, because of the existence of close, but not perfect, substitutes, the firm is faced with a fairly elastic, but not perfectly elastic, demand curve.

The oligopolistic market structure is characterized by very few producers, whose pricing decision are interdependent, producers who sell either a homogenous or a differentiated product, and considerable barriers to entry into the industry. The critical characteristic of oligopolistic firms if that their pricing decisions are interdependent. That is, the pricing decision of any one firm can substantially affect the sales of the others. Therefore, each firm watches very closely the pricing and output decisions of the other producers. The demand curve the oligopoly faces will be investigated in Chapter 24.

b.

	Number of Firms	Freedom of Entry	Type of Product
Perfect competition:	many	very easy	homogenous
Pure monopoly:	one	barred	single product
Monopolistic competition:	many	relatively easy	differentiated
Oligopoly:	few	difficult	either standardized or differentiated

c. i. Diagram (b) because the demand curve D_b is horizontal (perfectly elastic).

ii. Diagram (a) because the demand curve D_a looks most like a market demand curve.

iii. Diagram (c) because the demand curve D_c is very elastic but not perfectly elastic.

2. a. The demand curve facing a perfectly competitive firm is perfectly elastic (horizontal) at the market price because the firm can sell all it wishes at that price. The firm is so small in relation to the market (there are many competitors) that any attempt to charge a higher price results is a loss of sales. Furthermore, there is no need to lower price to sell more. This constant price facing the firm means that the marginal revenue from any unit sold is equal to the price and is constant. Therefore, the firm's demand curve is also its marginal revenue curve.

b. If demand or supply changes in the market, then the market price and therefore the demand facing the firm changes.

c. Any firm (whether perfectly competitive or not) will maximize profits (minimize losses) by producing where marginal revenue equals marginal cost ($MR = MC$). This occurs graphically where the *MR* and *MC* curves intersect. Therefore, this firm should produce q_1 units. (*Note:* A firm should not produce where average total costs are at a minimum. This would result in a sacrifice of some profits.)

d.
   i. Total revenue (*TR*) equals price per unit (*P*) multiplied by the number of units produced (*Q*). That is, $TR = P \times Q$. Price equals $0P_1$. The number of units produced equals $0Q_1$. So, total revenue equals area $0P_1Cq_1$.
   ii. Total fixed costs average fixed costs (per unit fixed costs) multiplied by the number of units produced. That is, $FC = AFC \times Q$. AFC at q_1 equals the vertical distance between the *ATC* and *AVC* curves, which is *fe*, and also equals *ab*. The number of units produced is $0q_1$, which is also equals *af; ab* × *af* equals area *abef*. So, total fixed costs equal area *abef*.
   iii. Total variable costs (*VC*) equal average variable costs (*AVC*) multiplied by the number of units produced (*Q*). That is, $VC = AVC \times Q$. At q_1, *AVC* equals $0a$. So $VC = 0a \times 0q_1 = 0afq_1$. So, total variable costs equal area $0afq_1$.
   iv. Total costs (*TC*) equal average total costs (*ATC*) multiplied by the number of units produced (*Q*). That is, $TC = ATC \times Q$. At q_1, *ATC* equals $0b$. So $TC = 0b \times 0q_1 = 0beq_1$. So, total costs equal area $0beq_1$. (Alternatively, $TC = VC + FC$. Therefore, $TC = 0afq_1 + abef = 0beq_1$.
   v. Total economic profits (or losses) equal total revenue (*TR*) minus total costs (*TC*). That is, profit = *TR* - *TC*. $TR = 0P_1cq_1$. $TC = 0beq$. Economic profits are earned because the area given by *TR* exceeds the area given by *TC* and is equal to area bP_1ce. Alternatively, total economic profit equals profit per unit multiplied by the number of unities produced. The profit per unit produced equals the revenue per unit ($0P_1$) minus per unit total costs ($0b$). Therefore, the profit per unit is bP_1. The number of units produced, $0q_1$, equals *be*. Therefore, total economic profits $= bP_1 \times be = bP_1ce$.

e. Because the perfectly competitive market is characterized by complete freedom of entry, in the long run any short-run economic profits encourage more investors to enter the market. This increases market supply (shifting the curve from S_1 to S_2). The market price falls (from P_1 to P_2) but the market quantity demanded and supplied rises (from Q_1 to Q_2). As the market price falls, the demand (marginal revenue) curve facing the firm falls (from d_1 to d_2). This causes the firm's production level to fall (from q_1 to q_2). As all this occurs, the firm's economic profits are zero . That is to say, this process continues until market price just equals minimum average total costs (at price P_2).

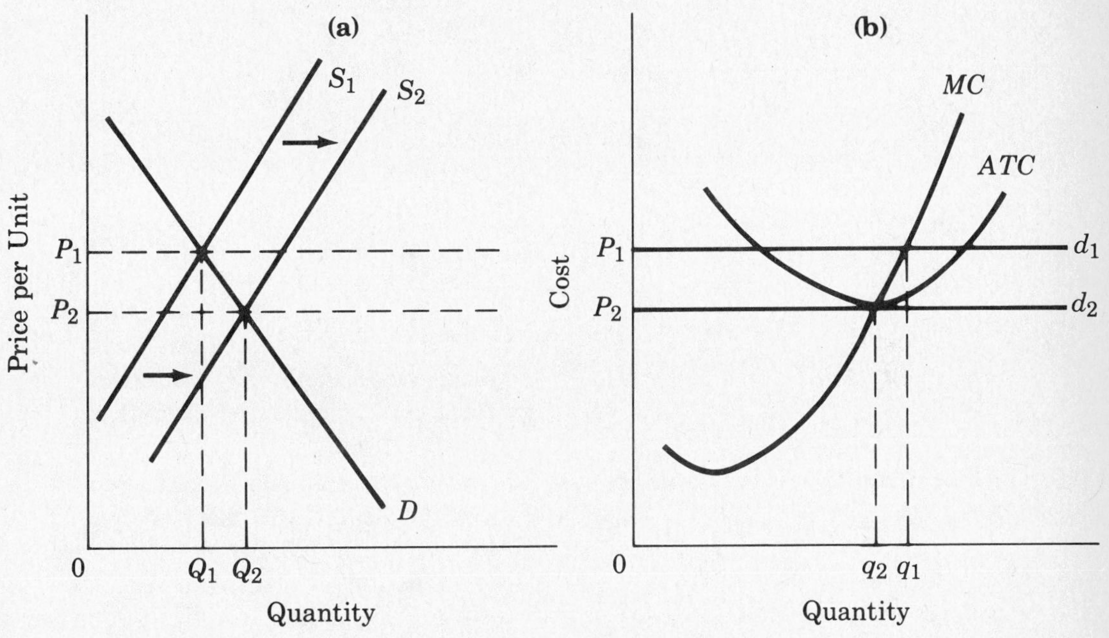

f. Yes.

g. We can conclude that if price exceeds average total costs at the profit-maximizing production level, economic profits will be earned. However, if price just equals minimum average total costs at the profit-maximizing production level, then economic profits equal zero.

3. a. All firms should produce where $MR = MC$ to maximize profits or minimize losses. A perfectly competitive firm's demand curve is also it MR curve. So, the firm should produce q_1 units where $MR = MC$ (where the two curves intersect).

   b. For a review of how to calculate these areas graphically, see the answer to question 2d.

      i. $0P_1fq_1$
      ii. abce
      iii. $0aeq_1$
      iv. $0bcq_1$
      v. Economic losses equal area P_1bcf because total costs exceed total revenue by that amount.

   c. This firm should shut down because total revenue ($0P_1fq_1$) is insufficient to cover total variable costs ($0aeq_1$). This firm is not even able to cover its out-of-pocket costs. Alternatively, this firm should shut down because losses (P_1bef) are greater than total fixed costs (*abce*). If the firm shuts down, its losses (equal to total fixed costs) are lower.

   d. No. Because total revenue would be sufficient to cover total variable costs. Therefore, some revenues can be applied toward the payment of fixed costs. Alternatively, if price is above minimum average variable costs, then losses are less than total fixed costs and the firm should remain in operation to minimize its losses (losses would equal total fixed costs if it shut down).

   e. Because the perfectly competitive market is characterized by complete freedom of exit from the industry, in the long run losses discourage some investors from remaining in the market. As some investors leave the market, this decreases market supply (shifting the curve from S_1 to S_2). The market price rises (from P_1 to P_2) but the market quantity demanded and supplied falls (from Q_1 to Q_2). As the market price rises, the demand (marginal revenue) curve facing the firm rises (from d_1 to d_2). This causes the firm's production level to rise (from q_1 to q_2). As all this occurs, the firm's losses fall. This process continues until losses are zero (until economic profits are zero). That is to say, this process continues until market price just equals minimum average total costs (at price P_2). (See graph on page 409.)

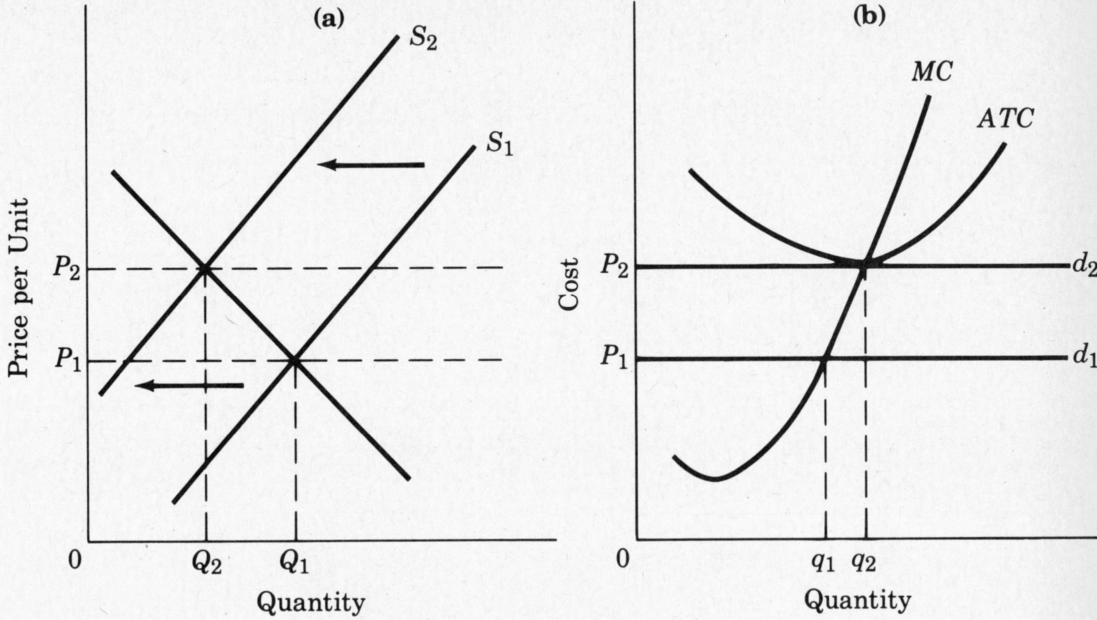

f. Yes

g. Losses are zero (economic profits are zero) when price equals minimum average total costs, but losses are incurred if price drops below minimum average total costs. If losses are incurred and price is above minimum average variable costs, the firm is losing money but should remain in operation to minimize losses. However, if price falls below minimum average variable costs, the firm should shut down to minimize losses.

h. Recall that a supply curve tells us how much will be produced at various prices. Also recall that a perfectly competitive firm produces where price (marginal revenue) equals marginal cost, and produces as long as price is above the minimum point on the average variable cost curve. Therefore, we can conclude that the firm's short-run supply curve is its marginal cost curve above the minimum point on the average variable cost curve.

4. If a perfectly competitive firm produces on a larger, smaller-cost scale, it can earn short-run economic profits and be able to underprice its competitors. On the other hand, if a firm does not produce at the lowest possible long-run average total cost, then its competitors surely will, and it will be underpriced and driven out of the market. A firm's very survival depends on its ability to minimize its

costs. Therefore, in the long run, a firm is expected to choose that scale of operation (plant size) at the low point on its long-run average total cost (*LRAC*) curve. At this point, *LRAC* is at a minimum. Plant size *ATC* minimizes *LRAC* at C_1 when producing q_1.

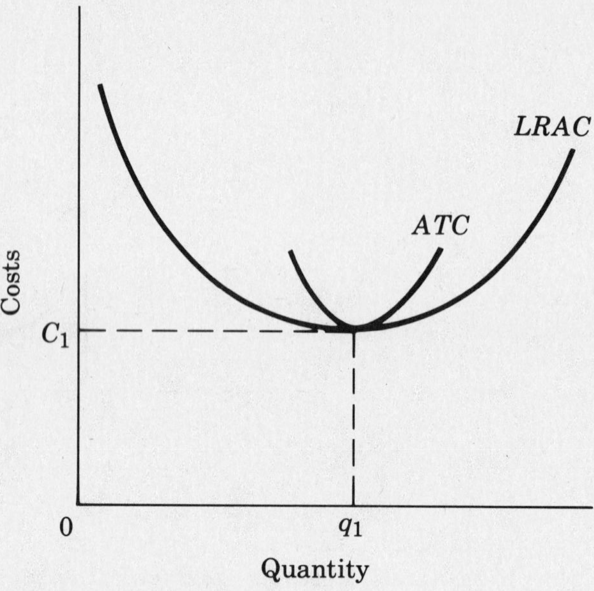

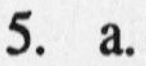
5. a.

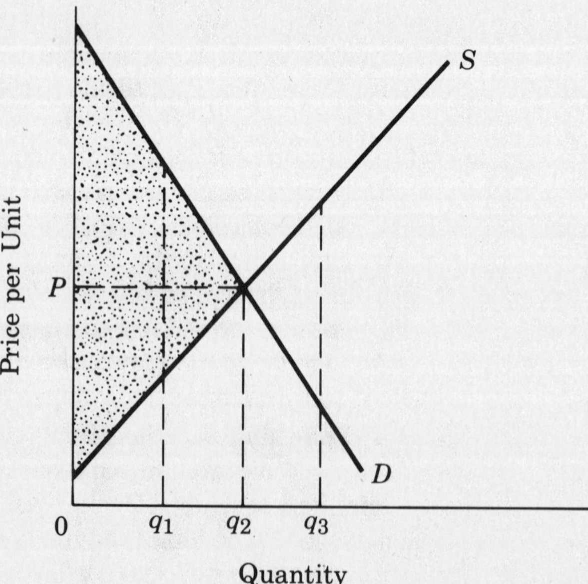

b. The demand curve. At any quantity, the demand curve indicates the price consumers are willing to pay. Price is an objective indication of the product's marginal benefits.
c. The supply curve. Recall that the supply curve is the sum of all firms' marginal cost curves above minimum average variable costs.
d. Below equilibrium (see q_1 in the preceding graph).
e. Above equilibrium (see q_3 in the preceding graph).
f. In a perfectly competitive market, q_2 (in the preceding graph) is produced. This is a quantity where the marginal benefits received form the last unit produced and consumed just equal the marginal cost of production. In other words, price equals marginal cost ($P = MC$). The perfectly competitive market is very efficient in this respect. To fully understand this, notice that at any quantity below q_2 marginal benefits exceed marginal cost ($P > MC$). Society values this product more than the cost (opportunity cost) of its production. A net gain to society (or surplus value) can be realized if production expands to q_2, as it does in a perfectly competitive market.
g. See the shaded area in the preceding graph.

True-False

1. T
2. F: The more monopolist is faced with a market demand curve that is downward-sloping.
3. F: A monopolistically competitive firm sells a differentiated product.
4. F: The critical characteristic of the oligopolistic market structure is that firms' pricing decisions are interdependent.
5. T
6. F: Any firm should produce that output level where marginal revenue equals marginal cost ($MR = MC$) to maximize profits or minimize losses.
7. T   8. T   9. T   10. T
11. F: A perfectly competitive firm's short-run supply curve is that portion of its marginal cost curve that lies above the minimum point on its average variable cost curve.

12. F: If a firm's losses are greater than its fixed costs, it should shut down to minimize short-run losses.
13. T 14. T
15. F: A perfectly competitive firm is expected to take advantage of any economies of scale.
16. F: If economic profits are earned in a perfectly competitive market, then we can expect market price and the production level of individual firms to fall.
17. T 18. T 19. T 20. T

Multiple Choice

1. b *(KQ3, 4)* 2. e *(KQ6)* 3. c *(KQ5)*
4. d *(KQ2, 3, 4)* 5. b *(KQ2, 3, 4)* 6. a *(KQ2, 3, 4)*
7. c *(KQ2, 3, 4)* 8. d *(KQ2, 3, 4)* 9. c *(KQ2, 3, 4)*
10. e *(KQ4)* 11. b *(KQ1)* 12. a *(KQ1)*
13. c *(KQ6)* 14. a *(KQ1)* 15. e *(KQ6)*
16. a *(KQ2, 3, 4)* 17. e *(KQ2, 3, 4)* 18. d *(KQ4)*
19. c *(KQ6)* 20. e *(KQ1)* 21. d *(KQ2, 3, 4, 5)*
22. e *(KQ5)*

CHAPTER 23

Pure Monopoly

Chapter Summary

Key Question 1: What is the source of monopoly power?

Key Question 2: What are the limits to monopoly power?

Key Question 3: How does a monopolist maximize profits?

Monopoly power results in a lower quantity produced and a higher price charged for a product. Monopoly power (the ability to control market price) varies considerably in the real business world. Its existence depends on barriers to entry into the industry. From whatever source barriers to entry arise, the stronger they are, the greater the degree of monopoly power. The pure monopolist possesses the greatest control over market price because it possesses the strongest barriers to entry. However, in the absence of government, the monopolist's market power is never complete. The monopolist is constrained by market demand, its cost structure, and by the fact that consumers can always choose substitute goods.

Because the monopolist is the only producer of a product, it faces the market demand curve for that product. The monopolist is a price searcher because it searches for the one price-quantity combination on its demand curve that maximizes its profits. The monopolist, like all other producers, maximizes profits by producing that quantity where marginal revenue equals marginal cost.

Because the monopolist faces the downward-sloping market demand curve, it must reduce its price on all units sold to sell greater quantities (assuming no price discrimination). Therefore, the marginal revenue from each additional unit sold decreases and is less than price (except for the first unit sold). This means that the marginal revenue curve facing the monopolist slopes downward and lies below the market demand curve. Where the marginal revenue curve intersects the marginal cost curve we get the profit-maximizing output level. Given that profit-maximizing quantity made available in the market, the monopolist charges the highest price market demand allows. This price is determined by reading off of the demand curve.

Key Question 4: What are monopoly profits?

The monopolist is not guaranteed short-run economic profits. The amount of profits (or losses) earned is calculated — as always — by subtracting total costs from total revenues. If the monopolist is losing money it will remain in operation (as would any other firm) as long as total revenue is sufficient to cover total variable costs (or alternatively, if losses are less than total fixed costs).

Key Question 5: What are the characteristics of long-run monopoly equilibrium?

In the long run, the monopolist produces where marginal revenue equals long-run marginal costs (*MR* = *LRMC*). Unlike a competitive firm, a monopolist can earn economic profits in the long run due to barriers to entry into the market. Furthermore, the monopolist does not necessarily produce at minimum long-run average total costs (*LRAC*). It simply produces that quantity where *MR* = *LRMC*. Because its marginal revenue curve is determined by market demand, the greater the demand (the farther it lies to the right), the greater the marginal revenue (the farther the *MR* curve lies to the right). If market demand increases enough, the monopolist may even produce in the range of diseconomies of scale. In short, in the long run, the monopolist may produce anywhere on its *LRAC* curve depending on the demand for its product.

Key Question 6: Is monopoly efficient?

Let's evaluate the efficiency of a monopoly by comparing it with the efficiency found in a perfectly competitive market. The price charged and quantity produced in a perfectly competitive market occurs at the point of intersection between market demand and supply. This means that marginal benefits from the last unit consumed equal its marginal costs of production. We know the monopolist faces the market demand curve and its marginal cost curve is the market supply curve, but it does not produce at the point of intersection between the two curves. Instead, it produces where marginal revenue equals marginal cost. Therefore, the monopolist charges a higher price and produces a lesser quantity (assuming no perfect price discrimination — which is very unlikely anyway). This means the marginal benefits from the last unit consumes (measured by price) are greater than its marginal costs of production. Therefore, some consumer welfare is sacrificed by the monopolist. This gives rise to what is sometimes called the deadweight loss of monopoly. Deadweight loss represents the inefficiency of a monopoly because it measures the net benefit (the amount by which marginal benefits exceed marginal costs) of those units not produced by the monopolist but that would otherwise by produced in a competitive market. The monopolist simply does not produce enough of the product. This means too few resources are devoted to the production of the monopolist's product and too many resources are used elsewhere (or they remain idle).

Key Question 7: What is monopolistic price discrimination?

A monopolist may have the ability to price-discriminate — that is, it may vary the price of its product according to how much is bought and who buys it. A monopolist may practice price discrimination if customers are unable to resell the produce they have purchased at a higher price, and if it can prevent competitors from entering the market and challenging the monopolist's market power by lowering the price of the good or service. Monopolists price-discriminate because it increases their economic profits.

There are two types of price discrimination. Perfect price discrimination is the practice of selling each unit of a good or service for the maximum possible price. This results in the monopolist's marginal revenue curve and the market demand curve it faces being one and the same. Under these conditions, because the monopolist produces where its marginal revenue curve (which, in this case is the same as the market demand curve) intersects its marginal cost curve (which is the same as the market supply curve because the monopolist is the only producer in the market), it produces the same output level as would a perfectly competitive market (where market demand and supply intersect). In this respect a perfect price-discriminating monopolist is efficient. That is, it produces up to the point where marginal benefits of consumption just equal marginal costs of production. (However, the surplus value that would go to consumers in a perfectly competitive market now goes to the monopolist as revenue.)

Perfect price discrimination is very rare, perhaps nonexistent. Most monopolists practice imperfect price discrimination, the practice of charging a few different prices for different consumption levels or different market segments. The monopolist may give discounts to those who buy a large volume. Or, if it is able to separate its market into segments based on customers' different willingness and ability to pay (a different demand curve in each segment), it will shift sales (its output level) from one market segment to another until the marginal revenue from the last unit sold in each segment is the same. Notice that because the demand curves across market segments are different, the price the monopolist charges is different. It will charge a higher price in a market segment with an inelastic demand. The practice of imperfect price discrimination results in greater profits. To find total profit, add the revenue collected in each market segment and subtract the total costs of production.

Key Question 8: What are the social costs of monopoly?

There are other inefficiencies, or social costs, of a monopoly than those mentioned earlier. First, it diverts resources away from the production of other products when it builds barriers to entry. Furthermore, resources used by the Antitrust Division of the Department of Justice in preventing monopoly power, or in breaking it up when it is acquired, are also diverted from the production of other products. Second, because the monopolist charges a higher than competitive price and usually earns economic profits in the long run (profits above what is necessary to keep investors in that business), this causes a redistribution of income away from consumers to monopoly owners (who are usually upper-income individuals). Many consider this redistribution of income socially undesirable. Third, this redistribution of income is likely to affect the demand for many products, causing a further misallocation of resources. Finally, because the monopolist may be able to earn economic profits indefinitely, it may not come under pressure to minimize its costs of production. If if does not, the result is an inefficient employment of resources.

Review Terms and Concepts

Perfect competition
Pure monopoly
Price searcher
Barriers to entry
Market demand
Market supply
Marginal cost
Average total cost
Average variable cost
Average fixed cost
Long-run average total cost
Long-run marginal cost
Marginal revenue
Economic profit
Total revenue
Total cost
Total variable cost
Total fixed cost
Marginal benefits
Economies of scale
Diseconomies of scale
Inelastic demand
Elastic demand
Surplus value

New Terms and Concepts

Monopoly power
Price discrimination
Perfect price discrimination
Imperfect price discrimination
Deadweight welfare loss of monopoly

Completion

less

higher

Monopoly power results in ____________________ (greater/less) production and a ____________________ (higher/lower) price charged than under competitive conditions. Monopoly power is a result of

barriers to entry	__________________ (barriers to entry/competition).
widely	Monopoly power varies __________ (little/widely) in the real
	business world. The degree of monopoly power is determined by the
strength	__________ (strength/number) of barriers to entry. The pure
strongest	monopolist has the __________ (strongest/weakest) barriers
greatest	to entry and therefore exercises the __________ (greatest/least)
	amount of market power. In the absence of government, monopoly
is never	power __________ (is/is never) complete. People do have
	other substitutes for the monopolist's product, and the monopolist must
	operate within market conditions. Furthermore, the monopolist's barriers
are not	to entry __________ (are/are not) insurmountable in the long run.
	Because the monopoly is the only producer of a product, its marginal
supply	cost curve is the market __________ (demand/supply) curve.
the market	The monopolist also faces __________ (a horizontal/the
does not produce	market) demand curve. The monopolist __________
	(produces/does not produce) at the intersection of market demand and
	supply curves. However, the perfectly competitive market does. The
above	price charged by a monopolist is __________ (above/at/below)
	the point of intersection of the market demand and supply curves. There-
higher	fore, a monopolist charges a __________ (higher/lower)
	price than a competitive market. The monopolist's output level is
below	__________ (above/at/below) the point of intersection between
	the market demand and supply curves. Therefore, a monopolist's output
lower	level is __________ (higher/lower) than in a competitive market.
	The monopolist charges a higher price and produces a smaller quantity
	than a perfectly competitive market because it produces where its

marginal revenue ______________________________ (marginal revenue/market demand) curve intersects its marginal cost curve. In other words, the monopolist charges a higher price and produces less because it will maximize profits

marginal by doing so. It simply produces that quantity where ________________

marginal (marginal/total) revenue and ________________ (marginal/total) costs are equal.

Because the monopoly faces the market demand curve, it must charge

lower a ________________ (higher/lower) price to entice consumers to buy more. When it reduces price, it must reduce the price of

all ________________ (the last/all) unity sold, assuming no perfect price discrimination. Therefore, the marginal revenue from each additional

decreases, less unit sold ________________ (increases/decreases) and is ___________ (greater/less) than price (except for the first unit sold). This means the

downward marginal revenue facing the monopoly is ____________________

below (downward/upward)-sloping and lies ________________ (above/below) the market demand curve it faces. When the marginal revenue and marginal cost curves intersect they are equal and this indicates the

output level ________________________ (price/output level) the firm should

produce ____________________ (charge/produce). After determining this profit-maximizing production level, the monopolist charges the

highest ________________ (lowest/highest) possible price market demand allows for this quantity to be sold. This is determined by reading off of

demand the ______________ (demand/marginal revenue) curve.

is not The monopolist ______________ (is/is not) guaranteed short-run

may economic profits. It ______________ (may/cannot) lose money in the

weak short run. If the demand for its product is relatively ______________ high | (strong/weak) and/or if its costs of production are relatively __________ (high/low), it may lose money. However, like any producer, it will remain in operation as long as total revenue is sufficient to cover total

variable | __________ (variable/fixed) costs. Alternatively stated, it will incur short-run losses and remain in operation as long as losses are

less | __________ (less/greater) than total fixed costs. However, the monopolist usually earns economic profits in the short run, as well as in the long run, because of its barriers to entry, which prevent competitors from entering the market.

In the long run, the monopolist produces where marginal revenue

long-run marginal costs | equals __________ (marginal costs/long-run marginal costs). The monopolist does not necessarily produce at minimum long-run average total costs (*LRAC*) of production. It

may even | __________ (may even/will never) produce in the range of

upward | diseconomies of scale. That is, it may produce in the __________ (upward/downward)-sloping portion of its *LRAC* curve. Whether the monopoly is producing in the range of economies of scale or diseconomies of scale or at the minimum of *LRAC* depends on the

demand for | __________ (demand for/supply of) its product.

A monopoly may be able to price-discriminate. Price discrimination

inability | requires some monopoly power and customers' __________ (ability/inability) to resell the product. Monopolies price-discriminate to

increase their profits | __________ (enhance consumer welfare/increase their profits).

rare | Perfect price discrimination is very __________ (common/rare).

highest | This is an ability to charge the __________ (highest/lowest)

possible price for each and every unit sold. It results in the firm's mar-
being identical to — ginal revenue curve ______________________ (lying below/
being identical to/lying above) the market demand curve it faces.
Because the monopolist's marginal cost curve is the market supply curve
and its marginal revenue curve is also the market demand curve and it
the same quantity as — produces where $MR = MC$, it produces ______________________
(a smaller quantity than/the same quantity as) a competitive market
would. This means that the perfectly price-discriminating monopolist is
efficient in that it produces where marginal benefits of the last unit con-
equal to — sumed are ________________ (greater than/equal to/less than) its
no — marginal costs of production. However, there is ______________
(some/no) surplus value going to consumers. All surplus value goes to
profits — the monopoly in the form of ________________ (profits/losses).

a few different prices — Imperfect price discrimination is charging ________________
different — (a few different prices/the same price) for ______________ (different/
the same) consumption levels or different market segments. For instance,
lower — the monopoly may charge a ______________ (higher/lower) price per
unit to those customers who buy a large volume. Or the monopolist may
different — segment its market according to __________________ (different/the
same) demand curves. It will charge a higher price in that market seg-
inelastic — ment that has a more ________________ (elastic/inelastic) demand.
The monopoly is able to increase profits by shifting sales among its
market segments until the marginal revenue from the last unit sold in
the same — each market is ________________ (maximized/the same).

When we evaluate the efficiency of the monopoly by comparing it
with the outcome of a competitive market we find that it charges a

higher	________________ (higher/lower) price and produces a
smaller	________________ (greater/smaller) quantity. This price-quantity
inefficiency	combination results in some ________________ (efficiency/
	inefficiency), measured by deadweight loss. Deadweight loss is the
exceed	amount by which marginal benefits ________________ (exceed/equal/
	fall short of) marginal costs of those units not produced by the monopo-
	list but that would otherwise by produced in a competitive market. The
little	monopolist simply produces too ________________ (much/little). This
few	results in too ________________ (many/few) resources used by the
many	monopoly and too ________________ (many/few) used elsewhere. A
a misallocation	monopoly causes ________________ (an efficient allocation/
	a misallocation) of resources.
other	There are ________________ (no other/other) inefficiencies associated
	with the monopoly. Barriers to entry divert resources away from other
	products, as do resources used in preventing monopolies from forming
	and in breaking them up once they are formed. This means we could
more	otherwise have ________________ (more/less) of other products.
undesirable	Monopolies may also cause a socially ________________
	(desirable/undesirable) redistribution of income. This in turn may change
	the composition of demand in our economy and therefore result in
a further misallocation	________________ (a more efficient
minimize	allocation/a further misallocation) of resources. Finally, the monopolist
inefficient	may not ________________ (minimize/maximize) its costs of
	production. If it does not, this may result in an ________________
	(efficient/inefficient) employment of resources.

Problems and Applications

1. What are the sources from which barriers to entry can arise and therefore enhance monopoly power?
2. Why is a monopolist's market power never complete in the absence of a government-granted franchise?
3. What are the relevant public policy questions when government considers breading up a monopoly?
4. a. Why does a monopoly face the market demand curve? What must the monopolist do if it wishes to sell a greater quantity? What happens to marginal revenue as more is sold and how is it related to price?

   b. Assume a monopolist faces a market demand curve that is expressed as a numerical table in columns (1) and (2) below. Fill in the total and marginal revenue columns — (3) and (4) — for this monopolist. (*Recall:* $TR = P \times Q$; MR = change in TR ÷ change in Q.)

Quantity Sold (1)	Price per Unit (2)	Total Revenue (*TR*) (3)	Marginal Revenue (*MR*) (4)
0	$15		
1	$14		
2	$13		
3	$12		
4	$11		
5	$10		

   c. Graph the demand and marginal revenue curves facing this monopolist. Does the *MR* curve slope downward and lie below the demand curve, illustrating that as additional units are sold marginal revenue decreases and is less than price (indicated by the demand curve) except for the first unit sold?

5. Answer this entire question before looking at the answers. Consider the graph on page 423 for a pure monopoly in the short run. (Assume the monopolist does not price-discriminate.)

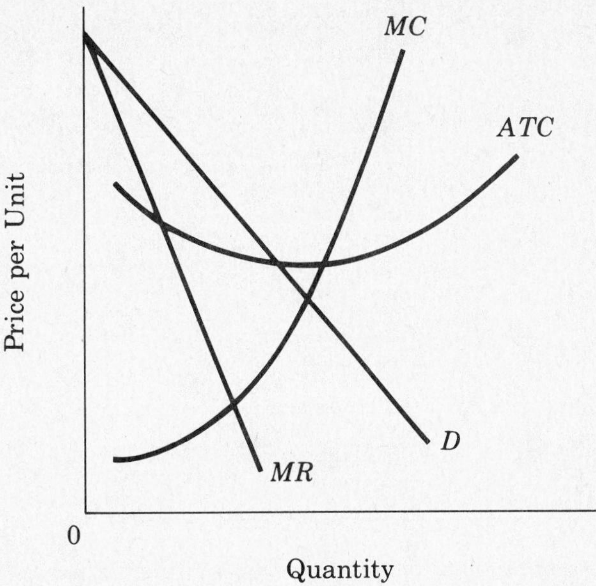

a. Indicate the quantity this monopoly should produce to maximize profits (or to minimize losses) and the price it would charge. Explain why the monopolist would produce this quantity and charge this price.

b. Indicate graphically the area expressing economic profits or losses. (For a review of how mathematically and graphically to determine economic profits, or losses, see "Problems and Applications," question 2d, in Chapter 22, and the corresponding answer.)

c. A monopolist is not guaranteed short-run economic profits. Under what conditions could a monopolist lose money in the short run?

d. If a monopolist is losing money in the short run, under what conditions should the firm shut down to minimize its short-run losses?

6. How long can a monopoly earn economic profits?

7. a. Assume a monopolist is in the long run. What quantity should the monopolist produce to maximize profits and what price will it charge? How are economic profits calculated?

b. What happens over the long run to the price charged, the output level produced, and the economic profits earned by a monopolist if the demand for its product increases?
c. Will a monopolist be forced to produce at minimum long-run average total costs *(LRAC)* in the long run? Would it ever produce in the range of diseconomies of scale?

8. Consider the following graph for a pure monopoly.

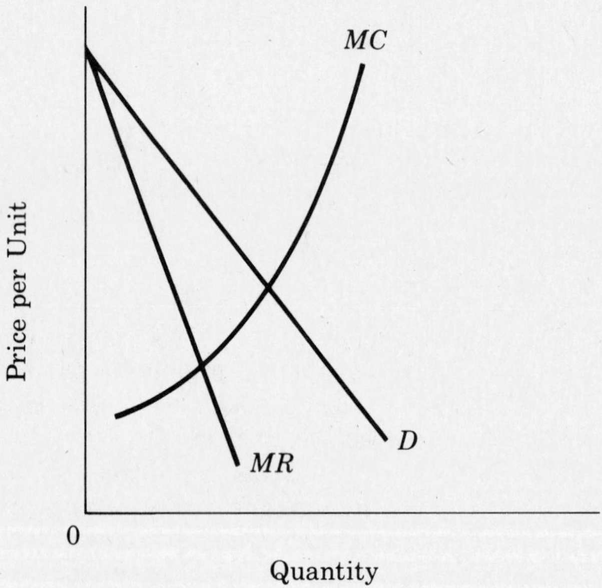

a. Is the demand curve facing a monopoly the market demand curve?
b. Does the market demand curve measure the marginal benefits to consumers from the last unit of any quantity consumed?
c. Is the monopoly's marginal cost *(MC)* curve the market supply curve? Why or why not?
d. Does the market supply curve (in the case of a monopolist, its *MC* curve) measure the marginal costs of producing the last unit of any quantity produced?
e. What quantity does a perfectly competitive market produce and what price does it charge? Indicate this as Q_c and P_c on the graph.
f. Does a perfectly competitive market produce an efficient output level? That is, does it produce an output level in which

marginal benefits to consumers of the last unit produced and consumed just equal its marginal costs of production?

g. Indicate on the graph above the quantity produced and the price charged by a monopolist as Q_m and P_m, respectively. Is this an efficient output level? Why or why not?

h. Indicate the area representing deadweight loss (the amount by which marginal benefits exceed marginal costs for those units not produced by the monopolist but that would otherwise be produced in a competitive market). In other words, indicate the area that represents the loss of consumer welfare that could otherwise be gained if this market was producing a competitive output level.

9. a. Why does a monopoly attempt to price-discriminate?

b. What conditions must be present for a monopoly to price-discriminate?

c. If a monopoly is a perfect price discriminator, what is the relationship between its demand and marginal revenue curves?

d. Given your answer to 9c above, consider again the graph in question 8. Where would a perfect price-discriminating monopolist produce and what price would it charge? Does a perfect price-discriminating monopolist produce an efficient output level?

e. Is perfect price discrimination very common among monopolies?

f. Is imperfect price discrimination very common among monopolies?

g. If a monopoly price-discriminates by segmenting its market based on different demand curves for its product, which market segment is charged the highest price?

h. On what basis does an imperfect price-discriminating monopolist based on market segmentation shift sales (its output level) among its market segments? How are profits calculated?

10. List the total social costs of monopoly.

True-False

For each item, determine whether the statement is basically true or false. If the statement is false, rewrite it so it is a true statement.

_____ 1. Market power results in restricted production and a higher price charged for a product.

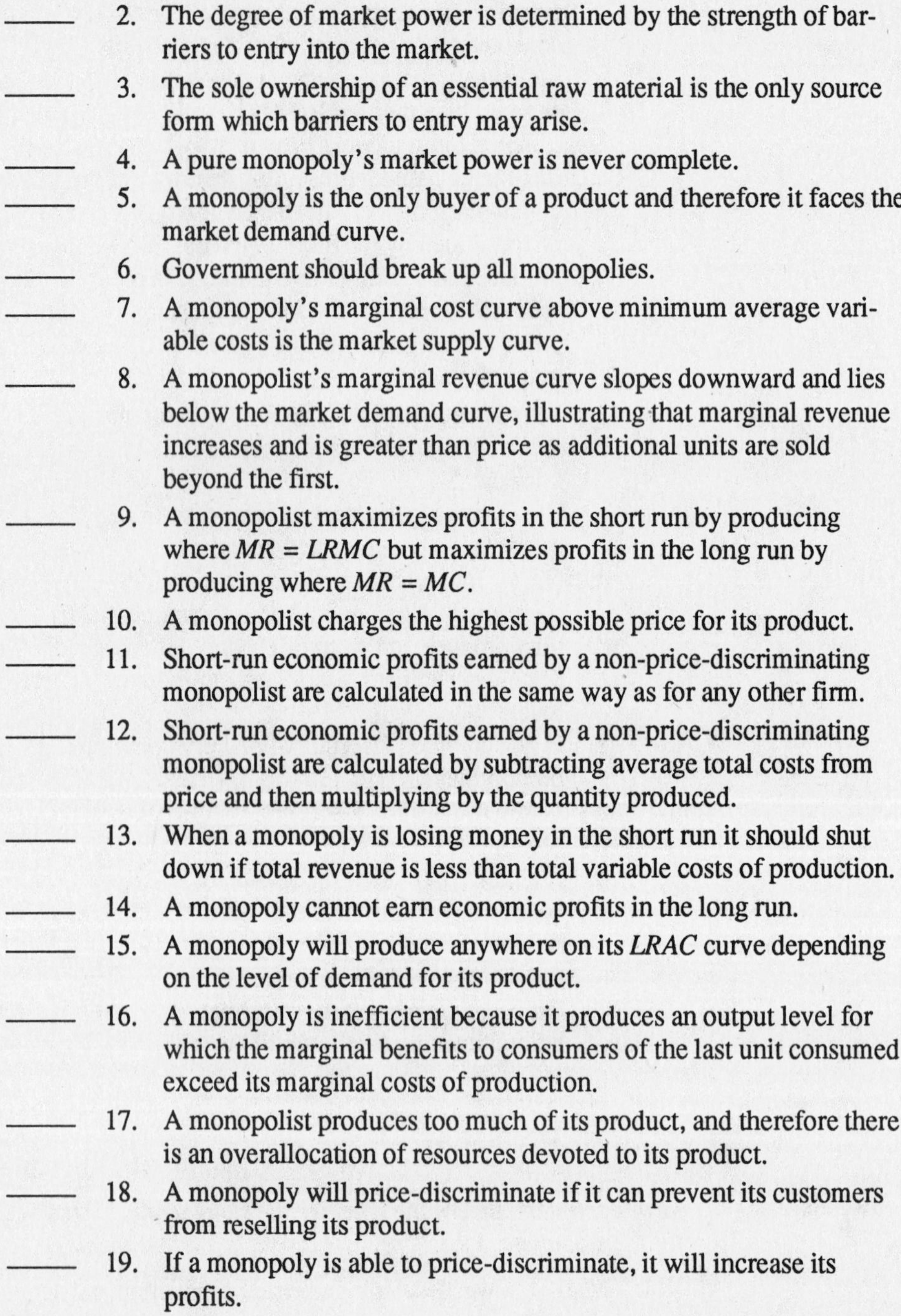

_____ 2. The degree of market power is determined by the strength of barriers to entry into the market.

_____ 3. The sole ownership of an essential raw material is the only source form which barriers to entry may arise.

_____ 4. A pure monopoly's market power is never complete.

_____ 5. A monopoly is the only buyer of a product and therefore it faces the market demand curve.

_____ 6. Government should break up all monopolies.

_____ 7. A monopoly's marginal cost curve above minimum average variable costs is the market supply curve.

_____ 8. A monopolist's marginal revenue curve slopes downward and lies below the market demand curve, illustrating that marginal revenue increases and is greater than price as additional units are sold beyond the first.

_____ 9. A monopolist maximizes profits in the short run by producing where $MR = LRMC$ but maximizes profits in the long run by producing where $MR = MC$.

_____ 10. A monopolist charges the highest possible price for its product.

_____ 11. Short-run economic profits earned by a non-price-discriminating monopolist are calculated in the same way as for any other firm.

_____ 12. Short-run economic profits earned by a non-price-discriminating monopolist are calculated by subtracting average total costs from price and then multiplying by the quantity produced.

_____ 13. When a monopoly is losing money in the short run it should shut down if total revenue is less than total variable costs of production.

_____ 14. A monopoly cannot earn economic profits in the long run.

_____ 15. A monopoly will produce anywhere on its *LRAC* curve depending on the level of demand for its product.

_____ 16. A monopoly is inefficient because it produces an output level for which the marginal benefits to consumers of the last unit consumed exceed its marginal costs of production.

_____ 17. A monopolist produces too much of its product, and therefore there is an overallocation of resources devoted to its product.

_____ 18. A monopoly will price-discriminate if it can prevent its customers from reselling its product.

_____ 19. If a monopoly is able to price-discriminate, it will increase its profits.

_____ 20. Perfect price discrimination is more common than imperfect price discrimination.

_____ 21. A monopolist that imperfectly price-discriminates by segmenting its market will shift its sales from one market segment to another until the marginal revenue from the last unit sold is the same in all market segments.

_____ 22. A perfect price-discriminating monopolist's demand curve is also its marginal revenue curve and therefore produces a competitive output level.

Multiple Choice

Choose the one best answer for each item.

_____ 1. Which of the following market structures is likely to possess some market power because of the presence of barriers to entry?
   a. Pure monopoly
   b. Monopolistic competition
   c. Oligopoly
   d. All of the above
   e. None of the above

_____ 2. A monopolist's market power is never complete because
   a. there still exist some substitutes for the monopoly's product.
   b. consumers are not forced to buy from the monopoly.
   c. it must still operate within its cost structure and the level of demand it faces.
   d. its barriers to entry are not insurmountable in the long run.
   e. all of the above are true.

_____ 3. A monopoly
   a. faces the market demand curve.
   b. must reduce its price to sell more, and therefore marginal revenue is less than price for all units sold beyond the first.
   c. is the only producer of its product, and therefore its marginal cost curve above minimum average variable costs is the market supply curve.
   d. charges a higher price and produces a smaller quantity than if its market was competitive.
   e. is described by all of the above.

_____ 4. Assume a monopolist is producing the profit-maximizing output level. The price it charges is determined by
   a. the intersection of its marginal revenue and marginal cost curves.
   b. reading off the demand curve.
   c. reading off its average total cost curve.
   d. the intersection of market demand and supply.
   e. the marginal costs of producing the last unit.

_____ 5. A monopoly will maximize profits in the long run by producing
   a. at minimum long-run average total costs.
   b. where $MR = MC$.
   c. where $MR = LRMC$.
   d. the greatest possible amount.
   e. in the range of economies of scale.

_____ 6. A monopolist's marginal revenue decreases and is less than price as additional units are sold beyond the first
   a. and therefore its marginal revenue curve is the same as its demand curve.
   b. and therefore its marginal revenue curve lies above its demand curve.
   c. because the monopolist faces the market demand curve.
   d. because the monopolist must reduce its price to increase its sales.
   e. because of both c and d.

_____ 7. A monopoly can lose money if
   a. the demand for its product is relatively weak.
   b. its costs of production are relatively high.
   c. its costs of production are relatively low.
   d. the demand for its product is relatively strong.
   e. both a and b are true.

_____ 8. A monopoly usually
   a. practices perfect price discrimination.
   b. earns economic profits in both the short and long run.
   c. produces an output level in which price equals marginal cost.
   d. incurs losses in the short run.
   e. produces a greater quantity and charges a lower price than if it were a competitive producer.

Use the following graph for a non-price-discriminating monopolist to answer questions 9-13.

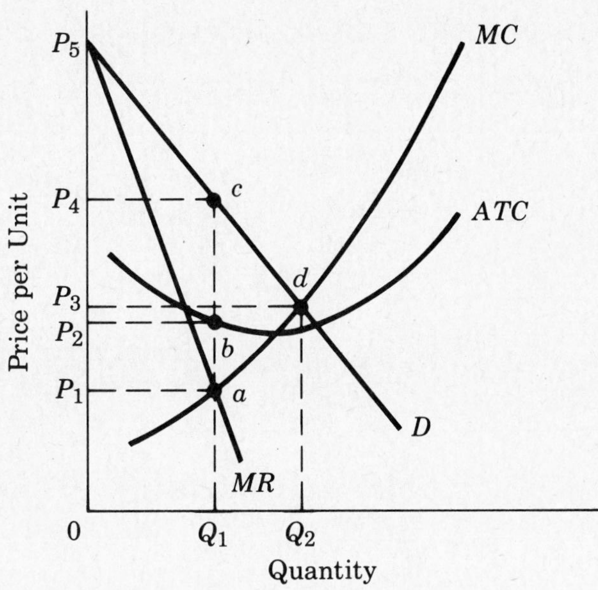

____ 9. This monopoly will produce
   a. Q_1 units and charge a price of P_4.
   b. Q_1 units and charge a price of P_3.
   c. Q_1 units and charge a price of P_2.
   d. Q_1 units and charge a price of P_1.
   e. Q_2 units and charge a price of P_3.

____ 10. If this market was perfectly competitive, it would produce
   a. Q_1 units and charge a price of P_4.
   b. Q_1 units and charge a price of P_3.
   c. Q_1 units and charge a price of P_2.
   d. Q_1 units and charge a price of P_1.
   e. Q_2 units and charge a price of P_3.

____ 11. If this monopoly was a perfect price discriminator
   a. it would produce Q_1 units.
   b. it would produce Q_2 units.
   c. its demand curve would lie below its marginal revenue curve.
   d. it would charge a price of P_5.
   e. it would charge a price of P_1.

_____ 12. The area of deadweight loss is
a. Q_1cdQ_2.
b. Q_1adQ_2.
c. *acd.*
d. P_2P_4cb.
e. P_3P_5d.

_____ 13. Which of the following statements is true?
a. Total revenue equals area $0P_4cQ_1$.
b. Total costs equal area $0P_2bQ_1$.
c. Economic profits equal area P_2P_4cb.
d. This monopolist is producing too little by the amount $Q_2 - Q_1$.
e. All of the above statements are true.

_____ 14. Which of the following statements about a monopoly is true?
a. It may produce anywhere on its long-run average total cost curve depending on the level of demand for its product.
b. If it is able to imperfectly price-discriminate by segmenting its market, it will charge a higher price in that market segment with an elastic demand.
c. The weaker the barriers to entry, the greater its market power.
d. It should always be broken up by government.
e. It never comes about because of inventions.

_____ 15. Which of the following is a social cost of monopoly?
a. It causes an undesired redistribution of income.
b. It may result in an inefficient employment of resources.
c. It causes a misallocation of resources.
d. It diverts resources away from the production of other products when it builds barriers to entry into its market.
e. All of the above.

Discussion Questions

1. What are some examples of price discrimination other than those listed in your book? *(KQ7)*
2. List some brand-name products to which you are very loyal. Why are you loyal to these brand names (why do you contribute to the producers' barriers to entry)? *(KQ1)*
3. Monopolists enjoy strong barriers to entry. However, assume an innovative competitor motivated by high profits has found a way into the monopolist's market. How is the monopolist likely to retaliate in the short run to attempt to drive this new competitor out of the

market? Now that the monopolist realizes its barriers to entry are not insurmountable, what type of long-run strategy is it likely to adopt — at least with respect to its output level, the price it charges, and the economic profits it earns? Will monopolies with relatively weak barriers to entry always attempt to maximize their profits? In either case, what would be the implications for the efficiency of monopolies over the short and long run? *(KQ1, 2, 5, 6, 8)*

4. Does a monopolist charge a price in the elastic or inelastic range of its demand curve? (*Hint:* Consider marginal revenue.) *(KQ2)*
5. What are the similarities and differences between perfectly competitive and monopolistic producers? *(KQ1)*
6. Overnight mail is most expensive when shipped through the post office. Why? Could the post office be operating in the range of diseconomies of scale? *(KQ5)*
7. Why was the American Telephone and Telegraph Company (AT&T) broken up? *(KQ5, 6, 7)*
8. Is there any surplus value going to consumers in a perfectly price-discriminating market? *(KQ6, 7)*
9. Increases in technology provided by firms that undertake research and development (R & D) provide numerous benefits to society over time. However, only those firms that earn substantial economic profits over time — such as monopolies — can afford R & D. Technological breakthroughs may also act as barriers to entry when this information is not shared with competitors. So we can see the monopoly may have an incentive to undertake R & D, and it may result in some technological breakthroughs that benefit society. Therefore, the monopolist may not be so "bad" after all. Under what conditions may a monopolist actually prevent the introduction of a new technology in its market? How important would the consequences of this prevention be for society? What alternative methods of financing R & D does society have? *(KQ8)*

Answers

Problems and Applications

1. Barriers to entry can arise from at least five sources. First, the monopolist may have sole ownership of an essential strategic resource for which there are no good substitutes. Second, it may be protected from competition by possessing a patent or copyright. Third, the monopolist may have an exclusive franchise (often granted by

government) to sell a given product in a specific geographical area. Fourth, the monopolist may own the rights to a well-known brand name with a highly loyal group of customers. Finally, there may be financial barriers that prevent potential competitors from entering the market. That is, it may be difficult to raise the enormous amounts of money required just to get started.

2. Because even if there are no good substitutes available for the monopolist's product, there still exist some substitutes, and the consumer is not forced to buy from the monopolist. Also, the monopolist is restricted by market conditions in that it must still operate within its cost structure and the level of demand for its product. (*Note:* A monopolist doesn't charge the highest possible price – that would result in the sale of just one unit. Instead, it will charge the highest possible price that market demand allows, given the profit-maximizing quantity the monopolist is producing.) Furthermore, although the monopolist's barriers to entry are very strong, they are not insurmountable in the long run. If profits are very high, then potential competitors will find a way into the market. But just how high profits have to be and how long it may take is, at best, indeterminate in the absence of additional information.
3. The relevant public policy questions are how long the monopoly is likely to persist if left alone (recall that its market power may be threatened in the long run if profits are high enough to encourage potential competitors to find a way around the barriers to entry into the market) and how costly it will be while it lasts (in terms of lost efficiency and the redistribution of income it may cause) as compared to the costs of breaking it up.
4. a. The monopoly faces the market demand curve because it is the only producer of the product. Because the market demand curve is downward-sloping, if the monopolist wishes to sell more, it must reduce its price. Therefore, the marginal revenue from each additional unit sold will decrease and be less than price (except for the first unit sold).

b.

Total Revenue *(TR)* (3)	Marginal Revenue *(MR)* (4)
\$ 0	\$ 0
\$14	\$14
\$26	\$12
\$36	\$10
\$44	\$ 8
\$50	\$ 6

c. Yes.

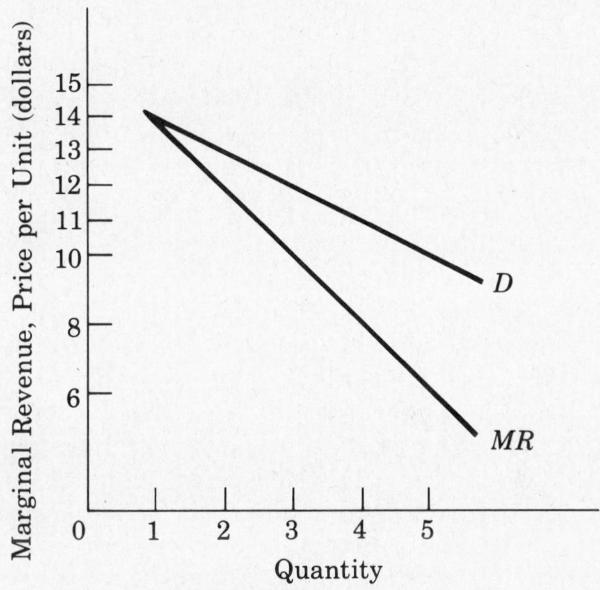

5. a. The monopolist, like any producer, should produce that quantity where marginal revenue equals marginal cost *(MR = MC)* to maximize profits or to minimize losses. When the *MR* curve intersects the *MC* curve they are equal, and this indicates the profit-maximizing (loss-minimizing) output level. Therefore, this monopolist should produce Q_1 units. A monopolist charges the highest price market demand allows after it has determined the profit-maximizing output level. Therefore, this monopolist will charge a price of P_1 (obtained by reading off of the demand curve). (See graph on page 434.)

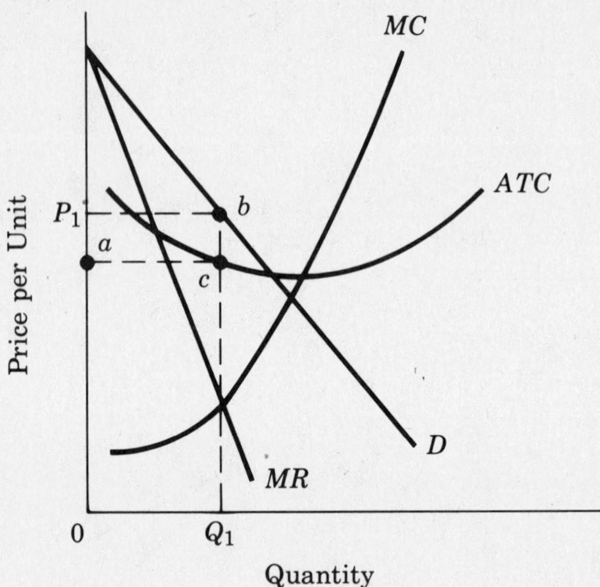

b. Economic profits are earned equal to the area aP_1bc. This is because profit equals total revenue *(TR)* minus total costs *(TC)*. In other words, profit = *TR* - *TC*. *TR* equals price received per unit *(P)* multiplied by the number of units sold *(Q)* — that is, $TR = P \times Q$. Total cost equals average, or per unit, total costs *(ATC)* multiplied by the quantity produced *(Q)* — that is, $TC = ATC \times Q$. Therefore, $TR = 0P_1 \times 0Q_1 = 0P_1bQ_1$, and $TC = 0a \times 0Q_1 = 0acQ_1$. Because *TR* exceeds *TC* by aP_1bc, economic profits equal aP_1bc. Alternatively, profit equals the profit per unit multiplied by the number of units produced and sold. Profit per unit equals the price received per unit ($0P_1$) minus average total costs ($0a$), or aP_1. The number of units produced and sold is $0Q_1$, which is also equal to *ac*. Therefore, economic profit = $aP_1 \times ac = aP_1bc$.

c. A monopolist can lose money in the short run if its costs of production (its cost curves) are relatively high and/or if the demand for its product (the market demand curve it faces) is relatively low.

d. Like any firm, a monopolist should shut down if its revenues are less than total variable costs, or alternatively, if its losses are greater than total fixed costs.

6. A monopolist can earn economic profits in the long run. Indeed, a monopoly can earn economic profits as long as the barriers to entry into its market are strong enough to prevent potential competitors from entering.
7. a. A monopolist will maximize profits in the long run by producing that quantity where marginal revenue equals long-run marginal costs *(MR = LRMC)*. Likewise, in the short run, the monopoly will charge the highest possible price market demand allows, given the profit-maximizing quantity supplied in the market. Economic profits can be earned by the monopoly in the long run. They are most easily calculated by subtracting long-run average total costs *(LRAC)* from price *(P)* to arrive at per unit profit and then multiplying by the number of units produced.
   b. If the demand for a monopolist's product increases in the long run, then the market demand curve facing the monopolist shifts to the right. This means it can receive a higher price for any given quantity produced. Therefore, marginal revenue increases and graphically shifts to the right as well. Because a monopoly produces where *MR = LRMC*, and the *MR* curve has shifted to the right, the monopoly produces a greater quantity using a larger scale of operation (plant size). This may result in either economies or diseconomies of scale. Economic profits earned by the monopoly also increase because the difference between price and *LRAC* (per unit profits) increase and are multiplied by a greater quantity. Note that economic profits increase whether economies or diseconomies of scale are experienced. In sum, if demand increases for a monopolist's product, then in the long run the price charged, the output level produced, and the economic profit earned all increase, whether economies or diseconomies of scale are experienced. Therefore, a monopoly may produce anywhere on its long-run average total costs curve. Exactly where it produces is determined by the demand for its product.
   c. A monopolist, unlike a perfectly competitive firm, will not be forced by competitive conditions to produce at the minimum of *LRAC* in the long run. Furthermore, because there is no competition the monopolist may even produce in the range of diseconomies of scale if the demand for its product is great enough.

8. a. Yes.
   b. Yes.
   c. Yes. Recall that the market supply curve is the horizontal sum of all firms' *MC* curves above minimum average variable costs *(AVC)* in the market. Because the monopoly is the only producer in the market, its marginal cost curve above minimum *AVC* is the market supply curve.
   d. Yes.
   e. A perfectly competitive market produces that quantity where market demand and market supply (the monopolist's *MC* curve) intersect. This also indicates the price that prevails in a perfectly competitive market.

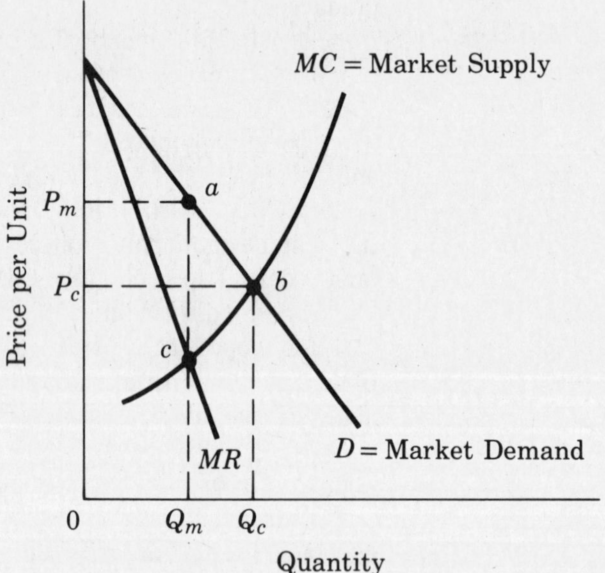

   f. Yes. Price is an objective measure of the marginal benefits of the last unit consumed, and a perfectly competitive market produces where price equals marginal cost *(P = MC)*.
   g. The monopolist does not produce an efficient output level, because it produces where marginal revenue equals marginal cost *(MR = MC)* and this results in price (an objective measure of the marginal benefits to consumers of the last unit consumed) exceeding marginal costs of the last unit produced. In short, the monopolist in inefficient because it produces too little.

h. Deadweight loss (or the loss of consumer welfare because this market is monopolized) equals area *abc*. This is because the marginal benefits of lost production that would otherwise be produced in a competitive market is given by area $Q_m abQ_c$. But the marginal costs of lost production is only area $Q_m cbQ_c$. Therefore, the net benefits lost by the monopolist's restricted output is area *abc*.

9. a. A monopoly price-discriminates to increase its profits.
   b. First, it must have some monopoly power — it must have some control over its price. Second, it must be difficult or impossible for customers to resell the product.
   c. They are one and the same because the monopoly is able to receive the highest possible price market demand will allow for each additional unit sold.
   d. Any firm will produce where $MR = MC$ to maximize profits — even a perfect price-discriminating monopolist. $MR = MC$ at the competitive output level of Q_c. The price charged would be a competitive price of P_c. Notice that the perfect price-discriminating monopoly produces where the marginal benefits from the consumption of the last unit produced and consumed equal its marginal costs of production and is therefore efficient in this regard. However, any consumer surplus that would go to consumers under competitive market conditions now goes to the monopolist as revenue.
   e. No, it is very rare, if not impossible, in the real world.
   f. Yes.
   g. The market segment with the most inelastic demand will be charged the highest price.
   h. First, the monopolist will shift sales among its market segments until the marginal revenue from the last unit sold in each segment is the same. Then the revenue of each market segment is added together and total costs of production are subtracted from this total revenue to arrive at the profit level earned.

10. First, it restricts production and charges a higher price, giving rise to some deadweight loss. Therefore, too few resources are used by a monopoly and too many elsewhere (or they remain idle). Second, it diverts resources away from the production of other products (hence, other products are sacrificed) when it builds barriers to entry. Furthermore, additional products are sacrificed when government uses resources to prevent monopoly power from forming, and when it attempts to break it up once it exists. Third, because

monopolies are able to earn economic profits in the long run they redistribute income from consumers to owners of monopolies. This, in turn, causes a further misallocation of resources by altering the demand for other products. Finally, a monopoly may inefficiently employ resources if it does not minimize its cost of production.

True-False

1. T
2. T
3. F: The sole ownership of an essential raw material is one among many sources from which barriers to entry may arise.
4. T
5. F: A monopoly is the only seller of a product and therefore it faces the market demand curve.
6. F: Government should not necessarily break up all monopolies because the social costs of doing so may outweigh the social benefits of breaking them up.
7. T
8. F: A monopolist's marginal revenue curve slopes downward and lies below the market demand curve, illustrating that marginal revenue decreases and is less than price as additional units are sold beyond the first.
9. F: A monopolist maximizes profits in the short run by producing where $MR = MC$ but maximizes profits in the long run by producing where $MR = LRMC$.
10. F: A monopolist does not charge the highest possible price for its product because this would result in the sale of only one unit. (However, it does charge the highest possible price market demand allows for the profit-maximizing quantity it produces to be sold.)
11. T
12. T
13. T
14. F: A monopoly can earn economic profits in the long run because of barriers to entry that prevent potential competitors from entering the market.
15. T
16. T
17. F: A monopolist produces too little of its product and therefore there is an underallocation of resources devoted to its product.
18. T
19. T

20. F: Imperfect price discrimination is more common than perfect price discrimination.
21. T
22. T

Multiple Choice

1. d *(KQ1)*
2. e *(KQ2)*
3. e *(KQ3)*
4. b *(KQ3,4)*
5. c *(KQ5)*
6. e *(KQ3)*
7. e *(KQ4)*
8. b *(KQ3, 4, 5, 7)*
9. a *(KQ3, 4)*
10. e *(KQ3, 4, 6)*
11. b *(KQ7)*
12. c *(KQ6)*
13. e *(KQ4,6)*
14. a *(KQ1, 2, 5, 7)*
15. e *(KQ6, 7)*

CHAPTER 24

Imperfect Competition

Chapter Summary

Key Question 1: What are the main characteristics of monopolistic competition?

Most real-world businesses approximate either the monopolistically competitive or the oligopolistic market structures. A monopolistically competitive firm exercises some monopoly power, which is reflected in the fact it faces a downward-sloping demand curve. However, its monopoly power is relatively weak, and therefore its demand curve is relatively elastic. Because its demand curve slopes downward, its marginal revenue curve also slopes downward and lies below the demand curve. Like all firms, the monopolistically competitive firm produces where $MR = MC$ in the short run. The actual level of profits (or losses) earned in the short run is calculated as before. If the firm is losing money, it will shut down under the same conditions as for any other firm. The quantity produced is slightly lower and the price charged is slightly higher than under perfectly competitive conditions. Therefore, market inefficiency (a measure of lost net benefits) is relatively small.

Because the barriers to entry into and exit from monopolistic competition are relatively weak, economic profits or losses will tend to disappear in the long run. For instance, if economic profits are earned in the short run, then investors will be attracted into the market. As the number of competitors increases, individual firms' demand and therefore marginal revenue curves shift down and become more elastic. As this happens, individual firms produce less and receive a lower price. This process continues until economic profits are zero.

When economic profits are zero in the long run, monopolistically competitive firms do not produce at minimum long-run average total costs (*LRAC*). In this respect the monopolistically competitive firm produces below capacity — it uses a plant size smaller than that which takes advantage of all economies of scale and therefore minimizes *LRAC*. This means monopolistic competition is not as efficient as a perfectly competitive market because smaller plant size results in less production and a higher price charged. However, the fact that monopolistic competition results in a larger variety of products from which consumers can choose may translate into greater benefits for society than those that result from perfectly competitive markets, where only standardized products are produced.

Key Question 2: How are price and output determined under oligopoly?

An oligopoly exercises more monopoly power (the ability to charge a higher than competitive price) than monopolistic competition because of stronger barriers to entry. Therefore, its demand and marginal revenue curves are less elastic. Because of this, and the fact that an oligopolist produces where $MR = MC$ (like all firms), market inefficiency is greater under oligopolistic conditions.

An oligopoly's pricing policies are not completely clear. This is because oligopolists' pricing decisions are interdependent. That is, the price charged by one firm significantly affects the others' sales. Each firm may second-guess how the others will react to a price change. This element of uncertainty causes theories of oligopolistic price determination to be almost exclusively confined to the short run. (In the long run, virtually anything can happen.) Nonetheless, there are two major theories of price determination.

First, an oligopolist may behave as a monopolist and produce where $MR = MC$ and charge the highest price the demand for its product allows. Alternatively, one of the firms may act as a price leader either because it has the lowest cost of production or because it dominates industry sales. A price leader produces where $MR = MC$ and then charges a price that enables its output to be sold. All other firms then charge the same price.

Secondly, there is the kinked demand curve theory. This theory does not explain how oligopolistic prices are established but, instead, why they appear to be quite stable. According to this theory, no matter how the market price may be established, the demand curve is kinked around that price. That is, it is inelastic below the market price but elastic above the market price. This is because it is assumed that a price reduction by one firm will cause all other firms to follow suit (to prevent an erosion of their market shares), while a price increase will not be followed by the other firms. This theory suggests that price changes by one firm will cause its total revenue and profits to fall. (See Chapter 18, "Problems and Applications," questions 6 and 7 and the accompanying answers.) Furthermore, because the demand curve is kinked, the marginal revenue curve is discontinuous. Therefore, only if marginal costs are very high would a firm be motivated to increase price above the market level — and then only slightly. This theory has been the accepted reasoning behind the apparent "stickiness" of oligopoly prices. However, it has been cast into doubt by recent evidence that suggests oligopoly prices are no more stable than those in monopolistic competition.

Because most oligopolies in the national market enjoy substantial financial barriers to enter, they may earn economic profits in the long run. However, if these profits are high enough we would expect other large corporations with financial capability to move into the market over time. This does not mean, however, that all oligopolies are large firms. Some of the best examples of oligopolistic markets are found in local markets. Therefore, we cannot judge the degree of competition by the absolute size of firms in a market. Instead, the basis for competition is the relative ability of firms to enter a market where profits can be made.

Key Question 3: How do cartels operate?

Firms can reduce competition among themselves and therefore enjoy greater profits if they form a cartel. However, cartels are not expected to last for very long, because each member has an incentive to chisel in an attempt to earn still greater profits. That is, each member has an incentive to move into another's designated market area, or to produce a greater quantity than its designated limit, or to lower its price below the designated level. Furthermore, each member knows the other members may try. So before the others chisel, one firm may. If this happens, other firms are likely to retaliate, and then the cartel destroys itself. Because of the built-in incentives first to collude and form a cartel, and then to chisel, the history of cartels tends to be cyclical. How long one is expected to last depends on the number of firms in the industry and the freedom with which other firms can enter.

Government can either encourage or discourage a cartel. Often, government regulatory agencies that set prices, determine market shares, and enforce the rules actually manage the cartel. Firms may welcome the regulation because it adds stability to the industry, and they may reason that it's easier to attempt to control the government agency than the chiseling that would otherwise occur.

Key Question 4: What is the U.S. government's antitrust policy?

Monopoly power results in underproduction and therefore an underallocation of resources devoted to those products where it exists. The lost net benefits associated with the underproduction could be captured, and therefore consumer welfare could be increased, if the monopoly power was dissolved. Thus, the United States government's antitrust policy is designed, ostensibly, to improve market efficiency by dissolving monopoly power and encouraging competition. Antitrust policy is based on three major laws, which have been amended and modified by court decision over the years: the Sherman, Clayton and Federal Trade Commission acts.

The Sherman Act of 1890 outlaws any form of monopoly or any attempts to acquire monopoly power. The Clayton Act of 1914 forbids certain forms of price discrimination, tying contracts and exclusive dealerships, horizontal mergers, and interlocking directorates. The Federal Trade Commission Act of 1914 empowers the Federal Trade Commission to investigate "unfair methods of competition."

There are some problems with detecting and dissolving monopoly power. The arbitrary use of concentration ratios as an indication of monopoly power can be misleading. One cannot judge the level of competition by the number or relative size of producers in an industry. Furthermore, once monopoly power has been detected, it requires a great deal of time and government resources to break it up. We must also realize that although government antitrust policy is ostensible designed to enhance consumer welfare, it has in some instances been employed actually to reduce competition. Indeed, because private firms have the power to initiate antitrust suits, the threat of a suit may prevent large firms from competing actively through better product design and lower prices. Finally, we must realize that the proper governmental policy question in determining whether monopoly power warrants government action is whether the benefits of antitrust suits exceed their cost.

Review Terms and Concepts

Perfect competition
Pure monopoly
Monopolistic competition
Oligopoly
Market power
Barriers to entry
Average total cost
Total cost
Average variable cost
Total variable cost
Average fixed cost
Marginal benefits
Inelastic demand
Elastic demand
Total fixed cost
Marginal cost
Long-run average total cost
Long-run marginal cost
Economies of scale
Diseconomies of scale
Market demand
Market supply
Marginal revenue
Total revenue
Economic profit
Monopoly power
Deadweight loss of monopoly power

New Terms and Concepts

- Cartel
- Duopoly
- Tying Contract
- Exclusive dealership
- Horizontal merger
- Vertical merger
- Conglomerate
- Interlocking directorate
- Price leadership
- Kinked demand curve
- Antitrust legislation
- Sherman Act
- Clayton Act
- Federal Trade Commission Act

Completion

	A monopolistically competitive firm enjoys some monopoly power.
downward-sloping	Therefore, its demand curve is ________________ (perfectly
	elastic/downward-sloping). But because its monopoly power is relatively
weak	________________ (weak/strong), its demand curve is relatively
elastic	________________ (elastic/inelastic). Because the monopolistically
	competitive firm faces a downward-sloping demand curve, its marginal
downward-sloping	revenue curve is ________________ (horizontal/downward-
below	sloping) and it lies ________________ (above/below) the demand curve.
$MR = MC$	The monopolistically competitive firm produces where ________________
will not	($MR = MC/ATC$ is at a minimum). It ________________ (will/will not)
	always earn economic profits. If the monopolistically competitive firm is
less	losing money, it should shut down if total revenue is ________________
	(greater/less) than total variable costs. The quantity produced is slightly
lower	________________ (higher/lower) and the price charged is slightly
higher	________________ (higher/lower) than under perfectly competitive
small	conditions. Therefore, market inefficiency is relatively ________________
	(small/large).
	In the long run, a monopolistically competitive firm will tend to incur
zero	________________ (positive/zero/negative) economic profits. This is

weak — because the barriers to entry are relatively __________________ (weak/strong). For instance, if a monopolistically competitive market is

leave — incurring losses, then some firms will _________________ (enter/leave) the market. A decrease in the number of competitors will cause individual firms' demand and therefore marginal revenue curves to shift

up, less — ______________ (up/down) and become ______________ (more/less) elastic. As this happens, individual firms left in the market produce

more, higher — ______________ (less/more) and receive a _________________ (higher/lower) price. This process continues until the losses disappear

zero — and economic profits are _______________ (zero/positive).

When economic profits are zero in the long run, monopolistically com-

do not produce — petitive firms _________________________ (produce/do not produce) at minimum long-run average total costs *(LRAC)*. Therefore, we can say

below — the monopolistically competitive firms produce _______________ (above/below) capacity. This means that monopolistic competition is

not as — _________________ (more/not as) efficient as a perfectly competitive

less — market because it results in _______________ (more/less) produced and

higher — a ____________________ (higher/lower) price charged. However, this inefficiency may not be so severe after we consider the fact that monopo-

greater — listically competitive markets produce a _________________ (greater/ smaller) variety of products for consumers to choose from. Indeed, society may benefit more from this type of market structure as compared

standardized — to perfectly competitive markets, wherein only ___________________ (differentiated/standardized) products are produced.

few — An oligopoly consists of relatively ______________ (many/few)

greater — producers. The market power enjoyed by each firm is ______________

	(less/greater) than for monopolistically competitive firms. Therefore,
inelastic	oligopolistic producers are faced with a more ____________________
	(elastic/inelastic) demand (and marginal revenue) curve. Because of this,
$MR = MC$	and the fact that an oligopolist produces where __________________
greater	($P = MC/MR = MC$), market inefficiency is __________________
	(greater/less) than under monopolistic competition. In other words, the
higher	price charged by an oligopolist is ________________ (higher/lower)
smaller	and the quantity produced is ____________________ (greater/smaller)
	under oligopolistic market conditions than under monopolistically com-
	petitive conditions.
are not	The pricing policies of an oligopoly__________________ (are/
	are not) completely clear. This is because pricing decisions are
interdependent	________________________ (independent/interdependent). In other
will	words, the price charged by one firm ________________ (will/will not)
uncertain	significantly affect the other firms' sales. Each firm is ______________
	(certain/uncertain) as to how the other firms will react to a price change.
	This element of uncertainty causes theories of oligopolistic price deter-
short	mination to be almost exclusively limited to the ________________
	(long/short) run. Nonetheless, there are two major theories of price deter-
	mination. One of them predicts that the oligopolist will price its product
monopolist	as would a ______________________ (monopolist/perfectly competi-
	tive firm). The other theory predicts that one firm will act as a price
leader	__________________ (leader/follower), either because it has the
lowest	__________________ (lowest/highest) costs of production or because
	it dominates industry sales. The price leader produces where
$MR = MC$, highest	____________ ($MR = MC/P = MC$) and charges the ______________

(highest/lowest) price the demand for its product allows. Then all other firms follow by charging the same price.

does not explain — The kinked demand curve theory ______________________ (explains/does not explain) how prices are determined. This theory explains why oligopolistic prices have tended to be quite ____________ (stable/unstable). Once market price is established, this theory assumes demand is ____________ (elastic/inelastic) above market price but ____________ (elastic/inelastic) below market price. This is because it assumes firms will follow a price ______________ (increase/decrease) but not a price ______________ (increase/decrease). This varying elasticity also implies that any attempt by one firm to either increase or decrease price will result in a decline in its ______________ (total revenue/losses). Furthermore, because the demand curve is kinked, the marginal revenue curve will be ________________ (continuous/discontinuous). Therefore, only very high costs of production could motivate firms to increase their price. For all of these reasons, we would expect firms' prices to be quite ________________ (stable/unstable). However, this theory has been cast into doubt by recent evidence that suggests oligopoly prices are ______________ (more/no more) stable than those for monopolistic competition.

Because most oligopolies are characterized by substantial ________________ (barriers/freedom) to entry, economic profits ______________ (may/may not) be earned in the long run. However, if profits are large enough, we would expect other firms to overcome the barriers and enter the market.

Answers (margin): stable; elastic; inelastic; decrease; increase; total revenue; discontinuous; stable; no more; barriers; may

are not We know that oligopolies ______________ (are/are not) very competitive. Examples of oligopolies are found in both local and national
markets. That is, oligopolies consist of both small and large producers.
cannot Therefore, we ________________ (can/cannot) judge the degree of
competition by the relative size or number of firms in the market.

decrease The purpose of cartels is to ______________ (increase/decrease)
increase competition among members and thereby to ________________
are not (increase/decrease) profits. Cartels ________________ (are/are not)
expected to last for a long time. This is because there is an incentive for
chisel on each member to ________________ (abide by/chisel on) the agreement, and each member knows it. Once one firm begins chiseling, other
firms are likely to retaliate and the cartel destroys itself. The
smaller ________________ (greater/smaller) the number of firms in the in-
stronger dustry and the ________________ (stronger/weaker) the barriers to
entry into the market, the longer the cartel should last.

Government antitrust policy is ostensibly designed to break up
monopoly power. If government can dissolve monopoly power, then a
greater ________________ (greater/smaller) quantity of products will be
increased produced and consumer welfare will be ________________
(increased/decreased). Antitrust policy is based on the Sherman, Clayton,
and Federal Trade Commission acts.

There are some shortcomings associated with antitrust policy. First,
it may be difficult to detect monopoly power. This is because we
cannot ______________ (can/cannot) easily determine the degree of competi-
a lot of tion by using concentration ratios. It also takes ________________
(little/a lot of) time and government resources to break up monopoly

power. Also, private firms may threaten their competitors with an antitrust suit. Furthermore, government antitrust policy

does not always enhance

_______________ (does not always enhance/always enhances) consumer welfare. In some instances, it has been used to reduce competition.

Problems and Applications

1. Which market structures do most real-world businesses approximate?
2. a. What determines the degree of monopoly power (the ability to charge a higher than perfectly competitive price) and therefore the degree of elasticity of demand for a monopolistically competitive firm's product?
   b. How much monopoly power does a monopolistically competitive firm have and how is this reflected in the demand curve it faces?
   c. What determines the degree of monopoly power and therefore the degree of elasticity of demand for an oligopolistic firm's product?
   d. How much monopoly power does an oligopolist firm have and how is this reflected in the demand curve it faces?
3. Consider the graph shown on page 450 for a monopolistically competitive firm.

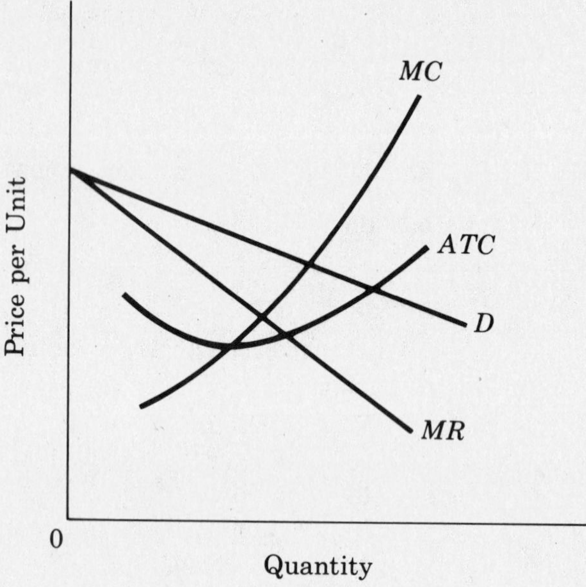

a. Indicate the quantity the monopolistically competitive firm would produce and the price it would charge.
b. Indicate the quantity produced and the price charged under perfectly competitive conditions.
c. What does market inefficiency measure?
d. Indicate the area of market inefficiency on the part of this monopolistically competitive firm.
e. Indicate the area expressing the level of economic profits or losses incurred.
f. Given your answer to 3e above, what would we expect to happen in the long run to: the number of firms in the market, the demand facing an individual firm, the quantity produced and the price received by a firm, and the economic profits (or losses) initially incurred?
g. Does a monopolistically competitive firm produce at minimum *LRAC* in the long run? Does this mean the monopolistically competitive firm is efficient or inefficient? Why?
h. How could one argue that the benefits from monopolistic competition sometimes outweigh its shortcomings?

4. Consider the following graph for an oligopolistic firm.

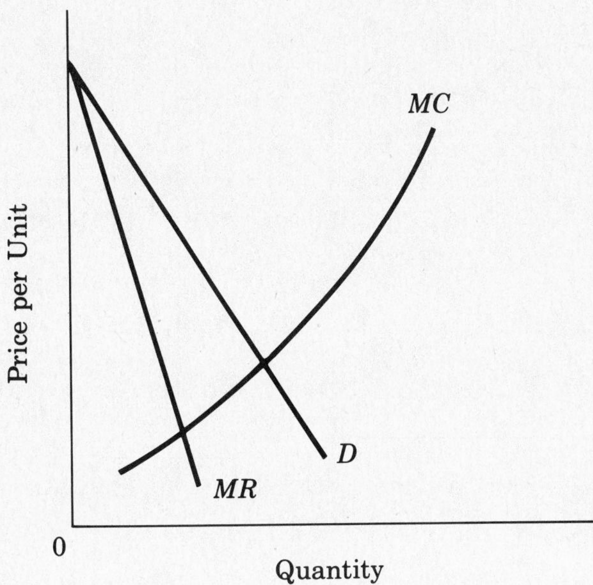

a. Indicate the quantity this oligopolist would produce and the price it would charge if it behaved as a monopolist.
b. Indicate the quantity produced and the price charged under perfectly competitive conditions.
c. Why is an oligopolist able to restrict production more, and charge a higher price, than a monopolistically competitive firm?
d. Indicate the area of market inefficiency on the part of this oligopolist. Is this greater or less than that for the monopolistically competitive firm?
e. Can we conclude that the greater the market power a firm enjoys, the more inelastic the demand for its product, and therefore the greater the market inefficiency?
f. Rank the four basic market structures according to their barriers to entry. Is this also the order in which monopoly power and market inefficiency are associated with firms in each of these market structures?

5. How does an oligopolistic price leader determine its price (the price all other firms follow)?

6. Assume on oligopolist faces a kinked demand curve around the market price.
   a. Which portion of the demand curve is inelastic? Why is it assumed to be inelastic? What would happen to a firm's total revenue if it reduced its price? Is it likely that price will be reduced?
   b. Which portion of the demand curve is elastic? Why is it assumed to be elastic? What would happen to a firm's total revenue if it increased its price? Is it likely that price will be increased?
   c. Under kinked demand curve conditions would we expect price to change very often? What motivated this theory?
   d. In light of recent evidence, are oligopoly prices any more stable than monopolistically competitive prices? What does this recent evidence mean for the kinked demand curve theory?
7. What motivates the formation of a cartel and what ultimately destroys it? Under what conditions is a cartel expected to last longest?
8. Determine whether the Sherman Act, the Clayton Act, or the Federal Trade Commission Act declared each of the following actions illegal:
   a. The practice of having the same people serve as directors of two or more competing firms
   b. The joining of two or more firms in the same market into a single firm
   c. An attempt to buy out all other competitors in the market
   d. An agreement between seller and buyer that requires the buyer of one good or service to purchase some other product or service
   e. The bribing of a competitive firm's employee to obtain a trade secret (such as a formula)
   f. An agreement between a manufacturer and its dealers that forbids the dealers from handling other manufacturers' products
9. What policy question should the government ask when it is considering antitrust action against a monopoly?

True-False

For each item, determine whether the statement is basically true or false. If the statement if false, rewrite it so it a true statement.

_____ 1. The greater the ability of a monopolistically competitive firm to differentiate its produce from its competitors, the greater the demand, and the inelasticity of demand, for its product.

_____ 2. A monopolistically competitive firm produces less and charges a greater price than a perfectly competitive firm, but market inefficiency is relatively small.

_____ 3. In the long run, a monopolistically competitive firm produces below capacity because it does not produce at minimum average total costs.

_____ 4. Relatively few firms in the real world approximate monopolistic competition and oligopoly market models.

_____ 5. A monopolistically competitive firm results in greater market inefficiency than an oligopolistic firm.

_____ 6. A monopolistically competitive firm faces a more inelastic demand curve than an oligopolistic firm because of greater barriers to entry.

_____ 7. An oligopoly is characterized by price interdependence.

_____ 8. An oligopoly that prices its product as a monopolist produces where marginal revenue equals marginal cost and then charges the highest price its demand allows.

_____ 9. Monopolistically competitive and oligopolistic firms maximize short-run profits by producing where marginal revenue equals marginal cost.

_____ 10. An oligopolist that prices its product as a price leader will produce and charge a price at minimum average total costs.

_____ 11. A kinked demand curve is elastic in the lower portion and inelastic in the upper portion.

_____ 12. A kinked demand curve assumes that a price decrease will be followed by the other firms but a price increase will not.

_____ 13. An oligopoly's barriers to entry are insurmountable in the long run.

_____ 14. A monopolistically competitive market results in a greater variety of products from which consumers can choose.

_____ 15. Cartels sow the seeds of their own destruction.

_____ 16. The greater the number of firms in a cartel, the longer it is expected to exist.

_____ 17. The Clayton Act declared as illegal price discrimination for the purpose of driving competitors out of the market.

____ 18. The Sherman Act declared any attempt to formulate a monopoly illegal.

____ 19. The Federal Trade Commission Act outlawed concentration ratios.

____ 20. Vertical mergers are illegal.

____ 21. The proper government policy question when considering antitrust action against a monopoly is whether the benefits of such action will outweigh its costs.

Multiple Choice *Choose the one best answer for each item.*

____ 1. Which of the following market structures results in the greatest market inefficiency?
a. Pure monopoly
b. Perfect competition
c. Oligopoly
d. Monopolistic competition
e. Cartel

____ 2. A monopolistically competitive firm
a. produces at minimum average total costs.
b. charges a high price and produces a greater quantity than a perfectly competitive firm.
c. will maximize short-run profits by producing where $MR = MC$.
d. produces in the range of diseconomies of scale in the long run.
e. results in a smaller variety of products from which consumers can choose.

____ 3. An oligopoly
a. is always associated with big business.
b. is characterized by less monopoly power than monopolistic competition.
c. faces a more inelastic demand curve than a monopoly.
d. charges a higher price and produces a smaller quantity than perfectly competitive and monopolistically competitive markets.
e. that is characterized by a kinked demand curve is likely to experience price instability.

____ 4. Which type of firm faces the most elastic demand curve and therefore experiences the least monopoly power?
a. Monopolistic
b. Perfectly competitive

c. Monopolistically competitive
d. Oligopolistic
e. A price leader

_____ 5. If short-run economic profits are earned in monopolistic competition, then over time we would expect
a. a smaller number of firms in the market.
b. a cartel to be formed.
c. individual firms' demand curves to shift to the left and become more elastic.
d. economic profits to increase.
e. individual firms' output levels to rise.

_____ 6. A kinked demand curve assumes
a. price instability.
b. that a price increase will be followed by other firms but a price decrease will not.
c. that a price decrease will result in a relatively larger percentage increase in the quantity sold.
d. that demand is inelastic in the lower portion but elastic in the upper portion.
e. that small changes in marginal costs will result in large changes in the price charged by a firm.

_____ 7. An oligopolistic price leader
a. will estimate its demand curve, produce where $MR = MC$, and charge the highest price its demand allows.
b. will price its product like a monopolist.
c. always produces at minimum average total cost.
d. usually accounts for a small percentage of industry sales.
e. usually has the highest costs of production in the market.

_____ 8. A cartel
a. is an agreement between a manufacturer and its dealers that forbids the dealers from handling other manufacturers' products.
b. is a kind of vertical merger.
c. is the joint regulation of market shares, production levels, and prices in order to increase consumer welfare.
d. is expected to last longest when it has a large number of members with differing cost structures.
e. has built-in incentives for its members to chisel and therefore to destroy it.

_____ 9. Antitrust policy has been ostensibly designed to
   a. reduce competition.
   b. encourage cartels.
   c. increase lost net benefits.
   d. dissolve monopoly power and therefore increase market efficiency.
   e. do all of the above.

_____ 10. The Clayton Act outlaws certain forms of
   a. price discrimination.
   b. interlocking directorates.
   c. tying contracts.
   d. horizontal mergers.
   e. all of the above.

_____ 11. An exclusive dealership is
   a. the only dealership in a certain locality.
   b. a dealership that caters to those with expensive tastes.
   c. an agreement between a manufacturer and its dealers that forbids the dealers from handling other manufacturers' products.
   d. an agreement between buyer and seller that requires the buyer of a product to purchase some other product.
   e. the joining of two or more firms in the same stage of a production process.

_____ 12. Concentration ratios measure
   a. interlocking directorates.
   b. the number of cartels in the economy.
   c. the number of horizontal and vertical mergers that are formed in a given industry during a specified period of time.
   d. the output level of the four largest firms in an industry as a percent of the total output in the industry.
   e. the ratio of monopolized industries to the total industries in the economy.

_____ 13. The Sherman Act
   a. declared any attempt to acquire monopoly power illegal.
   b. declared the Clayton act null and void.
   c. empowered the Justice Department to investigate unfair methods of competition.
   d. declared horizontal mergers illegal.
   e. declared certain forms of price discrimination illegal.

_____ 14. A horizontal merger is
  a. the formation of a conglomerate.
  b. the joining of two or more firms in the same market into a single firm.
  c. the joining of two or more firms that perform different stages of the production process into a single firm.
  d. the governmental process of measuring the expected benefits of antitrust suits against their costs.
  e. the practice of having two or more people serve as directors of two or more competiting firms.

Discussion Questions

1. What are some real-world examples of monopolistically competitive and oligopolistic market? *(KQ1, 2)*
2. Why do monopolistically competitive and oligopolistic firms rely so heavily on nonprice competition? *(KQ1, 2)*
3. What effect would an advertising campaign have on the level of demand and the elasticity of demand for a monopolistically competitive firm's product? What would happen to the firm's profits? *(KQ1)*
4. Under what conditions could a monopolistically competitive firm earn economic profits even in the long run? Why might an entrepreneur operating a monopolistically competitive firm be willing to suffer losses (a profit level less than what he or she could earn in another line of business) in the long run? *(KQ1)*
5. Why might an oligopolist purposefully not minimize its costs of production and therefore not maximize its profits? *(KQ2)*
6. Why do monopolistically competitive firms not produce at minimum long-run average total costs in the long run? *(KQ1)*
7. What could cause a monopolistically competitive or an oligopolistic firm to lose money in the short run? *(KQ1, 2)*
8. Why can't we judge the degree of competition in an industry by the number and size of firms in that industry? *(KQ4)*
9. Assume a kinked demand curve characterizes an oligopoly. Why would competition on the basis of price be detrimental to all firms in the industry? How would the firms be expected to compete? *(KQ2)*

10. What can be expected to happen to the OPEC cartel over time? What has already happened? *(KQ3)*
11. Why would a government regulatory agency be devised to encourage a cartel? *(KQ3, 4)*
12. How could government antitrust policy be employed to reduce, rather than promote, competition? Why do many firms encourage government regulation of their industry? *(KQ4)*

Answers

Problems and Applications

1. The monopolistically competitive and the oligopolistic.
2. a. The degree of monopoly power and therefore the degree of elasticity of demand for its product depends on: (1) the number of competitors, (2) the cost of expansion, (3) the cost of entry, (4) the cost of differentiation, and (5) the public's cost of gaining information of price differences.
   b. A monopolistically competitive firm's monopoly power is relatively weak, and therefore the demand curve it faces is relatively elastic.
   c. Basically, the barriers to entry into the oligopolist's market, which often are financial, determine the degree of monopoly power.
   d. An oligopolistic firm's monopoly power is relatively strong and therefore its demand curve is relatively inelastic.
3. a. Refer to the graph on page 459. The monopolistically competitive firm would produce Q_{mc} units (because $MR = MC$) at a price of P_{mc} (because this is the highest price its demand will allow).

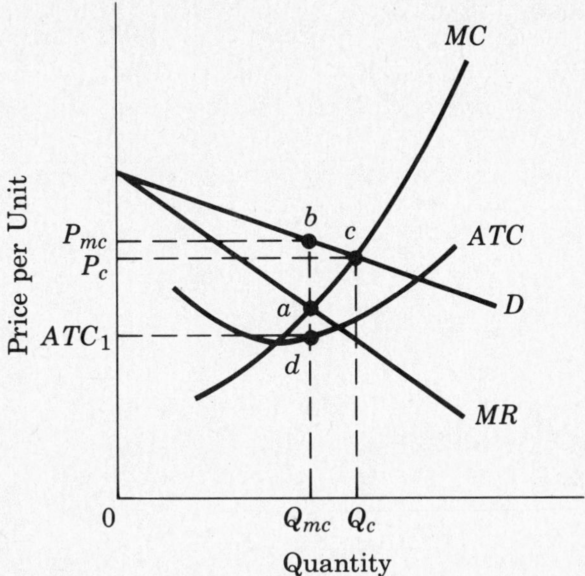

b. A perfectly competitive firm produces where $P = MC$. That is, it would produce Q_c units at a price of P_c. So, a monopolistically competitive firm charges a slightly higher price and produces a slightly lower quantity.

c. Market inefficiency measures lost net benefits. That is, it measures the amount by which marginal benefits from consumption exceed the marginal costs of production of those products not produced, but that would otherwise be produced under perfectly competitive market conditions.

d. This monopolistically competitive firm underproduces (as opposed to the perfectly competitive ideal) by $Q_c - Q_{mc}$ units. The lost marginal benefits of this underproduction is $Q_{mc}bcQ_c$. The marginal cost of these units not produced, but that would otherwise be produced under competitive conditions, is only $Q_{mc}acQ_c$ — less than $Q_{mc}bcQ_c$. Therefore, the lost net benefits (the market inefficiency) is *abc*.

e. Economic profits equal $ATC_1P_{mc}bd$.

f. A monopolistically competitive firm's barriers to entry are relatively weak. Therefore, when economic profits are incurred, investors will move into the market. The greater number of competitors will squeeze a firm's market share, decreasing the demand for its product. Its demand curve will also become more elastic as more firms enter the market because there is a greater number of substitutes from which consumers can choose. As this occurs, a firm's marginal revenue curve also decreases and becomes more elastic. Therefore, the profit maximizing quantity decreases and the price a firm receives decreases (because its demand curve has shifted down). This continues until economic profits are zero.

g. A monopolistically competitive firm (like all firms) produces where $MR = LRMC$ in the long run. However, this does not result in production at minimum *LRAC* (if economic profits are to be zero). Therefore, it produces below capacity. This results in a higher price charged and a smaller quantity produced than under perfectly competitive conditions (where production and price occur at minimum *LRAC*).

h. Although the price charged is higher and production is lower under monopolistic competition than under perfect competition, monopolistic competition may do a better job of satisfying the desires of consumers because it results in a greater variety of products from which consumers can choose.

4. a. An oligopolist behaving as a monopolist produces where $MR = MC$ and charges the highest price possible for its product, given demand. Therefore, it would produce Q_1 units at a price of P_1.

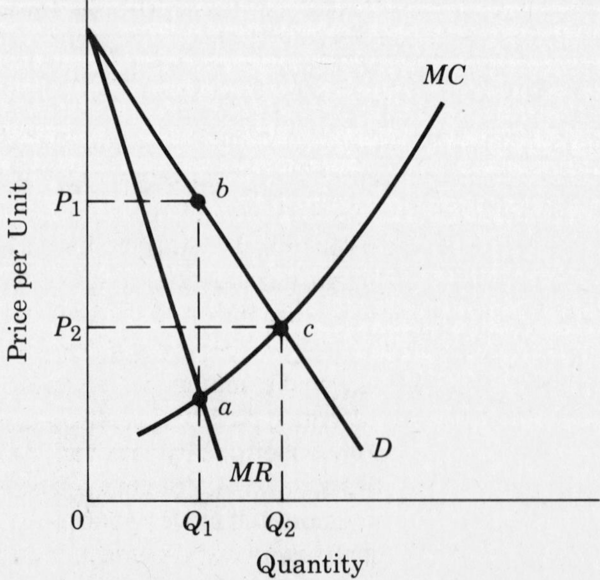

b. A perfectly competitive firm produces where $P = MC$. That is, it would produce Q_2 units at a price of P_2. So, an oligopolist produces well below the competitive output and charges a much higher price.

c. Because it enjoys greater monopoly power due to its stronger barriers to entry. This translates into a more inelastic demand curve. If the demand curve is more inelastic, then the *MR* curve is more inelastic, and output is restricted to a greater degree. (Recall that all firms produce where $MR = MC$, and if the *MR* curve is steeper, it intersects the *MC* curve at a lower output.) Not only that, but because demand is more inelastic (it's steeper), a greater price can be charged. (Recall that any non-competitive firm will charge the highest price its market demand allows for its profit-maximizing output level to be sold.)

d. Market inefficiency measures the lost net benefits of *abc*. Market inefficiency is greater for an oligopolist.

e. Yes.

f. The pure monopoly enjoys the strongest barriers to entry and therefore the greatest amount of monopoly power, followed by oligopoly and then monopolistic competition. The perfectly competitive market does not experience any barriers to entry or monopoly power — firms in this market are price takers. This is the same order in which monopoly power and market inefficiency are associated with these market structures. (*Note:* The perfectly competitive market is efficient.)

5. A price leader first estimates the demand for its product by determining the quantity it can expect to sell at various prices (the quantity it expects to sell at each of these various prices also depends on the amount sold by its competitors at these prices). Its estimated demand curve will have an accompanying marginal revenue curve associated with it. The price leader then produces that quantity where $MR = MC$ and charges a price that enables all of its output to be sold. (That price is determined by reading off the price leader's demand curve.) All other firms then charge the same price.

6. a. The lower portion of a kinked demand curve is assumed to be inelastic because a price reduction by one firm would cause rival firms to reduce their prices to prevent an erosion of their market shares. Therefore, there would be no shifting of market shares. Although each firm will sell more in its own market share (because price has been reduced), the percentage increase

in the quantity sold would be less than the percentage decrease in the price, and therefore total revenue would fall. Recall that $TR = P \times Q$. Hence, demand is inelastic and, therefore, it is unlikely for price to be reduced.

b. The upper portion of a kinked demand curve is assumed to be elastic because a price increase will not be followed by rival firms. They will instead keep their prices down in order to move in on the higher-priced firm's market share. A firm that increases its price by any percentage will find its quantity sold falling by a larger percentage. Therefore, its total revenue will fall. Hence, demand is elastic, and it is unlikely for price to be increased.

c. No. What motivated this theory was an attempt to explain why oligopoly prices appeared quite stable. Indeed, if a kinked demand curve existed, we would not expect price to change very often.

d. No. This theory is, at best, still searching for reasonable evidence to support it.

7. Cartels are formed to increase members' profits. However, the desire for still greater profits creates an incentive to chisel. Once chiseling begins, retaliatory responses bring on price wars, and the cartel eventually collapses. A cartel is expected to last longest when there is a small number or firms with similar cost structures in the cartel, and these firms are able to prevent potential competitors from entering the market.

8. a. Clayton Act
   b. Clayton Act
   c. Sherman Act
   d. Clayton Act
   e. Federal Trade Commission Act
   f. Clayton Act

9. The proper question is: "Will the benefits of the antitrust action outweigh the costs?"

True-False

1. T   2. T   3. T

4. F: Most firms in the real world approximate monopolistic competition and oligopoly market models.

5. F: An oligopolistic firm results in greater market inefficiency than a monopolistically competitive firm.
6. F: An oligopolistic firm faces a more inelastic demand curve than a monopolistically competitive firm because of greater barriers to entry.
7. T 8. T 9. T
10. F: An oligopolist that prices its product as a price leader will produce where $MR = MC$ and charge the highest price its demand allows.
11. F: A kinked demand curve is inelastic in the lower portion and elastic in the upper portion.
12. T
13. F: An oligopoly's barriers to entry are not insurmountable in the long run.
14. T 15. T
16. F: The smaller the number of firms in a cartel, the longer it is expected to exist.
17. T 18. T
19. F: The Federal Trade Commission Act outlawed "unfair methods of competition."
20. F: Horizontal mergers are illegal.
21. T

Multiple Choice

1. a *(KQ1, 2)* 2. c *(KQ1)* 3. d *(KQ2)*
4. b *(KQ1, 2)* 5. c *(KQ1)* 6. d *(KQ2)*
7. a *(KQ2)* 8. e *(KQ3)* 9. d *(KQ4)*
10. e *(KQ4)* 11. c *(KQ4)* 12. d *(KQ3)*
13. a *(KQ4)* 14. b *(KQ4)*

CHAPTER 25

Business Regulation

Chapter Summary

Federal, state, and local government regulation of business affects virtually all aspects of production and distribution in almost every industry in the economy. Currently, regulation is very controversial. The major concern is the extent to which regulatory agencies may benefit the regulated industries rather than the general public, for which they were ostensibly designed.

Key Question 1: What are the major federal regulatory agencies?

Some of the more important federal regulatory agencies include the Interstate Commerce Commission (ICC), Federal Trade Commission (FTC), Federal Communications Commission (FCC), Federal Energy Regulatory Commission (FERC), Nuclear Regulatory Commission (NRC), Securities and Exchange Commission (SEC), Food and Drug Administration (FDA), and Occupational Safety and Health Administration (OSHA). By studying their origins and functions, we can learn much about the regulatory process.

Key Question 2: What is the evidence of the public interest theory of regulation?

There are three major theories of public regulation. First, the public interest theory justifies regulation on the grounds that some commonly acknowledged national goals may be pursued through regulation. These may include a more democratic allocation of the nation's resources, an increase in market efficiency, and the enhancement of the nation's ability to pursue certain essentially political objectives (such as national defense). Economists' theories of regulation tend to be based on the goal of increasing market efficiency.

Market efficiency will be enhanced if regulation effectively incorporates external costs and benefits into the market. For instance, regulation may increase the safety of products. Market efficiency is also increased when industries that exercise monopoly power are forced to produce and price their products at perfectly competitive levels. By doing so, the lost net benefits of underproduction will be captured. That is, the marginal benefits of the last unit produced will equal the marginal cost of its production. Furthermore, forcing non-competitive firms to produce and price their products competitively may prevent them from otherwise earning excess economic profits in the long run. Therefore, regulation may help prevent an otherwise inequitable or unjust redistribution of income away from consumers to owners of noncompetitive firms. To accomplish this market efficiency, all government regulators need to do is to require that firms charge no more than what is considered the perfectly competitive price. However, determining that price may be very difficult, if not impossible. Nonetheless, requiring an industry to produce more by regulating the price it can charge will increase market efficiency even if the perfectly competitive ideal cannot be realistically obtained. In attempting to promote market efficiency through regulation we must never overlook its costs. That is, if we are to increase the efficiency of the overall social system, the benefits of regulation must exceed its costs.

So far our discussion of regulating monopoly power has assumed rising marginal costs. But if marginal costs in an industry decrease in the long run over the relevant range of production — that is, if an industry experiences economies of scale — it may be characterized by a natural monopoly. (Examples of natural monopolies include electric utilities.) Natural monopolies are seen as prime candidates for regulation, for their dominance in the market allows them to exert considerable monopoly power. However, many economists question the need for regulation. They point out that the substantial economic profits earned by restricting output and charging a higher price only invite potential competitors. Therefore, the fear of competition may restrain a natural monopoly's monopolistic tendencies. Furthermore, requiring a natural monopoly to price at the competitive level may force it to lose money. If this happens, then government subsidization and/or the allowance of price discrimination may be required, and this can create still further problems.

The public interest theory is not applicable to all forms of government regulation. Clearly, environmental, traffic, and other safety rules promote public goals. However, research has raised especially serious doubts about the usefulness to the public of economic regulation. Indeed, some empirical evidence suggests that economic regulation has served the regulated industry, as opposed to the general public.

Key Question 3: What is the economic or private theory of regulation?

The second theory of regulation is the economic (or private) theory. This theory does not view regulation as something imposed on firms by a government intent on serving the public interest. Instead, regulation is viewed as a service frequently sought by those who are regulated. Government is seen as a supplier of regulatory services that may decrease the industry's need to compete. However, these regulatory services come at a cost — campaign contributions, lucrative consulting jobs, or votes and volunteer work for political campaigns. But firms still demand regulation because the formation and maintenance of a cartel may be more costly.

According to the economic theory, the benefits of regulation are enjoyed by everyone in the industry. But the organizational and political costs of procuring regulation fall only on those who seek it. When large groups seek regulation they may entail a free-rider problem, which can cause the costs to exceed the expected benefits for those who seek regulation. For this reason collective action may not be pursued and therefore regulation may not be secured by large groups (although there have been some exceptions). Instead, small groups are more likely to secure regulation.

The economic (or private) theory of regulation is supported by much historical evidence. But because it is such a general theory, it is not equipped to predict which industries are likely to seek or achieve government regulation. Furthermore, it does not explain the current movement to deregulate some industries and to regulate the environment, where there is no particular business interest group demanding it.

Key Question 4: In what way is regulation like taxation?

The third major theory of regulation views regulation as a form of taxation — in the sense that taxation is the government's means of extracting money to pay for what are viewed as public good and services. In other words, if having lower prices for some goods and services is considered socially beneficial, then government regulation can force consumers to pay higher prices for other products so that these items' prices may be lowered.

Key Question 5: Why has the U.S. economy become increasingly deregulated in recent years?

Recently there has been a widespread movement toward deregulating American industry. Because much is yet to be learned about what motivates regulation and who benefits from it, any assessment of this trend must be considered tentative.

The public interest and economic theories of regulation presented in this chapter are not mutually exclusive explanations of real-world behavior. Instead, a combination of the two theories may go a long way in explaining the complex sources of regulation. Furthermore, probably the most important lesson to be learned from the study of regulation is that while the pursuit of the public's interest is valid basis for regulation, it can easily be exploited. Quite often those who argue in favor of regulation for public interest are promoting their own interest instead.

Review Terms and Concepts

External benefits
External costs
Public good
Monopoly power
Marginal benefits
Marginal cost
Market inefficiency
Deadweight loss of monopoly power
Economies of scale
Natural monopoly

New Terms and Concepts

Subadditive costs
Natural monopoly
Contestable market
Free-rider problem
Interstate Commerce Commission (ICC)
Federal Trade Commission (FTC)
Federal Communications Commission (FCC)
Federal Energy Regulatory Commission (FERC)
Nuclear Regulatory Commission (NRC)
Securities and Exchange Commission (SEC)
Food and Drug Administration (FDA)
Occupational Safety and Health Administration (OSHA)
Public interest theory of regulation
Economic theory of regulation
The theory of regulation as taxation

Completion

Federal, state, and local government regulation of business affects
virtually all ____________________ (virtually all/very few) aspects of production and
distribution in most industries in the economy. Currently, regulatory
very, Many policies are ________________ (not/very) controversial. ____________
(Many/Few) economists are concerned that regulatory agencies may be
benefiting the regulated industries as opposed to the general public.

There are three major theories of public regulation. One of them is the
public ______________________ (public/business) interest theory of regulation.
may This theory states that regulation ____________ (may/may not) make it

market efficiency

possible to pursue some commonly acknowledged national goals. One of these national goals, which is of particular concern to economists, is obtaining ________________________________ (a viable national defense/market efficiency).

externalities
increased
safety

One of the inefficiencies of a market economy is the presence of ____________________ (public goods/externalities). If external costs and benefits can be controlled by regulation, then market efficiency will be __________________ (increased/decreased). One external benefit that regulation may effectively incorporate into the market is __________________ (pollution/safety).

curtailed
greater
lower
greater
lost
gained
charge a perfectly competitive price
decrease

Market efficiency can also be increased through regulation if monopoly power can be ____________________ (curtailed/enhanced). If noncompetitive firms are forced to produce at perfectly competitive levels, then a __________________ (smaller/greater) quantity of products will be produced at a __________________ (lower/higher) price. The marginal benefits of this increased production will be __________________ (less/greater) than its marginal costs. Therefore, these net benefits, which would otherwise be _____________ (lost/gained) under noncompetitive market conditions, will be _____________ (lost/gained) when regulatory agencies force noncompetitive firms to produce and price their products at competitive levels. All regulatory agencies need to do to ensure that production occurs where the marginal benefits from the last unit consumed equal its marginal cost is to require noncompetitive firms to ________________________________ (charge a perfectly competitive price/produce where $MR = MC$). This will also __________________ (increase/decrease) the economic profits noncompetitive firms can earn, a decrease — which causes ____________________ (an increase/a decrease) in the inequitable redistribution of income away from consumers to owners of noncompetitive firms. In reality, determining the perfectly competitive

difficult — price is __________________ (simple/difficult).

Not all — ____________ (All/Not all) regulation that increases market efficiency should be undertaken, because if we are to increase the efficiency of

benefits — the overall social system, the _________________ (costs/benefits) of

costs — regulation must exceed its _________________ (costs/benefits).

Not all — _______________ (All/Not All) monopoly power should be dissolved. A natural monopoly may be socially beneficial because it is able

economies — to take advantage of ___________________ (economies/diseconomies) of scale. However, natural monopolies are seen as prime candidates for regulation because of their market dominance. Many economists

disagree — _________________ (agree/disagree) with the notion that regulation of natural monopolies is necessary, because a natural monopoly's tendency

restrained — toward exercising market power will be _______________________ (encouraged/restrained) by the fear of competition. Furthermore, regula-

only invite more — tion of a natural monopoly may ____________________________ (discourage/only invite more) government bureaucracy if the regulation forces the firm to lose money.

is not — The public interest theory ___________ (is/is not) applicable to all forms of government regulation. Many economists have reservations

economy — about the use of regulation in the _________________ (environment/economy). Some recent evidence suggests that economic regulation has

regulated — served the _________________ (public/regulated) at the expense of the

public — _________________ (public/regulated).

According to a second theory of regulation, government regulation is viewed as a service frequently sought by those who are regulated. This is

economic — the ____________ (taxation/economic) theory of regulation.

decreases — Businesses may seek regulation because it ____________ (increases/decreases) competition. They may reason that the cost of

cheaper — securing the regulation is ____________ (cheaper/more costly) than the cost of forming and maintaining a cartel. However, it is usually

small — ____________ (large/small) groups that are more likely to secure regulation.

is — The economic theory of regulation ____________ (is/is not) supported by much historical evidence. But because it is such a general

does not — theory it ____________ (does/does not) lend itself to concrete predictions. However, it points out an important lesson in the study of regulation: although the public interest is valid basis for regulation, it

can — ____________ (can/cannot) be easily exploited by those who are promoting their own interest.

Finally, there is also a theory of regulation that views regulation as a

taxation — form of ____________ (taxation/market efficiency). In other words, regulation may be a means of extracting money to pay for what

public — are viewed as ____________ (private/public) goods and services.

Problems and Applications

1. Determine which of the major federal regulatory agencies discussed in the textbook is being referred to in each of the following descriptions.
   a. In 1931 it became part of the Department of Health, Education, and Welfare.
   b. It regulates the use of some natural resources.

c. For decades economists have advocated reducing its power because it has tended to benefit those who are regulated, at the expense of consumers.
d. It issues licenses for three-year periods, and it requires firms to provide some public service.
e. It was established in 1934 in response to many instances of fraud, as well as to the conditions that helped cause the Great Depression.
f. It investigates tendencies toward greater industrial concentration and advises the president and Congress on antitrust law.
g. It is currently the most controversial government regulatory agency.

2. What is the overriding condition that must be met for regulation to increase the efficiency of the overall social system?
3. How can regulation that keeps price above competitive levels be socially beneficial?
4. Use the following graph based on a cartelized industry to answer questions a-g.

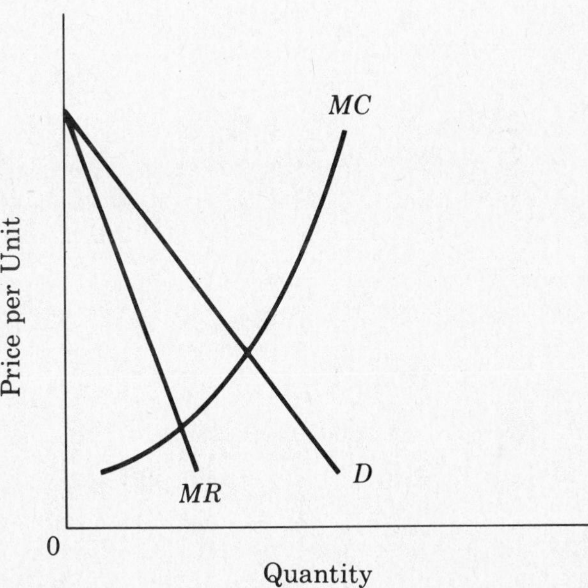

a. Assume this cartel prices its products as a monopolist. Indicate the quantity that will be produced and the price that it will charge.

b. Assume this was a perfectly competitive industry. Indicate the quantity that would be produced and the price that would be charged.
c. Why is the perfectly competitive outcome efficient?
d. Why is the cartel's noncompetitive outcome inefficient? Indicate the area of market inefficiency caused by this noncompetitive outcome.
e. How could government regulation increase market efficiency in this industry? What effect would this have on industry profits?
f. Given your answer to the preceding questions, what effect would regulation have on the inequitable redistribution of income away from consumers to owners of the cartel?
g. What problems might the regulatory agency encounter in attempting to force a competitive outcome from this industry?

5. a. How can a natural monopoly come into existence?
b. Why is a natural monopoly a prime candidate for regulation?
c. Why do many economists argue that regulation of natural monopolies may not be necessary?
d. What are some arguments in favor of regulating natural monopolies? (See the appendix to this chapter in the textbook.)
e. What are some arguments against regulating natural monopolies? (See the appendix to this chapter in the textbook.)

6. Why has regulation so often had little effect in reducing the profitability (market power) of regulated industries?
7. In the economic theory of regulation, government is seen as a supplier of regulatory services to industry. What are some of these services?

True-False

For each item, determine whether the statement is basically true or false. If the statement is false, rewrite it so it is a true statement.

_____ 1. Small groups are more likely to secure regulation than large groups.

_____ 2. Many economists question whether regulatory agencies as a group have been pursuing the public interest in any systematic way.

_____ 3. Government regulatory agencies have little effect on the production and distribution of products in most industries.

_____ 4. The ICC has tended to benefit consumers, at the expense of the regulated.

_____ 5. According to many economists, regulation of the economy in the pursuit of the public interest has almost always benefited consumers.

_____ 6. Regulation is socially worthwhile as long as it reduces market inefficiency.

_____ 7. The SEC can be viewed as a public service because it increases the public's confidence in the stock market.

_____ 8. Evidence seems to support economic theory of regulation.

_____ 9. Regulation to capture externalities may benefit consumers by leading to safer products.

_____ 10. Regulation to increase market efficiency can be obtained by requiring firms to charge a price for their product that equals the marginal cost of the last unit produced.

_____ 11. Regulation of industries that exercise monopoly power contributes to an inequitable distribution of income.

_____ 12. To accomplish market efficiency, all government regulators need to do is require firms to produce where $MR = MC$.

_____ 13. Natural monopolies are often seen as prime candidates for regulation because their dominance in the market allows them to exert considerable monopoly power.

_____ 14. Many economists question the need for regulating natural monopolies.

_____ 15. Requiring a natural monopoly to price at the competitive level may force it to lose money.

_____ 16. Businesses are very unlikely to argue for regulation of their industry.

_____ 17. Quite often those who argue in favor of regulation for the public interest are promoting their own interest instead.

_____ 18. A contestable market is a market where there are strong barriers to entry which promotes monopolistic behavior.

Multiple Choice *Choose the one best answer for each item.*

_____ 1. Which of the following federal regulatory agencies investigates tendencies toward greater industrial concentration?

a. Interstate Commerce Commission
b. Federal Trade Commission
c. Federal Energy Regulatory Commission

d. Securities and Exchange Commission
e. Food and Drug Administration

_____ 2. The public interest theory of regulation is founded in part on the need
a. for a more democratic allocation of the nation's resources.
b. to capture external benefits, like safety.
c. to reduce market inefficiency in those industries where monopoly power exists.
d. to avoid unnecessary or destructive competition.
e. for all of the above.

_____ 3. Which of the following is expected to occur if a noncompetitive market is regulated to increase market efficiency?
a. Economic profits will rise.
b. A more inequitable redistribution of income away from consumers to owners of noncompetitive firms will occur.
c. Firms will produce where $MR = MC$.
d. A greater quantity of the product will be produced and a lower price will be charged.
e. Lost net benefits will increase.

_____ 4. A natural monopoly
a. exists when long-run marginal costs decrease over the relevant range of production.
b. can be easily regulated without the presence of complicating side effects.
c. requires regulation, according to all economists, because it is protected by very strong barriers to entry.
d. will never earn economic profits in the long run.
e. never exists in the real world.

_____ 5. One of the problems in requiring firms that exert monopoly power to charge a competitive price is
a. they must produce a competitive output level.
b. the cost of determining that price may be very high.
c. firms are likely to underestimate their costs of production when no other competitor's cost estimates exist.
d. the firms' profits are likely to rise.
e. none of the above.

_____ 6. Evidence of economic regulation
a. is inconclusive.
b. suggests that more regulation is needed.

c. suggests that regulatory agencies as a group may not be systematically pursuing the public interest.
d. suggests that all forms of regulation should be abolished.
e. is yet to be gathered and analyzed.

_____ 7. The economic theory of regulation suggests that
a. if firms in an industry do not wish to compete, they will demand protective regulation.
b. regulation is a form of taxation.
c. regulation should be increased to increase market efficiency.
d. large groups are more likely to secure regulation than small groups.
e. regulation is almost always imposed on firms by a government intent on serving the public interest.

_____ 8. To maximize social efficiency, regulation should be undertaken only if
a. the benefits outweigh the cost.
b. competition is increased.
c. market efficiency is increased.
d. the number of firms in a market increases.
e. the quality of products is increased.

_____ 9. Regulation as a method of taxation is designed to
a. increase the price of those products that are considered socially beneficial.
b. increase government tax revenues by taxing monopoly profits.
c. increase the price of some goods and services so that other goods and services will be cheaper.
d. minimize government influence over natural monopolies.
e. promote a more fair or equitable corporate income tax structure.

_____ 10. According to the economic theory of regulation, a firm's profits may be increased if government regulation
a. builds barriers to entry.
b. taxes the production of a complementary product.
c. subsidizes the production of a substitute product.
d. abolishes price fixing.
e. does all of the above.

_____ 11. Regulation based on a "fair" rate of return has resulted in
a. lower profits.
b. greater amounts of labor and capital employed in the production process.
c. lower production costs.

d. greater amounts of capital but less labor employed in the production process.
e. less production.

Discussion Questions

1. Under what conditions would you argue that regulation increases freedom? Decreases freedom? *(KQ2)*
2. We know there is an economic problem with regulation that actually decreases competition because it contributes to market inefficiency. What are some potential problems that may result from firms paying the price for securing this type of regulation? *(KQ3)*
3. Under what conditions may it be in the public's best interest for government to provide regulatory services to an industry even if it decreases competition? (*Hint:* What are some of the social costs associated with a cartel?) *(KQ2)*
4. What changes would you propose in the major federal regulatory agencies discussed in the textbook to increase their inefficiency? *(KQ1)*
5. Why might a natural monopoly be socially beneficial? What are some of the problems associated with regulation that forces a natural monopoly to produce and price its product at a competitive level? *(KQ2)*

Answers

Problems and Applications

1. a. Food and Drug Administration (FDA)
   b. Federal Energy Regulatory Commission (FERC)
   c. Interstate Commerce Commission (ICC)
   d. Federal Communications Commission (FCC)
   e. Securities and Exchange Commission (SEC)
   f. Federal Trade Commission (FTC)
   g. Occupational Safety and Health Administration (OSHA)
2. The benefits of regulation must outweigh its costs. Therefore, not all market inefficiency can be expected to be controlled.
3. Regulation that keeps price above competitive levels may be socially beneficial if it increases the level of safety in an industry. In other words, if firms are unable to attract more customers by lower prices, they may compete through better quality and safety.

Examples include the airline and nuclear power industries, where price competition puts pressure on firms to control costs. This may result in cutting corners on safety. However, like all regulation, it is recommended only when the benefits (in this case, safety) are expected to outweigh the costs (costs include the usual organization and enforcement costs, and in this case some market inefficiency this type of regulation may cause because price is kept above the competitive level).

4. a. It will produce where $MR = MC$ and charge the highest price its demand allows. Therefore, it produces Q_m units at a price of P_m.

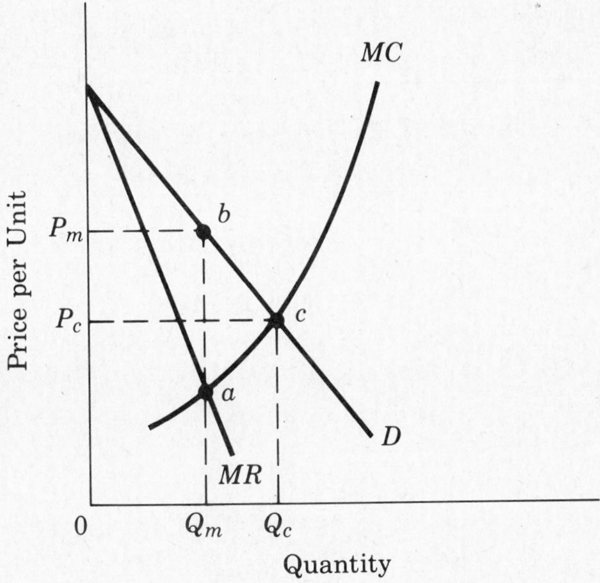

b. A perfectly competitive outcome in this industry would be a production of Q_c units sold at a price of P_c.

c. The perfectly competitive outcome is efficient because production occurs where $P = MC$. In other words, the marginal benefits of the last unit consumed (measured by price) equal the marginal cost (MC) of its production.

d. The cartel's noncompetitive outcome is inefficient because it produces where $P > MC$. In other words, the marginal benefits of the last unit consumed exceed its marginal cost of production. Therefore, the cartel produces too little equal to Q_c - Q_m

units. The marginal benefits of this underproduction equal the area under the demand curve, Q_mbcQ_c. This is greater than the marginal costs of the units underproduced, which is equal to the area under the *MC* curve, Q_macQ_c. Therefore, lost net benefits associated with the cartel's underproduction is area *abc*. Area *abc* equals the market inefficiency.

e. Market efficiency is increased when lost benefits associated with underproduction are captured. Regulation can capture these lost net benefits associated with underproduction by forbidding the cartel to charge a price above P_c. P_c becomes its marginal revenue curve for all units sold up to Q_c. At Q_c, $MR = MC$, and the firm will produce the competitive output level. This output level results in an equality between marginal benefits and marginal cost (i.e., $P = MC$). Therefore, market inefficiency is dissolved (the lost net benefits are captured). This competitive outcome also reduces the profits of the cartel owners.

f. Because excess economic profits going to the cartel (which could have otherwise been earned in the long run) have been reduced, this decreases the inequitable redistribution of income away from consumers to owners of the cartel.

g. First, the cost of determining the perfectly competitive price-quantity combination can be extraordinarily high, if not prohibitive. Second, regulated firms may lose their incentives to control costs. As costs rise (the *MC* curve rises), what is considered a competitive price will rise.

5. a. A natural monopoly can come into existence if long-run marginal costs (*LRMC*) decrease over the relevant range of production — that is, if the industry experiences economies of scale over the output that can be expected to be sold to satisfy industry demand. Therefore, one firm is expected to produce for the entire industry because it is able to produce at a lower cost.

b. Because it may exercise its monopoly power after it has secured its dominance over the industry.

c. Because the fear of competition may restrain the natural monopoly's tendency to earn substantial economic profits by restricting output and charging a higher price.

d. First, the financial barriers to entry are so great that a natural monopoly does not have to worry about potential competitors and will therefore exercise substantial monopoly power if unregulated. Second, a natural monopoly requires a large quantity of fixed assets, which become sunk costs when purchased and have to be ignored in short-run production and pricing decisions. Therefore, price wars brought about by any potential competitors could cause firms to destroy themselves and thereby contribute to industry instability. Finally, natural monopolies do not produce the efficient output level.

e. First, the barriers to entry to a natural monopoly are not so great as to keep potential competitors out of the market. Therefore, the fear of competition may restrain a natural monopoly's tendency to exercise its power. Second, it is not likely that natural monopolies will be unstable industries. Third, requiring a natural monopoly to produce an efficient competitive output level may force it to lose money. This would require a subsidy and/or permission to price-discriminate. This can result in higher costs of production and a need for greater government involvement, which is costly in and of itself. Consumers could end up getting less at a higher price.

6. First, perhaps regulators have been inept at carrying out their responsibilities. Or, regulation may be too difficult for any agency to handle properly. Second, perhaps while regulators are concentrating on prices and barriers to entry, firms may maintain profits by reducing the quality (and therefore the cost) of their products and services. Third, regulators may determine prices on the basis of a "fair" rate of return of profitability on investment. This encourages firms to substitute plant and equipment for labor so they can keep prices and profits up. Therefore, by making production more capital intensive, firms can circumvent the intent of regulation. Finally, regulators may be co-opted by the firms they are supposed to regulate.
7. Price fixing, restrictions on market entry, subsidies, and even suppression of substitute products (or promotion of complementary products) are services a regulatory agency could supply an industry.

True-False

1. T   2. T
3. F: Government regulatory agencies have a substantial effect on the production and distribution of products in most industries.

4. F: Regulation by the ICC has tended to benefit the regulated, at the expense of consumers.
5. F: According to many economists, regulation of the economy in the pursuit of the public interest has quite often benefited the regulated, at the expense of the public.
6. F: Regulation is socially worthwhile as long as its benefits outweigh its costs.
7. T 8. T 9. T 10. T
11. F: Regulation of industries that exercise monopoly power reduces the tendency toward an inequitable redistribution of income.
12. F: To accomplish market efficiency, all government regulators need to do is to require that firms charge no more than what is considered the perfectly competitive price.
13. T 14. T 15. T
16. F: Businesses often argue for regulation of their industry if they benefit more from the regulation than from its absence.
17. T
18. F: A contestable market is a market where ultrafree entry (and exit) constrain potential monopolistic behavior.

Multiple Choice

1. b *(KQ1)* 2. e *(KQ2)* 3. d *(KQ2)*
4. a *(KQ2)* 5. b *(KQ2)* 6. c *(KQ5)*
7. a *(KQ3)* 8. a *(KQ2, 5)* 9. c *(KQ4)*
10. a *(KQ3)* 11. d *(KQ2)*

CHAPTER 26

The Competitive Labor Market

Chapter Summary

Key Question 1: What determines the wage rate?

In any market, the interaction between the buyers (demand) and the sellers (supply) of a commodity determines its price. Labor too is a commodity, although a special kind, and employers buy it at a price: the wage rate laborers receive in exchange for their efforts.

The market demand for labor curve is downward-sloping, expressing the inverse relationship between the real wage rate (or, simply, wage rate) and the quantity of labor businesses wish to employ. In other words, as the wage rate decreases (increases), the quantity of labor (or labor hours) businesses wish to employ increases (decreases).

When analyzing a firm's demand for labor we must first consider how much each worker is worth to the firm. That is, we must first calculate the value of the marginal product of labor for each worker. The value of marginal product of labor for any worker tells us how much revenue that particular worker will generate for the firm. The value of marginal product of labor of any worker equals the price of the good or service produced, multiplied by the worker's marginal product (the extra output associated with that worker). The value of marginal product of labor of each additional worker employed decreases as more workers are employed. This happens because the law of diminishing returns causes the marginal product of each additional worker to fall. If we were to graph the value of marginal product of labor of additional workers employed, it would be a downward-sloping curve.

A firm will employ workers as long as their value of marginal product of labor at leasts covers the wage it has to pay them (which is a constant wage rate in a competitive labor market). If the value of marginal product of labor of a worker is greater than the wage rate, then the firm will earn a profit off of that worker. This means that a firm will continue to hire workers until the value of marginal product of labor of the last worker employed just equals the wage rate. If the wage rate decreases, then the firm will find it profitable to employ additional workers until the lower value of marginal product of labor of an additional worker just equals the lower wage rate. Therefore, a firm's demand for labor curve is downward-sloping, implying the inverse relationship between the real wage rate and the quantity of labor it employs. Note that the firm's demand for labor curve is really its value of marginal product of labor (VMP_L) curve. Furthermore, because the VMP_L curve slopes downward, due to diminishing returns, the market demand for labor curve also slopes downward due to diminishing returns. (Likewise, the demand curve for any resource is downward-sloping because of diminishing returns.)

The market demand curve for labor shows the quantity of labor (or labor hours) that would be employed at each of the various possible real wage rates. Alternatively, it shows the value of marginal product of labor of the last worker employed at each of the various quantities of labor that could be employed.

One must distinguish between a change in the quantity demanded of labor (represented by movement along a given demand curve caused by a change in the wage rate) and a change in the demand for labor. An increase (a decrease) in the demand for labor is expressed graphically as a rightward (leftward) shift of the demand curve and could be caused by an increase (a decrease) in the price of the product workers are producing or an increase (a decrease) in the marginal product of workers. An increase (a decrease) in the demand for labor means that employers are willing and able to employ more (fewer) workers at any given real wage rate, or alternatively, that the value of marginal product of labor has increased (decreased) for all of the various quantities of labor that could be employed.

The market supply of labor curve is upward-sloping, expressing the positive (or direct) relationship between the real wage rate and the quantity of labor (or labor hours) seeking employment. In other words, as the real wage rate increases (decreases), the quantity of labor (or labor hours) seeking employment also increases (decreases).

The supply of labor curve slopes upward because of the cost-benefit (or work-leisure) tradeoff. People allocate their time so that the marginal benefit of an hour spent at work (equal to the real wage rate) is just equal to the marginal benefit of an hour spent at leisure activity. Therefore, the only way employers can entice more workers into the labor market, or entice those currently in the market to work longer hours, is to increase the opportunity cost of workers' leisure time — that is, to increase the real wage rate.

One must distinguish between a change in the quantity supplied of labor (represented by a movement along a given supply curve caused by a change in the wage rate) and a change in the supply of labor. An increase (a decrease) in the supply of labor is expressed graphically as a rightward (leftward) shift of the supply curve and could caused by a decrease (an increase) of the valuation of workers' leisure time or a decrease (an increase) in the wage rate workers could earn elsewhere.

In a competitive labor market, no one employer or employee has the ability to affect the wage rate. The wage rate is determined by the interaction between the market demand for and supply of labor and exists at the point of intersection between the two curves. This is because there is neither a shortage nor a surplus of labor at the point of intersection — that is, we have an equilibrium quantity of labor, which defines the equilibrium real wage rate. In other words, those workers willing and able to work at the going market wage rate will be able to find employment. If the real wage rate is above (below) equilibrium, a surplus (shortage) exists, and the real wage rate will fall (rise).

Key Question 2: Why do wage rates differ?

Because wage rates are determined by the interaction between demand and supply, wage differentials can be explained in terms of demand and supply.

If the nonmonetary benefits of a job are quite attractive, then the supply of labor will be greater than otherwise, and therefore the wage rate will be lower than otherwise. (Although workers may complain about their relatively low wage rate, when they consider their full wage rate — money wage plus nonmonetary benefits — they may be better off than they think.) On the other hand, if the supply of some workers is relatively scarce, then they can command relatively higher wages. Or if the demand for some workers is relatively high because they are more productive (their marginal product is greater), they will earn a relatively higher wage. Some workers may be more productive because they have acquired a skill (human capital). Wages may also differ because of a lack of competition on either the demand or the supply side of the market. Finally, wages may differ because of social discrimination.

Key Question 3: What are the effects of the minimum wage?

The use of demand and supply analysis enables us to predict the effects of a minimum wage. A minimum wage will increase unemployment (it creates a surplus in the labor market). Indeed, it prevents some workers from finding employment who otherwise would, and at the same time it increases the number of people seeking employment who otherwise would not. It may also displace some workers from their preferred line of employment, reducing their full wage rate. Furthermore, it tends to make employment more difficult for those for whom it was designed — the least skilled. Of course, those who are able to remain employed will be better off. However, their improved status comes at a cost to society of higher unemployment.

Strictly from an economic point of view, minimum wage laws can be said to have several social effects. They may increase the number of people on welfare and unemployment compensation. They may increase the level of criminal activity. They may also increase discrimination in the job market because they increase the competition for jobs. Finally, because employers are forced to pay a higher wage, the nonmonetary aspects of jobs may be decreased to the extent that full wage rates fall. And because the minimum wage creates a surplus of labor, employees can do little about it.

Why do minimum wage laws attract so much political support? Possibly for two reasons. First, the public (especially those it hurts most) may be unaware of the results. Second, minimum wage laws benefit the more productive workers and the unionized sectors of the labor force.

Review Terms and Concepts

Land
Labor
Capital
Entrepreneur
Technology
Positive economics
Normative economics
Circular law of income
Market
Demand
Law of demand
Market demand
Change in market demand
Supply
Law of supply
Market supply
Change in market supply
Price
Equilibrium price
Change in equilibrium price
Equilibrium quantity
Change in equilibrium quantity
Quantity demanded
Change in quantity demanded
Quantity supplied
Change in quantity supplied
Surplus
Shortage
Law of diminishing marginal returns
Marginal product
Real wage rate
Opportunity cost
Cost-benefit analysis
Marginal benefit

New Terms and Concepts

Demand for labor
Supply of labor
Full wage rate
Human capital
Productivity of labor
Value of the marginal product of labor
Wage differentials
Nonmonetary benefits
Minimum wage

Completion

downward
inverse
quantity demanded
decreases
downward
VMP_L
is worth to
multiplied
marginal product of labor of the worker
decreases
diminishing returns

The market demand for labor curve is ________________________ (downward/upward)-sloping. This expresses the ________________ (positive/inverse) relationship between the real wage rate (or, simply, wage rate) and the ______________________________ (quantity demanded/quantity supplied) of labor. That is, as the real wage rate increases, the quantity demanded of labor ________________ (increases/decreases), and vice versa. We know this must be the case in the market because the demand for labor curve for an individual firm slopes ________________________ (downward/upward).

An individual firm's demand for labor curve is really its ______________ (VMP_L /MC) curve. The value of the marginal product of labor for a particular worker tells us how much the worker ________________________ (is worth to/produces for) the firm. The value of marginal product of labor for any worker is equal to the price of the product produced ________________ (multiplied/divided) by the ____ (marginal product of labor of the worker/number of workers). The MP_L of each additional worker employed ________________ (increases/decreases) because of the law of ____________________________ (diminishing marginal utility/ diminishing returns). If we were to graph the value of marginal

product of labor of additional workers employed, it would be a
downward ____________________ (downward/upward)-sloping curve.

do not have any — In a competitive labor market, firms ____________________ (do not have any/have some) control over the real wage rate. Firms will take the wage rate as given and will continue to hire workers up to the point where the value of marginal product of labor of the last worker is
equal to — ____________________ (greater than/equal to/less than) the wage rate. The firm will earn a profit from workers whose value of marginal
greater than — product of labor is ____________________ (greater than/equal to/less than) the wage rate. If the market wage decreases, then the firm will find
profitable — it ____________________ (profitable/unprofitable) to employ more workers. The firm will continue to hire additional workers until the
lower — ____________________ (lower/higher) value of marginal product of labor is equal to the lower wage rate. Because a single employer will hire addi-
decreases — tional workers as the wage rate ____________________ (increases/decreases), the same must be true for the market. Therefore, the market
downward — demand for labor curve must be ____________________ (upward/downward)-sloping.

The demand for labor curve will shift to the right, expressing
an increase — ____________________ (an increase/a decrease) in the demand for labor
increases — if the price of workers' output ____________________ (increases/
increases — decreases) or if the marginal product of workers ____________________ (increases/decreases).

upward — The market supply of labor curve is ____________________
a positive — (downward/upward)-sloping, expressing ____________________ (an inverse/a positive) relationship between the real wage rate (or, simply,

quantity supplied	wage rate) and the ______________________ (quantity demanded/
	quantity supplied) of labor. In other words, if the wage rate decreases,
fewer	then ____________ (more/fewer) workers will be seeking employment.
	The supply of labor curve slopes upward because of
the cost-benefit tradeoff	____ (the cost-benefit
	tradeoff/rising marginal costs of production). The opportunity cost of
the wage rate	leisure time is ________________________ (work/the wage rate).
	Therefore, the only way an employer can entice more workers into the
	market, or entice those currently employed to work longer hours, is to
increase	__________________ (increase/decrease) the wage rate.
	The supply of labor curve will shift to the right, expressing
an increase	__________________ (an increase/a decrease) in the supply of labor if
decreases	the valuation of workers' leisure time _________________ (increases/
	decreases) or if the wage rate workers can receive elsewhere
decreases	__________________ (increases/decreases).
competitive	In a _____________________ (competitive/noncompetitive) labor
	market, no one individual employer or employee has the ability to affect
	the wage rate. Therefore, the market wage rate is determined by the inter-
demand for	action between the ______________________ (demand for/price of the
supply	product produced) and the _____________________ (supply/value of
	the marginal product) of labor. Graphically, the wage rate is shown by
the point of inter-section between	____ (adding/the
	point of intersection between) the demand and supply curves. If the wage
surplus	rate is above equilibrium, a _______________ (surplus/shortage) exists,
down	and the wage rate will be competitively bid _____________ (down/up)
workers	by _________________ (businesses/workers).

Wage rates differ among workers because of differences in the
demand for and supply of their services and because of nonmonetary
benefits. If some workers are very productive, their marginal product is
greater ________________ (lower/greater) than otherwise. This means that the
demand for ____________________ (demand for/supply of) their services is greater
higher than otherwise, and they will therefore earn a ____________________
(higher/lower) wage than otherwise. Their higher productivity may have
human been a result of __________________ (human/money) capital. If a job
takes place in comfortable surroundings coupled with prestige — that is,
more if the nonmonetary benefits are attractive — then _______________
(fewer/ more) workers will be attracted to this type of work. This means
supply of that the __________________ (demand for/supply of) this type of labor
greater will be ________________ (greater/less) than otherwise. Therefore, the
lower wage rate will be ______________ (lower/higher) than otherwise. Although these workers may complain of their relatively low wage rate,
full they may be better off than they think if they consider the ____________
(real/full) wage rate they are earning.

above A minimum wage is a wage rate set by government that is __________
(above/below) the equilibrium level. Therefore, it causes a
surplus ________________ (shortage/surplus) of labor. In other words, it
unemployment causes some _______________________ (unemployment/employment).
fall It may also cause some workers' full wage rates to _______________
also some (rise/fall). There are __________________ (no/also some) undesirable
social side effects associated with a minimum wage.

Problems and Applications

1. What are the similarities and differences between the market for goods and services discussed in Chapter 3 and the market for a resource (such as labor) discussed in this chapter?
2. a. Use the following table to determine the value of the marginal product of labor for each worker a firm could possibly employ.

Number of Workers	Marginal Product of each Worker (Per Hour)	Price Per Unit of Output	Value of the Marginal Product of Labor
1	4	$3	
2	3.5	$3	
3	3	$3	
4	2.5	$3	
5	2	$3	

   b. What does the value of the marginal product of labor of any worker tell us?
   c. Why does the value of marginal product of labor of each worker fall as more workers are employed?
   d. Graph the value of the marginal product of labor (VMP_L) for these workers. Does the curve slope downward or upward? Why?
   e. Will this firm be able to influence the market wage rate in a competitive labor market?
   f. If the market wage rate is $7.50 per hour, how many workers will this firm employ? Why? Express this on the graph drawn for question 2d.
   g. If the wage rate is reduced to $6 per hour, how many workers would this firm employ? Express this on the graph drawn for question 2d. Is there a change in the quantity demanded of labor or a change in the demand for labor? Is this VMP_L curve the firm's demand for labor curve?
   h. What can we conclude about the relationship between the wage rate and the quantity of labor demanded by this firm? Will the same relationship exist in the market — that is, for all firms considered together?
   i. Why does the market demand for labor curve slope downward? Will the demand curve for any resource slope downward for the same reason?
3. What is the relationship between the real wage rate and the quantity supplied of labor? Does the supply of labor curve slope upward or downward? Why?

4. Consider the following demand and supply curves for labor. Assume this market is perfectly competitive.

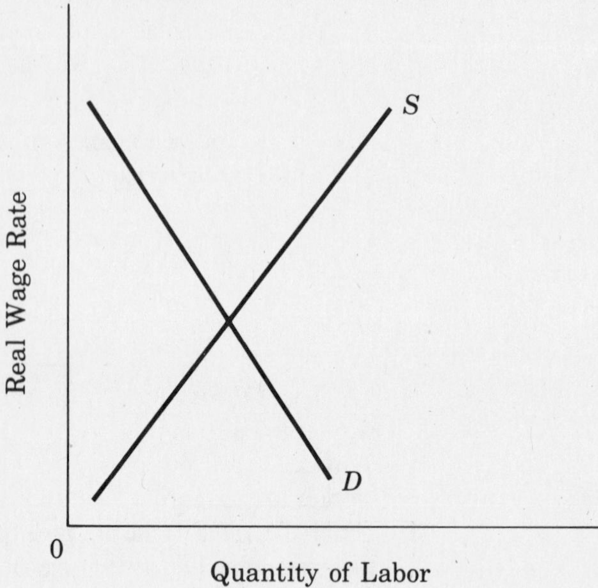

a. Indicate the equilibrium wage rate and the equilibrium quantity of labor. Why is this an equilibrium?
b. Indicate a wage rate below the equilibrium level. Indicate the quantity demanded and the quantity supplied of labor. Does this cause a shortage or a surplus of labor? What is expected to happen to the wage rate and the shortage or surplus? Why?
c. Indicate a wage rate above the equilibrium level. Indicate the quantity demanded and quantity supplied of labor. Does this cause a shortage or a surplus of labor? What is expected to happen to the wage rate and the shortage or surplus? Why?
d. Assume the wage rate is held above equilibrium by a minimum wage law. How does your answer to 3c change?

5. For each of the following situations, determine whether there is a change in the demand for or supply of labor. Also determine what happens to the wage rate and the level of employment. (*Hint:* It is always helpful to draw demand and supply curves and analyze these situations graphically.)
a. The demand for the product workers are producing rises.
b. It is Christmas Day, and workers value their leisure time more highly.

c. The other factory in town is now offering a higher wage rate.
d. Workers have invested in human capital.
e. The nonmonetary benefits of jobs in this market have just increased substantially.

True-False

For each item, determine whether the statement is basically true or false. If the statement is false, rewrite it so it is a true statement.

_____ 1. The demand for labor is the assumed positive relationship between the real wage rate and the quantity of labor business (employers) wish to employ.

_____ 2. The demand curve for any resource slopes upward because of the law of diminishing returns.

_____ 3. The demand curve in the resource market reflects businesses' point of view, whereas the supply of labor curve is seen from resource owners' point of view.

_____ 4. The value of the marginal product of labor of any worker equals the price of the product produced multiplied by the marginal product of the worker.

_____ 5. An increase in the price of the product produced or the marginal product of workers will decrease the demand for labor because it takes fewer workers to produce a lower output.

_____ 6. The value of the marginal product of labor decreases as additional workers are employed because the marginal product of additional workers employed decreases.

_____ 7. A firm will continue to hire workers as long as the wage rate the firm has to pay them is greater than their value of marginal product of labor.

_____ 8. A change in the quantity demanded of labor is caused by a change in the wage rate and is expressed graphically as movement along a given demand curve.

_____ 9. An increase in the wage rate will increase the opportunity cost of leisure and therefore more workers will seek employment or will work longer hours.

_____ 10. A decrease in the wage rate will decrease the quantity supplied of labor.

_____ 11. The supply of a labor curve will shift to the right if the price of the product workers are producing increases.

_____ 12. In a competitive labor market, no one individual employer or employee has the ability to affect the wage rate.

_____ 13. If the wage rate is too high for equilibrium, this means the quantity supplied exceeds the quantity demanded of labor, and workers will competitively bid down the wage rate.

_____ 14. If some workers are more productive than others, then the supply curve of this type of labor will lie farther to the right than otherwise.

_____ 15. If the demand for labor increases, then the wage rate and the quantity of workers employed increases.

_____ 16. The full wage rate is the wage rate plus the monetary equivalent of the nonmonetary benefits of a job.

_____ 17. If a particular group of people is discriminated against, then their wages will be lower because the supply of those workers is greater than otherwise.

_____ 18. A minimum wage law will increase employment.

_____ 19. A minimum wage law benefits unskilled workers as a group.

Multiple Choice *Choose the one best item for each answer.*

_____ 1. The demand for labor curve is
   a. downward-sloping because of the law of diminishing returns.
   b. downward-sloping because increasingly inferior workers are employed as the level of employment expands.
   c. upward-sloping because the wage rate must be increased to entice more workers into the labor market.
   d. upward-sloping because of the cost-benefit, or work-leisure, tradeoff.
   e. upward-sloping, expressing the inverse relationship between the real wage rate and the quantity of labor employers wish to hire.

_____ 2. The value of the marginal product of labor may fall if
   a. the price of workers' output rises.
   b. the productivity of workers rises.
   c. more workers are employed.
   d. the supply of labor decreases.
   e. the demand for the product workers are producing rises.

Use the table on page 493 to answer questions 3 through 5.

Number of Workers	Marginal Product of Each Worker (Per Hour)	Price of the Product
1	10	$2
2	8	$2
3	6	$2
4	4	$2
5	2	$2

_____ 3. The value of the marginal product of the
  a. first worker is $10.
  b. second worker is $16.
  c. third worker is $18.
  d. fourth worker is $2.
  e. fifth worker is $10.

_____ 4. If the wage rate is $8 per hour, how many workers should this firm employ?
  a. 1
  b. 2
  c. 3
  d. 4
  e. 5

_____ 5. If the wage rate is $8 per hour, what is the profit on the first worker per hour?
  a. $2
  b. $8
  c. $4
  d. $20
  e. $12

_____ 6. The demand for labor curve shows
  a. the quantity of labor (or labor hours) that would be employed at each of the various possible wage rates.
  b. the value of the marginal product of labor of the last worker employed at each of the various quantities of labor that could be employed.
  c. that a decrease in the real wage rate will cause the demand for labor to rise.
  d. that an increase in the real wage rate will cause the demand for labor to rise.
  e. both a and b.

_____ 7. Which of the following could cause an increase in the demand for labor?
  a. A decrease in the value of the marginal product of labor
  b. An increase in the marginal product of workers
  c. A decrease in the real wage rate
  d. A decrease in the price of the product workers are producing
  e. An increase in the workers' valuation of leisure time

_____ 8. The supply of labor curve shows that
  a. an increase in the real wage rate will cause an increase in the quantity of workers seeking employment.
  b. a decrease in the real wage rate will cause an increase in the quantity of workers seeking employment.
  c. an increase in the real wage rate will cause an increase in the quantity of workers businesses are willing to hire.
  d. a decrease in the real wage rate will cause an increase in the quantity of workers businesses are willing to hire.
  e. an increase in the real wage rate will cause an increase in the supply of labor.

_____ 9. The supply of labor curve will increase if the
  a. marginal product of workers increases.
  b. real wage rate increases.
  c. nonmonetary benefits of jobs in the market increase.
  d. valuation of worker's leisure time increases.
  e. wages workers could earn elsewhere increase.

_____ 10. An increase in the supply of labor
  a. will cause a decrease in the wage rate and an increase in the level of employment.
  b. will cause an increase in the quantity of labor seeking employment.
  c. means that a greater number of workers are willing to work at any given wage rate.
  d. means that workers do not require as high a wage rate to work the same quantity of hours.
  e. means all of the above.

_____ 11. If the wage rate is below equilibrium, then
  a. the quantity supplied exceeds the quantity demanded of labor.
  b. the wage rate will be competitively bid up by employers.
  c. a surplus of labor exists.
  d. this could have been caused by a minimum wage law.
  e. all of the above will be true.

_____ 12. Wage rates may differ because of
   a. social discrimination.
   b. differences in the productivity of workers.
   c. differences in the supply of different types of workers.
   d. differences in the demand for different types of workers.
   e. all of the above.

_____ 13. The full wage rate
   a. cannot be increased if workers receive nonmonetary benefits.
   b. will always be increased with the imposition of a minimum wage.
   c. measures the difference between monetary and nonmonetary payments for worker's services.
   d. is the sum of the wage rate and the monetary equivalent of the nonmonetary benefits of a job.
   e. is the wage rate earned before taxes are deducted.

_____ 14. Which of the following is an investment in human capital?
   a. Businesses purchase more workers.
   b. Businesses purchase machines to replace workers.
   c. Businesses purchase machines to increase the efficiency of workers.
   d. Workers purchase more training or education.
   e. Workers purchase more home equipment, such as dishwashers and riding lawn mowers, to increase their leisure time.

_____ 15. A minimum wage law
   a. increases employment opportunities for unskilled workers.
   b. is usually opposed by unions.
   c. increases the quantity of workers seeking employment but decreases the quantity of workers finding employment.
   d. will most likely decrease the number of people on welfare and the level of criminal activity.
   e. causes a shortage of labor.

Discussion Questions

1. What would happen to the elasticity of demand for labor if firms began selling their output in a noncompetitive product market? (*Hint:* What must happen to the price of a product in a noncompetitive market if more is to be sold?) Given the supply of workers, what can we conclude about the employment opportunities in this labor market? *(KQ1)*

2. Are workers paid what they are worth in a perfectly competitive labor market? Why or why not? *(KQ1)*
3. If the minimum wage creates so many problems, how else could government attempt to relieve poverty among low-income individuals? (*KQ3*. See also Chapter 29.)
4. How will changes in a labor market affect the prices of the goods and services the workers produce? Will there be a feedback effect on this labor market? (*KQ1*. See also Chapter 21.)
5. Why do construction workers earn a higher wage than bank tellers even though each can do the other's job? *(KQ2)*
6. What can cause the real wage rate to rise and fall other than changes in the demand for supply and labor? (*KQ1*. See also Chapter 10.)

Answers

Problems and Applications

1. If a market exists for some item (whether it be a good, service, or resource), then there are both buyers (demanders) and sellers (suppliers) of the item. The interaction between buyers (demand) and sellers (supply) determines the equilibrium price (going market price). An equilibrium price exists only when an equilibrium quantity exists (one implies the other). An equilibrium quantity exists when there is neither a surplus nor a shortage of the item. Therefore, an equilibrium price exists when there is neither a surplus (hence, no tendency for price to fall) nor a shortage (hence, no tendency for price to rise). On a graph, equilibrium price and quantity exist at the point of intersection between the downward-sloping demand curve and the upward-sloping supply curve. Note that the laws of demand and supply hold in all markets.

   Because we are now interested in resource markets (as opposed to markets for goods and services), we must realize that the buyers are now businesses (as opposed to consumers) and the suppliers are now resource owners (as opposed to businesses). Therefore, a demand curve in a resource market must be interpreted from the business's (employer's) point of view, and a supply curve must be interpreted from the resource owner's point of view.

   The resource categories (and therefore resource markets) we will concentrate on are labor, land, and capital. All we need to do to determine the prices of these resources (the price of labor is the wage rate, the price of land is the rental rate, the price of capital is the interest rate) is to investigate their determinants of demand and supply. The determinants of the demand for and supply of labor discussed in this chapter are basically the same for land and capital, which makes our investigation easier. In other words, the demand curve for any resource slopes downward because of diminishing marginal returns (whereas the demand curve for any good or service slopes downward because of diminishing marginal utility), and the supply curve of any resource slopes upward because of increasing opportunity costs of alternative uses of the resource (whereas the supply curve of any product slopes upward because of increasing marginal costs).

2. a.

Value of the Marginal Product of Labor
$12.00
$10.50
$ 9.00
$ 7.50
$ 6.00

b. The value of the marginal product of labor tells us how much each worker is worth to the firm. That is, it tells us how much revenue a particular worker will generate for the firm.

c. The value of the marginal product of labor of each worker falls as more workers are employed because the marginal product of labor falls as more workers are employed, due to diminishing returns.

d. The VMP_L curve slopes downward because of the law of diminishing returns. (See graph on page 498.)

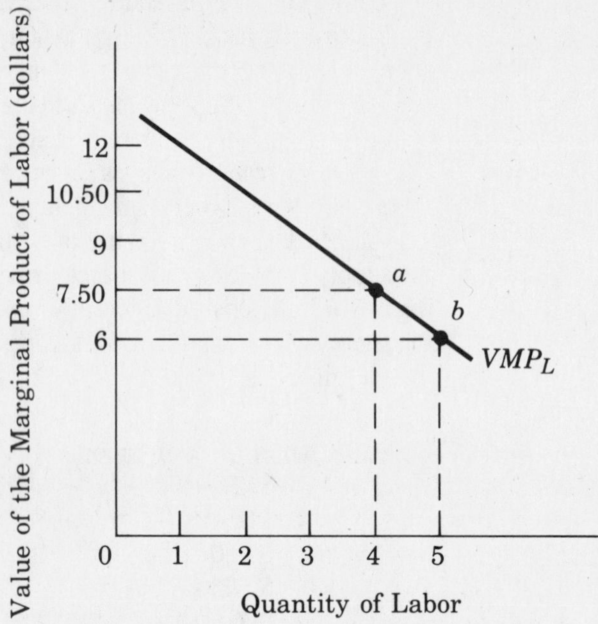

e. No. In a competitive labor market no one employer or employee has the ability to influence the market wage rate. Everyone is a price taker.

f. See the preceding graph. The firm will employ four workers because the value of the marginal product of labor of all workers, up to the fourth, is greater than the wage rate. We will assume that the firm hires the fourth worker because this worker is able to pay for himself or herself. The firm is earning a profit from the employment of the first three workers equal to the difference between the value of the marginal product of labor of each worker and the wage rate (shown graphically by the vertical distance between the VMP_L curve and the wage rate). For instance, the profit from employing the second worker is $3.

g. See the preceding graph. The firm will now find it profitable to employ five workers. The reduction in the wage rate from $7.50 per hour to $6 per hour increased the quantity demanded by one. A change in the quantity demanded of labor is always caused by a change in the wage rate and is expressed graphically as movement along a given demand curve — such as from point *a* to point *b* in this case. (Note that a change in the demand for labor that is caused by something other than a change in the wage rate is expressed graphically as a shift of the demand curve.) The VMP_L curve for this firm is its demand for labor curve because it shows how many workers it would employ at any given wage rate, or, alternatively, it shows the value of the marginal product of labor of the last worker employed out of each of various quantities of labor that could be employed.

h. There is an inverse relationship between the wage rate and the quantity demanded of labor for this firm. In other words, whatever the wage rate does, the quantity demanded of labor does the opposite. By logical extension, the same inverse relationship will exist in the market.

i. The VMP_L curve slopes downward, because of the law of diminishing marginal returns, so the demand for labor in the market slopes downward for the same reason. Indeed, the demand for any resource will always slope downward — that is, there will exist an inverse relationship between its price and the quantity demanded — because of diminishing returns associated with its increased use.

3. There is a positive (or direct) relationship between the real wage rate and the quantity supplied of labor. This is the definition of the supply of labor. In other words, as the wage rate rises (falls), the quantity of labor seeking employment also rises (falls). Therefore, the supply of labor curves slopes upward. This positive relationship exists because of the cost-benefit (or work-leisure) tradeoff.

4. a. The equilibrium wage rate is W_2 and the equilibrium quantity of labor is Q_3. This is an equilibrium because at this point of intersection between the demand and supply curves there is neither a surplus of labor (hence, no tendency for the wage rate to fall) nor a shortage of labor (hence, no tendency for the wage rate to rise). In other words, at W_2 the quantity of workers seeking employment just equals the quantity of workers finding employment. (See graph on page 500.)

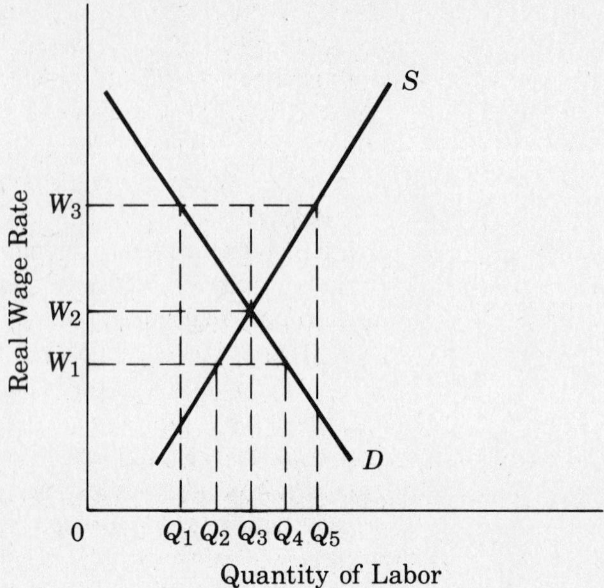

b. A wage rate such as W_1 is below the equilibrium of W_2. The quantity demanded of labor is Q_4, while the quantity supplied is Q_2. Because the quantity demanded (the amount of workers, or labor hours, employers would like to have) is greater than the quantity supplied (the number of workers, or labor hours, seeking employment), there is a shortage of labor at W_1 equal to Q_4 - Q_2. This shortage of labor will cause employers to bid up the wage rate competitively (some businesses will pay a higher wage rate just to get some of these workers). As the wage rate rises, the quantity demanded decreases and the quantity supplied increases. In this way, the shortage begins to disappear. This process continues until the quantity demanded just equals the quantity supplied at W_2. At W_2 there is no shortage (or surplus) of labor.

c. W_3 is above the equilibrium of W_2. The quantity demanded of labor is Q_1, while the quantity supplied is Q_5. Because the quantity supplied exceeds the quantity demanded, a surplus of labor exists equal to Q_5 - Q_1. This surplus is unemployment. Therefore, workers will competitively bid down the wage rate (some workers will be willing to work for a wage less than W_3 just to get a job) toward W_2. As the wage rate is competitively bid down, the quantity demanded rises (employers will hire more workers) and the quantity supplied falls (fewer workers will seek employment). The surplus (unemployment) begins to disappear. This process continues until the quantity demanded just equals the quantity supplied at W_2. At W_2 there is no surplus (or shortage) of labor.

d. If a minimum wage is set at W_3, then the surplus (unemployment) of Q_5 - Q_1 will persist. It will persist for as long as the minimum wage is held at W_3.

5. a. An increase in the demand for the product workers are producing will cause the price of the product to rise. Therefore, the value of the marginal product of labor of workers will rise. This means that the demand for labor increases — it shifts to the right. (This is because the demand for labor curve indicates the value of the marginal product of labor of the last worker employed at each of the various quantities of labor that could be employed. If the value of marginal product of labor increases for all workers who could be employed, then the demand for labor curve shifts to the right.) Therefore, the wage rate rises and the quantity of workers employed also rises.

b. An increase in workers' valuation of leisure time decreases the supply of labor — it shifts to the left. (This leftward shift indicates that a higher wage would have to be paid to keep the same quantity of workers on the job.) Therefore the wage rate rises and the quantity of labor employed falls. (Notice that on Christmas Day fewer people are working but those that are get paid a premium.)

c. An increase in the wage rate that could be earned elsewhere will cause the supply of labor curve under consideration to decrease. Therefore, the wage rate in the market under consideration will rise, and the level of employment will fall.

d. An increase in human capital means workers are more skilled. This will cause workers to be more productive — their marginal products are greater. This means the value of marginal product of labor for these workers will rise. Therefore, the demand for these workers rises. Their wage rate rises as well as their employment.

e. If the nonmonetary benefits of a job are more attractive, a greater quantity of labor will seek this type of employment at any given wage rate. In other words, the supply of labor seeking the jobs in this market will increase — the supply curve shifts to the right. Therefore, the wages paid for these jobs drop but the quantity of workers finding employment in this market rises. Although these workers are earning a lower wage rate, they may be better off than they think because their full wage rate is higher than the wage they could earn in the absence of the nonmonetary benefits. (See the following graph. Before the nonmonetary benefits were offered, the supply curve of labor in this market was S_1. After nonmonetary benefits are offered, the supply curve shifts to S_2. The wage rate drops from W_2 to W_1. Employment increases from Q_1 to Q_2. But because the vertical distance between S_1 and S_2 (equal to W_3 - W_1) indicates the monetary equivalent of the nonmonetary benefits, the full wage rate of W_3 is higher than the wage rate of W_2, which could be earned in the absence of the nonmonetary benefits.)

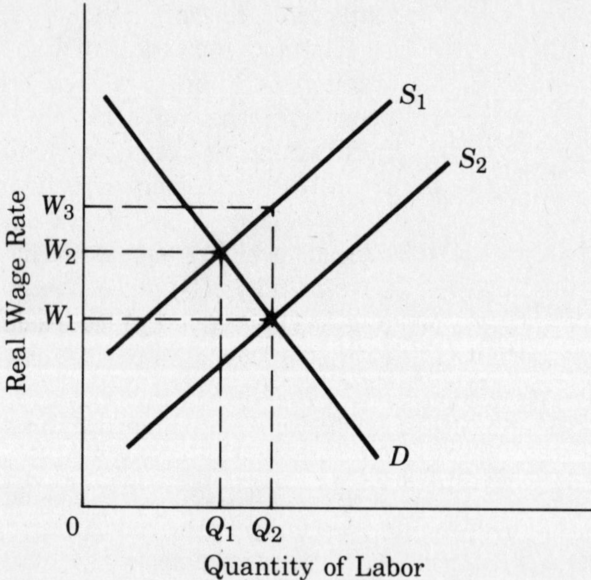

True-False

1. F: The demand for labor is the assumed inverse relationship between the real wage rate and the quantity of labor businesses (employers) wish to employ.

2. F: The demand curve for any resource slopes downward because of the law of diminishing returns.

3. T 4. T

5. F: An increase in the price of the product produced or the marginal product of workers will increase the demand for labor.

6. T

7. F: A firm will continue to hire workers as long as their VMP_L exceeds the wage rate the firm has to pay them.

8. T 9. T 10. T

11. F: The supply of labor curve will shift to the right if workers' valuation of their leisure time decreases or if there is a decrease in the wage rate workers can earn elsewhere.

12. T 13. T

14. F: If some workers are more productive than others, then the demand curve of this type of labor will lie farther to the right than otherwise.

15. T 16. T

17. F: If a particular group of people is discriminated against, then their wages will be lower because the demand for these workers is lower than otherwise.

18. F: A minimum wage law should cause some unemployment.

19. F: A minimum wage law does not benefit unskilled workers as a group but instead benefits the more productive workers and unionized workers.

Multiple Choice

1. a *(KQ1)* 2. c *(KQ1)* 3. b *(KQ1)*
4. d *(KQ1)* 5. e *(KQ1)* 6. e *(KQ1)*
7. b *(KQ1)* 8. a *(KQ1)* 9. c *(KQ1)*
10. e *(KQ1)* 11. b *(KQ1)* 12. e *(KQ2)*
13. d *(KQ2)* 14. d *(KQ2)* 15. c *(KQ3)*

CHAPTER 27

Monopsonies and Unions

Chapter Summary

This chapter examines the noncompetitive labor market. Power may be exerted in a noncompetitive market on either the demand side (by employers) or the supply side (by employees), or both. When employers have the ability to affect the market wage rate, they posses monopsony power. Employers who possess monopsony power hire fewer workers and suppress wage rates below competitive levels. Employees try to increase their wages either by differentiating their skills or by forming unions.

Key Question 1: How are wages and employment determined under conditions of monopsony?

A monopsony is the only employer (or, at least, the dominant employer) of labor in a given market. Therefore, the monopsonist's demand for labor curve is the market demand for labor curve. Furthermore, the monopsonist faces the market supply curve of labor. This is because the only way a monopsonist can entice more labor to work, or entice currently employed workers to work longer hours, is to increase the wage rate. And this higher wage rate must be paid to all other currently employed workers. So, the marginal cost of labor is the higher wage paid an additional worker plus the increase in the wage rate that must be paid to all other currently employed workers. Therefore, the marginal cost of labor is greater than the wage rate (except for the first worker employed), and the difference between the two increases as the monopsonist increases employment. Graphically, then, the marginal cost of labor curve *(MC)* lies above the market supply curve, and the vertical distance between them increases as employment increases.

Unlike the perfectly competitive employer who must accept the market wage rate as given, the monopsonist searches for that one wage-quantity combination on the market supply of labor curve that maximizes its profits. However, like any employer, a monopsonist will find it profitable to hire additional workers as long as each additional worker employed contributes more to the firm's revenues than to its costs. Therefore, a monopsonist will employ that quantity of workers where the last worker's marginal value just equals his or her marginal cost. (The marginal value of a worker is the value of the marginal product of that worker — in other words, the extra revenue generated by employing that worker.) The firm's demand curve measures the marginal value of each worker as employment is expanded. (Recall that the value of the marginal product curve is the firm's demand for labor curve, and it slopes downward.) Therefore, the profit-maximizing quantity to employ is shown graphically by the intersection of the *MC* of labor curve and the demand for labor curve. Because the monopsonist faces the market supply of labor curve, which indicates the wage rate that must be paid to get various quantities of labor, the monopsonist only need pay that wage rate indicated by the market supply of labor curve to entice the profit-maximizing quantity into the market. The quantity of labor employed and the wage rate paid by the monopsonist are both below the perfectly competitive levels (indicated by the point of intersection between the market demand and supply curves).

Competitive employers may behave as monopsonists to lower wages and increase profits if they are able to collude and form an employer cartel. The usual method of lowering wages to increase profits is to establish restrictive employment rules that limit the movement of workers from one job to another. This effectively reduces the demand for labor, which reduces both employment and the wages employers have to pay workers.

Economically, a monopsony is inefficient because it misallocates employment: too few people are employed by a monopsony or cartelized labor market and too many are employed elsewhere (or are unemployed). This result can be seen graphically. First, compare the quantity of labor that would be employed in a competitive market with the quantity employed in a monopsony. Given this underemployment by the monopsonist, the area under the supply curve measures the market value of output from employment elsewhere. However, the area under the demand — which is larger — measures the market value of output that could be produced by the monopsonist but is not. The difference between these areas indicates the net value that could be gained by society if the monopsonist increased employment to the competitive level. Furthermore, this inefficiency created by the monopsonist may be even greater, because of the productive resources the monopsonist must use the erect and maintain barriers to entry into its labor market.

Employer cartels are inefficient for the same reasons. However, like all cartels, they are not expected to last for very long because of the incentives to chisel. Those with the smallest number of members or with government blessing are likely to exist the longest.

Key Question 2: How do individual workers acquire market power?

On the supply side of the labor market, employees attempt to increase their wages by differentiating their skills or by forming unions. Workers can differentiate themselves from others by moving to a more favorable market with few competitors, or, more often, by investing in themselves (human capital) through education and training. The higher wages earned by acquiring more skills may be short-lived because other workers are most likely doing the same thing. But usually the benefits of doing so outweigh the costs. Furthermore, consumers tend to benefit from all this because higher-quality goods and services are produced over time.

Key Question 3: What are the economic effects of labor unions?

Historically, unions have been viewed as an important force in increasing workers' economic power. However, over the last three decades union membership as a percentage of the labor force has been falling.

Unions can increase wage rates in three general ways. First, they can restrict their membership. This limits their supply and pushes their wage rate up. However, it also decreases the employment opportunities in that particular market. Second, through the threat of a strike, unions may demand and receive a higher wage rate by effectively limiting the supply of labor to zero below the wage rate demanded. On a graph, the supply and the marginal cost of labor curves become one and the same and are horizontal at this wage rate (until they meet the upward-sloping portion of the supply curve). If this method of attempting to increase wages is imposed on a monopsonist or employer cartel, it can actually increase both wages and employment opportunities for workers. It is in the case of a monopsony or employer cartel that a minimum wage may be most beneficial. However, minimum wage laws are imposed on all markets and therefore the overall effect is a reduction in employment.

A third way in which unions may increase wages for their members is to promote union-made goods and services. This may increase the demand for the product they are producing. In turn, it may increase the demand for their labor services, increasing their wages and employment opportunities.

Union efforts do not necessarily increase employment for all workers. Furthermore, although unions may increase wages for their members, they may decrease wages in nonunionized labor markets if they restrict employment in unionized markets (fewer workers employed in unionized industries means a greater supply of workers seeking employment elsewhere).

Small unions are usually more successful in acting as a unified force in limiting their supply than large unions. Free-riding is less of a problem in small unions. Therefore, large unions are more likely to use the threat of force to keep members in line.

Government laws may support union-organizing efforts. For instance, the Wagner Act permits the organization of a union shop by a simple majority of worker votes.

Although unions may help combat employer cartels, they can have negative effects as well. They may not foster hard work or improved skills.

Review Terms and Concepts

Demand for labor
Supply of labor
Value of the marginal product of labor
Wage differentials
Full wage rate
Human capital
Cartel

New Terms and Concepts

Monopsony
Monopsony power
Marginal cost of labor
Employer cartel
Right-to-work laws
Union shop

Completion

A monopsony is the only employer of labor in a given market. A

is — monopsony's demand for labor curve ______________ (is/is not) the market demand for labor curve. The monopsonist also faces the market

increase — supply of labor curve. Therefore, a monopsonist must ______________ (increase/decrease) the wage rate to entice more workers into the market. This higher wage rate that must be paid to obtain additional workers

also has to be — __________________ (is not/also has to be) paid to all other currently employed workers. This means that the marginal cost of labor equals

plus — the extra wage paid an additional worker ______________ (plus/multi-

increase — plied by) the __________________ (increase/decrease) in the wage rate that must paid to all currently employed workers. Therefore, the mar-

greater than — ginal cost of labor is __________________ (greater than/less than) the

increases	wage rate. Furthermore, the difference between the two ____________
	(increases/decreases) as employment expands. This means that the mar-
above	ginal cost of labor curve lies ____________ (below/above) the supply
	of labor curve.
searcher	A monopsonist is a wage ______________ (taker/searcher). In other
	words, it will search for that one wage-quantity combination on the
supply of	market __________________ (demand for/supply of) labor curve that
its profits	maximizes _________________ (its profits/employment). The quantity
	of labor a monopsonist will employ is found when the marginal cost of
equal to	the last worker hired is _________________ (greater than/equal to/less
	than) the marginal value of that worker. The marginal value of the last
demand for	worker employed is given by the ___________________ (demand for/
	supply of) labor curve. Graphically, the quantity of labor a monopsonist
demand	will employ is shown where the ________________ (demand/marginal
MC	product) and _____________ (*MC*/supply) curves intersect. The wage
supply	rate that is paid is determined by reading off of the ________________
	(*MC*/demand/supply) curve of labor. The monopsonist will pay
a lower	_______________ (a greater/the same/a lower) wage rate and employ
fewer	_______________ (more/the same/fewer) workers than is the case in a
	perfectly competitive labor market.
inefficient	Monopsony is economically ______________________ (efficient/
few	inefficient). It results in a misallocation of employment. Too ________
many	(few/many) people are employed by the monopsonist and too ________
can	(few/many) people are employed elsewhere. We ________ (can/cannot)
	measure the inefficiency of the monopsonist graphically. The area under
	the demand curve for those workers who would be employed under com-

petitive conditions, but are not, measures the market value of output
that the monopsonist could produce ______________________ (from employment
elsewhere/that the monopsonist could produce). The area under the supply curve for those workers who would be employed under competitive
conditions, but are not, measures the market value of employment else-
is larger than — where. The area under the demand curve ______________
(is larger than/is less than) the area under the supply curve; this is the
area of inefficiency created by the monopsonist. It represents the net
loss — __________ (value/loss) to society caused by the monopsonist's
underemployment — ______________ (underemployment/overemployment).

inefficent — An employer cartel is economically ____________ (efficient/
underemployment — inefficient) because it results in ______________ (under-
employment/overemployment). Furthermore, an employer cartel results
lower — in a ___________ (higher/lower) wage rate than that paid under
competitive conditions. An employer cartel is able to lower wages and
decreasing — increase profits by ___________ (increasing/decreasing) the
restrictive — demand for labor. It does this by establishing ____________
limit — (liberal/restrictive) employment rules that __________ (enhance/
limit) movement of workers from one job to another.

Workers attempt to receive higher wages by differentiating themselves
from other workers and by forming unions. A union can effectively in-
decreasing — crease wages by ___________ (decreasing/increasing) the supply
of labor. If a union threatens to strike if it does not receive a particular
supply of — wage rate, then it is effectively limiting the _______________
below — (supply of/demand for) its labor services to zero ____________

(above/below) that wage rate. If a union does this to a monopsonist, it can increase both wages and employment for its workers.

A minimum wage law imposed on a monopsonist will most likely
increase ________________ (increase/decrease) employment. It will also most
increase likely ________________ (increase/decrease) the wage rate. Minimum
almost all wage laws are imposed by government on ________________ (only monopsonistic/almost all) labor markets. The overall effect of minimum
decrease wage laws is to ________________ (increase/decrease) employment.

Unions may also increase their members' wages by promoting union-made goods and services. If this type of campaign is successful, it will
increase ________________ (increase/decrease) the demand for the products the
increase unions are producing and ________________ (increase/decrease) their
increase prices. This in turn will ________________ (increase/decrease) the marginal value of all workers. This means that the demand for their labor
increase will ________________ (increase/decrease) and cause their wages to
rise rise. It will also cause their employment opportunities to ____________ (fall/rise).

Problems and Applications

1. a. Given the information in the following table, determine the total wage bill and the marginal cost of labor for this firm.

(1) Number of Workers Willing to Work	(2) Value of the Marginal Product of Each Worker	(3) Annual Wage of Each Worker	(4) Total Wage Bill	(5) Marginal Cost of Each Additional Worker
1	$20,000	$12,000		
2	$18,000	$14,000		
3	$16,000	$16,000		
4	$14,000	$18,000		
5	$12,000	$20,000		

b. Why does the marginal cost of each additional worker employed rise?
c. Is the monopsonist's demand for labor curve the market demand curve? Does a monopsonist face the market supply curve? Which columns express the demand and market supply schedules?
d. How many workers will this firm employ? Why? What annual wage will this firm pay each of its workers?
e. How many workers would be employed and what wage rate would be paid all workers employed if this were a perfectly competitive labor market?
f. Does a monopsonist employ fewer workers and pay them a lower wage rate than under perfectly competitive conditions?

2. Consider the following graph for a monopsonistic employer.

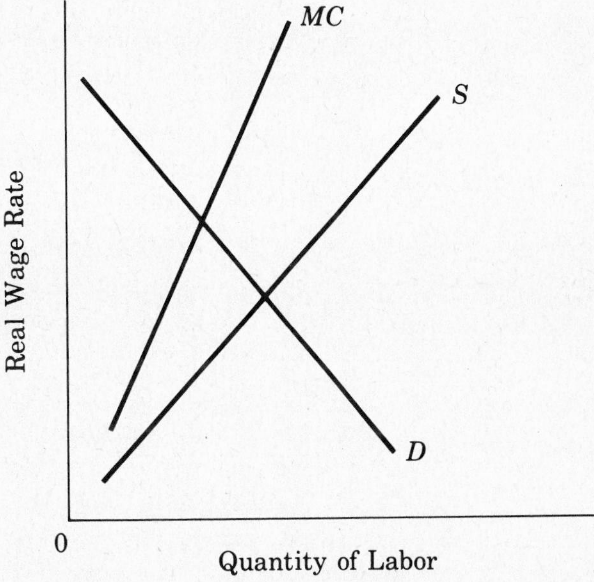

a. Indicate the quantity of labor employed and the wage rate paid by this monopsonist.
b. Indicate the quantity of labor employed and the wage rate paid by this monopsonist if this were a perfectly competitive labor market.
c. Does a monopsonist employ too many or too few workers? What is this equal to graphically?

d. What area on the graph measures the market value of output from employment elsewhere caused by the monopsonist's underemployment?
e. What area measures the market value of output that could be produced by the monopsonist but is not?
f. What is the area of market inefficiency — that is, what is the area that shows the net value that could be gained by society if the monopsonist increased employment to the competitive level?

3. Consider again the graph for a monopsonistic employer in question 2. Now assume a union is formed and threatens to strike if it does not receive a higher wage rate.
   a. Indicate the higher wage the union could receive without lowering employment below that which the monopsonist would otherwise employ.
   b. Indicate the wage rates between which a union-negotiated wage rates would actually increase employment opportunities for the union.
   c. Can market power on both sides of the market — in this case, a union facing a monopsony — result in a competitive outcome?
4. Why has union membership as a percentage if the total labor force decreased in the last three decades?

True-False

For each item, determine whether the statement is basically true or false. If the statement is false, rewrite it so it is a true statement.

_____ 1. Because a monopsonist faces the market supply curve, the marginal cost of labor increases and is greater than the wage rate as additional workers are employed beyond the first.

_____ 2. The marginal cost of labor curve *(MC)* slopes upward and lies above the market supply curve of labor, indicating that the marginal cost of labor is greater than the wage rate except for the first worker employed.

_____ 3. A monopsonist, like all employers, will hire additional workers as long as each worker's marginal cost exceeds its marginal value.

_____ 4. A monopsonist determines the wage it must pay at the profit-maximizing output level by graphically reading off its demand for labor curve.

_____ 5. A monopsonist will employ fewer workers and pay a higher wage rate than an employer in a perfectly competitive labor market.

_____ 6. An employer cartel attempts to pay a lower wage and increase its profits by establishing restrictive employment rules that reduce the demand for labor.

_____ 7. A monopsonist employs more workers than is socially optimal.

_____ 8. The National Football League is an example of an employer cartel.

_____ 9. The greater the number of members, the longer an employer cartel is likely to last.

_____ 10. When workers attempt to increase their skills to differentiate themselves from other workers, higher-quality goods and services and therefore increased consumer welfare may result.

_____ 11. Because of right-to-work laws, unions are no longer as prevalent as they used to be.

_____ 12. A union may increase wages and employment if it is able to decrease the supply of its labor services.

_____ 13. A union-negotiated wage increase in a monopsonistic labor market will always increase the wage rate and decrease employment opportunities.

_____ 14. A minimum wage imposed on a monopsonistic labor market may increase employment.

_____ 15. Unions can create economic inefficiencies.

Multiple Choice *Choose the one best answer for each item.*

_____ 1. A monopsonist's marginal cost of labor curve
   a. slopes upward and lies above the market supply curve.
   b. slopes upward and lies below the market supply curve.
   c. is horizontal at the market wage rate.
   d. is the same as the supply of labor curve.
   e. is its demand for labor curve.

_____ 2. A monopsonist
   a. is the only buyer of a good, service, or resource.
   b. must pay a higher wage to entice more workers into the market.
   c. is faced with a rising marginal cost of labor curve that lies above the wage rate it must pay workers.

d. employs fewer workers and pays a lower wage than a perfectly competitive employer.
e. is described by all of the above.

______ 3. If the marginal value of a worker exceeds his or her marginal cost, then the employer
a. is losing money from the employment of that worker.
b. should reduce the employment level until the marginal cost of the last worker employed exceeds his or her marginal value.
c. is employing the proper quantity of workers.
d. should continue to increase the employment of these workers.
e. is a monopsonist.

______ 4. A monopsony will employ a quantity of labor
a. indicated by the intersection of the marginal cost of labor curve and the market supply of labor curve.
b. indicated by the intersection of the demand for labor curve and the marginal cost of labor curve.
c. indicated by the intersection of the market demand and supply curves.
d. below the competitive level and pay a higher than competitive wage rate.
e. that minimizes the employment of labor.

______ 5. Market inefficiency of a monopsonist
a. is below that of a competitive employer.
b. is graphically indicated by the area under the demand curve but above the supply curve for that quantity of labor under-employed by the monopsonist but that would otherwise be employed in a competitive labor market.
c. is graphically indicated by the area under the supply curve for that quantity of labor underemployed by the monopsonist but that would otherwise be employed in a competitive labor market.
d. is graphically indicated by the area under the demand curve for that quantity of labor underemployed by the monopsonist but that would otherwise be employed in a competitive labor market.
e. may not be so great after considering the resources it uses to build and maintain its barriers to entry into the labor market.

______ 6. An employer cartel
a. does not exist in the real world.
b. increases the demand for labor.

c. decreases the demand for labor.
d. increases the supply of labor.
e. decreases the supply of labor.

______ 7. A union may increase the wage rate for its members by
a. restricting membership.
b. decreasing the supply of labor.
c. increasing the demand for labor.
d. threatening to strike.
e. doing all of the above.

______ 8. When a union threatens to strike if it does not receive a particular wage rate, it
a. is increasing the demand for its members.
b. causes the marginal cost of labor and supply curves to become horizontal at that wage rate.
c. causes the marginal cost of labor and supply curves to become vertical at that wage rate.
d. is increasing the supply of its labor.
e. is causing the marginal cost of labor curve to shift leftward.

______ 9. A union shop means that
a. workers are unionized in that market.
b. workers must join the union as a condition of employment.
c. workers may enjoy the benefits of union membership without having to join the union.
d. unionized workers are employed by a monopsonist.
e. unionized workers are employed by a competitive employer.

______ 10. Union membership in the United States has decreased in the last three decades in part because of
a. monopsony power.
b. fewer nonmonetary benefits offered by employers.
c. right-to-work laws.
d. competition from labor markets that are nonunionized.
e. all of the above.

______ 11. A minimum wage law imposed on a monopsonistic labor market will most likely cause
a. greater employment.
b. less employment.
c. lower wages.
d. criticism from union members.
e. both b and d to occur.

Discussion Questions

1. Can we judge the degree of monopsony power by the number of employers in a market? *(KQ1)*
2. What does the supply curve of labor look like facing a perfectly competitive employer? What is the relationship between the marginal cost of labor curve and the supply of labor curve facing a perfectly competitive employer? *(KQ1.* See Chapter 26.)
3. Why would a monopsonist hire more union workers if it must pay these workers a higher wage? *(KQ3)*
4. We know that a minimum wage can increase employment when imposed on a monopsonist. Can we conclude that because the overall effect of minimum wage laws is a reduction in unemployment that most labor is employed in competitive markets? Or is it that the minimum wage is too high to increase employment even in monopsonistic labor markets? *(KQ3)*
5. How do craft (or trade) unions (such as barbers, bricklayers, printers, plumbers) limit the supply of their labor services? How do industrial unions (such as the United Auto Workers, United Mine Workers, Teamsters) limit their supply? *(KQ3)*

Answers

Problems and Applications

1. a.

(4) Total Wage Bill	(5) Marginal Cost of Each Additional Worker
$ 12,000	$12,000
$ 28,000	$16,000
$ 48,000	$20,000
$ 72,000	$24,000
$100,000	$28,000

   b. Because the higher wage paid to attract each additional worker must also be paid to those already employed.
   c. A monopsonist's demand for labor curve is the market demand for labor curve. Furthermore, a monopsonist faces the market supply of labor curve. Column 2 expresses the market demand for labor and column 3 the market supply of labor.
   d. This monopsonist will employ two workers because this is the closest it can come to equating the marginal cost of labor with its marginal value. (If it employed the third worker, it would add more to its costs than to its revenues.)

e. A perfectly competitive labor market will employ that quantity and pay that wage rate given by the intersection of the market demand and supply curves. Because columns 2 and 3 express the market demand and supply schedules, three workers would be employed, each at a wage rate of $16,000. In other words, the quantity demanded of labor and the quantity supplied of labor are equal when three workers are employed at a wage of $16,000.

f. Yes. Note that the monopsonist hires one worker less and pays a wage rate $2,000 less than under competitive conditions.

2. a. This monopsonist will employ Q_1 workers and pay a wage rate of W_1.

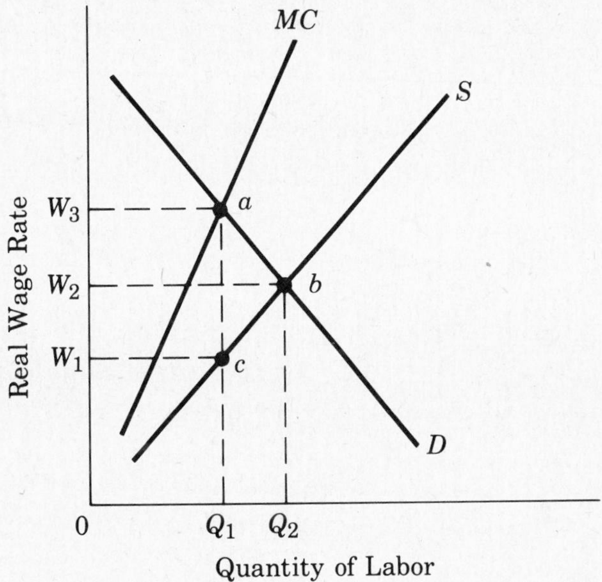

b. A perfectly competitive market would employ Q_2 workers and pay a wage rate of W_2.

c. A monopsonist employs too few workers — below the perfectly competitive ideal — equal $Q_2 - Q_1$.

d. Q_1cbQ_2

e. Q_1abQ_2

f. *abc*

3. a. Union members could receive a wage rate of W_3 without causing employment to fall below what the monopsonist would otherwise employ.

b. A union-negotiated wage rate between W_1 and W_3 would increase employment opportunities for the union.
c. Yes it can, but this will not necessarily happen. Notice that a union-negotiated wage rate of W_2 would cause Q_2 workers to be employed — the competitive outcome.

4. This is a reflection of several factors. First, the increased competition as foreign markets are opened up means that union strikes are less of a threat. People can more easily turn to other, nonunion suppliers. Second, most recent growth in employment opportunities has been in the services and high-technology industries, where unions have not been established. It is costly to organize a union, and it may be even more difficult now, since many of these new white-collar workers associate themselves with management. Third, workers are following job opportunities to the southern and western states, which have right-to-work laws. Finally, management has increased nonmonetary benefits to reduce the incentives for unionization.

True-False

1. T 2. T
3. F: A monopsonist, like all employers, will hire additional workers as long as each worker's marginal value exceeds his or her marginal cost.
4. F: A monopsonist determines the wage it must pay at the profit-maximizing output level by graphically reading off its market supply of labor curve.
5. F: A monopsonist will employ fewer workers and pay a lower wage rate than an employer in a perfectly competitive labor market.
6. T
7. F: A monopsonist employs fewer workers than is socially optimal.
8. T
9. F: The smaller the number of members, the longer an employer cartel is likelly to last.
10. T 11. T
12. F: A union may increase wages and employment if it is able to increase the demand for its product.

13. F: A union-negotiated wage increase in a monopsonistic labor market will always increase the wage rate, and it may also increase employment opportunities.

14. T 15. T

Multiple Choice

1. a *(KQ1)* 2. e *(KQ1)* 3. d *(KQ1)*
4. b *(KQ1)* 5. b *(KQ1)* 6. c *(KQ1)*
7. e *(KQ3)* 8. b *(KQ3)* 9. b *(KQ3)*
10. c *(KQ3)* 11. a *(KQ1)*

CHAPTER 28

Rent, Interest, and Profit

Chapter Summary

In this chapter we turn our attention to price determination in the land and capital markets, which are assumed to be competitive. This chapter also briefly evaluates the various explanations for the existence of business profits.

Key Question 1: How is the demand for a productive resource determined?

A firm's demand for land, like any other resource, is derived by multiplying the price of the final product *(P)* by the marginal product *(MP)* of each unit (acre) that could be used. This gives us the value of the marginal product *(VMP)* of each acre. The marginal product of additional acres used decreases because of the law of diminishing marginal returns. Therefore, the value of the marginal product of additional acres used decreases. Graphically, the downward-sloping *VMP* of land curve becomes the firm's demand curve for land. This is because, given the price of land, a firm will find it profitable to increase the use of land until the value of the marginal product of the last acre used is equal to its price. If the price decreases (increases), then it will be profitable to use more (less) land. This is shown by reading off the *VMP* of land curve (which is the firm's demand curve for land). (*Note:* The *VMP* curve for any resource is derived in the same manner and is the firm's demand curve for that resource.)

The market demand for a resource like land and labor is not, as one might expect, equal to the horizontal summation of all firms' *VMP* curves. Instead, the market demand curve is steeper than a horizontal summation of all firms' *VMP* curves. Nevertheless, the market demand curve for a resource slopes downward, reflecting the inverse relationship between its price and the quantity demanded.

The market supply of land may be upward-sloping if it has alternative uses, or it may be vertical (perfectly inelastic) if it does not have any alternative uses. Nevertheless, given the supply and demand curves for land, we can determine its use price, which is usually thought of as rent. However, in economics, rent has a special meaning, either economic rent or common economic rent (also known as quasi-rent).

Key Question 2: What is economic rent?

Economic rent is associated with resources that have a zero opportunity cost. This means that they are fixed in quantity, regardless of their price. That is, their supply curves are vertical, or perfectly inelastic. Some land fits this category because it has no alternative uses. Given the demand for its use, we can determine the economic rent earned. If demand increases, then the economic rent earned by the owner increases — even though the owner does nothing to improve his or her property. For this reason, economic rent may be viewed as unearned profit. Furthermore, the selling price of this land, which is a reflection of the present value of its future use — the economic rent it can earn over time — is entirely captured by the owner when sold, not the buyer. However, the pricing of the land determines who will use it and how it will be used.

Common economic rent (or quasi-rent) is associated with resources (like land or labor) that have alternative uses, and therefore their use is associated with some positive opportunity cost. The supply curve of a resource measures the opportunity cost of the last unit used for any given quantity used and it slopes upward, expressing increasing opportunity costs. Therefore, given the demand and supply for the resource, we can determine its price and the common economic rent earned. *Note:* Common economic rent is really payment above what is necessary to get units employed up to the last.

Resources may differ in their opportunity cost, and therefore the amount of common economic rent that may be earned, because of differences in their quality, location, and mineral deposits (applicable only to landed resources).

Noncompetitive producers may also earn common economic rent in the form of economic profits if they are able to secure protective legislation that limits competition. But recent evidence suggests that any surplus income earned may have already been spent for advertising, lobbying, and other activities directed at securing protective legislation.

Key Question 3: How is the rate of interest determined?

A firm's demand for capital is derived in the same manner as for any other resource. But in this case the value of marginal product of capital is called the rate of return on investment. When an additional unit of capital is purchased and employed, its value of marginal product is called the marginal rate of return on investment. The marginal rate of return on investment, expressed as a percentage of the purchase price of capital, decreases as more capital is employed. It not only decreases because of diminishing returns (decreasing marginal productivity of capital) but because profitable opportunities decrease as more investment in capital is undertaken. The marginal rate of return on investment curve slopes downward (just like the *VMP* curves for the other resources) and is the firm's demand for capital curve (its investment demand curve). By logical extension, the market demand for capital curve (or investment demand curve) is also downward-sloping for the same reasons.

The interest rate is considered the cost (or price) of acquiring capital because it is the price that must be paid for money borrowed to finance the purchase of capital. Even if the funds required to purchase capital are internally financed by the firm, it must consider the interest rate that could be earned by putting these funds in the bank. If the marginal rate of return on investment in capital is greater than the interest rate, then the firm will purchase capital because it gives a higher rate of return, or because it more than covers the cost of borrowing. Therefore, a firm will continue to purchase and employ more capital until the marginal rate of return on investment is just equal to the interest rate. If the interest rate decreases (increases), then more (fewer) investment opportunities will be profitable and more (less) capital will be purchased. Therefore, there is an inverse relationship between the interest rate and the level of investment (the quantity of capital purchased and employed). This inverse relationship is expressed in the downward-sloping demand for capital curve. So, to determine the level of investment, all we need to know is the interest rate. But before we derive the market demand and supply curves that determine the interest rate we must first see why it exists.

In order to raise the money necessary for investment to take place, people must forgo current consumption. Current consumption will be forgone only if people are compensated for doing so, and people are compensated for deferring consumption — that is, for loaning money — by receiving a rate of interest. Indeed, the cost of a loan — the price that must be paid for money — is the interest rate. Therefore, the interest rate exists as a payment for deferring consumption. It enables investment to be undertaken.

We can see that the cost of investment (money spent on capital) is really the interest rate. Alternatively stated, the opportunity cost of money loaned (and spent on capital) is deferred consumption. As one might expect, the opportunity cost of loaning money increases as more is loaned. That is, the interest rate must rise if more money is to be loaned out. This happens for two reasons. First, a greater amount of consumption will have to be deferred. Second, when larger amounts of current consumption is foregone, increasingly more valuable (desirable) goods and services are deferred. Therefore, the market supply of lendable funds curve slopes upward, reflecting increasing opportunity costs.

The market demand for lendable funds is the market demand curve for capital (or market investment demand curve). We know this because as the interest rate comes down, the level of investment goes up. That is, as the interest rate decreases, the quantity demanded of lendable funds increases to finance the greater quantity of capital that firms find profitable to purchase and employ. When the demand for and supply of lendable funds are brought together, we get the equilibrium interest rate in the market. If a usury law is imposed on the market, however, a shortage of funds will result.

The market or nominal interest rate consists of three components: a pure interest rate (the return one can expect from an investment in the absence of risk and inflation), a risk cost, and an anticipated inflation rate. The real interest rate equals the nominal (or market) interest rate minus the anticipated rate of inflation. If the risk of loaning money increases, then the supply of lendable funds curve shifts upward (or leftward), reflecting the fact that lenders will require a higher interest rate to be compensated for the increased risk of default on their loans. If a higher rate of inflation is anticipated, it causes the demand for lendable funds to rise as investors wish to purchase more now rather than waiting for prices to rise. At the same time, the supply of lendable funds shifts leftward, reflecting that lenders require a higher interest rate for any quantity loaned to compensate for devalued dollars when loans are repaid. (*Note:* The market interest rate — or simply the interest rate — equals the real interest rate plus anticipated inflation.) These combined effects cause the interest rate to rise equal to the amount of the anticipated inflation.

Key Question 4: How do business firms earn economic profits?

In the realm of economics, profit is a highly controversial concept. Nevertheless, profits can arise because of innovation, market accidents, entrepreneurship, monopoly power, or exploitation of labor or other resources.

Review Terms and Concepts

Labor
Land
Capital
Entrepreneur
Opportunity cost
Law of diminishing marginal returns
Marginal product
Value of marginal product
Horizontal summation
Anticipated inflation
Risk cost
Monopoly power
Barriers to entry
Shortage
Surplus

New Terms and Concepts

Economic rent
Common economic rent
Interest
Interest rate
Market (nominal) interest rate
Pure interest rate
Real interest rate
Rate of return on investment
Marginal rate of return on investment
Usury law

Completion

Answer	Text
the same	A firm's demand curve for land or capital is derived in _______________
	(a different/the same) way as for labor. A firm's demand curve for any
VMP	resource is its _______________ (*VMP*/*MC*) curve. The value of marginal
decreases	product of any resource _______________________ (increases/decreases)
	as additional units are purchased and employed. A firm will continue to
	purchase more of any resource until its value of marginal product is
equal to	_______________________ (greater than/equal to/less than) its price. The
	value of marginal product for all units purchased and employed up to
	the last means that the value of marginal product for these units is
greater than	_______________________ (greater than/equal to/less than) its price. The
earns a profit	firm ______________________ (earns a profit/loses money) off of these
value of marginal product minus price	units equal to the ____
	(price minus value of marginal product/value of marginal product minus
downward	price) for each unit. Graphically, the *VMP* curve slopes _______________
firm's	(upward/downward) and is the ______________________ (firm's/market)
	demand curve.
is not	The market demand curve for a resource _______________ (is/is not)
	obtained by horizontally summing all individual firms' *VMP* curves. The
is	market demand curve for a resource _________________ (is/is not)

Answers	
an inverse	downward-sloping. This implies that there is ____________________
	(an inverse/a positive) relationship between the price of a resource and
quantity demanded	the ____________________ (quantity demanded/quantity supplied).
	The supply curve for any resource that is not fixed in quantity is
upward	____________________ (downward/upward)-sloping, reflecting
increasing	____________________ (increasing/decreasing) opportunity costs.
a positive	The supply curve for any resource implies ____________________
	(an inverse/a positive) relationship between the price of a resource and
quantity supplied	the ____________________ (quantity demanded/quantity supplied).
	In competitive resource markets the price of a resource is determined
the intersection between	by ____________________ (summing/the intersection
demand	between) the ____________________ (demand/*VMP*) curve and the
supply	____________________ (demand/supply) curve. If the demand or supply
	curve changes, this changes the equilibrium price.
	Economic rent is earned by land when its opportunity cost is
zero	____________________ (positive/zero/negative). This means that the
does not	land ____________________ (does/does not) have any alternative uses.
	Given this supply, the interaction with demand determines the rental rate.
multiplying	Economic rent is calculated by ____________________ (adding/
	multiplying) the rental rate and the fixed quantity used. If demand
increases	____________________ (increases/decreases), then the economic rent
	earned by the owner of the land increases. This is usually viewed as
unearned	____________________ (earned/unearned) profit. The price of the land
will not	____________________ (will/will not) determine its use.

Common economic rent is associated with the resources whose supply
upward-sloping curves are ________________________ (vertical/perfectly inelastic/
do upward-sloping). This means that they __________ (do/do not) have
difference between alternative uses. The __________________________ (addition of/
difference between) the price and the opportunity cost of a resource
measures its common economic rent (or quasi-rent).

marginal rate A firm's demand for capital is its ______________________ (rate/
downward marginal rate) of return on investment curve. It slopes ____________
(upward/downward) because of diminishing returns and because of
decreasing ____________________ (increasing/decreasing) profit opportunities
from investment as investment increases. The marginal rate of return on
downward investment curve slopes __________________ (upward/downward)
firm's and is the ______________ (firm's/market) demand curve for capital.
market The cost of acquiring capital is the _______________ (market/price)
interest rate. The market interest rate consists of the pure interest rate and
anticipated the risk cost and a premium for ____________________ (anticipated/
unanticipated) inflation. As the market interest rate (or, simply, interest
more rate) decreases, a firm will purchase and employ ____________ (more/
less) capital, until the marginal rate of return on investment is
equal to ________________ (greater than/equal to/less than) the interest rate.
This means that the marginal rate of return from the use of all units of
greater than capital up the last is _____________________ (greater than/less than)
the interest rate.

downward The market demand curve for capital is ______________ (upward/
an inverse downward)-sloping. This means that there is __________________
(a positive/an inverse) relationship between the interest rate and the level

investment	of __________________ (investment/opportunity costs). Because
	the market demand curve for capital is downward-sloping, the market
downward	demand for lendable funds is ______________ (upward/downward)-
	sloping.
	The market supply curve of lendable funds is upward-sloping, reflect-
increasing	ing the ______________ (decreasing/increasing) opportunity costs
lending	of __________________ (borrowing/lending) money. When we
	bring the demand for and supply of lendable funds together we get
the equilibrium interest rate	________________________________ (a surplus/the equilibrium
	interest rate/a shortage).
	The market interest rate may change if there are changes in risk costs
supply of	that shift the ____________________ (demand for/supply of/demand
	for and supply of) lendable funds curve(s). The market interest rate may
anticipated	also change if there is a change in the ____________________
	(anticipated/unanticipated) inflation rate. This is because we know that
	the market (or nominal) interest rate equals the real interest rate
plus	__________ (plus/minus) anticipated inflation. Changes in anticipated
demand for and supply of	inflation will cause changes in the __________________________
	(demand for/supply of/demand for and supply of) lendable funds
	curve(s). An increase in anticipated inflation will cause
an increase	________________ (an increase/a decrease) in the market (or
	nominal) interest rate equal to the anticipated inflation.
is	In the realm of economics, profit ___________ (is/is not) a very
	controversial concept. Nevertheless, it can occur because of innovation,
	market accidents, entrepreneurship, monopoly power, or exploitation of
	labor or other resources.

Problems and Applications

1. a. What do all resources have in common when it comes to deriving a firm's demand curve for those resources?
   b. What do all resources have in common in terms of the quantities a firm chooses to employ?
   c. What do all resources' supply curves have in common?
2. How is the market demand curve for a resource (like land and labor) derived?
3. a. What does the supply curve look like for a resource that earns pure economic rent?
   b. How is economic rent calculated?
   c. What condition must be met for resources to earn common economic rent (or quasi-rents)? How is common economic rent calculated? Draw a graph and indicate the areas of common economic rent.
   d. How can producers of goods and services earn common economic rent?
4. a. Why does a firm's marginal rate of return on investment decrease?
   b. Is a firm's marginal rate of return on investment curve its demand for capital curve? What is its slope? What does its slope tell us?
   c. Given the market interest rate, how much capital will a firm purchase and employ? What can be said about all the quantities of capital purchased up to the last?
   d. How is a firm's demand for capital curve related to the market demand curve for lendable funds?
5. Why is the supply of lendable funds curve upward-sloping?
6. For each of the following situations, determine what effect there would be on either the demand for or the supply of lendable funds and what would happen to the market interest rate.
   a. People anticipate an inflation rate of 5 percent in the coming year.
   b. The chances of a political upheaval seem greater than ever before.
7. What are the economic consequences of usury laws?

True-False

For each item, determine whether the statement is basically true or false. If the statement is false, rewrite it so it is a true statement.

_____ 1. The demand curve for any resource is derived in the same manner as any other resource.

_____ 2. The demand curves for all resources slope upward because of increasing opportunity costs.

_____ 3. A market demand curve for a resource is derived by horizontally summing all firms' *VMP* curves for the resource.

_____ 4. A firm will continue to employ additional units of a resource until the value of marginal product of the last unit employed just equals its price.

_____ 5. Economic rent is earned by a resource that does not have any alternative uses.

_____ 6. Common economic rent is associated with resources that have upward-sloping supply curves because upward-sloping supply curves measure positive and increasing opportunity costs.

_____ 7. Resources may differ in their opportunity costs because of differences in their quality or location.

_____ 8. Firms that secure government legislation to limit competition receive all of the higher economic profits the government protection generates.

_____ 9. A firm's demand for capital curve is its marginal resource cost curve.

_____ 10. The market interest rate is almost always greater than the pure interest rate.

_____ 11. An increase in anticipated inflation of 5 percent will increase the pure interest rate by 5 percent.

_____ 12. Borrowers in high-crime areas have to pay a higher interest rate on loans because the demand for these types of loans is greater than otherwise, reflecting a greater risk cost.

_____ 13. A decrease in anticipated inflation will cause the demand for lendable funds to decrease but the supply of lendable funds to increase.

_____ 14. There is an inverse relationship between the interest rate and the level of investment.

_____ 15. Any given level of investment receives a rate of return equal to the interest rate, or more.

_____ 16. The supply for lendable funds is upward-sloping because the marginal productivity of capital decreases and because the profitability of increased investment decreases.

_____ 17. If the marginal rate of return on investment is 10 percent and the interest rate is 8 percent, the firm should purchase the capital.

_____ 18. Business profits are unearned profits.

_____ 19. The real interest rate is equal to the nominal interest rate plus an anticipated rate of inflation.

Multiple Choice *Choose the one best answer for each item.*

_____ 1. Which of the following resources has an upward-sloping supply curve?
   a. Land
   b. Labor
   c. Capital
   d. All of the above
   e. None of the above

_____ 2. For a resource, if a firm's value of marginal product
   a. curve slopes downward, it is because of increasing opportunity costs.
   b. curve is horizontally summed with all firms' *VMP* curves, we obtain the market demand curve.
   c. curve is upward-sloping, we get the firm's supply curve of the resource.
   d. is greater than its price, then too many units of the resource are employed.
   e. decreases as more units of the resource are employed, then the law of diminishing returns has set in to the production process.

_____ 3. Economic rent
   a. is the same as quasi-rent.
   b. is derived by multiplying the price of the final product by the marginal product of the resource.
   c. is earned by resources that have zero economic costs.
   d. is viewed as earned income.
   e. is associated with a resource that has an upward-sloping supply curve.

_____ 4. Common economic rent will be earned
   a. by a worker who would work for a lower wage than he or she is currently receiving.
   b. by a worker who would work only if the wage rate were higher than it currently is.
   c. when the opportunity cost of a worker is just equal to the wage rate.
   d. when the opportunity cost of a worker is greater than the wage rate.
   e. by workers when total compensation is less than workers' opportunity cost.

_____ 5. The demand for lendable funds
   a. slopes downward because the marginal rate of return on investment decreases as investment increases.
   b. is the market demand curve for capital.
   c. will increase if investors anticipate a higher rate of inflation.
   d. slopes downward because of diminishing returns to capital.
   e. is described by all of the above.

_____ 6. The market interest rate
   a. compensates businesses for forgone investment.
   b. equals the real interest rate minus anticipated inflation.
   c. is the cost of capital.
   d. determines the pure interest rate.
   e. is unearned income on the part of lenders.

Use the graph on page 532 to answer questions 7-10.

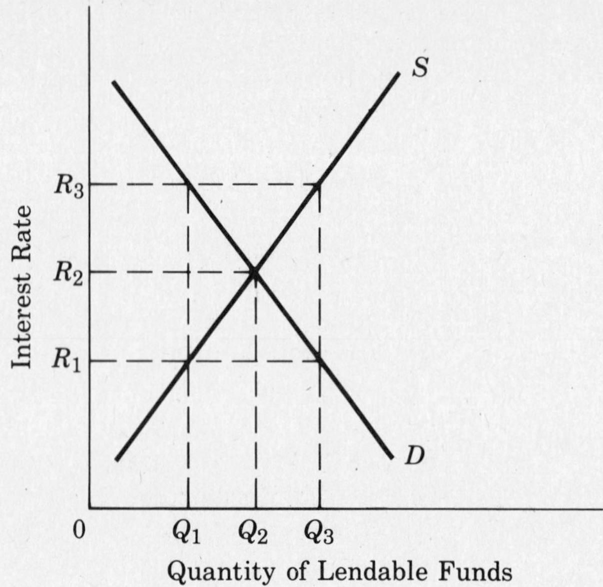

_____ 7. Which of the following statements is true?
a. Equilibrium exists at R_2 and Q_2.
b. A shortage of Q_3 - Q_1 exists at R_1.
c. A surplus of Q_3 - Q_1 exists at R_3.
d. At the equilibrium investment level Q_2 all of the quantities of capital purchased below Q_2 have a rate of return of R_2 or more.
e. All of the above are true statements.

_____ 8. If the interest rate is R_1
a. a shortage of Q_3 - Q_1 exists, and the interest rate will rise.
b. a surplus of Q_2 - Q_1 exists, and the interest rate will fall.
c. a surplus of Q_3 - Q_1 exists, and the interest rate will rise.
d. demand will shift to the left.
e. supply will shift to the left.

_____ 9. An interest rate of R_3 could become an equilibrium if
a. the risk cost of loans increased.
b. anticipated inflation decreased.
c. the demand for loans decreased.
d. the productivity of capital decreased.
e. the opportunity cost of foregone consumption decreased.

_____ 10. The supply curve of lendable funds slopes upward because of
a. the law of diminishing returns.
b. increasing opportunity costs associated with greater amounts of deferred consumption.
c. increasing risk costs as more funds are loaned.
d. increased inflation as more investment is undertaken.
e. all of the above.

_____ 11. Which of the following conditions under which business profits may be earned is most likely to have the least desirable social effects?
a. Innovation
b. Market accidents
c. Entrepreneurship
d. Monopoly power
e. Government protection

Discussion Questions

1. What will cause the quantity supplied of land for a particular use to increase? Can you think of some examples? *(KQ2)*
2. How much common economic rent do you think professional athletes make? *(KQ2)*
3. Under what conditions could a firm that is able to secure protective legislation receive some common economic rent? Under what conditions would it not receive any common economic rent? Under what conditions could it actually lose money? *(KQ2)*
4. How does the interest rate help allocate society's scarce resources between the production of consumer goods and services and capital products? What can change the interest rate, hence this allocation? How will a change in this allocation affect economic growth? (*KQ3*. See also Chapter 2.)
5. Why would government wish to impose a price ceiling on the market interest rate? What would the economic consequences be? Who would be hurt most by a usury law? *(KQ3)*
6. Will an unanticipated change in inflation affect the market interest rate? Why or why not? *(KQ3)*

Answers

Problems and Applications

1. a. A firm's demand for any resource, whether it be labor, land, or capital, is derived in part from the price of the final product and in part from its marginal productivity. That is, each unit used has a value of marginal product associated with it. The value of marginal product of any unit of a resource equals the price of the final product multiplied by that unit's marginal product. Because the marginal productivity of additional units employed decreases, due to the law of diminishing marginal returns, the value of marginal product of additional units employed decreases. Graphically, the *VMP* curve for any resource is downward-sloping and is the firm's demand curve for that resource.
   b. A firm will find it profitable to continue to increase the employment of any resource until the value of marginal product (or marginal value) of the last unit employed just equals its price (or marginal cost). If the price of the resource decreases, a firm will find it profitable to increase the employment of the resource. If the price rises, the firm will employ fewer units. So we can see that there is an inverse relationship between the price of any resource and the quantity demanded (the quantity the firm wishes to purchase and employ). Indeed, its demand curve is downward-sloping.
   c. The market supply curve of any resource that is not fixed in quantity slopes upward, reflecting increasing opportunity costs associated with greater quantities made available in the market. Because the supply curve of a resource is upward-sloping, it shows that there is a positive (or direct) relationship between its price and the quantity supplied.
2. The market demand for a resource is not, as one might expect, equal to the horizontal summation of all firms' *VMP* curves. This is because as more of a resource is used in a market, the output of the final product increases. This pushes its market price down. Therefore, a lower price multiplied by the marginal product decreases the value of marginal product of these additional units employed. A lower value of marginal product means that fewer units of the resource will be employed as its price falls than otherwise. There is still an increase in the quantity employed in the market but not by as much as would be expected by summing individual firms' *VMP* curves. Therefore, the market demand for a resource will be steeper

than a horizontal summation of all firms' *VMP* curves because it is obtained by allowing for a fall in the value of marginal product as more goods and services are produced at lower prices.

3. a. It is vertical, or perfectly inelastic, illustrating that there is zero opportunity cost associated with its use. That is, regardless of its price, the same quantity will be supplied in the market.
   b. It is calculated by multiplying the rental rate (or price) by the fixed quantity used.
   c. The supply curve must be upward-sloping, reflecting increasing opportunity costs for its use. When increasing opportunity costs are present, this means that the resource has alternative uses, and its supply curve slopes upward. When the supply curve of a resource slopes upward, then common economic rent can be earned. Because the supply curve indicates the opportunity cost of each additional unit supplied in the market, and because common economic rent is the difference between the price of the resource and its opportunity cost, when we are given the demand for the resource we can determine the price and therefore the common economic rent earned by all units supplied in the market up to the last. In the graph, area $0W_2aQ_2$ is the total compensation paid to the units of the resource. The area under

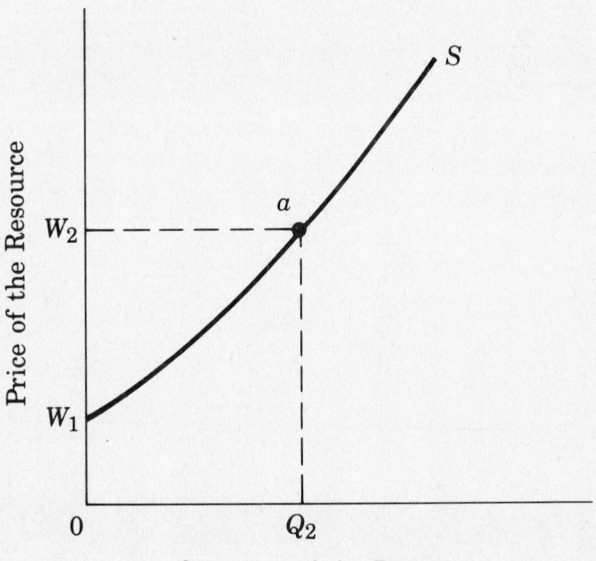

the supply curve indicates the total opportunity cost of all units. Therefore, the area W_1W_2a is the area indicating common economic rent earned by all units supplied in the market up to the last.

d. Noncompetitive firms may earn common economic rent in the form of economic profits above what is necessary to keep them in the market (i.e., above a zero economic profit, which is their opportunity cost) if they are able to secure government protection from competition. However, this common economic rent (economic profit) may not actually be received by these firms. That income may have already been spent on securing the government protection. It may be the lobbyists or politicians who actually receive this rent.

4. a. First, because of diminishing returns that cause the marginal productivity of additional units of capital purchased and employed to decrease. Second, because as more investment in capital is undertaken, each investment project is less profitable.

   b. Yes. It is downward-sloping, reflecting the inverse relationship between the interest rate (the cost of acquiring capital) and the quantity of capital purchased and employed.

   c. A firm will continue to purchase and employ capital until the marginal rate of return on the last unit purchased just equals the market interest rate. All quantities of capital purchased up to the last have a higher marginal rate of return than the market interest rate. So, the total unit of capital purchased has a rate of return on investment equal to the market interest rate, *or more*.

   d. Because a firm will increase the quantity of capital purchased as the interest rate falls — shown by reading off its demand for capital curve — the quantity of lendable funds it requires to purchase this greater amount of capital also increases. This means that the demand for lendable funds curve must be downward-sloping also. Indeed, the demand for lendable funds curve is the market demand curve for capital.

5. For two reasons. First, a greater amount of consumption will have to be foregone to increase the quantity supplied of lendable funds. Second, when larger amounts of current consumption are foregone, increasingly more valuable goods and services will have to be deferred. In sum, the supply of lendable funds slopes upward because of increasing opportunity costs (just like all other supply curves).

6. a. Demand increases and supply decreases. The interest rate rises equal to the amount of the anticipated inflation of 5 percent — or approximately so.
   b. Supply decreases and the interest rate rises.
7. Shortages of lendable funds. Usury laws can make loans more difficult to be secured by those who may need them the most.

True-False

1. T
2. F: The demand curves for all resources slope downward because of diminishing returns.
3. F: A market demand curve for a resource is not derived by horizontally summing all firms' *VMP* curves for the resource.
4. T 5. T 6. T 7. T
8. F: Firms that secure government legislation to limit competition may receive much, but not necessarily all, of the higher economic profits the government protection generates.
9. F: A firm's demand for capital curve is its marginal rate of return on investment curve.
10. T
11. F: An increase in anticipated inflation of 5 percent will increase the market interest rate by 5 percent.
12. F: Borrowers in high-crime areas have to pay a higher interest rate because the supply of those types of loans is lower than otherwise, reflecting a greater risk cost.
13. T 14. T 15. T
16. F: The supply for lendable funds curve is upward-sloping because of the increasing opportunity costs of loaning money.
17. T
18. F: Business profits are not always unearned profits.
19. F: The real interest rate is equal to the nominal interest rate minus an anticipated rate of inflation.

Multiple Choice

1. d *(KQ1)*	2. e *(KQ1)*	3. c *(KQ2)*
4. a *(KQ2)*	5. e *(KQ3)*	6. c *(KQ3)*
7. e *(KQ3)*	8. a *(KQ3)*	9. a *(KQ3)*
10. b *(KQ3)*	11. d *(KQ4)*	

CHAPTER 29

Poverty and Poverty Relief

Chapter Summary

Key Question 1: How would the distribution of income in the United States be described?

Key Question 2: How is poverty determined?

Key Question 3: What causes poverty?

The distribution of income in the United States is quite uneven. It results in a large number of lower-income people in poverty. Poverty may be one of the most apparent and severe shortcomings of capitalism. In the United States, we have not only a poverty problem but also a problem of providing relief to the many who need it.

The official government definition of poverty is given by the poverty income threshold, which defines the minimum income believed necessary for basic subsistence. But there are some shortcomings associated with official government statistics, which tend both to overstate and understate the number of poor.

The causes of poverty are at least as complicated as the question of how to define it. Currently, four factors are emphasized. First, workers who are uneducated or unskilled are not very productive in today's economy, and their wages reflect that fact. Those who are physically or mentally handicapped are also at a disadvantage. Some suggest that a "cycle of poverty" may entrap the poor in an environment that is not conducive to upward mobility. Second, statistical evidence suggests that sexual and racial discrimination also contribute to poverty. Third, low aggregate demand or total spending in the economy brings recession, unemployment, and therefore poverty. Furthermore, it is usually minorities and women who are the last hired and the first fired. Finally, poverty sometimes stems from a person's lifestyle. Some people put job satisfaction above monetary reward, while others may speculate in the pursuit of high incomes and fail.

Many factors have contributed to the government's increased effort to relieve poverty. The presence of poverty imposes external costs on other

Key Question 4: What are the justifications for government programs to relieve poverty?

members of society, and aid to the poor may benefit not just the poor but everyone in the community (the external benefits of aid are the benefits provided to members of the community other than the poor). But because there is a free-rider problem associated with contributing aid, it can only be provided in adequate amounts through government public service programs and the accompanying forced taxation to pay for them. Government poverty relief can also be viewed as a form of social insurance because people cannot be certain they will not end up among the ranks of the poor. Government poverty relief may also be one outcome of practical politics.

Key Question 5: What methods are used to relieve poverty?

There are four broad categories of aid to the poor: in-kind transfers, cash transfers, minimum wage and rent controls, and job training. Regardless of their purpose, all tend to change people's incentives to work, invest, and buy subsidized goods and services. Most have two distinguishable effects, an income effect and relative price (substitution) effect.

In-kind transfers — goods or services provided by the government to a select group of citizens — consist of food, housing, medical care, and education. All in-kind transfers increase the total effective income (purchasing power) of recipients. They also cause the relative prices of these subsidized items to fall. Therefore, the poor are expected to purchase and consume more of them than they otherwise would — that is, given that their earned income was as high as their total effective income created by government assistance.

Food stamps are available to all who need them, unlike many of the other in-kind transfers. The food stamp program is also unique among in-kind transfers because there is an implicit marginal income tax rate (a take-back rate) within the system up to the break-even level. This creates a slight disincentive to work. Unlike food stamps, the benefits provided by public housing go to a relatively small portion of the people who need it. The tax-paying public is unwilling to meet the demand at controlled rent prices because the cost of providing that quantity of public housing is considered too high. Although the benefits of public education are available to everyone, not just the poor, evidence suggests it is really the upper-income individuals who benefit most. (This becomes most apparent when higher education is considered.) This may suggest public education is a kind of upside-down welfare program.

The second broad category of aid to the poor is cash transfers. The poor prefer cash grants over in-kind transfers because cash grants offer greater choice. Therefore, for the same dollar amount of tax dollars, cash transfers offer greater benefits to the poor. Cash grants can be made to the poor in many ways. One method is by way of a negative income tax. Instead of paying taxes, those families below a break-even level would receive cash grants. The lower a family's income, the greater the grant. If its income is zero, it would receive a guaranteed income. As a family's income rises, some of the cash grant is taken back. Because of this implicit marginal income tax rate (take-back rate), the negative income tax creates a disincentive to work. And to keep program costs down and to concentrate benefits on the truly poor, any negative income tax system is likely to bear a rather high marginal income tax system.

Minimum wages and rent controls are also designed to help the poor, but they are very inefficient. The minimum wage tends to make jobs more difficult to find for the less productive. Furthermore, the poor are the first laid off when the minimum wage rates are raised. Rent controls cause a shortage of low-income housing. Worse yet, they intensify a shortage once it exists. Landlords let their buildings deteriorate, and fewer housing units are constructed over time.

Finally, the government may administer job training and job placement services. In a changing economy it is inevitable for skills that once were in demand to become obsolete. Therefore, government programs aimed at retraining or continuing education should offer some relief. On the other hand, if a particular skill is no longer demanded in one location it may still be needed elsewhere. Government employment agencies attempt to increase the flow of information on job openings from employers to employees.

Key Question 6: What is a basic problem with poverty programs?

In sum, all aid tends to reduce the incentive for the poor to work. The amount of aid lost by working is given by the implicit marginal income tax rate. Furthermore, because people receive aid from various sources, the take-back rate is compounded by working — sometimes to the extent that the poor are better off not working. Also, because the combined implicit marginal income tax rate for most poor who are receiving many programs is so very high, it creates what is sometimes called a poverty wall. Finally, policymakers are advised to keep a close eye on incentives and disincentives when they establish the qualifications for aid based on special characteristics such as income or family size. If they don't, they may promote undesirable social side effects.

Key Question 7: How can day-care contribute to overcoming poverty?

Escaping the cycle of poverty is certainly not an easy task, especially for women with dependent children. However, it has been suggested that subsidizing day-care centers, or parents, or relaxing some of the regulations governing day-care centers may help. But, of course, the social benefit of relaxing the regulation of day-care centers as compared to the cost is a debatable issue.

Review Terms and Concepts

Income effect
Substitution effect
Consumer price index
Real income
Productivity
Aggregate demand
External cost
External benefit
Subsidy

New Terms and Concepts

Median family income
Mean family income
Poverty income threshold
In-kind transfer
Break-even income level
Cash transfer
Negative income tax
Guaranteed income level
Implicit marginal income tax
Implicit marginal income tax rate
"Cycle of poverty"
Poverty wall

Completion

poverty income threshold — The official definition of poverty is given by the ________________ (median family income/poverty income threshold). This defines the

minimum — ________________ (minimum/maximum) income believed neces-

some — sary for basic subsistence. There are ______________ (no/some) real problems in statistically determining the actual number of people living in poverty. The official government statistics tend to

underestimate and overestimate — ________________________________(underestimate/overestimate/underestimate and overestimate) the poverty level in this country.

complicated — The causes of poverty are ______________________ (simple/

low — complicated). One major cause is related to ___________ (high/low)

and — productivity. There is also evidence that racial _________ (but not/and) sexual discrimination may account for some poverty. If aggregate

low — demand is ____________ (high/low), we may experience some

	unemployment and therefore some poverty. Finally, poverty may have its
lifestyle	roots in some people's ____________________ (laziness/lifestyle).
increased	Government has ______________________ (increased/decreased) its efforts at poverty relief in the last 85 years. This has been done in part to correct for some externalities associated with poverty. In this way we
public	may view poverty relief as a ________________ (private/public) good.
four	There are ______________ (two/four) broad categories of aid to the poor. One category provides goods and services to the poor. This category is
in-kind transfers	called _________________________ (in-kind transfers/cash grants).
negative	Almost all of these forms of aid tend to have a __________________ (positive/negative) effect on incentives to work. Almost all have an
income	______________________ (income/implicit) effect and a relative
price	____________________ (productivity/price) effect.
to everyone who needs them	Food stamps are available ___________________________________ (only to a few/to everyone who needs them). Public housing is not. There
shortage	is a ______________________ (shortage/surplus) of public housing. This means that the benefits of public housing go to
only a few who need it	____ (too many/only a few who need it). Public education appears to benefit those who need it
least	________________ (most/least).
more	Cash grants provide _______________ (more/fewer) benefits to the poor than in-kind transfers. This means that for the same amount of tax
greater	money spent on the poor, _____________________ (greater/fewer) benefits can be derived. One method of providing cash grants is the
negative	________________________ (negative/progressive) income tax. This is
implicit marginal income tax rate	similar to the food stamp program in that an ________________________

(in-kind transfer/implicit marginal income tax rate) is present. This means that some of the cash grants are ____________________ (taken back/given away). Therefore, there is ____________________ (a disincentive/an incentive) to work. This is a problem with almost all forms of poverty relief.

taken back

a disincentive

Another method of poverty relief is government control over the wage rate and rents. The minimum wage causes some ____________________ (employment/unemployment). Rent controls cause a ________________ (surplus/shortage) of low-income housing. Both are ________________ (inefficient/efficient) forms of poverty relief. Finally, government attempts to relieve poverty through job placement and job training.

unemployment

shortage

inefficient

To have effective poverty relief programs, government needs to keep a close eye on the ______________________________ (incentives/disincentives/incentives and disincentives), especially when it is designing qualifications for aid based on special characteristics, such as income or family size. Furthermore, government programs seem to ______________ (inhibit/promote) a wall of poverty.

incentives and disincentives

promote

Escaping the cycle of poverty is ________________________ (an easy/a difficult) task. One way that is highly recommended is ______________________ (crime/education).

a difficult

education

Problems and Applications

1. What is the poverty income threshold based on and why does it change over time?
2. What are some of the reasons official government statistics tend to overstate the extent of poverty? Understate the extent of poverty?
3. What are the benefits and costs of poverty relief and how can it be viewed as a public service? How can poverty relief be viewed as a form of social insurance?

4. How does the food stamp program work? What effect does it have on the total adjusted income (total purchasing power) of recipients? How does it affect the incentive to work? Why do some taxpayers prefer food stamps over cash grants?
5. Does the in-kind transfer of public education benefit everyone? Who really benefits, the low-income student or the more well-to-do student?
6. a. What effect would the subsidization of day-care centers have on the price and quantity of children served and therefore the ability of parents to pursue more education or training in order to escape the poverty trap? Is there any difference between subsidizing the centers and subsidizing the parents?
   b. What would be the economic benefits of relaxing day-care center regulation?

True-False

For each item, determine whether the statement is basically true or false. If the statement is false, rewrite it so it is a true statement.

____ 1. The poverty income threshold is based primarily on the cost of a nutritionally adequate but economically thrifty food plan.

____ 2. The poverty income threshold is adjusted each year for changes in the cost of living, as measured by the consumer price index.

____ 3. Some people are not counted in the poverty statistics because they are homeless.

____ 4. Poverty statistics are adjusted for regional differences in the cost of living.

____ 5. The cycle of poverty refers to the fact that the poor socialize with people in the same socioeconomic class.

____ 6. Sexual and racial discrimination do not account for much poverty.

____ 7. Recessions, or downturns in economic activity, account for some temporary poverty.

____ 8. Aid to the poor brings many external benefits.

____ 9. A cash grant is more valuable to the poor than an equal dollar amount of in-kind transfers.

____ 10. Anyone above the break-even level is eligible for food stamps.

____ 11. There is too much public housing, causing the costs of the program to exceed its benefits.

_____ 12. Government money spent on public education appears to benefit those in low-income brackets more than those in high-income brackets.

_____ 13. The negative income tax is characterized by the conflicting goals of poverty relief, minimizing disincentives to work, and keeping program costs down.

_____ 14. There is an implicit marginal income tax rate in both the food stamp program and the negative income tax.

_____ 15. The poverty wall refers to the built-in disincentives to work in most poverty relief programs.

_____ 16. The minimum wage and rent controls most help those who are the least productive and the most impoverished.

Multiple Choice *Choose the one best answer for each item.*

_____ 1. The twenty percent of U.S. families with the highest incomes earned approximately what percentage of the nation's total family income?
a. 5 percent
b. 11 percent
c. 17 percent
d. 25 percent
e. 43 percent

_____ 2. Which of the following statements about the percentage of families below the poverty line is true?
a. Most are there voluntarily.
b. The percentage has increased in the last decade.
c. The percentage has decreased in the last decade.
d. The percentage has been around 5 percent.
e. The percentage has been around 20 percent.

_____ 3. One of the shortcomings of poverty statistics, which tends to underestimate the extent of poverty, is that
a. those who are homeless are not counted.
b. some of the poor may be earning substantial incomes in the black market.
c. some of the poor may be underreporting their legal incomes.

d. the government multiplies an economical food budget by a factor of three.
e. most poverty is temporary.

____ 4. Which of the following causes of poverty contributes most to the "cycle of poverty"?
a. Low aggregate demand
b. Low productivity
c. High tax rates
d. Choice of lifestyle
e. High university tuition costs

____ 5. Cash transfers
a. are a form of in-kind transfers.
b. include the minimum wage and rent controls.
c. provide more benefits for the money spent by government than in-kind transfers.
d. provide for food stamps.
e. are least preferred by the poor.

____ 6. The minimum wage
a. makes it more difficult for the least productive to find employment.
b. may cause the poor to be the first laid off when the minimum wage increases.
c. may perpetuate sexual and racial discrimination.
d. causes some unemployment.
e. is described by all of the above.

____ 7. Which of the following statements about poverty relief programs is true?
a. They change incentives to work and invest.
b. Almost all in-kind transfers subsidies cause both an income and relative price effect.
c. Policymakers should watch closely how qualifications for aid are designed.
d. Cash transfers are more efficient than in-kind transfers.
e. All of the above are true statements.

____ 8. Public education
a. raises the real incomes of the poor.
b. raises the real incomes of the rich.
c. benefits the rich more than the poor.
d. is a form of in-kind transfer.
e. is described by all of the above.

_____ 9. An implicit marginal income tax rate is
   a. the amount of taxes lost by government when people are impoverished.
   b. the difference between tax rates for the poor and the rich.
   c. the percentage by which a government subsidy increases when income rises.
   d. a negative income tax.
   e. the amount by which a government subsidy is reduced when earned income rises, stated as a percentage of the additional earned income.

_____ 10. To increase the incentives for the poor to seek out further education and training, cheaper day-care service may be required. Which form of government action is likely to reduce the price of day-care services?
   a. A decrease in subsidies of day-care centers
   b. A decrease in tax rates for unwed mothers with dependent children
   c. A subsidy to day-care centers
   d. More stringent regulations governing day-care centers
   e. Both b and d

_____ 11. A guaranteed income level
   a. is an increase in the minimum wage.
   b. is a government income subsidy at the poverty income threshold.
   c. is a government income subsidy at a zero income level.
   d. exists in the food stamp program.
   e. is an income level at which a government subsidy is no longer available.

_____ 12. Which of the following is a major problem with the U.S. welfare system?
   a. It does not relieve poverty to any noticeable degree.
   b. We have an enormous problem determining who is poor.
   c. Those who need assistance least are receiving most of it.
   d. The combined implicit marginal income tax rates of the various programs create a poverty wall.
   e. All of the above.

Discussion Questions

1. What are the relative benefits and costs of the negative income tax system as compared to the current poverty relief systems? We know the minimum wage creates unemployment for the relatively unproductive and unemployment creates a lack of personal esteem, not to mention the many other undesirable side effects. Would a minimum wage be necessary under a negative income tax system? *(KQ5)*
2. Many states have state employment services. How effective are they in transmitting job information? Do you think a national employment service would be beneficial? *(KQ5)*
3. What is meant by the "cycle of poverty"? What could or should government do to break the cycle? *(KQ5, 6)*
4. What is meant by a poverty wall and how does this contribute to poverty? *(KQ5, 6)*
5. What could cause the unemployed to be unwilling to move where they may be able to get a job even if they knew it existed? *(KQ5)*
6. We know that most welfare programs are administered by the states and that states differ in both their benefits and their implicit marginal income tax rates. How could states with generous welfare programs be "punished" for their concern for the poor? *(KQ5, 6)*

Answers

Problems and Applications

1. It is based primarily on the cost of a nutritionally adequate but economically shifting food plan. It is adjusted each year for changes in the cost of living as measured by the consumer price index.
2. Government statistics can overstate the extent of poverty for several reasons. First, government poverty figures are based solely on money income received as earnings or government grants. They do not include welfare assistance received by the poor, which can push some of them above the threshold. Second, government statistics overlook the fact that some people considered to be poor have access to additional income or accumulate wealth. And still others are employed in the underground economy, or they underreport their legal income. Third, poverty statistics are not adjusted for regional differences in the cost of living, which leads to both over- and underestimates. Fourth, the use of the consumer price index as an adjustment for the poverty threshold level may have resulted in an increase in the real purchasing power of the poor. Fifth, because the

poor typically spend more than one-third of their incomes on food, the method of calculating the poverty income threshold overstate the minimum income required to escape poverty. Finally, government statistics do not allow for the fact that most poverty is temporary. Many people have savings to draw on during relatively short periods of hard times.

Government statistics may also understate the extent of poverty in three important ways. First, some people are simply uncounted. Second, children under fifteen who live alone are uncounted. Finally, poverty statistics do not account for sudden drains on people's incomes — for example, when they have accidents or become sick.

3. Whether out of benevolence or guilt, some people may have come to view poverty relief as having such large external benefits that government has been called to provide the various public services to relieve poverty we now have. Still, other, less benevolent factors may have come into play. The presence of poverty can impose heavy external costs on a community. For instance, unpleasant sights of poverty can depress property values. This may cause some to move to neighborhoods where strict zoning laws have been imposed. But the rich pay handsomely for escaping the unpleasant sights of poverty. Government aid to the poor can reduce the costs to the rich of escaping those who do not live as they do. Thus, government aid can benefit everyone in the community. However, not everyone is necessarily willing to pay for it. There is likely to be a free-rider problem, and therefore aid would be underprovided in the absence of government-forced taxation. Finally, poverty relief programs may be construed as a form of social insurance people purchase from government. Because no one can be certain that he or she will not become impoverished too, people may benefit from the fact that poverty relief is there "just in case." Furthermore, poverty relief can make for good politics.
4. The food stamp program issues government coupons, or "stamps," which recipients use in buying food. As a family's income increases, the allotted value of the stamps decreases. Eventually a break-even income level is reached in which the government subsidy is no longer available. The effect of the food subsidy is to increase families' total adjusted income (or total purchasing power). But the increases in total adjusted income are greater for low-income levels than for high-income levels. Therefore, this program slightly reduces the incentive of the poor to work and earn income. Many people favor the food stamp program over cash grants

because it ensures that tax dollars are spent on food — as opposed to tobacco or liquor. But it does not enable the poor to spend money on something they may want more than extra food — for instance, continuing education. For that reason food stamps are less valuable to the poor than cash grants.

5. Public education benefits everyone, not just the poor. Studies suggest, in fact, that it is really the upper-income individuals who benefit most. Innate abilities and home experiences affect how much students learn, and in these areas children from high-income families have an advantage. When it comes to higher education, especially, low-income individuals are at a disadvantage. They may not meet the entrance requirements or they may go to smaller, less academically qualified schools on which the state spends little money. Public education, then, may be an upside-down welfare system. But, government subsidies of higher education do raise the real incomes (purchasing power) of those who are aided. Although some of this aid for higher education may be spent on better housing, entertainment, or spring vacations, it does reduce the relative price of education and induce parents and students to purchase more.

6. a. If government subsidized day-care centers, the supply would increase and the price would fall. Therefore, more parents could afford to put their children in day-care centers and pursue more education or training. If the parents were subsidized, the only difference is that demand would increase — the effective price after the subsidy is considered would be the same as with subsidization of the centers.
   b. The supply of day-care centers would increase more than demand would decrease (there would be some decrease in demand because of the decline in quality). The result is a reduction in price and therefore more children placed in day-care centers so parents could continue their education or training. And this would occur at no cost to taxpayers. Of course, whether relaxing day-care regulations is a good idea is a debatable issue.

True-False

1. T 2. T 3. T
4. F: Poverty statistics are not adjusted for regional differences in the cost of living, and this leads to both over- and underestimates.
5. F: The cycle of poverty refers to unproductive poor who received inadequate education and are unable to earn enough to afford a good education for their children.
6. F: Sexual and racial discrimination accounts for some poverty.
7. T 8. T 9. T
10. F: Everyone below the break-even level is eligible for food stamps.
11. F: There is a shortage of public housing, which means its benefits go to a small portion of those who need it.
12. F: Government money spent on education appears to benefit those in high-income brackets more than those in low-income brackets.
13. T 14. T 15. T
16. F: The minimum wage and rent controls most hurt those who are the least productive and the most impoverished.

Multiple Choice

1. e *(KQ1)* 2. b *(KQ2)* 3. a *(KQ2)*
4. b *(KQ3)* 5. c *(KQ5)* 6. e *(KQ5)*
7. e *(KQ6)* 8. e *(KQ5)* 9. e *(KQ5, 6)*
10. c *(KQ7)* 11. c *(KQ5)* 12. d *(KQ6)*

CHAPTER 30

Market Failures: External Costs and Benefits

Chapter Summary

There are several sources of market failure. Among those sources are external costs and external benefits. This chapter looks at the consequences of external costs and benefits and how government attempts to correct for them.

The competitive market produces at the point of intersection between demand and supply, where the quantity demanded exactly equals the quantity supplied at the going market price. It does not overproduce or underproduce any good or service. In other words, an ideal competitive market continues to produce a product until the marginal cost (extra cost) to producers of producing the last unit just equals its marginal benefit to consumers (measured by the price consumers are willing to pay). To the extent that these ideal conditions are not met, the market fails.

Key Question 1: What are the effects of external costs and external benefits?

Externalities (or spillovers) are third-party effects associated with the production and/or consumption of a good or service. In other words, they affect people not directly involved in the trades. An externality either has a negative effect upon society (external cost) or a positive effect (external benefit). Products that have external costs are overproduced: there is an overallocation of resources (too many resources) devoted to their production if the total costs are considered. External benefit products are underproduced. There is an underallocation of resources devoted to their production if total benefits are considered. We would simply like to have more of them from society's point of view than are being provided in the market. We know this is the case when we analyze externalities graphically.

When external costs are internalized (when private plus social costs are brought to bear on the market), the true marginal costs are higher. This means that the real supply curve (incorporating private and social marginal costs of production) lies above the supply curve incorporating private marginal costs alone. Therefore, after the external costs are internalized in the market, the price of the product is higher, and the quantity demanded (and the quantity supplied) is lower. We simply would not want as much of the product, as a society, if the price we had to pay covers both private and social costs of production. The amount by which equilibrium quantity drops indicates the amount of overproduction. Furthermore, the amount by which the supply curve lies above the demand curve for those units overproduced indicates the area for which total marginal costs exceed marginal benefits. In sum, an external cost good or service is overproduced. The market fails to produce the socially optimal quantity.

When external benefits are internalized (when both private and social benefits are incorporated in the market), the true marginal benefits are greater. This means that the read demand curve for the product (incorporating private plus social marginal benefits of consumption) lies above the demand curve incorporating private marginal benefits alone. Therefore, after the external benefits are internalized in the market, the price we are willing to pay and the quantity we are willing to consume both increase. We are simply willing to pay a higher price and buy more, as a society, when both private and social benefits from consumption are considered. The amount by which the equilibrium quantity increases indicates the amount of underproduction. Furthermore, the amount by which the demand curve lies above the supply curve for those units underproduced indicates the area for which total marginal benefits exceed marginal costs. In sum, an external benefit good or service is underproduced in the absence of government intervention.

Key Question 2: When should government intervene?

Government can correct for the over- and underproduction associated with externalities, thereby increasing the efficient allocation of our nation's scarce resources. However, government should intervene only if the social benefits from correcting externalities outweigh the social costs of government intervention. After all, government bureaucracies are expensive to administer. Some external costs may be so small they don't warrant government action. Furthermore, government intervention may impose external costs of its own. For instance, government intervention may limit individual freedom. Finally, some of the externalities that cause market distortions may be internalized by competitive forces in the market over time.

Key Question 3: What are the methods of reducing externalities?

When the benefits of government intervention obviously outweigh the costs, then only the form of government intervention remains to be determined. Government action may take several forms: persuasion; assignment of communal property rights to individuals; government production of goods and services; control of product prices through taxes, fines, and subsidies; and regulation of production through published standards.

Key Question 4: What are the advantages of selling rights to pollute?

Selecting the most efficient and least costly method of minimizing externalities can be a complicated process. For example, the most efficient way to limit the external cost of pollution in many industries is not by setting limits, but instead by selling rights (tickets) to pollute. A market will then be established for these rights with a downward-sloping demand curve. This shows that if the price of the ticket decreases, firms will pollute more. But the supply curve will be vertical (perfectly inelastic), reflecting that regardless of the demand (the price firms may be willing to pay to pollute), the same quantity of pollutants will be allowed to be emitted. By letting a market develop for rights to pollute, we minimize the total social costs of limiting pollution to some acceptable level. Selling rights to pollute is simply more efficient. More money, and therefore resources, go into production and less into cleanup, for any given level of pollution that is allowed.

Review Terms and Concepts

Private sector
Public sector
Private goods
Public goods
Externalities
Demand
Supply
Law of demand
Law of supply
Increase in demand
Decrease in demand
Increase in supply
Decrease in supply
Quantity demanded
Market failure
External benefit
External cost
Monopoly power
Common-access resources
Quantity supplied
Change in quantity demanded
Change in quantity supplied
Equilibrium price
Equilibrium quantity
Market equilibrium
Marginal benefits
Marginal costs

Completion

efficient

A competitive market, in the absence of externalities, is ____________ (efficient/inefficient). This because it produces at the point of

	intersection between demand and supply. The demand curve indicates
benefits	________________ (costs/benefits). In other words, the demand curve
consumers are willing to pay	indicates the price ________________ (consumers are willing to pay/producers must receive) for any given quantity. This
benefit	price is a measure of the marginal ________________ (benefit/cost) from consuming that last unit. The supply curve indicates the marginal
cost	________________ (cost/benefit) of producing each additional unit of a good or service. At the point of intersection between the demand and supply curves, the marginal benefit from the last unit consumed equals
marginal cost	its ________________ (quantity/marginal cost). For all quantities
greater than	below this equilibrium, the marginal benefits are ________________ (less than/equal to/greater than) the marginal costs of production. We
demand	know this because the ________________ (demand/supply) curve lies
supply	above the ________________ (demand/supply) curve. These excess
are	benefits ____________ (are/are not) realized by consumers. When externalities are present, the marginal benefits from the last unit consumed
do not equal	________________ (equal/do not equal) its marginal cost.
negative	External costs are ________________ (negative/positive) third-
overproduced	party effects. Products that have external costs are ________________ (underproduced/overproduced). If the external costs of a good or service
supply	are internalized into the market, this causes the ____________ (demand/
up	supply) curve to shift ____________ (up/down). This happens because the
plus	private ____________ (plus/minus) the social marginal costs of produc-
included	tion are ________________ (included/excluded). The result in the
increases	market is that the price ________________ (increases/decreases) and
decreases	the quantity ________________ (increases/decreases). Because

the quantity decreases, we know that the external cost good or service
overproduced — was ________________________ (overproduced/underproduced) before
the external costs were internalized.

positive — External benefits are ____________________ (positive/negative)
third-party effects. Products that have external benefits are
underproduced — ______________________ (underproduced/overproduced). Because of
too few — this, we can say that ________________ (too many/too few) of our
nation's resources are devoted to their production. When we internalize
demand — the external benefits, this causes the __________________ (demand/
up — supply) curve to shift ____________ (up/down). This indicates that the
greater — demand for the product is ________________ (greater/less) when we
add — __________ (add/subtract) the social benefits from its consumption to
increase — the private benefits. The effect in the market is to ________________
(increase/decrease) the quantity produced. Therefore, we can conclude
underproduced — that external benefit goods and services are ______________________
(underproduced/overproduced) in the absence of governmental
intervention.

should not — Government ______________________ (should/should not) necessarily correct for externalities because some external costs may be
so small — ___________________ (so large/so small) that intervening in the
marketplace may not be worthwhile. Also, government may impose
costs — external __________________ (benefits/costs) of its own. Therefore,
benefits — government should intervene only if the expected social ____________
costs — (costs/benefits) from doing so exceed their ________________ (costs/
benefits).

many ways

Government can correct for externalities in ____________________ (one way/many ways). Out of the methods available, government should

minimizes costs

select the one that ______________________________ (minimizes costs/ maximizes government involvement) in obtaining market efficiency. If we are concerned with pollution, for example, it is best for government

sell pollution rights

to ____________________________ (set standards/sell pollution rights).

Problems and Applications

1. What are some examples of external costs and benefits other than those mentioned in the text?
2. If the marginal benefit from the last unit consumed exceeds its marginal cost, should production be increased, decreased, or held constant for market efficiency to be realized?
3. Use the following graph of demand and supply curves for some good or service to answer the following questions. Complete this entire problem before you look at the answers.

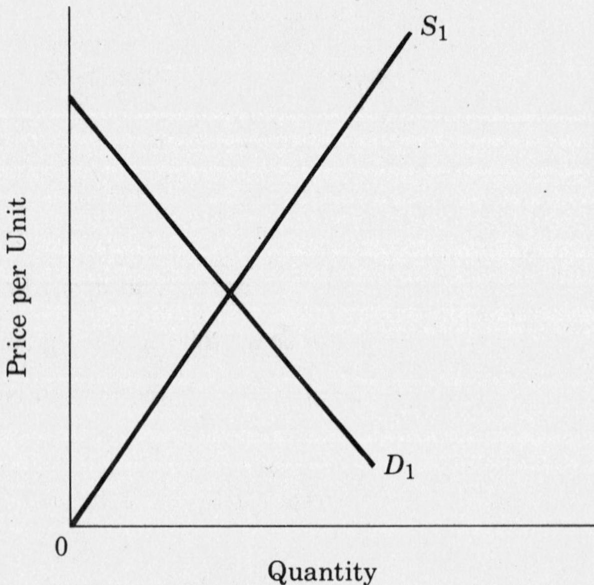

a. Assume that there is neither an external cost nor an external benefit associated with the production and/or consumption of this product. Indicate the equilibrium price and quantity.
b. Indicate the area of excess benefits.
c. Now assume that an external cost is associated with this product, and it is internalized within the market. What happens to demand and/or supply? Indicate this change.
d. What can we say about the marginal costs and benefits at the initial equilibrium now that the external cost has been internalized? What will happen to the price and quantity in the market? Indicate this change.
e. Indicate by how much this product was overproduced or underproduced before the external costs were internalized. What can we say about the marginal costs and benefits of this overproduction or underproduction? Indicate that area.
f. Would a tax or subsidy correct for the presence of these external costs?
g. What would happen to a market if we assumed that external benefits were present and internalized rather than external costs?

4. What gives rise to the presence of external costs like pollution on the part of producers of goods and services?
5. For each of the following situations, determine whether an external cost or an external benefit is associated with the good or service.
   a. Aerosol cans have just been declared illegal in California.
   b. Asbestos as an insulator has just been declared illegal.
   c. Smokey the Bear warns against playing with matches.
   d. Government-recommended daily allowances of vitamins and minerals are stamped on some food items.
   e. Handguns must be registered with the Department of Tobacco, Firearms, and Alcohol.
6. Why does the government produce some goods and services to prevent underproduction? That is, why does it provide some public goods and services?

True-False

For each item, determine whether the statement is basically true or false. If the statement is false, rewrite it so it is a true statement.

_____ 1. A litterbug is someone who contributes to an external benefit.

_____ 2. There is an underallocation of resources devoted to an external cost good or service.

_____ 3. Price is an indication of the marginal benefits.

_____ 4. If the private plus social marginal benefits of a good or service exceed marginal costs, then this good or service has external benefits associated with it.

_____ 5. A competitive market system produces inadequate amounts of some goods and services and excess amounts of others in the absence of government.

_____ 6. Government should correct for all externalities if they are benefits but not if they are costs.

_____ 7. If a product's marginal benefits are less than its marginal costs, then external costs may be present.

_____ 8. Government action may create an external cost of its own.

_____ 9. Persuasion is usually very effective in controlling externalities.

_____ 10. The assignment of property rights may correct for some external benefits.

_____ 11. Government production of some goods and services may correct for some external costs and benefits at the same time.

_____ 12. If the social benefits of government intervention in correcting for externalities outweigh the costs of doing so, then intervention should be undertaken.

_____ 13. Production standards, such as those imposed on sewage-treatment plants, are less efficient than the selling of pollution rights.

_____ 14. Choosing the most efficient government method of minimizing externalities is a complicated process.

Multiple Choice

Choose the one best answer for each item.

_____ 1. Which of the following methods of correcting for externalities is the most effective?
   a. Production standards
   b. Taxes and subsidies
   c. Government production

d. Persuasion
e. We cannot judge without more information

_____ 2. External costs of a good or service, if internalized in the market, will cause
a. marginal benefits to exceed marginal costs at market equilibrium.
b. overproduction of the good or service.
c. underproduction of the good or service.
d. the supply curve to shift up equal to the social marginal costs.
e. the demand curve to shift up equal to the social marginal costs.

_____ 3. External benefits of a good or service
a. cause negative third-party effects.
b. cause an overproduction of the good or service.
c. are benefits that accrue to others than the buyers and sellers of the product.
d. when internalized cause the supply curve to shift up and to the left.
e. cause society to desire less of the good or service it is associated with.

_____ 4. Government can correct for external benefits of a good or service by
a. requiring that the good or service be produced without emitting pollutants.
b. increasing taxes on its production.
c. increasing subsidies to its production.
d. declaring it illegal.
e. doing all of the above.

Use the graph on page 562 to answer question 5. Assume that the demand and supply curves are uncorrected for any externalities.

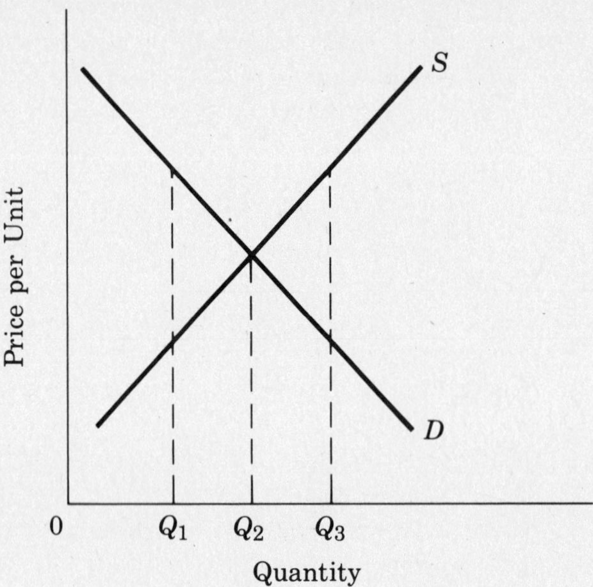

_____ 5. If an external benefit is internalized in this market, then an efficient output will be realized at
   a. Q_1 if supply is decreased.
   b. Q_1 if demand is decreased.
   c. Q_2 if demand is increased and supply is decreased.
   d. Q_3 if demand is increased.
   e. none of the above.

_____ 6. Externalities, when internalized, affect
   a. market price.
   b. the amount consumed.
   c. the allocation of our nation's resources.
   d. the amount produced.
   e. all of the above.

_____ 7. Government involvement in the economy to correct for external benefits
   a. may require an increase in taxes on the production of the good or service.
   b. will decrease the amount of resources devoted to the good or service.
   c. will decrease the price if consumers are subsidized.

d. will cause the private plus social marginal benefits to exceed the marginal costs at the initial market equilibrium.
e. all of the above.

_____ 8. If a product has an external cost associated with it, then
a. the demand curve is too high.
b. the demand curve is too low.
c. the supply curve is too high.
d. the supply curve is too low.
e. government should increase demand for the product by subsidizing consumers.

_____ 9. Which of the following is a form of market failure?
a. The internalization of external costs
b. The internalization of external benefits
c. Government involvement in the economy
d. Competition
e. Externalities

Discussion Questions

1. Can external costs and benefits arise from the production and/or consumption of a good or service? *(KQ1)*
2. What effect would a tax on the consumption of an external cost product have on the market for the good or service? Is this preferable to a tax on production? Why or why not? *(KQ1, 3)*
3. Do you think government should intervene more or less in correcting for externalities? What are some of the external costs it creates by intervening in the market? *(KQ1, 2, 3)*
4. What are the external costs or benefits of an ever-growing population? *(KQ1)*
5. Some goods and services have external costs or benefits associated with them. What do you think are some goods and services for which the government should increase its efforts to correct the misallocation of resources? *(KQ1, 2, 3)*
6. Can we economically measure the social benefits and costs of government intervention in correcting for externalities? Why or why not? *(KQ2)*

Answers

Problems and Applications

1. Examples of external benefits and costs include social behavior beyond that found in legal markets. External costs may include prostitution, gambling, drug trafficking, noisy neighbors, neighbors who let their property deteriorate, the burning of trash, possession of firearms, smoking in public places, and the like. Some external benefits are etiquette or friendly attitudes, well-groomed people, neighbors who keep up their property, and the like. Note that not all of these external costs and benefits require government intervention to decrease or increase their production and/or consumption.
2. Production should be increased. This may be shown graphically as a quantity below equilibrium where the demand curve (indicating marginal benefit from the last unit consumed) lies above the supply curve (indicating marginal cost of the last unit).
3. a. Equilibrium exists at the point of intersection. In the following graph, given D_1 and S_1, equilibrium exists at P_1 and Q_2.

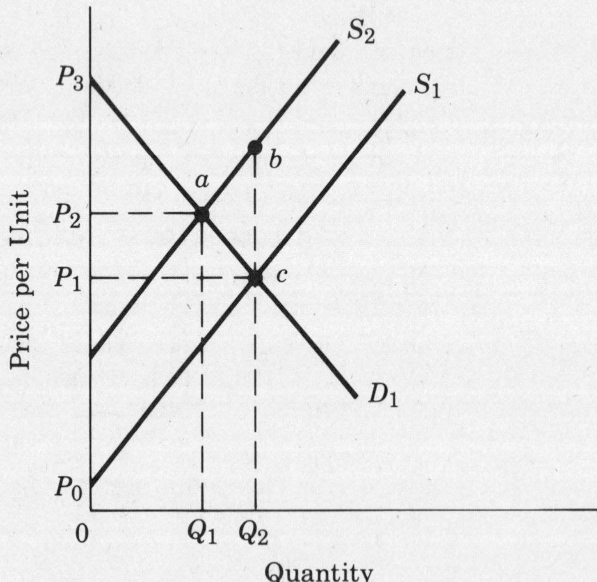

   b. Area P_0P_3c shows the amount by which marginal benefits exceed marginal costs up to the last unit produced (Q_2). Therefore, this area measures the excess benefits.
   c. Demand remains the same at D_1. The supply curve shifts up, such as S_1 to S_2, by the amount of the social marginal costs. The vertical distance between S_1 and S_2 measures social marginal costs.
   d. True marginal costs (private plus social marginal costs) exceed marginal benefits at Q_2. We know this because S_2 lies above D_1 at Q_2. Therefore, the price will rise to P_2 and the quantity will fall to Q_1. We reach a new equilibrium at P_2 and Q_1 after the external costs are internalized.
   e. The product was overproduced by Q_2 - Q_1 units. Marginal costs exceeded marginal benefits for this overproduction by area *abc*.
   f. A tax equal to *cb* would shift the supply curve up equal to the social marginal costs. (A subsidy would increase supply if given to producers and increase demand if given to consumers.)
   g. The demand curve would shift up. The price and quantity would increase. Because the quantity increased, there was underproduction before the external benefit was internalized.
4. Producers may not care about the physical or social environment. But even if they do care, they cannot afford to care too much, because competitive forces require that costs be kept to a minimum.
5. a. External cost (ozone may be destroyed).
   b. External cost (it may cause cancer).
   c. External benefit (fewer children playing with matches helps prevent fires).
   d. External benefit (it perpetuates good health).
   e. External cost (it may prevent some dangerous people from possessing firearms).
6. Because the external benefits are so large. That is, these goods and services would be underproduced to a very large extent in the absence of government. Examples include the military; police and fire departments; city, state and national parks; sewage-treatment plants; highways, roads and bridges, and dams. But this does not necessarily mean that government has to provide all these goods and services by itself. It could subsidize private firms, for example, fire departments or penal institutions.

True-False

1. F: A litterbug is someone who contributes to an external cost.
2. F: There is an overallocation of resources devoted to an external cost good or service.
3. T
4. T
5. T
6. F: Government should not necessarily correct for all external benefits or costs.
7. T
8. T
9. F: Persuasion is usually not very effective in controlling externalities.
10. F: The assignment of property rights may be correct for some external costs.
11. T
12. T
13. T
14. T

Multiple Choice

1. e *(KQ3)*
2. d *(KQ1)*
3. c *(KQ1)*
4. c *(KQ3)*
5. d *(KQ1, 3)*
6. e *(KQ1, 3)*
7. d *(KQ1, 3)*
8. d *(KQ1)*
9. e *(KQ1)*

CHAPTER 31

Government Controls: Price Controls and Consumer Protection

Chapter Summary

Government intervenes in the market system in an attempt to correct for some market failure, such as monopoly power or externalities. This chapter investigates how excise taxes, price controls, and consumer protection play a role in that attempt.

Key Question 1: Who bears the burden of an excise tax?

An excise tax (or per unit tax) imposed on producers of a product will decrease supply equal to the amount of the tax. Given a downward-sloping demand curve, only part of the tax is passed on to consumers in the form of a higher price for the product. Because the equilibrium price rises, the equilibrium quantity falls — which may have been the purpose of the tax (to correct for an external cost). Who actually bears the biggest burden of the tax depends on the elasticity of demand. The more inelastic the demand, the larger the percentage of the tax passed on to consumers.

Key Question 2: What are the economic effects of price controls?

The second type of government control over the market, price controls (or legal prices) set by government, is controversial. A price control can be set either above or below market equilibrium. If it is set above market equilibrium, it is called a price support or price floor (because the price would otherwise fall as a result of the surplus it creates). This chapter is concerned with the other type of price control — price ceilings.

Price ceilings generally have popular appeal because government is holding prices down. They may be viewed as a way of protecting citizens, especially those on fixed or low incomes, form the harmful effects of inflation. They also appeal to those who believe that monopoly power is a dominant force in many markets. For instance, some people believe that without price ceilings large, unearned profits may accrue to producers, or that producers no longer respond to the forces of demand and supply. Instead, they exercise their market power by forcing a contrived cutback in production, which drives prices and profits up. They may also increase demand for their product through effective advertising campaigns, which drive prices and profits up further. Finally, market theory suggests that price ceilings imposed on monopolistic firms will increase their output level — a definite plus.

Arguments against price controls are based primarily on the competitive market model. They also question whether government always acts with the best interests of the general public in mind. That is, government officials may subjectively determine what is "just." Or, price controls may be subject to clever political maneuvering, which may not result in what is best for society as a whole.

We can predict the economic effects of price ceilings in terms of a competitive market model. Because a price ceiling is a legal price set by government that is below equilibrium, it causes a shortage. Indeed, it is called a price ceiling because the price would otherwise rise as a result of the shortage it creates. Shortages can cause the effective price one has to pay to be above the price ceiling set by government because of time spent in line or the decline in quality producers can afford. Shortages create other problems. Businesses may engage in fraud or black markets. To assure a fair means of distributing the good or service, some form of rationing may be required. Otherwise, it will be rationed on a first-come, first-served basis. The usual method of rationing is to issue coupons. By limiting coupons the government limits demand and thereby eliminates the shortage and relieves the congestion problem. But then there is the problem of how to distribute the coupons fairly. The price system is markedly more efficient in eliminating a shortage. Indeed, under a coupon system the effective price of the product will be greater than the price established under free market conditions. To make matters worse, the higher effective price is not received by producers but by those fortunate enough to get coupons. This means that there is no incentive for producers to provide more of the product.

Key Question 3: What are the arguments for and against consumer protection?

The third type of government intervention in the market to correct for external benefits, external costs, and monopoly power is consumer protection laws. Protecting consumers by setting product standards may internalize external benefits, thus correcting for underproduction (although there is a limit to how much government should impose product standards if net benefits to society are to be realized). The argument for consumer protection can also be applied to external cost products. Because overproduction will occur, government can tax those items to bring greater market efficiency. Consumer advocates contend that monopolistic forces restrict consumer welfare in terms of price, quantity, quality, safety, and effectiveness.

Finally, social welfare may be increased by government providing public information concerning the various aspects of goods and services.

There are many arguments against consumer protection. First, competition acts as a form of consumer protection. No firm can last long if it does not accede to the wishes of the consumer. Second, people differ in their aversion toward risk. Let those averse to risk purchase safer products if they will, but this does not necessarily mean that all others should. Furthermore, the welfare of many may be impaired by requiring them to do so. Simply put, consumer protection standards may reduce consumer preferences. Furthermore, the burden of consumer protection may fall disproportionately on the poor.

Review Terms and Concepts

Price ceilings
Price floors (supports)
Market demand
Market supply
Law of demand
Increase in demand
Decrease in demand
Law of supply
Increase in supply
Decrease in supply
Equilibrium price
Equilibrium quantity
Market equilibrium
Inflation
Quantity demanded
Change in quantity demanded
Quantity supplied
Change in quantity supplied
Shortage
Surplus
Elasticity of demand
Elasticity of supply
External benefits
External costs
Monopoly power
Excise tax
Market failure

New Terms and Concepts

Effective price
Rationing by coupons

Completion

a per unit

supply

An excise tax is ________________ (a per unit/an income) tax. When an excise tax is imposed on producers it causes ________________

decrease	(demand/supply) to ____________ (increase/decrease). The
equal to	curve shifts up (or to the left) by an amount ____________
	(greater than/less than/equal to) the tax, which causes the market price
increase	to ____________ (increase/decrease) by an amount
less than	____________ (greater than/less than/equal to) the amount of
	the tax. This is because the demand curve for most goods and services is
downward	____________ (downward/upward) sloping. That is, as the price
decreases	rises the quantity demanded ____________ (increases/decreases),
unable	which means that producers are ____________ (able/unable) to pass
	the entire tax on to the consumers. The only time producers are able to
	pass the entire tax on to consumers is when the demand curve is perfectly
inelastic	____________ (elastic/inelastic). When demand is inelastic it
not very	means that consumers are ____________ (very/not very) responsive
	to a change in the price of the good or service. Therefore, the greater the
larger	inelasticity of demand for a product, the ____________
	(larger/smaller) the percent of the excise tax paid by consumers.
	There are two kinds of price controls. There is a legal price set by
	government that is above the market price called a price support (or price
ceilings	floor). This chapter, however, is concerned with price ____________
below	(freezes/ceilings), legal prices set by government that are ____________
	(above/below) market equilibrium. They are called price ceilings because
rise	prices would otherwise ____________ (rise/fall).
	Price ceilings are generally popular because they hold prices
down	____________ (up/down). One of the arguments in favor of price
inflation	ceilings is that they may combat the consequences of ____________
	(deflation/inflation). for instance, price ceilings are viewed as an aid to

those on fixed incomes. It is also perceived that large corporations may
unearned — accrue large ______________ (unearned/earned) profits in the absence
of price controls. Another argument in favor of price ceilings, which
monopolistic — many economists sympathize with, is that ______________________
increase — (competitive/monopolistic) firms will __________________ (increase/
decrease) output above levels that would occur in the absence of price
ceilings.

competitive — Arguments against price ceilings rest heavily on _________________
(competitive/monopolistic) market models. They also question whether
government always acts with the best interests of the general public in
mind.

We can predict the economic effects of price ceilings in terms of a
shortage — competitive market model. A price ceiling will cause a _____________
quantity demanded — (surplus/shortage). That is, at the controlled price the _______________
quantity supplied — (quantity demanded/quantity supplied) exceeds the ________________
(quantity demanded/quantity supplied). Shortages may cause the effec-
greater than — tive price one has to pay for the product to be __________________
(greater than/less than) the controlled price. Shortages create many other
problems. For instance, they may require the issuing of coupons, which
creates problems of its own — ______________ (is efficient/creates problems of its own). The use of
coupons as a rationing device will cause the price of the product to be
greater — ______________ (less/greater) than under a free market system, but
do not receive — producers ____________________ (receive/do not receive) this higher
no — price. This means that there is ______________ (an/no) incentive for
producers to provide more of the product.

Answers	
and	There are arguments for______________ (and/but not) against consumer protection. The arguments for consumer protection view this type
correcting for	of government intervention as ______________________ (correcting for/contributing to) externalities and monopoly power. The arguments
acts	against consumer protection state that first, competition ____________ (acts/does not act) as a form of consumer protection, and second, people
different aversions	have ____________________________________ (the same aversion/ different aversions) to risk. This may cause consumer protection to
decrease	______________ (increase/decrease) consumer welfare. Consumer
hurt	protection may especially ______________ (help/hurt) the poor, who
more	are usually ______________ (more/less) risk-averse.

Problems and Applications

1. a. Given supply, if demand for a product is inelastic and government imposes an excise tax on its production, who bears the largest percentage of the tax, consumers or producers? How can we graphically estimate who bears the burden of the tax?
   b. Why might government impose an excise tax on the production of a good or service other than to increase tax revenues?
2. Consider the graph on page 573 for a monopolistic producer.

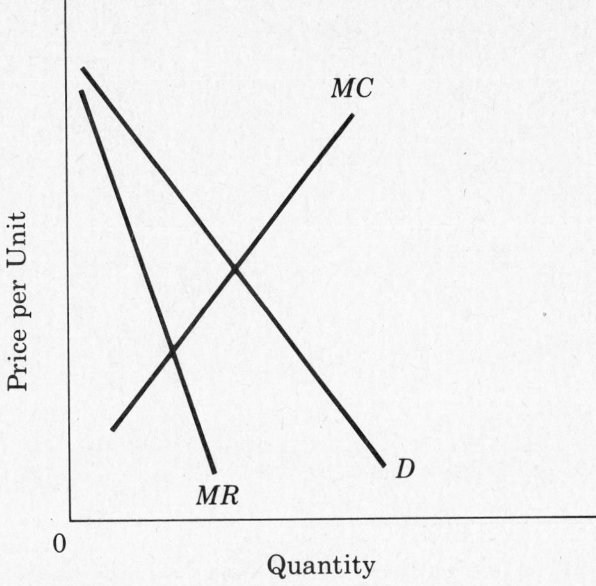

a. Indicate the quantity this monopolist would produce and the price it would charge.
b. Indicate a price ceiling (price control) that could cause this monopolist to increase output. Why will the ceiling result in the monopolist producing a greater output?
c. Can we conclude that a price ceiling imposed on a monopolistic producer will increase output and therefore increase market efficiency?

3. Consider the graph on page 574, which represents a competitive market for a good or service.

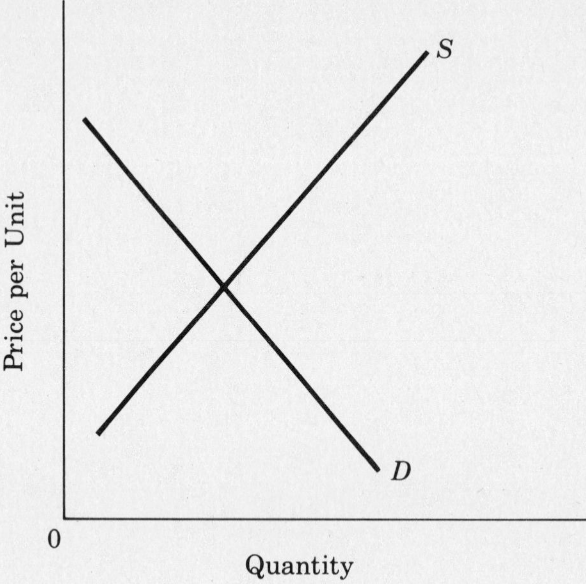

a. Indicate the equilibrium price and quantity. Why is there an equilibrium in this market?
b. Suppose this equilibrium price is considered too high, and government imposes a price ceiling on the product. Indicate a price ceiling on this market. What will happen in this market?
c. Can we conclude that a price ceiling imposed on a competitive producer will create some market inefficiency?
d. How does the government usually respond to the consequences of price ceilings? Is this response as efficient in allocating the product as the market system?

4. What is an effective price as it relates to a shortage?
5. Why might a shortage created by a price ceiling become more acute over time?
6. Consumer protection through product standards (for instance, safety standards) may correct for external benefits, which is socially beneficial. Is there a limit, however?

True-False

For each item, determine whether the statement is basically true or false. If the statement is false, rewrite it so it is a true statement.

_____ 1. When an excise tax is imposed on the production of a product, its supply curve decreases and the vertical distance between the original and new supply curves equals the amount of the tax.

_____ 2. The largest percentage of an excise tax is borne by producers when demand is elastic.

_____ 3. Rent controls are an example of price controls.

_____ 4. One argument is favor of price controls is that they protect business profits.

_____ 5. One argument in favor of price controls is that they increase competition among large firms.

_____ 6. Price controls can cause firms that exercise market power to expand production.

_____ 7. Opponents of price controls argue that government always acts with the public's general welfare in mind.

_____ 8. Price ceilings cause the quantity supplied to exceed the quantity demanded.

_____ 9. Shortages caused by price ceilings may result in an effective price above the controlled price.

_____ 10. Coupons as a method of rationing are a more equitable allocation of the product than the market system they replace.

_____ 11. Consumer protection by way of production standards may correct for external benefits or costs.

_____ 12. Those who argue for consumer protection emphasize the competitive market's lack of ability to respond to consumer demand.

_____ 13. Competition may be a form of consumer protection in and of itself.

_____ 14. Consumer protection may increase the social costs to society by imposing blanket rules that protect the safety of all products in a particular category.

_____ 15. Safety standards tend to hurt the poor more than the rich.

Multiple Choice *Choose the one best answer for each item.*

_____ 1. The external benefits of consumer protection can be captured efficiently only if the production level occurs
a. below the intersection of the market demand and supply curves.
b. above the point of intersection of the market supply curve and the demand curve, measuring the private plus the social benefits.
c. at the point of intersection between the market supply curve and the demand curve, measuring the private plus the social benefits.
d. at the level where the social benefits equal the social costs.
e. at a lower price.

_____ 2. If the demand curve for a product is perfectly inelastic and government imposes an excise tax on its production, then the burden of the tax will be
a. equally shared by consumers and producers.
b. principally paid by consumers, but some of the tax will be paid by producers.
c. principally paid by producers, but some of the tax will be paid by consumers.
d. entirely paid by producers.
e. entirely paid by consumers.

_____ 3. When an excise tax is imposed on the production of a good or service
a. supply increases and the price falls.
b. supply decreases and the price rises.
c. demand increases and the price rises.
d. demand decreases and the price falls.
e. producers always pass the tax on to consumers in the form of a higher price.

_____ 4. A price ceiling imposed on natural gas will cause
a. the quantity demanded to rise.
b. the quantity supplied to fall.
c. a shortage of natural gas.
d. producers' profits to fall.
e. all of the above to occur.

_____ 5. A price ceiling causes
a. a surplus.
b. an overallocation of resources devoted to the product.
c. competitive producers to reduce production.

d. monopolistic producers to increase production.
e. both c and d.

_____ 6. Those who argue against price controls
a. emphasize noncompetitive producers' ability to control prices.
b. emphasize noncompetitive producers' ability to accrue unearned profits.
c. emphasize that the pricing decisions made by any government agency will reflect the will of its staff.
d. emphasize the need for consumer control over the quality of products.
e. emphasize all of the above.

_____ 7. When a price ceiling is imposed on the market for a good or service, government rationing
a. may be a consequence of the resulting shortages.
b. is a black market.
c. results in a surplus.
d. is a more efficient allocative system than the market system.
e. results in higher profits for producers through the use of coupons.

_____ 8. Consumer protection may
a. correct for external benefits but not external costs.
b. limit the amount of public information available to consumers.
c. impose costs on society that fall disproportionately on the poor.
d. cause different aversions toward risk.
e. cause price ceilings.

_____ 9. The fact that government coupons may have a market value if people are allowed to exchange them shows that the price ceiling
a. is held above equilibrium.
b. causes longer lines.
c. creates a surplus of the product.
d. causes the effective price to be lower than the price ceiling.
e. causes a shortage, and the shortage has not been eliminated.

_____ 10. An increase in an excise tax on liquor will
a. not affect the demand curve for liquor.
b. decrease the supply of liquor.
c. decrease the quantity demanded and the quantity supplied.
d. cause consumers, producers, retailers, and tavern owners to pay a higher price for liquor.
e. do all of the above.

Discussion Questions

1. Do price ceilings cause an overallocation or an underallocation of resources devoted to the good or service? *(KQ2)*
2. Given demand, if a product has an inelastic supply curve, and an excise tax is imposed on the product, who principally bears the burden of the tax? *(KQ1)*
3. If government wished to maximize its collection of excise tax revenues, would it be best for it to impose the tax on products with an elastic or an inelastic demand? *(KQ1)*
4. What would we expect to happen over time to the supply of a product that has a price ceiling imposed on it? *(KQ1)*
5. What would a domestic price ceiling imposed on the price of world oil do to a country's oil imports? Can it be argued that the country could bring on its own "oil crisis"? *(KQ1)*
6. How can society get too much of a good thing? *(KQ3)*

Answers

Problems and Applications

1. a. Given supply, if demand is inelastic and government imposes an excise tax on the production of a product, then its supply curve shifts upward equal to the amount of the tax (supply decreases equal to the amount of the tax.) Consumers bear the largest percentage of the tax. This can be determined graphically by first noting that the vertical distance between the supply curves is equal to the tax. Now, at the new equilibrium quantity, compare the vertical distance between the original equilibrium price and the new equilibrium price with the vertical distance measuring the tax (the vertical distance between the supply curve at the new equilibrium quantity). If demand is inelastic, we can see that the price increase is a relatively large percentage of the vertical distance between the supply curves (the tax). Therefore, consumers pay the largest percentage of the tax.

   b. Government might impose an excise tax to correct for the external costs associated with the production and/or consumption of a good or service — that is, to correct for its overproduction. Examples of products with inelastic demand curves that have external costs associated with them and also have excise taxes imposed on them include cigarettes, gasoline, liquor, and tires.

(Can you explain what the external costs associated with these items are and why they have inelastic demands?)

2. a. See the following graph. A monopolist (like all producers) will produce that quantity where marginal revenue equals marginal cost ($MR = MC$). It will charge the highest possible price market demand will allow in order for the profit-maximizing quantity to be sold. Therefore this monopolist will produce Q_m units at a price of P_m.

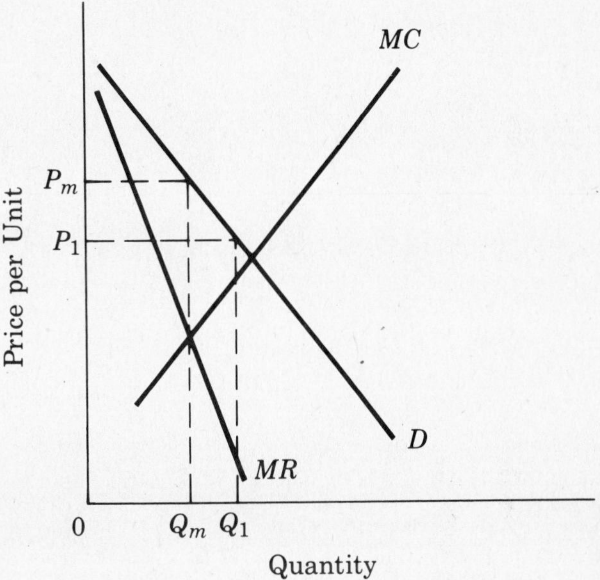

b. A price ceiling means that it is illegal for the product to be bought and sold above that level. Therefore, a price such as P_1 means that the MR and the demand curve become horizontal at that price — until the price intersects the original demand curve. The firm will attempt to equate marginal revenue and marginal cost. In this case the closest the firm can come is an output level of Q_1. (The firm will not produce more because market demand indicates that the price would have to be reduced below the price ceiling of P_1.) *Note:* The price ceiling results in an increase in production.

c. Yes.

3. a. See the following graph. The equilibrium price is P_2 and the equilibrium quantity is Q_2. Equilibrium exists in this market because at the price of P_2 the quantity demanded exactly equals the quantity supplied of Q_2. (In other words, the quantity demanded equals the quantity supplied of Q_2 by a price of P_2.) Because the quantity demanded exactly equals the quantity supplied, there is neither a surplus (hence, no tendency for the price to rise), and therefore the market is in equilibrium.

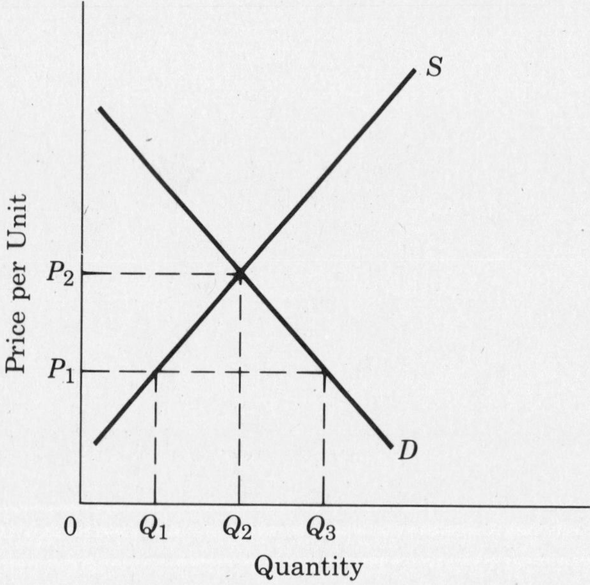

b. A price ceiling is a legal price set by government that is below market equilibrium. A price such as P_1 is below market equilibrium. The effect of a price ceiling is to cause the quantity demanded to rise from Q_2 to Q_3. The quantity supplied will fall from Q_2 to Q_1. Therefore, a shortage is created equal to $Q_3 - Q_1$.

c. Yes.

d. The government usually issues coupons to ration the product. That is, it attempts to eliminate the congestion created by shortages by reducing demand to where it equals the supply at the controlled price. The coupon method of allocating the product is not as efficient as the market system.

4. When a shortage exists (the quantity demanded exceeds the quantity supplied at the controlled price) and coupons have not been issued to limit demand, people will have to wait in line for the product. An effective price is the sum of the price of the product plus the value of time lost waiting in line. Therefore, the real price to consumers (the effective price) actually rises when a price ceiling is imposed on a product.
5. Because the lower price limits the profits businesses can earn in that market. Over time we would expect businesses to move into more profitable markets. As some businesses leave the market, the market supply decreases (shifts to the left) and the shortage becomes more acute.
6. Yes. The limit is reached when the quantity of the product government requires to be produced is so great that the social benefits are equal to the social costs of continued production. It is possible, if government goes beyond this limit, that society is buying too much of a good thing.

True-False

1. T 2. T 3. T
4. F: One argument in favor of price controls is that they can prevent businesses from accruing unearned profit.
5. F: One argument in favor of price controls is that they increase the output of large firms.
6. T
7. F: Opponents of price controls argue that government does not always act with the public's general welfare in mind.
8. F: Price ceilings cause the quantity demanded to exceed the quantity supplied.
9. T
10. F: Coupons as a method of rationing are a less equitable allocation of the product than the market system they replace.
11. T
12. F: Those who argue for consumer protection emphasize that monopolistic forces in the economy have the ability to manipulate consumer demand through advertising.
13. T 14. T 15. T

Multiple Choice

1. c *(KQ3)*
2. e *(KQ1)*
3. b *(KQ1)*
4. e *(KQ2)*
5. e *(KQ2)*
6. c *(KQ2)*
7. a *(KQ2)*
8. c *(KQ3)*
9. e *(KQ2)*
10. e *(KQ1)*

CHAPTER 32

Agriculture and Government Agricultural Policy

Chapter Summary

This chapter looks at the short-run and long-run problems of farmers and how government can help solve them.

Key Question 1: Why do farm prices and incomes fluctuate in the short run?

Farmers' short-run problem is that small changes in the production (supply) of agricultural products result in large changes in prices and therefore farm incomes because there is an inelastic demand *and* an inelastic supply of agricultural commodities. Demand is inelastic because food is a necessity. If price increases (decreases) then the quantity demanded decreases (increases) by a much smaller percent. That is, because there are few substitutes for the staple food commodities, when prices rise people can't cut back much on their consumption. On the other hand, there is a limit to how much food we can eat when prices go down. Supply is inelastic because most costs of production are sunk costs and because of the interest costs on storing the commodity in speculation of higher prices. For these reasons, unforeseen changes in weather conditions can result in large changes in farm incomes.

Key Question 2: Why has agriculture declined relative to other industries?

Farmers' long-run problem is that their relative prices — that is, the ratio of farm prices to nonfarm prices — have fallen. In other words, farmers' real incomes in relation to nonfarm incomes have fallen. The relative price of farm commodities has fallen because the increases in the supply of agricultural commodities have outstripped the increases in demand. Demand increases over time because of population growth and because of increases in people's real incomes associated with economic growth. Supply has increased because of improvements in technology stimulated by government and university research programs. This growth in productivity has benefited those who have adopted the new technology at the expense of those who have lagged behind the latest developments. But even the most aggressive farmers today are hard pressed to keep pace with the technological advances the competitive farming industry requires.

Government has tried in various ways to control the supply or prop up the low prices (and therefore incomes) of farmers created by these advances in productivity. This chapter examines three types of government programs: price supports, acreage allotments and set-asides, and target prices.

Key Question 3: How does the price support program work?

Under a price-support program, government supports the price of the commodity above market equilibrium by buying up the surplus that is created, which naturally causes higher prices for food. (These higher prices for food can be particularly burdensome for the urban poor.) It also causes taxes to increase to pay for the purchase of the surplus. Government can dispose of the surplus in many ways. First, government can give it away through various domestic and foreign aid programs. But it must be sure not to give food away to those who would otherwise buy it. If it did, this would decrease the demand for the commodity and thereby increase the surplus government would have to purchase. Government can also sell surplus food abroad. But this action may depress farm prices abroad. Foreigners may retaliate by dumping their surplus commodities in the United States or by imposing higher tariffs on U.S. exports. Furthermore, domestic consumers may object to the sale of agricultural commodities abroad for less than the going market price at home. Second, government could destroy the surplus. However, when millions of people are starving worldwide, this solution may not be politically or morally palatable. Finally, government could store the commodities to soften shortages created by natural disasters. But over time the surpluses would build up beyond what is necessary, and the storage costs can be extremely high.

Key Question 4: What are the purposes of acreage allotment and set-aside programs?

Because surpluses create problems, government also attempts to restrict the supply of agricultural commodities to increase prices and therefore the incomes of farmers. Government gets involved because there are so many farmers that they are unable to form a cartel and reduce production themselves. Government can restrict supply in three ways: acreage allotments, production quotas, or paying farmers to produce less. Each method is a means of dividing the restricted quantity among individual farmers.

Through acreage allotment, government restricts the number of acres of a given crop that can be planted. However, farmers are free to farm other acres as intensively as they wish. The result has been only a mild reduction in supply. For this reason, acreage allotment programs are less desirable than outright production quotas. Furthermore, costs of production will be lower (and incomes higher) under production quotas because the primary objective is to minimize costs in producing the quota. The now-defunct soil bank program paid farmers to take part of their land out of production. However, supply did not decrease much because usually the least productive land was taken out of production (some of the land was never farmed). Today, to qualify for price supports farmers must set aside (hence, set-aside program) or take out of production a certain number of productive acres. Because price supports are a form of money payment, the set-aside program has much the same effect as the old soil bank program. It restricts supply and raises the price of the supported commodities. The short-lived payment-in-kind (PIK) program paid farmers in kind for their set-asides. They were paid with surplus commodities that were accumulating. The purpose was to decrease price-support payments and storage costs.

Key Question 5: How does the target price program differ from traditional price supports?

In 1973, the federal government began to move from price supports to target prices. Under this program, government guarantees farmers a certain price for a commodity. Farmers produce accordingly. The price is then allowed to fall to clear the market of the output level produced. Notice that consumers are able to get more food at cheaper prices under the target price program. This program also reduces government purchases of surplus commodities and therefore storage costs. However, this system has continued to contribute to over-production and the need for tax revenues to finance farm incomes because the target price is above market equilibrium.

Key Question 6: Have government programs helped farmers?

Government involvement to increase farm incomes may be beneficial in the short run. However, in the long run, the incomes of farmers do not change because of the effects of government programs on the price of land. Government programs simply escalate the price of land and therefore the costs of farming along with the boost in commodity prices.

Key Question 7: What are the distributional effects of government policies toward agriculture?

In sum, the effect of government agricultural programs has been to redistribute income from consumers and taxpayers to farmers but the income redistribution has been inefficient. Most tax dollars spent benefit rich farmers more than poor farmers (who usually run small family farms) because rich farmers usually operate on a larger scale, which results in lower per-unit costs of production. Furthermore, government agricultural policy creates higher prices of food for the poor on and off the farm — a regressive form of "taxation." Also, government policy has restricted the supply of food, driving world prices up, and it may have contributed to some starvation.

Because government farm programs are not effective in increasing farmers' incomes in the long run, a more equitable alternative may be to give income grants to the truly needy.

Review Terms and Concepts

Price ceilings
Price floors (supports)
Market demand
Market supply
Law of demand
Increase in demand
Decrease in demand
Law of supply
Increase in supply
Decrease in supply
Equilibrium price
Real income
Cartel
Marginal cost
Equilibrium quantity
Market equilibrium
Quantity demanded
Change in quantity demanded
Quantity supplied
Change in quantity supplied
Shortage
Surplus
Elasticity of demand
Elasticity of supply
Sunk cost
Marginal benefit
Subsidy
Regressive tax

New Terms and Concepts

Price-support program
Acreage allotment program
Set-aside program
Payment-in-kind (PIK) program
Target price program
Soil bank program

Completion

small | large | inelastic | inelastic | supply | demand, increases | government research

The short-run problem of farmers is that ________________ (small/large) changes in the production of agricultural products result in ________________ (small/large) changes in prices and therefore farm incomes. This is because there is an ______________________ (elastic/inelastic) demand for agricultural commodities and an ______________ (elastic/inelastic) supply. The long-run problem of farmers is that ________________ (demand/supply) has been increasing faster than ________________ (demand/supply) due to ________________ (increases/decreases) in productivity. The technological breakthrough in the production of crops has been due to ________________________

(farmers/government research). The long-run increases in productivity
fall — have caused the ratio of farm prices to nonfarm prices to ____________
fallen — (rise/fall). In order words, the real income of farmers has ___________
(risen/fallen).

support — Government can prop up farm prices with a price _________________
surplus — (support/ceiling). This results in a _____________________ (shortage/
surplus) of farm commodities. The agricultural price-support program
higher — causes _________________ (lower/higher) prices for food. It also causes
rise — taxes to ______________ (fall/rise) to finance government purchases of
agricultural commodities. Government can dispose of the surplus by sell-
foreign — ing it in the _________________ (domestic/foreign) market. Or it could
would not — give the surplus to those who __________________ (would/would not)
otherwise buy it. Government could also destroy the surplus. This solu-
would not — tion, most likely, _________________ (would/would not) be politically
popular. Finally, government could store the surplus. Over time, storage
rise — costs are likely to ______________ (fall/rise).

Because surpluses are a problem with price supports, government can
decrease — instead try to _________________ (decrease/increase) supply. It can do
production — this through an acreage allotment program or through _______________
(consumption/production) quotas. It may also require farmers to
set aside — _________________ (set aside/soil bank) some of their land as a condition for receiving money payments under the price-support program.

Under the target price program, government guarantees farmers a cer-
price — tain ________________ (price/profit). The farmers will then produce
accordingly. This output level can be determined by reading off the
supply — _______________ (demand/supply) curve. Given this production level,

fall	the price consumers have to pay will then ________________ (rise/fall)
	to clear the market of the output. This price can be determined by read-
demand	ing off the ____________________ (demand/supply) curve. This program
different from	is ______________________ (exactly the same as/different from) the price-
lower	support program. The price consumers have to pay is ________________
smaller	(higher/lower). Government has to purchase and store a _____________
decrease	(larger/smaller) surplus. These factors should _____________________
	(increase/decrease) program costs. The target price program is similar
	to the price support program, however, in that both cause an
overproduction	______________________________ (overproduction/underproduction) of
rise	agricultural commodities. Also, both cause taxes to __________________
	(rise/fall).
may be	Government involvement in agriculture __________________ (may be/
but not	is not) beneficial in the short run __________________ (and also/but not)
	in the long run. One reason is that government involvement causes the
rise	price of land to ________________ (rise/fall). The higher costs of produc-
more or less the same	tion cause farmers' incomes to be ______________________________
	(higher/lower/more or less the same) in the long run.
inefficient	Government agricultural policy has been an ______________________
	(efficient/inefficient) method of income redistribution. It causes
higher	_________________ (higher/lower) food prices for the poor. Furthermore,
rich	it really benefits the ____________________ (rich/poor) farmers the most.
inability	Given these considerations and the long-run _____________________
	(ability/inability) of government agricultural policy to help, it may be
needy	more equitable simply to give cash grants to the truly ________________
	(efficient/needy).

Problems and Applications

1. Assume that government is not involved in the agricultural market.
   a. Why is the demand for agricultural commodities inelastic?
   b. Graphically express an inelastic demand curve.
   c. Why is the supply of agricultural commodities inelastic?
   d. Graphically express an inelastic supply curve.
   e. Graphically express the equilibrium price and quantity, given the demand and supply curves you have drawn.
   f. Assume that farmers have a bumper crop. What happens in the market for this commodity? What happens to farm incomes? Are bumper crops good or bad for farmers?
   g. Does this analysis illustrate some of the problems of farmers?
2. a. Draw demand and supply curves for an agricultural commodity in the absence of government intervention. Indicate the equilibrium price and quantity in the market.
   b. Now assume that the price is not considered adequate to provide farmers with a decent living. Therefore, government supports a price above equilibrium. Indicate price support on the graph. What happens in the market when this price support is imposed?
   c. What happens to the price that consumers have to pay for this commodity?
   d. What happens to taxes when government purchases this commodity (when government acts as a buyer of last resort)? Indicate the amount by which taxes change.
   e. If supply could be decreased (shifted to the left) until it intersected the demand curve at point *a*, would a surplus result (and all the problems created by a surplus)? Would taxes have to be increased to purchase the surplus?
   f. Given your answer to question 2e, is this why government has undertaken the acreage allotment and set-aside programs? If supply can be restricted, what will happen to farm incomes?
3. Use the graph you drew for question 2 and assume that the market is initially in equilibrium and government is not involved. Now suppose that government sets a target price at the same level at which it established the price-support level.
   a. What happens to the quantity supplied, the quantity demanded, and the price consumers pay? Is there a surplus?
   b. What can we say about the market efficiency of this target price system? In other words, what can we say about marginal costs *(MC)* of the last unit produces as compared to its marginal benefits *(MB)*?

c. What, if anything, happens to taxes in the target price program?

4. What are the basic differences and similarities between a price support program and a target price program?

True-False

For each item, determine whether the statement is true or false. If the statement is false, rewrite it so it is a true statement.

_____ 1. There are too many farmers to form a workable cartel.

_____ 2. The short-run problem of farming is that small changes in production result in relatively small changes in prices and farm incomes.

_____ 3. Most of the costs of farming have been incurred in the past and are ignored in current production decisions.

_____ 4. The long-run problem is simply too much production, driving farm prices and incomes down in relation to nonfarm prices and incomes.

_____ 5. The price-support program causes the quantity demanded to exceed the quantity supplied at the price-support level.

_____ 6. The price-support program leads to lower food prices for consumers.

_____ 7. The target price program causes lower food prices for consumers than the price-support program.

_____ 8. Taxes must be raised to finance both the price-support and target price programs.

_____ 9. Government storage costs of surplus farm commodities are insignificant.

_____ 10. Government should sell surplus farm commodities in the domestic market.

_____ 11. Production quotas would be more effective than acreage allotments in limiting the supply of agricultural commodities.

_____ 12. Government agricultural policy benefits the large farmers more than the small farmers.

_____ 13. Government agricultural policy is not effective in the long run because it simply pushes up costs along with prices.

Multiple Choice *Choose the one best answer for each item.*

_____ 1. The short-run problem facing farmers is that
a. demand is elastic.
b. supply is elastic.
c. changes in weather conditions can have substantial effect on prices and farm incomes.
d. government agricultural policy is unable to affect the price of farmers' crops.
e. All of the above are short-run problems facing farmers.

_____ 2. The supply of farm commodities
a. is highly elastic because of relatively high interest costs on storage.
b. has been increasing faster than demand.
c. is perfectly elastic at a price-support level.
d. is perfectly inelastic in the long run.
e. decreases when weather conditions are favorable.

_____ 3. One similarity between the price-support and target price programs is that they both cause
a. higher prices for consumers.
b. taxes to decease.
c. marginal costs of production to exceed marginal benefits.
d. a decrease in the price of land and other costs of production in the long run.
e. the poor to benefit from lower prices.

_____ 4. Which of the following would *not* be recommended as a means of disposing of a government surplus?
a. Letting the crop rot in the field
b. Destroying the crop after it has been harvested
c. Giving the crop away to those who would otherwise buy it
d. Selling the crop abroad
e. Storing the crop

_____ 5. Under a target price program
a. government guarantees a price below market equilibrium.
b. the quantity demanded exceeds the quantity supplied.
c. the price is allowed to fall until the market clears.
d. surpluses must be purchased by government as a buyer of last resort.
e. all of the above result.

_____ 6. The long-run farm problem is that
   a. demand has been increasing faster than supply.
   b. productivity increases have decreased supply.
   c. productivity increases have decreased demand.
   d. relative commodity prices for farmers have been too low.
   e. technological breakthroughs have made it difficult for many farmers to keep pace.

_____ 7. Which of the following government attempts to restrict supply would be most effective?
   a. Production quotas
   b. Farm subsidies
   c. Acreage allotments
   d. Soil banking
   e. All of the above would be equally effective.

_____ 8. The long-run effect of government agricultural policy has been
   a. an increase in the price of farmland.
   b. a redistribution of income away form consumers and taxpayers to farmers.
   c. a greater increase in subsidies to larger farmers.
   d. an increase in the price of food.
   e. all of the above.

_____ 9. The acreage allotment program
   a. pays farmers to take part of their land out of use.
   b. discourages farmers from taking their worst land out of production.
   c. sets production quotas.
   d. is not very effective in restricting supply because farmers may more intensely farm the acres left in production.
   e. supports the price of commodities above equilibrium.

_____ 10. Farm programs
   a. help the poor.
   b. benefit those farmers who need it most.
   c. cause the world price of food to be higher than otherwise.
   d. cause decreases in the federal deficit.
   e. do none of the above.

Discussion Questions

1. What can we say about the market efficiency of the price-support program? In other words, what can we say about the marginal cost of producing the last unit under a price-support system as compared to its marginal benefit to consumers? (*KQ1*. See also Chapter 22.)
2. What are the similarities and differences between price-support programs and target price programs? (*KQ5*)
3. We have seen throughout the textbook that government price controls (whether they be price supports or price ceilings) cause undesirable economic side effects. Why then does government undertake such policies? (*KQ1, 2*)
4. If the past and present government agricultural programs are not solving the long-run farm problem, is there anything else the government can do? (See Chapter 29.)
5. Why have the farmers been able to secure so much government support? (See Chapter 33.)
6. Who benefits most and who is hurt most under an agricultural price-support program? (*KQ7*)

Answers

Problems and Applications

1. a. Because food is a necessity.
   b. See the graph on page 594. An inelastic demand curve (such as D_1) is relatively steep, expressing that as price rises (falls), the quantity demanded falls (rises) by a relatively smaller percentage.

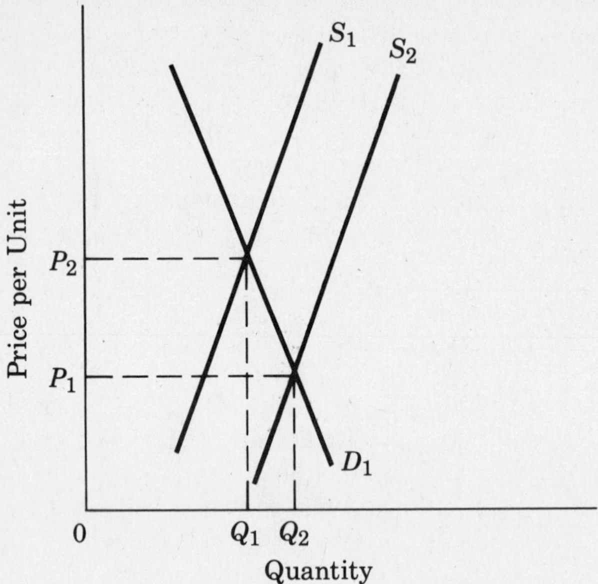

c. Because most costs of production are sunk costs and because of interest rate costs on storing the commodity in speculation of higher prices (which may not come to pass).
d. See the preceding graph. An inelastic supply curve (such as S_1) is relatively steep, expressing that as price rises (falls), the quantity supplied rises (falls) by a relatively smaller percentage.
e. See the preceding graph. Equilibrium exists at the point of intersection between the demand and supply curves because at that price the quantity demanded exactly equals the quantity supplied. Given the original demand and supply curves of D_1 and S_1, equilibrium exists at P_2 and Q_1.
f. The supply of the commodity increases, such as from S_1 to S_2. The equilibrium price falls from P_2 to P_1, and the equilibrium quantity increases form Q_1 to Q_2. Because demand is inelastic, total revenue to farmers falls. Total revenue *(TR)* equals price *(P)* multiplied by quantity *(Q)*: $TR = P \times Q$. If demand is inelastic, given some percentage decrease in price, the quantity demanded increases by a smaller percentage. Hence, total revenue falls. If a few farmers have a bumper crop, and other farmers do not, market supply is left unaffected (each farmer is small in relation to the market) and those farmers' incomes will

rise. However, if every farmer has a bumper crop, this increases supply, and farmers experience a fall in income. Therefore, bumper crops may be a mixed blessing.

g. Yes.

2. a. See the following graph. In the absence of government, market equilibrium exists at P_2 and Q_2.

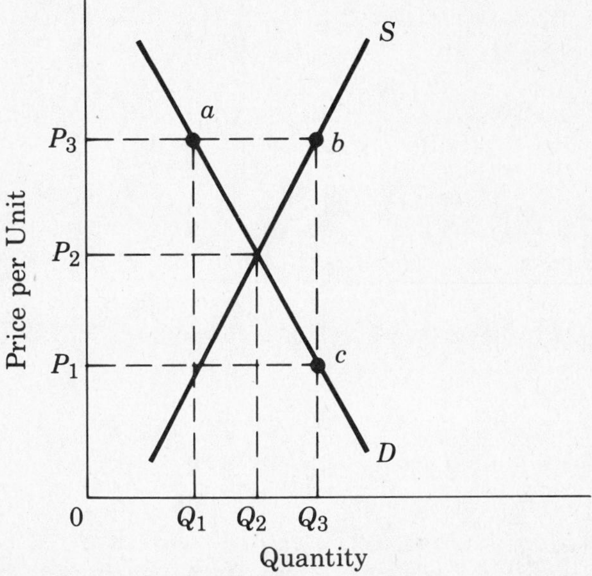

b. A price support may be shown by a price such as P_3. At P_3 the quantity demanded decreases from Q_2 to Q_1; the quantity supplied increases from Q_2 to Q_3. therefore, a surplus of Q_3 - Q_1 results. Any price support creates a surplus.

c. The price increases from P_2 to P_3.

d. Taxes increase by the cost of purchasing the surplus. The cost of purchasing the surplus is P_3 (the price government pays farmers per unit) multiplied by Q_3 - Q_1. (Q_3 - Q_1 equals the surplus.) The area Q_1abQ_3 represents the amount taxes increase.

e. If supply could be decreased until it intersects demand at point *a*, there would be no surplus for government to purchase at the price of P_3. Therefore, there would be no need to increase taxes to finance the purchase of a surplus, because it wouldn't exist.

f. Yes. Farm income would rise if supply could be restricted because demand is inelastic.

3. a. See the preceding graph. The price farmers can expect is P_3 (a higher price than P_2 and therefore farmers' incomes will be higher). The quantity supplied increases form Q_2 to Q_3. However, because the price consumers pay is allowed to fall to clear the market, for the quantity demanded to be Q_3 (to clear the market) the price is allowed to fall to P_1. (To purchase Q_3 units consumers are willing only to pay P_1 — shown by reading off the demand curve.) *Note:* Because the quantity supplied and the quantity demanded are both Q_3, there is no surplus under the target price system. This should eliminate the costs of storage (which can be very expensive to taxpayers) that exist under a price-support system.
   b. An efficient market results in a production level where the marginal cost of the last unit produced just equals its marginal benefit. The target price system creates market inefficiency because marginal costs exceed marginal benefits for all units produced above Q_2. (We know this because the *MC* curve lies above the demand curve — which indicates the marginal benefit of the last unit of any given quantity produced — for the Q_3 - Q_2 units.)
   c. Taxes will increase by the difference between the price promised to farmers and the price they receive multiplied by the number of units sold. Taxes increase by the area P_1P_3bc.
4. Under a target price program, the price of an agricultural commodity is lower, the quantity consumers get is higher, and the purchases of surplus crops and therefore storage costs are lower than under a price-support program. However, both programs impose a social cost in the form of the higher taxes needed to finance them, as opposed to no government intervention. Furthermore, they both create an overproduction of crops (and therefore and overallocation of resources devoted to agriculture) because the marginal cost of an additional unit exceeds its marginal benefit.

True-False

1. T
2. F: The short-run problem of farming is that small changes in production result in relatively large changes in prices and farm incomes.

3. T   4. T
5. F: The price-support program causes the quantity supplied to exceed the quantity demanded at the price-support level.
6. F: The price support program causes higher food prices for consumers.
7. T   8. T
9. F: Government storage costs of surplus farm commodities are significant.
10. F: Government should not sell surplus farm commodities in domestic markets because this would decrease demand and increase the surpluses it must purchase.
11. T   12. T   13. T

Multiple Choice

1. c *(KQ1)*   2. b *(KQ1)*   3. c *(KQ5)*
4. c *(KQ3)*   5. c *(KQ5)*   6. e *(KQ2)*
7. a *(KQ3)*   8. e *(KQ6)*   9. d *(KQ4)*
10. c *(KQ7)*

CHAPTER 33

Public Choice: The Economics of Government

Chapter Summary

Throughout the textbook we have used the tools of economics to study the private sector of the economy. We have seen that the market system fails in a few respects (monopoly power, externalities, inequitable distribution of income, lack of public goods and services, and macroeconomic instability). We then introduced government and investigated what, if anything, government could do to alleviate some of these shortcomings. But, as has been pointed out, government itself may have some shortcomings. In this chapter we analyze the efficiency of government action using economic principles.

Key Question 1: Why do candidates in two-party political systems tend to move toward the "middle of the road"?

First, we must realize that in a two-party democratic system, elected officials typically take middle-of-the road positions, which tends to moderate the differences between the two political parties. Political success in the campaign process through competition for votes requires that politicians cater to the median voter group.

However, not all political decisions are made by a simple majority rule — nor should they be. Some issues are simply too trivial. The voting rule that government follows helps determine the size and scope of government activities. The smaller the number of people required to come to an agreement, the easier it is for the slope of government activities to increase. But if the voting rule required unanimity, very few proposals will be implemented. Furthermore, the type of voting rule used determines the particular interest government represents, and the extent to which it represents them.

Key Question 2: How does the rule for determining winners in elections affect the decisions that are made in a political system?

Democracy is efficient in that it disperses power. It creates a competitive environment in which individual whims and capriciousness play a small role, thus protecting individual liberties. Competition for votes also requires

Key Question 3: What are the sources of inefficiency in democratic political systems?

that candidates reveal what they are willing to do for various interest groups. But democracy is less than efficient as a producer of some goods and services. This is not to say it should be replaced, any more than the market system should be replaced it fails in some respects. We must carefully weigh the costs and benefits of each system and choose the most efficient.

Democracy is inefficient in producing some goods and services because collective action is required. The voting role determines how much will be produced, and it is the median voter group that determines the quantity. Individuals cannot adjust their consumption of public goods or services, as in a marketplace, but must accept whatever quantity of service the collective decision-making process yields. If you are not a member of the median voter group, the compromise that is necessary inflicts a cost on you — at least in the form of taxes. Even though the costs of a proposed project may exceed its benefits to society, the majority may vote for it, because they feel that their costs are less than the benefits they receive. This feeling may not be shared by the minority, however. Simply put, the democratic system can be less than cost efficient.

Other problems exist in a democratic system. One of them is that simple majority rule can result in the passage of measures for which the total costs exceed the total benefits to all voters. Another closely related problem is political ignorance. Many people are simply not informed about legislative proposals and their implications. Therefore, government may not make the decisions it should. In this sense greater political information could be viewed as a public good that benefits everyone. But, as we have seen, people in large groups have little incentive to become actively involved in the decision-making process. Therefore, government may cater to special-interest groups: politicians are likely to bend an ear toward those who watch their actions closely. Therefore special interest groups are likely to receive a disproportionate share of government benefits. Another problem with democracy is that logical people can make perfectly consistent personal decisions and yet make inconsistent collective choices when acting as a group. This problem of cyclical majorities may result in inconsistent or even contradictory policies.

Key Question 4: How can competition among governments improve the effectiveness of government programs?

We can also analyze government using the concepts of competition, economies of scale, and monopoly power. Competition among different levels of government has many benefits, but local governmental units may not be able to take advantage of the economies of scale (lower costs) associated with consolidated. On the other hand, government consolidation may result in some abuses of power; government may behave as a monopolist.

Key Question 5: How do government bureaucracies determine their levels of production?

Government bureaucracies may be analyzed using market models, but we must remember that the primary objective of business is to earn a profit. With government bureaucracies, however, different bureaucracies may pursue different objectives, such as monopolistic profit maximization, size maximization, and waste maximization.

Although some bureaucracies are regional monopolies (such as the police) it is unlikely they would behave as profit maximizers because it is unlikely they would be able to hide their costs. Also, they are unable to pocket the money. Nonetheless, they would produce where marginal revenue equals marginal cost and charge the highest price market allows. This results in a smaller quantity of services provided at a higher price to the public.

Since a government bureaucracy is unlikely to take profit as its main objective, size maximization is more likely. Bureaucrats will attempt to increase their prestige, salaries, offices, or amount of equipment, assuming they are able to hide their costs. The result is a greater than competitive quantity of the service provided until all consumer surplus is gone.This in turn also increases costs to taxpayers. Finally, instead of maximizing size, bureaucrats may choose to maximize waste by reducing their workloads, increasing their salaries, or improving their working conditions — again, assuming they are able to hide their real costs. The result of waste is an increase in costs, resulting in a higher price charged for any quantity of service provided. This continues until all consumer surplus is gone. In reality, a combination of size and waste maximization is most likely, but there is a tradeoff between the two. The result may be positive consumer surplus. That is, there may be some net benefit to society.

Key Question 6: How can bureaucracies be made more competitive and efficient?

One way to make bureaucracy more efficient is through managerial expertise at the congressional level to encourage more accurate measurements of the costs and benefits of government service. As long as special-interest groups exist, however, the potential for waste will be substantial. Another way to increase efficiency is to introduce more competition into bureaucracy, which can be done in several ways. First, proposals to consolidate departments should be carefully scrutinized. Second, government services could be provided and competitively bid for by private producers. Finally, dividing a bureaucracy into smaller departments with separate budgets may increase competition and thus reduce costs and increase the quantity and quality of government services.

Review Terms and Concepts

Private sector
Public sector
Opportunity cost (or, simply, cost)
Cost-benefit analysis
Competition
Monopoly power
Economies of scale
Marginal benefit
Marginal cost
Marginal revenue
Market demand
Law of demand
Monopoly
Consumer surplus

New Terms and Concepts

Median voter
Simple majority voting rule
Unanimity voting rule
Special-interest groups
Cyclical majority

Completion

Democracy is efficient in many respects. It tends to respond to the
median ________________ (median/fringes) of political thought. However, it is
inefficient in a few other respects. It may impose the costs of collective
decisions concerning the production of some goods and services on those
not in ________________ (in/not in) the median voter group because individuals
are not ________________ (are/are not) able to adjust the consumption of public
goods and services. Even if the total social costs exceed the social
may pass benefits of a program, it ________________ (may pass/is sure to fail),
majority due to the ________________ (majority/minority) voting rule. The
some majority, acting out of its own self-interest, may enact ________________
(some/no) social programs that are less than cost efficient.

ignorance Another problem with democracy is political ________________
(awareness/ignorance), which may result in government providing
more proportionately ________________ (more/less) benefits to special-interest

inconsistent	groups. There may also be some problems with ________________
logical	(consistent/inconsistent) policies because otherwise ______________
	(logical/illogical/ignorant) people, when acting as a group, may make
contradictory	____________ (logical/illogical/contradictory) collective decisions.
cyclical	This phenomenon happens because of ________________ (stable/
	cyclical) majorities.
	Government programs and services are usually more efficient the more
competitive	______________ (competitive/monopolistic) they are. Government
monopolistic	bureaucracies tend to be ____________ (competitive/monopolistic).
do not necessarily	Government actions ______________________ (do not neces-
	sarily/always) result in an increase in social welfare. In this market sys-
earn a profit	tem the primary objective of business is to ___________________
can	(earn a profit/serve the public good). This ___________ (can/cannot)
can	be easily measured. We _____________ (can/cannot) predict with
	reasonable accuracy how businesses will behave. With government,
are no	there __________ (are/are no) clearly designed ways to measure suc-
are not	cess in obtaining its objectives. Further, these objectives __________
cannot	(are/are not) often clearly defined. We ______________ (can/cannot)
many	easily predict government behavior. In sum, there are ____________
	(only a few/many) objectives of government, and the success of these
are not	objectives _____________ (are/are not) easily measured. However,
	there may be three possible objectives of bureaucracies.
	One possible objective of bureaucracies is monopolistic profit
maximization	________________ (minimization/maximization), which results in
fewer, higher	___________ (more/fewer) services provided and a __________
decreases	(higher/lower) price charged. It therefore ____________ (increases/

decreases) consumer surplus. This type of bureaucracy is the one that is
least — ____________ (most/least) likely in the real world. Another possible
maximize — objective of a bureaucracy is to ______________ (minimize/maximize)
greater — its size. This results in a ________________ (greater/smaller) quantity
above — of the service provided but _____________ (above/below) the optimum.
increase — It causes costs to _________________ (increase/decrease) as compared
to a competitive outcome. A third objective of a bureaucracy may be to
increase — maximize waste. This also causes costs to _______________ (increase/
decrease), so that a competitive quantity is provided but at a
higher — ____________________ (lower/higher) price. In reality, a bureaucracy
size — is most likely to be both a __________________ (profit/size) and a
waste — ___________________ (competitive/waste) maximizer. In sum,
big — bureaucracies have a tendency to be too ______________ (small/big)
more competitive — and their costs too high. What we need is to make bureaucracies
_______________________ (more competitive/less controlled).

We could make bureaucracies more competitive by
dividing them up — _________________________ (consolidating them/dividing them up).
increase — We could also ____________________ (increase/decrease) the amount
of public services that private industry bids for.

Problems and Applications

1. Given a normal distribution (or bell-shaped curve) representing the varying degrees of liberal and conservative political views, where in the distribution will we find winning candidates?
2 Consider the graph on page 604 for a bureaucracy.

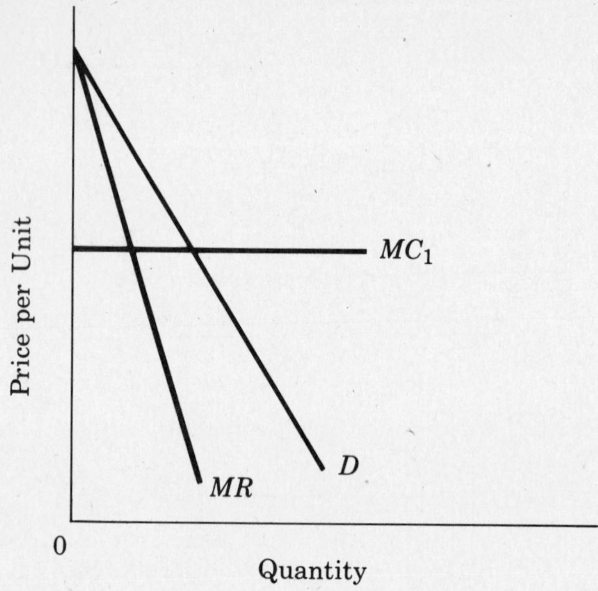

a. Indicate the price and quality supplied if this bureaucracy behaved competitively.
b. Indicate the area of consumer surplus.
c. Indicate the price and quantity supplied if this bureaucracy behaved as a profit-maximizing monopolist.
d. Indicate the area of consumer surplus. Is there more or less consumer surplus when the bureaucracy behaves as a profit-maximizing monopolist as opposed to competitive behavior? Are consumers better or worse off?
e. Is it likely a bureaucracy will behave as a profit-maximizing monopolist? Why or why not?
f. Indicate the price and quantity supplied if this bureaucracy behaved as a size maximizer.
g. Compare total costs of a size maximizer with a competitive bureaucracy.
h. Is a size-maximizer bureaucracy likely?
i. How would a waste maximizer behave?
j. Compare the costs of the waste-maximizing bureaucracy with the competitive bureaucracy.
k. Is a waste-maximizing bureaucracy likely?
l. Are bureaucracies likely to be both waste-maximizing and size-maximizing? Why or why not?

True-False

For each item, determine whether the statement is basically true or false. If the statement is false, rewrite it so it is a true statement.

_____ 1. The median voter group is the large group of voters in the middle of the political distribution.

_____ 2. A unanimity voting rule can be exploited by small groups of voters.

_____ 3. The larger the percentage of voters required to make a decision, the greater the costs of the decision-making process.

_____ 4. The preferences of a few almost always determine the quantity of public goods produced.

_____ 5. The simple majority voting rule always results in the production of public goods whose social benefits outweigh their costs.

_____ 6. Rational people have little incentive to be politically ignorant.

_____ 7. Special-interest groups receive a disproportionately large share of government benefits because they are more politically aware and active.

_____ 8. Politicians do not cater to special interests because their political reputations could be damaged.

_____ 9. There is a tradeoff between a bureaucracy attempting to maximize waste and attempting to maximize size.

_____ 10. *Cyclical majority* refers to the changes made in the efficiency of government elections.

_____ 11. Government services should always be consolidated for greater efficiency because of economies of scale.

_____ 12. Different bureaucracies pursue different objectives.

_____ 13. A monopolistic profit-maximizing bureaucracy results in the loss of all consumer surplus.

_____ 14. A size-maximizing bureaucracy produces more and at higher total costs than a competitive bureaucracy.

_____ 15. In reality most bureaucracies are size and waste maximizers.

_____ 16. Some government goods and services could be provided by private industry at lower costs to government and lower prices to consumers.

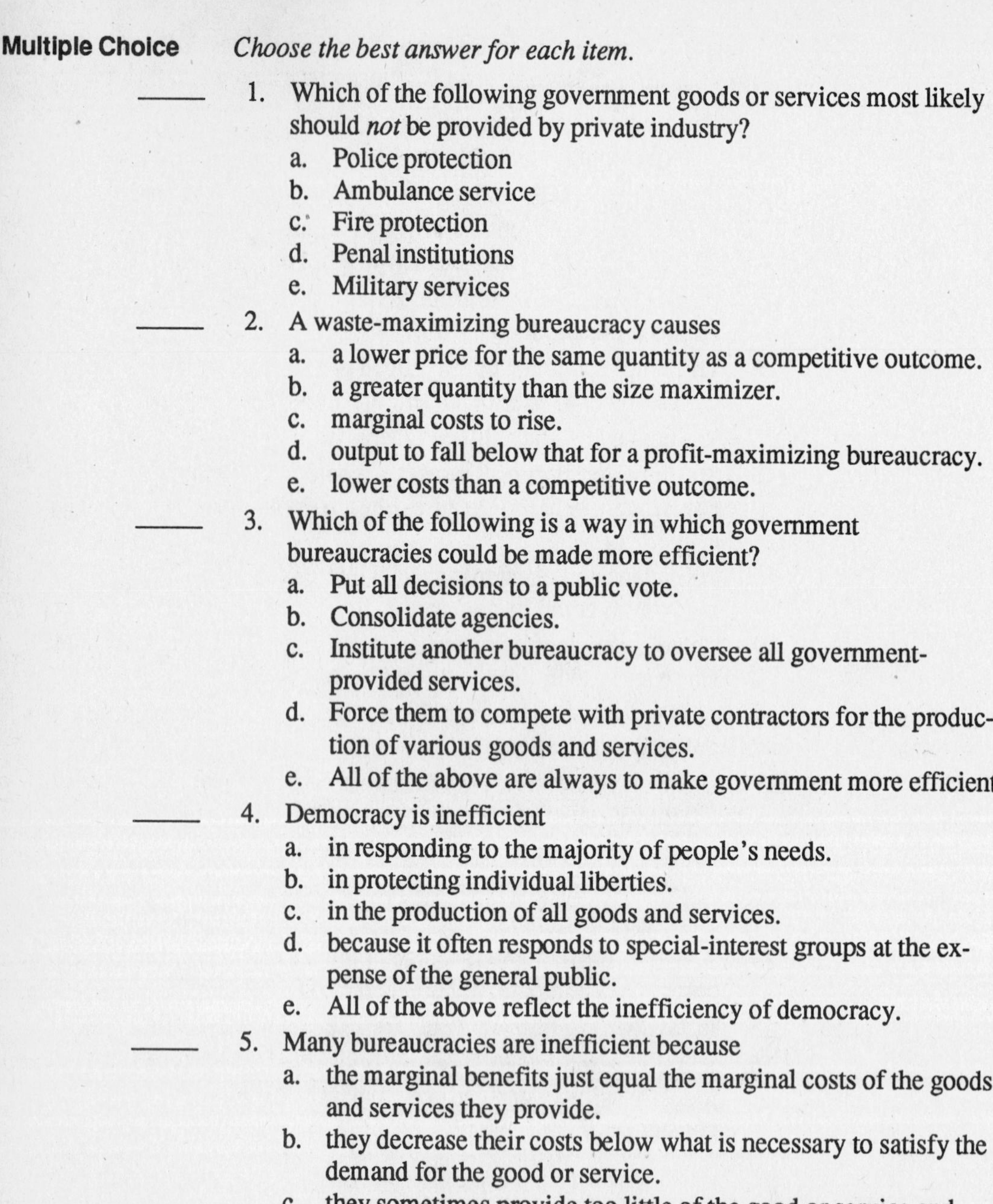

Multiple Choice *Choose the best answer for each item.*

_____ 1. Which of the following government goods or services most likely should *not* be provided by private industry?
   a. Police protection
   b. Ambulance service
   c. Fire protection
   d. Penal institutions
   e. Military services

_____ 2. A waste-maximizing bureaucracy causes
   a. a lower price for the same quantity as a competitive outcome.
   b. a greater quantity than the size maximizer.
   c. marginal costs to rise.
   d. output to fall below that for a profit-maximizing bureaucracy.
   e. lower costs than a competitive outcome.

_____ 3. Which of the following is a way in which government bureaucracies could be made more efficient?
   a. Put all decisions to a public vote.
   b. Consolidate agencies.
   c. Institute another bureaucracy to oversee all government-provided services.
   d. Force them to compete with private contractors for the production of various goods and services.
   e. All of the above are always to make government more efficient.

_____ 4. Democracy is inefficient
   a. in responding to the majority of people's needs.
   b. in protecting individual liberties.
   c. in the production of all goods and services.
   d. because it often responds to special-interest groups at the expense of the general public.
   e. All of the above reflect the inefficiency of democracy.

_____ 5. Many bureaucracies are inefficient because
   a. the marginal benefits just equal the marginal costs of the goods and services they provide.
   b. they decrease their costs below what is necessary to satisfy the demand for the good or service.
   c. they sometimes provide too little of the good or service and sometimes too much.
   d. they are too concerned with the public welfare.
   e. they are operated by private firms.

_____ 6. A cyclical, or revolving, majority refers to
   a. the median voter group, which alternates its political preferences between the two political parties.
   b. changes in the leadership of bureaucracies where in directors of agencies simply switch jobs.
   c. the group of individuals who hold political power.
   d. the large percentage of special-interest groups that change their preferences for the two political parties whenever it is in their interest to do so.
   e. the fact that rational choices made by individuals may appear inconsistent when they act as a group.

_____ 7. Which of the following statements is true?
   a. Political information on the part of those in the median voter group is very sophisticated.
   b. Political information on the part of those in the median voter group is relatively low.
   c. The right-wing fringe of the political spectrum controls the decisions about the types and quantities of public goods and services produced.
   d. A unanimity rule is most likely to be exploited by special-interest groups.
   e. A profit-maximizing bureaucracy results in a loss of all consumer surplus.

_____ 8. Which type of government bureaucracy is most likely to exist in the real world?
   a. Profit maximizing
   b. Waste maximizing
   c. Size maximizing
   d. Waste and size maximizing
   e. Profit and waste maximizing

_____ 9. A bureaucracy that is waste and size maximizing will
   a. attempt to increase its size and budget at the same time.
   b. have to trade off between waste and size.
   c. result in some net benefits to society.
   d. produce greater quantity of the good and service to be provided and charge a higher price than otherwise.
   e. do all of the above.

_____ 10. Democracy is faced with
   a. an imperfect market system.
   b. an imperfect governmental system.

c. the need for politicians to cater to the median voter groups for political success.
d. a choice between the market system and government, and should choose the one that is most efficient.
e. all of the above.

_____ 11. Special-interest groups
a. always get their way.
b. very rarely get their way.
c. can limit benefits to society as a whole.
d. contribute to political ignorance.
e. are catered to by the general public.

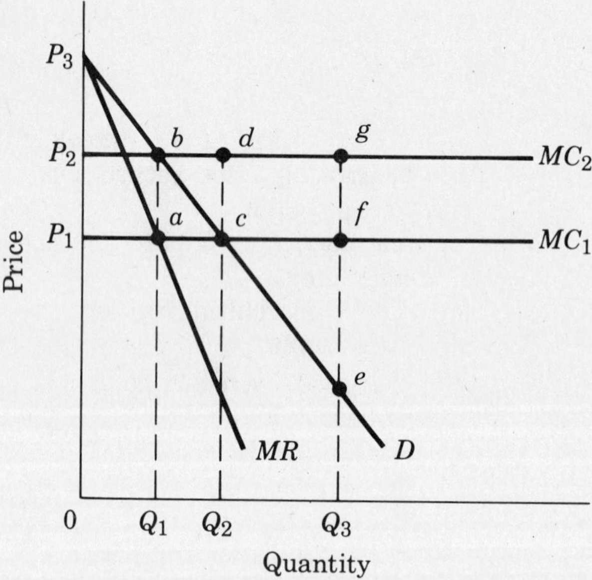

_____ 12. Using the preceding graph for a bureaucracy, and assuming a marginal cost curve of MC_1, which of the following statements is true?
a. A profit-maximizing monopolist will charge a price of P_1 and produce Q_1.
b. The consumer surplus left by a size maximizer is area *cfe*.
c. The total cost of a size maximizer is area $0P_1fQ_3$.
d. A waste maximizer will shift the marginal cost curve to MC_2 and will charge a price of P_2 for Q_3 units of service.
e. The area of waste for a size maximizer is area P_1P_3c.

Discussion Questions

1. There is an old adage that states, "To the squeaky wheel goes the oil." How would you respond in the context of the benefits various sectors of the electorate are likely to receive from government officials? *(KQ2, 3)*
2. Winston Churchill once said, "Democracy is the worst form of government — except for all others." Do you agree or disagree? Why? *(KQ1, 2, 3)*
3. Why do bureaucracies sometimes tend not to serve the public interest? *(KQ3, 5)*
4. If government responds to the median voter group, does this make the tendency toward mass behavior more or less likely? *(KQ1, 2)*
5. Is it possible government would respond to the wishes of the median voter group even when that is not in its best interests — at least in the long run? *(KQ1, 2, 3)*

Answers

Problems and Applications

1. Those near the middle of the distribution.
2. a. See the following graph. A competitive bureaucracy would charge P_1 and provide Q_2 services.

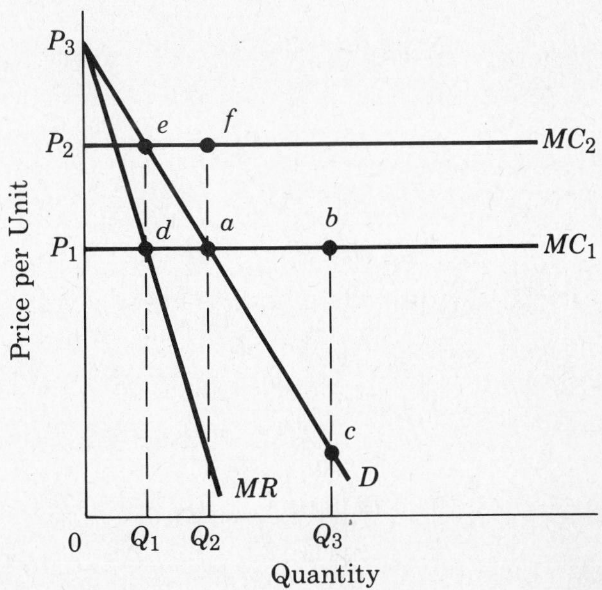

b. P_1P_3a is the area of consumer surplus because it is the amount by which marginal benefits (measured by reading price off of the demand curve) exceed marginal costs for all units supplied up to the last.
c. P_2 would be charged for Q_1 services because the monopolist would maximize profits by equating marginal revenue with marginal costs.
d. P_2P_3e is the area of consumer surplus, and it is less than if the bureaucracy behaved competitively. Therefore, consumers are worse off. They have to pay more for less service.
e. No, because it is unable to pocket the money. It is also unlikely that the bureaucracy will be able to hide its costs.
f. P_1 would be charged for Q_3 services. Note that the size maximizer will continue to expand services until the net waste (area *abc*) just offsets the consumer surplus (area P_1P_2a).
g. A competitive bureaucracy would incur total costs of the service provided equal to area $0P_1bQ_3$. The size maximizer would naturally incur greater costs — equal to area $0P_1bQ_3$.
h. Yes.
i. It will pad its costs, shifting the marginal cost curve. It will continue to cause costs to rise until all consumer surplus has evaporated. That is, MC_1 will continue to shift up until it reaches MC_2, where the area P_2P_3e (the area indicating consumer surplus at a price of P_2) equals *efa* (the area representing waste).
j. The waste-maximizing bureaucracy will incur costs equal to $0P_2fQ_2$, greater than the competitive bureaucracy costs of $0P_1aQ_2$.
k. Yes.
l. Yes, because for each unit of service a bureaucracy provides, it will try to expand both the size of its operation and the funds spent on it. But tradeoffs between the two objectives will have to be made: both size and per unit cost of service cannot increase at once. Therefore, it is likely that some surplus will go to consumers. In other words, the net social benefits are expected to be positive.

True-False

1. T
2. T
3. T
4. F: The preferences of the median voter group almost always determine the quantity of public goods produced.
5. F: The simple majority voting rule does not always result in the production of public goods whose social benefits outweigh their costs.
6. F: Rational people have little incentive to be politically aware.
7. T
8. F: Politicians do cater to special interests because they know they are being watched carefully.
9. T
10. F: *Cyclical majority* refers to the continual change in policy based on collective decision making.
11. F: Government services should not necessarily always be consolidated for greater efficiency.
12. T
13. F: A monopolistic profit-maximizing bureaucracy decreases consumer surplus but does not cause the loss of all consumer surplus.
14. T
15. T
16. T

Multiple Choice

1. e *(KQ3)*
2. c *(KQ5)*
3. d *(KQ6)*
4. d *(KQ3)*
5. c *(KQ5)*
6. e *(KQ3)*
7. d *(KQ2)*
8. d *(KQ5)*
9. e *(KQ5)*
10. e *(KQ1, 2, 3)*
11. c *(KQ2, 3)*
12. c *(KQ5)*

CHAPTER 34

International Trade

Chapter Summary

Key Question 1: What does the balance of payments measure?

Key Question 2: How do nations gain from international trade?

Key Question 3: What are the distributional effects of international trade?

International trade is an extension of marketplace models already developed, although there are some differences between international and domestic trade.

The gains from international trade can be seen in the balance of payments statistics, summarizes of all transactions between one nation and the rest of the world. Nations trade because it increases their welfare. Specialization and trade based on comparative advantage are mutually beneficial to all economies involved because each is able to escape the confines of its own production possibilities. This can be shown graphically by a point representing a combination of goods and services outside a nation's production possibilities curve. And all this occurs even if a nation has an absolute advantage in the production of all goods and services.

Although nations as a whole gain from international trade, some individuals within nations lose. Firms that export their product tend to gain because foreign markets open up. This increases the demand for their product, thereby increasing their revenues and profits. Workers in these industries also gain because the demand for their services increases, causing their wages earned and employment opportunities to rise. Domestic consumers may complain of the higher prices the increased exports cause, but without exports a nation cannot afford imports. Trade is ultimately a two-way street. If exports are restricted, then imports of other goods will also be restricted.

Some firms lose if foreigners export goods and services to the domestic economy — that is, if the domestic economy imports these goods and services. Supply increases, driving prices and profits down for domestic firms.

As price decreases, the firms produce less. Therefore, the demand for workers falls, causing wages earned and employment opportunities to fall. Once again, some may object, but the total social benefit from trade outweighs these costs.

Key Question 4: What do trade restrictions such as tariffs and quotas do to international trade?

Because foreign competition hurts some businesses and workers, they have an incentive to seek government protection. If they are successful, then government will impose either a tariff or a quota on an imported product.

Tariffs can be ad valorem or specific. Tariffs shift the supply (domestic plus foreign) curve up — or to the left — equal to the tax. Price rises, as does domestic production. Domestic firms' profits rise, and workers' wages and employment opportunities increase. Quotas have the same general effect. However, there are three important differences between them. First, quotas firmly restrict importation. Tariffs do not. If demand rises, tariffs allow greater importation. Second, quotas invite more government enforcement because each imported foreign product is limited to a specific amount. Tariffs place no such restriction on foreign producers. Finally, quotas enable domestic firms to raise their prices (therefore their profits rise). Tariffs encourage foreign firms to decrease their prices to offset the tax. Furthermore, tariffs add revenue to the government. Quotas do not.

We would expect domestic firms to seek government protection as long as the increased profits outweigh the political costs (campaign contributions, etc.) of obtaining it. On the other hand, consumers have reason to oppose protection because it causes higher prices. Consumers, however, are usually unaware of these effects and are poorly organized. Businesses are more organized and therefore able to secure government protection from foreign competition. This, however, causes both imports and exports to fall — our imports (foreigners' exports) pay for foreigners' imports (our exports) and vice versa. Because our trade falls, our nation's income falls, although the incomes of protected businesses rise. This means that the size of the economic pie is reduced, but the protected few get a bigger slice.

Key Question 5: What is good about free international trade?

The case for free trade is a strong one. The nation as a whole is simply better off. But individual firms and industries, especially those that are most politically adept, are likely to receive the protection they want. The arguments for restricted trade are usually disguised as some national goal. But in reality, it is firms' or labor unions' self-interest that motivates them to seek protection. There is one notable exception, the maintenance of national security. Even this reason, however, may be abused.

Key Question 6: What arguments in favor of restricted international trade are valid?

There are other arguments for restricted trade, or protectionism, but they are weak from both a practical and a theoretical perspective. First, it is argued that workers are paid less in foreign countries, and U.S. industries are therefore unable to compete. Trade, however, depends on the relative costs of production, not on absolute wages in various nations.

Second, some argue that the United States loses money when it flows overseas in payment for imports. But, recall trade is a two-way street and, as we have seen, our real income increases with trade — we are able to escape the confines of our own production possibilities curve.

Third, it is often argued that foreigners impose tariffs and quotas on our output, so we must retaliate or lose sales in both our domestic and our foreign markets. But foreigners need American dollars to buy from us. To get those dollars, we must buy from them. So, foreign tariffs on our exports ultimately hurt the foreign nation that imposed them as well as America. If America retaliates, trade is reduced even further. The harm is compounded, not negated. However, the threat of a retaliatory tariff may act as a bargaining chip in international trade conferences.

Fourth, it is argued that tariffs increase workers' employment opportunities. This may be effective in the short run, but in the long run reduced imports will result in reduced exports, which will increase unemployment.

Finally, it is argued that new industries deserve protection (the so-called infant industry argument). But it is very difficult for government to determine which new industries may be able to compete with foreign rivals.

Review Terms and Concepts

Production possibilities curve
Opportunity cost
Comparative advantage
Specialization
Cost-benefit analysis
Demand
Law of demand
Change in demand
Supply
Law of supply
Change in Supply
Equilibrium price
Equilibrium quantity

New Terms and Concepts

International balance of payments
Merchandise trade balance
Current account
Current account deficit
Current account surplus
Capital account
Capital account surplus
Capital account deficit
Absolute advantage
Comparative advantage
Terms of trade
Tariff
Quota
Ad valorem duty
Specific duty

Completion

all	International trade is beneficial to __________ (some/all) nations that
comparative	participate. The basis of international trade is ____________________
	(absolute/comparative) advantage. Countries should specialize in their
comparative	________________________ (absolute/comparative) advantage and then
escape	trade. When they do, they are able to _______________ (capture/escape)
	the confines of their own production possibilities curves, shown graphi-
outside	cally as a point _______________ (inside/outside) their production pos-
occurs	sibilities curve. This __________________ (occurs/does not occur) if a
	nation has an absolute advantage in the production of all goods and ser-
	vices.
	Nations as a whole gain from trade. Individuals within nations
do not necessarily	____________________________ (also/do not necessarily) gain. Those
gain	who are able to export more, _____________ (lose/gain) because the
demand for	________________________ (demand for/supply of) their product
increases	____________________ (increases/decreases). The price of the product
rises, rise	___________ (rises/falls), and profits __________ (rise/fall). Workers
benefit, demand for	_________________ (lose/benefit) because the ____________________
rises	(demand for/supply of) their services ______________ (rises/falls), as do
	their incomes.
lose	Industries that are faced with increased imports ______________
supply	(lose/gain) because the ____________________ (demand/supply) curve
rises	in affected industries ___________ (rises/falls), which causes their price
fall, lose	to ___________ (rise/fall), as do their profits. Workers ___________
demand for	(lose/gain) because the _________________ (demand for/supply of)
falls	their services __________ (rises/falls), as do their incomes. Therefore,

encourage — we would expect these firms and workers to ____________________
(resist/encourage) government protectionism.

tariff — If government restricts trade, it does so by either a ______________
tax on — (tariff/capital account) or a quota. A tariff is a ______________ (tax
tariffs — on/a limit on the quantity of) an import. Generally, ______________
(tariffs/quotas) have more favorable results.

Most of the time, businesses and workers argue for restricted trade out
their own self-interest — of a concern for ______________________________ (their own
one — self-interest/the nation's welfare). However, there is ____________
(no/one) good argument for restricted trade. The argument for national
valid — security is a ___________ (flawed/valid) argument. All the other
arguments are flawed. Generally, any restriction on trade means
a decrease — ______________ (a decrease/an increase) in real incomes. In other
smaller — words, the economic pie gets ______________ (smaller/larger).
larger — Those who are protected by tariffs receive a ______________
(larger/smaller) piece of that pie.

Problems and Applications

1. Consider the production possibilities curve for some country, shown on page 617. Assume that it is not engaging in international trade. We see that it could produce the combination X_1Y_2 or X_2Y_1, or many other combinations along its production possibilities curve. What happens to the combination of products X and Y this country could have if it specialized in the production of either X or Y, for which it has a comparative advantage, and then traded with another country?

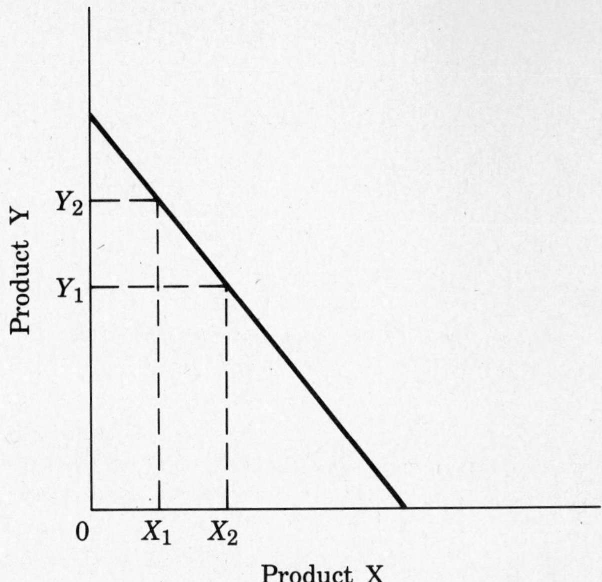

2. Consider the following graph for a domestic firm in the absence of foreign competition.

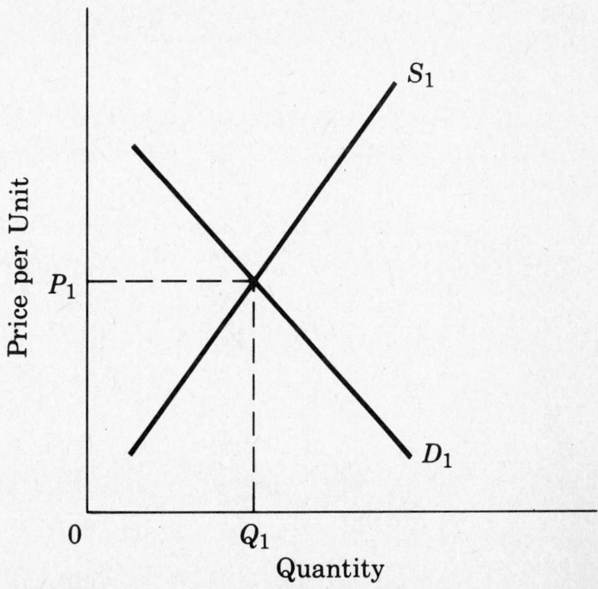

a. Assume that a foreign market opens up for this product. What happens to demand or supply and the price and quantity?
b. Indicate the change in revenues for this firm.
c. Indicate the change in costs of production. Do workers gain or lose?

3. Consider the following graph for a domestic firm in the absence of foreign competition.

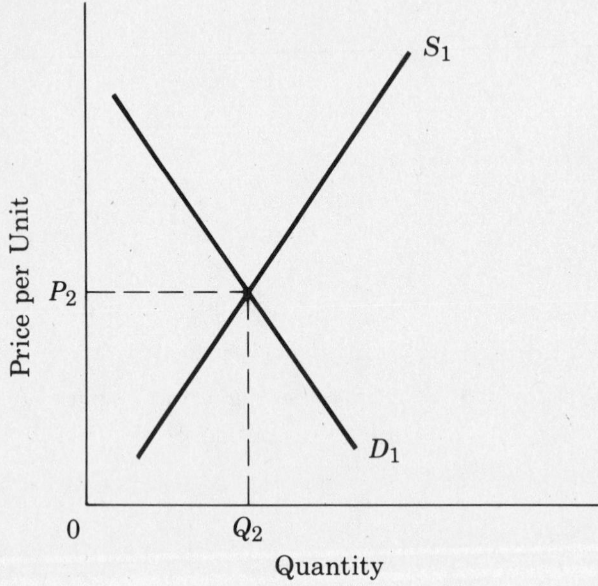

a. Assume that more of this product is imported. What happens to demand or supply and the price and quantity?
b. Indicate the change in revenues for this firm.
c. Indicate the change in costs of production. Do workers gain or lose?

True-False

For each item, determine whether the statement is basically true or false. If the statement is false, rewrite it so it is a true statement.

_____ 1. Trade is based on absolute advantage.

_____ 2. Nations should specialize in the production of the goods or services they have a comparative advantage in, and then trade.

_____ 3. International trade is beneficial to all economies involved.

_____ 4. Any restriction to trade is beneficial to some but not to the nation as a whole.

_____ 5. International balance of payments is the dollar value of goods imported and exported.

_____ 6. A capital account is the record of U.S. investments abroad and foreign investments in the United States.

_____ 7. A tariff is a physical limitation on the amount of a good that is allowed in a nation.

_____ 8. If firms are able to sell more abroad, this increases their market supply curve and their profits.

_____ 9. Workers who experience an increase in competition from foreign producers experience a decline in incomes and job opportunities.

_____ 10. Foreign producers may be able to move in on another country's market if that country increases its tariffs.

_____ 11. One of the differences between quotas and tariffs is that quotas enable an increase in tax revenues collected by government.

_____ 12. One valid argument against free trade is the infant industry argument.

_____ 13. One positive attribute of tariffs is that they may strengthen a country's bargaining position in international trade conferences.

Multiple Choice *Choose the one best answer for each item.*

_____ 1. An absolute advantage means that a country
   a. has a lower opportunity cost in the production of a good.
   b. has a higher opportunity cost in the production of a good.
   c. can produce more of any good with fewer resources.
   d. has imposed a tariff on goods form another country and that country has not retaliated.
   e. can sell in other countries but other countries can't sell in its markets.

_____ 2. Differences between quotas and tariffs include the fact that tariffs
   a. restrict output.
   b. are specified for each important foreign producer.
   c. enable firms to raise their price and earn higher profits.
   d. are not desired by businesses.
   e. enable government to collect revenue.

_____ 3. International trade
   a. is based on specialization and absolute advantage.
   b. benefits industrialized nations at the expense of underdeveloped countries.
   c. is not necessary for rich nations such as the United States.
   d. barriers such as tariffs benefit the country imposing them.
   e. is mutually beneficial for every economy involved.

_____ 4. Foreign producers can gain a foothold in a domestic economy if they
   a. can impose a quota on the domestic economy's exports.
   b. can impose a tariff on the domestic economy's exports.
   c. produce too much at home.
   d. introduce a product the domestic economy does not have.
   e. discover a surplus of their product in the domestic economy.

_____ 5. Exports of one country
   a. finance tariffs of that country.
   b. finance quotas of that country.
   c. finance imports of that country.
   d. cause a decrease in that country's balance of payments.
   e. do all of the above.

_____ 6. Which of the following statements about international trade is true?
   a. It can be represented by a point outside a country's production possibilities curve.
   b. Tariffs and quotas are damaging only in the short run.
   c. Tariffs and quotas increase the supply of the product they are imposed on.
   d. Tariffs cause higher real incomes for all nations.
   e. All of the above

_____ 7. Tariffs cause
   a. the price of imports to fall.
   b. the supply of products to consumers to increase.
   c. domestic prices to decrease.
   d. domestic production to increase.
   e. all of the above.

_____ 8. If a firm now has to compete with foreign producers, then
   a. demand for its product increases.
   b. revenues to the firm will increase.
   c. employment opportunities of workers decrease.
   d. consumers are likely to object to the higher prices.
   e. the firm's production level will increase.

Use the following graph to answer questions 9 and 10.

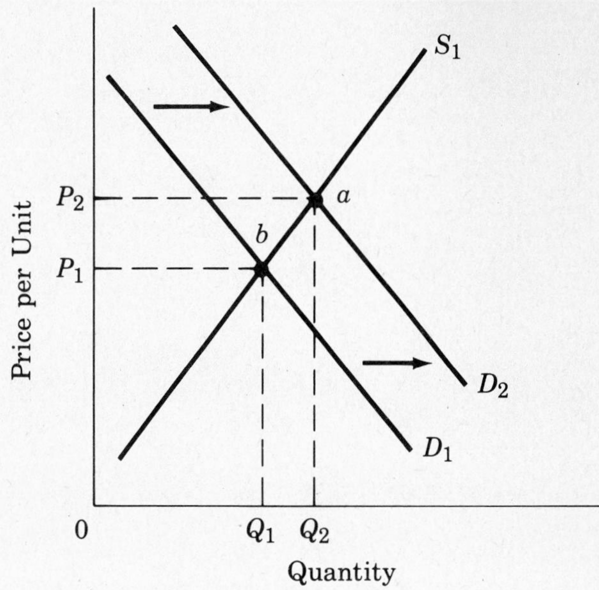

_____ 9. Which of the following statements is true?
  a. A quota has been imposed on this product.
  b. The firm is able to sell in a foreign market that was not previously available.
  c. A tariff has been imposed equal to P_2 - P_1.
  d. Employment opportunities will fall.
  e. The firm's revenues and profits will fall.

_____ 10. If demand increases from D_1 to D_2, this industry will experience an increase in
  a. revenues of $P_1P_2aQ_2Q_1b$.
  b. costs of Q_1baQ_2.
  c. profits equal to P_1P_2ab.
  d. workers' income.
  e. all of the above.

_____ 11. Which of the following is a valid argument for restricted trade?
  a. It increases competition for nations that pay their workers lower wages.
  b. It is needed for national security.
  c. It will enable infant industries to become competitive over time.

d. We lose money when goods and services flow abroad.
e. It is necessary to encourage competition.

Discussion Questions

1. Why has the United States operated with a large balance of payments deficit in the last few years? *(KQ1)*
2. How do specialization and trade in our economy differ from specialization and trade in the international economy? *(KQ2)*
3. How important is international trade for our economy? *(KQ2, 5)*
4. How effective are trade restrictions, or economic sanctions, in "punishing" countries? Whom do they hurt? *(KQ4)*
5. If it is true that trade depends on the relative costs of production and not on absolute wage rates in other nations, why do businesses build new plants in countries with low wages? *(KQ3)*

Answers

Problems and Applications

1. If a country specializes in its comparative advantage (whether it is in X or Y), then trade will enable it to escape the confines of its own domestic production possibilities curve. For instance, this country could possibly have the combination X_2Y_2, which was unobtainable before trade. See the graph on page 623.

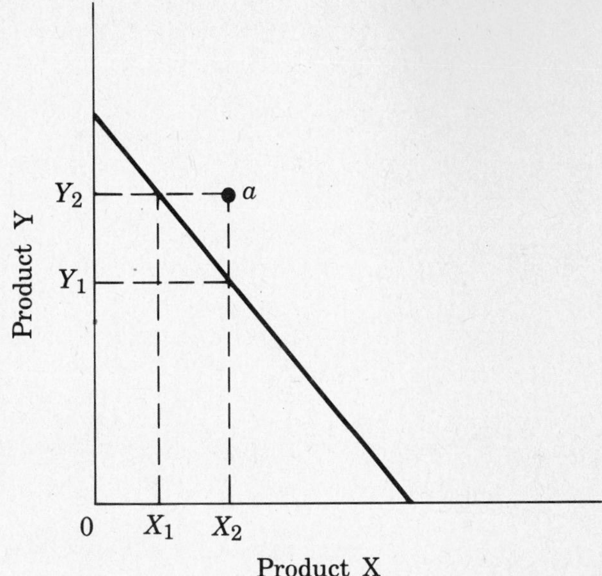

2. a. Demand increases from D_1 to D_2; price increases from P_1 to P_2; and quantity increases from Q_1 to Q_2.

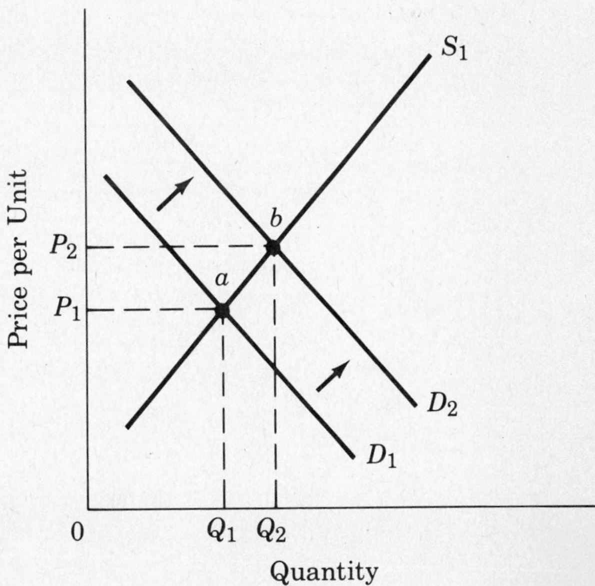

b. Revenues increase equal to area $P_2bQ_2Q_1aP_1$.
c. The cost of producing additional units for export is area Q_1abQ_2. This is the area by which workers gain additional income.

3. a. See the graph below. Supply increases from S_1 to S_2; price decreases from P_2 to P_1; and quantity increases from Q_2 to Q_3.
b. Revenues lost to foreign producers equal area $P_2aQ_2Q_1bP_1$. Of this loss, owners of domestic firms lose the area above the supply curve of P_2abP_1.
c. Because the firm has lost sales of Q_2 - Q_1, costs decrease equal to area Q_2abQ_1, which is the area under the supply curve. Workers lose income by this same amount.

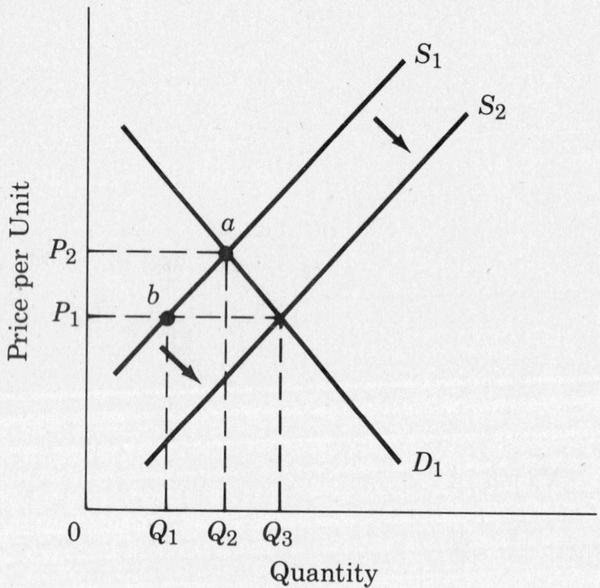

True-False

1. F: Trade is based on comparative advantage.
2. T 3. T 4. T
5. F: International balance of payments is a summary statement of all transactions between one nation and the rest of the world.
6. T
7. F: A tariff is a special tax on imported goods.

8. F: If firms are able to sell more abroad, their market demand curve and their profits are increased.
9. T
10. F: Foreign producers may be able to move in on another country's market if that country decreases its tariffs.
11. T
12. F: One valid argument against free trade is the need to preserve national defense.
13. T

Multiple Choice

1. c *(KQ2)*	2. e *(KQ4)*	3. e *(KQ2, 5)*
4. d *(KQ2)*	5. c *(KQ2)*	6. a *(KQ2)*
7. d *(KQ4)*	8. c *(KQ3)*	9. b *(KQ3)*
10. e *(KQ3)*	11. b *(KQ6)*	

CHAPTER 35

International Finance

Chapter Summary

This chapter looks at the international exchange system whereby importers pay for the goods they buy in their own currency, but the exporters they deal with receive payments in their currency.

Key Question 1: What are international exchange rates?

Dollars must be converted because foreigners want payment in their own currency — just as we do. The international exchange rate is the dollar price one must pay for each unit of a foreign currency. This, in turn, determines the relative price (dollar price of the foreign goods) of the goods one wishes to purchase. And, as always, we can predict from the law of demand what changes will occur in the amount purchased, given a change in the dollar price of the foreign currency.

A depreciation of the dollar means that the dollar will not buy as much foreign currency. In other words, the dollar's value has decreased, and the foreign currency's value has increased. Therefore, the relative price of foreign goods increases, and we will not purchase as much — we will import less. An appreciation of the dollar means that the dollar price of the foreign currency decreases, and we will import more.

From a foreign country's point of view, if the dollar depreciates, it means that the foreign currency price of the dollar has fallen — it now takes less of the foreign currency to buy a dollar. Therefore, the relative price of U.S. products falls, and foreigners will buy more, which means we will export more. An appreciation of the dollar means that the foreign currency price of the dollar has risen, and we will export less.

Key Question 2: How are international exchange rates determined?

Let's look at a specific foreign currency, the French franc. The exchange rate for dollars and francs is the relative prices of francs in terms of dollars (hence, the dollar price of a franc), and vice versa.

Francs can be thought of as another good or service to be purchased. The exchange rate for francs, then, is simply the price of francs in dollars (just as we think of the price of anything else in dollars). Just as with any other commodity, their price is determined by demand and supply. It's important to remember that we (Americans) are the demanders, and we demand francs to purchase French goods — to import them. So the demand for francs really reflects our demand for French imports. As the dollar price of francs decreases, we will import more. According to the J-curve phenomenon this may take some time. But, we will import more over time. (As the dollar price of francs decreases, we will buy more francs so we can buy and import more French goods over time). If the dollar price of francs rises, we will import less. Indeed, the demand for francs, like all demand curves, is downward-sloping.

It is also important to realize that the French are the suppliers of francs. If the dollar price of francs rises, they will buy more of our goods, which means we will export more. But to buy U.S. goods they must first buy dollars. To buy more dollars, they will need to increase the quantity supplied of francs. On the other hand, if the dollar price of francs falls, the quantity supplied will fall — we will export less. Therefore, the supply curve of francs is upward-sloping, like all supply curves. Note that the supply curve indicates our exports. In sum, the demand curve for Francs reflects our demand for imports, whereas the supply curve reflects our supply of exports.

Key Question 3: How do floating, flexible, or freely fluctuating international exchange rates work?

Under a floating, flexible or freely fluctuating international exchange rate system, when we bring the demand for and supply of francs together, we get the equilibrium exchange rate (*ER*) for francs, just as we get the equilibrium price for any commodity. If the *ER* is below equilibrium, the quantity demanded exceeds the quantity supplied. Therefore, we are importing more than we are exporting. That is, we are incurring a balance of payments deficit. This shortage of francs is eliminated as people competitively bid up the dollar price of francs. In other words, the relative price of French goods is so low that some people will be willing to pay a higher price (dollar price for francs) just to get the francs necessary to purchase those French goods. Thus the shortage is eliminated as the *ER* rises toward equilibrium. Note that in the process, U.S. imports fall while exports rise until the balance of payments is reestablished at the equilibrium *ER*. Likewise, if the *ER* is above equilibrium, it will create a balance of payments surplus (exports exceeding imports), which will be eliminated as the *ER* is reestablished. We can see that in a freely floating exchange rate system such as this, the imbalances between imports and exports will not persist for long. Competitive conditions will not allow it.

The equilibrium exchange rate under a floating system will change only if there are changes in demand and/or supply. Demand will increase if (1) American preferences for French goods increase; (2) Americans' real incomes rise; (3) the U.S. inflation rate rises or real interest rates fall; or (4) people expect the exchange rate value of the franc to rise. This will cause an increase in the exchange rate and the equilibrium quantity of francs trading in international money markets. (Supply will increase for the same reasons, but with respect to the French.)

Key Question 4: What is a fixed or pegged international exchange rate system?

Not until 1971 were exchange rates allowed to float — reach equilibrium in response to market conditions. (Even after 1971, many countries allowed their exchange rates to change only within prescribed limits. This is known as a pegged system.) Before then, they were fixed and maintained by governments. The fixed exchange rate system has one advantage over the floating rate: it is stable. This reduces the risks involved in international trade, which translates into lower prices for foreign goods. However, if market conditions change, a fixed system can result in surpluses or shortages of a currency.

Key Question 5: How does monetary adjustment operate under a fixed rate system?

Historically, many methods have been used to fill the gap between the quantity demanded and the quantity supplied which could result under a fixed rate system. Government currency reserves can fill a gap if a shortage exists. Government sells its reserves to keep the exchange rate down. But this assumes that reserves are sufficient. If they are not, then a liquidity problem is created. The shortage can be remedied in several ways. These include selling gold reserves, or currency reserves, borrowing from the IMF, swapping currencies, or using Special Drawing Rights (SDRs).

If the shortages persist too long — that is, if a nation continues to import more than it exports because the exchange rate is held below equilibrium — then inflation is likely to result. To correct this problem, taxes may have to be increased, and government spending or the growth of the money stock may have to be reduced. This may help for a while, but at the cost of a decrease in real income (a recession). The lower inflation makes U.S. goods more attractive, increasing our exports. We would also import less because of the decrease in real income.

Tariffs or restrictions on the flow of funds into foreign investment may also help correct persistent balance of payment deficits. Finally, if all else fails, a country can arbitrarily depreciate its currency (raise the exchange rate toward equilibrium).

Key Question 6: How does a persistent balance of payments problem get solved?

The demise of the fixed (or pegged) exchange rate system in 1971 was inevitable. Although a fixed rate system lessens the risk, uncertainty, and instability in trade, it tends to create balance of payments problems. For instance, the United States large balance of payments deficit caused it to lose billions of dollars in gold reserves, and the dollar was saturating foreign bank accounts. Furthermore, people began to expect a floating system to be announced, which created much speculation. It disrupted international markets and created an even more severe shortage as people began to demand an undervalued currency such as the franc.

Review Terms and Concepts

International balance of payments
Barter
Money
Inflation
Real income
Change in demand
Supply
Law of supply
Change in supply
Quantity demanded
Change in quantity demanded
Quantity supplied
Change in quantity supplied
Equilibrium price
Equilibrium quantity
Surplus
Shortage

New Terms and Concepts

Foreign exchange
International exchange rate
Depreciation
Appreciation
J-curve phenomenon
Dirty or managed float exchange rate system
Purchasing power parity theory
Floating, flexible, or freely fluctuating exchange rate system
Fixed or pegged exchange rate system
Devaluation (revaluation)
Gold reserves
Currency reserves
International Monetary Fund (IMF)
Currency swap
Special Drawing Rights (SDRs)

Completion

The international exchange rate is the price of one currency stated in

another national

terms of ______________________________ (the international/another national) currency. For instance, the dollar price of a franc is the cost of a

franc, dollar — ____________ (dollar/franc) in terms of a ____________
(dollar/franc).

A depreciation of the dollar means that the dollar will

not buy as many — ____________ (not buy as many/buy more) francs.
a decrease — In other words, ____________ (a decrease/an increase) has
an increase — occurred in the value of the dollar, and ____________ (a decrease/
an increase) has occurred in the dollar price of the franc. Therefore, the
increased — relative price of French goods has ____________ (increased/
will not, as many — decreased). We ____________ (will/will not) purchase ____________
less — (more/as many) French goods. So, we'll import ____________
(more/less). In sum, if the dollar depreciates, the dollar price of the franc
increases — ____________ (decreases/increases), and we will import
less — ____________ (less/more).

On the other hand, an appreciation of the dollar means that the dollar
decreases — price of the franc ____________ (increases/decreases), and we
more — will import ____________ (more/less).

This analysis shows, then, that the demand curve for francs is
downward — ____________ (upward/downward)-sloping. It also shows that
imports — the demand for francs really reflects our demand for ____________
(exports/imports).

Let's look at this from France's point of view. If the dollar depreciates,
then the dollar price of the franc increases. But to the French, this means
fallen — that the franc price of the dollar has ____________ (risen/fallen). In other
fewer — words, it now takes ____________ (more/fewer) francs to buy a dollar.
fallen — The relative price of U.S. product has ____________ (risen/
more — fallen), and the French will buy ____________ (fewer/more) U.S. products.

more	This means that we will export ________ (less/more). In sum, if the
increases	dollar depreciates, then the dollar price of the franc ________
more	(increases/decreases), and we will export ________ (more/less).
	On the other hand, an appreciation of the dollar means that the dollar
increases	price of the franc ________ (increases/decreases), and we
less	will export ________ (more/less).
	This analysis shows that the supply curve for francs is
downward	________ (downward/upward)-sloping. It also shows that
exports	the supply of francs really reflects our supply ________
	(imports/exports).
	When we bring the demand for and supply of francs together we can
exchange rate	determine the equilibrium ________ (exchange rate/
francs	balance of payments deficit) for ________ (dollars/francs).
imports	If the exchange rate is below equilibrium, then ________
exports	(imports/exports) exceed ________ (imports/exports). We
deficit	will experience a balance of payments ________ (surplus/
exports	deficit). If the exchange is above equilibrium, then ________
imports	(imports/exports) exceed ________ (imports/exports).
surplus	We will experience a balance of payments ________
	(deficit/surplus). Whenever either a balance of payments surplus or
floating	deficit exists, then under a ________ (fixed/floating) exchange
	rate the surplus or deficit will disappear as the exchange rate moves
	toward equilibrium.
	The equilibrium exchange rate will change if demand and/or supply
rise	change. Demand will increase if Americans' real incomes ________

rises (fall/rise), if U.S. inflation ____________ (falls/rises), or if American

increases preference for French goods ________________ (increases/decreases).

The floating exchange rate did not exist in recent times until

1971 _____________ (1950/1971). At that time we were taken off the

fixed ________________ (fixed/international) exchange rate system. Before 1971, the United States experienced large balance of payments

deficits ________________ (surpluses/deficits). This happened because the

below exchange rate was held ___________ (above/below) equilibrium, which

created ____________________ (created/did not create) many problems. It

was _____________ (was/was not) inevitable that we would be taken off the fixed exchange rate system.

Problems and Applications

1. a. Why does the demand curve for a foreign currency, such as the franc, slope downward?
   b. Does the demand curve reflect our demand for French goods — our imports?
   c. Graph a demand curve for francs.
2. a. Why does the supply curve for a foreign currency, such as the franc, slope upward?
   b. Does the supply curve reflect the French people's demand for our goods — our exports?
   c. Graph a supply curve for francs on the graph drawn for question 1c.
3. a. Indicate an equilibrium exchange rate on the preceding graph. Why is this an equilibrium?
   b. What would happen in the market for francs if the exchange rate was below or above equilibrium? How is this related to a balance of payments deficit or surplus? What happens to the balance of payments deficits or surpluses over time?
   c. Indicate a balance of payments deficit and surplus on the graph.
4. What could cause the equilibrium exchange rate to change?

True-False

For each item, determine whether the statement is basically true or false. If the statement is false, rewrite it so it is a true statement.

_____ 1. The international exchange rate is the price of one national currency stated in terms of another national currency.

_____ 2. Depreciation of the dollar means an increase in its purchasing power with respect to other currencies.

_____ 3. A fixed exchange rate system is still in existence.

_____ 4. A decrease in the dollar price of a franc means that the purchasing power of the dollar has increased.

_____ 5. An increase in the dollar price of a franc may result in a balance of payments surplus.

_____ 6. A depreciation of the dollar discourages exports.

_____ 7. U.S. exports increase the dollar holdings of foreign banks.

_____ 8. As the dollar price of the franc rises, the price of U.S. goods to the French falls.

_____ 9. The demand for francs reflects a demand for French imports.

_____ 10. An increase in American preference for French goods will reduce the exchange rate.

_____ 11. A fixed exchange rate reduces the risks involved in international trade.

_____ 12. A fixed exchange rate may cause either a balance of payments deficit or surplus.

_____ 13. The IMF was created to expand reserves to help alleviate shortages of currencies.

_____ 14. SDRs are sometimes called black gold.

_____ 15. Persistent shortages of a nation's currency may require the nation to decrease its taxes and increase the growth of the money stock.

_____ 16. The J-curve phenomenon indicates that when depreciation occurs, then for a short while importers will accept lower profit margins before increasing prices in order to maintain their market share.

Multiple Choice

Choose the one best answer for each item.

_____ 1. One way to help alleviate the shortage of a currency that causes persistent balance of payments deficits is to
   a. trade gold for currency.
   b. let loose some currency reserves.

c. borrow from the IMF.
d. swap currencies.
e. do all of the above.

_____ 2. If the exchange rate for francs is above equilibrium, this means that
a. the dollar price of francs is too low.
b. exports exceed imports.
c. a balance of payments deficit will be incurred.
d. the exchange rate will rise in the near future.
e. a shortage has developed and the country will lose reserves.

_____ 3. To say that a country is losing reserves means that
a. the dollar price of foreign currencies is too high.
b. the country is running a balance of payments surplus.
c. there is a shortage of the currency.
d. the exchange rate will rise.
e. all of the above are or will be true.

_____ 4. The demand for francs will rise if
a. the dollar price of francs falls.
b. the supply of francs falls.
c. the supply of francs rises.
d. the real income of Americans rises.
e. inflation falls in the United States.

_____ 5. An appreciation of the dollar
a. may have been caused by a balance of payments surplus.
b. means a decrease in the purchasing power of the dollar.
c. will cause the relative price of U.S. goods to rise.
d. is not allowed in a floating exchange rate system.
e. is described in all of the above.

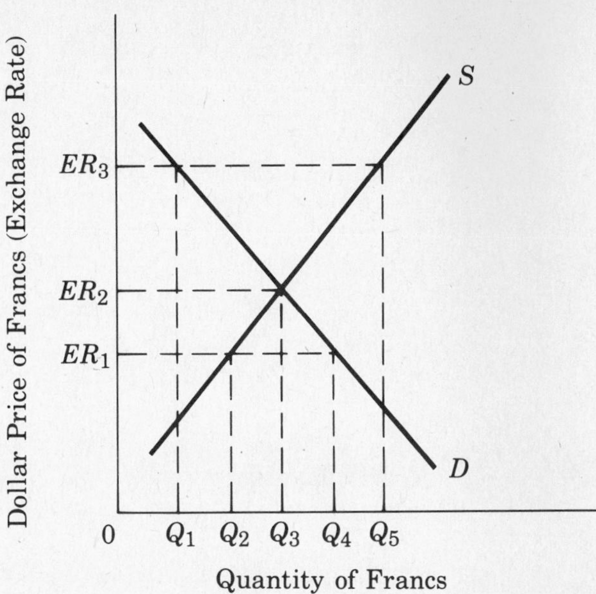

____ 6. Based on the preceding graph, which of the following statements is true?
   a. The demand for francs reflects the price of U.S. products to the French.
   b. A balance of payments deficit of $(Q_5 - Q_1)$ exists at ER_3.
   c. A balance of payments deficit exists at ER_2.
   d. If ER_1 is a fixed exchange rate, then currency holdings may have to be increased by $Q_4 - Q_2$.
   e. The supply curve of francs shows U.S. exports at various exchange rates.

____ 7. Any U.S. export will
   a. increase our holdings of foreign currency.
   b. increase our holdings of our currency.
   c. increase foreign holdings of the dollar.
   d. cause the exchange rate to fall.
   e. cause the exchange rate to rise.

____ 8. If the dollar price of a franc decreases
   a. the dollar has appreciated.
   b. the relative price of French goods has fallen.
   c. the French will buy fewer U.S. products.

d. Americans are likely to buy more and sell less abroad.
e. all of the above are apt to be true.

_____ 9. If the supply of francs increased, the exchange rate would
a. rise, and demand would decrease.
b. fall, and demand would remain stable.
c. remain unchanged.
d. fall, and demand would increase.
e. do none of the above.

_____ 10. A decrease in Americans' real income will cause which effect in the market of the francs?
a. An increase in demand
b. A decrease in demand
c. An increase in supply
d. A decrease in supply
e. An increase in demand and an increase in supply

Discussion Questions

1. What has caused our persistent balance of payments problem in the last few years? (*Hint:* Think in terms of what can shift demand.) *(KQ3, 6)*
2. Do you think the U.S. abandonment of the fixed exchange rate system was related to the rising price of oil? In other words, the world price of oil was tied to the value of the dollar. If the dollar depreciated, then the real price of oil decreased. Do you think this played a role? *(KQ4, 5, 6)*
3. What could cause the supply curve in the market for francs to shift? *(KQ3)*

Answers

Problems and Applications

1. a. The demand curve for a foreign currency slopes downward because as the dollar price of a franc, for instance, decreases, we will wish to buy more francs because the relative price of French goods decreases. Therefore, as the dollar price of the franc falls, the quantity demanded for francs will rise. Note that the demand curve reflects our desire for imports.
b. Yes.
c. See the graph on page 637.

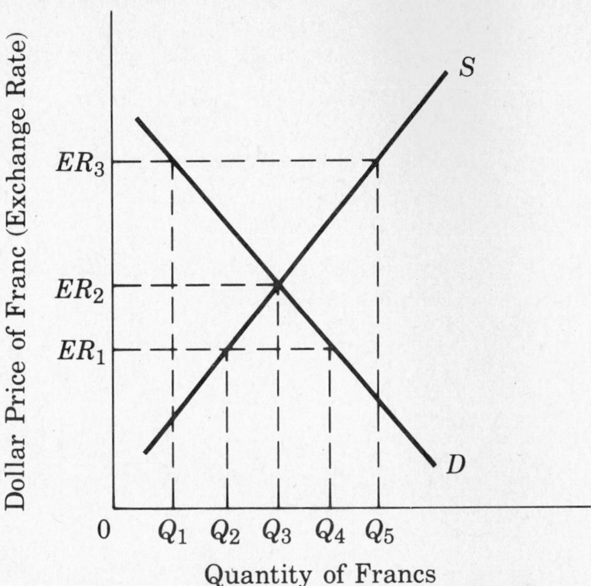

2. a. The supply curve reflects the French people's demand for U.S. exports. If the dollar price of the franc increases, the franc increases in value (the relative price of U.S. goods decreases), and the French will wish to purchase more U.S. goods. But to do so they will have to convert francs into dollars. They will offer more on the market. That is, the quantity supplied of francs increases as the dollar price of francs increases. Note that the supply curve is foreigners' desire for our exports.
   b. Yes.
   c. See the preceding graph.
3. a. In the preceding graph, the equilibrium exchange rate is ER_2, and the quantity demanded and the quantity supplied are the same at Q_3. This is an equilibrium because there is no balance of payments deficit or surplus.
   b. If the exchange rate is below equilibrium, the quantity demanded of francs exceeds the quantity supplied. Our imports will exceed our exports, and the dollar price of francs will rise (the value of the dollar will fall). If we are importing more than we are exporting then we are running a balance of payments deficit. On the other hand, if the exchange rate is above equilibrium, the quantity supplied (French purchases of our exports) will exceed the quantity demanded (our imports of French products), and the dollar price of francs will fall. This corrects

for the balance of payments surplus. In sum, the exchange rate reaches equilibrium as any price would in any other market. Note that an equilibrium there are no imbalances between imports and exports. Therefore, in a freely floating exchange rate system all imbalances will be corrected over time.

c. A balance of payments deficit occurs when the exchange rate is below equilibrium. This occurs at ER_1, where imports of Q_4 exceed exports of Q_2. The balance of payments surplus could be shown at ER_3, where exports of Q_5 exceed imports of Q_1.

4. Changes in the equilibrium exchange rate occur for the same reasons as equilibrium changes in any other market — because of changes (shifts) in demand and supply curves.

True-False

1. T
2. F: Depreciation of the dollar means a decrease in its purchasing power with respect to other currencies.
3. F: A fixed exchange rate system was abandoned in 1971.
4. T 5. T
6. F: A depreciation of the dollar encourages exports.
7. F: U.S. exports reduce the dollar holdings of foreign banks.
8. T 9. T
10. F: An increase in American preferences for French goods will increase the exchange rate because it increases the demand for francs.
11. T 12. T 13. T
14. F: SDRs are sometimes called paper gold.
15. F: Persistent shortages of a nation's currency may require the nation to increase taxes and decrease the growth of the money stock.
16. T

Multiple Choice

1. e *(KQ5)* 2. b *(KQ3, 4, 5)* 3. e *(KQ3, 4, 5)*
4. d *(KQ1, 2)* 5. c *(KQ1, 2)* 6. e *(KQ1, 2, 3)*
7. a *(KQ1, 2)* 8. e *(KQ1, 2)* 9. b *(KQ3)*
10. b *(KQ3)*

CHAPTER 36

International Trade and the Macroeconomy

Chapter Summary

In this chapter we are concerned with how international trade — the volume of exports *(Ex)* and imports *(Im)* — and the domestic macroeconomy interact. We investigate this interaction from the perspective of the Keynesian, monetarist, and supply-side macroeconomic schools of thought.

Key Question 1: How do international transactions fit into the Keynesian model of the macroeconomy?

Recall from Chapter 11 that from the Keynesian perspective of the macroeconomy there are two ways of viewing how an equilibrium level of economic activity (or, simply, income level) can be achieved and how it may change. There is the total planned expenditures approach (also known as the total spending-total output approach), and there is the leakages-injections approach. Furthermore, recall that if total spending equals total output, then an equilibrium income level is established. If total spending exceeds (falls short of) total output then the income level will rise (fall) until total spending is just sufficient to clear total output off the market. Alternatively, if leakages equal injections then we get an equilibrium income level. If leakages fall short of (exceed) injections then the income level will rise (fall) until the leakages out of the circular flow of income are just offset by an equal amount of injections.

In terms of the total spending-total output approach, and in the absence of international trade, total spending simply equals the sum of consumption (C), investment (I), and government expenditures (G). That is, $TS = C + I + G$. However, when we consider international trade, we must add exports *(Ex)* and subtract imports ***(Im)*** in determining the total spending level. In mathematical notation, the total spending equation becomes: $TS = C + I + G + Ex - Im$. From this perspective it is easy to see that an increase in exports or a decrease in imports will result in an increase in total spending (all other things held constant). Assuming the economy was initially in equilibrium, total spending will now exceed total output. This will cause the income level to expand by a multiple of the increase in total spending because of the multiplier effect. However, with the inclusion of international trade into our analysis the multiplier effect is not quite as large as before. In other words, the multiplier is now smaller.

The effects of a change in exports and imports can be summarized in terms of aggregate demand and supply. Recall that whatever causes an increase (decrease) in total spending will cause an increase (decrease) in aggregate demand. Therefore, if exports increase or imports fall then total spending rises and the aggregate demand curve shifts to the right. This causes a multiple increase in income and an increase in the general price level. Conversely, a movement in the direction of a trade deficit (an increase in imports or a decrease in exports) will cause a multiple decrease in income and a decrease in the general price level.

In terms of the leakages-injections approach, and in the absence of international trade, leakages from the circular flow of income simply consist of savings (S) plus taxes (T). Injections simply consist of investment expenditures (I) plus government expenditures (G). However, when we include exports (Ex) and imports (Im) into our analysis, total leakages become $S + I + Im$, and total injections become $I + G + Ex$. Imports are a leakage because they represent spending abroad that otherwise would have been spent domestically. Exports are an injection for the opposite reason. Because equilibrium in the macroeconomy can be defined when $S + T + Im = I + G + Ex$ then changes in exports or imports (holding all other things constant) will have the predicted effects on the economy. For instance, assume the economy is initially at equilibrium and the only thing that changes is an increase in imports or a decrease in exports. This will cause total leakages to exceed total injections and a multiple contraction in the income level will take place. However, the multiple contraction in income will be smaller now that international trade is considered.

The foregoing analysis has implicitly assumed that the exchange rate has been fixed (or maintained) by government. In other words, any change in exports or imports will not induce any offsetting change in the other. However, under a flexible exchange rate system changes in exports or imports will likely have offsetting effects on the other. For example, an initial exogenous increase in exports will cause an increase in the demand for the dollar (foreigners will need more dollars to buy our exports) and, therefore, an increase in the exchange rate value of the dollar. This, in turn, increases the relative price of American exports and decreases the relative price of American imports, causing American exports to fall and imports to rise. The end result is little, if any, change in total spending (or leakages and injections) and therefore the level of economic activity.

Whether we have a fixed or flexible exchange rate system also determines the effectiveness of Keynesian fiscal and monetary policies. Under a fixed exchange rate system, Keynesian fiscal policy is effective in changing total spending (or injections and leakages) and therefore the income level, as discussed in earlier chapters. (In particular, see Chapter 13.) This is because changes in government expenditures or taxes will not have any offsetting effects on exports or imports. However, under a fixed exchange rate system, Keynesian monetary policy may be largely ineffective. Suppose, for example, the money supply increases. This will decrease domestic interest rates and increase the demand for foreign currencies as individuals rush to place their money in other economies where interest rates are relatively higher. In other words, a capital (money) outflow takes place. The increase in the demand for foreign currencies pushes their exchange rate values up. This will cause a depreciation of the dollar. (Alternatively viewed: a reduction in U.S. interest rates will cause an increase in the supply of the dollar in international exchange rate markets as more Americans attempt to buy more foreign currencies. Therefore, the dollar depreciates). In order to keep the value of the dollar from falling, the government will be forced to buy dollars in international exchange rate markets. In essence, the government will be buying back the dollars it initially sought to add to the money supply.

Under a flexible exchange rate system we get opposite results in terms of the effectiveness of Keynesian fiscal and monetary policies. That is, under a flexible exchange rate system fiscal policy is ineffective in changing the level of economic activity whereas monetary policy is effective. As before, these results are due to the predicted effects of changes in capital flows.

Consider an increase in the government's budget deficit under a flexible exchange rate system. This will cause an increase in domestic interest rates due to an increase in the demand for loanable funds. Higher interest rates here will cause foreigners to demand more dollars in order to save here. The dollar appreciates causing American exports to fall and imports to rise leaving total spending (aggregate demand) and, therefore, the income level unchanged. (Furthermore, because of the predicted effects of changes in capital flows, an increase in consumption and investment spending will also push up interest rates and cause offsetting effects on imports and exports leaving the income level unchanged).

Now consider an increase in the money supply under a flexible exchange rate system. This will cause domestic interest rates to fall causing a capital outflow (because U.S. investors will want to save and invest at relatively higher interest rates abroad) and a depreciation of the dollar. As the dollar depreciates, U.S. exports rise and imports fall resulting in a further increase in total spending (aggregate demand) and an increase in income and a reduction in unemployment.

Key Question 2: How do international transactions fit into the monetarist model of the macroeconomy?

Monetarists emphasize the effects of changes in the money stock on the price levels in different countries and on international exchange rates in effecting exports and imports in different countries.

The monetarists argue that the equation of exchange is not only applicable to the domestic economy but the world economy as well. Therefore in a gold standard world, in which all currencies are valued in terms of gold, an increase in the world money supply (gold) will cause a higher world price level. However, the distributional effects of gold flows between nations is a matter of supply and demand. For instance, if the quantity of money demanded (representing exports) exceeds the quantity supplied (representing imports) for a particular nation then gold flows in until equilibrium is established. That is, a trade surplus (exports exceeding imports) will eventually be eliminated when enough gold flows in.

The simple quantity theory model, which emphasizes the equation of exchange, must be altered when we apply it to a world where each nation has its own currency (and no single international currency such as gold exists). Under these conditions, international prices are no longer stated in terms of gold but in terms of exchange rates between different currencies. In turn, exchange rates are determined by purchasing power parity — which can be viewed absolutely or relatively. Absolute purchasing power parity tries to explain the level of exchange rates whereas the relative purchasing power parity tries to explain the changes in an exchange rate. In either event the monetary approach to exchange rates assumes that long-run changes in exchange rates are determined by differences in foreign and domestic rates of inflation. Suppose the United States increases its money supply and the U.S. price level rises relative to another country. It will now take more dollars to buy that foreign currency. The value of the dollar falls; exports increase and imports fall. That is, the quantity demanded of dollars (representing U.S. exports) will now exceed the quantity supplied of dollars (representing U.S. imports). This short-run shortage of dollars will then cause the value of the dollar to rise again over time. As the value of the dollar rises in the long run, then exports fall and imports rise offsetting the short-run gains. According to the monetarists, over the long run, attempting to manipulate exchange rates and, therefore, exports and imports and the national income level, will not be effective.

Supply-siders emphasize aggregate supply as the key determinant to the level of economic activity. They argue that a reduction in tax rates and the elimination of inefficient government regulations will stimulate aggregate supply, thereby increasing income (reducing unemployment) and decreasing the price level.

Key Question 3: How do international transactions fit into the supply-side model of the macroeconomy?

However, when international trade is considered, an increase in the income level due to a tax rate cut is expected to increase imports and decrease exports creating a trade deficit — at least in the short run. This will occur for two reasons. First, a greater after-tax return in the domestic economy will cause a greater demand for the dollar and, therefore, value of the dollar as more capital flows into the economy and less flows out. Second, the greater real income and production can be expected to lead to greater imports. However, over time, supply-siders argue that greater domestic productivity can help reduce a trade deficit. Other remedies called for by some, but certainly not all supply-siders, is a return to some fixed exchange rate system. Some have even called for a return to the gold standard.

Review Terms and Concepts

Macroeconomics
Keynesian
Monetarist
Supply-side
Aggregate demand
Aggregate supply
Production possibilities curve
Total planned expenditures (Total expenditures, Total spending)
The circular flow of income
Injections (Inflows)
Leakages (Outflows)
Private investment *(I)*
Government expenditures *(G)*
Savings *(S)*
Marginal Propensity to Save *(MPS)*
Marginal Propensity to Consume *(MPC)*
Taxes *(T)*
National income *(Y)*
Consumption expenditure
Exports
Imports
Equilibrium in the macroeconomy
Fiscal policy
Monetary policy
Federal budget deficit
Federal budget surplus
International trade deficit
International trade surplus
Multiplier effect
Multiplier *(m)*
Exchange rate
Fixed exchange rate system
Flexible exchange rate system
Current account deficit
Current account surplus
Crowding-out effect
Appreciation
Depreciation
Quantity theory of money
Equation of exchange
Cambridge equation of exchange
Absolute purchasing power parity
Relative purchasing power parity

Completion

	The Keynesian macroeconomic school of thought emphasizes aggregate
demand	________________ (demand/supply) as the key determinant to the
	level of economic activity. A synonym for aggregate demand is total
spending	________________ (output/spending). If total spending equals total
be in equilibrium	output then the income level will ________________
	(fall/be in equilibrium/rise). If total spending is greater than total output
rise	then the income level will ________________ (fall/be in equilibrium/
	rise). The converse is also true. In the absence of international trade, total
plus	spending equals consumption spending ____________ (plus/minus)
plus	investment spending ____________ (plus/minus) government spend-
	ing. When international trade is considered then exports will have to be
added to	____________ (added to/subtracted from) total spending, whereas
subtracted from	imports will have to be ______________ (added to/subtracted from)
	total spending. Therefore, in mathematical notation we get: $TS = C + I +$
an increase	$G + Ex - Im$. From this perspective we can see that ____________
a decrease	(an increase/a decrease) in exports or ______________ (an increase/
	a decrease) in imports will increase total spending. If this occurs then the
	international sector of the economy is moving in the direction of a
surplus	balance of payments ____________ (deficit/surplus). The total spend-
increase	ing level will, therefore, ______________ (increase/decrease) and the
rise	equilibrium income level will __________ (rise/fall). The income level
greater	will change by a dollar amount ______________ (less/greater) than
	the dollar change in total spending. However, the multiplier effect on the
smaller	income level given any change in total spending is ____________
	(larger/smaller) than before when international trade was ignored.

are	Changes in total spending that are due to a change in *any* of its com-
	ponents ____________ (are/are not) reflected in the aggregate demand-
	aggregate supply model. An increase in total spending is reflected in the
an increase	model as ____________________ (a decrease/an increase) in aggregate
demand	____________________ (demand/supply). This means the curve will shift
right, rise	to the _____________ (left/right). The level of income will __________
fall	(rise/fall) and unemployment will ______________ (rise/fall). The effect
	of an increase in total spending and the accompanying rightward shift of
increase	the aggregate demand curve is to ________________ (increase/decrease)
	the general price level.
	Another way to look at how an equilibrium income level is established
leakages	and how it may change is to look at the total ______________________
injections	(spending/leakages) and total ____________________ (output/injections)
	approach. In this approach, when international trade is considered,
imports	savings *(S)* and taxes *(T)* are supplemented by adding _______________
	(exports/imports) to obtain total leakages from the circular flow of in-
	come. When international trade is considered then the total injections be-
plus	come investment spending *(I)* ____________ (minus/plus) government
plus	spending ____________ (minus/plus) exports. We know that equilibrium
equal	in the macroeconomy is determined when total leakages ____________
	(exceed/equal/fall short of) total injections. In mathematical notation
=	equilibrium occurs when $S + T + Im$ _________ $(< / = / >)$ $I + G + Ex$.
	If total leakages exceed total injections, then the income level will
fall	____________ (fall/rise), and vice versa. From this perspective it is then
easy	_______________ (easy/difficult) to predict the effects of changes in in-
	ternational trade on the macroeconomy. For example, if exports fall and

exceed imports rise then total leakages will now __________ (exceed/equal/fall short of) total injections and the income level will experience a
contraction multiple __________ (expansion/contraction).

The foregoing analysis in terms of both the total spending-total output and total leakages-total injections approaches have implicitly assumed a fixed exchange rate. Under a fixed exchange rate system any change in
will not either exports or imports __________ (will/will not) have an offsetting effect on the other. However, under a flexible exchange rate system
an increase an increase in exports for example, will likely cause __________ (an increase/a decrease) in imports over time. This means that changes in international trade under a flexible exchange rate system will likely
not have __________ (have/not have) much impact on the level of economic activity over the long run.

Whether a nation has a fixed or flexible exchange rate system
will also __________ (will also/does not) determine the effectiveness of Keynesian fiscal and monetary policies. Under a fixed exchange rate
effective system fiscal policy is __________ (effective/ineffective) and
ineffective monetary policy is __________ (effective/ineffective) in changing the national income level. Under a flexible exchange rate sys-
effective tem fiscal policy is __________ (effective/ineffective) and
ineffective monetary policy is __________ (effective/ineffective). These con-
are clusions __________ (are/are not) due to capital flows and the resulting effects on exchange rates and therefore exports and imports.

the money supply The monetarist perspective emphasizes changes in __________ (aggregate demand/aggregate supply/the money supply) and the effects on the price levels of different countries, and, therefore, exchange rates

	in effecting international trade and the macroeconomy. In particular, the
equation of exchange	monetarists emphasize the ______________________________ (total
	spending equation/equation of exchange). They believe this equation
both, and	holds for __________ (only/both) the domestic economy __________
	(but not/and) the world economy. This means an increase in the money
	supply (within a domestic economy or a world economy) will cause the
rise	price level to ______________ (rise/fall).
	Essentially the monetarists believe that changes in a nation's money
will not	stock designed to effect the level of economic activity ______________
	(will/will not) be effective in the long run. For example, an increase in
increase	the U.S. money stock will __________________ (increase/decrease)
	the U.S. inflation rate. This, in turn, will cause the dollar to
depreciate	__________________ (depreciate/appreciate). If the value of the dollar
rise	falls, this causes exports to _____________ (rise/fall) and imports to
fall	_____________ (rise/fall). This means that the quantity demanded of
exceed	dollars (representing U.S. exports) will now _____________ (exceed/
	be less than) the quantity supplied of dollars (representing U.S. imports).
	The short-run result of an increase in the money supply then is an in-
	crease in exports, a decrease in imports, and a shortage of dollars.
	However, in the long run, the shortage of dollars will cause the value of
rise	the dollar to ___________ (rise/fall). As the dollar appreciates, then ex-
fall, rise	ports will _________ (rise/fall) and imports will _________ (rise/fall).
offsets	This long-run result _________________ (enhances/offsets) the short-
	run effect. In sum, the monetarists argue that changes in the money sup-
	ply in order to change real economic activity may be effective in the
short run, long run	_______________ (short run/long run) but not in the _____________

essentially the same (short run/long run). This is ______________________ (essentially the same/a different) conclusion the monetarists have about the discretionary use of monetary policy in the domestic economy. That is, changes in the money supply are not effective in the long run.

The supply-side macroeconomic school of thought emphasizes the
supply aggregate ________________ (demand/supply) side of the economy.
increase They attempt to ______________(increase/decrease) aggregate supply
decreasing by ________________ (increasing/decreasing) marginal tax rates and
reducing ________________ (increasing/reducing) government regulation. An
increase increase in aggregate supply is expected to _____________ (increase/
decrease decrease) national income and ________________ (increase/decrease) the general price level.

However, when international trade is included, an increase in the in-
decrease come level due to a tax rate cut is expected to _________________
increase (increase/decrease) exports and _______________ (increase/decrease)
deficit imports. This movement in the direction of a trade ________________ (deficit/surplus) will occur in part because lower marginal tax rates will
encourage _________________ (encourage/discourage) capital (money) inflows into the country. Another reason for a decrease in exports and an increase in imports is that as income rises (due to an increase in aggregate supply)
rise the demand for imported products by Americans will __________ (fall/
an increase rise). Nonetheless, __________________ (an increase/a decrease) in productivity due to tax cuts may reduce the trade deficit over time. This
decrease is because greater productivity will ________________ (increase/ decrease) the relative price of American products to foreigners and

increase

________________ (increase/decrease) the relative price of imported products to Americans.

In sum, if a supply-side tax rate cut creates a trade deficit, this will

less

render the tax cut ____________ (more/less) effective in controlling the level of income and prices.

Problems and Applications

1. Consider the Keynesian macroeconomic school of thought. Furthermore, consider the total spending-total output approach to equilibrium national income and how it may change. Also assume a fixed exchange rate system.
   a. What is the key determinant to the levels of economic activity?
   b. What is total spending equal to mathematically when international trade (exports and imports) is considered?
   c. Why are exports added to total spending and imports subtracted from total spending?
   d. How is equilibrium in the macroeconomy determined in terms of the total spending-total output approach? How is equilibrium expressed mathematically?
   e. If the value of the dollar appreciates, what happens to U.S. exports and imports? What happens to the balance of payments?
   f. If exports fall and imports rise what happens to total spending and the income level? How is this situation reflected in terms of the aggregate demand-aggregate supply model?
   g. Can we conclude that an appreciation of the dollar and the consequent balance of payments deficit it creates will cause a contraction in the macroeconomy (holding all other things constant)?
2. What is expected to happen to imports as income expands? How is this related to the multiplier effect? What happens to the size of the multiplier when international trade is taken into consideration?
3. Consider the Keynesian macroeconomic school of thought. Furthermore, consider the leakages-injections approach to equilibrium national income and how it may change. Also assume a fixed exchange rate system.
   a. What are total leakages from the circular flow of income when international trade is considered? Express this in mathematical notation.

b. What are total injections into the circular flow of income when international trade is considered? Express this in mathematical notation.
c. How is equilibrium defined in terms of the leakages-injections approach? How is equilibrium defined mathematically?
d. Is it necessary to have a balance of payments (exports equal imports) in order to have equilibrium in the macroeconomy?
e. Suppose exports rise and imports fall due to a depreciation of the dollar. What will happen to the balance of payments and the macroeconomy in terms of the leakages-injections approach?
f. Are the total spending-total output and leakages-injections approaches simply two different ways of looking at the same thing?

4. Consider the Keynesian macroeconomic school of thought. Assume a fixed exchange rate system and an initial balance of payments. For the two following situations, determine what will happen to exports, imports, the balance of payments, and the domestic equilibrium income level.
   a. An appreciation of the dollar.
   b. A depreciation of the dollar.
5. Consider the Keynesian school of thought and assume a flexible exchange rate system in answering the following questions.
   a. What effect will an exogenous increase in exports have on the demand for the dollar?
   b. Given your answer in part a above, what happens to the value of the dollar?
   c. Given you answer to part b above, what will happen to U.S. imports?
   d. Does this illustrate that under a flexible exchange rate system that a change in either exports or imports will cause an offsetting effect on the other?
6. Consider the Keynesian perspective and assume a fixed exchange rate system in answering the following questions.
   a. Is fiscal policy effective? Why or why not?
   b. Is monetary policy effective? Why or why not?
7. Consider the Keynesian perspective and assume a flexible exchange rate system in answering the following questions.
   a. Is fiscal policy effective? Why or why not?
   b. Is monetary policy effective? Why or why not?

8. Consider the monetarist macroeconomic school of thought. Assume the United States increases its money supply and the inflation rate rises to 7 percent. Also assume the Japanese are experiencing an inflation rate of 4 percent.
   a. According to the relative purchasing power parity, how much would the dollar depreciate (and the exchange rate rise)?
   b. If the dollar depreciates, what happens to U.S. exports and imports in the short run?
   c. In the short run, if U.S. exports rise and imports fall what happens to the quantity demanded and supplied of dollars in international exchange rate markets? Is the quantity demanded of dollars now greater, or less than the quantity supplied of dollars? Is there a shortage or surplus of dollars?
   d. What is expected to happen to the total spending level in the U.S. and, therefore, the level of economic activity?
   e. In the long run, if a shortage of dollars exists what happens to the value of the dollar?
   f. What happens to U.S. exports and imports when the value of the dollar rises (appreciates) and, hence, the level of economic activity in the United States?
   g. According to the monetarists, will an increase in the U.S. money supply cause any substantial gains for the U.S. economy in the long run?
9. Consider the supply-side macroeconomic school of thought.
   a. What two basic policies do the supply-siders recommend to increase aggregate supply (and therefore increase national income and reduce the general price level)?
   b. What effect would a reduction in U.S. marginal tax rates have on U.S. exports and imports and therefore U.S. balance of payments? Why?
   c. Would a trade deficit help or hinder supply-side policy?

True-False

For each item determine whether the statement is basically true or false. If the statement is false, rewrite it so it is a true statement.

____ 1. From a Keynesian perspective, if the international balance of payments moves in the direction of a deficit then the equilibrium income level will fall.

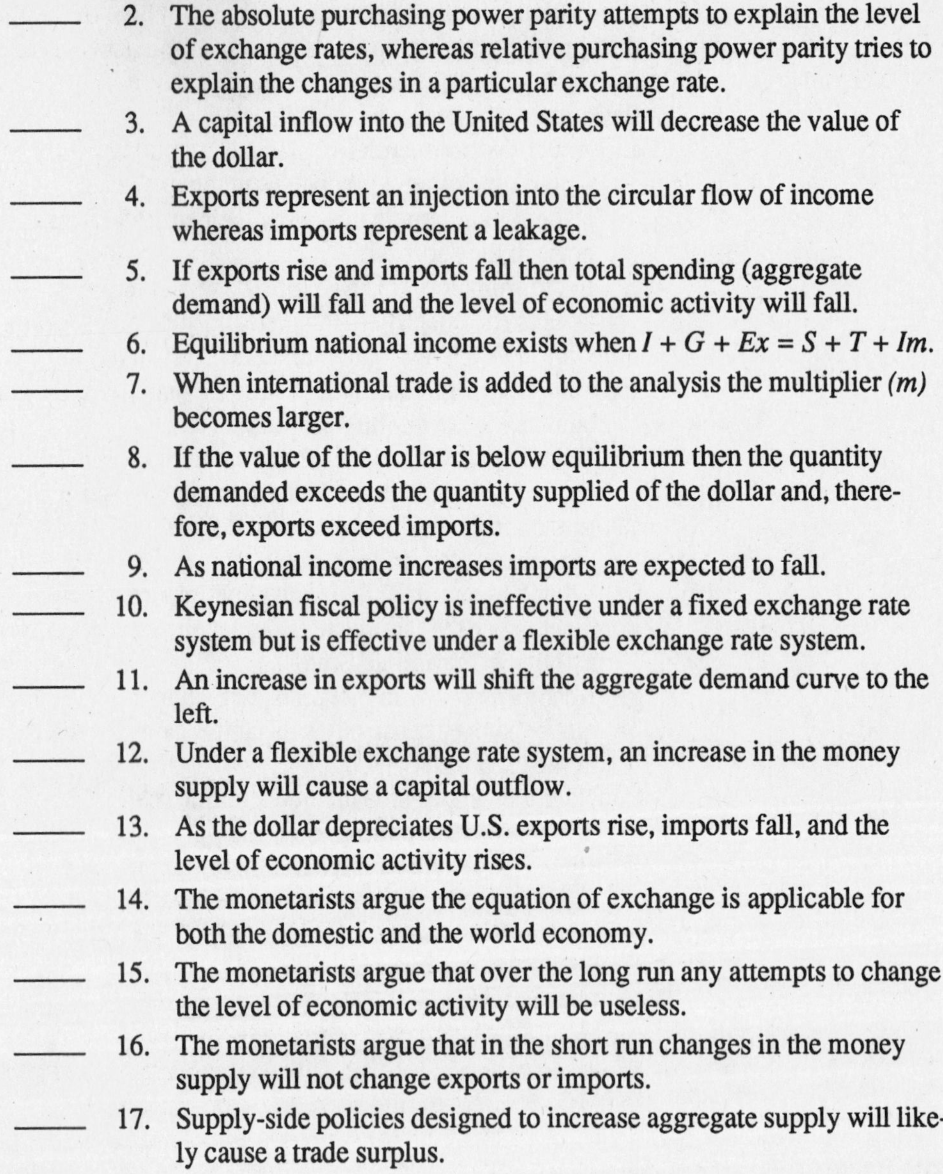

____ 2. The absolute purchasing power parity attempts to explain the level of exchange rates, whereas relative purchasing power parity tries to explain the changes in a particular exchange rate.

____ 3. A capital inflow into the United States will decrease the value of the dollar.

____ 4. Exports represent an injection into the circular flow of income whereas imports represent a leakage.

____ 5. If exports rise and imports fall then total spending (aggregate demand) will fall and the level of economic activity will fall.

____ 6. Equilibrium national income exists when $I + G + Ex = S + T + Im$.

____ 7. When international trade is added to the analysis the multiplier (m) becomes larger.

____ 8. If the value of the dollar is below equilibrium then the quantity demanded exceeds the quantity supplied of the dollar and, therefore, exports exceed imports.

____ 9. As national income increases imports are expected to fall.

____ 10. Keynesian fiscal policy is ineffective under a fixed exchange rate system but is effective under a flexible exchange rate system.

____ 11. An increase in exports will shift the aggregate demand curve to the left.

____ 12. Under a flexible exchange rate system, an increase in the money supply will cause a capital outflow.

____ 13. As the dollar depreciates U.S. exports rise, imports fall, and the level of economic activity rises.

____ 14. The monetarists argue the equation of exchange is applicable for both the domestic and the world economy.

____ 15. The monetarists argue that over the long run any attempts to change the level of economic activity will be useless.

____ 16. The monetarists argue that in the short run changes in the money supply will not change exports or imports.

____ 17. Supply-side policies designed to increase aggregate supply will likely cause a trade surplus.

Multiple Choice *Choose the one best answer for each item.*

_____ 1. Which of the following statements is correct with respect to the Keynesian perspective of macroeconomics and international trade?
   a. An increase in imports will increase national income.
   b. An increase in exports will increase national income.
   c. Imports are an injection into the circular flow of national income whereas exports are a leakage.
   d. Equilibrium national income can be defined to exist when $S + T + Ex = I + G + Im$.
   e. Exports must equal imports in order to have an equilibrium national income level.

_____ 2. Which of the following is a leakage from the circular flow of income?
   a. Consumption spending
   b. Taxes
   c. Exports
   d. Government expenditures
   e. Investment spending

_____ 3. Aggregate demand (or total spending) will increase if
   a. imports fall.
   b. exports fall.
   c. government expenditures fall and taxes rise.
   d. total leakages increase while total injections remain the same.
   e. a trade deficit increases.

_____ 4. Which of the following could cause a capital inflow?
   a. An increase in the government's budget deficit.
   b. An increase in domestic interest rates.
   c. A reduction in tax rates.
   d. A reduction in the domestic money stock.
   e. All of the above could cause a capital inflow.

_____ 5. From the Keynesian perspective, an increase in unemployment in the United States would most likely be caused by
   a. a greater U.S. balance of payments surplus.
   b. a greater U.S. balance of payments deficit.
   c. a depreciation of the dollar.
   d. a capital outflow.
   e. total injections exceeding total leakages.

_____ 6. A U.S. trade deficit will most likely be caused by
   a. a depreciation of the dollar.
   b. a capital inflow into the United States.

c. a decline in the U.S. government's budget deficit.
d. an increase in the U.S. money stock.
e. any of the above.

_____ 7. When international trade is taken into consideration, the multiplier effect of a change in total spending (or aggregate demand) on national income will now be
a. zero.
b. larger because as income rises imports fall.
c. larger because as income rises imports rise.
d. smaller because as income rises imports fall.
e. smaller because as income rises imports rise.

_____ 8. If the dollar appreciates then
a. the relative price of American exports to foreigners will rise and the relative price of imports to Americans falls.
b. the United States will experience a balance of payments deficit.
c. aggregate demand falls.
d. the level of national income falls and unemployment rises.
e. all of the above will be true.

_____ 9. From a Keynesian perspective, under a fixed exchange rate system
a. an exogenous increase in exports will cause a decrease in imports over time.
b. fiscal policy is effective in changing national income but monetary policy is not.
c. fiscal and monetary policies are effective in changing the level of national income.
d. an increase in the domestic supply of the dollar will force the U.S. government to sell dollars in the international exchange rate market in order to maintain the fixed exchange rate.
e. an increase in government expenditures will cause exports to fall and imports to rise.

_____ 10. From a Keynesian perspective, under a flexible exchange rate system,
a. a capital inflow will appreciate the dollar creating a trade deficit.
b. a capital inflow will depreciate the dollar creating a trade surplus.
c. a capital outflow will appreciate the dollar creating a trade surplus.

d. a capital outflow will depreciate the dollar creating a trade deficit.
e. none of the above will occur.

_____ 11. An increase in a trade surplus means
a. imports are rising or exports are falling.
b. aggregate demand will rise.
c. national income will fall.
d. the value of the currency must have appreciated.
e. all of the above.

_____ 12. According to the monetarist, the most fundamental variable effecting exports and imports is
a. the price levels in different countries.
b. the exchange rates.
c. aggregate demand.
d. aggregate supply.
e. the growth rate in the domestic money supply.

_____ 13. According to the monetarists, in a world economy in which gold constitutes the international currency then
a. the equation of exchange no longer holds for the world economy as it does for the domestic economy.
b. if the quantity demanded exceeds the quantity supplied in some nation, that nation will experience gold flowing out.
c. if the quantity demanded falls short of the quantity supplied in some nation, that nation will experience gold flowing in.
d. as the world supply of gold increases the world price level rises.
e. as the world supply of gold increases the world price level falls.

_____ 14. According to the theory of relative purchasing power parity, if the rate of inflation in the United States is 8 percent and the rate of inflation in Japan is 3 percent then
a. the dollar will appreciate 11 percent.
b. the dollar will appreciate 5 percent.
c. the dollar will depreciate 5 percent.
d. the U.S. will experience an increase in imports and a decrease in exports.
e. none of the above will occur.

_____ 15. According to the monetarists which of the following statements is true?
a. Movements in exchange rates are determined by the demand and supply of money.

b. The exchange rate will depreciate if the quantity of money supplied exceeds the quantity of money demanded.
c. Attempting to manipulate the domestic national income level by changing exchange rates may have some short-run effects but no long-run effects.
d. Any changes in the domestic or international sectors of an economy are a monetary phenomenon.
e. All of the above are true.

_____ 16. Supply-side theory and international trade theory both focus on
a. aggregate demand.
b. aggregate supply.
c. growth rates in the money stock.
d. fiscal policy.
e. expectations.

_____ 17. Supply-side policy is likely to be more effective if
a. consumers buy more imports as national income expands.
b. producers import more raw materials as national income expands.
c. higher after-tax returns from investment did not create a capital inflow and the consequent increase in the value of the dollar.
d. it increases marginal tax rates.
e. all of the above.

_____ 18. All supply-side theorists agree that
a. a return to the gold standard would be helpful.
b. a reduction in marginal tax rates would decrease aggregate supply.
c. an increase in government regulation would increase aggregate supply.
d. an increase in productivity due to lower taxes and less government regulation would lower a trade deficit over time.
e. aggregate demand management is more effective in controlling the economy than aggregate supply management.

Discussion Questions

1. How would the rational expectations macroeconomic school of thought incorporate international trade into their theory of macroeconomics? *(KQ1, 2, 3)*

2. Why has the United States been incurring such large and unprecedented balance of payments deficits throughout the 1980s? *(KQ1, 2, 3)*
3. Which model of the macroeconomy has U.S. trade policy been based on in recent years? *(KQ1, 2, 3)*
4. What types of trade policies would the monetarists recommend? *(KQ2)*
5. Which school of macroeconomic thought would most likely recommend a fixed exchange rate system? A flexible exchange rate system? *(KQ1, 2, 3)*
6. What are the similarities between supply-side theory and international trade theory? *(KQ3)*
7. If the simple Keynesian multiplier *(m)* is equal to the reciprocal of the marginal propensity to save then what would a more sophisticated multiplier that takes into account taxes and imports be equal to? *(KQ1)*
8. How can an increase in a nation's productivity reduce its trade deficit? *(KQ3)*
9. Are there any parallels between the large increases in the U.S. government's budget deficit and the U.S. trade deficit? *(KQ3)*

Answers

Problems and Applications

1. a. The level of total spending (aggregate demand; total planned expenditures).
   b. $TS = C + I + G + Ex - Im$.
   c. Exports are added to domestic total spending because exports represent foreigner demand (spending) on our domestic output. Imports are subtracted from the domestic total spending level because imports represent spending abroad which could have potentially been undertaken domestically.
   d. Equilibrium in the macroeconomy is established when total spending $(= C + I + G + Ex - Im)$ is just sufficient to clear total output (Y) off the market. Therefore, equilibrium exists when $Y = C + I + G + Ex - Im$.
   e. An increase in the value of the dollar means that greater quantities of a foreign currency will be required to purchase a single dollar. Therefore the relative price of U.S. exports to foreigners

will rise and the United States will export less. On the other hand, as the dollar appreciates, then fewer dollars are required to buy a single unit of a foreign currency. Therefore, the relative price of foreign products to Americans is lower. The United States will import more. In sum, as the dollar appreciates U.S. exports fall while U.S. imports rise. This creates a movement in the direction of a U.S. balance of payments deficit. If the United States is already experiencing a trade deficit it will get larger.

f. Total spending will fall (because $TS + C + I + G + Ex - Im$). As total spending falls the economy will experience an unplanned accumulation of inventories, a cutback in production, an increase in unemployment, a decline in national income, and the decline in income will cause a further decline in total spending, and so on. This process continues until total spending is once again just sufficient to clear total output off the market. Note there will be a multiple contraction in output and income greater than the initial decline in total spending because of the multiplier effect.

   A decline in total spending is reflected as a leftward shift of the aggregate demand curve in the aggregate demand-aggregate supply model. This creates a lower equilibrium income (output) level and a lower general price level.

g. Yes.

2. Imports are expected to rise as income expands for two reasons. First, because as domestic producers seek to satisfy the greater demand for their output they will import more raw materials. Second, with rising incomes, consumers will want to supplement their domestic purchases with goods and services from foreign countries. The result of rising imports as income expands means that the multiplier effect of an increase in total spending (from whatever source) on the income level will be smaller. Simply put, just like savings and taxes (the other leakages from the circular flow of income), imports also drain away purchases that would otherwise be realized by domestic producers. Therefore, we can conclude that the multiplier is smaller when international trade is taken into consideration.

3. a. Total leakages consist of savings *(S)* plus taxes *(T)* plus imports *(Im)*. Mathematically, total leakages = $S + I + Im$.

b. Total injections consist of investment spending *(I)* plus government spending *(G)* plus exports *(Ex)*. Mathematically, total injections = $I + G + Ex$.

c. Equilibrium exists when the income level is such that total leakages from the circular flow of income are just matched by an equal amount of total injections. Mathematically equilibrium in the macroeconomy exists when: $S + T + Im = I + G + Ex$.

d. No. What is necessary is that *total* leakages equal *total* injections.

e. This will cause a movement in the direction of a balance of payments surplus. Total injections will now exceed total leakages and the national income level will expand.

f. Yes.

4. a. Exports will fall, imports will rise. A movement in the direction of a balance of payments deficit. Because total spending falls (or total leakages now exceed total injections) then the national income level will fall.

b. Exports will rise, imports will fall. A movement in the direction of a balance of payments surplus. An increase in national income.

5. a. It will cause an increase in the demand for the dollar. This is because foreigners must first buy dollars in order to purchase goods from American producers. (*Note:* The demand for the dollar represents the demand for U.S. exports).

b. Like any other commodity if demand rises its value rises. The value of the dollar increases — it appreciates.

c. U.S. imports will rise. This is because as the value of the dollar increases (appreciates) the relative price of imported products to Americans falls enticing Americans to buy more imports.

d. Yes. (Note that we use the term "offsetting" because an increase in exports alone would increase total spending and the income level. However, an accompanying increase in imports will decrease total spending and the income level.)

6. a. Yes. Because a change in government spending or taxes will not have an offsetting effect on exports and imports. Exports and imports will not change because the exchange rate is indeed fixed — it will not change.

b. No. Suppose the money stock is increased and domestic interest rates fall. Because interest rates are relatively more attractive abroad, investors will remove their funds from the United

States and place them abroad. There will be a capital (money) outflow, but, first, dollars must be exchanged for foreign currencies. This causes an increase in the supply of dollars (an increase in the demand for foreign currencies) decreasing the value of the dollar. However, the exchange rate under a fixed exchange rate system is not allowed to fall. Therefore, the government will have to buy back the dollars it initially intended to add to the domestic money supply.

7. a. No. Suppose a fiscal deficit is incurred. The government deficit will be financed by borrowing (issuing more U.S. government debt) which increases U.S. interest rates. This, in turn, causes a capital (money) inflow. That is, foreigners will want to invest in the United States where interest rates are relatively higher. But, first, these foreigners must buy dollars. This increases the demand for dollars increasing the value of the dollar. As the dollar appreciates exports fall, imports rise, offsetting the initial increase in total spending caused by deficit spending. The economy may well be unaffected (except for resource reallocative effects).
   b. Yes. Suppose the money supply is increased and interest rates fall. The value of the dollar falls because of capital outflows ("Problems and Applications" question 6b above). As it falls (and it is allowed to fall under a flexible exchange rate system) exports rise, imports fall and this further stimulates total spending and the income level in the domestic economy.
8. a. 3 percent.
   b. U.S. exports rise and imports fall initially (in the short run).
   c. When U.S. exports rise the quantity demanded for dollars in international exchange rate markets has to rise. This is because foreigners (for example, the Japanese) must purchase more dollars first in order to purchase a greater quantity of products from the United States (our exports). (*Note:* The demand for the dollar really represents U.S. exports.)

   When U.S. imports fall the quantity supplied of dollars in international exchange rate markets has to fall. One must understand that in order for Americans to purchase imported products they must first purchase the foreign currency associated with the imported product. In order to buy foreign currencies, dollars are supplied in exchange rate markets. Therefore, if fewer products are imported into the United States then a smaller quantity of dollars are supplied in exchange rate markets. (*Note:* The supply of dollars really represents U.S. imports).

The quantity demanded of dollars will exceed the quantity supplied of dollars whenever the dollar depreciates. There will be a shortage of dollars.

d. When exports rise and imports fall the total spending (or aggregate demand) level rises causing national income to rise and unemployment to fall.

e. The dollar will increase in value. It will appreciate.

f. U.S. exports will fall and imports will rise causing total spending and therefore national income to fall (unemployment to rise).

g. No. The short-run gains (rising exports, falling imports, a rising total spending and national income level, and falling unemployment level) will be offset by long-run corrections in the exchange rate markets (the shortage of dollars increases the value of the dollar pushing exports back down and imports back up causing total spending to fall, returning national income and unemployment to their original levels).

9. a. Reduce marginal tax rates and eliminate inefficient government regulations.

b. A tax rate cut is expected to increase imports and decrease exports creating a U.S. balance of payments deficit. This will occur for two major reasons. First, greater after-tax returns on investment in the U.S. will encourage more foreigners to invest in the U.S. There will be a capital inflow into the United States. In order to do so they must first buy dollars. This increases the demand for the dollar pushing up its value. Therefore, an appreciated dollar will stimulate imports but curtail exports. Second, lower tax rates should increase national income. As income rises Americans will buy more imports.

c. A trade deficit will render supply-side policy less effective because a trade deficit decreases total spending and therefore the national income level.

True-False

1. T 2. T
3. F: A capital inflow into the United States will increase the value of the dollar.
4. T
5. F: If exports rise and imports fall then total spending (aggregate demand) will rise and the level of economic activity will rise.
6. T
7. F: When international trade is added to the analysis the multiplier *(m)* becomes smaller.
8. T
9. F: As national income increases imports are expected to rise.
10. F: Keynesian fiscal policy is effective under a fixed exchange rate system but is ineffective under a flexible exchange rate system.
11. F: An increase in exports will shift the aggregate demand curve to the right.
12. T 13. T 14. T 15. T
16. F: The monetarists argue that in the short run changes in the money supply will change exports and imports but not in the long run.
17. F: Supply-side policies designed to increase aggregate supply will likely cause a trade deficit.

Multiple Choice

1. b *(KQ1)*	2. b *(KQ1)*	3. a *(KQ1)*
4. e *(KQ1, 2, 3)*	5. *b (KQ1)*	6. b *(KQ1)*
7. e *(KQ1, 3)*	8. e *(KQ1)*	9. b *(KQ1)*
10. a *(KQ1)*	11. b *(KQ1)*	12. e *(KQ2)*
13. d *(KQ2)*	14. c *(KQ2)*	15. e *(KQ2)*
16. b *(KQ3)*	17. c *(KQ3)*	18. d *(KQ3)*

CHAPTER 37

Comparative Economic Systems

Chapter Summary

Present-day economic systems, as well as those of times past, exist on a spectrum ranging from strong government control to nearly unbridled free enterprise. This chapter looks at some of the economic systems in which government control and free enterprise blend in the modern world. Although there are important differences among the world's various economies, there are also significant similarities.

Key Question 1: What are the principal economic systems?

The Industrial Revolution brought production out of the home and into factories, where large amounts of capital were required to finance large-scale production. A new economic system, called capitalism, began to emerge. Capitalism is based on private property and competition through free enterprise. It is the philosophical basis for the free market system that exists today in the United States and elsewhere. However, in its pure form, it has never enjoyed unqualified support anywhere. Furthermore, the market capitalism in America during the nineteenth century has given rise to mixed capitalism in America today. Two other principal economic systems besides market and mixed capitalism are planned socialism and market socialism. The principal division in the world, however, is between capitalism and socialism.

Key Question 2: What is the basis of the Marxian critique of capitalism?

One of the most popular critics of capitalism was the German economist Karl Marx. Writing toward the end of the nineteenth century, Marx did not favor a return to the traditional economy. He believed instead that capitalism was a traditional phase with a fatal weakness — the unemployment created by business cycles. Marx, like Hegel, believed that history could be viewed as a series of events in which a thesis (or idea) is pitted against an antithesis (or contrasting idea) to form a synthesis, or new idea. This process, as Marx interpreted it, is called "dialectical materialism." Marx saw specific social classes taking on the roles of the opposing forces in the dialectical process. Workers (the proletariat) would be pitted against bourgeois capitalists. Marx argued that only the workers created value. The capitalists were simply exploiters of the workers. As Marx saw it, capitalism would continue to increase the "reserve army of the unemployed." (He failed to see that workers would benefit from the improved productivity created by new equipment purchased by capitalists over time.) So many workers would be replaced by machines (and therefore the capitalists would absorb an even greater share of national income) that eventually the workers would rise up and overthrow the system. What would emerge would be communism, a classless society governed by workers. In this economic system, virtually all means of production would be owned and controlled by the state. Production and distribution would be efficient because they would be based on the principle of "from each according to his ability, to each according to his need."

Marx may have been wrong about the threat capital posed to labor, and naive to believe that a totally classless society was possible, but his description of a communistic utopian state has provided many revolutionaries with hope and inspiration. The real-world outcome of revolutions inspired by followers of Marx, however, has been far from what Marx himself envisioned.

Key Question 3: How does Soviet Communism work?

One of these revolutions occurred in Russia in October 1917, led by Lenin and his Bolsheviks. During his short reign of power, economic difficulties forced Lenin to grant greater freedom to farmers and businessmen in an attempt to restore the economy. In 1928, Stalin came to power and rejected Lenin's policies. His overriding goal was the rapid industrialization of the Russian economy through national economic planning. To approach this goal, Stalin set up Gosplan, the Soviet central planning agency. Five-year plans were instituted and enforced by the Soviet police. Private farms were abolished, replaced by huge collectives. Food was earmarked primarily for workers in urban areas to support their construction and factory work. Farmers were forced to accept subsistence wages. Stalin's desire for higher productivity on the farm backfired as many farmers retaliated by destroying their produce. Stalin responded by shooting several thousand of them.

Stalin's policies did not last, but production problems have continued to plague the Soviet economy. In recent years, some of the stringent rules and production quotas have been replaced with free market incentives in an attempt to increase productivity. However, Marx's classless Communist society has not yet emerged in the Soviet Union. The ruling class has privileges that the workers do not have.

Between the planned socialist economy of the Soviet Union and the market system of the United States lies market socialism. Market socialism involves less government control of the economy than planned socialism. But all socialist governments actually get involved in the production of goods and services. The idea is to prevent "unearned" capitalist profits, eliminate the exploitation of labor by improving working conditions, and promote a more equitable distribution of income.

Key Question 4: What elements of democratic socialism can be found in mixed capitalist economies?

Many governments in Western Europe own and operate enterprises in their mixed capitalist economies. Indeed, even certain limited forms of socialism exist in the United States, examples of which are the postal system, public schools, and railroads like Amtrak. In Europe, however, socialism plays a much larger role. Although socialization of industry was initially intended to prevent exploitation of workers and to distribute unearned profits, many governments have come to control companies because they were failing. This aspect of socialism may contribute to a continued inefficient use of resources or the production of products consumers are no longer pleased with. Furthermore, often the profit motive is replaced by political motives, which can cause mismanagement and greater problems in the long run. Socialist economies do attempt to realize goals beneficial to the general public by using economic planning, but some economists question the effectiveness of this planning.

Review Terms and Concepts

Exports
Imports
Balance of payments deficit
Balance of payments surplus
Monopoly power
Inflation

New Terms and Concepts

Economic System
Mercantilism
Capitalism
Communism
National economic planning
Democratic socialism (or, simply, socialism)
Market capitalism
Mixed capitalism
Planned socialism
Market socialism
Dialectical materialism

Completion

a mixture of	All modern economies are characterized by ____________________
and	(either/a mixture of) government control ______________ (and/or)
	free enterprise.
	Market capitalism means resources are owned by
private individuals	________________________ (government/private individuals) and
markets	resource allocation is determined by __________________ (markets/
	government). Mixed capitalism means resources are predominantly
private individuals	owned by __________________________ (government/private
	individuals) and resources are predominantly allocated by
markets	_______________ (markets/government). The difference between
	market and mixed capitalism is that government is more heavily involved
mixed	in _______________ (market/mixed) capitalism. The real difference
	between planned socialism and market socialism is that government
planned	plans determine resource allocation in ___________________
market	(planned/market) socialism but not __________________ (planned/
	market) socialism.
has never enjoyed	Capitalism in its pure form __________________________ (has
	never enjoyed/enjoys) unqualified support. One of the most popular
Marx	critics of capitalism was _______________ (Stalin/Marx). He wrote
communism	about the downfall of capitalism and the birth of _______________
	(socialism/communism). He believed that capitalism would cause un-
rise	employment to _____________ (rise/fall) over time as workers were
overlooked	replaced by machines. Marx ______________ (overlooked/believed)
	the fact that productivity of workers could be enhanced by the use of
	more capital. Marx also argued that workers would be paid a

subsistence	____________________ (handsome/subsistence) wage. Over time there
workers	would be a redistribution of income away from ____________________
capitalists	(capitalists/workers) to ____________________ (capitalists/workers).
	Eventually, workers would overthrow capitalism and replace it with a
	classless society governed by workers. This system is known as
communism	____________________ (socialism/communism). The type of system
has never existed	envisioned by Marx ____________________ (does exist
	/has never existed).
much different from	The Soviet form of communism is ____________________
	(very similar to/much different from) that conceived by Marx.
1917	The Soviet revolution took place in _______________ (1937/1917). It
Lenin	was led by _______________ (Lenin/Stalin), who came to believe that
necessary	greater freedom in production and distribution was _______________
	(necessary/unnecessary) for a more productive economy. When Lenin
Stalin	lost control in 1928, _______________ (Trotsky/Stalin) took his place.
disagreed with	He ____________________ (agreed with/disagreed with) Lenin's
	philosophy of granting greater freedom to provide incentives for greater
Gosplan	productivity and established the ____________________ (Gosplan/kulak)
five-year	to institute _______________ (five-year/ten-year) national production
	plans. Stalin believed that national economic planning was necessary.
decreased	His economic plans and production quotas ____________________
	(increased/decreased) incentives. The incentive problems of the Soviet
still	Union _______________ (still/no longer) exist. Free market incentives
adopted	have been ____________________ (adopted/abolished) in recent years.
has not yet	Marx's classless society ____________________ (has/has not yet)
	emerged in the Soviet Union.

Another form of political economy is socialism. It relies more heavily on government control than does ____________________ (capitalism/communism). Under socialism, government actually owns and operates some industries. The main goal of socialism is to prevent ____________________ (profits/unearned profits) and the ____________________ (one of capital/exploitation of workers). It has also been used to control companies that were ____________________ (earning large profits/losing money). This, however, usually creates ____________________ (greater/less) efficiency in the production of these goods and services. Also, many decisions have become more ____________________ (business/politically) oriented, which has tended to create ____________________ (greater efficiency/many problems) in the long run.

Socialist economies also attempt to realize common goals through economic planning. Many economists ____________________ (question whether/agree that) this is efficient. Much evidence suggests that it ____________________ (is/is not).

capitalism
unearned profits
exploitation of workers
losing money
less
politically
many problems
question whether
is not

Problems and Applications

1. What did Karl Marx mean by "dialectical materialism"?
2. What is the basic difference between communism and socialism?
3. What are the two primary objectives of socialism?

True-False

For each item, determine whether the statement is basically true or false. If the statement is false, rewrite it so it is a true statement.

_____ 1. Market capitalism is characterized by private ownership of resources and market determination over resource allocation.

_____ 2. Market capitalism characterizes the modern American economy.

______ 3. Many advocates of socialism, either market or planned, believe that the authoritarian political system of the Soviet Union does not have to accompany a socialist economy.

______ 4. Marx argued that only labor created value.

______ 5. Marx felt that the fundamental problems with capitalism were its inability to employ workers and the income inequalities it created.

______ 6. Communism is any attempt by government to gain ownership of the private means of production.

______ 7. Communism as conceived by Marx exists in the Soviet Union.

______ 8. Stalin believed that more centralized planning was necessary to modernize the Soviet Union.

______ 9. National economic planning is undertaken only by communist regimes.

______ 10. One of the primary objectives of socialism is a more equitable distribution of income.

______ 11. One of the effects of nationalization is an increases politicization of the production process.

______ 12. The public school system in the United States could be considered a form of socialism.

______ 13. All forms of government have elements of both free enterprise and government control of economic affairs.

Multiple Choice *Choose the one best answer for each item.*

______ 1. Democratic socialism is a system of economic organization that
  a. can only be acquired by a violent revolution.
  b. is designed to cause a more equitable distribution of income.
  c. is designed to inhibit government influence.
  d. is uncommon in capitalist nations.
  e. increases the wealth of a few at the expense of the general public.

______ 2. Capitalism in its pure form
  a. does not exist and has never existed.
  b. sows the seeds of its own destruction, according to Stalin.
  c. is based on public ownership of essential raw materials.
  d. once existed in the United States.
  e. discourages competition.

_____ 3. Communism as conceived by Marx
 a. would precede capitalism in the dialectical process.
 b. is a classless society governed by workers.
 c. sows the seeds of its own destruction.
 d. would be a government ruled by a few knowledgeable individuals with workers' best interests in mind.
 e. would rely heavily on the concept of property.

_____ 4. Adam Smith
 a. was a socialist.
 b. was overthrown by Lenin as the leader of Russia in 1918.
 c. is known for his use of the term "invisible hand."
 d. argued in favor of communism.
 e. wrote about the labor theory of value.

_____ 5. National economic planning
 a. is done by the Gosplan in the Soviet Union.
 b. is designed to redistribute income.
 c. always results in greater economic efficiency.
 d. is not undertaken in socialist countries.
 e. is always communistic.

_____ 6. Which of the following countries best exemplifies market socialism?
 a. United States
 b. Soviet Union
 c. Japan
 d. Norway
 e. Yugoslavia

_____ 7. To Marx the labor theory of value meant
 a. from each according to his ability, to each according to his need.
 b. that the world's output was rigidly fixed and could not increase.
 c. that workers' wages would rise if greater amounts of capital were used in the production process.
 d. that only labor created value.
 e. all of the above.

Discussion Questions

1. If Marx believed that the process of "dialectical materialism" was an ongoing force throughout history, why did he argue that it would stop with the development of communism? *(KQ2)*

2. Do you think a true communist system as conceived by Marx could ever exist? Why or why not? *(KQ2, 3)*
3. What are the differences between the incentives in the Soviet Union and in the United States? *(KQ3)*
4. How could one argue that Marx was wrong in concluding that capitalism sows the seeds of its own destruction? Has the American government done anything to prevent these "seeds" from growing? If so, what? *(KQ2)*

Answers

Problems and Applications

1. A dialectical process is one in which a thesis (or existing idea) is confronted by an antithesis (a conflicting idea) and out of the conflict emerges a synthesis (a consensus of thought consisting partly of the thesis and partly the antithesis). Marx applied this idea of Hegel's to specific social classes, which he saw as the opposing forces in the dialectical process. Thus the dialectical process had a distinctly economic, or material, base. Hence, "dialectical materialism."
2. There is much debate over the differences between communism and socialism. Most debates center around the definitions of the terms. However, in describing the differences between communism and socialism as they now exist in nations around the world, most Westerners would argue that socialism is collective ownership through democratic means, while communism is not democratic.
3. First, to prevent unearned profits from being earned — or at least to redistribute them more equitably. Second, to ensure that workers are not exploited, that their work environment is adequate.

True-False

1. T
2. F: Mixed capitalism characterizes the modern American economy.
3. T 4. T 5. T
6. F: Communism is an economic system in which virtually all the means of production are owned and controlled by the state.

7. F: Communism as conceived by Marx does not exist in the Soviet Union.
8. T
9. F: National economic planning is undertaken by many nations, not just communist regimes.

10. T 11. T 12. T 13. T

Multiple Choice

1. b *(KQ4)* 2. a *(KQ1)* 3. b *(KQ2, 3)*
4. c *(KQ1)* 5. a *(KQ3, 4)* 6. e *(KQ1)*
7. d *(KQ2)*

CHAPTER 38

Economic Growth and Development

Chapter Summary

Key Question 1: What is the difference between economic growth and economic development?

This chapter examines why countries vary in their level of economic growth and development. Economic growth is the expansion of a nation's capacity to produce the products its people want. Economic development is the enhancement of a nation's capacity to produce through the creation of new kinds of output. (The distinction is similar to the differences between growth and development in human beings.) An economy can have economic growth without economic development, but not vice versa.

There are number of prerequisites for economic growth and development. These include a sufficient quantity and quality of labor, capital, and natural resources. A sufficiently high level of technology and favorable sociocultural factors are also required. The more developed countries have at least several of these factors present.

Key Question 2: What are some important differences between less developed countries and developed countries?

Three-fourths of the world's population lives in less developed countries. Economic growth is particularly important for these countries because it increases the quantity of goods and services available, it expands the supply of resources available for capital formation, and it gives government the resources it needs to discharge its social responsibilities. Characteristics common to all these countries include a relatively low per capita income and an inequitable distribution of income. Also, economic growth is more difficult for countries with large populations because most their productive capacities are exhausted just by making enough consumer products to feed and clothe their people. This means that very few resources can be devoted to the production of the capital products necessary for economic growth. Furthermore, economic growth is also made more difficult because both social overhead capital (the structure and equipment required to support and develop human resources) and physical capital (directly productive capital) require savings, but because incomes are low, savings are low. Another one of the most fundamental characteristics of the less developed countries is a high percentage of the population employed in agriculture. Finally, technological development may be hindered by the customs of diverse cultures.

Key Question 3: How can a less developed country become a developed country?

There are several theories about the conditions necessary for economic development. The classical theory emphasized technological development, which depended on the accumulation of capital and ultimately on profits. The Marxist theory agreed, but added that eventually capitalism would collapse, giving way to the new communist society.

Rostow's takeoff theory is the most prominent of recent theories on economic development. According to Rostow, nations pass through five stages. First, there is the traditional society, in which most resources are concentrated in agriculture. Second, there must be prerequisites for takeoff. For this to occur, some members of society must abandon their fatalistic outlook on life. Social respect must come to depend on economic achievement rather than on inherited status. And a leading industry must propel the takeoff. Third, there is the takeoff stage. This stage may last twenty to thirty years. Economic and social change occurs quite rapidly in this stage, fueled by an increase in the percentage of gross national product that is saved and invested. The fourth stage in development is the drive to maturity. This stage lasts about sixty years and is characterized by the acquisition of the most advanced technology available. The final stage is the stage of mass consumption. During this stage, most of the population is able to attain a high standard of living.

Rostow's theory has been criticized because it does not fit historical fact very closely. The theory is also vague on what causes growth in each stage, and what distinguishes one stage from the next.

Another theory of economic development is the big push theory, which argues that a large infusion of investment, primarily from foreign sources, will stimulate growth. The dependency theory argues that nations become so dependent on their mother countries that economic development is hampered.

Key Question 4: What are the economic problems faced by less developed countries?

There are several obstacles to economic development. First, overpopulation creates problems because of urbanization and food shortages. Second, a lack of an infrastructure such as schools, roads, and other facilities discourages both economic and social development. Third, low savings rates mean low levels of investment and low rates of capital accumulation, which hinders economic development. Fourth, the less developed countries tend to export primarily raw materials and agricultural products. Some countries rely very heavily on just one product for export revenues, increasing their vulnerability to changes in economic activity. Finally, sociocultural factors can inhibit economic development if individuals and groups are unwilling to yield to change.

Key Question 5: How can less developed countries solve their economic problems?

There are no easy remedies for economic underdevelopment. Overpopulation can be very difficult to deal with. If tariffs and quotas could be reduced by developed nations, the income of the less developed nations might increase. Foreign aid may also help. There are numerous international agencies as well as individual nations that provide foreign aid. Military aid may also be considered a form of foreign aid. It is helpful, however, only if it diverts the country's defense funds to more productive uses. Furthermore, if aid is used for consumption rather than investment, it will generate few lasting economic benefits. There may be other solutions to economic development, which may or may not incorporate industrialization. But generally, a greater reliance on market incentives in the allocation of scarce resources is recommended.

Review Terms and Concepts

Production possibilities
Capital
Imports
Gross National Product
Investment
Consumer products
Exports
Technology
Saving
Diminishing returns

New Terms and Concepts

Economic growth
Economic development
Social overhead capital
Technological dualism
Foreign aid

Completion

different from — Economic growth is ____________________ (the same as/different from) economic development. It is possible to have economic

growth — ______________ (growth/development) without economic

development — ___________________ (growth/development) but not the other way

a number of	around. There are ____________________ (a number of/only two)
	prerequisites for economic growth and development.
low	Less developed countries are characterized by a __________ (low/
inequitable	high) per capita income and a more ________________ (equitable/
	inequitable) distribution of income. The problems of less developed
overpopulation	economics stem from ____________________ (overpopulation/
low	underpopulation). Another problem is __________ (low/high) rates of
low, low	savings. This means _________ (low/high) investment and ________
	(low/high) capital accumulation, which translates into low rates of
growth	economic ____________ (growth/development). Another problem is
high	that less developed countries have a _________ (high/low) percentage
	of the population employed in agriculture.
too little	There are also problems with _____________ (too little/too much)
few	infrastructure, exporting too _________ (many/few) kinds of products
	and raw materials, and the inhibiting of economic development by
	sociocultural factors.
	There are several theories about the conditions necessary for economic
	development. The classical and Marxist theories emphasize
technological advances	____________ (technological advances/low rates of savings).
	Rostow's theory analyzes the five stages of growth, from the
traditional	____________ (traditional/mass consumption) society to the
mass consumption	____________ (traditional/mass consumption) society.

Problems and Applications

1. Determine whether each of the following items is associated with a high or a low level of economic growth and development.
   a. High quantity and quality of labor
   b. Overpopulation
   c. High savings rate

d. Inequitable distribution of income
e. Low rate of capital formation
f. High level of technology
g. Low per capita GNP
h. High percentage of the population employed in agriculture
i. High profit levels
j. Technological dualism
k. Traditional society
l. Low productivity
m. Infrastructure in place
n. Limited range of exports
o. Limited social roles of women
p. Military aid that does not release funds for the development of an infrastructure

True-False

For each item, determine whether the statement is basically true or false. If the statement is false, then rewrite it so it is a true statement.

____ 1. Foreign aid is the transfer of income from rich nations to poor nations with the goal of providing them with military security.

____ 2. Economic growth is the expansion of a nation's capacity to produce the goods and services its people want.

____ 3. A high per capita GNP is associated with high ratios of economic growth and development.

____ 4. A sufficient quantity and quality of labor does not guarantee growth and development.

____ 5. An inequitable distribution of income is associated with high rates of economic growth.

____ 6. One of the fundamental characteristics of less developed countries is that a low percentage of the population is employed in agriculture.

____ 7. The classical theory of development saw technological progress as the key to development.

____ 8. Rostow's takeoff theory divides growth into five stages, from the early mass consumption society to the traditional society.

____ 9. Marxist theory divides growth into five stages.

Multiple Choice *Choose the one best answer for each item.*

____ 1. Economic development is
a. the expansion of a nation's capacity to produce the goods and services its people want.
b. the enhancement of a nation's capacity to produce through the creation of new kinds of output.
c. associated with strict social roles for women.
d. successful only in traditional economies.
e. limited to countries that have a large population.

____ 2. Economic growth is most likely a result of
a. an inequitable distribution of income.
b. overpopulation.
c. technological dualism.
d. high savings rates.
e. economic development.

____ 3. Low rate of savings can cause
a. low rates of economic growth.
b. low rate of economic development.
c. low capital accumulation.
d. low income.
e. all of the above.

____ 4. Which stage in Rostow's growth theory lasts about sixty years?
a. The traditional society
b. Prerequisites for takeoff
c. Takeoff
d. The drive to maturity
e. Mass consumption

____ 5. Remedies for economic problems of less developed economies include
a. increased population growth.
b. lower rates of savings.
c. greater reliance on market incentives.
d. less foreign aid.
e. exporting fewer products.

____ 6. The big push theory of economic development explains economic development as stemming from
a. a country's dependence on its former colonial status.
b. low productivity.
c. a lack of technological developments.

d. a large infusion of foreign investment.
e. technological breakthroughs.

Discussion Questions

1. How could economic growth be illustrated using a production possibilities curve? Can economic development be shown in the context of a production possibilities curve? *(KQ1)*
2. What factors would most likely give rise to the fastest rate of economic growth? Economic development? *(KQ3, 5)*
3. Why does the United States have an interest in helping poorer nations grow and develop? *(KQ2)*
4. Do you think economic growth and development are always positive outcomes for a given nation? Under what circumstances would you argue that growth and development should not necessarily be undertaken? *(KQ2, 4)*
5. Do you think revolutions or social disorder are primarily caused by political factors or by changes in economic growth and development? *(KQ2, 3, 4, 5)*

Answers

Problems and Applications

1. a. high
   b. low
   c. high
   d. low
   e. low
   f. high
   g. low
   h. low
   i. high
   j. low
   k. low
   l. low
   m. high
   n. low
   o. low
   p. low

True-False

1. F: Foreign aid is the transfer of income from rich nations to poor nations with the goal of promoting their economic development.
2. T   3. T   4. T
5. F: An inequitable distribution of income is associated with low rates of economic growth.
6. F: One of the fundamental characteristics of less developed countries is that a high percentage of the population is employed in agriculture.
7. T
8. F: Rostow's takeoff theory divides growth into five stages, from the early traditional society to the mass consumption society.
9. F: Marxist theory focuses on the role of expanding technology and the capitalist incentive to accumulate ever-increasing amounts of capital.

Multiple Choice

1. b *(KQ1)*   2. d *(KQ1, 3)*   3. e *(KQ4)*
4. d *(KQ3)*   5. c *(KQ5)*   6. d *(KQ3)*